Crowell's Handbook of

CLASSICAL

DRAMA

Crowell's Handbook of

CLASSICAL

DRAMA

By RICHMOND Y. HATHORN

Professor, State University of New York, Stony Brook

Thomas Y. Crowell Company

NEW YORK / ESTABLISHED 1834

L. C. Card 67-12403
ISBN 0-690-22501-6
4   5   6   7   8   9   10

Preface

THERE HAS BEEN NOTHING quite like this handbook in any language heretofore; this announcement will doubtless arouse various kinds of thankfulness in users. The customary summaries and background materials are here; in addition, more notice than customary has been taken of lost and fragmentary works. A unique feature is the attempt to offer an explanation for every proper name in the complete extant plays, with these exceptions: Persian warriors mentioned by Aeschylus, of whom nothing is known but that they are mentioned by Aeschylus; various Greeks mentioned by Aristophanes, of whom nothing is known, et cetera; some abstract deities whose names are universally Englished in translations; and some places and persons occurring in extremely conjectural readings. The explanations themselves—of myths, for instance—are slanted toward ancient drama, not necessarily toward epic, lyric, or the like.

Line references in plays come from the Loeb Library texts; other references are in the form standard among classicists. Translated phrases, from Greek, Latin, or whatever, are the author's own.

To the innumerable scholars whose work I have plundered, I can only declare that silent gratitude exists; if the plundering itself has been ill-considered or ill-executed, the blame must be mine. Explicit thanks are due to my editors, Edward Tripp—his were the initial conception and the choice of executor—and Rhoda Tripp, who patiently, perspicaciously, and profitably disputed many a passage.

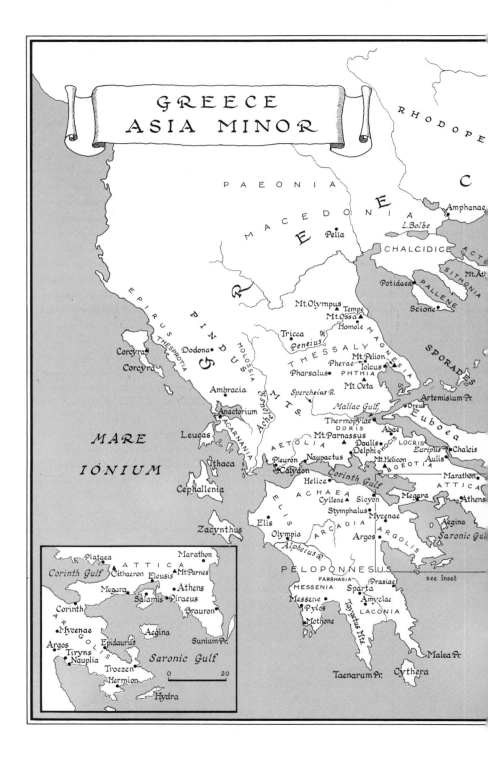

OCEANUS

ATLANTICUS

GERMANIA

GALLIA

HISPANIA

Tagus R.

Genua

Massilia

Mare
Liguriae

Ravenna

Mare
Adriatticum

Salonae

ILLYRICU

Axios

Tarraco

CORSICA

ITALIA

Epidamnus

BALEARES

SARDINIA

Roma

Capua
Neapolis

Brundisium
Tarentum

GR

Baetis R.

Gades Tartessus

Mt. Calpe

Mt. Abyla

Carthago Nova

MARE

Mare
Tyrrhenum

SICILIA

Enna

Mt. Aetna

Aetnae

MAURETANIA

Caesarea

Carthago

Agrigentum
Camarina

Syracusae

AFRICA

GAETULIA

Barc

Cinyphus R.

LI

MEDITERRANEAN
WORLD

0   200   400   600

Miles

deFontaine

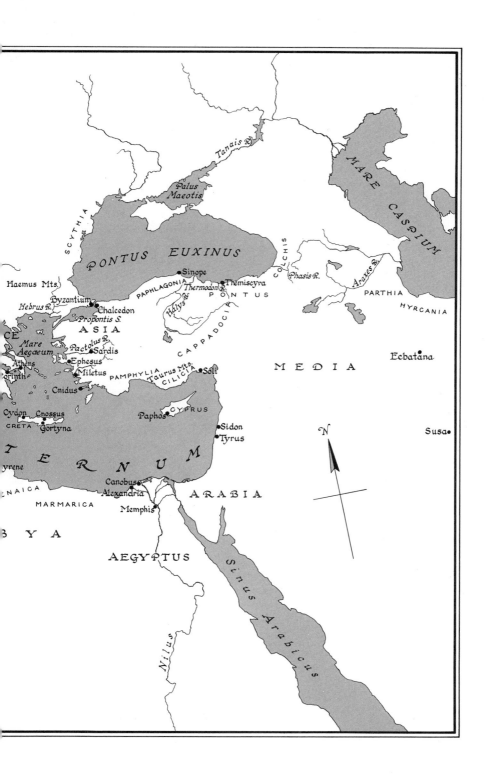

Crowell's Handbook of

CLASSICAL

DRAMA

A

Abae (Gk. **Abai**). City in northeast Phocis known for its temple and oracle of Apollo.

Abas. *Myth.* King of Euboea and a son of Poseidon.

Absyrtus (Gk. **Apsyrtos**). *Myth.* Brother of Medea. Absyrtus was murdered by his sister after she had helped Jason to capture the golden fleece. Medea scattered bits of Absyrtus' body over the water to delay her father, Aeëtes, in his pursuit of the fleeing *Argo.* In Seneca's *Medea* (line 963 ff.) Absyrtus' silent ghost appears seeking vengeance just as Medea is preparing to kill her children. According to some versions of the myth, Absyrtus was murdered by Jason.

Abydus (Gk. **Abydos**). Greek city on the Hellespont colonized by Miletus.

Abyla. Mountain on the African side of the Strait of Gibraltar. Abyla was one of the Pillars of Hercules.

Academy or **Academe** (Gk. **Akademeia**). Grove on the outskirts of Athens named for the hero Academus. In Aristophanes' time it was only a place for exercises, but it later became the site of Plato's philosophical school.

Acamas (Gk. **Akamas**). *Myth.* Son of Theseus and brother of Demophon. Acamas appears as a mute character in Euripides' *Heraclidae.*

Acarnania (Gk. **Akarnania**). Section of central Greece extending northward from the Corinthian Gulf along the western coast; through it flows the river Achelous. Acarnania was regarded by the ancient Greeks as somewhat primitive.

Acastus (Gk. **Akastos**). *Myth.* Brother of Alcestis and son of Pelias, whom he succeeded as king of Iolcus. Acastus' wife, Hippolyte (also called Astydameia), made advances to the hero Peleus, who had taken refuge in the court of Iolcus. Peleus repulsed Hippolyte, whereupon she denounced him to the king as a would-be adulterer. Acastus accordingly abandoned Peleus in the mountains, asleep and disarmed, to be eaten by wild beasts. But Peleus, rescued by the centaur Chiron, returned to kill both husband and wife. Another version holds that in his old age Peleus was harried out of the land by King Acastus.

Accius, Lucius. Roman writer of tragedies (170–c. 84 B.C.). Accius shared with Pacuvius the reputation of being foremost in this field. Born in Pisaurum of slave ancestry, Accius was educated in Rome. His patron was Decimus Brutus, in whose honor Accius wrote an historical tragedy, *Brutus,* about the expulsion of the kings from Rome. Accius' career began in about 140 B.C., and he lived long enough to have literary conversations with young Cicero.

His pride was considerable: although he was very short, Accius set up a tall statue of himself in the Temple of the Muses; and he refused to stand for Julius Caesar Strabo at a meeting of the College of Poets, remarking that this was one situation where Strabo was definitely outranked. Yet when Accius read his *Atreus* to Pacuvius, he accepted the older man's criticisms meekly. Praised for his skillful handling of argument in plays and asked why he had not become a lawyer, Accius replied that in the courtroom he could never make his opponent say what he wanted him to.

Of Accius' tragedies on Greek mythological themes, more than forty titles and numerous fragments survive. The saying from *Atreus* "Let them hate, so long as they fear" has become proverbial.

Accius also wrote two plays on Roman history that are lost: the above-named *Brutus,* and *Decius,* which was about the self-sacrifice of Decius Mus in battle. Two lost poems dealing with dramatic poetry are: *Didascalica,* a kind of poetics treating both Greek and Roman plays, among many other subjects; and *Pragmatica,* a manual of dramaturgic technique, in which Accius blamed the public for the poet's shortcomings.

Acestor (Gk. **Akestor**). 1. Writer of tragedy contemporary with Aristophanes. The comedians nicknamed Acestor SACAS.

2. (Gk. "healer"). Epithet of Apollo as patron god of medicine.

Achaea (Gk. **Achaia**). 1. Region on the north coast of the Peloponnesus; also a region in southeast Thessaly. By extension, all of the Peloponnesus or all Greece. Hence, in Homeric and later poetic usage, "Achaean" meant "Greek."

2. Epithet of Demeter. The name was said by the ancients to be derived from the Greek word *ache,* "sorrows."

Achaeans' Banquet, The (Gk. **Achaion Syndeipnon**). Lost play by Sophocles, possibly a satyr play. Apparently it described a dinner, involving drunkenness and revelry, which Agamemnon gave at Tenedos on the way to Troy. Achilles was not invited and required much soothing.

Achaeus (Gk. **Achaios**). 1. *Myth.* Son of Xuthus and Creusa and ancestor of the Achaeans.

2. Writer of tragedies and satyr plays (5th century B.C.). Of Achaeus' works about twenty titles are known. The Alexandrian critics ranked Achaeus directly after the three great tragedians Aeschylus, Sophocles, and Euripides. He was said to be second only to Aeschylus as a writer of satyr plays.

Acharnae (Gk. **Acharnai**). A country deme of Attica and the most populous of all demes. Acharnae's chief activities were agriculture and charcoal making. Its inhabitants were considered rustic and belligerent, but honest.

Acharneus. A mountain of the Attic deme Acharnae.

Acharnians, The (Gk. **Acharnes**). Extant comedy by Aristophanes, his earliest surviving play. It was produced at the Lenaea of 425 B.C. under the name of Aristophanes' friend Callistratus and was awarded first prize over the works of Cratinus and Eupolis. Translations: John Hookham Frere, 1839; Benjamin B. Rogers, 1924; Arthur S. Way, 1927; Patric Dickinson, 1957; Lionel Casson, 1960; Douglass Parker, 1962.

S C E N E. Athens, a street by the Pnyx, meeting place of the Assembly.

S U M M A R Y. Dicaeopolis, ("Good Government"), a man from the country, impatiently awaits the arrival of the dilatory members of the Assembly. He expresses his determination to force the citizens to discuss the negotiation of peace with Sparta. When the meeting finally begins, Amphitheus offers to go himself to make peace, but he is forcibly silenced. The Athenian ambassadors to Persia and Thrace then report on their missions and introduce some rather dubious examples of the wonders of those barbarian lands. The meeting is hastily adjourned when Dicaeopolis feels a drop of rain and declares that it is an omen.

Amphitheus, whom Dicaeopolis has sent to conclude a private treaty with Sparta for himself and his family, returns with various proposals. Dicaeopolis immediately seizes the offer of a thirty-year truce and announces that he will now celebrate the Rural Dionysia. But a Chorus of Acharnians who are hostile to the idea of peace threaten to stone him. At this Dicaeopolis engages to convince them that neither side in the conflict is wholly wrong and offers to argue his case with his head on a block. In order to arouse their pity, he goes to Euripides and borrows the beggar's rags of Telephus, whom the playwright represented in his lost tragedy of that name.

In his speech Dicaeopolis says that he hates the Spartans but that the Athenians must bear part of the blame for the war since they forbade trade with Megara on a flimsy pretext, forcing the Megarians to appeal to Sparta for aid. Some of the Acharnians are convinced by his arguments, but the others call in the general Lamachus for help. Dicaeopolis is, however, not impressed by Lamachus, an aristocrat to whom war is a benefit. After Lamachus withdraws, Dicaeopolis announces that henceforth his own market will be open to the Spartans, Megarians, and Boeotians.

The Chorus of Acharnians, addressing the audience directly, praise the poet for daring to speak the truth to the Athenians instead of misleading them with deceit and flattery. The Athenians are reproved for permitting the mistreatment of the white-haired veterans who have won so many victories for them.

Dicaeopolis now declares himself ready to trade with everyone except Lamachus. First enters a Megarian with two starving daughters, whom he stuffs into a sack and sells as pigs. Next comes a Boeotian, who is willing to trade eels for some product unobtainable at home. In exchange Dicaeopolis crates up the informer Nicarchus.

After the Acharnians express their admiration for Dicaeopolis' wisdom and the prosperity it has brought him, various persons come and beg a portion of Dicaeopolis' peace, the most coveted of all commodities. A Herald announces the start of the Feast of Jugs (the second day of the Anthesteria), but Lamachus is summoned to battle against the Boeotians and is unable to participate. As the general reluctantly departs with his weapons and his meager soldier's fare, Dicaeopolis goes off in the opposite direction to enjoy the celebration with a basketful of tasty foods. At the end of the play Lamachus, the man of war, hobbles in from the battlefield and goes to bed with a wound, while Dicaeopolis, the man of peace, staggers off to bed with a courtesan on either arm.

C O M M E N T A R Y. *The Acharnians* did not have much influence on later drama, nor has it evoked much criticism. It is generally recognized as fore-shadowing Aristophanes' chief attitudes: his sympathy with rustic, old-fashioned men as models of the good citizen; his persistent desire for peace; and his hatred of demagogues, extravagant and pretentious deceivers of the populace (includ-ing poets especially), warmongers, and advocates of a ruthless foreign policy. Aristophanes is not so much a hidebound conservative as a voice raised in be-half of common sense, humaneness, and moderation in an age when, as Thucyd-ides shows in *The Peloponnesian War*, men of all sides were slipping into a vicious circle of extremism.

Acheloïdes. Descendants of Achelous (2).

Achelous (Gk. **Acheloos**). 1. Largest river in Greece, forming the border between Acarnania and Aetolia. By extension, all fresh water, or all water.

2. *Myth.* God of the river and suitor of the reluctant Deianira, daughter of Oeneus of Calydon. Deianira was saved from this marriage by Heracles, who fought and overcame Achelous in spite of the many forms that the god assumed. In art Achelous was given a horned head and a serpent's body.

Acheron. *Myth.* One of the rivers of the underworld; by association, the whole land of the dead or death itself. "Acheruntian," as applied to people, meant "aged and ripe for death."

Achilles or **Achilleus.** *Myth.* One of the greatest of Greek heroes (hence "Achillean" meant "of the first rank"), son of Peleus and the sea goddess Thetis. After Achilles' mother returned to the sea, the child was reared and educated by the centaur Chiron. When the Trojan War broke out (according to the plan of the gods, the purpose of the war was to bring Achilles fame, as well as to disburden the earth of surplus population), his parents learned from an oracle that their son would not survive the fighting. Achilles was accordingly disguised as a girl and sent to Sycros, where he lived among King Lycomedes' daughters. There the princess Deidamia bore him a son, Neoptolemus (also called Pyrrhus). Achilles' disguise was pierced by Odysseus, who, coming as a peddler laden with women's clothes and men's weapons, noted which one of the "maidens" showed interest in the weapons.

On the first voyage against Troy, the Greek fleet strayed to Mysia, and in the ensuing battle Achilles wounded King Telephus. When Telephus' wound did not heal, he was obliged to follow Achilles back to Greece to be healed, according to divine decree, by the same weapon that had hurt him. The second voyage to Troy left from Aulis. It was here that Iphigenia was lured to the sacri-fice on the promise that she would be Achilles' bride. (Achilles' only appear-ance in extant classical drama is in Euripides' *Iphigenia in Aulis*, where he is indignant to learn of the deception and swears to protect the deluded girl.)

After nine years of war at Troy, Achilles quarreled with Agamemnon, who had robbed him of the captive girl Briseis to compensate for the loss of his own captive girl, Chryseis. Achilles withdrew his Myrmidons from battle and sulked in his tent, rejecting Agamemnon's embassy of reconciliation. At last, however, Patroclus, Achilles' dearest friend, was killed by Hector, whereupon Achilles returned to the fray. Clothed in the divine armor that his mother had brought from Hephaestus, he killed Hector and dragged his body around Troy. When King Priam stole through the Greek lines with a wagonload of ransom, Achilles returned Hector's corpse to the Trojans.

Among the allies of Troy killed by Achilles were the Amazon queen Penthesilea and the Ethiopian prince Memnon. Soon after Hector's death, Achilles was himself fatally shot by Paris, who was aided by Apollo. Some say that Achilles had been waiting unarmed to negotiate a marriage with Polyxena, Priam's daughter. After a debate between Ajax and Odysseus as to which should receive Achilles' armor, it was awarded to Odysseus. On the fall of Troy, Achilles' ghost demanded that Polyxena be sacrificed on his tomb. The spirit of the hero then went to live on one of the Islands of the Blessed by the White Coast of the Euxine Sea.

Plays named *Achilles* were written by Aristarchus (1), Accius, and Ennius.

Achilles' Lovers (Gk. **Achilleos Erastai**). Lost satyr play by Sophocles about the boyhood of Achilles. Fragments indicate that in the play Peleus described the metamorphoses through which Thetis tried unsuccessfully to evade his wooing, that Phoenix fought off lustful satyrs from his charge Achilles, and that more noble lovers taught the boy to become a hero.

Acragas. See AGRIGENTUM.

Acrisius (Gk. **Akrisios**). *Myth.* King of Argos, twin brother of Proetus, and father of DANAË. Hearing that Danaë's son, Perseus, was returning to Argos after having killed the Gorgon, Acrisius fled to Larissa to escape the prophecy that his grandson would kill him. But Perseus arrived in Larissa to participate in games there, and a discus that he threw swerved and killed Acrisius, who was among the spectators. The flight and accidental death of Acrisius may have been the subject of a lost play by Sophocles called *Acrisius*. The play may, however, have dealt with the birth of Perseus.

Actaeon (Gk. **Aktaion**). *Myth.* Son of Aristaeus and Autonoë. Actaeon offended Artemis, either by boasting that he could hunt better than the goddess or by accidentally coming upon her as she bathed in a woodland pool. Artemis changed Actaeon into a stag, letting his own hounds run him down and tear him to pieces on Mt. Cithaeron.

act division. Early Greek dramatic performances, both tragic and comic, were continuous, punctuated only by the choric songs that separated the episodes. With the decline of the chorus in the fourth century B.C., its function must have been felt to be more and more simply divisional (see CHORUS). When artistic drama came to Rome in the third century B.C., the prevailing Greek custom of dividing tragedies by choric songs and comedies by flute solos or other entertainments came with it. The introduction of the curtain by the end of the second century B.C. probably rendered the divisions unmistakable.

Whether or not the number of acts was regularly five remains a controversial question. No proof can be drawn from the manuscripts of Plautus and Terence; the act divisions evident in some of them could have been supplied by later editors. The manuscript of Menander's *Arbitrants* has such indications of division as "Here a song by the chorus." Similar guides in his *Dyskolos* are so spaced as to provide for five convenient acts. Horace is positive in his pronouncement "Let the play be no less and no longer than five acts" (*Ars Poetica,* line 189). The theory of the five-act play may have gone back to the Alexandrian age and even to the period of New Comedy. (See also THEOPHRASTUS.)

Acte (Gk. **Akte,** "seacoast"). **1.** Name for any coastal district but especially for the coast of Attica at the Piraeus. Hence the adjective "Actaean" meant "Attic."

2. A long, narrow, and mountainous peninsula, the easternmost of three nearly parallel peninsulas that jut southeastward into the Aegean Sea from the coast of Macedonia. Mt. Athos is at its tip. Aeschylus called it "sacred to Zeus" (*Agamemnon,* line 285).

Actor (Gk. **Aktor**). *Myth.* Theban hero, son of Oenops and brother of Hyperbius.

actors and acting. The earliest actors must have been amateurs, in Athens as well as in the regions where Doric farce held sway. Originally there was only one actor, probably the author himself, and he might take more than one role in his play. In the first century of its existence, however, Greek drama began to be played by professionals, for the performances came to be state occasions and performers were paid by the state. While Aeschylus did not retire from acting until later life, Sophocles said farewell to the stage while still young— because of a weak voice, some said. For a time the poet chose the actors himself, but after about 449 B.C. the leading role was assigned on the basis of a competition.

Aeschylus added a second actor, Sophocles a third. Some scholars think that there were never more than three actors and that they handled all the roles; others say that the so-called rule of three actors was not fixed until the fourth century B.C. The leading actor was called the protagonist; the terms deuteragonist and tritagonist for the second and third actor are not so well attested but are probable enough. As for *hypokrites,* the general Greek word for "actor," there is no agreement as to whether its primary meaning was "answerer" or "explainer." Because of the use of masks and stylized costume and because of the ritual character of drama and the large size of the theater, the Greek actor had to depend chiefly on his voice for dramatic effects; moreover, his gestures had to be broad and grand. A good singing voice and a good memory were requisites.

From earliest times, actors must have altered and interpolated lines. Evidence of this practice is shown by Lycurgus' efforts in the later fourth century B.C. to establish definitive texts of the works of the great tragedians (see LYCURGUS 4). By Aristotle's time the actor overshadowed the playwright. In this and succeeding ages there were performers who were idols of the Hellenic world, making triumphal tours and amassing large fortunes. There were, too, breach-of-contract suits and fines levied on actors who failed to appear. Actors' guilds, called "Dionysiac artists," were organized in the third century B.C. Guilds of actors were also formed in Rome.

In Rome, as in Greece, roles were first taken by amateurs, and in ATELLAN FARCE it was common for the players to be dilettantes even in later periods. According to tradition, the first trained actors came from Etruria (the Latin word *histrio*, "actor," is of Etruscan origin). Livius Andronicus and Plautus were said to have appeared on stage, but in Rome, as in Greece, the playwright very soon retired behind the scenes. Most actors in Rome were slaves educated for that purpose; a few of the more famous ones were freed and became respectable. Nevertheless, there was always in Rome a stigma attached to the profession, for actors were *infames*, "without civic rights or reputation."

In Greece women never appeared on the stage. In Rome they could be only mimes, pantomimes, stage dancers, and the like, and they were legally classified with prostitutes. Only very late did actresses begin to appear in comedy.

Adeimantus (Gk. **Adeimantos**). Athenian military leader during the Peloponnesian War who was suspected of pro-Spartan sympathies. Adeimantus was a friend of Alcibiades and was involved in the scandal of the profanation of the mysteries.

Adelphoe (Gk. **Adelphoi, The Brothers**). Extant comedy by Terence (produced at the funeral games in honor of Lucius Aemilius Paulus, 160 B.C.). The author's last play, it was adapted from the *Adelphoi* of Menander (who apparently wrote two plays so entitled), with the addition of a scene from the *Synapothnescontes* (*The Suicide Pact*) of Diphilus. Translations: John Sargeaunt, 1912; W. Ritchie, 1927; Lionel Casson, 1960; Frank O. Copley, 1962. Adaptations and works influenced by *Adelphoe*: Molière, *The School for Husbands*, 1661; Thomas Shadwell, *The Squire of Alsatia*, 1688; Richard Steele, *The Tender Husband*, 1705; Henry Fielding, *The Fathers*, 1778.

S C E N E. A street in Athens: before the houses of Micio and Sostrata.

S U M M A R Y. The prologue is Terence's means of replying to the usual two accusations leveled at him by the opposing literary clique: one, that he intermingled two Greek originals, using material that had been presented before; and two, that he was helped in his writing by prominent men (who presumably would not have wanted to appear before the public under their own names). The first charge is countered with the admission that one episode of the play, that of the young man carrying off the prostitute from the pimp, occurred in Diphilus' *The Suicide Pact*, Latinized by Plautus, but that it was an episode Plautus omitted. The second charge is simply denied.

The beginning of the action finds Demea coming in from the country to berate his brother Micio, a city bachelor, for his indulgent rearing of Aeschinus, Demea's elder son whom Micio has adopted. Demea contrasts the spoiled boy's behavior with that of his model younger brother, Ctesipho, whom he has reared with the proper sternness. Aeschinus' latest escapade has been to carry off a girl from Sannio's brothel and to install her in his own house, claiming that she is freeborn. Demea does not know that Aeschinus abducted the girl as a favor to Ctesipho, who is in love with her.

In the meantime, Sostrata, the widowed mother of the girl Pamphila, who is about to bear Aeschinus' child, fears that her daughter has been abandoned by her lover. Sostrata calls in a kinsman to champion their cause. Micio, learning of the situation, immediately gives his consent to the marriage of Aeschinus and Pamphila, but he reproaches his nephew for his folly and negligence. Demea, still ignorant of Ctesipho's involvement with the courtesan, is shocked at Micio's unruffled acceptance of this new evidence of Aeschinus' licentiousness. When he does at last learn the truth about Ctesipho, Demea accuses Micio of encouraging the youth's debauchery by permitting the courtesan to remain in his house. But the old bachelor expresses his conviction that both of his nephews are decent, honorable fellows who will soon outgrow their waywardness.

Demea then realizes that Micio's liberality and unfailing good humor have made him loved by all, while his own frugality and harshness have earned him universal dislike. Deciding, therefore, to imitate his brother's conduct, he showers money everywhere and frees slaves. He promises to take Ctesipho's girl into his own house, prevails on the reluctant Micio to marry her mother, and proposes that the wall between the two houses be knocked down and that they all become one happy family. At the play's end all realize that the right way of life must be a balance between indulgence and discipline.

C O M M E N T A R Y. The critical consensus—aside from that of the anti-Terentians—has been that *The Brothers* is Terence's masterpiece. First, it is a serious comedy in the best sense of the words, since it deals with the significant theme of education and works out the consequences of opposing theories in ways that are simultaneously logical and amusing. Second, it is a tour de force of double-plotting hardly equaled in drama: there are two systems of upbringing, two young products thereof, with their two love affairs, as well as the two brothers of the older generation who are the cause of it all. Lastly, in spite of the play's clever plot, its characters remain complex and humanly variable; perhaps this is because doubling is of the very essence of *The Brothers*. The characters themselves have double natures: Demea, whose inflexibility conceals humorous shrewdness; Micio, whose kindliness, viewed from another angle, is only self-indulgence; and Aeschinus, who is forward in another's cause but backward in his own. Terence, in typical Roman and classical fashion, gave discipline its due. Treatments of this theme from the eighteenth century onward have weighted the balance toward permissiveness.

Admetus (Gk. **Admetos**). *Myth.* King of Pherae. When Apollo killed the Cyclopes, who had indirectly caused the death of Asclepius, Zeus condemned him to serve Admetus as a shepherd. Admetus treated Apollo kindly, and the god helped him to win Alcestis, who later sacrificed her life for him. He appears as one of the chief characters in Euripides' *Alcestis*. A lost play by Sophocles called *Admetus* was possibly about the servitude of Apollo.

Adonia. See **Adonis**.

Adonis. *Myth.* A hunter of great personal beauty loved by Aphrodite. Adonis was gored to death by a wild boar when he rejected the goddess' advances. The celebration of his cult, which was of Syrian-Mesopotamian origin and was honored chiefly by women, culminated in the Adonia, an annual festival of lamentation, which was not officially prominent until Hellenistic times. At Athens, however, even in the classical age, women sang the ritual lament for Adonis' death from the rooftops. Tragedies entitled *Adonis* were written by Nicophon and Dionysius of Syracuse.

Adrasteia (glossed by the Greeks as "not to be run from"). An epithet of NEMESIS, or Necessity.

Adrastus (Gk. **Adrastos**). *Myth.* King of Argos. Discovering the heroes Tydeus (an exile from Calydon) and Polyneices (an exile from Thebes) fighting outside his palace one stormy night, Adrastus recalled Apollo's oracle that he should wed his daughters to a lion and a boar and accordingly married them to Polyneices and Tydeus, who wore shield devices representing those animals. Adrastus promised to restore his sons-in-law to their native cities and, intending to reinstate Polyneices first, organized the expedition of the Seven against Thebes. He appears in Euripides' *Suppliants,* after the failure of this expedition, begging the help of Theseus in obtaining the bodies of the slain for burial; later he leads the dirge over the recovered corpses and eulogizes each hero. In his old age Adrastus, according to some versions of the myth, led the sons of the Seven, the Epigoni, on a successful expedition against Thebes.

Adria, Hadria, or **Adrian Sea.** The Adriatic Sea.

Adulescens (Lat. "young man"). The young lover, a stock character in New Comedy.

Aeacus (Gk. **Aiakos**). *Myth.* Father of Peleus, grandfather of Achilles, great-grandfather of Neoptolemus. (Hence Aeacides, "descendant of Aeacus," referred to any one of the foregoing.) After death, Aeacus became a judge of souls in the underworld. He appears in burlesque guise as Pluto's doorkeeper in Aristophanes' *Frogs.*

aediles. Roman officials. The plebeian aediles, elected from the lower body of the national assembly, had, among other duties, charge of the Plebeian Games. The curule aediles, chosen from among the patricians, directed the Roman Games. (See LUDI.)

Aeëtes (Gk. **Aietes**). *Myth.* King of Colchis, son of the sun god Helios, and father of Medea. When Phrixus arrived in Colchis flying on the golden ram, Aeëtes welcomed him and hung up the ram's fleece in a sacred grove. On Jason's appearance in search of the golden fleece, Aeëtes tried to foil the young man, giving him seemingly impossible preliminary tasks to perform. The fleece gained with the aid of Aeëtes' daughter Medea, Jason sailed off with it, accompanied by Medea. Aeëtes' angry pursuit was halted by the necessity of collecting the pieces of his son Absyrtus, whom Medea had murdered.

Aegeus (Gk. **Aigeus**). *Myth.* King of Athens, son of Pandion (2), and father of Theseus (hence "Aegeides" meant "Athenians"). Having no children, Aegeus consulted the Delphic oracle, which told him: "Pour no wine from the goatskin until you return to Athens." On his way home, Aegeus stopped at Corinth, lent a sympathetic ear to Medea's troubles, and promised her refuge if she would cure his sterility. (Aegeus appears in this role in Euripides'

Medea.) He then paid a visit to his friend King Pittheus of Troezen, who, comprehending the oracle—"Aegeus" means "goat"—made his guest drunk and caused him to bed with his (Pittheus') daughter Aethra. The result of this union was Theseus.

Medea, after killing her children by Jason, joined Aegeus in Athens and bore him a son, Medus. When Theseus appeared, having grown to manhood, Medea tried to remove him, first by sending him against the monster bull of Marathon and afterward by poison. These plots failed, and when Aegeus finally recognized and acknowledged his son, Medea fled. Later Theseus departed to the court of King Minos at Crete, promising Aegeus that if he should return, having overcome the Minotaur, he would hoist a white sail. But Theseus forgot to make the sign, and Aegeus, sighting a black sail, threw himself into the sea, thenceforth called the Aegean.

A lost play by Sophocles called *Aegeus* probably treated Medea's attempt to kill Theseus; and a lost play of the same name by Euripides, presumably composed before *Medea* (431 B.C.), dealt with much the same material as Sophocles' play. Euripides' *Aegeus* may have formed the first of a trilogy, followed by *Theseus* and the earlier version of *Hippolytus*.

Aegialeus (Gk. **Aigialeus**). *Myth.* Son of Adrastus. According to some versions of the myth, Aegialeus was one of the leaders of the EPIGONI, the "Afterborn," on the second, and successful, expedition against Thebes.

Aegicores (Gk. **Aigikores**). One of the four original tribal divisions in Athens.

Aegina (Gk. **Aigina**). **1.** Island in the Saronic Gulf, directly south of Salamis.

2. *Myth.* Daughter of the river god Asopus and mother, by Zeus, of Aeacus.

Aegiplanctus (Gk. **Aigiplanktos**). Probably Mount Geraneia on the Saronic Gulf in Megara. Aegiplanctus is possibly not a proper name at all, but a descriptive adjective: "wandered over by goats."

aegis (Gk. **aigis**, "goatskin"). *Myth.* Goatskin cuirass, fringed with snakes and decorated with the Gorgon's head in the center, worn usually by Athena. The aegis was, however, sometimes described as an emblem of Zeus or of an Erinys or of Persephone. According to one story, it was the skin of the goat that suckled the infant Zeus on Crete; according to another, it was the skin of the Gorgon herself, stripped off by Athena during the battle of the gods and the Giants.

Aegisthus (Gk. **Aigisthos**). *Myth.* Son of Thyestes. Thyestes had been told by an oracle that vengeance on his brother Atreus could be effected only if he had a son by his own daughter, the priestess Pelopia. So Thyestes ravished Pelopia under cover of darkness, although she managed to snatch away his sword. After Pelopia had borne Aegisthus, she exposed him, but by chance she caught the attention of King Atreus, who married her. The exposed child was recovered from the shepherds who had saved him, and he was reared as a prince. When Thyestes was subsequently brought to the palace as a captive, he recognized the sword which Aegisthus was wearing, revealed their kinship, and inspired the youth to kill Atreus.

Later, while Agamemnon was away at Troy, Aegisthus seduced his wife, Clytemnestra, and, according to one account, murdered Agamemnon at a banquet on his return. In Seneca's *Agamemnon* Aegisthus merely assists Clytemnestra in the murder, and in Aeschylus' *Agamemnon* he slinks in after the deed is done. Eventually Aegisthus was himself killed by Orestes. In Euripides' *Electra* this latter murder is described by a messenger; in Aeschylus' *Choephori* Aegisthus makes a brief appearance, goes into the palace, and is killed before Clytemnestra meets her death; in Sophocles' *Electra* Aegisthus, after Clytemnestra's murder, is driven off the stage to his death. Of a lost play by Sophocles called *Aegisthus* nothing is known. The title itself may be incorrect.

Aegoceros (Gk. **Aigokeros**). The constellation of Capricorn.

Aegyptus (Gk. **Aigyptos**). *Myth.* Eponymous hero of Egypt, son of Belus and brother of Danaüs. Aegyptus' fifty sons, acting on their father's wish, forcibly married Danaüs' fifty daughters. (See DANAÏDES.)

Aemilius Scaurus, Mamercus. See Mamercus Aemilius SCAURUS.

Aeneas (Gk. **Aineias**). *Myth.* Trojan hero, collateral descendant of the royal line of Troy. Aeneas managed to lead away a remnant of Trojans after the fall of the city. According to Roman tradition, he brought them to Italy, where their descendants became the Roman race. Aeneas appears in Euripides' *Rhesus,* where he persuades Hector to send someone out to spy on the enemy.

Aenianes. Tribe scattered throughout Thessaly and other parts of northern Greece.

Aeolosicon (Gk. **Aiolosikon**, "Aeolus as Sicon"). Lost comedy by Aristophanes. It was brought out in 387 B.C., with *Cocalus,* by the poet's son Araros. *Aeolosicon* had no choric songs, no political satire, and no parabasis and was thus one of the plays marking the transition from Old Comedy to Middle Comedy. Although little is known of its plot, the fact that Sicon was a typical slave's name indicates the titular hero's position. It is known that some tragedy entitled *Aeolus* was parodied in the play and that the familiar comic figure of the gluttonous Heracles appeared. Evidence indicates that there may have been two versions of this comedy.

Aeolus (Gk. **Aiolos**). **1.** *Myth.* Ruler of the winds and father of Melanippe.

2. *Myth.* Son of Hellen and ancestor of the Aeolians. Aeolus was the father of Sisyphus, Athamas, Salmoneus, Macareus, Canace, Alcyone, and others. He was sometimes identified with Aeolus (1). Because his son Sisyphus was the mythical founder of Corinth, "Aeolian" sometimes meant "Corinthian." *Aeolus* was the title of a lost tragedy by Euripides.

Aeolus (Gk. **Aiolos**). Lost tragedy by Euripides (written before 423 B.C.). Fragments show that the plot is concentrated on the incestuous love of Aeolus' son Marcareus for his sister Canace, who is about to bear his child. Aeolus, ignorant of the whole affair, is busy finding a wife for Macareus and a husband for Canace. Macareus tries unsuccessfully to persuade his father to mate all his sons with all his daughters; in his plea occurs the famous line "Is anything shameful if those who do it do not think it so?" (The immorality of the sentiment, it is said, caused a riot in the audience, and explanations had to be offered before the show could go on.) On learning the truth about his son and daughter, Aeolus sends a sword to Canace. She commits suicide, and Macareus follows suit. The play was long notorious and often parodied by the comedians. The emperor Nero liked to perform the lament of the pregnant Canace.

Aërope. *Myth.* Granddaughter of King Minos of Crete and mother, by Atreus, of Agamemnon and Menelaus. Aërope fell in love with Thyestes, Atreus' brother, and managed to give him the golden fleece, which carried the kingship with it. But Atreus discovered the plot and threw her into the sea. (See ATREUS.)

Aeschines (Gk. **Aischines**). **1.** An unscrupulous, venal, and loudmouthed politician in Aristophanes' Athens. Aeschines eventually became one of the Thirty who tyrannized the city after Athens' defeat by Sparta.

2. An orator and political opponent of Demosthenes (389–314 B.C.). Before entering politics Aeschines had pursued a career in acting.

Aeschylus (Gk. **Aischylos**). Earliest of the three great Athenian writers of tragedy (c. 525–c. 456 B.C.).

L I F E. Aeschylus was born at Eleusis of a noble and wealthy family. In March 499 B.C., he produced his first tragedies, competing against Choerilus and Pratinas. He must have fought in the battle of Marathon in 490. During the battle his brother Cynegeirus caught hold of the prow of a Persian ship; his arm was cut off, and he died. When Aeschylus entered a competition the next year for the best elegy on those fallen in the battle, he lost to Simonides. In March 484, however, his entry won first place in the dramatic contest.

Four years later Aeschylus took part in the battle of Salamis, and he may have fought elsewhere during the Persian wars. Sometime during the 470's he visited Sicily under the patronage of Hiero of Syracuse; this was one of several visits. In Sicily Aeschylus produced *The Persians* (perhaps for the first time but more likely as a revival) and *The Aetnaeans,* the latter written to celebrate the founding of Hiero's colony of Aetna or Aetnae.

In March 472 the playwright was in Athens, where he won a first prize with the tetralogy *Phineus, The Persians, Glaucus of Potniae,* and the satyr play *Prometheus the Fire-Kindler.* Perhaps the Sicilian productions of *The Persians* and *The Aetnaeans* followed this. Aeschylus was defeated by Sophocles in the dramatic competition of 468 but won first place the following year with the tetralogy *Laius, Oedipus, The Seven Against Thebes,* and the satyr play *The Sphinx.* Somewhere in the mid-460's, most probably in 463, he won again with the tetralogy *The Suppliants, The Egyptians, Danaïdes,* and the satyr play *Amymone.* His last victory was in 458 with the *Oresteia.*

Not much else is known. Aeschylus was friendly with Ion of Chios and possibly with Pindar. His son was a tragedian, and descendants of his sister were also tragedians. At one point Aeschylus stood trial for divulging the secrets of the Eleusinian mysteries but was acquitted because he had done so inadvertently. In his last years the playwright retired to Sicily. For this various reasons are given: disgust with the Athenian public, jealousy of Sophocles, the uproar in the theater during the *Eumenides*. The traditional story of his death is that an eagle, wanting to split open a turtle, dropped it on Aeschylus' bald head, mistaking it for a boulder. His tomb at Gela in Sicily became a place of pilgrimage, and his self-composed epitaph is remarkable in that it mentions military exploits while ignoring his literary career.

E X T A N T   W O R K S (see under individual entries). *The Persians, Prometheus Bound, The Seven Against Thebes, The Suppliants,* and the trilogy *Oresteia,* consisting of *Agamemnon, Choephori,* and *Eumenides.*

L O S T   W O R K S (see under individual entries). *Proteus* was the satyr play for the *Oresteia.* Four other tetralogies were almost certainly written by Aeschylus: the *Persians Tetralogy,* consisting of *Phineus, The Persians* (extant), *Glaucus of Potniae,* and *Prometheus the Fire-Kindler;* the *Theban Tetralogy,* consisting of *Laius, Oedipus, The Seven Against Thebes* (extant), and *The Sphinx;* the *Lycurgeia,* consisting of *The Edonians, The Bassarids, The Youths,* and *Lycurgus;* and the *Danaïd Tetralogy,* consisting of *The Suppliants* (extant), *The Egyptians, Danaïdes,* and *Amymone.* For the *Prometheia* only the satyr play is disputed; the titles, but not the order, of *Prometheus Bound* (extant), *Prometheus Unbound,* and *Prometheus the Fire-Bringer* are unquestioned.

The following titles cannot be grouped with certainty: *The Aetnaeans, Alcmena, The Argives, The Argo, Atalanta, Athamas, The Award of Armor, Bacchae, The Bone-Gatherers, The Builders of the Bridal Chamber, Cabiri, Callisto, The Carians, Cercyon, Circe, The Conjurors of the Dead, The Cretan Women, Cygnus, Dictyulci, The Eleusinians, Epigoni, Eurytion, Glaucus the Sea God, Heliades, Heraclidae, The Heralds, The Huntresses, Hypsipyle, Iphigenia, The Isthmiasts, Ixion, The Lemnians, The Lion, Memnon, The Myrmidons, The Mysians, Nemea, The Nereids, Niobe, The Nurses, Oreithyia, Palamedes, Penelope, Pentheus, The Perrhaebians, Philoctetes, Phorcides, Polydectes, The Priestesses, The Processional, The Ransom of Hector, Semele, Sisyphus the Stone-Pusher, Telephus, Tenes, The Thracian Women, The Weighing of Souls, The Women of Salamis,* and *Xantriai.*

C R I T I C I S M. Ever since the staging of Aristophanes' *Frogs,* in which Aeschylus appears in order to defend his works against those of Euripides, Aeschylus has been praised for austere morality, deep religiousness, grandeur of language, and seriousness of thought; he has also been censured for bombast and for occasional obscurity. His plays were not much to the taste of Greek audiences in later classical times, and they were less often revived than those by other tragedians.

Aeschylus was most often cited for his contributions to the development of drama in introducing a second actor and in making changes in scenery and costume. Since, however, a recent discovery proves that *The Suppliants,* long considered the earliest extant tragedy, was really written late in the playwright's career, much that has been written of his dramatic development, and indeed of the development of drama in general, must be revised. Aeschylus has always been called the master of the satyr play, a judgment difficult to evaluate now, although *Dictyulci* and *The Isthmiasts* furnish enough fragments for credible reconstructions.

Modern critics have been interested in Aeschylus as the master of the "genuine," as opposed to the "spurious," trilogy (see TRILOGY); as a skillful handler of rich, consistent imagery and symbolism; and as a controversial religious thinker. Although the influence of the Eleusinian mysteries on his work has been discounted, Aeschylus was undoubtedly deeply concerned with the mystery of cosmic justice. His conception of Zeus is more provocative for its theodicy, its justifying the ways of God to man, than for its monotheism; but that the notion of a "developing godhead" forms part of Aeschylus' thinking is much to be doubted. There are probably depths of religious thought still to be plumbed in the works of Aeschylus. Those who think of him as primitive in any respect can only be considered guilty of philological arrogance and theological ignorance.

Aesculapius. Roman form of ASCLEPIUS.

Aesimus (Gk. **Aisimos**). A penurious, illiterate, and unprincipled Athenian. Aesimus was ridiculed by Aristophanes in *Ecclesiazusae* (line 208).

Aeson (Gk. **Aison**). *Myth.* Father of JASON.

Aesop (Gk. **Aisopos**). Semilegendary composer of fables. Aesop was thought by the Greeks to have lived at about the end of the seventh century B.C. Almost any current fable was attributed to him.

Aesopus, Clodius. Tragic actor in Rome (1st century B.C.). Aesopus was a friend of Cicero.

Aethiopes or **Aethiopians** (Gk. **Aithiopes**, "bright-faced" or "burnt-faced"). A mythical people on the eastern edge of the world. The Aethiopes were said by Homer to be the most pious of all races and hence on friendly terms with the gods. They lived on the banks of the river Aethiops (Gk. *Aithiops*), where the sun rose. The probability is that in later Greek times the historical Ethiopians were simply identified with them and given their name.

Aethra (Gk. **Aithra**). *Myth.* Daughter of Pittheus, king of Troezen, and mother, by AEGEUS, of Theseus. According to one story, Aethra was raped by Poseidon on the same day that Pittheus gave her to Aegeus, with the result that Theseus passed as the son of both the mortal and the god. Aethra appears as an old woman in Euripides' *Suppliants,* begging her son Theseus to help retrieve the bodies of the slain heroes, the Seven against Thebes, for burial.

Aetna (Gk. **Aitna**). 1. Large volcanic mountain in the northeast corner of Sicily. In myth Aetna was said to pin down the defeated monster Typhon or the Titan (or Giant) Enceladus. Hephaestus had a smithy in its summit, and the Cyclopes lived nearby.

2 (also **Aetnae**). City at the base of Mt. Aetna founded by Hiero of Syracuse. The region was noted for a large variety of beetle and a famous breed of horse.

Aetnaeans, The (Gk. **Aitnaiai**). Lost play by Aeschylus. It was a festival drama written in the 470's B.C. to celebrate the founding of the city of Aetna, or

Aetnae, by Aeschylus' occasional patron, the tyrant Hiero of Syracuse. A fragment of the play's hypothesis shows that *The Aetnaens* was unusual in having several parts, at least three of which were laid in different localities in Sicily. At some point the goddess Dike made a speech. The ancient list of Aeschylus' plays mentions a spurious *Aetnaeans* as well as a genuine one.

Aetolia (Gk. **Aitolia**). Section of Greece east of Acarnania on the northern coast of the Corinthian Gulf.

Aexone (Gk. **Aixone**). Town in Attica. Aexone was said to have produced a disproportionate share of informers.

Afranius, Lucius. Roman writer of a type of comedy called FABULA TOGATA (fl. second half of 2nd century B.C.). Afranius was a friend of the younger Scipio and an admirer of Menander and Terence. His works held the stage at least until the time of Nero and gained attention from commentators and grammarians for even longer. Of his works many fragments and more than forty titles survive; some of the better known plays were *Thais, The Cousins, The Impostor,* and *The Fire.*

Agamemnon. *Myth.* King of Argos and Mycenae. Agamemnon was the son of Atreus and Aërope, the brother of Menelaus, the husband of Clytemnestra, and the father of Iphigenia, Chrysothemis, Electra, and Orestes. In order to get possession of Clytemnestra, he was said to have killed her first husband and her newborn child.

After embarking for Troy, the Greek fleet, which Agamemnon commanded, was becalmed at Aulis. In order to gain a wind, Agamemnon was forced to sacrifice his daughter Iphigenia to Artemis. His doubt and torment before coming to this decision are portrayed in Euripides' *Iphigenia at Aulis.* At Troy Agamemnon had his famous quarrel with Achilles, recounted in Homer's *Iliad.* In Sophocles' *Ajax* Agamemnon at first forbids Ajax's burial but at last relents. Seneca's *Trojan Women* shows him objecting to the sacrifice of Polyxena, only giving way at the soothsayer's demand. In Euripides' *Hecuba* Agamemnon demonstrates his sense of justice by giving the captive Trojan queen her due. His murder is the theme of Aeschylus' *Agamemnon,* and he is the titular hero of a tragedy by Seneca.

Agamemnon. Extant tragedy by Aeschylus. (See ORESTEIA.)

Agamemnon. Extant tragedy by Seneca. Translation: Frank J. Miller, 1929.

S C E N E. Argos, the palace.

S U M M A R Y. The ghost of Thyestes rises up and rouses to vengeance his son Aegisthus, whom he begot on his own daughter. Thyestes recalls the crimes of his house since he was fed the flesh of his own children by his brother Atreus, Agamemnon's father. The ghost vanishes. Aegisthus, who had become the lover of Agamemnon's wife, Clytemnestra, during the latter's absence in Troy, wants to kill the king upon his return to Argos, but Clytemnestra vacillates, for she is willing to be reconciled with her husband, who is ignorant of her adultery. Aegisthus, however, strengthens her resolve by reminding her that Agamemnon brings with him the Trojan princess Cassandra, of whom he is enamored and with whom Clytemnestra will have to share both bed and throne.

Before the Greek fleet arrives, a Herald enters and describes the horrible storm that buffeted the ships. A group of captive Trojan women is brought in, among them Cassandra. In a prophetic frenzy she foretells Agamemnon's death. Agamemnon himself passes into the palace after a word with Cassandra. As he celebrates his triumphal banquet inside, she is able to see what ensues: tangled in his robe, Agamemnon falls beneath the blows of Aegisthus but continues to struggle against his assailant until Clytemnestra, wielding the double axe, severs his head from his shoulders. After the murder, Agamemnon's daughter Electra entrusts her little brother, Orestes, to King Strophius of Phocis, asking him to keep the boy hidden from his foes. She refuses to reveal the boy's whereabouts to Clytemnestra and is taken away to imprisonment, as Clytemnestra pronounces the death sentence on Cassandra.

    COMMENTARY. Most criticism simply contrasts the play, to its detriment, with Aeschylus' masterpiece. This is probably unfair and almost certainly irrelevant. Although there are doubtless scenes reminiscent of Aeschylus' *Agamemnon* in Seneca's drama—in the Herald's speech, in the treatment of Cassandra, and in the description of Agamemnon's entanglement in his robe at the moment of murder—they are probably filtered through an unknown number of intervening versions, both Roman and Greek.

    On the whole, Seneca is following an entirely different tradition of the myth, one in which Aegisthus is the leader in the murder plot. This change necessarily results in an entirely different role for Clytemnestra. While she is no longer a match for Medea and Lady Macbeth, she is not without interest: although hesitant in her relations with men, she is implacable toward her own sex, even toward her own daughter. Granted that Seneca's plays are better called melodramas than tragedies, *Agamemnon* seems a melodrama of considerable power. The plot is straightforward and the psychological-moral study of Clytemnestra holds it together very well. The conjecture that it was Seneca's first venture into drama was offered mostly as an excuse for its being a poor play, but it is a poor play only in not having been written by Aeschylus.

    Agatharchus (Gk. **Agatharchos**). Greek painter (5th century B.C.). Agatharchus was said to have been the first to paint scenery; it was used for Aeschylus' plays.

    Agathocles (Gk. **Agathokles**). Tyrant of Syracuse (317–289 B.C.). Agathocles was noted for his military audacity, especially against the Carthaginians.

    Agathon. Writer of tragedies (c. 447–c. 400 B.C.). Agathon came of a rich and aristocratic family. He cultivated Socrates and the Sophists Gorgias and Prodicus and was himself handsome, sociable, and elegant in manner. Toward the end of his life he, like Euripides, visited the Macedonian court of King Archelaus.

    Agathon's style was noted for its wit and elaboration. He had a tendency to prefer the seductive "new music," and, like Euripides, he apparently influenced the development of tragedy by inserting choric odes that lacked organic relevance and by turning from genuinely tragic subjects to melodramatic ones. The fictional setting of Plato's *Symposium* is Agathon's house, where the host's first victory in dramatic tragedy (416 B.C.) is being celebrated, where love is the topic of conversation, and where Aristophanes, Alcibiades, and Socrates are among the guests. In *Thesmophoriazusae* Aristophanes brings Agathon on the stage, where he appears at his dressing-table decked out as a woman, assuring Euripides and his father-in-law Mnesilochus that he is appareled this way to get the feeling of the woman's role he is writing. Agathon warbles parts for both chorus and chorus leader, probably in parody of the highly artificial style of his own works. Although he refuses to go as a woman to the women's meeting, he helps to deck out Mnesilochus in female garb. Aristophanes' lost *Gerytades* treated Agathon even more roughly.

Aristotle mentions Agathon with respect, remarking on his *Anthos,* or *Antheus,* as a rare instance of an invented tragic plot. Other works by Agathon were *Aërope, Alcmeon, The Mysians, Telephus,* and *Thyestes.*

Agave (Gk. **Agaue**). *Myth.* Daughter of Cadmus, king of Thebes. When her sister Semele was consumed by a lightning blast, Agave spread the story that this was Semele's punishment for having tried to hide a sordid love affair by pretending to be the beloved of Zeus. In revenge Dionysus, Semele's son by Zeus, drove Agave mad and caused her to roam the woods as a maenad. In this condition she appears in Euripides' *Bacchae,* leading her sisters, Autonoë and Ino, and the maenad band in the dismemberment of her own son, Pentheus. In the last scene Agave enters cradling Pentheus' head in her arms, exulting over her success in the "lion hunt." On coming to her senses, Agave is horrified to discover her error and is grief-stricken over the loss of her son. Dionysus appears at the play's end and banishes Agave as further punishment.

Agbatana. Variant of ECBATANA.

Agen. Lost satyr play attributed to Python (2). There is a dispute as to whether *Agen* was performed for the soldiers of Alexander the Great encamped on the Hydaspes in 326 B.C. or two years later at Susa or Ecbatana. The character Pallides (a pun on "phallus") represented Harpalus, Alexander's treasurer and governor of Babylonia, who absconded with a great deal of money in about 325 B.C. While governor, Harpalus had built a temple in Babylon to a dead harlot, Pythionice, who was worshiped there as an incarnation of Aphrodite. The play depicted an attempt by Pallides to call her up from the dead; he was assisted by Persian Magi, who probably formed the satyr chorus.

The title *Agen* may mean "leader" and may refer to Alexander, whose claim to be an incarnate divinity would certainly have been put in a bad light by his treasurer's deification of a whore. For this reason some ancient Greeks thought that Alexander himself was the real author, satirizing Harpalus in order to save his own reputation.

Agenor. *Myth.* Phoenician king, father of Cadmus and Europa.

Aglaurus. See AGRAULUS.

Agnoia (Gk. "ignorance" or "misunderstanding"). Personification of misapprehension who speaks the prologue of Menander's *Perikeiromene.*

agon (Gk. "contest"). 1. A contest of any kind. The word agon referred especially to an event in athletic games (for example, those held at Olympia,

Delphi, Corinth, and Nemea) but also to a dramatic contest (*skenikos agon*) in tragedy or comedy at the festivals. In Athens a tragic playwright submitted his tetralogy to the official in charge of the festival; if found acceptable, it was produced at state expense (see CHOREGUS). A comic poet similarly submitted a single comedy. At the most important festival, the City Dionysia, three tetralogies and five comedies were given productions throughout most of the fifth century B.C. (see DIONYSIA; LENAEA).

A board of ten judges, one from each Athenian tribe, took an oath to render a fair and impartial decision; they awarded first, second, and third prizes in each of the two categories. (Beginning about the middle of the fifth century, the chief actors, or protagonists, were also ranked first, second, and third.) A herald announced the winners. All received a sum of money, and their names and other pertinent data were carved in the official inscriptions (see DIDASCALIAE). The poets who won first prizes were crowned with ivy.

2. In tragedy, a prolonged dispute, particularly a rather formal debate. An example is the debate between Hecuba and Polymestor in Euripides' *Hecuba*.

3. One of the elements of Old Comedy. (See EPIRRHEMATIC AGON.)

agora. Market place of a Greek city. The agora was the center of commercial, social, and often political activity. Before the slopes of the Acropolis were used, the earliest dramatic performances in Athens were given in the agora.

Agoracritus (Gk. **Agorakritos**). 1. Famous sculptor (5th century B.C.). Agoracritus was a pupil of Phidias. Aristophanes hints that he was a professional informer (*The Knights*, line 1257).

2. Name assumed by the sausage-seller in Aristophanes' *Knights*. The word means "choice of the market place."

Agoraios (Gk. "he of the market place or assembly place"). 1. Epithet of Zeus as patron of public speaking.

2. Epithet of Hermes as patron of business.

Agraulus (Gk. **Agraulos**). *Myth.* 1. Wife of Cecrops and mother of the Agraulidae, or Cecropidae.

2. Usually **Aglaurus** (Gk. **Aglauros**). Daughter of the above and one of the CECROPIDAE. Either mother or daughter (probably a confusion of the two) was venerated as an Attic earth goddess. Her name appeared in several formulas for oaths.

Agrigentum (Gk. **Akragas**). Greek colony in Sicily, modern Girgenti.

Agrippa, Marcus Vipsanius. Henchman of the emperor Augustus, especially in military matters (c. 63–12 B.C.). Agrippa was one of the husbands of Augustus' daughter, Julia, and was the father of Agrippina the Elder.

Agrippina. 1. The Elder, daughter of Agrippa, granddaughter of Augustus, and wife of Germanicus (c. 14 B.C.–A.D. 33). Because of her outspoken opposition to the emperor Tiberius, Agrippina was banished and starved to death.

2. The Younger, daughter of the above, mother of Nero by Domitius Ahenobarbus, and wife of the emperor Claudius (A.D. 15–59). Claudius was

supposedly poisoned by Agrippina, and Nero succeeded to the throne. After a few years Nero tired of his mother's control and had her killed. In the pseudo-Senecan play *Octavia*, Agrippina's ghost appears and curses the marriage of Nero and Poppaea.

Aguieus or **Agyieus** (Gk. "he of the streets"). Epithet of Apollo, in whose honor pointed columns or altars were set up at house doors. The altar that was a regular furnishing of the classical stage, which very often represented a street, was generally regarded as sacred to Apollo Aguieus.

Agyrrhius (Gk. **Agyrrhios**). Athenian politician. Agyrrhius was a target of ridicule in Old Comedy because of his youthful effeminacy and because he instituted a law by which citizens were paid to attend the Assembly.

Aidoios (Gk. "he of the sense of honor"). Epithet of Zeus as overseer of oaths and obligations.

Aidoneus. Variant form of HADES.

Aidos (Gk. "sense of shame, reverence, and honor"). Personification of modesty and honor.

Ailinon (Gk. "alas for Linus"). Refrain in the dirge for LINUS (2), or in any mournful song, and by extension the name of the dirge itself.

Aisa. Greek deity, personification of fate or destiny.

Ajax (Gk. **Aias**). 1. *Myth.* Son of Telamon (king of Salamis); called Ajax the Greater. At Troy, Ajax was the strongest and bravest of the Greeks after Achilles. When the latter died, Ajax's lack of skill in speech caused him to lose to Odysseus the debate over who should inherit Achilles' armor. This injustice led Ajax to blasphemy and schemes of treachery, for which Athena drove him mad. The sequel to the story is told in Sophocles' *Ajax*.

2. *Myth.* Son of Oïleus of Opuntian Locris; called Ajax the Lesser. Ajax distinguished himself by an act of impiety during the sack of Troy. When Cassandra took refuge at the shrine of Athena, embracing the statue of the goddess, Ajax dragged both statue and woman out of the sanctuary and raped Cassandra. Because the other Greeks did not protest the outrage, Athena took revenge by enlisting Poseidon's aid in wrecking much of the Greek fleet on its way home. Ajax himself was pierced by a lightning bolt and dashed to pieces on a cliff. A lost play by Sophocles called *Ajax of Locris* told of the crime and punishment of Ajax the Lesser.

Ajax (Gk. **Aias**). Extant tragedy by Sophocles. *Ajax* is thought by virtually all scholars to antedate the playwright's *Antigone;* hence it was written before 442 B.C. Translations: Thomas Francklin, 1759; Edward H. Plumptre, 1865; Richard C. Jebb, 1904; F. Storr, 1912; Robert C. Trevelyan, 1919; E. F. Watling, 1953; John Moore, 1957. Adaptation: Ugo Foscolo, *Aiace*, 1811. *Aiace* was suppressed by the police and not published until 1828. In it Agamemnon represented Napoleon; Ajax, General Moreau; Ulysses, Fouché; and the cynical atheist Calchas, Pope Pius VII.

S C E N E. The Greek encampment before Troy.

S U M M A R Y. Because the Atreidae (Agamemnon and Menelaus, leaders of the Greek host) had awarded the divine armor of Achilles to the glib Odysseus, passing over the claims of the far braver Ajax, the latter had formed a plan to kill his fellow Greek chieftains in the night. But the goddess Athena drove Ajax insane, and he killed only the cattle and sheep that the Greeks had captured in raids.

As the play opens, it is morning, and Athena explains to Odysseus the cause of Ajax's mad behavior. Calling Ajax, she exhibits his derangement, encouraging him to recite his imagined exploits.

A Chorus of Ajax's men from his home island of Salamis grieve over their leader's shame. His captive concubine, the Phrygian princess Tecmessa, informs them that Ajax has now come to his senses and is sitting anguished in his tent, knowing that he has become the laughingstock of the army. She begs the Chorus to comfort him.

Ajax, refusing to be consoled, calls for his son Eurysaces and, after taking leave of the child, vows to cure his malady by desperate measures. Overhearing Ajax, Tecmessa begs him not to kill himself and not to abandon her and Eurysaces. Ajax pretends to give way, saying that he is leaving only to appease Athena's anger and to hide his stained sword in the ground.

After Ajax's departure, a Messenger reports that the hero's half brother, Teucer, has been warned by the seer Calchas that Ajax, for having boasted of not needing the gods' aid, is in danger from Athena's wrath for this one day and must be kept in his tent. Alarmed, Tecmessa sends men to look for Ajax, and all leave.

Alone by the seashore, Ajax fixes his sword firmly in the ground, prays to Zeus and Hermes, and calls on the Erinyes to bring ruin on the Atreidae. He then falls on his sword, Hector's gift to him after their duel. Tecmessa finds the body, and Teucer arrives to join her in mourning; he realizes that he will be blamed and probably banished by their father for not 'preventing Ajax's fate. Yet he does one last service for his brother; when Menelaus, seconded by Agamemnon, refuses to let the body have proper burial and orders it to be thrown to the birds, Teucer opposes them valiantly. Finally Odysseus, laying aside his enmity, intervenes and prevails on them to allow the burial to proceed.

C O M M E N T A R Y. Several minor flaws of plot construction, especially in comparison with *Antigone,* which *Ajax* greatly resembles in general outline, have strengthened the impression that this is Sophocles' earliest surviving play. Some of these flaws are: the doubling of the Messenger's report (he tells his news first to the Chorus, then to Tecmessa); the awkwardness with which the concluding scenes with Teucer are incorporated; and the clumsiness of the dispute between Teucer and the Atreidae. But as *Antigone,* Sophocles' first datable play, came some twenty-five years after he began writing, there is no reason to look on *Ajax* as a piece of apprentice work. On the contrary, the probable reason for its preservation was the emergence in it of the typical Sophoclean hero and a typical Sophoclean issue.

The hero is a man who is brought to ruin by his limitations and fatally hurt by what he does not know. Ajax is a hero in the old sense: he is stubbornly committed to a purely external code of honor, the warrior code which puts complete emphasis on the kind of figure that one cuts in the eyes of others. (Ajax belongs to a "shame-culture," as contrasted to a "guilt-culture," to use the anthropological terms that E. R. Dodds, in *The Greeks and the Irrational*, has made current in Greek studies.) In this code, to lose face is to be annihilated. Nevertheless, the code is, for all its stress on valor, an offense to Athena, who by her nature looks before and after, planning, weighing, and calculating. She is, in fact, the very spirit that must lead to an internalization of morality.

Heroes of the old code—it would be a mistake to call them Homeric heroes, since Homer by no means stamps them with unreserved approval—have for their greatest enemy Time, which brings them to the impotence of old age and causes their militaristic ethic to become obsolete in a more subtle and complex society. The best that can happen to such heroes is early, glorious death and honored burial. The hero cult is essentially a cult of the tomb and a cult of the past. It was the transition from the primitive code of the warrior to the ethic of the polis, with its intellectuality, its calculation, and its rationality, that continued to interest Sophocles.

Something might be lost in this transition: courage, magnanimity, transcendence of self. But precisely because Sophocles viewed the process in terms of the symbolic personages of myth, he saw clearly that the change of code was not merely historical, but individual, psychological, and moral—a danger and a potential gain in the development of every self. Honor might be lost in the use of intellect, Sophocles says, but it need not be; it is possible to preserve the best of the old code while espousing the new. This was precisely Sophocles' and Pericles' ideal for fifth-century Athens. Significantly, then, it is Odysseus, the new man of rationalism, who is finally responsible for rendering due honor to the heroism of Ajax.

Akraia (Gk. "of the heights"). Epithet of Hera. At her sanctuary in Corinth was celebrated a ritual of mourning connected with the death of Medea's children.

Alastor. Personification of a curse. Alastor was regarded as a spirit of vengeance; hence the word meant any malevolent spirit or a wicked and ruthless individual.

alazon (Gk. "vagabond," later "charlatan" or "braggart"). 1. One of the three perennial character types of comedy, the other two being BOMOLOCHOS and EIRON. (This classification has been employed more by modern critics than it was by the ancient Greeks.) The *alazon* is pretentious and is therefore a balloon to be pricked. He takes the form of many subtypes: the quack doctor, the quack prophet, the religious fanatic, the affected aesthete, the humorless politician, the lover who is in love with love, the romantic dreamer, the swaggering soldier, the pedantic scholar, the tradition-bound old man—anyone who thinks himself above the ordinary and whose self-importance and lack of realism may be exposed to ridicule. His is a *hybris* with comic rather than tragic results. The type may have descended from primitive ritual (compare the quack doctor in the English mummers' play), and it has even been suggested that he represented the Old Year, who had to be eliminated as an obstacle before the arrival of spring and the triumph of the new generation.

2. Title of the Greek play on which Plautus' *Miles Gloriosus* was based. The author is unknown.

Alcaeus (Gk. **Alkaios**). 1. *Myth.* Son of Perseus, father of Amphitryon, and grandfather of Heracles.

2. Lyric poet of Lesbos (late 7th to early 6th century B.C.). Alcaeus was a friend of Sappho and deeply involved in the political turmoils of his island. Only fragments of his work survive.

3. Writer of Old Comedy (fl. c. 400 B.C.). Alcaeus' *Pasiphaë* appeared in 388 B.C. Of about ten titles known, almost all, except *The Comedotragedy* and *Sisters in Adultery*, suggest parodies of myth.

Alcestis (Gk. **Alkestis**). *Myth.* Daughter of Pelias, king of Iolcus. Alcestis' father refused to give her to any suitor who could not yoke a lion and a wild boar to a chariot. With Apollo's help Admetus was able to do this. Alcestis' story after her marriage to Admetus is told in Euripides' *Alcestis*.

Alcestis (Gk. **Alkestis**). Extant play by Euripides (produced in 438 B.C.). *Alcestis* formed the afterpiece (thus taking the place of a satyr play) of the trilogy *The Cretan Women, Alcmeon in Psophis,* and *Telephus.* This tetralogy won second prize, an unknown tetralogy by Sophocles taking first. Translations: Arthur S. Way, 1912; Richard Aldington, 1930; Augustus T. Murray, 1931; D. W. Lucas, 1951; Philip Vellacott, 1953; Richmond Lattimore, 1955; Alistair Elliott, 1965. Adaptations and works influenced by *Alcestis:* Hans Sachs, *Alcestis,* 1531; Alexandre Hardy, *Alceste,* 1602; Philippe Quinault, *Alceste* (opera), 1674; Handel, *Admeto,* 1727; Gluck, *Alceste,* 1767; Vittorio Alfieri, *Alceste Seconda,* 1798; Johann Gottfried von Herder, *Admetus' Haus,* 1803; Robert Browning, *Balaustion's Adventure,* 1871.

S C E N E. Pherae, the palace.

S U M M A R Y. Apollo speaks the prologue: In revenge for the death of his son Asclepius, killed by Zeus's lightning blast, Apollo killed the Cyclopes, who had fashioned the thunderbolts. For this act Zeus forced Apollo to become a shepherd in the service of King Admetus. Finding Admetus a pious man, Apollo tricked the Fates into promising that when Admetus' day came to die, he might escape if he found a willing substitute. Such a substitute, however, no one would consent to be, except his wife Alcestis.

Thanatos (Death) approaches to claim Alcestis and, paying little attention to Apollo's scornful and threatening words, disappears into the palace and Apollo vanishes. The people of Pherae ask after the queen, and a Servant Girl tells them of Alcestis' preparations for death, her leave-taking of marriage bed, attendants, and husband. The long farewell continues as Admetus and Alcestis come on the scene. On his wife's request that he not marry again, Admetus promises to remain a widower, mourning her for the rest of her life. He declares that he will have an image made of Alcestis which he can embrace now and then. Alcestis dies and is borne away.

Into the ensuing scene of grief bursts Heracles, who is engaged in his labor of fetching King Diomedes' man-eating horses. Seeing the melancholy of the household, Heracles begs Admetus to let him go on his way; Admetus, however, forces his guest to partake of his hospitality. While Heracles is inside, Pheres, Admetus' father, comes with offerings for the funeral, but Admetus taunts him for his cowardice in refusing to be the substitute in death. Pheres retorts that Admetus himself is a coward and virtually his wife's murderer.

The funeral procession leaves and a Servant enters the empty stage, complaining of Heracles' boisterous behavior. Shortly afterward Heracles appears and extracts from the Servant the information that it is the mistress of the household who has died. Dismayed, Heracles goes off to wrest Alcestis from Death. Admetus returns from the obsequies, beginning to realize the magnitude of his loss and the worthlessness of his life. Presently Heracles returns with a veiled woman, whom he claims to have won as a prize in athletic games. He asks Admetus to keep her while he is away. The king is strongly opposed to keeping the woman, but finally, and with reluctance, Admetus takes her by the hand. At this, Heracles throws back her veil, revealing Alcestis; he tells how he wrestled with Death and overcame him. As husband and wife embrace, Heracles speeds on his way.

COMMENTARY. There is no getting around it: the character of Admetus in this play has been a scandal and an embarrassment to critics and adapters alike ever since the Renaissance. It is difficult to imagine how the play could have caught on even with a Greek audience. That it was a substitute for a satyr play is surprising enough; that Heracles is the stock comic figure here that he always was in comedy and satyr play confirms one's impression that some kind of joke was intended—but it seems a very sorry joke, and the more comic individual effects that one notes, the more jarring is the effect of the whole.

There is no doubt that the character of Alcestis is the reason for which readers, critics, and revisionists return to the play again and again. Few figures in literature are nobler or more memorable. This seems to render her husband all the less heroic, excuse him how we may: his too-late regrets convict him of an insensitivity almost as contemptible as his previous lack of chivalry. As for the scene where Admetus quarrels with his father, critics have usually been struck speechless regarding it. Perhaps the best thing to do would be to put Admetus into a coma before the action, as some of the eighteenth-century adapters did. In this way we would probably get a lesser drama but a more understandable one. No critic yet—and the play evokes several essays a year—has shown that he understood what Euripides was trying to do.

Alcibiades (Gk.**Alkibiades**). Athenian politician, general, and prototype of gilded youth (c. 450–404 B.C.). Alcibiades was a nephew of Pericles and an admirer of Socrates. He was chiefly responsible for the ill-fated Sicilian expedition, from command of which he was recalled to stand trial for having mutilated the herms of Athens and profaned the Eleusinian mysteries. Considering this treatment unjust, Alcibiades deserted to Sparta and then went over to Persia.

He returned to Athens, however, in 411 B.C. and won several naval victories. Exiled again in 406, he was murdered by the Persians, who were prompted by his enemies in Greece.

Alcides. Epithet of Heracles meaning "descendant of Alcaeus." (See ALCAEUS 1.)

Alcmena (Gk. **Alkmene**). *Myth.* Daughter of Electrus, or Electryon, and virtuous wife of AMPHITRYON. Alcmena became mother of Heracles by Zeus, who deceptively took the form of her husband and made love to her throughout a night that he prolonged beyond its normal span. She is a principal character in Plautus' *Amphitryon* and appears as an old woman in Euripides' *Heraclidae* and Seneca's *Hercules on Oeta*.

Only one word survives of a lost play by Aeschylus called *Alcmena*. Euripides' lost play of the same name apparently dealt with Zeus's deception. In it there was a well-known scene in which Amphitryon, on his return, is about to burn the wife whom he regards as faithless. His act is prevented by Zeus, who sends a sudden storm. A character in Plautus' *Rudens* (line 86) says: "That wasn't a wind; it was a regular Euripides' *Alcmena*."

Alcmeon or **Alcmaeon** (Gk. **Alkmaion**). *Myth.* Son of AMPHIARAUS and ERIPHYLE. To avenge his father's death in the expedition of the Seven against Thebes, Alcmeon led the EPIGONI on a second campaign, which was successful. He then killed his mother, whose greed had caused Amphiaraus' death. Pursued by the Erinyes, Alcmeon first took refuge at Psophis, where he married the princess Arsinoë (or Alphesiboea). He gave her Eriphyle's notorious necklace and robe.

The land becoming barren on account of his matricide, Alcmeon went to Delphi and was told by the oracle that he must settle in a land that had not existed when his mother died. He slipped away to the newly formed delta of Achelous, where the river god purified him and gave him his daughter Callirhoë in marriage. But Callirhoë coveted the necklace and robe, and so Alcmeon returned to Psophis and got possession of them, pretending that he had to dedicate them at Delphi. Arsinoë's brothers learned the truth, however, and murdered Alcmeon. When Arsinoë protested the killing, they shut her in a chest and sold her into slavery; or, judging from a fragment of one of Accius' works, they shut her in a cave. (See also ALCMEON IN CORINTH.)

Alcmeon was the title of a lost play by Sophocles. It is not known which part of the hero's adventures it dealt with.

Alcmeon in Corinth. Lost play by Euripides. It was produced posthumously in 406 B.C. with *Iphigenia in Aulis* and the *Bacchae*. *Alcmeon in Corinth* told how the hero, driven mad after killing his mother, had two children by Manto, daughter of Tiresias. These two, Amphilochus and Tisiphone, were left with Creon of Corinth to rear. But as the years went by, Creon's wife grew jealous of Tisiphone's beauty and sold her as a slave to her own unsuspecting father, Alcmeon. Recognition took place when Alcmeon went to Corinth to recover his children: Amphilochus identified the slave girl as his sister.

Alcmeon in Psophis. Lost play by Euripides. It dealt with the hero's return to Psophis and his death (see ALCMEON). *Alcmeon in Psophis* was produced in 438 B.C. with *The Cretan Women, Telephus,* and *Alcestis.* Ennius' *Alcmeon* was perhaps based on this play.

Alcumeus. Name meaning "madman," derived from Alcmeon, whose name was a byword for insanity.

Alcyone or **Halcyone** (Gk. **Alkyone** or **Halkyone**). *Myth.* Wife of Ceyx. Alcyone and her husband, as king and queen, styled themselves Zeus and Hera. The gods punished their presumption by changing them into sea birds. To enable Alcyone to nest on the waves, it was divinely decreed that the two weeks on either side of the winter solstice would be marked by calm each year ("halcyon days").

Aleadae (Gk. **Aleadai,** "sons of Aleos"). Lost play by Sophocles. Its plot was based on one of the many stories about TELEPHUS. Auge, daughter of Aleos, had been made a priestess of Athena by her father to thwart an oracle which predicted that her son would kill Aleos' sons. Auge was nevertheless seduced by Heracles and bore Telephus, whom she exposed on a mountain. The babe was suckled by a doe and found by shepherds. Much later, after Telephus had killed the sons of Aleos and was about to kill Aleos himself, all was set straight in a scene of mutual recognition. The play may have formed part of a trilogy, the TELEPHEIA.

Aletes. *Myth.* Son of Aegisthus. On receiving the false news that Orestes and Pylades had been sacrificed in the land of the Taurians, Aletes seized the throne of Mycenae. Electra fled to Delphi and there came upon Iphigenia, who was pointed out to her as the priestess who had performed the sacrifice. Snatching a brand from the altar, Electra was about to attack her long-lost and unrecognized sister when Orestes entered and made them known to each other. They then formed a plot to go to Mycenae, and there Orestes killed Aletes. A lost play by Sophocles called *Aletes* was based on this myth.

Alexander (Gk. **Alexandros**). 1. *Myth.* Name given to PARIS by shepherds as meaning "the protected man." While Queen Hecuba of Troy was pregnant with Paris, she dreamed that she had given birth to a firebrand. This dream was taken to indicate that the child would ruin his country, and so he was exposed on Mount Ida. There he was found and reared by shepherds. Many years later, when games were held in Troy to commemorate the infant's supposed death and Alexander's fine bull was requisitioned as a prize, the indignant young shepherd entered the contests and won them all. Hector and Deiphobus, feeling their honor offended, pursued Alexander to the altar of Zeus, where the prophetess Cassandra revealed that he was Paris, their long-lost brother. Paris was thereupon welcomed into the palace as a prince of Troy.

Lost plays by Sophocles and Euripides entitled *Alexander* were based on the foregoing myth. Euripides' play was produced with *Palamedes* and *The Trojan Women* in 415 B.C. Ennius' lost *Alexander* was probably modeled on that of Euripides.

2. Alexander the Great. King of Macedonia (356–323 B.C.). Alexander became King in 336 B.C. He conquered the Persian empire, his invasion beginning in 334 B.C.

3. Tyrant of Pherae from 369 to 358 B.C. Alexander was murdered by his brother-in-law. His name became a byword for cruelty and despotism.

4. Alexander the Aetolian. Critic, writer of tragedies, and member of the Alexandrian PLEIAD (born c. 315 B.C.). He went to Alexandria and became an official in its famous library, occupying himself chiefly with scholarly work on the drama. Alexander wrote in both scholarly and literary fields. His plays include *Antigone* (possibly) and *The Players at Knucklebones*, the latter dealing with Patroclus' early life. Alexander was a friend of Theocritus, and may appear as Tityrus in one or more of Theocritus' *Idyls*.

Alexeterios (Gk. "defender"). Epithet of Zeus as protector of Thebes.

Alexis. Perhaps the most important writer of Middle Comedy (c. 370–c. 270 B.C.). Alexis' long life lasted well into the period of New Comedy. Born at Thurii, he came early to Athens. Menander, a native Athenian, was one of his relatives, probably a nephew. Alexis wrote 245 plays, of which fragments and 130 titles survive; a few of these were adapted from plays by Antiphanes. Although he parodied mythical stories, Alexis did not often burlesque tragedy. He seems to have been chiefly responsible for the large role played by parasites in comedy.

Many titles of Alexis' plays were typical of Middle and New Comedy. Examples are: *The Nurse, The Heiress, The Deceiver, The Lyre-Player, The Changeling*, as well as the usual *The Girl from* series (supply *Athens, Achaea, Olynthus, Cnidus*, etc.); others are names of professions, courtesans, and mythical characters. Such titles as *The Wall-Eyed Man, The Trick Rider, The School for Debauchees, The Matriarchy, Drummed Out of the Service, The Woman Drugged with Mandrake,* and *Odysseus the Weaver* are more unusual. Alexis' works were well known to the Romans. Caecilius apparently adapted *The Exile, The Letter* and *The Syracusans*.

Alimus. See HALIMUS.

Alis. See ELIS.

Aloadae. *Myth.* Otus and Ephialtes, giant sons of Iphimedia and Poseidon. (See OSSA.)

Alope. *Myth.* Daughter of Cercyon, robber king of Eleusis. By Poseidon Alope had a son, whom she exposed; he was, however, suckled by a mare and discovered by shepherds. From them Cercyon learned of his daughter's transgression and was about to put her to death when Theseus arrived on the scene and killed him. *Alope* was the title of a play by Euripides based on the foregoing myth. In one scene the shepherds who discovered the child quarreled over his clothes. This scene was imitated by Menander in *The Arbitrants*.

Alphesiboea. *Myth.* Wife of ALCMAEON.

Alpheus or **Alpheius** (Gk. **Alpheios**). **1.** River of the western Peloponnesus. On its banks was Olympia.

2. *Myth.* The god of the above river. Alpheus fell in love with the nymph Arethusa and pursued her under the sea to an island in the harbor of Syracuse, where he mingled his waters with hers.

altars. The orchestra, or dance place, of the Greek theater contained an altar (see THYMELE) sacred to Dionysus; it was often the focus of the chorus' movements. There was also an altar forming a permanent fixture on the stage. It was sometimes regarded as sacred to Apollo Aguieus and used for his worship, sometimes regarded as sacred to another god appropriate to the play, sometimes —perhaps—used as a tomb, and sometimes ignored.

Althaea (Gk. **Althaia**). *Myth.* Queen of Calydon and mother of Deianira and Meleager. For the story of how Althaea caused her son to die, see MELEAGER.

Amazons. *Myth.* Race of warrior women. Thought by some to be cannibalistic, the Amazons were always represented as fierce manhaters. They were located vaguely in the north or the east, in Colchis or on the banks of the Thermodon. They were skilled at archery and used crescent-shaped shields. The Amazons' main exploits concerned the Trojan War and their invasion of Attica; the chief heroes with whom they dealt were Heracles, Theseus, and Achilles.

Ambivius Turpio, Lucius. Noted Roman actor and producer (2nd century B.C.). In his old age, Turpio appeared in the premieres of all of Terence's plays. As a character, he speaks the prologue of Terence's *Self-tormentor,* as well as that added to a later production of *The Mother-in-Law.* In the latter play Turpio tells the audience that he formerly made Caecilius' plays popular after much opposition and is determined to do the same for those of Terence.

Ambracia (Gk. **Ambrakia**). City in Epirus, capital of King Pyrrhus.

ambrosia (Gk. "immortality"). Food of the gods. Ambrosia conferred youth and immortality on those partaking of it.

Ameipsias. Writer of Old Comedy (later 5th century B.C.). Of Ameipsias' works seven titles and a few fragments remain. His *Connus* (Gk. *Konnos,* 423 B.C.) was named after a music teacher. The chorus consisted of Connus' pupils, who were all Sophists, the chief of them being Socrates, who was satirized in much the same way as in Aristophanes' *Clouds.* Other titles of Ameipsias' plays were *The Last Throw at Cottabus, The Glutton, The Adulterers, The Sling,* and *Sappho.* His *Roisterers* (Gk. *Komastai*) won first place over Aristophanes' *Birds* in 414 B.C. Ameipsias was said to have remarked of Aristophanes' custom of producing plays under other men's names that this showed he was born to be a slave and to work for others. Aristophanes accordingly scored off Ameipsias' vulgar type of humor in *The Frogs* (line 14).

Ammon. The Egyptian god Amon. He was regarded, during the great imperial period of Egyptian history, as king of the gods and was consequently identified by the Greeks with their Zeus. Ammon's oracle in the Libyan desert near Cyrene was famous throughout the Greek world.

Amor (Lat. "love"). CUPID.

Amorgus (Gk. **Amorgos**). Small island in the south-central Aegean Sea, southeast of Naxos.

Amphanae (Gk. **Amphanai**). City on the coast of Thessaly.

Amphiaraus (Gk. **Amphiaraos** or **Amphiareos**). *Myth.* Prophet and warrior. Amphiaraus quarreled with his cousin Adrastus but married the latter's sister Eriphyle, swearing to abide by her decision in any later disagreement. When Adrastus planned the expedition of the Seven against Thebes, Amphiaraus was asked to be one of the Seven. At first he refused, foreseeing the failure of the expedition and his own death. But Adrastus (or, some say, Polyneices) bribed Eriphyle with the necklace and robe of HARMONIA, and she accordingly pronounced her decision in favor of her husband's going. Amphiaraus, on setting out, made his sons swear to avenge him on Eriphyle. In the rout that followed the defeat of the Seven, Zeus sent a thunderbolt that opened a chasm on the banks of the river Ismenus, and Amphiaraus plunged in, chariot and all.

Amphiaraus was the title of a lost satyr play by Sophocles. It may have shown the hero hiding in his house to avoid going on the campaign, having posted satyrs as lookouts. At some point an illiterate character managed to convey a message by dancing the shape of its letters. A lost comedy by Aristophanes, also called *Amphiaraus,* was produced at the Lenaea of 414 B.C. under the name of a friend, Philonides. The play seems to have had something to do with the famous shrine of Amphiaraus, located at the scene of his supposed engulfment. This shrine was the gathering place of a healing cult, whose ceremonies involved sleeping in the temple and having dreams interpreted by an oracle. The comedy's plot may have included the rejuvenation of an old man at the shrine.

Amphion. *Myth.* Son of Antiope, by Zeus, and twin brother of Zethus. (For Amphion's early life, see ANTIOPE 2). He was a miraculous musician: at his playing, stones leaped into place to form the walls of Thebes. Amphion eventually became the husband of Niobe and father of her ill-fated children. He, like his sons, was killed by Apollo.

Amphis or **Amphias.** Writer of Middle Comedy (second half of 4th century B.C.). Of Amphis' works only fragments and titles remain; they show the usual range of Middle Comedy. Most interesting of his plays must have been *Opora* (perhaps, however, the work of Alexis). In it Sirius, the Dog Star, rejected by Opora, the harvest season, burned earth so badly that Boreas, the north wind, had to send his sons to force Opora to yield to Sirius' advances.

Amphitrite. *Myth.* One of the chief Greek sea goddesses. Amphitrite was the wife of Poseidon.

Amphitryon. *Myth.* Son of Alcaeus, king of Tiryns. By accident Amphitryon killed Electryon, father of ALCMENA, whom he loved. He consequently had to retire to Thebes, where he was purified of guilt by King Creon. Alcmena stipulated as a condition of marriage that Amphitryon take vengeance on the Teleboans, who had killed her brothers. He accordingly set out on this campaign after their wedding, leaving his wife pregnant. While Amphitryon was gone, Zeus took his form, wooed Alcmena, and begot Heracles, who was nevertheless often called Amphitryonides, "son of Amphitryon." Heracles' twin brother, Amphitryon's real son, was named Iphicles.

Amphitryon appears as an old man in Euripides' *Heracles* and Seneca's *Hercules Furens.* He was the titular hero of a lost play by Sophocles which probably dealt with Zeus's deception. In it Amphitryon apparently learned of his wife's extramarital affair from Tiresias. An extant play by Plautus is also entitled *Amphitryon.*

Amphitryon (Lat. **Amphitruo**). Extant comedy by Plautus (variously dated from 215 to 186 B.C.). *Amphitryon* was based on an unknown Greek play. Translations: Bonnell Thornton, 1769–1774; Henry T. Riley, 1852; Edward H. Sugden, 1893; Robert Allison, 1914; Paul Nixon, 1916; Lionel Casson, 1963; E. F. Watling, 1964. Adaptations: Thomas Heywood, *The Silver Age,* 1612; Jean de Rotrou, *Les Sosies,* 1638; Molière, *Amphitryon,* 1668; John Dryden, *Amphitryon,* 1690; Heinrich von Kleist, *Amphitryon,* 1807; Jean Giraudoux, *Amphitryon 38,* 1929.

S C E N E. Thebes, a street.

S U M M A R Y. In the prologue, Mercury informs the audience that they had better behave well if they want him to favor their business. He proceeds to unfold the dramatic situation: Amphitryon, an Argive hero, is off at war, leaving behind his pregnant wife, Alcmena. Jupiter, desiring Alcmena for himself, has put on the appearance of Amphitryon and is even now lying in her arms, having prolonged his night of ecstasy and gotten her with a second child. Mercury, as lookout, has taken on the guise of Sosia, Amphitryon's slave. To distinguish himself from his counterpart, Mercury wears a golden tassel.

Sosia comes up from the harbor to bring news of victory, but Mercury bars him from entering the house and beats him. The slave goes away in bewilderment, having been persuaded by Mercury's looks and his knowledge of Sosia's secret actions that Mercury is the real Sosia.

Alcmena finally emerges with Jupiter, who says that he must go back to his troops; he gives her the golden drinking bowl that he supposedly won from the enemy king and departs. At once the real Amphitryon appears, indignantly listening to Sosia's tale of how he was beaten by himself and kept out of the house by himself. Amphitryon's anger is increased when Alcmena answers his greeting by pointing out that he spent the night just past with her. To prove it, she produces the golden bowl, and when Amphitryon in turn unseals the chest in which he was bringing the selfsame gift, it turns out to be empty. He goes to fetch Alcmena's kinsman Naucrates to substantiate the story that he has been away for ten months and has spent the night on shipboard. In the meantime, Jupiter-Amphitryon returns and convinces Alcmena and Sosia that his former suspicions of Alcmena were only a test and a joke. On his exit, the real Amphitryon appears, only to be insolently refused entrance by Mercury-Sosia.

In the lacuna that follows this scene, the real Sosia probably gets beaten by Amphitryon for his supposed insolence, and Amphitryon is probably confronted by his double, Jupiter-Amphitryon, who, leaving the husband in despair, re-enters the house to assist in Alcmena's childbirth.

An old Maidservant comes out to describe her mistress's labor: twin boys have been born to the accompaniment of thunder and lightning. Raising Amphitryon, who has been flattened by the thunderbolt, the Servant tells him how two serpents, creeping toward the babies' cradle, were strangled by the stronger of the twins, at which Jupiter's voice from the sky proclaimed that he was this child's father. The much-chastened Amphitryon is about to go to consult the soothsayer Tiresias when he is stopped by a vision of Jupiter in all his glory. The god explains all and Amphitryon reverently acquiesces in the situation.

COMMENTARY. There are dozens and dozens of Middle Comedy (and even Old Comedy) play titles that were obviously parodies of myth.

Amphitryon is the only surviving instance of a parody of this kind, but it is impossible to say whether the unknown Greek original came from the period of Middle Comedy. Some have thought not, on the ground that much of the plotting and atmosphere is that of New Comedy. This argument is, however, questionable: after all, almost nothing exists of Middle Comedy, and so it is not known how far later specimens of it may have gone in the transition to New Comedy.

The undeniable thing is that *Amphitryon* is unique. Mercury, speaking the prologue, calls the play a tragicomedy, since kings and gods are not proper characters for comedy, nor slaves proper for tragedy. Critics have always ranked it high among Plautus' works, admiring especially the comic scene between Mercury and Sosia and the consistent nobility in the portrait of Alcmena.

Amyclae (Gk. **Amyklai**). Town in Laconia south of Sparta. Amyclae was famous for its sanctuary of Apollo.

Amycus (Gk. **Amykos**). *Myth.* Giant king of the Bebrycians in Bithynia. Challenging all strangers to box, Amycus defeated and killed every one. When the Argonauts landed, he was overcome by Polydeuces. *Amycus* was the title of a lost satyr play by Sophocles, which was based on this myth.

Amymone. *Myth.* One of the DANAÏDES. Poseidon, jealous of the Argives' devotion to Hera, had dried up all the springs in the land. When Danaüs arrived in Argos, he sent his daughters, among them Amymone, to look for food and water. Chasing a deer, Amymone threw a javelin and hit a sleeping satyr, who awakened and tried to rape her. Poseidon came to the maiden's rescue and then made love to her himself, after which he pointed out to her the spring of Lerna. The result of Amymone's union with the god was Nauplius.

A lost satyr play by Aeschylus called *Amymone* was based on the foregoing myth. It formed the conclusion of the DANAÏD TETRALOGY.

Amynias. An impoverished but dandified and effeminate informer, gambler, and moneylender of Aristophanes' time.

Amynon. An orator, mocked by Aristophanes for effeminacy.

Amynus (Gk. **Amynos**, "the averter"). *Myth.* Athenian hero-physician, in whose cult Sophocles was honored after death.

Anacreon (Gk. **Anakreon**). Lyric poet of Teos (fl. 6th century B.C.). Anacreon was famous for short love poems and drinking songs. In later classical times a number of trifles of this kind, called "Anacreontics," were falsely attributed to him.

Anactorium (Gk. **Anaktorion**). City on the coast of Acarnania.

anagnorisis (Gk. "recognition"). Anagnorisis, as defined by Aristotle in the POETICS, denotes the discovery of the true identity of a character in drama, for example, the recognition of Orestes by Electra in *Choephori* or the establishment of the courtesan heroine as a freeborn Athenian in New Comedy. Some modern critics have interpreted anagnorisis in a wider sense: the recognition by a character of his own or another's true condition or of the true meaning of his actions, for example, Oedipus' gradual self-recognition in *Oedipus the King*.

Anagyra. Attic deme. (See also ANAGYRUS.)

Anagyrus (Gk. **Anagyros**). *Myth.* Hero-patron of the deme Anagyra, where there were a grove and altar sacred to him. According to legend, a farmer once desecrated the place. The farmer's punishment began when his second wife fell in love with her stepson. The boy repulsed his stepmother and she denounced him for attempted seduction, whereupon the father blinded his son. When the truth came out, the farmer hanged (or burned) himself, and his wife drowned herself in a well. A slough (some say a malodorous plant) in the Attic deme was called Anagyrus. When stirred up, it emitted a bad smell. "To stir up anagyrus" came to mean "to raise a stink," or "not to let sleeping dogs lie." *Anagyrus* was the title of a lost comedy by Aristophanes.

Anagyrus (Gk. **Anagyros**). Lost comedy by Aristophanes. It has been suggested that the play was produced in 399 B.C. The matter of the profanation of the Eleusinian mysteries of 415 was revived in 399 (compare Andocides' *On the Mysteries*). Accordingly, the legend of Anagyrus (see preceding entry) would have provided the framework for Aristophanes' play: the farmer representing Demos (a personification of the Athenian citizenry), the stirring-up of the smelly slough representing the profanation, and the subsequent misfortunes representing the disastrous Sicilian expedition. But perhaps the play was a warning against stirring up such a smelly business after so long a time.

Some scholars think that *Anagyrus* was written between 419 and 412 B.C. Fragments from it show that Aristophanes was carrying on a running feud with Eupolis, whom he accused of snipping up one of his plays and making three out of it. According to some ancient sources, Aristophanes' comedy was a parody of Euripides' *Phoenix,* which used a myth closely paralleling that of Aristophanes' hero Anagyrus.

Ananke (Gk. "necessity"). Personification of necessity or destiny.

Anaphlystia. Attic deme. In *Ecclesiazusae* (line 979) Aristophanes puns on the name to suggest *anaphlan,* "to masturbate."

anapiesma (Gk. "something pressed upward"). A kind of stage device by which persons were made to appear on the scene from below, as if from the depths of the earth.

Anaurus (Gk. **Anauros**). Small stream on the Magnesian peninsula in Thessaly. Jason lost a sandal in crossing the Anaurus when it was flooded.

Anaxandrides. Writer of Middle Comedy (middle 4th century B.C.). Although he was not a native Athenian, Anaxandrides won at least ten first prizes for drama in that city. He was said to have been the first to make love affairs and seductions common elements of plot. Handsome and dandified, he was so vain and irritable that if one of his plays did not win a prize, he either burned the manuscript or gave it to shopkeepers for wrapping paper. Anaxandrides once rode a horse into the theater and recited a dithyramb. Politically he was a supporter of Philip of Macedon.

Many of the thirty-odd surviving titles of Anaxandrides' plays are of myth parodies and names of professions and nationalities. More interesting are *An Old Man's Madness; The Cities*, in which Egypt and Demos were characters; and *Lycurgus*, which was probably a satire of the theater reformer LYCURGUS (4), using the myth of LYCURGUS (1), the defier of Dionysus.

Anaxilas. Writer of Middle Comedy (4th century B.C.). Anaxilas ridiculed the philosopher Plato in several plays, among them *Circe* and *The Rich Women*. Other representative titles by Anaxilas are *The Chicken, The Cooks, The Misanthropist, The Pimp,* and *The Men's Beauty Contest.*

Ancaeus (Gk. Ankaios). *Myth.* Hero of Arcadia and an Argonaut. Ancaeus was one of the hunters of the Calydonian boar, by which he was killed. (See MELEAGER.)

Andria (Lat. **The Girl from Andros** or **The Woman of Andros**). Extant comedy by Terence. *Andria* was produced at the Megalensian Games of 166 B.C. under the management of Lucius Ambivius Turpio. It was based on two Greek plays, *Andria* and *Perinthia,* by Menander. This was Terence's first play. Translations: John Sargeaunt, 1912; W. Ritchie, 1927; F. Perry, 1929; Frank O. Copley, 1949; Robert Graves and Laurence Echard, 1962. Adaptations and works influenced by *Andria:* Richard Steele, *The Conscious Lovers,* 1722; Thornton Wilder, *The Woman of Andros* (novel), 1930.

S C E N E. Athens, a street.

S U M M A R Y. Terence uses the prologue, as he himself says, not for the traditional purpose of explicating the plot, but in order to answer the criticisms of rivals. An old playwright, Luscius Lanuvinus, has charged that Terence is guilty of "contamination" in combining Menander's *Andria* and *Perinthia* into one Latin play. Terence appeals to the precedents of Ennius, Naevius, and Plautus and says that he prefers to emulate their negligence rather than the purism of his critics.

Simo has engaged his son Pamphilus to marry Philumena, the daughter of Chremes. For a time he had thought the marriage blocked by Pamphilus' involvement with Chrysis, a woman who had moved to Athens from Andros and had slipped into harlotry under pressure of poverty. Simo's relief at learning that there was no real involvement has been ruined by Pamphilus' behavior at Chrysis' recent funeral where the young man rescued Glycerium, Chrysis' reputed sister, from falling into the flames of the funeral pyre in her distraction and grief. No spectator could remain unaware of the love between Pamphilus and Glycerium. Actually Pamphilus regards Glycerium as his wife, since she is about to bear his child. To make their alliance respectable, the pair have concocted a dubious tale that Glycerium is really the daughter of an Athenian.

Chremes is indignant over this state of affairs. Davus, Pamphilus' slave, thinking that Chremes will now refuse to hand over his daughter Philumena, advises Pamphilus to please his father by consenting to the marriage. Unfortunately, Simo manages to subdue Chremes' opposition, and Pamphilus finds himself a traitor, not only to Glycerium, but to his friend Charinus, who is in love with Philumena. To arouse Chremes' wrath again, Davus arranges to have the baby that Glycerium has just borne placed on Pamphilus' doorstep.

Once more Simo is soothing Chremes, convincing him that it is all a plot of Glycerium and Davus, when a stranger from Andros arrives. The stranger tells a story of how an Athenian, Phania, was long ago shipwrecked on Andros with his brother's small daughter Pasibula, and how after Phania's death the girl was reared by Chrysis and grew up to be Glycerium.

Since Phania was Chremes' brother, all is now resolved. Glycerium, as Chremes' daughter, may now marry Pamphilus, and Charinus may have Philumena. (There is an alternative ending, about a page long. Although it does not materially alter the plot, it has given rise to much scholarly discussion.)

COMMENTARY. With *Andria* Terence reveals, at the outset of his career, his interest in plot-making—in fact, in double-plot-making. The doubling here is, however, not as well integrated as it was to be in later efforts. Particularly admired by critics are the clever new turns given to well-worn situations: it is the *senex* here who is *dolosus,* while the *servus* is about as inept as an intriguer can be (see SENEX and SERVUS).

Androcles (Gk. **Androkles**). Athenian of Aristophanes' time. Androcles was a parasite, satirized in *The Wasps* (line 1187) for his effeminacy and vulgarity.

Andromache. *Myth.* Wife of Hector. During the Trojan War Andromache's father, brothers, and husband were all killed by Achilles. In Euripides' and Seneca's plays entitled *The Trojan Women,* set immediately after the fall of Troy, Andromache plays a considerable role. Her little son Astyanax is torn from her to be thrown to his death, and she herself is taken to the ship of Neoptolemus, Achilles' son, as part of the booty. According to the myth, Andromache was carried to Epirus or Phthia, where she became Neoptolemus' concubine. Her further adventures are told in Euripides' *Andromache.* She was the titular heroine of a lost tragedy by Sophocles; its exact subject is unknown.

Andromache. Extant play by Euripides (written between 430 and 424 B.C.). The scholiast on *Andromache* says that it was not produced in Athens. Translations: Edward P. Coleridge, 1891; Arthur S. Way, 1912; Hugh O. Meredith, 1937; Van L. Johnson, 1955; John Frederick Nims, 1956. Adaptation: Racine, *Andromaque,* 1667.

SCENE. Before the palace of Neoptolemus, in Phthia, Thessaly.

SUMMARY. Hermione, Helen's daughter, and her father, Menelaus, are plotting to kill the child that Andromache, the Trojan concubine of Neoptolemus, has borne; for Hermione, Neoptolemus' lawful wife, blames her own childlessness on evil spells allegedly cast by Andromache.

In the absence of Neoptolemus (who is at Delphi doing penance to Apollo for having defied the god, who had helped Paris kill his father, Achilles), Andromache has taken sanctuary at the altar of the sea goddess Thetis, Achilles' mother. She sends for help to Peleus, Achilles' aged father, who is still alive and ruling.

Hermione enters and berates Andromache for having turned Neoptolemus against her. Andromache answers that it is not witchcraft but Hermione's own arrogance that has alienated her husband. Menelaus now produces Andromache's son Molossus, who has been discovered in hiding; he asks Andromache to choose between her own life and her son's. The mother leaves the altar to save her child, but she has been tricked, and both are condemned.

Their execution is halted by Peleus' entry, and after a bitter clash of words, Menelaus announces his intention to leave the country. Hermione, abandoned by her father and fearful of her husband's anger, contemplates suicide, but is stopped by the arrival of her cousin Orestes, to whom she was originally betrothed. He is still eager for vengeance on his successful rival, Neoptolemus, and persuades Hermione to run away.

Soon a Messenger brings news that Orestes has achieved Neoptolemus' death by rousing a mob of Delphians with a false rumor that Neoptolemus has come to plunder Apollo's oracular sanctuary. The body of the prince is brought in, but the ensuing lamentations are interrupted by Thetis, who appears from above. She foretells that Andromache will marry Helenus, Hector's brother, and that Molossus will found a dynasty of Molossian kings. The aged Peleus is instructed to bury the body of Neoptolemus at Delphi and then to join Thetis, his erstwhile bride, in the depths of the sea, where he will become a god.

C O M M E N T A R Y. An anonymous ancient commentator, whose words are preserved in the manuscripts of the play, says, in effect: "Some parts are good, and some parts are not bad, but the whole is unremarkable." Modern critics agree, most of them pointing out that there is a serious lack of unity in what amounts to a succession of melodramatic themes. One of the chief characters, Neoptolemus, never appears except as a corpse, and the other "hero," Orestes, is little better than contemptible. Perhaps the chief feature of the work is its anti-Spartanism—natural in the first years of the Peloponnesian War—particularly the disgust for Spartan perfidy that is embodied in the characters of Menelaus and Hermione.

Andromeda (Gk. **Andromede**). *Myth.* Daughter of Cepheus and Cassiopeia, king and queen of Ethiopia. Because Cassiopeia boasted that she was more beautiful than the Nereids, Poseidon sent a monster out of the sea to ravage the land. The oracle pronounced Andromeda to be the only fitting propitiation, and so Cepheus chained her to a rock to await the monster. When Perseus flew by, after having killed the Gorgon, he saw Andromeda and fell in love with her. On receiving Cepheus' promise of the maiden as his bride, Perseus killed the monster with his sword or turned it to stone with the Gorgon's head. Cepheus' brother Phineus, who had been betrothed to Andromeda, plotted to rid himself of his rival, but Perseus discovered the conspiracy and turned Phineus and his confederates into stone by showing them the Gorgon's head.

Andromeda was the titular heroine of lost plays by Sophocles and Euripides.

Andromeda (Gk. **Andromede**). Lost play by Euripides (produced in 412 B.C.). It began with a famous scene in which Andromeda, chained to the rock, lamented her fate, the last word of each of her lines being repeated by Echo. (This scene is burlesqued in Aristophanes' *Thesmophoriazusae*, line 411 ff., where Euripides echoes the captive Mnesilochus.) Later on in the play, Cepheus went back on his promise to betroth his daughter to Perseus; the issue was, however, probably decided at the appearance of Athena, who promised all of the family immortality among the stars. Euripides' *Andromeda* completely eclipsed Sophocles' play of the same name; it was the model for plays by Livius Andronicus, Ennius, and possibly Accius.

Andromeda (Gk. **Andromede**). Lost play by Sophocles (produced sometime before 412 B.C.). It was based on the myth of Andromeda. After the maiden's rescue, Phineus (or Agenor), an effeminate Oriental prince and former suitor of Andromeda, led an armed attack to keep her from Perseus, but he and his retinue were turned to stone by the Gorgon's head. Accius may have modeled his Roman play *Andromeda* on Sophocles' drama.

Andronicus. 1. See LIVIUS ANDRONICUS, LUCIUS.

2. (Gk. **Andronikos**). Actor (fl. 3rd century B.C.). Andronicus was said to have given the orator Demosthenes lessons in acting techniques.

Andros. Aegean island directly east of Attica and southeast of Euboea.

angelos. See MESSENGER.

angiportum or **angiportus.** It was once thought that the *angiportum* was a passageway, representing an alley, that ran between the two permanent house fronts on the Roman stage. Scholars now tend to doubt that such a passageway was ever a part of the stage set. They conclude that *angiportum* simply meant a street of any kind and that the two Roman stage houses were adjoining.

Angry Old Man, The. See DYSKOLOS.

Animula. Small, poor town in Apulia, Italy.

Antaeus (Gk. **Antaios,** "adversary"). *Myth.* Libyan giant who compelled all strangers to wrestle to the death with him. Heracles, discovering that Antaeus drew fresh strength from the earth whenever he was thrown, held the giant up above his shoulders and strangled him.

Antenor. *Myth.* A Trojan who advocated conciliation with the Greeks during the Trojan War. Antenor and his sons were consequently spared during the sack of Troy. (See ANTENORIDAE.)

Antenoridae (Gk. **Antenoridai,** "The Sons of Antenor"). Lost play by Sophocles. *Antenoridae* told how, at the fall of Troy, the Greeks hung up a pantherskin at the door of the house of ANTENOR. This was a signal that he and his fifty sons (who probably constituted the chorus) should be spared. Later, according to myth, the whole family migrated to a new home near the Adriatic Sea.

antepirrhema. See EPIRRHEMATIC AGON.

Anthesteria. Athenian annual festival held in early March in honor of Dionysus. The three days of the Anthesteria were: the Pithoigia, breaking out the new wine; the Choes, feast of jugs, when the new wine was drunk; and the Chytroi, feast of pots, when cooked fruits were presented to the dead. There was no drama at this festival. Two features were a ritual marriage between the priest-king and priestess-queen and a mystery rite held at night in the old temple of Dionysus at Limnae, a swampy part of Athens. The latter rite is burlesqued by the chorus in Aristophanes' *Frogs* (line 215 ff.).

Antigone. *Myth.* Daughter of Oedipus and Jocasta. Antigone was the sister of Ismene, Eteocles, and Polyneices. She appears with Ismene as a mute character at the end of Sophocles' *Oedipus the King*, where Oedipus, disgraced and blinded, takes leave of the young girls. In Seneca's *Phoenician Women*, Antigone plays an important role at Thebes during its siege by the Seven. Her part in Euripides' *Phoenician Women* is similar; at the play's end, however, she goes out to accompany her blind father in his wandering as an exile. In Sophocles' *Oedipus at Colonus* Antigone is again her father's companion, though in this play Oedipus is about to disappear from earth and the expedition of the Seven is only being prepared. At the close of Aeschylus' *Seven Against Thebes*, Antigone threatens to defy Creon's decree that Polyneices' body must not be buried; this is the theme of Sophocles' drama in which Antigone takes the title role. She was also the titular heroine of a lost play by Euripides. (See the entries following.)

Antigone. Lost play by Euripides. It was written later than Sophocles' tragedy of the same name, and it differed radically in its ending. Haemon, in love with Antigone, seems to have helped her to bury Polyneices; the punishment of both at the play's end seems to have been prevented by the *deus ex machina*, Dionysus. Although there was an interesting clash of ideas between Creon and Antigone about tyranny, the play paled beside Sophocles' version. Even the *Antigone* of Astydamas apparently found more favor with the public.

Antigone. Extant tragedy by Sophocles (produced 442 or 441 B.C.). Translations: G. H. Palmer, 1899; Richard C. Jebb, 1904; F. Storr, 1912; Shaemas O'Sheel, 1931; Dudley Fitts and Robert Fitzgerald, 1938; Gilbert Murray, 1941; Theodore H. Banks, 1950; F. Kinchin Smith, 1950; Elizabeth Wyckoff, 1954; Paul Roche, 1958; C. W. E. Peckett, 1958; H. D. F. Kitto, 1962. Adaptations and works influenced by *Antigone*: Jean de Rotrou, *Antigone*, 1638; Racine, *La Thébaïde*, 1663; Vittorio Alfieri, *Antigone*, 1782; Houston Stewart Chamberlain, *Der Tod der Antigone*, 1917; Jean Anouilh, *Antigone*, 1946.

S C E N E. Thebes, the palace.

S U M M A R Y. Antigone has summoned her sister Ismene outside the palace gates to tell her of the latest calamity to befall the afflicted family of Oedipus: Of their two brothers who killed each other in the recent siege, Eteocles, defender of the city, has been placed in the earth with all due rites, whereas

Polyneices, the attacker, must, according to the edict of the new ruler, Creon, be left unwept and unburied as food for the birds. The penalty for transgressing this decree is death by stoning.

Antigone proposes that the two sisters bury Polyneices together, for it is not their uncle Creon's right to keep a person from his own family. But Ismene, begging the dead for forgiveness, cites all the past sufferings of the house; pleading her weakness as woman and as subject, she shrinks from the task, saying that she will obey those in control, "for to pass beyond the usual is to show a lack of sense." Antigone receives her sister's excuses with contempt, for she herself is resolved that it will be good to die in such an act, pleasing those who lie in death, where she herself will soon forever lie. Ismene, she says, fails to honor what the gods honor, and now, even if she wished to help, her help would not be wanted. The timid Ismene promises to keep Antigone's deed secret, but Antigone tells her to speak it out, to proclaim it to everyone. She leaves her sister bewildered and awed.

The Chorus, old men of Thebes, enter singing a song of victory, followed by Creon, whose speech emphasizes the priority of the state over private concerns. Creon repeats his decree about the treatment of Polyneices.

One of the guards who was posted over the body suddenly appears. He is hesitant and frightened, having been chosen by lot to convey the bad news that someone has strewn dust on Polyneices as a token of the burial rite. Creon is furious, and, as he is accustomed to suppose that human beings are motivated solely by desire for gain, suspects that malcontents have bribed the guard. He orders that they catch the culprit or suffer torture and death.

The Chorus, left alone, meditate on the human condition: there are many wonderful and terrible things, but nothing more wonderful and terrible than man, who is master of the waves, the earth, the birds, the beasts, speech, thought, and social life and has remedies for every ill except death. The Chorus continue, expressing their disdain for the wicked who stand outside society. Presently Antigone is led in by the Guard, who says, "She is the very one who did the deed." He describes how he and his fellows had swept away the dust from Polyneices' body and had sat through the night in watch, when a sudden whirlwind obscured the morning sun. After it had subsided, they saw this maiden, who wailed her indignation and began to pour a libation for the dead.

To Creon's questions Antigone admits that she is guilty and that she knew of the decree. To Creon's query: "And yet you dared to overstep these regulations?" she replies: "It was not Zeus or Dike [Justice] who proclaimed those laws; mortal proclamations cannot outrun the unwritten and untouched laws of the gods, which are not of now nor of yesterday, but forever, and no one knows where they emerged." It is these laws that Antigone obeys, even if her disobedience brings death. She adds: "And if I perhaps seem to you now to be acting the fool, then it is a fool, almost, that convicts me of folly."

Creon declares that Antigone must pay the full penalty, not only for her crime, but for her pride in the crime. Suspecting that Ismene is implicated, he has her brought in. Ismene claims that she helped in the burial, but Antigone denies that her sister has a right to share the credit. Creon concludes that both are insane, and his low opinion of women is confirmed. When Ismene asks whether he will put his own son's intended bride to death, Creon answers that there are other fields to plow.

After the sisters have been led away, Haemon, Antigone's betrothed, comes to plead with his father, but his appeals to reason are received by Creon with the reply that he will allow no mutiny in his household or anywhere else. Their dispute is so intense that Haemon rushes off crying that his father will never see him again, and Creon, enraged, orders that Antigone be walled up in a cave at once, with only a little food and water.

The Chorus' song to "Eros, invincible in battle," Eros that drives men mad and rules even the gods, preludes Antigone's march to her death, a kind of wedding procession with Hades as the bridegroom. Creon re-enters to hurry on the execution. In almost her last words, Antigone points out that she might not have defied the state by burying a child or a husband, who could have been replaced, but that she would never have another brother and so was justified in burying him. At her exit, the Chorus compare Antigone's fate to that of other heroines of story. At the end of their song the blind prophet Tiresias is led in and warns Creon that ill omens have revealed plainly the gods' displeasure with his actions. When Creon answers that prophets are frauds who act only from greed, Tiresias proclaims that the present pollutions will be paid for by the life of Creon's own offspring.

Deeply disturbed by Tiresias' words, the king orders his men to free Antigone and to bury Polyneices. He himself hurries off to Antigone's cave. A Messenger soon arrives, however, with news that, after Polyneices was duly buried, the cave was discovered broken into and Creon and his men found Haemon clasping Antigone, who had hanged herself. At his father's approach, Haemon rushed at him with his sword and then fell on it himself. Hearing this tale, Haemon's mother, Queen Eurydice, goes into the palace without a word. When Creon comes back contrite and broken, escorting his son's body, it is only to receive the further report that Eurydice has also killed herself. At the play's end, Creon acknowledges his guilt, realizing that his life is now no more than nothingness.

COMMENTARY. Antigone's action in repeating the burial ceremony has puzzled commentators. The second burial hardly seemed necessary, since it was no closer to being an actual interment than the first, and the first served the religious purpose adequately. Answers to the puzzle have ranged all the way from the psychological (she had a martyr complex and wanted to get caught, she was remarkably stiff-necked, and so forth) to the literary-technical (Sophocles revised the play and overlooked the resulting inconsistency, as he did also the detail about Creon's threatening death by stoning but carrying out the punishment with immurement; all authors who revise, according to this theory, revise with amazing carelessness). No solution yet offered has satisfied anyone but the proposer, nor is it any more satisfactory to say, as some do, that there is no need of an answer.

Nevertheless, this last judgment could certainly be passed on the question of whether the play belongs to Antigone or Creon; this kind of question might interest actors, but hardly critics. The opposition between Creon and Antigone is, of course, at the heart of the drama; everyone since Hegel has had his theory about it. Hegel's concept of thesis (Creon representing love of country) versus antithesis (Antigone representing love of family) is still influential. It is, however, inadequate in itself, since it results in no easily comprehensible synthesis. The use made of Hegel's theory has been unfortunate, since out of it has come a notion that tragedy results when one good principle clashes with another equally good. This is certainly not what is said by Sophocles in *Antigone;* the playwright leaves no doubt that the final verdict goes against Creon and what he represents. Yet Hegel at least performed the service of putting the discussion on a serious basis.

The confrontation of Antigone and Creon forms the scene that the playwright obviously regarded as central. But it is a mistake to say that here Creon represents love of country. His patriotism is too narrow and negative and his conception of justice is too exclusive—it does not extend to women or to foreigners—to be dignified by the name of love for the state. Creon's comprehension of order and legality is based on a system of low calculation. He considers only what is visible, palpable, and practical, and in his system of psychology every human being is motivated solely by the love of gain. Creon's vulgar notion of common-sense practicality, as opposed to what he regards as impractical idealism, is shown in the long run to be most impractical, since it is brought up short by the very real fact of death. "Man has conquered everything, but he cannot conquer death," the Chorus sing in one stasimon, and then they proceed to sing the praises of unconquerable Love.

Antigone's love, on the other hand, which the Creons of this world must necessarily look upon as bafflingly idealistic, even lunatic, is shown to be most realistic, since it takes into consideration death and the reality that may be beyond death. This thought is presented most beautifully in her final, "Bride of Death," scene.

There is, accordingly, an opposition, not between one good principle and another one equally good, but between one limited principle and another that transcends and includes it.

antikatakeleusmos. See EPIRRHEMATIC AGON.

antilabe (Gk. "interruption"). In dramatic dialogue, the division of a single line between two speakers.

Antileon. An Athenian of Aristophanes' time. Antileon was a busybody of low character.

Antilochus (Gk. **Antilochos**). *Myth.* Son of Nestor. Antilochus was killed in the Trojan War by Hector, or, according to another version of the myth, by Memnon.

Antimachus (Gk. **Antimachos**). Patron, or choregus, for Aristophanes' *The Banqueters,* which won second prize in the dramatic contest. It seems that

Antimachus offended Aristophanes by failing to invite him to the victory dinner. In retaliation the poet mocked Antimachus' effeminate manners and his habit of spraying out saliva when he talked (compare *The Acharnians,* line 1150 ff.).

Antiochus (Gk. **Antiochos**). Name of several kings of the Seleucid (or Greco-Syrian) empire, especially Antiochus III, or the Great (242–187 B.C.). The latter was defeated by the Romans.

Antiope. 1. *Myth.* An Amazon, also called Hippolyta. Theseus carried off Antiope, thereby causing the war between the Amazons and the Athenians. In some versions of the myth, she is the mother of Hippolytus.

2. *Myth.* Daughter of Nycteus, king of Thebes. Ravished by Zeus in the form of a satyr, Antiope took refuge with Epopeus, king of Sicyon. Her father committed suicide for shame, laying on his brother Lycus the duty of punishment. Lycus accordingly defeated and killed Epopeus and carried off Antiope. On the way back to Thebes, she bore twin sons, Amphion and Zethus, whom she was forced to expose on Mt. Cithaeron. They were found and reared by a shepherd. Amphion became a great player on the lyre, Zethus a herdsman and warrior. Antiope, meanwhile, was a slave to the cruel Dirce, Lycus' wife, who was jealous of her beauty. As Dirce was having Antiope bound to a bull to be dragged to death, Amphion and Zethus appeared, freed their mother, and tied Dirce to the bull instead.

Antiope. Lost tragedy by Euripides (produced c. 408 B.C.). Extensive fragments survive. Early in the play there was a famous scene, referred to by Plato in *Gorgias,* where Amphion and Zethus argued the merits of the contemplative and the active life. It is perhaps the earliest occurrence of this debate in world literature. The setting must have been the hut of the shepherd who reared Amphion and Zethus. Their mother flees here from Dirce, and through the shepherd she is reunited with her sons. Dirce comes in leading a band of maenads to celebrate Dionysiac rites. Her seizure of Antiope is thwarted, and she is killed. Lycus is then lured into a cave, and the twins are about to kill him when Hermes appears as *deus ex machina* and stops the killing. He tells Amphion and Zethus to build the walls of Thebes and to rule there and orders that Dirce's ashes be thrown into the spring that is to bear her name. Pacuvius' Latin play *Antiope* was modeled on Euripides' tragedy.

Antiphanes. Writer of Middle Comedy (c. 385–c. 314 B.C.). Antiphanes was said to have written the astonishing total of 260 plays, of which 119 titles are known. A few titles that are of more than routine interest are *The Creation of Man, Sappho, The Athletic Traineress,* and *As Much Again;* there are numerous titles of parodies on myth. Antiphanes was praised for his wit, charm, and elegant language. Demetrius of Phalerum and Dorotheus wrote critical works on his plays.

antipnigos. See EPIRRHEMATIC AGON.

Antisthenes. A stingy and effeminate physician contemporary with Aristophanes.

antistrophe. See STASIMON.

Antonius, Marcus (**Mark Antony**). Roman politician and general (82–

30 B.C.). Mark Antony was a henchman of Julius Caesar, colleague and later opponent of Augustus, and ancestor, through his marriage with Augustus' sister Octavia, of several members of the imperial Julio-Claudian family.

Aonian. Boeotian.

Apaturia (Gk. **Apatouria**). Three-day Athenian festival. In it the children born in the preceding year were enrolled in the proper phratry, or clan. The Apaturia began with a communal banquet.

Apelles. Renowned Greek painter (4th century B.C.).

Aphidna or **Aphidnae** (Gk. **Aphidnai**). Deme, originally a village, of Attica.

Aphiktor (Gr. "suppliant"). Epithet of Zeus as protector of suppliants.

Aphrodisia. Festival of Aphrodite. The Aphrodisia was celebrated particularly by courtesans, who dressed in their best and made sacrifice to the goddess.

Aphrodite. *Myth.* Greek goddess of love, identified by the Romans with their goddess Venus. Some called Aphrodite the daughter of Zeus and Dione. Others said that when Cronus castrated Uranus the genitals fell into the sea, which boiled and foamed; out of the foam sprang Aphrodite. She was wafted to the islands of Cythera (whence her title "Cytherea") and Cyprus (whence her title "Cypris" or "the Cyprian"). Although Aphrodite was married to Hephaestus, she had many lovers. Among them were the god Ares, the hunter Adonis, and the Trojan prince Anchises, to whom she bore Aeneas.

Aphrodite was especially worshiped by prostitutes, and her altars and statues were common sights in brothels. Her intervention in mortal affairs was cruel, capricious, and calamitous: she helped Paris carry Helen off to Troy as reward for his giving her the golden apple in the beauty contest of the goddesses (see PARIS). And when Aphrodite speaks the prologue of Euripides' *Hippolytus,* she vows vengeance on Hippolytus for slighting her, even though this entails the ruin of the inoffensive Phaedra. At the end of this play Artemis hints that she will retaliate by destroying Aphrodite's favorite, Adonis.

Apia. Old, poetic name for the Peloponnesus as a whole, or for the land of Argos in particular.

Apidanus (Gk. **Apidanos**). River in Thessaly.

Apis. *Myth.* Son of Apollo. Apis was a seer who came into the land of Argos and freed it of serpents.

Apollinaris, Sulpicius. See SULPICIUS APOLLINARIS.

Apollo (Gk. **Apollon**). *Myth.* Greek god of many functions. Apollo was the son of Zeus and Leto and the brother of Artemis. His cult was transferred almost unchanged to Rome, where it became very prominent. Most sacred to Apollo were his reputed birthplace, the island of Delos, where every four years a great festival was held in his honor, and the city of Delphi, where older gods turned over to him a shrine of prophecy. In seizing Delphi, he killed the monster Python, which guarded the oracle of Themis. But in penance for this deed Apollo established the Pythian Games, named the Delphic priestess Pythia, and retired every winter to the land of the Hyperboreans in the far north, returning in the spring.

Apollo's Delphian oracle plays a large part in numerous myths, particularly in the stories of Ion, Oedipus, and Orestes. It was at Apollo's command that Orestes committed matricide, and in Aeschylus' *Eumenides* Apollo appears in order to conduct Orestes' defense at his trial in Athens. At the end of Euripides' *Orestes,* Apollo is the *deus ex machina;* he raises Helen to immortality and resolves other complications of the plot.

One of Apollo's original functions may have been to act as male counterpart to his sister Artemis in her role of mistress of animals. Apollo was god of wolves, swans, dolphins, sheep and other domesticated flocks, rats, and mice. In connection with the last, he was god of plague and disease and, consequently, of healing too. Asclepius, the great healer, was Apollo's son. Taking vengeance on the Cyclopes, who were indirectly responsible for Asclepius' death, Apollo was forced, in punishment, to become a shepherd in the service of Admetus. Hence he appears at the beginning of Euripides' *Alcestis* to remind Death that for Admetus he wrested from the Fates a promise that Admetus might live on if a substitute could be found.

Only occasionally was Apollo associated with the sun, driving fiery steeds and golden chariot across the sky. This association was, however, neither late nor unclassical, and it harmonized very well with Apollo's gift for revealing the future, since the sun sees all. As god of light, he was directly opposed to the realm of death. Apollo was also the archetypal musician; he led the Muses' dance on Cithaeron or Parnassus, playing on his lyre. Poets, prophets, and musicians were his mouthpieces. In Aeschylus' *Agamemnon* Apollo drives to frenzy the Trojan prophetess Cassandra, who spurned his love; she cries out in pain, and, associating him with the wolf, puns on his name, calling him *Apollon emos* ("my destroyer").

Apollo's association with Troy and the East was strong. He had helped Poseidon to build Troy, and he favored the Trojans in their war. Furthermore, his skill with bow and arrow was un-Greek; neither Greeks nor Romans cared much for archery. Apollo's connection with Dionysus, another god of un-Greek associations, was close. Their cults were interwoven strangely at Delphi, and it is possible that some bringing-together of Apollonianism and Dionysianism preceded the emergence of classical drama.

Apollodorus (Gk. **Apollodoros**). **1.** Writer of New Comedy (fl. c. 300 B.C.). Apollodorus came from Carystus. His *Lawsuit* was the model for Terence's *Phormio,* and his *Mother-in-Law* for Terence's drama of the same name. Of his plays twenty-odd titles survive, among them *The Notebook-Maker, The Priestess* (c. 313 B.C.), and *The Slanderer.*

2. Another writer of New Comedy, from Gela. This Apollodorus lived about a generation later than Apollodorus (1). It is, however, not always possible to distinguish between the two.

3. Athenian critic and grammarian (1st century B.C.). Apollodorus produced editions of works by Epicharmus and Sophron and commentaries on these writers.

Apollogenes. Tragic actor (3rd century B.C.). Almost equally renowned as a boxer, Apollogenes won numerous contests in both professions.

Apollophanes. Writer of Old Comedy (late 5th century B.C.). Known titles of Apollophanes' plays are *Dalis, Danaë, The Cretans, Old Man Mighty,* and *The Centaurs* (who doubtless formed the chorus).

Apotropaios (Gk. "turning aside"). Epithet of Apollo as averter of evil.

Apulia. Section of southeastern Italy. Its inhabitants were regarded as being particularly provincial.

Aquilo. Roman equivalent of BOREAS.

Arachnaeum (Gk. **Arachnaion**). Mountain ridge of the northeast Peloponnesus, now called Arna.

Arai (Gk. "curses"). Curses regarded as avenging spirits and sometimes equated with the Erinyes. A curse once pronounced was thought to lead a kind of life of its own until vengeance was attained. This idea is especially prominent in the works of Aeschylus, for example, the *Oresteia* and *The Seven Against Thebes.*

Araros. Son of Aristophanes. In 387 B.C., Aristophanes allowed his own *Aeolosicon* and *Cocalus* to be brought out under Araros' name so as to introduce the young man to the public. Araros was himself a writer of Middle Comedy, producing his first works in the 370's. Some extant titles are *The Birth of Pan, Hymenaeus, Adònis,* and *The Little Girl.*

Araxes. River in Armenia.

Arbitrants, The, or **The Arbitration** (Gk. **Epitrepontes**). Comedy by Menander (possibly produced soon after 304 B.C.). Translations: L. A. Post, 1929; Francis G. Allinson, 1930; Gilbert Murray, 1945; Lionel Casson, 1960.

The play has been pieced together from several sources. Of an estimated original 1,100 to 1,200 lines, only about half remain in connected passages of any length; the rest are missing or much mutilated.

S U M M A R Y. In Act One, which is extremely fragmentary, Smicrines, who is old, miserly, and bad-tempered, comes to investigate a report that his son-in-law Charisius is carrying on with a harp girl, carousing with boon companions, and shamefully neglecting his wife, Pamphila. But somewhere in the plot it develops that Charisius is purposely misbehaving in order to provide his wife with an excuse to leave him, for he has learned that before their marriage she bore a child conceived of an unknown father. Charisius is too fond of Pamphila to disgrace her with denunciation and divorce.

Act Two, apparently almost complete, contains the scene from which the play takes its title: the slaves Davus and Syriscus submit a dispute to Smicrines' arbitration. Davus had given Syriscus an infant he had found but had kept for himself the jewelry and tokens found with it. Syriscus is demanding that he be given the trinkets. Smicrines rules that they must go to the one who rears the child. As the ornaments are being examined, Charisius' slave Onesimus enters and, recognizing a ring belonging to his master, takes it away.

The remaining three acts are dominated by the music girl, Habrotonon. Hearing Onesimus speak of the ring that his master lost at the festival of Artemis Tauropolos, she remembers that while she was playing for the ceremonies a young girl wandered off and came back shortly afterward with clothes torn, weeping in great distress. Habrotonon puts on the ring, intending, when Charisius recognizes it, to say that she was the girl raped at the festival and is the mother of the foundling. In remorse Charisius will then buy her and set her free.

To carry out her plan, Habrotonon borrows the baby and its trinkets. However, she meets Pamphila, Charisius' wife, who sees by the trinkets that the baby is her own. Habrotonon in turn realizes that Pamphila is the wronged girl whom she is impersonating. Charisius is then made aware of the truth, and when Smicrines comes at last to insist that his daughter leave her husband, he finds a reconciled and happy family.

COMMENTARY. An ancient writer, Alciphron, calls this play one of Menander's masterpieces. Agreement or disagreement is impossible, since the text is so fragmented. Resemblances to Euripides' *Alope* and *Auge* are obvious. Menander's use of the Chorus is interesting: they are a *komos*, a band of revelers wandering the streets, passing as fellow merrymakers of Charisius. Although their entrances are prepared for in the dialogue, the songs or entertainment they provide (the manuscript has no indication of its nature) served simply to separate what might well be called acts.

Arcadia (Gk. **Arkadia**). Central section of the Peloponnesus. Arcadia is mountainous, inaccessible, and unspoiled; it was a repository of ancient simplicity and antique myths and customs. In *Phaedra* (line 786) Seneca calls the Arcadians "older than the moon."

Arcas (Gk. **Arkas**, related to *arktos,* "bear"). *Myth.* King of Arcadia, which took its name from him. Arcas' mother, Callisto, had made a vow of chastity to Artemis but was tricked and seduced by Zeus and and gave birth to Arcas. For this Artemis changed Callisto into a bear. When Arcas was grown, he was on the point of accidentally killing his mother, when Zeus saved the situation by putting mother and son into the sky as the Great and Little Bears (or as the Bear and Arctophylax, "the bear's guardian").

Archedemus (Gk. **Archedemos**). Politician of Aristophanes' time. In *The Frogs* (lines 588 and 417) Aristophanes gibes at Archedemus' weak eyesight and at his difficulties in getting enrolled as a citizen. Archedemus was, however, an excellent orator, had considerable influence, and was praised by many.

Archelaus (Gk. **Archelaos**). 1. *Myth.* Alleged descendant of Heracles. Driven from Argos by his brothers, Archelaus went to Macedonia and there led the troops of King Cisseus to victory. Cisseus had promised to give the hero his daughter and half of his kingdom but treacherously decided to get rid of him. Digging a pit, Cisseus spread the bottom with hot coals and covered over the top lightly, intending that Archelaus should fall in. Archelaus learned of this trick and pushed Cisseus in instead. Then he founded Aegae, becoming ancestor of the kings of Macedonia.

2. King of Macedonia. Archelaus usurped the throne in 413 B.C. Euripides spent his last years at this king's court. *Archelaus,* a lost play by Euripides, was written during the poet's sojourn in Macedonia. It is thought to have been based on the myth of Archelaus (1), but that story may have been invented

by Euripides to satisfy his patron's desire to provide the half-barbaric Macedonian royal family with a respectable Greek ancestry.

Archeptolemus (Gk. **Archeptolemos**). Politician of Aristophanes' time. Archeptolemus was a member of the peace party, was suspected of oligarchic tendencies, and was opposed by Cleon and the democrats.

Archilochus (Gk. **Archilochos**). Greek satiric poet of Paros (7th century B.C.). Archilochus was traditionally the first to use iambic verse and to turn it to the purposes of lampoon, satire, and personal invective. One of his fragments says: "I know how to lead the dithyramb, the fair song in honor of Lord Dionysus, when my wits are muddled with wine." According to tradition, Archilochus introduced a phallic cult of Dionysus into Paros. If so, he may have anticipated Arion in leading satyr choruses in the dithyramb, thus breaking a path for the development of drama. Some of his lines, especially those about throwing away his shield and running from battle, became almost proverbial. Aristophanes often echoes him.

archimime (Lat. **archimimus** or **archimima**). Chief actor (or actress) in a mime. The archimime was often, too, the director of a troupe of actors of mime.

Archippus (Gk. **Archippos**). Writer of Old Comedy, all of whose plays are lost. Archippus was contemporary with Aristophanes. His imitativeness of the latter was shown in his *Fishes*, probably inspired by Aristophanes' *Birds;* in it the Chorus of Fishes argued with the Athenians about being eaten. Other plays were *Amphitryon, The Marriage of Heracles, The Donkey's Shadow,* and *Rhinon* (an Athenian general). In some ancient sources several of Aristophanes' plays (now lost) are assigned to Archippus.

archon (Gk. "ruler"). Athenian official. During the classical period there were nine archons holding office at one time. One of them had charge of celebrating the DIONYSIA and one the LENAEA.

Arctophylax (Latinized Gk. "guardian of the bear"). ARCAS as translated to the sky. Arctophylax is, however, the same constellation as Boötes.

Arctos (Gk. **Arktos**, "bear"). The constellation of the Great Bear. (See ARCAS.)

Arcturus (Gk. **Arktouros**, "the bear's tail"). A bright star considered by the ancients as forming part of the Great Bear. In Plautus' *Rudens* an actor representing Arcturus wears a star on his forehead and speaks the prologue; he has caused the storm that precedes the action. The star Arcturus, rising in September, was associated with the stormy period of the autumnal equinox.

Areopagus (Gk. **Areios pagos**, "hill of Ares"). A hill in Athens; also the advisory, administrative, and judicial assembly that met there. The trial of Orestes is represented as taking place on the hill of Ares. Two explanations were given for the name: one, that the Amazons encamped there when they made war (see ARES) on Athens; the other, that on this hill Ares had to defend himself, in the archetype of all trials, against the charge of having murdered Halirrhothius.

Ares. *Myth.* Greek god of war, son of Zeus and Hera. Ares was identified by the Romans with their god Mars. He was the spirit of bloodlust, which he breathed into warriors. Associating with Phobos (Rout), Eris (Quarrel), and Enyo (Strife), he delighted in a harvest of men and feasted on slaughter. Ares' favorite haunts were Thrace and Thebes; at the latter place it was his spring that was guarded by the dragon killed by Cadmus. The Thebans, descended from the dragon's teeth, were regarded also as Ares' descendants. The hill Areopagus in Athens was named for him; it was there in the archetypal murder trial that he was acquitted for killing Halirrhothius, Poseidon's son, who had assaulted his daughter. Ares was the lover of Aphrodite, wife of Hephaestus. On one occasion a man whom he had posted as lookout while meeting the love goddess failed in his task; Ares changed him into a cock.

Arethusa (Gk. **Arethousa**). Usually said to be a fountain and its nymph in the Peloponnesus (see ALPHEUS). Arethusa was, however, sometimes located in Euboea.

Argades. One of the four original tribal divisions in Athens.

Argives (Gk. **Argeioi**). Inhabitants of Argos or Argolis. The name was sometimes used to mean all the Greeks. *The Argives* was the title of a lost play by Aeschylus of which almost nothing is known. Its correct title may be *The Argive Women*.

Argo. *Myth.* The miraculous ship on which the Argonauts ("sailors of the *Argo*") sailed to get the golden fleece. The *Argo* was sometimes thought of as the first ship ever built.

Of a lost play by Aeschylus called *The Argo*, the only extant fragment mentions the speaking beam of the ship that was taken from the prophetic oak of Dodona. The tragedy may have been the first of a tetralogy, followed by *The Lemnian Women, Hypsipyle,* and the *Cabiri.* If Accius' *Argonauts* was modeled on this play, there was in it a scene in which a terrified shepherd had his first sight of a ship.

Argolis or the **Argolid.** See ARGOS.

Argos (adj. Argive, Argolic, or Argolian). Prominent city of the northeastern Peloponnesus. Argos was noted for its cult of Hera. In myth it alternated with Mycenae as the city of Agamemnon and his family. By extension, the name Argos was used to designate the whole surrounding region, which was, however, more properly known as Argolis. In English the region is also referred to as the Argolid.

Argus the All-Seeing (Gk. **Argos Panoptes**). *Myth.* An earthborn monster with eyes all over his body. When Zeus turned Io into a cow so that she would escape Hera's notice, Hera, who was not deceived, set Argus to watch over her rival. But Hermes, under orders from Zeus, lulled the monster to sleep and killed him. Hera changed Argus into her attendant bird, the peacock, but his ghost became the gadfly that continued to torment Io.

Aria or **Areia.** Province of Persia.

Ariadne. *Myth.* Cretan princess, daughter of Minos and Pasiphaë. Ariadne fell in love with THESEUS, helped him kill the Minotaur, and fled with him from

Crete. But Theseus deserted her on the island of Naxos while she was sleeping. Dionysus found Ariadne shortly afterward and made her his goddess-bride. The coronet he gave her as a wedding present became the constellation of the Northern Crown.

Arignotus (Gk. **Arignotos**). Harper, contemporary with Aristophanes. In *The Knights* (line 1278) Aristophanes praises Arignotus but (line 1281 ff.) attacks his brother Ariphrades for his vile practices. Again in *The Wasps* (line 1275 ff.) Arignotus' cleverness and musicianship are praised.

Arimaspians. *Myth.* A people located north of the Scythians and south of the Hyperboreans. Handsome but one-eyed, they owned many horses and accumulated much wealth by stealing gold from griffons.

Arion. Poet and musician. Although Arion was said to have come from Lesbos and to have been active at Corinth in about 600 B.C., his very existence is disputed. According to legend, he was rescued by a dolphin after having been flung from a ship. Arion was said to have been the first (1) to use and train choruses, (2) to sing dithyrambs and call them by that name, (3) to costume choristers as satyrs and provide them with verses to deliver, (4) to give the name of the chorus to what was sung, and (5) to employ the tragic mode. This may mean that Arion, if he existed, raised the native Corinthian satyr dance to the status of art, widened the scope of subject matter in the Dionysiac cult song, and gave choric song and dance a more serious tone. In the process, he brought about a closer connection between the rituals of Dionysus and Apollo.

Ariphrades. See ARIGNOTUS.

Aristaeus (Gk. **Aristaios**). *Myth.* Son of Apollo and the nymph Cyrene. Aristaeus was the husband of Autonoë and the father of Actaeon.

Aristarchus (Gk. **Aristarchos**). **1.** Writer of tragedies in Athens (5th century B.C.). Aristarchus was originally from Tegea. He was said to have been the playwright who established the traditional length of plays. Of seventy tragedies and satyr plays, the only titles known are *Tantalus, Asclepius* (written as a thank offering after recovery from illness), and *Achilles*. The last was adapted by Ennius and referred to by Plautus at the beginning of his *Poenulus*.

2. One of the most noted of ancient critics and philologists (c. 217–c. 145 B.C.). Aristarchus was a pupil of Aristophanes of Byzantium and became director of the Library of Alexandria. His editorial work on Homer was his most famous; he may have edited Aristophanes also.

Aristias. Writer of tragedies and satyr plays (middle 5th century B.C.). Aristias was the son of Pratinas. After his father's death he produced three of Pratinas' works, *Perseus, Tantalus,* and *The Wrestlers,* winning a second prize in the dramatic contest (467 B.C.). Shortly thereafter Aristias won a first prize with a tetralogy of his own. He was especially admired for satyr plays, titles of which included *Antaeus, Keres, Orpheus,* and *Cyclops*. The last probably influenced Euripides in his play of the same name.

Aristides (Gk. **Aristeides**). Athenian statesman and military leader (c. 525–

c. 467 B.C.). Aristides, known as "the Just," was a commander at Marathon.

Aristodemus (Gk. **Aristodemos**). Famous tragic actor (fl. middle 4th century B.C.). An Athenian, Aristodemus was invited to act at the Macedonian court, where he also served as an ambassador.

Aristogeiton. See HARMODIUS.

Aristomenes. Writer of Old Comedy (career c. 440–c. 388 B.C.). Aristomenes competed against Aristophanes several times in dramatic contests and won several prizes. Some known titles of his plays are *The Scabbard-Wearers, Admetus, The Assistants, The Wood-Carriers, Masters of Hocus-Pocus,* and *Dionysus the Would-Be Athlete.*

Aristonymus (Gk. **Aristonymos**). Writer of Old Comedy. Aristonymus was a younger contemporary of Aristophanes. Of his plays only two titles are known: *Theseus* and *The Sun Grows Cold.* The latter perhaps referred to an eclipse.

Aristophanes. 1. Only writer of Old Comedy whose plays are extant (c. 445–c. 385 B.C.).

L I F E. Aristophanes was born of a wealthy family; his father had property and connections in Aegina. His poetical career began at a very early age, with the production of *The Banqueters* in 427 B.C. This play and the next two, *The Babylonians* and *The Acharnians,* were produced under the name of a friend, Callistratus. Although Aristophanes seems to indicate that this was due to a feeling of unsureness because of his immaturity (compare *The Clouds,* line 530 ff.: he "exposed his first-born for others to adopt"), he probably had a life-long aversion to handling the details of production. This would account for the fact that, later on, *The Birds* and *Lysistrata* also appeared under the name of Callistratus, and *The Wasps, Amphiaraus,* and *The Frogs* were presented by another friend, Philonides.

Aristophanes' last two plays were produced toward the end of his life by his son ARAROS; however, this was done specifically to provide the young man with a dramatic debut. Araros went on to write comedies of his own, as did Aristophanes' two other sons, Philippus and Nicostratus. Nothing more is known of Aristophanes' life. He appears in Plato's *Symposium* as a member of aristocratic society and on amiable terms with Socrates and Agathon. This last is surprising in view of the rough handling that these two get in Aristophanes' comedies; it would be useless, however, to speculate on personal relations that we know nothing of.

E X T A N T   W O R K S (see under separate headings). *The Acharnians, The Birds, The Clouds* (second version), *Ecclesiazusae, The Frogs, The Knights, Lysistrata, Peace* (first version), *Plutus* (second version), *Thesmophoriazusae* (first version), *The Wasps.*

L O S T   W O R K S (see under separate headings). *Aeolosicon* (two versions), *Amphiaraus, Anagyrus, The Babylonians, The Banqueters, The Clouds* (first version), *Cocalus, Daedalus, Danaïdes, Dionysus Shipwrecked* (doubtfully described to Aristophanes), *Dramas or The Centaur, Dramas or Niobus* (doubtful), *The Farmers, The Friers, Gerytades, The Heroes, The Islands* (doubtful), *The Lemnian Women, The Merchantmen, Peace* (second version), *The Phoenician Women, Plutus* (first version), *Poetry* (doubtful), *Polyidus, The Rehearsal, The Seasons, The Seat-Grabbers, The Storks, The Telemessians, Thesmophoriazusae* (second version), *The Three-Phallus Man.*

CRITICISM. Since the extant plays of Aristophanes are all that is left of Old Comedy aside from fragments, most discussion of Old Comedy—its form, its style, and its qualities—is discussion of his work. Thus the juxtaposition of lyricism and fantasy with slapstick and obscenity may have been typical of all Old Comedy, or only typically Aristophanic. Treatments of his individual plays have, for the greater part, been aimed at relating the works to the social and political events of the time. This is justified, since in satire of this kind the relation is close. Aristophanes' own outlook, everyone admits, was conservative; but the suspicion arises that the definition of "conservatism" here depends more on the critic than on what is criticized, for the poet has been called everything from the farmer's friend to a despiser of the mob. Certainly he sincerely longed for peace and sincerely deplored the intellectual and social movements that he thought tended toward decadence. Certainly, too, his attitudes toward Socrates and Euripides seem unfair and superficial. The catastrophe that Aristophanes warned against did indeed come about; but whether, as he seemed to think, every current of the age, however fair appearing, was sweeping toward the abyss is an historical-philosophical problem that no one has ever yet solved. In a realm more properly that of literary criticism, interesting work has begun to be done on Aristophanes' symbolism. (See also COMEDY: *Old Comedy.*)

2. Aristophanes of Byzantium (c. 257–c. 180 B.C.). One of the greatest of ancient critics. Aristophanes was a pupil of Eratosthenes and Callimachus; he became director of the Alexandrian Library in his old age. He edited the works of Euripides and Aristophanes and probably those of Aeschylus and Sophocles as well. Several of the extant hypotheses to tragedies may be his work. Aristophanes and Aristarchus were probably the ones chiefly responsible for setting up the "Alexandrian Canon," a listing of principal writers in every field. In it Aeschylus, Sophocles, and Euripides were acknowledged as the greatest tragedians. Other works of Aristophanes, all lost, were: *Additions to Callimachus' "Tablets," Characters in Comedy, The Courtesans of Athens,* and *Menander's Literary Thefts.*

Aristotle (Gk. **Aristoteles**). Renowned Greek philosopher (384–322 B.C.). Aristotle was a pupil of Plato and the teacher of Alexander the Great. He founded in Athens a school of philosophy called the Lyceum or the Peripatetic School. The latter name was given either because he taught in a covered walk (*peripatos*), or because he taught while walking the grounds (*peripatein,* to walk). Aristotle's partially extant POETICS is the most influential work ever written on literary criticism in general and the theory of tragedy in particular. His lost works pertaining to drama were DIDASCALIAE, *Victories at the City Dionysia and Lenaea,* and *Treatise on Tragedies.*

Aristoxenus (Gk. **Aristoxenos**). **1.** Corrupt demagogue of Aristophanes' time. On one occasion Aristoxenus' property was confiscated. He was a needle-seller by trade.

2. Greek philosopher and scholar (late 4th century B.C.). Aristoxenus was a pupil of Aristotle. He was noted chiefly for his works on music, now only partially extant. Two of his lost works dealt with drama: *Writers of Tragedy* and *The Dance in Tragedy*.

Aristyllus (Gk. **Aristyllos**). Disreputable contemporary of Aristophanes. Aristyllus was accused by the playwright of various perversions (compare *Plutus*, line 314).

Arsinoë. *Myth.* Wife of ALCMAEON.

Ars Poetica (Lat. **The Art of Poetry**). Discussion of poetic principles in the form of a verse epistle of some 475 lines by Horace. Although historically the *Ars* has had an influence on dramaturgic theory and practice second only to Aristotle's *Poetics,* almost everything about it is controversial. It has been dated from 28 to 8 B.C., with 20 as perhaps the likeliest compromise. It is sometimes called *Epistle to the Pisos,* sometimes *Book Two, Epistle Three* of the *Epistles,* though neither of these titles has ancient authority. Furthermore, the Piso and his two sons who are addressed have never been identified to everyone's satisfaction. The most intense dispute has raged over whether the poem is planless or systematically arranged and, if the latter, over what the system is. A *poesis-poema-poeta* scheme has been the favorite choice. Supposedly derived from a Hellenistic critic, Neoptolemus of Parium, the scheme is as follows: the prerequisites of *poetry,* the technical problems of a *poem,* the characteristics of a *poet.*

Luckily the settling of the question has little to do with the various influential pieces of advice about playwriting. The most important of these (contained chiefly in lines 89–294) follow:

The principle of *decorum* (fitness) must always be kept in mind; the comic style, with certain exceptions, is not suitable for tragedy, and vice versa. The sentiments expressed must be fitted to the emotion that the author desires to arouse ("If you wish me to weep, you must first be in pain yourself"). Furthermore, the style must suit the character. The best way to achieve this is to follow well-established models: Medea must be implacable, Ixion treacherous. If an untraditional character is brought on the boards, he should be consistently portrayed throughout. The playwright should carefully observe the traits typical of each period of life. Although events acted out on the stage are more affecting, bloody and grotesque incidents should be reported, not shown. Have neither more nor fewer than five acts and no more than three actors. Use a *deus ex machina* only if there is a knot worth his cutting. Employ the chorus for some purpose; make it integral to the action. Keep the music within the bounds of taste. As for the satyr play, consider that it accompanies tragedy, and do not descend too quickly or too far from the tragic heights either in action or diction. Pay attention to metrical correctness; the earlier Roman dramatic poets were allowed too much license in this respect.

The part of the *Ars* that deals purely with the history of drama ends with the much-fought-over passage on origins:

> Thespis is said to have discovered the as-yet-unknown literary genre of tragedy and to have mounted his compositions on carts, where men who had their faces stained with dregs from grape vats could sing and act. After him Aeschylus introduced masks and dignified robes, had a wooden stage built of modest size, and taught drama to speak in elevated style and to prance in the buskin. Old Comedy came next, praiseworthy to be sure, but its liberty slipped into license and its excesses cried out for regulation: the law was passed; the chorus fell into a cowardly silence when it lost its power to hurt. Our own Roman poets have left nothing untried, and not least of their accomplishments is their daring to stop following in the steps of the Greeks, so as to celebrate our own native life and history in the *togata* and the *praetexta*.

Artemis. *Myth.* Greek goddess of the woodland and mistress of wild animals. Artemis was identified by the Romans with their goddess Diana. Daughter of Zeus and Leto and sister of Apollo, Artemis was a virgin huntress, armed with bow and arrow and attended by a train of nymphs, whose sins against chastity she swiftly punished. For various offenses she also took vengeance on Actaeon, Niobe, and the king of Calydon, and she caused the sea winds to fail and becalm the Greek fleet at Aulis. Artemis was often associated with the moon; she was especially the patroness of young girls but was also appealed to by women in childbirth. Arcadia and Laconia were major centers of her cult. In Ephesus Artemis was identified with an Asian fertility goddess with whom she had little in common. She appears at the end of Euripides' *Hippolytus* to take leave of the dying hero, her special devotee; but, as death approaches, she typically and somewhat indifferently withdraws.

Artemisia. Queen of Halicarnassus (5th century B.C.). Artemisia had great influence with Xerxes. During the Persian invasion of Greece, she furnished five ships for Xerxes' fleet. At the Battle of Salamis, according to Herodotus, she sank a ship on her own side while being pursued by a Greek ship. This act convinced the Greeks that Artemisia's ship was fighting for them; it also brought praise from Xerxes, who thought she had sunk an enemy vessel.

Artemisium (Gk. **Artemision**). Promontory on the island of Euboea. Here Greek and Persian fleets fought in 480 B.C.

Artemon. Military engineer employed by Pericles and mocked in Aristophanes' *Acharnians* (line 850). Artemon was lame and had to be carried in a litter, thus recalling a rich and lazy man of the same name about whom Anacreon had written satirical poems.

Asclepiades (Gk. **Asklepiades**). Greek philologian (4th century B.C.). Asclepiades' lost *Tales from the Tragedians* did not summarize plots but gave straightforward accounts of the myths used in tragedy.

Asclepius (Gk. **Asklepios**). *Myth.* Greek hero-god of healing, borrowed by the Romans as Aesculapius. Asclepius was the son of Apollo and a pupil of Chiron. He gained such skill in medicine that he could raise the dead, and Zeus had to strike him with a thunderbolt in order to preserve the natural order of things. His father, Apollo, outraged at this injustice, killed the Cyclopes who forged the thunderbolts, since he could not touch Zeus himself. For this deed Apollo was forced to go to earth and serve as a slave for a time.

Asclepius was regarded as a god after death. His cult, which spread far and wide during classical times, was welcomed into Athens by Sophocles. The chief centers of the cult were Cos and Epidaurus; Euripides mentions a "rock of Asclepius" near Epidaurus (*Hippolytus*, line 1209). Groups of physicians called themselves Asclepidae or Asclepiadae, "descendants of Asclepius." His temples were used for "incubation," that is, sleeping-in with the hope of a miraculous cure or at least of having a dream that, when interpreted, would tell a person how to be cured.

Ascondas (Gk. **Askondas**). Athenian of Aristophanes' time. In *The Wasps* (line 1191) Aristophanes mocks Ascondas for his cowardice and effeminacy.

Asinaria (Lat. **The Comedy of Asses**). Extant comedy by Plautus (variously dated 212 or 207 B.C.) *Asinaria* was adapted from a Greek play, *Onagos* (*The Ass-Driver*) or *Onagros* (*The Wild Ass*), by Demophilus, an obscure dramatist. Translations: Henry T. Riley, 1852; Edward H. Sugden, 1893; Paul Nixon, 1916.

S C E N E. Athens, a street.

S U M M A R Y. Demaenetus, an older man, is thoroughly under the thumb of his wife, Artemona, whose control is based on the large dowry she brought to the marriage. The henpecked husband encourages his slave Libanus to devise some way of cheating him or his wife or her steward, Saurea, out of enough money to enable his son Argyrippus to enjoy his ladylove, Philaenium. Argyrippus has been banished from Philaenium's house by her mercenary mother, Cleareta, because he cannot put up the sum of twenty minae.

Libanus and his fellow slave Leonida try to extract some money from a merchant who has come to pay for some asses he bought through a servant of Saurea, the steward. Although Leonida tries to pose as Saurea, he is unsuccessful until Demaenetus himself confirms his story. Leonida and Libanus then give the twenty minae to the lovers, Argyrippus and Philaenium, but Libanus makes clear that Demaenetus, the ultimate donor, must have an evening with the lady first. This evening of merrymaking is, however, interrupted by Diabolus, a young man who has come to buy Philaenium for his own use during one year. Finding Argyrippus already in possession of her, Diabolus sends his parasite to inform Artemona, the shrewish wife, of the debauchery of her husband and son. The play ends with her attack on the brothel, and old Demaenetus is dragged away in disgrace.

C O M M E N T A R Y. *Asinaria* is utterly innocent of morals, and criticism of it has varied in accordance with the critic's reaction to this fact. To some, the whole story is a steady descent into bad taste; others, probably in a spirit of opposition, have stressed their delight. In the play as objectively viewed, the action seems to have a moderate amount of drive and verve; the sentimental scenes show effective contrast; the henpecked husband and the termagant wife are fairly well-drawn specimens of common enough types; and the plot is midway between Plautus' best and worst.

Asopus (Gk. **Asopos**). **1.** River in Boeotia.

2. *Myth*. God of this river, father of Aegina.

Aspasia. Famous Athenian courtesan. Aspasia was the mistress of Pericles.

Assaracus (Gk. **Assarakos**). *Myth*. Member of the royal house of Troy. Assaracus was the brother of Ganymede and an ancestor of Aeneas.

Assembly of the Achaeans, The (Gk. **Achaion Syllogos**). Lost play by Sophocles. It dealt with much the same material as Aeschylus' and Euripides' *Telephus*. However, the episode where Telephus threatened Orestes was perhaps omitted, and Odysseus may have been used as a go-between. *The Assembly of the Achaeans* may have been the third play of Sophocles' supposed trilogy TELEPHEIA.

Astacus (Gk. **Astakos**). *Myth*. Theban hero. Astacus was a descendant of the *Spartoi* (men sprung from the teeth of the dragon slain by Cadmus) and the father of Melanippus.

Astraea (Gk. **Astraia**). *Myth*. Goddess daughter of Zeus and Themis. During the Golden Age Astraea lived among men and saw that justice prevailed. But with the increasing degeneration of mankind, she withdrew to the sky and became the constellation later known as Virgo, "the maiden."

Astyanax (also **Scamandrius**; Gk. **Skamandrios**). *Myth*. Child of Hector and Andromache, called "prince [*anax*] of the city [*asty*]" by the common people. In Euripides' *Trojan Women*, Astyanax is a mute character. He is torn from his mother's arms to be dashed to his death from the walls of Troy, because the Greek leaders are afraid that the son of such a hero as Hector will grow up to be a danger to them. Hecuba mourns over his corpse, which is borne out for burial on Hector's shield. In Seneca's *Trojan Women*, Astyanax's mother hides him in Hector's tomb, but she is forced to give him up for execution when Ulysses threatens to demolish and desecrate the tomb.

Astydamas. 1. Son of Morismus and a writer of tragedies (fl. early 4th century B.C.). Among Astydamas' play titles are *Achilles, Alcmeon, Antigone, Athamas, Hector, Hermes, Nauplius,* and *Lycaon.*

2. Writer of tragedies, son of the above, from whose works his cannot always be distinguished. Astydamas wrote 240 tragedies and satyr plays, won fifteen first prizes in dramatic contests, and gained such fame that his image was set up in the Theater of Dionysus sometime after 338 B.C. For this image Astydamas wrote such a flattering inscription that his name became a byword for vanity. Some of his play titles were *Alcmene, Bellerophon, Epigoni, Heracles, Mad Ajax, Palamedes, Parthenopaeus, Phoenix,* and *Tyro.*

Atalanta (Gk. **Atalante**). *Myth*. Maiden huntress. A follower of Artemis, Atalanta was remarkable for her speed in running and her prowess in the hunt. For stories relating to her, see MELANION, MELEAGER, and PARTHENOPAEUS. *Atalanta* was the title of a lost play by Aeschylus; of it no fragments survive. If the *Atalanta* of Pacuvius was an adaptation of Aeschylus' play, the latter's plot included a foot race with Atalanta's hand as the prize. It was won by Parthenopaeus, the son whom she had borne to Meleager and had abandoned. Incest between mother and son was barely averted.

Ate. *Myth.* Greek goddess of stupidity and error, of "not being oneself" in respect to being out of one's senses. Banished from Olympus by Zeus, Ate wandered among men, ensnaring them and bringing them to ruin.

Atellan farce (Lat. **fabula Atellana**). A type of native Italian farce. Atellan farce was associated with the Campanian town Atella and was imported into Rome some time before the introduction of Greek-influenced drama in 240 B.C. It was first performed in the Oscan dialect but was soon Latinized. In origin it seems to have been an Italic parallel to the Italian-Greek PHLYAKES plays. The action was slapstick, jokes were crude, and the language was that of everyday life. Plot complications, called *tricae,* were negligible, and much use was made of beatings, ghosts, and scenes of drunkenness. All female roles were taken by men. The actors, who were sometimes amateurs, did not suffer the loss of reputation that usually went with appearance on the stage. Masks were always used, providing for at least four stock characters. Most often seen was Maccus, a stupid buffoon or guzzler; his name occurs in many play titles: *Maccus the Maiden, Maccus the Innkeeper, Maccus the Soldier.* Bucco, whose name may have meant "fat cheeks," was apparently a glutton and a boaster; Pappus (called Casnar in Oscan) was a gullible and fussy old man; Dossenus, who may have been the same as Manducus (a later version of Bucco), was perhaps a greedy trickster. (The exact nature of all of these characters is, however, much disputed.)

Although Atellan farce was influenced by the Greek-derived comedy of Rome, it rose in popularity during the anti-Greek reaction of the late second century B.C., when it was regularly used as an EXODIUM (afterplay) for a comedy in Roman setting. It reached something like artistic stature in the following century with the writers POMPONIUS and NOVIUS, and was still performed in early imperial times. With the rise of the mime, Atellan farce declined steadily, except for a revival in the archaizing second century A.D.

Athamas. *Myth.* King of Boeotia. Many conflicting stories were told of Athamas. By his first wife, Nephele, "Cloud," he had a son, Phrixus, and a daughter, Helle. But Athamas tired of Nephele and put her away, whereupon she caused a drought in the land. This drought could be removed only by a royal sacrifice, and so Phrixus and Helle were led to the altar. Their mother, however, sent a golden ram with a human voice which bade her children climb on its back. They did so, and the ram flew into the sky toward the east. On the journey, Helle fell off into the strait afterward called the Hellespont, but Phrixus continued to Colchis, where he sacrificed the ram, whose fleece Jason later appropriated. Meanwhile, Athamas was substituted for the sacrifice, but as he waited, all garlanded and ready to be killed, Heracles rescued him. Euripides used a slightly different version of this story in his *Phrixus* (see PHRIXUS 2).

According to another myth, Athamas took as a second wife Ino, one of Cadmus' daughters. Hera drove him mad because he allowed Ino to bring up Dionysus, whom the goddess hated. Thinking his son Learchus a wild animal, Athamas killed him and chased Ino and his other son, Melicertes, into the sea. The mother and son were metamorphosed into the sea goddess Leucothea and the sea god Palaemon. Euripides treated still another story in his INO.

In again a different myth, Athamas' second wife was named Demodice. According to this version, Demodice fell in love with her stepson Phrixus, slandered him to his father when her proffered love was disdained, and thus brought about the intended sacrifice of the boy and his sister.

Athamas was the title of a lost tragedy by Aeschylus. It was based on the story of Ino, Learchus, and Melicertes, with the possible variation that Ino, also driven mad, threw Melicertes into a boiling caldron and then leaped with him into the sea. There were two lost plays by Sophocles called *Athamas*. One (probably produced before 423 B.C., since it seems to be referred to in Aristophanes' *Clouds*) dealt with the story of Nephele, Phrixus, and Helle. The other may have been a revision of the first or may have dealt with the story of Ino, Learchus, and Melicertes.

Athena or **Athene.** *Myth.* Patron goddess of Athens. Worshiped throughout the Greek world, Athena was identified by the Romans with their goddess Minerva. Athena was a protectress of cities and of civilization and its arts; she was also regarded as the personification of wisdom, strategy, and technique. Having sprung in full armor out of the head of Zeus, Athena remained always a militant virgin, carrying a shield, a spear, and a breastplate in the form of the aegis. Although she patronized weaving and olive culture, her favorites were neither women nor farmers, but warriors: Heracles, Theseus, Diomedes, Perseus, and above all the wily Odysseus.

Not surprisingly, Athena appears more often than any other deity in extant Athenian plays. In Euripides' *Rhesus,* she helps Odysseus and Diomedes and deceives Paris; in the poet's *Suppliants, Ion,* and *Iphigenia among the Taurians* she is the *dea ex machina;* in the prologue of Euripides' *Trojan Women* she discusses with Poseidon the punishment that must be visited on the homegoing Greeks for their outrages at Troy. At the beginning of Sophocles' *Ajax,* she taunts Ajax, whom she has driven mad for his insolent remarks about the gods; and in Aeschylus' *Eumenides,* she brings the whole *Oresteia* trilogy to a conclusion when she presides over Orestes' trial, casting the deciding vote in his favor and reconciling the Erinyes to their role as guarantors of civic justice.

Athenaeus (Gk. **Athenaios**). Author of *Deipnosophistae* (*The Banquet of the Learned*) (c. A.D. 200). It is an almost inexhaustible source of quotations and random information relative to Greek drama, especially comedy.

Athenodorus (Gk. **Athenodoros**). Famous actor (second half of 4th century B.C.). Athenodorus went with Alexander the Great on his Asian campaigns. In 332 B.C. he defeated Thettalus in an acting contest at Tyre, and in 324 B.C. he took part in the plays celebrating Alexander's marriage at Susa.

Athmonia or **Athmonon**. Attic deme, famous for its vineyards.

Atilius, Marcus. Roman adapter of Greek comedy (fl. middle 2nd century B.C.). Only one of Atilius' play titles is known: *The Woman-Hater*. He seems also to have produced a bad version of Sophocles' *Electra*. Cicero considered him very rough and unpolished, but other Romans ranked him highly. (See FABULA PALLIATA.)

Atlantides. Daughters of ATLAS, *i.e.*, the Pleiades.

Atlas or **Atlans**. *Myth*. Titan (or Giant), a brother of Prometheus. Atlas was one of those who participated in the war of the Titans (or Giants) against the gods. For this he was punished, according to Aeschylus, by being made to support the column of earth and sky. The later conception was that Atlas stood in northwest Africa and held up the sky on his back and shoulders.

Atossa. Persian empress, wife of Darius, mother of Xerxes (6th–5th centuries B.C.). Atossa is a leading character in Aeschylus' *Persians*.

Atreides (Gk. "son of Atreus"). Designation for Agamemnon. The plural form, *Atreidai* (Lat. *Atreidae*), was used to mean both Agamemnon and Menelaus.

Atreus. *Myth*. Son of Pelops and Hippodamia and brother of Thyestes. Atreus and Thyestes were cursed by their father for the death of CHRYSIPPUS, and so took refuge in Mycenae. There Atreus vowed to sacrifice to Artemis the finest animal born in his flocks, but when a golden lamb appeared, he killed it and hid the fleece in a chest. When the oracle advised that the vacant throne of Mycenae should go to a son of Pelops, Atreus' wife, Aërope, having fallen in love with Thyestes, stole the fleece away and proposed that the brother producing a golden fleece should be king. Atreus agreed, but it was naturally Thyestes who produced the fleece. Atreus then asked Thyestes to yield him the throne whenever the sun should travel from west to east. Thyestes consented, whereupon Zeus caused the whole heaven to revolve in the opposite direction. Atreus took over the kingdom but still meditated revenge. He caused his wife to commit suicide (or threw her into the sea), and he invited Thyestes to a banquet at which the chief dish was three of Thyestes' murdered sons. (For the story of Atreus' death, see AEGISTHUS.)

Atreus is one of the chief characters in Seneca's *Thyestes,* where there is a lurid description of his murder of his nephews in a gloomy wood. Sophocles' lost play *Atreus* treated the events in his career up to his revenge on Thyestes; this play was also called *The Mycenaean Women*. Accius may have modeled his *Atreus* on it and may have also drawn elements from Euripides' *Thyestes*.

Atridae. See ATREIDES.

Atropos. One of the MOIRAE.

Atta, Titus Quinctius. Writer of Latin comedy on Roman themes (died 77 B.C.). Atta was admired for his character portrayals of women. Some of his plays' titles are *The Spa, Lady Go-between, The Megalensian Games, Off to War*. (See FABULA TOGATA.)

Attalus (Gk. **Attalos**). The name of three kings of Pergamum during the third and second centuries B.C.

Attis. *Myth.* Central figure of an orgiastic cult imported into the Greco-Roman world from Asia Minor. Attis bore much the same relation to Cybele as Adonis to Aphrodite; he was supposed to have been killed by a lion after rejecting the goddess's advances or to have died after castrating himself. Attis was served by eunuch priests, who were often itinerant beggars.

Auainos. Proper name invented by Aristophanes, suggesting "drying" or "withering" (*The Frogs*, line 194).

audience. Ancient theaters were as large as their cities could afford, and they usually had excellent acoustics. Because plays were official ceremonies and were staged only a few times each year, houses were always packed and audiences were multitudinous. Plato's mention in the *Symposium* of 30,000 people applauding Agathon's tragedy at the Theater of Dionysus in Athens must, however, have been an exaggeration, and the number should be reduced to about half. The theater at Epidaurus must have held about 14,000. Its acoustics are always described admiringly.

Only citizens and resident aliens could attend the Lenaea in Athens (women and children were admitted on all occasions), but at the City Dionysia spectators flocked to Athens from all over Greece. Although there was a general scramble for seats, actual fights in the theater were controlled by specially appointed ushers. Ticket agents charged outrageous amounts, but this abuse was suppressed by Pericles, who presumably fixed the price. It is known that in his time a ticket cost two obols and that, in accordance with his decree, this fee was paid to poorer citizens out of the "theoric fund" (a fund established to furnish the poor with money for admission fees). It seems that particular blocks of seats were allotted to the Attic tribes (see TICKETS). Repair of the theater, distribution of the seats, and assignment of places of honor were the business of an entrepreneur who contracted with the state for these tasks. The front-row seats always went to the Priest of Dionysus, lesser priests, other officials, and ambassadors. Some sixty inscribed designations still appear on the seats in the front row of the Theater of Dionysus.

Audience reactions to drama were intense, judging from accounts of riots, hissing, fainting, and the pelting of actors with fruit. Discussion about the intelligence level of the Athenian audience is probably bootless. While there might have been a Socrates and a Pericles in the theater, Aristophanes' complaints make it clear that a great many people were there, in Hamlet's phrase, "for a jig or a tale of bawdry, or they fell asleep." Whether, as some think, the close parodies of tragedy in Aristophanes' works prove that the spectators had phenomenal memories is hard to say; the comic actor may have provoked laughter just by putting on tragic airs. Even though Aeschylus and Euripides were said to have retired from Athens in disgust with Athenian audiences, it should nevertheless be pointed out, paraphrasing Walt Whitman, that the Greeks had great poets and so must have had great audiences too.

Auge. *Myth.* Daughter of Aleos, king of Tegea in Arcadia. Hence Seneca, in *Hercules on Oeta* (lines 366–67), calls her "the Arcadian maid." Auge was a virgin priestess of Athena but was made pregnant by Heracles during a nocturnal festival. The son she bore, Telephus, was exposed; however, he was found and reared by shepherds. Auge's indignant father gave her to Nauplius to drown, but he sold her as a slave and she was brought to the court of Teuthras, king of Mysia, who became fond of her and considered her as his adopted daughter.

When Telephus grew up, he went to the oracle of Delphi and asked where he might find his mother. The oracle directed him to go to Mysia. Arriving there, Telephus rescued King Teuthras from an invading army and was given the hand of Auge as a reward. But Auge disdained to mate with anyone less than Heracles and on the wedding night would have killed her bridegroom with a sword that she had concealed if the gods had not sent a huge serpent into the chamber. Both murder and incest were thus prevented. Auge and Telephus then recounted their life stories and, in so doing, recognized each other. Telephus was designated as heir to the throne of Mysia (see TELEPHUS).

Auge was the title of a lost play by Euripedes (c. 413–410 B.C.), based on the foregoing myth. That it was long a favorite is shown by Menander's reference to it in *The Arbitrants*. The two plays had in common the motif of a rape during a nocturnal festival and a subsequent recognition. At one point in *The Arbitrants* the slave girl Sophrone quotes two lines from *Auge* and adds: "If you don't understand, Smicrines, I'll declaim a whole tragedy speech from *Auge*."

Augeas or **Augias** (Gk. **Augeias**). King of Elis in the Peloponnesus. Augeas' stables had not been cleaned out for many years. To clean them—some say in one day—was one of Heracles' twelve labors. He accomplished this task by diverting one or two rivers through the stables.

Augustus (Lat. "propitious" or "revered"). Title conferred on the first Roman emperor, Caesar Octavian, and assumed by succeeding emperors. Hence, in the pseudo-Senecan play *Octavia*, "Augustus" is used for both Tiberius and Nero, and "Augusta" for Agrippina.

aulaeum. Latin word for curtain. (See CURTAINS.)

Aulis. Port on the northern coast of Boeotia, opposite the island of Euboea at the narrowest point of the strait (the Euripus). Aulis was the assembly place for the Greek fleet that sailed against Troy.

Aulularia (Lat. **The Pot of Gold**). Extant comedy by Plautus (dated variously c. 200 or c. 186 B.C.). It is thought that *Aulularia* might have been based on a Greek play by Menander, perhaps his *Apistos*, "The Suspicious Man." Translations: Henry T. Riley, 1852; Edward H. Sugden, 1893; Paul Nixon, 1916; Lionel Casson, 1963. Adaptations and works influenced by *Aulularia*: QUEROLUS; Ben Jonson, *The Case Is Altered*, c. 1597; Molière, *L'Avare* (*The Miser*), 1668.

S C E N E. Athens, a street.

S U M M A R Y. The prologue is spoken by the Lar, or household god, of Euclio, a parsimonious old Athenian who is supposedly a poor man. The god explains that he has revealed to Euclio a pot of gold buried by his grandfather, who was equally stingy, so that Euclio's devout daughter, Phaedria, may make a suitable marriage. Ten months earlier Phaedria had been ravished by young Lyconides during a festival of Ceres; she does not, however, know the identity of her seducer, and her father is completely ignorant of the whole affair.

As the action begins, Euclio, who suspects everyone of having discovered the existence of his secret hoard, drives the old slave woman Staphyla from the house for her supposed snooping. After he himself reluctantly leaves the house to get his share of a small public dole lest anyone suspect him of having become rich, Euclio is met by a wealthy neighbor, Megadorus, the uncle of Lyconides. Megadorus is eager to marry Phaedria despite her poverty, and Euclio reluctantly consents to the match on condition that no dowry be required. His house is immediately overrun with cooks, slaves, and music girls hired by Megadorus to prepare for the wedding celebration. When Euclio hears the cooks mention pots, he assumes that his treasure has been found and cudgels them out into the street.

Afraid that the gold is unsafe inside the house, Euclio smuggles it out under his cloak. On the street he shakes off Megadorus, whose every attempt to be friendly he takes for a design on his gold. He intends to leave the treasure in the Temple of Fides (Faith), but when he realizes that Strobilus, a slave of Lyconides, has heard him mention the hiding place, he is forced to go elsewhere. Euclio finally hides the pot in a grove, not knowing that he has been followed by Strobilus, who soon makes off with the treasure.

Meanwhile, Phaedria is going into labor with Lyconides' child. Euclio appears, driven almost insane by the loss of his gold. Lyconides, on encountering him, interprets his grief as indignation at Phaedria's betrayal. After this misunderstanding is cleared up, Lyconides explains that his uncle Megadorus is willing to step aside so that he may marry the girl.

Just as Lyconides learns from his slave where the gold is, the manuscripts break off. Presumably the treasure was returned, the marriage of the young people was arranged, and perhaps Euclio, realizing the eternal misery that the gold would bring him, gave it to his daughter as her dowry.

COMMENTARY. Humorous, lively, well-constructed—an almost Aristotelian demonstration of the logical consequences of situation and character—out of Plautus' top drawer: this is the general verdict on *Aulularia,* and it has met with little disagreement. Thanks partly to Molière's adaptation of the play, the character of the miser emerges as a considerable figure in world literature.

Aurora. *Myth.* Roman goddess of the dawn, identified with Eos.

Ausonia. Italy.

Autochthons (Gk. **Autochthones,** "those born from the earth"). Designation claimed for themselves by several Greek peoples whose traditions maintained that "they had always been there."

Autolycus (Gk. **Autolykos**). *Myth.* A son of Hermes. Autolycus' feats of thievery and trickery were proverbial. Euripides' lost satyr play *Autolycus* may have dealt with his tricks, such as the stealing of Sisyphus' cattle, and those of

Sisyphus, who seduced Autolycus' daughter (and thus was the real father of Odysseus). In the only extant fragment of length, there is criticism of the overrating of athletics.

Automenes. Father of Arignotus.

Autonoë. *Myth.* Daughter of Cadmus and mother of Actaeon. Driven mad by Dionysus, Autonoë helped her sisters Agave and Ino tear Pentheus to pieces. (See AGAVE.)

Avernus. Miasmic Italian lake, thought to be an entrance to the underworld and hence used also to designate the underworld.

Award of Armor, The (Gk. **Hoplon Krisis**). Lost play by Aeschylus. It dealt with the contest between Ajax and Odysseus over Achilles' armor (see AJAX 1). Trojan captives seem to have been the judges. The tragedy must have been the first of an Ajax trilogy, followed by *The Thracian Women* and *The Women of Salamis.* Pacuvius' *Armorum Iudicium* was a free adaptation of this play.

Axios. River in Macedonia.

Azania. One of the three main divisions of Arcadia. The Azanians inhabited the northwestern part.

B

Babylonians, The (Gk. *Babylonioi*). Lost comedy by Aristophanes (427 or 426 B.C.). *The Babylonians,* though produced under the name of the author's friend Callistratus, was the play that inspired the lifelong enmity between Aristophanes and the demagogue Cleon. The chorus consisted of the so-called allies of the Athenian empire, who were actually oppressed subjects; they were eventually sent off to the treadmill by the character Demos (the Athenian people). Because Cleon was personally satirized, he prosecuted Aristophanes on charges of injustice to the Athenian citizenry and insolent behavior toward the people and their advisory body. Judging from a choric speech in *The Acharnians* (line 377 ff.), the poet was acquitted.

Bacchae (Gk. *Bakchai*). *Myth.* Female celebrants of the Dionysiac orgies (see MAENADS). *Bacchae* was the title of a lost tragedy by Aeschylus of which only two lines survive. Its relationship to his *Pentheus* is therefore impossible to determine. Euripides wrote an extant tragedy called *Bacchae,* which was adapted by Accius.

Bacchae; also **The Bacchantes** or **The Bacchanals** (Gk. *Bakchai*). Extant tragedy by Euripides (produced c. 405 B.C.). Translations: Henry Hart Milman, 1865; Gilbert Murray, 1911; Arthur S. Way, 1912; D. W. Lucas, 1930; Philip Vellacott, 1954; Henry Birkhead, 1957; William Arrowsmith, 1958. Adaptations: Pacuvius, *Pentheus;* Accius, *Bacchae:* Hans Werner Henze, *Die Bassariden* (opera), 1966, based on libretto by W. H. Auden and Chester Kallman.

S C E N E. Thebes, the palace.

S U M M A R Y. The sanctuary and tomb of the Theban princess Semele is still smoldering from the lightning blast that killed her when Hera tricked her into requesting that Zeus appear to her as he appeared to his consort in the full panoply of heaven. Dionysus, Semele's son by Zeus, speaks the prologue. He announces that he has come from Asia to Thebes to make his first Hellenic conquest and is assuming human form in order to wreak vengeance on Cadmus' people. His anger is directed at Cadmus' daughters (Agave, Ino, and Autonoë) in particular, for in declaring that their sister Semele lied when she claimed that her pregnancy was due to an immortal lover they have denied that Dionysus is a god. In revenge, Dionysus has driven the women of Thebes to a frenzy in which they continuously celebrate his rites. They are even now wandering in the mountains. In order to make his conquest complete, Dionysus must teach Pentheus, grandson of Cadmus and present occupant of the throne, that his cult is not to be rejected. Making way for the chorus of female followers that he has led with him from many lands, Dionysus—or the mortal whose form he has taken—retires to join the bacchanalian dances on Mount Cithaeron.

The Chorus of Bacchanals enter, singing of their progress from Asian Mount Tmolus and from Phrygia and Lydia, where the orgies of the Great Mother, Rhea Cybele, are celebrated by the wild Corybantes. Their hymn refers to all the trappings and dogmas of Dionysian and similar rites: the fawnskin cloak, the beaten timbrel, the shrilling flute, the thyrsus wand, the ivy garlands, the purifying mysteries, the Curetes' dance for the infant Zeus, the pinning of the unborn Dionysus in Zeus's thigh to conceal him from Hera, the birth of the bull-horned god, the ecstatic orgies in the wilderness, the tracking down and tearing to pieces of the goat victim at the three-year feast.

Blind Tiresias, the seer, now bids old Cadmus to provide himself with fawnskin, thyrsus, and ivy. Cadmus expresses his willingness to have a try at the practices of the cult, in spite of his age. As they totter toward the mountains, Tiresias discourses on man's ability to reason away ancient religious tradition. This discourse is interrupted by King Pentheus, who is outraged by what he considers the allurements, the drunkenness, and sexual immorality of this foreign cult being preached by a Stranger, who is no more than a master of hocus-pocus. Pentheus is out on a foray to imprison all adherents of the sect, but he is brought up short at the sight of Tiresias and his grandfather making fools of themselves in what seems a blasphemous manner.

To Pentheus' expostulation, Tiresias rejoins that it is not blasphemy at all: for as the earth goddess Demeter gives nourishment to men in the domain of the dry, so Dionysus provides it in the wet, and his provision, the stream of the vine, is a respite from grief, it is a sleep and a forgetfulness. Tiresias goes on to say that the story of the god's stay in Zeus's thigh (*meros*) simply arose from the fact that he was kept a hostage (*homeros*) in heaven, safe from Hera's jealous wrath; that Dionysus is akin to Apollo in prophecy and to Ares in frenzy, and that he makes men neither virtuous nor unvirtuous, but must be welcomed as he is. Cadmus adds that even if the whole Dionysian story is a fraud it will confer honor on the family, and besides, Pentheus should bear in mind the fate of his cousin Actaeon, who was torn to pieces by his own dogs for insulting Artemis.

Pentheus' reaction is to thrust away the hand that extends the ivy, to order Tiresias' place of soothsaying razed and despoiled, and to spur his guard after the effeminate Stranger, who, when caught, is to be stoned. Tiresias expresses the hope that the name Pentheus may not bring suffering (*penthos*) to the Cadmian house, but the king pays no heed. The Chorus then contrasts the folly of the overwise with the simple faith that, in the case of Bacchic worship, leads to joy, peace, ecstasy, and holiness.

At this point the Stranger is led in captive and presented to Pentheus. An attendant tells the king that the man yielded easily to capture, but that his followers were mysteriously released from prison. After some gibes at the man's delicate appearance, Pentheus learns that he came from Lydia, where, he says, he was initiated into the mysteries by Dionysus himself. The Stranger assures Pentheus that Dionysus is watching from near at hand and that if the king persists in his persecutions, he will soon learn that he is named Pentheus ("the Sufferer") for good reason.

Nevertheless, the Stranger is ordered to be imprisoned in the stables, whereupon the Chorus prophesies that Thebes, which rejects Dionysus now, will one day receive him, since it was at Thebes that Zeus rescued the unborn babe, put him into his male womb, and saluted him as "Dithyrambus" (perhaps in allusion to the idea that he twice, *dis*, came through the door, *thyra*, of birth).

This ode is interrupted by the voice of Dionysus from inside, calling on the earth to quake and fire to destroy the palace. Flames rise everywhere. The Stranger then appears and tells his followers how he teased Pentheus so that in his delusion the king tied up a bull thinking that it was his prisoner, and how Bacchus invented a phantom stranger, which Pentheus tried desperately to attack.

Now the king hurls himself out of the palace in a frenzy, but he has hardly begun to vent his rage when a Herdsman comes in to report that he has seen three bands of maenads in the wilds led by Agave, Pentheus' mother, and her sisters, Ino and Autonoë. At dawn, the Herdsman continues, the women rested quietly, fondling serpents, suckling wolf cubs and fawns, causing the earth to gush with water, wine, and milk, and making their thyrsi drip with honey. But, roused by the attempted capture of Agave, they gave chase, and the herdsmen barely escaped with their lives. Meanwhile the women proceeded to tear the herds to pieces with their bare hands—calves, heifers, bulls—and to invade the villages. Although no weapon could harm them, their wands inflicted wound after wound on the men.

The enraged Pentheus is about to marshal his army, when the Stranger offers to lead the women back to the city without violence. But Pentheus suspects a trick. Then with a ringing cry, the Stranger puts Pentheus under a spell so that he becomes intensely eager to see the women at their drunken revels and is persuaded to dress himself as a woman in order to spy on the Bacchae undetected. The Chorus sing of their longing for the bacchanalian dance and of wise submission to heaven's will. Presently the Stranger leads away the hypnotized Pentheus, pleased with his disguise and prattling like a child. As the king departs, the Chorus call down punishment on him for his unbelief.

A Messenger, Pentheus' servant, now returns to tell of the subsequent events: how on Cithaeron the Stranger miraculously bent down a large pine tree so that the king might mount and view the maenads' lewdness, and how the Stranger disappeared and the voice of Dionysus cried repeatedly from the sky, bidding the women to avenge him. With Agave leading, they obeyed, tearing up the pine by its roots. Pentheus, brought crashing to the ground, pleaded with his mother to recognize him, but in her madness she wrenched his arm from its socket. The other women then fell on the king and tore him to pieces.

Agave enters, cradling her son's head in her arms, under the delusion that she has taken part in a successful lion hunt. But when Cadmus enters, bringing with him the fragments of Pentheus' torn body which he has been collecting, Agave gradually comes to her senses.

The text breaks off, and when it resumes after the lacuna, Dionysus himself is pronouncing judgment. He ordains that Cadmus and his wife, Harmonia, will become serpents and will lead a barbarian army against Greece, though Ares at the end will establish them in the Islands of the Blessed. Agave, for her tardiness in believing, must leave Thebes forever. The god withdraws, and the drama ends with father and daughter lamenting their sentences and preparing for exile.

C O M M E N T A R Y. Modern critics have generally recognized that an understanding of the *Bacchae* is crucial for an understanding of Euripides' work as a whole. Accordingly, modes of interpretation of this play can be grouped along the lines of general Euripidean criticism.

There was little to support the nineteenth-century view that the play represents Euripides' "recantation" of an earlier hostile attitude to religion, and so, around the turn of the century, the "Euripides the Rationalist" line began to prevail. According to it the author expected the audience to realize that the Dionysus cult was a piece of hocus-pocus, in which the Stranger-Dionysus figure was a transparent charlatan. After this view was discredited, interpreters tended to shift toward the kind of pseudocriticism which asserts that the *Bacchae*— and by implication all literature—had no "meaning" but was simply a good piece of theater (though what "good theater" might mean in this connection must go unspecified). Still later came advocates of the opinion that the *Bacchae* was a warning against the horrors of barbaric excess in orgiastic religion, the poet having observed such cults in Macedonia.

There is, however, a more comprehensive interpretation, and one more conformable to the structure of the play. It is that Euripides was emphasizing the wide scope of the religious sphere—which is wider than the human mind or spirit can grasp or endure—as well as the astounding and terrifying impingement of the divine element on the human, toward which it is perilous to take any attitude other than that of recognition, participation, and submission.

Bacchides (Lat. **The Two Bacchides** or **The Two Bacchises**). Extant comedy by Plautus (variously dated between 189 and 184 B.C.). *Bacchides* was based on a Greek play, *The Double Deceiver*, by Menander. Translations: Henry T. Riley, 1852; Edward H. Sugden, 1893; Paul Nixon, 1916.

S C E N E. Athens, before the houses of Bacchis and Nicobulus.

S U M M A R Y. A few lines have been lost from the beginning of the play. In the first surviving scene, the prostitute Bacchis of Athens welcomes her sister of the same name and profession, who has been brought to Athens from Samos by the soldier Cleomachus, to whom she owes a year of service. But Bacchis of Samos is in love with young Mnesilochus, whom she met in Ephesus, where he had gone with his servant Chrysalus to collect money owed his father. To help her sister gain her freedom from Cleomachus, Bacchis of Athens decides to make use of Mnesilochus' friend Pistoclerus, who has been sent to find his friend's beloved. Pistoclerus quickly becomes infatuated with Bacchis of Athens, and in a short while he returns with provisions for a feast in the prostitutes' house, ignoring the shocked protests of his old pedagogue, Lydus.

When Mnesilochus' slave Chrysalus arrives in Athens, he is told that money will be needed to repay Cleomachus the two hundred gold pieces he gave for the Samian Bacchis. Chrysalus accordingly holds back from his master's father, Nicobulus, the money that he (Chrysalus) and Mnesilochus had gone to Ephesus to collect, telling Nicobolus that the gold has been deposited in the Temple of Diana in Ephesus to keep it safe from pirates.

Upon arriving in Athens, Mnesilochus is overjoyed to learn that his sweetheart has been found and that the money to redeem her is available. He is, however, soon thrown into despair when he meets Lydus, who, amid complaints about the self-indulgence and vice of modern youth, reveals that Pistoclerus has been making love to a girl called Bacchis. Convinced that his friend has betrayed him, Mnesilochus gives his father the money that was due him, only to be informed shortly afterward that there are two Bacchises and that his jealousy is baseless. The wily Chrysalus now concocts a scheme for getting the money back from Nicobulus. When Cleomachus comes to fetch Bacchis of Samos, Chrysalus tells Nicobulus that the soldier is her husband and persuades the old man to promise two hundred gold pieces to prevent Cleomachus from killing Mnesilochus. The slave then extracts another two hundred on the strength of a letter from Mnesilochus, who vows to mend his ways and abjure bad company if only his father will give him the wherewithal to pay off the wicked woman from Samos.

As Chrysalus carries away this money for further merrymaking, Nicobulus meets Cleomachus and learns by chance that the woman in question is not the soldier's wife but a prostitute. Enraged, Nicobulus and Pistoclerus' father prepare to assault the house of ill fame. They are met at the door by the two Bacchises, who soothe and cajole the old men until they are enticed inside to enjoy a festive evening.

COMMENTARY. There is general agreement that this is one of the liveliest and most interestingly constructed of Plautus' plays. The Greek original is shown to be Menander's *Dis Exapaton* (*The Double Deceiver*) by the fact that the well-known line "Whom the gods love die young" is quoted from Menander's play. Furthermore, the double deception practiced by Chrysalus, one of the best examples of the *servus dolosus* in ancient drama, is reminiscent of the Menandrian title. The device in which a rather stupid young master frustrates the helpful schemes of his tricky slave, thus spurring him to greater heights of chicanery, was imitated in neoclassical comedy, for example, in Molière's *L'Étourdi*. Another favorite theme of later classical comedy was that of the two contrasting kinds of education, the overdisciplinary versus the permissive (compare Terence's *Adelphoe*). *Bacchides* was performed at the marriage festivities of Lucrezia Borgia in 1502; with it were staged *Epidicus, Asinaria, Miles Gloriosus,* and *Casina*.

Bacchus (Gk. **Bakchos** or **Bakchios**). One of the many names of DIONYSUS.

Bacchylides (Gk. **Bakchylides**). Greek choric poet (fl. middle 5th century

B.C.). In the 1890's the British Museum acquired an Egyptian papyrus that contained, among other poems by Bacchylides, a half-dozen called "Dithyrambs." They are the only specimens of significant length illustrating the genre that was alleged to have had a special relationship to the development of drama. The poems deal with scenes from heroic legend in a manner far from ecstatic or "dithyrambic"; only one has anything to do with Dionysus. In the poem called "Theseus," the chorus leader (*exarchos*) and the chorus sing alternately. This poem is said by some to be representative of the "missing link" between choric song and tragedy. Probably, however, it represents only one of several traditional dithyrambic types that may have resulted in tragic drama of some kind.

Bacis (Gk. **Bakis**). Soothsayer. The ancients identified at least three soothsayers of this name. By Aristophanes' time, apparently, the name Bacis had become almost a synonym for "fortuneteller" or "quack prophet."

Baetis. River in southern Spain.

Balbus, Lucius Cornelius. Spanish-Roman soldier, statesman, and playwright (1st century B.C.). Balbus wrote a *fabula praetexta* (historical play) about his services as a go-between in the civil war of Caesar and Pompey; he produced it himself in his native city of Cadiz. The stone theater which Balbus dedicated in the Campus Martius in 13 B.C. was one of the three most considerable in imperial Rome. It was converted into a fortress by the Cenci in the Middle Ages.

Banqueters, The (Gk. **Daitales**). Lost comedy by Aristophanes (427 B.C.). The author's first play, *The Banqueters* was produced under the name of his friend Callistratus; it won a second prize in the dramatic contest. The plot centered around an old man with two sons, one of them modest and self-controlled, the other a profligate representative of the new generation.

Barca (Gk. **Barke**; adj. Barcaean). City in Cyrenaica, Africa. Barca was noted for its horse training and chariot driving.

Basileia (Gk. "sovereignty"). Maiden in Aristophanes' *Birds*, the embodiment of the sovereignty of Zeus.

Bassarae or **Bassarids** (Gk. **Bassarai** or **Bassarides**). Maenads. *Bassarae* was the title of a lost tragedy by Aeschylus. (See LYCURGEIA.)

Bathyllus. Pantomimist (1st century B.C.). Bathyllus was a freedman and a favorite of the famous Roman patron of the arts, Maecenas. With Pylades (2) he established pantomime as a separate genre; his dramatic material tended toward comedy. So popular was Bathyllus in his own day that his partisans and those of Pylades clashed in riots. Through pupils and imitators he founded a tradition that lasted a century and a half.

Baton of Sinope. Writer of comedy (first half of 3rd century B.C.). Of Baton's works only four or five titles and a few fragments survive. His chief target seems to have been philosophers whose lives did not jibe with their teachings.

Batrachoi. See THE FROGS.

Battus (Gk. **Battos**). Founder of Cyrene, a Greek city on the north coast of

Africa. Cyrene was famous for its cultivation of silphium, an aromatic plant. The term "Battus' silphium" was used to mean anything rich and rare.

Belias. *Myth.* A descendant of Belus; specifically one of the Danaïdes.

Bellerophon or **Bellerophontes.** *Myth.* Corinthian hero. Exiled from Corinth for homicide, Bellerophon was purified by Proetus, king of Tiryns. Proetus' wife, Stheneboea (or Anteia, according to the *Iliad*, Book VI; and Anticleia, in other versions of the myth) tried to seduce him. Repulsed by the chaste youth, she denounced him to her husband as a would-be adulterer. Proetus then sent Bellerophon across the sea to Stheneboea's father, King Iobates, of Lycia or Caria, with a sealed message instructing Iobates to put the bearer to death. Rather than incur blood-guilt directly, the king sent Bellerophon on the seemingly hopeless mission of killing the monster Chimaera. With divine help, the hero was able to capture and tame the winged horse Pegasus and thus to accomplish his mission.

After performing various other feats and winning the hand of Iobates' daughter Philonoë, as well as half of his father-in-law's kingdom, Bellerophon returned to Tiryns. There he revenged himself on Queen Stheneboea by inviting her for a ride on Pegasus and then pushing her off into the sea. Finally, swollen with success, Bellerophon directed his winged steed toward Olympus, whereupon Zeus struck him down and he fell to the Aleian Plain, an outcast among men. There (possibly according to fragments of Euripides' *Bellerophon*) Megapenthes, son of Stheneboea, tried to kill Bellerophon, but he was rescued by his own son Glaucus and later died, old and lame but reconciled to the gods.

Bellerophon. Lost tragedy by Euripides (produced between 428 and 425 B.C.). It dealt with the last episodes of Bellerophon's life, from the time that he tried to fly Pegasus to heaven and was struck down by the gods. From gibes in Aristophanes' *Peace* it is learned that in Euripides' play the hero appeared flying over the stage (like Trygaeus on his dung beetle), and from Aristophanes' *Acharnians* that he later appeared as a lame beggar in rags. Certain atheistical speeches in *Bellerophon* were notorious, for example: "Does anyone say that there are gods in heaven? There are none, none: if anyone says there are, let him not foolishly use that obsolete word. Look at the facts, you who do not agree: I say that tyrants kill and rob multitudes, that perjurers ruin cities, and that those who behave so are far more prosperous than those who lead quiet and pious lives." These words were apparently spoken by the hero after his downfall. The play may have ended, however, with his reconciliation to his fate.

Bellona. Roman goddess of war, often thought of as resembling a Fury and inhabiting the underworld.

Belus (Gk. **Belos**). *Myth.* Father, by the daughter of the river god Nile, of the twins Aegyptus and Danaüs.

bema. Properly the speaker's platform in a political assembly. Sometimes these platforms were erected in theaters, and the term was occasionally applied to the stage itself.

Bessa. City of the eastern Locrians. See LOCRIS.

Bia (Gk.). Personification of force. Bia is a mute character in the first scene of Aeschylus' *Prometheus Bound.*

Birds, The (Gk. **Ornithes;** traditional Latin title, **Aves**). Extant comedy by Aristophanes (produced 414 B.C.). Translations: John Hookham Frere, 1839; Benjamin B. Rogers, 1924; Arthur S. Way, 1934; Gilbert Murray, 1950; Dudley Fitts, 1957; William Arrowsmith, 1961.

S C E N E. The countryside near Athens.

S U M M A R Y. With a jackdaw and a raven for guides, Peithetaerus, or, according to some manuscripts, Peisthetaerus (Persuasive), and Euelpides (Optimistic) have left Athens to seek out the hoopoe Epops, who was once Tereus, the wicked king of Thrace. The Athenians hope that Epops may direct them to a better land than Attica, where lawsuits and other abuses have made life unendurable. Epops is unable to help, but Peithetaerus hits on a plan whereby the birds would set up their own commonwealth in mid-air; it would base its power on control of the passing smoke of sacrifices that rises from earth to Olympus. The others fall in eagerly with the idea.

Epops then warbles a summons, and a Chorus of various kinds of birds flit in. At first they are hostile to the strangers, but when Epops gets permission for Peithetaerus to describe the project, they are won over. The birds, Peithetaerus says, are older than the gods, and therefore they ought to be the rulers of the universe. Let the birds, he continues, block off the mid-region of the air with a brick wall and demand overlordship of the gods, threatening to shut them off from earth and their love affairs with mortals; and let the birds subdue men, threatening to eat their seeds and pick out the eyes of their stock, while promising to keep down insects and to supply reliable omens. The birds accept the scheme with enthusiasm. Epops then takes Peithetaerus and Euelpides off to eat a root that causes wings to grow.

In their absence the bird Chorus sings a parody of the creation stories that must have been common in contemporary mystery cults and philosophical speculations. According to their version, birds are the offspring of Eros and Chaos; they are older than the Olympians and worthier of worship. They offer their commonwealth as a refuge for anyone tired of the restraints in human communities.

Peithetaerus and Euelpides, returning with their wings, choose the name Nephelococcygia, "Cloudcuckooland," for the new state. After the first state sacrifice to the bird gods, however, a bothersome succession of busybodies arrive, eager to interfere with the new government: a Poet with poems of dedication, a Soothsayer with made-to-order oracles, a Real Estate Agent who wants to parcel the air into lots, an Inspector from Athens anxious to take over as a kind of viceroy, and a Retailer of Government Decrees. All these pests are hustled off the scene in one way or another.

When the brick wall is completed, Iris, goddess of the rainbow and messenger of the Olympians, is dragged in as a trespasser. Peithetaerus answers her threats with insults and sends her on her way. A Herald from earth brings news that bird imitation has become all the rage and that a mob of men can soon be expected to arrive asking for wings. In comes a Young Man who wants to kill his father, followed by the dithyrambic poet Cinesias and an Informer; all present themselves for adoption into the bird kingdom, but Peithetaerus rudely gets rid of them.

Next Prometheus, masked for fear of Zeus, arrives to inform the birds that the blockade is bringing Olympus to its knees and that a deputation from the gods is on its way. He advises Peithetaerus to demand Basileia (the personification of Zeus's sovereignty) for his wife. The delegates arrive: they are Poseidon, Heracles, and Triballus, a clownish barbarian who speaks a foreign gibberish. At first Peithetaerus rudely ignores the Olympians, but when Heracles suggests that they begin to discuss peace, he demands Basileia and promises in return that the birds, if they become rulers, will act as spies of the gods and executors of their justice. He adds that Heracles, who is Zeus's heir, will have nothing to lose, since he is illegitimate and cannot inherit. After much bickering, the terms are agreed upon, and the barbarian's mutterings are interpreted as consent. The gods depart and the play ends with the joyous marriage procession of Basileia and Peithetaerus.

C O M M E N T A R Y. *The Birds* is a satire on utopianism, written a generation before the first literary Utopia, Plato's *Republic*, became as much as a gleam in Plato's mind. Discussions of governmental reform and ideal societies must have been commonplace in Greek intellectual circles from the days of Solon, and the fantasy of a model community midway between earth and heaven is one that might naturally rise from the universal ancient notion that all human order must strive to be a replica of harmony on the divine level. The play's satire cuts in two directions: although Aristophanes was lampooning utopianism, his chief object was to point up the shortcomings of contemporary Athens; but his sympathies, if they were anywhere, were on the side of the utopians. The fantastic nature of the theme held a special appeal, later, for the Romantic age, and the delicacy of the lyrics and general sprightliness of the episodes have made *The Birds* a favorite in every period. Yet on its first appearance it lost the prize to Ameipsias' *Komastai*.

bisellia. Front-row seats of double width in the Roman theater. They were reserved for officials.

Bistonians (Gk. **Bistones**). Thracian tribe that inhabited the coastal region near Abdera.

Boeotia. District in central Greece, northwest of Attica. Boeotia was supposed to have derived its name from the cow (*bous*) which the oracle told Cadmus to follow to the future site of Thebes. Most of Boeotia was usually opposed to Athens in any war; this fact may have contributed to the reputation for stupidity that the Boeotians enjoyed in Attic literature.

Boii. Gallic tribe.

Bolbe. Lake in Thrace.

bomolochos (Gk. "one who lurks by the altar"). The *bomolochos* waited for scraps from the sacrifices; hence he was a low, calculating person. According to ancient theorists of comedy, *bomolochos*, ALAZON, and EIRON were the three universal character types most commonly used for comic effects. The *bomolochos*, commonly portrayed as a sly old countryman or a flippant servant, is the typical Sancho Panza, literal-minded, limited in imagination, self-seeking, acquisitive, and full of practical common sense—a caricature of the "natural man." He punctures pretensions, scoffs at romantic vagaries, indulges in earthy and obscene jests, gives figurative expressions a literal turn, often breaks the dramatic illusion to address the audience, and sometimes seems the only sane figure in a multitude of eccentrics. In the last capacity he sometimes becomes the mouthpiece of the author. Some modern scholars think that the *bomolochos* may originally have been a personage in primitive ritual whose function was to punctuate ceremonies with irreverent or satirical observations in order to avert bad luck.

Some Aristophanic examples of this character type are Strepsiades in *The Clouds* and Trygaeus in *Peace*. In New Comedy two of its manifestations are the *servus dolosus* (see SERVUS) and the PARASITE. A few modern critics have used the term *bomolochos* to denote a character present in a comic agon who is either judge of the dispute or a helper of one of the disputants (see EPIRRHEMATIC AGON).

Bone-Gatherers, The (Gk. **Ostologoi**). Lost play by Aeschylus. Of it one scanty fragment remains. Apparently the play was one of an Odysseus cycle and depicted the relatives of Penelope's slain suitors coming to collect the bodies and to demand a reckoning of Odysseus.

Boötes. (Gk. The "oxen-driver," *i.e.*, wagon-driver). A constellation near the Pole Star.

Boreas. *Myth.* The deified north wind. Boreas carried off Oreithyia, an Athenian princess, and she bore him twin sons, Zetes and Calais.

Borraean, or **Borrhaean, Gates.** The northern (see BOREAS) gateway of Thebes.

Bosporus (Gk. **Bosporos**). Name applied both to the strait connecting the Sea of Azov to the Black Sea (the Cimmerian Bosporus) and, more commonly, to that connecting the Black Sea with the Aegean Sea (the Thracian Bosporus). In legend the name was interpreted as "the cow's passage" and was associated with the wanderings of Io in the form of a cow—as she appears in Aeschylus' *Prometheus Bound*.

Boupalos. "Hold my coat while I cut out Boupalos' eye" was a line from the poet Hipponax that had become proverbial. Aristophanes refers to it in *Lysistrata* (line 361).

Bouphonia. The "ox-killing," an odd Athenian ritual forming part of the festival Dipolieia. After a priest had killed an ox with an axe, he fled, and the axe was pronounced guilty and thrown into the sea. When the celebrants had feasted on the beef, they stuffed the oxskin and yoked it to a plough. This was a symbolic expiation of the guilt incurred in slaughtering domestic animals for food.

Braggart Soldier, The, or **The Braggart Warrior.** See MILES GLORIOSUS.

Brasidas. Spartan general. An able soldier, Brasidas was active in the early years of the Peloponnesian War. He was killed in the fighting around Amphipolis in 422 B.C.

Brauron. Village in Attica, home of the Brauronia, a festival of Artemis. The festival's chief feature was a dance performed in honor of the goddess by small girls, called bears, who wore yellow dresses that were perhaps an imitation of bearskins.

Briareus. *Myth.* In Homer's *Iliad* a hundred-armed monster who was Zeus's occasional bodyguard. According to Seneca, however, Briareus and his brother Gyas were among the Giants who tried to storm heaven (*Hercules on Oeta,* line 167).

Briseis. *Myth.* Achilles' concubine captured in the Trojan War. Agamemnon appropriated Briseis to compensate himself for having to give up his own captive woman, Chryseis. His act caused Achilles' angry withdrawal from battle.

Britannicus. Son of the emperor Claudius, named in honor of his father's conquest of Britain. In the pseudo-Senecan play *Octavia,* Britannicus is referred to as Octavia's brother, and his death is mourned. He was universally believed to have been poisoned by Nero in A.D. 55.

Bromius (Gk. **Bromios**). Epithet of DIONYSUS as "god of shouting and uproar."

bronteion (Gk.). Device for simulating thunder, probably by striking stones or clubs against metal. The *bronteion* may have been used quite early in the theater, for example, at the conclusion of *Prometheus Bound.*

Brothers, The. See ADELPHOE.

Brothers Menaechmus, The. See MENAECHMI.

Bruttium. Southernmost section of Italy, "the toe of the boot."

Brutus, Marcus Junius. The protégé of Julius Caesar. Brutus was, however, one of the chief instigators of Caesar's assassination in 44 B.C.

Bucco. See ATELLAN FARCE.

Builders of the Bridal Chamber, The (Gk. **Thalamopoioi**). Lost play by Aeschylus. Since only two lines are extant, virtually nothing is known about it. Some consider it an alternate title to *The Egyptians* (see DANAÏD TETRALOGY), thinking that the play dealt with the construction of the bridal chambers of the Danaïdes. Others think that it was a satyr play of unknown plot.

Bupalus. See BOUPALOS.

Busiris (Gk. **Bousiris**). *Myth.* Egyptian king who sacrificed a stranger to Zeus every year. When Heracles was captured and led to the altar as the victim, he broke his bonds and sacrificed Busiris. A lost satyr play by Euripides called *Busiris* was based on the foregoing myth.

Bybline. 1. (also **Bibline**) Adjective denoting some mountains of uncertain location mentioned by Aeschylus in *Prometheus Bound*. They were considered by the playwright to be near the first cataract of the Nile. The name may have come from *byblos,* "the papyrus plant."

2. Pertaining to Byblos, a city in Phoenicia.

Byzantium (Gk. **Byzantion**). Greek colony on the Thracian Bosporus, reputedly founded by Megarians in the seventh century B.C. In classical times Byzantium was an important commercial city, noted for its use of iron money. It was reconstituted in A.D. 330 as New Rome, or Constantinople.

C

Cabiri or **Cabeiri** (Gk. **Kabeiroi**). *Myth*. Vague deities of indefinite number connected with certain cult mysteries on the island of Samothrace. The Cabiri were either sons of Hephaestus or closely associated with him in some other way. They were either referred to mysteriously as "the Great Gods" or conflated with the pygmy spirits of the forge.

Cabiri was the title of a lost play by Aeschylus, probably the satyr play of an Argonaut tetralogy (the others being *The Argo*, *The Lemnians*, and *Hypsipyle*). In it, apparently, the Argonauts landed on Samothrace; there were comic scenes of drunkenness, the earliest known to have been on the stage.

Cadmus (Gk. **Kadmos**). *Myth*. Phoenician prince, founder of Thebes. In *The Phoenician Women* (lines 124–25) Seneca calls Cadmus an "Assyrian king." The latter was sent by his father, Agenor, in search of the lost Europa, and so wandered to Greece. But in obedience to the Delphian oracle, Cadmus abandoned his search and followed a cow to Boeotia, where he killed Ares' dragon. The dragon's teeth, when sown, produced warriors from the earth, called *Spartoi*, "sown ones." A fight arose among the *Spartoi* and they killed one another, but the five survivors helped Cadmus to found Thebes. Hence the Thebans were referred to as "children of Cadmus," "Cadmians," or "Cadmeians."

Cadmus married Harmonia, and of his four daughters—Autonoë, Agave, Ino, and Semele—three went mad under the influence of Dionysus (see AGAVE). Seneca, in *Hercules Furens* (line 750 ff.), depicts them as haunting the underworld. In Euripides' *Bacchae* Cadmus appears, as an old man, with the seer Tiresias; he has retired from rule and warns his grandson and successor, Pentheus, not to oppose Dionysus. At the end of the *Bacchae*, after Cadmus has collected the pieces of Pentheus' body, he is banished by Dionysus to Illyria, where he and his wife are destined to turn into serpents.

Caecilius Statius. Roman writer of comedy, FABULA PALLIATA (born 230–219 B.C.; died ?168 B.C.). Caecilius was ranked by some ancient critics as the equal, if not the superior, of Plautus and Terence. Of his forty known plays only about three hundred fragmentary lines survive. He was usually said to have been of Gallic origin, coming from northern Italy, but the story that he was captured in war, brought to Rome as a slave, and finally freed may have arisen from a misunderstanding. Not much is known of Caecilius' life aside from the fact that he was a good friend of Ennius and shared a house with him for a time. Although his death date has been given as 168 B.C., some modern scholars have put it a year or two later to authenticate the story that the young Terence read his *Andria*, which was produced in 166 B.C., to the older playwright.

Caecilius' poetical work was devoted entirely to adapting plays from Greek New Comedy, chiefly from Menander; most of his titles are Latinized Greek. Best known is *Plocium* (*The Necklace*), adapted from Menander's *Plokion*. In it the marriage plans of boy and girl are upset when the girl gives birth to a child of unknown paternity; the boy's mother suspects her husband, but all is resolved when a necklace provides proof that the boy himself is the father. Caecilius' Latin was adversely criticized by Cicero and his plots praised by Varro. It has been thought by some that his works provided a transition from the loosely knit plays of Plautus to the closely knit ones of Terence and that he was the first to use the prologue to express personal opinions. All that is certain is that, in the prologue to Terence's *Mother-in-Law* (*Hecyra*), Ambivius Turpio claims that by dint of presenting Caecilius' plays repeatedly he made them popular with the public.

Calais. *Myth.* Son of Boreas. (See ZETES.)

Calchas (Gk. **Kalchas**). *Myth.* Soothsayer with the Greek expedition against Troy. Although Calchas does not appear in Euripides' *Iphigenia at Aulis*, the play evolves from his prophecy that Iphigenia must be sacrificed before the Greek fleet can sail. Calchas speaks a few lines in Seneca's *Trojan Women*, confirming the pronouncement that Polyxena must be sacrificed.

Calchedon (Gk. **Kalchedon**). Greek city across the Bosporus from Byzantium.

calends. First day of the Roman month.

Callias (Gk. **Kallias**). 1. Athenian spendthrift and profligate. Callias was called the "evil genius" of his aristocratic family. Aristophanes ridiculed him in *Ecclesiazusae* (line 810). His house is the fictional scene of Xenophon's *Symposium* and Plato's *Protagoras*.

2. Writer of Old Comedy. Callias was the author of a lost *Alphabetic Tragedy*, which was actually a comedy. In it each member of the twenty-four-man comic chorus represented a letter of the Greek alphabet; by their varied groupings words were spelled out. The work was said in ancient times to have influenced Sophocles' *Oedipus the King* and Euripides' *Medea*, but evidence of this is extremely uncertain. The suggestion has been made that in the *Alphabetic Tragedy* the letters appeared in regular order, then in reverse, and that this prompted Sophocles and Euripides to make a chiastic arrangement of episodes in their plays (*a b c d e d c b a*). This idea is ingenious but hardly convincing, since a chiastic arrangement was common in Greek literature.

3. Writer of Old Comedy. This Callias is probably, but not certainly, identical with the foregoing playwright. He was the author of plays named *The Egyptian, The Atalanta Comedy, The Frogs, The Cyclopes, The Chain Gang, The Satyrs, The Idlers,* and *The Iron Pestles;* all are lost.

Callichorus (Gk. **Kallichoros**). River in Paphlagonia considered sacred to Dionysus.

Calligeneia (Gk. **Kalligeneia**, "mother of beautiful offspring"). Epithet of Demeter at the festival of the Thesmophoria.

Callimachus (Gk. **Kallimachos**). 1. Needy writer of choruses. Callimachus was mentioned by Aristophanes in *Ecclesiazusae* (line 809).

2. Poet, scholar, and librarian (middle 3rd century B.C.). Callimachus' poetry is famous, but his lost *Pinakes* (*Tablets*), an exhaustive descriptive catalogue of the Alexandrian Library, must have been the indirect source of much that is now known about ancient drama.

Calliope (Gk. **Kalliope**, "beautiful-voiced"). *Myth.* One of the Muses. Calliope was called, at various times, the mother of Orpheus, of the Sirens, of Linus, and of Rhesus.

Callippides (Gk. **Kallippides**). Athenian tragic actor (later 5th century B.C.). Callippides was a friend of Sophocles. Arrogant and vain, he was often ridiculed by the comedians and criticized for overacting. The Spartan Agesilaus refused to listen to his imitation of a nightingale, saying, "I have heard the real thing many times."

Callisto (Gk. **Kallisto**). *Myth.* Nymph in the train of Artemis and mother of Arcas by Zeus. Callisto became the constellation of the Great Bear (see ARCAS). *Callisto* was the title of a lost play by Aeschylus, who may have used the version of the myth in which Artemis, at Hera's prompting, shot and killed Callisto, who had been disguised as a bear to escape the notice of Hera. Zeus rescued the unborn child, Arcas, from the dying mother's womb.

Callistratus (Gk. **Kallistratos**). 1. Friend of Aristophanes and perhaps himself a writer of comedy. Under Callistratus' name Aristophanes produced *The Banqueters, The Babylonians, The Acharnians, The Birds,* and *Lysistrata.*

2. Critic of the Alexandrian age. Callistratus was so famous as a disciple of Aristophanes of Byzantium that he was called "the Aristophanian." He wrote commentaries on the three great tragedians (Aeschylus, Sophocles, and Euripides) and on Cratinus, Eupolis, and Aristophanes; all are lost.

Calpe. Mt. Gibraltar, one of the Pillars of Hercules.

Calydnae. Small island near the Trojan coast.

Calydon (Gk. **Kalydon**). City in Aetolia. Calydon was the scene of the famous mythical boar hunt involving MELEAGER and Atalanta. Plautus' *Poenulus* is also laid there.

Calypso (Gk. **Kalypso**, "the concealer"). *Myth.* Goddess of an enchanted isle. Calypso received the shipwrecked Odysseus on his way home from Troy and kept him for years as her lover until she was ordered by the council of the gods to let him go.

Camarina (Gk. **Kamarina**). Greek colony on the southern coast of Sicily.

Camicans, The (Gk. **Kamikoi**). Lost play by Sophocles. It probably told how King Minos tracked down DAEDALUS to the court of King Cocalus in Sicilian

Camicus and how the daughters of Cocalus killed Minos with scalding water. Perhaps this play was identical with Sophocles' lost *Minos*.

Campania. Section of Italy around Naples. Campania was known for prosperity and luxurious living.

Canephori (Gk. **Kanephoroi**, "basket-bearers"). Athenian girls who carried baskets of sacrificial objects and sacred symbolic materials on their heads in the processions of the great festivals.

Cannonus (Gk. **Kannonos**). Athenian politician (5th century B.C.). Cannonus was responsible for a decree by which anyone accused of wronging the people of Athens had to defend himself in chains.

Canobus or **Canopus** (Gk. **Kanobos** or **Kanopos**). City on the westernmost mouth of the Nile.

Cantharus (Gk. **Kantharos**). Elaborate pun made by Aristophanes in *Peace* (line 145). It involved (a) the western harbor of the Piraeus, named after a hero, (b) a kind of cup, (c) a kind of dung beetle, (d) a kind of boat.

canticum, pl. **cantica.** Solo song in Roman drama, as opposed to choric song. In a wider sense the word included all parts of the Roman play except the strictly dialogue parts written in the six-beat iambic line. *Cantica* were accompanied by flute music; if the actor could not sing well, a *cantor* might take over while the actor went through the motions of singing and acting.

In the sense of polymetrical elaborate monody, the *canticum* is found in extant drama only in the plays of Plautus. The question of where it came from has evoked the following answers: from New Comedy (but there is no evidence of it in Greek New Comedy or in Terence); from Greek tragedy as adapted by earlier Roman poets; from Etruria; from the popular dramatic entertainments of southern Italy; and from the dramatic *satura,* a kind of early amateur theatrical described by Livy (the existence of which is much doubted). All of these theories are speculative and inconclusive.

Capaneus (Gk. **Kapaneus**). *Myth.* One of the Seven against Thebes. Although Capaneus was described in Euripides' *Suppliants* (line 861 ff.) as wealthy but modest, and having many good personal qualities, his behavior on the battlefield was described by Aeschylus in *The Seven Against Thebes* (line 422 ff.) as boastful and impious. Capaneus declared that he would burn Thebes whether the gods were willing or not. As Capaneus mounted a scaling ladder, Zeus struck him dead with a thunderbolt.

Caphareus (Gk. **Kaphareus**). Promontory on Euboea. Here Nauplius set out misleading lights and wrecked many Greek ships on their way home from Troy.

Cappadocia (Gk. **Kappadokia**). Region in central Asia Minor.

Captives, The (Lat. **Captivi**). Extant comedy by Plautus. The play has been variously dated as follows: between 205 and 202 B.C.; c. 200 B.C.; between 193 and 189 B.C. It was adapted from a Greek original the name of which is a matter of guesswork but might be Alexis' *Thebans,* Philemon's *Aetolian,* Posidippus' *Captives,* or a play by Anaxandrides. Translations: Henry T. Riley, 1852; Edward H. Sugden, 1893; Paul Nixon, 1916; C. W. Parry, 1954.

Adaptations and works influenced by *The Captives:* Lodovico Ariosto, *I Suppositi,* 1509 (translation by George Gascoigne, *The Supposes,* 1566); Ben Jonson, *The Case Is Altered,* c. 1597; Thomas Middleton, *No Wit, No Help Like a Woman's,* 1613; Philip Massinger, *A New Way to Pay Old Debts,* 1625; Pedro Calderón de la Barca, *El Principe Constante,* 1629; Jean de Rotrou, *Les Captifs,* 1638.

SCENE. A city in Aetolia.

SUMMARY. The speaker of the prologue explains that Hegio, an old man of Aetolia, had two sons. One of them, Tyndarus, was stolen when four years old by a slave, who ran away to Elis and sold him to Philocrates' father. All his life since that time, Tyndarus has been Philocrates' personal slave as well as his friend. Many years later when war broke out between Aetolia and Elis, Hegio's other son, Philopolemus, was taken prisoner and had become the slave of a physician, Menarchus.

In order to have some prisoner whom he can exchange for his son Philopolemus, Hegio has begun to buy up Elean captives. In so doing he has unwittingly gained possession of his son Tyndarus and the son's master, Philocrates, who have, however, exchanged identities in the hope that the master will be freed. The ruse succeeds when Tyndarus, the supposed master, persuades Hegio to send Philocrates, the supposed slave, to Elis to arrange for Philopolemus' release.

As soon as Philocrates has gone on his mission, Hegio brings in another Elean captive, Aristophontes, who is a friend of Philocrates. When Aristophontes addresses the supposed Philocrates as "Tyndarus," the latter tries to convince Hegio that Aristophontes has long been known as a lunatic. But Aristophontes manages to prove to Hegio that he is not insane, and Tyndarus, though he makes a good impression by his proud assertion that he is glad to suffer for the sake of his master's liberty, is ordered to be shackled and sent to the stone quarries.

Shortly afterward Philocrates returns, as he had promised to do, bringing with him Philopolemus and, in addition, the very slave who had made off with Hegio's child long ago. The play ends happily when Tyndarus is recognized as that child.

COMMENTARY. From the time of Lessing, who considered it the finest play ever staged, *The Captives* has been one of the most highly praised of Plautus' works. One can discount some of the admiration of the eighteenth and nineteenth centuries—based as it was on a taste for sentimentalism and a distaste for obscenity—without losing sight of the play's genuine merits and peculiar points of interest. The prologue reflects the author's pride in its uniqueness: "here are no unquotable dirty lines, no pimp, no whore, no braggart soldier"; the short epilogue re-emphasizes the play's decency: "It is one of the few comedies that teach good people how to become better." These passages may not, however, have been by Plautus, but later additions.

From the standpoint of plot, the point of the exchange of roles is a little hard to grasp, but some humorous scenes are made possible by the exchange, and it certainly provides for the play's most distinguishing feature, the transformation of the stereotyped role of tricky slave into an admirable one portraying loyalty and friendship. Thus almost every character is both sympathetic and believable, and the female element and the usual love affair are not missed. Lessing's verdict can be sympathized with, if not echoed to the letter.

Captive Women, The (Gk. **Aichmalotides**). Lost play by Sophocles. Some scholars think that it dealt with the love of Achilles and Briseis, Achilles' captured slave girl; others think the plot was similar to that of Euripides' *Trojan Women*.

Capua. Large city in Campania.

Carcinus (Gk. **Karkinos**). **1.** General and writer of tragedies in Athens in the early years of the Peloponnesian War. Only one of Carcinus' play titles, *The Mice*, is known. His sons also wrote tragedies. In *The Wasps* (line 1501 ff.) Aristophanes puns on Carcinus' name (it means "crab" in Greek), and in *Peace* (line 781 ff.) ridicules the whole family for their diminutive stature and the fashionable new kinds of dances they affect.

2. Grandson of the above, also a writer of tragedy (fl. c. 376 B.C.). Carcinus was supposed to have written 160 plays. Because of the riddling speech of his *Orestes*, the term "Carcinus' poems" came to be a synonym for "riddles." Aristotle often mentions him.

Cardia (Gk. **Kardia**). City on the Thracian Chersonese. In Aristophanes' *Birds* (line 1474) its name is used to suggest the Greek word for "heart."

Cardopion (Gk. **Kardopion**). *Myth.* Obscure demigod. It seems that Cardopion mistreated Rhea, the great mother of the gods. Pherecrates wrote a play on the subject, and Aristophanes is thought to have quoted from this play in *The Wasps* (line 1178).

Caria (Gk. **Karia**). Region on the southwestern coast of Asia Minor. The Carians were said to have been the first to use crests on helmets. Their flutes, which gave a melancholy tone, were famous.

Carians, The. Lost play by Aeschylus having the alternate title of *Europa*. An extant fragment of twenty-five lines contains a description by Europa of her abduction by the divine bull and the birth of her three sons, Minos, Rhadamanthus, and the luckless Sarpedon, whose fate she mourns. The play's subject must therefore have been the killing of Sarpedon by Patroclus as told in the *Iliad*, Book XVI, the Carians being substituted for Homer's Lycians.

Carnea (Gk. **Karneia**). Feast in honor of Apollo. The Carnea was celebrated in Laconia during the month of the same name (August-September).

carrus navalis. See SHIP-WAGON.

Carthaginian, The. See POENULUS.

Carystius (Gk. **Karystios**). Critic of Pergamum (late 3rd century B.C.). Among other works now lost, Carystius wrote a *Didascalia*. It was in ancient times a valuable source of information about Sophocles.

Carystus (Gk. **Karystos**). City on the southern end of Euboea.

Casina. Extant comedy by Plautus. The play is dated by some before 186 B.C., but if line 980 refers to the Senate's decree against the bacchanalian orgies in that year, 185 or 184 B.C. is probably more correct. The Greek play from which *Casina* was adapted was Diphilus' *Allotment,* which can be dated shortly after Alexander's death in 323 B.C. because of the line "As if you didn't know how human Jupiters can up and die." Translations: Henry T. Riley, 1852; Paul Nixon, 1917; Lionel Casson, 1963. Adaptations and works influenced by *Casina:* Niccolò Machiavelli, *La Clizia,* 1525; Ben Jonson, *Epicoene or The Silent Woman,* 1609.

S C E N E. Athens.

S U M M A R Y. The prologue, obviously added for a revival after Plautus' time, informs the audience that the sixteen-year-old girl slave Casina, a foundling, has awakened desire in both her master, Lysidamus, and his son, Euthynicus. Lysidamus hopes to gain access to the girl by marrying her to his overseer, Olympio, while Euthynicus has concocted a similar scheme with his armorbearer, Chalinus. Lysidamus has sent his son away, but his wife, Cleostrata, has discovered the plot and is resolved to give Casina to Chalinus.

Lysidamus forces the rival slaves to draw lots for Casina, and Olympio wins her. But the master's plan to take the bridegroom's place on the wedding night is foiled when Cleostrata decks out Chalinus in bridal costume, complete with veil. Lysidamus escorts the wedding procession into the house of his neighbor, Alcesimus. Shortly afterward Olympio, who had hoped to beat Lysidamus to Casina's bed, runs out in great distress, saying that the bride had responded to his caresses by thrashing him soundly. Lysidamus, still ignorant of the deception, tries to win Casina's favors for himself but soon reappears in similar disarray. His disgrace is completed when Chalinus comes out and mockingly invites him to return to the marriage bed. After Cleostrata has forgiven the repentant old rake, the epilogue discloses that Casina will be revealed as the daughter of Alcesimus and that she will marry Euthynicus.

C O M M E N T A R Y. The fact that it was revived demonstrates *Casina's* popularity. Probably the girl's fortunes formed a much larger part of the Greek original. The prologue and epilogue that now exist tie up a few loose ends in this respect, but obviously Plautus' mind was on other things—on lively action, uproarious humor, and song (*Casina* has a greater proportion of *cantica* than any other extant Roman comedy). All pretense of moral edification is abandoned from the very outset: father and son lust after the same bit of flesh; the wronged wife is as unscrupulous as the old lecher; and the final substitution of the male bride is as bawdy and funny as anything else in drama.

Casket, The, or **The Casket Comedy.** See CISTELLARIA.

Casnar. Oscan name for the stock-character Pappus in ATELLAN FARCE.

Cassandra (Gk. **Kassandra**). *Myth.* Daughter of King Priam and Queen Hecuba of Troy. Cassandra promised her love to Apollo in return for the gift of prophecy, then rejected him. He punished her by decreeing that her prophecies would never be believed. Consequently, when Cassandra forewarned her people of the fall of Troy, she was ignored. During the sack of the city she took refuge in Athena's shrine but was impiously dragged out by Ajax the Lesser.

Cassandra appears in Euripides' *Trojan Women* after the city's fall.

Allotted to Agamemnon, she rejoices that her union with him will be bloodier than Helen's with Paris. In Aeschylus' *Agamemnon* she enters Argos in the king's chariot. When Agamemnon and Clytemnestra enter the palace, Cassandra, possessed and tormented by Apollo, sees in a trance the past and present calamities of Atreus' house. Her frenzied outburst leads to the play's climax, when the voice of the dying Agamemnon is heard from within. Soon afterward Cassandra goes inside to meet her own death. In Seneca's *Agamemnon* she enacts much the same role but is a more willing victim, having lived to see Troy avenged.

Castalia or **Castaly** (Gk. **Kastalia**). Spring near Delphi.

Castor (Gk. **Kastor**). One of the DIOSCURI.

Catamitus. Latin form of GANYMEDE.

catharsis (Gk. **katharsis**, "purging" or "purification"). This term was used by Aristotle in his famous definiton of tragedy in the POETICS, which concludes with the statement that tragedy arouses the emotions of pity and fear and brings about a "catharsis of these emotions." Since Aristotle offered no further explanation, and since his phrase is ambiguous in Greek, a considerable theorizing literature has grown up along the following lines: According to one theory, the statement means that pity and fear are undesirable and that by means of art the spectator may vicariously suffer these emotions and discharge them harmlessly. The view that pity is undesirable is not acceptable in the modern age; it was nevertheless held by some in classical times, when the attitude toward all strong emotion was likely to be disapproving, especially among the philosophers.

A second interpretation of Aristotle's statement is that, according to the philosopher, pity and fear are to be kept within bounds. This theory gains support from Aristotle's conception of moral virtue as a mean between extremes. Yet "moderate pity" is still a rather repellent idea. According to a third view, he was saying that the emotions are to be retained but purified, a theory supported by the parallel Aristotelian discussion, in the *Ethics*, of the various ascending qualities of pleasure, depending on the activity the pleasure accompanies. Critics holding the third view substitute "pity and fear" for "pleasure." In general, however, every reader of Aristotle must come to his own conclusion, for the works discussing catharsis now number in the thousands.

cavea. The auditorium of the Roman theater.

Caycus or **Caicus** (Gk. **Kaykos** or **Kaikos**). The principal river of Mysia.

Cayster (Gk. **Kaystros**). River in Lydia.

Cebriones (Gk. **Kebriones**). *Myth.* One of the Giants who tried to storm Olympus.

Ceceides, Cecides, or **Cedeides** (Gk. **Kekeides** or **Kedeides**). Composer of dithyrambs. In *The Clouds* (line 985) Aristophanes speaks of Ceceides as being archaic. The two men may, however, have been contemporaries, and the playwright may have been making a joke at Ceceides' expense.

Cecropidae or **Cecropids** (Gk. **Kekropidai**). 1. The Athenians, as the people of Cecrops.

2. One of the Attic tribes.

3. *Myth.* The daughters of Cecrops, also called Agraulids or Aglaurids. Athena gave the sisters a basket with instructions that they were not to open it, but the Cecropidae were overcome with curiosity and disobeyed the goddess. Inside the basket they found the child Erechtheus, or Erichthonius, who was part serpent. Driven mad at the sight, the sisters leaped to their deaths from the Acropolis.

Cecrops (Gk. **Kekrops**). *Myth.* King of Attica, born of the soil. Hence Attica was sometimes called "Cecropia" and the Athenians "Cecropidae" or "Cecropians." As a son of earth, Cecrops was serpent-shaped in the lower part of his body. His daughters were the Cecropidae (3).

Cedalion (Gk. **Kedalion**). *Myth.* A spirit of the forge and a fertility spirit (from *kedalon*, "phallus"). Cedalion was stolen away from Hephaestus' smithy by the blind Orion, who held him on his shoulders as a guide and walked straight toward the east, staring at the sun. In this way Orion recovered his sight. A lost satyr play by Sophocles called *Cedalion* was based on this myth.

Cedeides. See CECEIDES.

Celeus (Gk. **Keleos**). *Myth.* King of Eleusis. When Demeter was searching for her daughter Persephone, Celeus received the goddess kindly. He was usually said to be the father of Triptolemus, but Aristophanes jokingly calls the latter Celeus' grandfather (*The Acharnians*, line 48).

Cenaeum (Gk. **Kenaion**). Rocky peninsula on the northwestern corner of Euboea.

Cenchreae. See CERCHNEIA.

Centaurs. *Myth.* A race of creatures who were half men and half horse. Except for Chiron, the Centaurs were violent and bestial. They were sometimes thought of as roaming the wilderness and sometimes pictured among the monsters of the underworld.

centunculus (Lat.). Varicolored patchwork robe worn by mimes in the Roman period. Some costumes of the *commedia dell'arte* and of the Punch and Judy shows seem to have descended from the *centunculus*.

Ceos (Gk. **Keos**). Aegean island near the coast of Attica.

Cephalae (Gk. **Kephalai**). Attic deme. In *The Birds* (line 476) Aristophanes puns on its name, which suggests the Greek word for "head."

Cephallenia (Gk. **Kephallenia**). Large island off the western coast of Greece, near the entrance to the Corinthian Gulf.

Cephalus (Gk. **Kephalos**). **1.** *Myth.* Husband of Procris, an Attic princess. Procris hid in the underbrush to spy on Cephalus because the time he spent hunting had aroused her jealousy. Seeing a movement in the bushes, Cephalus threw his spear and accidentally killed his wife.

2. Demagogue of Aristophanes' time. Cephalus was a potter by trade.

Cepheus (Gk. **Kepheus**). *Myth.* King of Ethiopia, husband of Cassiopeia, and father of Andromeda.

Cephisodemus (Gk. **Kephisodemos**). Athenian politician and noisy orator.

Cephisodemus was accused of having Scythian blood. He succeeded in ostracizing Thucydides, rival of Pericles, in 444 B.C.

Cephisophon (Gk. **Kephisophon**). Allegedly a slave of Euripides. Several stories of doubtful origin were told of Cephisophon: one, that he helped Euripides write his plays; another, that Euripides resigned his own wife to him when he discovered the pair *flagrante delicto.*

Cephisus (Gk. **Kephisos**). 1. River in Attica.

2. *Myth.* The god of the river. Cephisus was pictured as a bull.

Ceramicus (Gk. **Kerameikos**, "pertaining to potters"). Two adjacent sections, one inside and one outside the walls of northwest Athens, called the Potters' Quarter. Here was held the annual torch race that honored Prometheus and brought fresh fire to the kilns.

Cerberus (Gk. **Kerberos**). *Myth.* Three-headed dog of the underworld having a mane and serpent's tail and serpents around its head. One of Heracles' twelve labors was to descend to the land of death—where the inhabitants were sometimes called "Cerberians" (as in Aristophanes' *Frogs*, line 187) —and to bring Cerberus to earth. *Cerberus* was the title of a lost play by Sophocles. It was presumably a satyr play portraying the labor of Heracles.

Cerchneia (Gk. **Kerchneia**). Variant form of Cenchreae, a small town in the Peloponnesus between Argos and Tegea.

Cercyon (Gk. **Kerkyon**). *Myth.* Brigand chieftain of Eleusis. Cercyon overcame and killed all passers-by, until young Theseus came that way and either choked him or threw him into the air and dashed him to death. A lost satyr play by Aeschylus called *Cercyon* was based on the foregoing myth. The bandit was also the titular hero of a lost play by Euripides thought to be the same as *Alope*.

Ceres. *Myth.* Roman goddess identified with DEMETER.

Ceyx (Gk. **Keyx**). *Myth.* Husband of ALCYONE.

Chaeremon (Gk. **Chairemon**). Writer of tragedies and satyr plays (4th century B.C.). Chaeremon's dramas were intended to be read, not acted; titles of about nine of them survive. His *Centaurus* seems to have been a tour de force that displayed all kinds of meters.

Chaerephon (Gk. **Chairephon**). Disciple of Socrates, ridiculed in Aristophanes' *Clouds*. Chaerephon was nicknamed "the Bat" because of his squeaky voice.

Chaeris (Gk. **Chairis**). Untalented flute player from Thebes who was contemporary with Aristophanes. Chaeris had the habit of appearing uninvited at banquets.

Chalcedon (Gk. **Chalkedon**). See CALCHEDON.

Chalcidice (Gk. **Chalkidike**). Large three-pronged peninsula projecting southward from Macedonia.

Chalcis (Gk. **Chalkis**). Large city of Euboea. Chalcis is near the narrowest part of the strait between Euboea and mainland Greece.

Chalcodon (Gk. **Chalkodon**). *Myth.* Euboean king and conqueror. Hence Chalcodontidae were "Euboeans."

Chalybes. A race in Pontus or Scythia noted for ironwork.

Chamaeleon (Gk. **Chamaileon**). Scholar (probably early 3rd century B.C.). Chamaeleon was a pupil of Theophrastus and a follower of Aristotle's Peripatetic school. He wrote works, now lost, on Thespis, Aeschylus, satyr play, and comedy. He is cited in ancient commentaries in a way which indicates that the classification of comedy into Old, Middle, and New may already have been current in his time.

Chaonia. Section of Epirus where Dodona was located.

Chaos (Gk.). *Myth.* The primeval yawning or gaping emptiness, the state of utter disorder out of which the created Cosmos emerged and back into which it always threatens to dissolve.

Charites (Gk. "joys, graces"). *Myth.* Goddesses of beauty, delight, and natural vitality. The Charites were usually thought of as three in number and pictured as dancing at springtime in a garden where nature existed in perfection. They were closely associated with the Muses.

Charition. Anonymous popular Greek mime of about 230 lines. Found on a papyrus, *Charition* was published in 1903. It tells the story of a girl, Charition, who is held captive by barbarians in India. Her brother gets them drunk and then helps her to escape. The piece is interesting because it shows what appealed to the public in the second century A.D.

Charixena. Supposed early Greek poet, who probably never existed. She was said to have been a writer of love poems. "This is not according to Charixena" meant "This is unusual, not as it should be."

Charminus (Gk. **Charminos**). Athenian commander. In 411 B.C. Charminus was defeated in a naval battle off Tyre by a Peloponnesian fleet.

Charon. *Myth.* Ferryman of the underworld. Charon punted the souls of the dead across the Acheron or the Styx. He was depicted as a hardy old man, gray-haired, surly, and dirty. He appears in Aristophanes' *Frogs.*

Charonian steps. Staircase leading up from a subterranean passage into the orchestra. It is usually said that the Charonian steps served for the appearance of ghosts from the underworld. Scholars have denied this, arguing that ghosts appeared on the raised stage, not in the orchestra, and therefore the steps must have been used by the chorus for some special purpose.

Charybdis. *Myth.* Monster on one side of the Strait of Messina. Three times a day Charybdis gulped down and spewed back up much of the water of the strait.

Chersonese or **Chersonesus** (Gk. **Chersonesos**). Narrow peninsula jutting down from Thrace and forming the northern coast of the Hellespont. It is now called Gallipoli.

Children of Heracles, The. See HERACLIDAE.

Chimaera (Gk. **Chimaira**, "she-goat"). *Myth.* Monster, part serpent, part lion, part goat. The Chimaera was overcome by BELLEROPHON.

Chionides. One of the earliest writers of Old Comedy. In 486 B.C., Chionides won a first prize at the introduction of comedy into the Greater Dionysia.

Of his plays only titles remain. *The Heroes* is certainly Chionides' work; however, *The Beggars* and *The Persians or The Assyrians* may not be his.

Chios. Large island in the east central Aegean. In the Peloponnesian War the Chians were at first faithful allies of Athens, but they fell away after the Sicilian expedition. Chios was famous for its wine.

Chiron (Gk. **Cheiron**). *Myth.* Wise and good centaur. Chiron lived in a cave on Mt. Pelion in Thessaly. He was a famous physician and the teacher of Asclepius, Jason, Achilles, and other heroes.

Chloë (Gk. "green tendril"). Epithet of Demeter as goddess of vegetation after the appearance of spring verdure.

Choephori or **Choephoroe.** See ORESTEIA.

Choerilus (Gk. **Choirilos**). Earliest of the Athenian writers of tragedy after Thespis (born c. middle 6th century B.C.). Choerilus began his dramatic career in the late 520's and contended against Aeschylus and Pratinas in the early 490's. He allegedly wrote 160 plays—a questionable figure, since his works were lost at an early period and only one title, *Alope*, has been preserved. In an extant anonymous line Choerilus is called "king of the satyr play." It was said that he contributed to the development of costume.

Choes. The Feast of Cups, or Pitchers, celebrated at Athens on the second day of the Anthesteria. The Choes was said to have been instituted in honor of Orestes, who, when he went to Athens, could find no one to share a cup with him.

Cholargus (Gk. **Cholargos**). Attic deme.

Cholleidae (Gk. **Cholleidai**). Attic deme.

choregus (Gk. **choregos**, "chorus-leader"). Despite the etymology, the choregus was not the leader of the chorus (who was the coryphaeus), but the man who paid the expenses of the dramatic production. Athenians whose fortunes went above a certain level were liable for a "liturgy," that is, the privilege of defraying the cost of a state function or piece of equipment, as for example the outfitting of a warship. One of the most burdensome of the liturgies was the *choregia,* the mounting of a dramatic production or dithyrambic chorus. The cost was so high, running into hundreds or thousands of drachmae, that it often had to be shared among two or three citizens.

The choregus represented his tribe. He had to hire a chorus trainer, pay the actors and choristers, provide a place for rehearsing, and foot the bill for costumes, special scenery, and properties. In reward he might march at the head of his chorus in the ritual procession. If his play won first prize, the choregus was crowned, had his name carved in the commemorative inscription, and was perhaps granted a tripod, which he could then erect on a pedestal at his own expense. See also AGON.

chorodidaskalos (Gk. "chorus teacher"). The trainer of a chorus. In early times this duty was performed by the poet, but long before 400 B.C. it had been taken over, for the most part, by a professional.

chorus (Gk. **choros,** "dance group"). The participation of singing, dancing, and processional groups of celebrants in festival rituals, sometimes costumed, sometimes not, is age-old and world-wide. Such groups, some in animal costume, are well-attested on Mycenaean artifacts. In spite of missing links in the evidence, there is no good reason to doubt that the choric odes, written for choric processionals, which appear in Greek literature from about 700 B.C., were continuations of that ancient ritual.

The most notable development before the appearance of actual drama was the attachment of a large part of these choric activities specifically to the cult of Dionysus. Tradition connected this development with the cities of Corinth and Sicyon and with the names of Arion and Cleisthenes (1), but the details are uncertain. At any rate, no one denies that at some time in the sixth century B.C. drama developed out of the chorus; precisely how the various dramatic genres emerged is the question that has provoked a thousand controversies (see COMEDY; SATYR PLAY; TRAGEDY). Although drama grew from the choric group, it certainly did not immediately supersede it. The purely nondramatic singing processional continued to be an important part of the celebration (see DITHYRAMB); such choruses were called "cyclic" or "circular" from their physical grouping, as opposed to the usual rectangular formation of the dramatic chorus.

The fact that there was only one actor until Aeschylus added another proves that for a long time the chorus dominated the dramatic performance. This is evident in the persistent tendency of playwrights to name both tragic and comic plays after the choristers—*The Trojan Women, The Persians, Eumenides, The Phoenician Women, The Birds, The Clouds.* The same tendency is shown in the dramatic terminology that became conventional: to submit one's play for the festival was to "request a chorus"; to have a play produced was to "obtain a chorus"; the playwright was originally the *chorodidaskalos,* "chorus teacher"; a satyr play was regularly called "satyrs"; and a tragedy was referred to more often than not as *tragoidoi,* "singers of tragedy."

The number of *choreutai,* or choristers, used in tragedy has been much disputed. Fifty took part in the cyclic (dithyrambic) chorus. Pollux (*Onomasticon,* Book IV, line 110) says that this was also the number for early tragedy until it was reduced by law because of the great havoc caused in the audience by the hideous choristers of Aeschylus' *Eumenides* in 458 B.C. Since it seems certain that for most of the classical period the number was twelve, increased at times to fifteen, most scholars have discounted Pollux's statement. But as several myths treated in plays before 458 are concerned with groups of fifty, for example the Danaïdes, Pollux may have spoken the truth.

The chorus of comedy had twenty-four members. It was often divided into two groups of twelve, each singing against the other; different groupings were also possible. Evidence indicates that in later centuries the comic chorus was sometimes reduced to seven. The chorus of the satyr play numbered twelve. Sometimes, as with the hunters in *Hippolytus* and the frogs in *The Frogs,* an auxiliary chorus (*parachoregema*) was used. Its members appeared by themselves on the stage (*Hippolytus*), were heard offstage (*The Frogs*), or joined the principal chorus onstage (finale of the *Eumenides*).

In comedy the decline in importance of the chorus was steady and final. Cratinus omitted choric odes in his *Odysseus Comedy,* and Aristophanes did the same in his last plays. In Middle Comedy the use of a chorus was more the exception than the rule; however, there is some evidence that as late as the 330's B.C. the chorus appeared in political satires and mythological parodies. By the time of New Comedy the chorus was reduced to singing interludes during pauses in the action, though Menander, in *The Arbitrants,* gave it back some of its old importance by introducing it as a *komos,* or band of revelers. In Roman comedy the chorus disappeared altogether.

The foregoing was never true of tragedy or satyr plays. Although it is sometimes said that the chorus was most integral in Aeschylus' plays, less so in Sophocles', and least so in Euripides', examination will hardly bear this out, for the latter's *Bacchae,* the latest extant Greek tragedy, has a more relevant chorus than almost any other. It is known that Agathon wrote choric odes which could be transferred from one play to another; in contrast, many an ode in the works of Sophocles and Euripides that seems extraneous on first reading turns out, on closer analysis, to have a subtle and profound relevance. The most probable conclusion is that use of the chorus did not decline in tragedy and that the degree of its integration into a play depended very much on the particular play and the particular author.

Chryse or **Chrysa. 1.** City of the Troad, supposedly sacked by the Greeks during the Trojan War.

2. Island near Lemnos that had disappeared by later classical times.

3. *Myth.* Nymph, guardian of the island. Philoctetes somehow profaned Chryse's roofless shrine and aroused her serpent, which bit him on the foot.

Chryseis. *Myth.* Captive maiden from a city near Troy. When her city was sacked by the Greeks, Chryseis fell to Agamemnon as his share of the loot. Her father, Chryses (1), came to ransom the girl, but Agamemnon refused to give her up until he was forced to do so by Apollo's vengeful acts. Chryseis became the mother of Chryses (2).

Chryses. 1. *Myth.* Priest of Apollo, father of Chryseis, and grandfather of Chryses (2).

2. *Myth.* Son of Agamemnon. Chryses' mother, Chryseis, pretended that he was the son of Apollo. When Orestes, Pylades, and Iphigenia were escaping from King Thoas (see IPHIGENIA AMONG THE TAURIANS), they came by the city in the Troad where Chryses was serving as priest. After Chryseis had revealed her son's true parentage, Chryses joined his half brother and half sister in killing Thoas. A lost play by Sophocles was based on the foregoing myth. *Chryses* was produced before Aristophanes' *Birds* (414 B.C.), which parodies a passage in it. Pacuvius' *Chryses* was modeled largely on Sophocles'. It contained a famous scene where Orestes was about to be sacrificed; when, however, Pylades claimed to be Orestes, King Thoas decided to sacrifice both together.

Chrysippus (Gk. **Chrysippos**). *Myth.* Son of Pelops and a nymph. Because of his great beauty, Chrysippus was carried off by King Laius of Thebes, whom Pelops accordingly cursed with childlessness. After Chrysippus was rescued, he aroused the jealousy of his stepmother, Hippodamia, who either stabbed him herself or inspired her own sons, Atreus and Thyestes, to stab him. Hippodamia then committed suicide. *Chrysippus* was the title of a lost play by Euripides (409 B.C.), which was probably based on the episode involving Laius. The *Chrysippus* of Accius seems to have told of Hippodamia's crime.

Chrysothemis. *Myth.* Daughter of Agamemnon and Clytemnestra. In Sophocles' *Electra* Chrysothemis is the weak sister and the favorite of their mother because of her complaisance. Presented by the playwright as a foil for Electra, she urges Electra to be more yielding but receives only scorn in return.

Chthon (Gk. "earth"). *Myth.* Earth as a deity. Chthon was sometimes identified with Ge (or Gaia) and sometimes thought of as the underworld— as in Chthonian Hermes (Hermes' as the conductor of the dead) and the Chthonians (the souls of the dead).

Cicynna (Gk. **Kikynna**). Attic deme.

Cilicia (Gk. **Kilikia**). Easternmost region along the south coast of Asia Minor.

Cilla (Gk. **Killa**). City in the Troad sacred to Apollo.

Cillicon (Gk. **Killikon**). Citizen of Miletus. When asked what he was planning, Cillicon said, "Nothing bad," though he actually intended to betray his country. The saying became proverbial.

Cimmeria (Gk. **Kimmeria**). Fabulous place described in the *Odyssey* as a land of darkness situated on the rim of Ocean near the realm of the dead. When a barbarian race from Scythia invaded Asia Minor in about 700 B.C., they were identified with the Cimmerians. Hence the "Cimmerian isthmus" was the isthmus of the Crimean peninsula.

Cimolus (Gk. **Kimolos**). Small island north of Melos. It produced a soil which was used as a soap.

Cimon (Gk. **Kimon**). Athenian general and statesman (c. 510–449 B.C.). Cimon led the naval attacks on the Persians after Xerxes' invasion had failed. He helped Sparta during a revolt of the helots in the 460's but was seriously embarrassed by the suspicion in which the Spartans held him.

Cincius Faliscus. Actor in Rome (late 2nd century B.C.). Cincius was said to have been the first to use masks in Roman comedy.

Cinesias (Gk. **Kinesias**). Composer of dithyrambs. Cinesias was a contemporary of Aristophanes, who ridiculed his thinness, his sickliness, his habit of wearing corsets, and especially his impiety as instanced by his deliberately giving dinners on unlucky days and his once defiling a shrine of Hecate. In *The Frogs* Cinesias' admirers are consigned to the underworld; in *The Birds* he comes, spouting dithyrambs, to join Cloudcuckooland but is finally put to flight. Cinesias was the subject of a play by Strattis.

Cinyphus or **Cinyps** (Gk. **Kinyphos** or **Kinyps**). River flowing into the

Mediterranean Sea near the Syrtes, the great quicksands of the North African coast.

Circe (Gk. **Kirke**). *Myth.* Daughter of the Sun and witch goddess of an enchanted isle. Circe changed Odysseus' men into swine. Odysseus himself evaded her spells, persuaded her to release his men, and lived with her for a time as a lover. *Circe* was the title of a lost satyr play by Aeschylus. Only two words survive, but it presumably dealt with the above myth and perhaps formed the end of an Odysseus tetralogy (with *The Conjurors of the Dead, Penelope,* and *The Bone-Gatherers*).

Cirrha (Gk. **Kirrha**). City in Phocis near Delphi.

Cisseus (Gk. **Kisseus**). *Myth.* Father of Hecuba.

Cissians (Gk. **Kissioi**). Inhabitants of the district in Persia around the city of Susa.

Cistellaria (Lat. **The Casket** or **The Casket Comedy**). Extant comedy by Plautus. This play has been dated 202–201 B.C., at the end of the Second Punic War, because of its line "Let the conquered Carthaginians suffer the penalty." The Greek play on which *Cistellaria* was based was Menander's *Women's Luncheon.* Translations: Henry T. Riley, 1852; Paul Nixon, 1917. Adaptations and works influenced by *Cistellaria:* Aeneas Sylvius Piccolomini (Pope Pius II), *Chrysis,* 1444; Molière, *Les Femmes Savantes,* 1672.

S C E N E. Sicyon.

S U M M A R Y. Selenium tells her friend Gymnasium, who has been forced into prostitution by her mother, the old bawd Syra, that she has fallen in love with Alcesimarchus. The young man's father has, however, picked out another bride for him. Gymnasium promises to take over Selenium's house while the latter visits her mother, Melaenis. In a drunken monologue Syra then tells the audience that Selenium was really a foundling whom she had given to her courtesan friend Melaenis to bring up as her own. This explanation is clarified further by the god Auxilium (Assistance or Succor), who comes on in a belated prologue and relates how Selenium was really the child of Demipho, a young man from Lemnos, and of a girl he had raped at a festival of Dionysus. Returning after some years and marrying the girl he had wronged, Demipho has been trying to recover their child. In the course of the play, Syra is recognized as the woman who took the baby, and under questioning she indicates Melaenis as the woman to whom the child was given.

As Melaenis brings her foster daughter to give her over to her real parents, along with the casket of rattles and baby toys that will prove her identity, Alcesimarchus attacks them, sword in hand, distracted because he has been kept from his beloved Selenium. He carries Selenium off to his house. All ends happily when Selenium's father and mother learn definitely that she is theirs.

C O M M E N T A R Y. Because the text of *Cistellaria* is in a very bad state, mutilated and full of gaps, judgment of it is difficult. The general opinion that it must be an unusually close rendering of the Greek original is borne out by the Menandrian cast of the plot and the Menandrian seriousness and predilection for sentiment. The play's only salient features are the romantic violence of Alcesimarchus and the variety of female roles.

Cisthene (Gk. **Kisthene**). City on the Aeolian coast of Asia Minor.

Cithaeron (Gk. **Kithairon**). Mountain separating Boeotia, the Isthmus of Corinth, and Attica. Here Oedipus was exposed as an infant.

cithara (Gk. **kithara**). Greek lyre. The general opinion is that the cithara was not used for accompaniment in drama except for special effects and in special scenes. The theory has been advanced, however, that flute music, which was peculiar to comedy, superseded lyre music as accompaniment to tragedy and dithyramb only in the fifth century B.C. and that there was considerable opposition to this change, symbolized in the pseudomyth of Athena's rejection of the flute because of its ugliness.

claques. There is no evidence that in the Greek theater people were hired to applaud. Plautus, however, mentions the practice in his prologue to *Amphitryon* (line 64 ff.) and implies that claques were illegal if employed for the purpose of winning a prize.

Claudia. Name applied to OCTAVIA in the pseudo-Senecan tragedy of that name.

Claudius. Emperor of Rome from A.D. 41 to 54. Claudius was the husband of Messalina and Agrippina, the father of Octavia and Britannicus, and Nero's stepfather.

Cleaenetus (Gk. **Kleainetos**). Father of Cleon.

Cleidemides (Gk. **Kleidemides**). Friend of Sophocles and leading actor in his plays.

Cleinias (Gk. **Kleinias**). Father of Alcibiades.

Cleisthenes (Gk. **Kleisthenes**). 1. Tyrant of Sicyon from about 600 to 565 B.C. Herodotos (Book V, sect. 67) says that in a war with Argos Cleisthenes took the "tragic choruses" away from the cult of Adrastus, an Argive hero, and gave them to Dionysus. There has been much debate on what this statement signifies in the development of Greek tragedy.

2. Leader of the antioligarchic party in Athens. Shortly before 500 B.C. this party succeeded in establishing a constitution that was the foundation of Athenian democracy.

3. Contemporary of Aristophanes, who never tired of ridiculing Cleisthenes' effeminacy. In *Thesmophoriazusae* Cleisthenes appears as an ally of the women, warning them against the plots of Euripides.

Cleitagora (Gk. **Kleitagora**). Name of a drinking song.

Cleitophon (Gk. **Kleitophon**). Athenian politician, disciple of Socrates, and friend of Plato.

Cleomenes (Gk. **Kleomenes**). King of Sparta. Cleomenes was active in the affairs of Greece in about 500 B.C. Called in by the antidemocratic faction to block the reforms of Cleisthenes (2) in Athens, he was besieged in the Acropolis and finally permitted to leave.

Cleon (Gk. **Kleon**). Athenian tanner and demagogue, son of Cleaenetus (died 422 B.C.). Of all politicians Cleon was the one most detested by Aristophanes. An opponent of Pericles and a leader of the antiaristocratic party, Cleon was under constant attack in all of Aristophanes' plays throughout the 420's B.C. After he was held up for ridicule in *The Babylonians*, the politician unsuccessfully prosecuted the playwright. It was Cleon's advocacy of the Peloponnesian War and his tyrannical policy toward the Athenian allies that most aroused Aristophanes' indignation, though his loud voice, his vulgar manners, and the stench of the tannery were the subjects of most of the individual jokes made in the plays.

Cleon gained control of Athens after Pericles' death. When the Spartans were blockaded at Sphacteria and sued for peace in 425, he caused their proposal to be rejected, mounted an expedition against them, and, to the amazement of all, captured the Spartan force himself. Not long afterward Cleon was killed at Amphipolis.

Cleonae (Gk. **Kleonai**). City in Argolis. Since Cleonae was near Nemea, the Nemean Lion killed by Heracles was sometimes called the Cleonaean Lion.

Cleonymus (Gk. **Kleonymos**). A favorite target of Aristophanes. In his plays the latter calls Cleonymus a glutton, a coward, a liar, an informer, and a parasite, and accuses him of throwing away his shield and running at the battle of Delium.

Cleopatra (Gk. **Kleopatra**). 1. *Myth.* Daughter of Boreas and Oreithyia and wife of Phineus. When Phineus decided to take a second wife, Cleopatra was thrown into prison. Her twin sons were blinded by their stepmother.

2. (68–30 B.C.) Queen of Egypt, last of the house of Ptolemy. Cleopatra was the mistress, first of Julius Caesar, then of Mark Antony.

Cleophon (Gk. **Kleophon**). Athenian politician. Cleophon was the leader of the democratic party from about 410 B.C., succeeding Hyperbolus. According to Aristophanes, he was a demagogue, a barbarian, a warmonger, and a madman.

Clepsydra (Gk. **Klepsydra**). 1. Spring near the grotto of Pan on the slope of the Acropolis.

2. (clepsydra). Water clock, used especially to time speakers in courts and assemblies.

Cloacina or **Cluacina** (Lat. "the purifier"). Epithet of Venus.

Clopides or **Clopidians** (Gk. **Klopides**). Deme name invented by Aristophanes, a pun on *klops*, "thief," and Cropides, a real deme (*The Knights*, line 79).

Clotho (Gk. **Klotho**). One of the MOIRAE.

Clouds, The (Gk. **Nephelai**; traditional Lat. title, **Nubes**). Extant comedy by Aristophanes, a revised version. The first version was produced at the City Dionysia of 423 B.C., where it took third place, after Cratinus' *Wine Flagon* and Ameipsias' *Connus*. The revision was done soon afterward but never produced; the only certain alteration is the rewritten parabasis. Translations: Benjamin B. Rogers, 1924; Arthur S. Way, 1934; Robert Henning Webb, 1960; William Arrowsmith, 1962; H. J. and P. E. Easterling, 1962.

SCENE. Athens, a street.

SUMMARY. Old Strepsiades (Twister) cannot sleep for worrying about impending bankruptcy, brought on by the passion of his son, Pheidippides, for keeping and racing horses. The boy (who is the offspring of Strepsiades' unhappy marriage with an aristocratic wife) shows no interest when his father proposes to save the situation by sending him to school next door, where there is a Phrontisterion, or Thinking School, held by Socrates and Chaerephon. Here are taught—among things such as a fantastic astronomy and meteorology—two ways of reasoning, a better and a worse; the latter, which can make false argument sound convincing, is what Strepsiades needs to know in order to trick his creditors out of the money due them. Pheidippides declining to be educated, the father himself knocks at the school door. He is met by one of the pupils, who discourses on Socrates' wisdom in solving such problems as "How far does a flea jump?" and "Does a gnat drone through its mouth or its rump?" When the door is opened, the class is revealed. With noses to the ground, they are searching out the secrets of earth while their rear ends are probing the heavens. Socrates himself is suspended in a basket, "walking the air and looking down on the sun."

He descends and, after questioning Strepsiades, admits him as a student. Socrates then invokes the Ether and the Clouds, the only deities he recognizes. As the Chorus of Clouds draw near, Socrates scouts the notion that there is such a personage as Zeus or that he sends rain, thunder, or lightning. Giving physical explanations of all these phenomena, Socrates bids Strepsiades subscribe to the creed: "I believe in Chaos, Clouds, and the Tongue, these three."

While teacher and pupil go inside for the lessons, the Chorus speak to the audience in the poet's behalf, asking favor for a work that disdains to use the cheap and borrowed tricks of Eupolis, Phrynichus, and Hermippus. Socrates then emerges quite vexed with Strepsiades for his stupidity and, after a few more attempts to instruct him, advises that he send his son over. Strepsiades parades his new-found knowledge for Pheidippides and coaxes him to become a student in his stead.

At this point two characters, Just Reasoning and Unjust Reasoning, have a debate as to which should take over the son's instruction. Just Reasoning advocates the old-style discipline and education but is defeated when, on a particular point, the disapproval of adultery, he realizes that most of the audience are on the other side.

Not long after Pheidippides has been entrusted to Socrates, he is returned to his father as an excellent Sophist, able to talk his way out of any kind of obligation. Thus encouraged, Strepsiades repels two creditors, but presently comes screaming into the street, having just been beaten by his son. Pheidippides proves by Sophist reasoning that it was perfectly right, for as a father whips his son for his own good, so should sons whip fathers, and mothers, too. This is too much for Strepsiades, who now sees the error of his ways. His final act is to lead his slaves in an assault on the Phrontisterion, setting it afire.

COMMENTARY. Discussion of *The Clouds* inevitably centers on an extraliterary question: How accurate is the portrayal of Socrates? The answer was, formerly, that the portrayal was both inaccurate and grossly unjust, as Socrates himself seemed to think a generation later, judging from what he is made to say in Plato's *Apology*. But when the play first came out, Socrates apparently found it inoffensive, for during the performance he good-humoredly stood up so that the audience might see whom the playwright was ridiculing. In Plato's *Symposium*, which is set about a decade later, it is taken for granted that good feeling between Socrates and Aristophanes is unimpaired.

There has recently been a reaction in favor of the accuracy and justice of Aristophanes' portrait. It must be realized that the Socrates of 423 B.C. may have been more like the character in *The Clouds* than the Socrates of the last decade of the century who appears in the works of Xenophon and Plato. He may have at first been concerned with physical and grammatical trivialities that he later outgrew. Without saying, as some have, that the playwright's representation is favorable (the whole tenor of the play denies this), one must acknowledge that a great deal of the distortion of Socratic thought is due to Strepsiades, who is stupidity and dishonesty personified. Furthermore, much of the play's obvious exaggeration is due simply to the requirements of comic art, for which Socrates had to be fitted into the trappings of the Wise Fool, a traditional subvariety of the *alazon* type. In this last respect Aristophanes might have admitted to inaccuracy but not to injustice, for it would be no more right to blame him for his audience's misconstruction of his intentions than it would be to blame Socrates for Alcibiades' or Critias' misapplication of Socraticism.

Finally, Aristophanes saw in his time the inescapable evidences of cultural decline, partly brought about by a war that was clearly a cultural, as well as a political, catastrophe. To his mind the chief cause of this decline was a new mode of analytic thought in which persistent questioning led to skepticism and moral relativism. Socrates, it is known, was against both of these latter developments, but his solution was to go beyond them by even more rigorous analysis; Aristophanes, however, viewed the philosopher's solution as "more of the same." A conservative himself, the artist was unlikely to subscribe to the belief that the earlier mythico-religious mode of thought could be supported, rather than supplanted, by the habit of analysis and uncommitted examination. In spite of all good will, Aristophanes and Socrates were unlikely ever to have agreed. It would be a very wise man who could judge which of them was right and which was wrong.

Clytemnestra (Gk. **Klytaimnestra**, preferably **Klytaimestra**). *Myth*. Daughter of Tyndareus and Leda and sister of Helen and the Dioscuri (Castor and Pollux). Agamemnon killed Clytemnestra's first husband, tore her baby from her breast, and dashed it against the rocks; the Dioscuri then forced him to marry her. Among their children were Iphigenia, Electra, Chrysothemis, and Orestes. In Euripides' *Iphigenia at Aulis*, Clytemnestra brings her eldest daughter to Aulis to be Achilles' bride, only to see the girl sacrificed at the demand of the army so that they might sail to Troy. The myth goes on to say that while Agamemnon was in Troy, his wife took as her lover his cousin Aegisthus. On

Agamemnon's homecoming, Clytemnestra revenged herself on him, not only for his sacrifice of Iphigenia, but also for his keeping of concubines while in camp.

Clytemnestra wholly dominates Aeschylus' *Agamemnon* (see ORESTEIA), where she is one of the great characters of all drama: a lioness, a spider spinning her web, a man-woman, and a veritable Mother Earth, who rejoices in receiving the warm rain of her dying husband's blood. Clytemnestra dispatches both Agamemnon and Cassandra and declares that the sight of their corpses adds relish to her own love-making. In Seneca's *Agamemnon* Aegisthus plays a larger role in the slaughter, and Clytemnestra a correspondingly smaller one.

After a reign of many years in Argos, Aegisthus and Clytemnestra were killed by the latter's son, Orestes. The various ways in which this deed was accomplished are the subjects of Aeschylus' *Choephori* (see ORESTEIA), Sophocles' *Electra*, and Euripides' *Electra*. In Aeschylus' *Eumenides* (see ORESTEIA), Clytemnestra's ghost rises up to awaken the Erinyes and speed them on after their prey, who has escaped them. Of a lost play by Sophocles entitled *Clytemnestra*, not a trace remains beyond the title. It may have been the model for Accius' *Clutemestra*.

Cnidus (Gk. **Knidos**). Greek city on the southwest coast of Asia Minor.

Cnossus (Gk. **Knossos**). Cretan city, Minos' capital.

Cocalus (Gk. **Kokalos**). *Myth*. King of Camicus in Sicily. DAEDALUS took refuge at Cocalus' court after escaping from the Labyrinth.

Cocalus (Gk. **Kokalos**). Lost comedy by Aristophanes. The play was produced under the name of Aristophanes' son Araros at the Dionysia of 387 B.C., with *Aeolosicon*. *Cocalus* was one of those plays transitional to Middle Comedy, having neither parabasis nor integral choric odes; it even foreshadowed New Comedy, since the plot included a rape, a recognition scene, and other typical devices used by Menander. (Philemon later used the same plot, with only minor alterations, for his *Changeling*.) Further evidence of Middle Comedy in Aristophanes' play is the fact that the whole was a parody on Sophocles' *Camicans*. It has been ingeniously suggested that in it Cocalus represented Dionysius of Syracuse and Daedalus represented that metaphysical highflyer, the philosopher Plato, who visited Sicily in 389–388 B.C.

Coclites (Lat. "one-eyed"). CYCLOPES.

Cocytus (Gk. **Kokytos**). *Myth*. One of the rivers of the underworld, the river of groaning and wailing.

Coesyra (Gk. **Koisyra**). Typical Athenian aristocratic female name.

Colaenis (Gk. **Kolainis**). Cult title of Artemis. There was a temple of this name, sacred to the goddess, in a deme in Attica.

Colchian Women, The (Gk. **Kolchides**). Lost play by Sophocles. It probably dealt with Jason's trials in Colchis, Medea's assistance, and the murder of Absyrtus. (See JASON; MEDEA; ABSYRTUS.)

Colchis (Gk. **Kolchis**). *Myth*. Magical land of the golden fleece. Colchis was sometimes called, also, the land of the Amazons. It was thought to be vaguely in the east or, more specifically, on the eastern coast of the Black Sea.

Colias (Gk. Kolias). *Myth.* Minor but ancient love goddess in Attica. Colias came to be associated with Aphrodite and was more or less identified with her.

Coloneus (Gk. Koloneus). *Myth.* Hero chieftain after whom Colonus was supposedly named.

Colonus (Gk. Kolonos). Northern section of Athens.

comedy. ORIGINS. All scholars agree in approving as the true etymology of *komoidia* "the song of the *komos*," that is, of a revel procession having something to do with Dionysianism. By no means all, however, would agree that comedy derives from *komos* in the sense of a formal Dionysiac fertility ritual or phallic dance (see KOMOS; PHALLOPHORIA). The latter interpretation may actually throw a good deal of light on the essence of comedy (always a victory of the new over the old and an expulsion from society of unassimilable or outworn elements) and, if not applied too rigidly, may throw equal light on the components of all ancient comic literature, for example, the obscenities, the emphasis on food and sexuality, the theme of love and marriage. Nevertheless, it does little to identify the direct antecedents of classical Athenian comedy. Theories about Athenian comedy might be classified as either Composite or Unitary.

The Composite theory, which is still the dominant one, holds that Old Comedy, as it is known from extant plays, had two separate origins. The more formal parts of the comedy (see below under *Old Comedy*) developed from native Attic Dionysiac practices, which were influenced by, or mixed with, some non-Attic practices. The comic dramatic episodes, on the other hand, came in from the Dorian sections of Greece. According to the Composite theory, the predecessors of the participants in the formal parts of the play (any combination is possible here, depending on the theorist) were: (1)· fertility dancers in the guise of animals—of general Hellenic and even Mycenaean origin; (2) fertility dancers in the guise of satyrs; (3) phallus-wearers or phallus-bearers in dance or procession; (4) "flyters," that is, those exchanging insults with, or dispensing insults to, the bystanders on occasions more or less ceremonious; and (5)· thick-bellied, phallus-wearing dancers or actors. The last-named are the best attested as having come from Dorian Greece; the exact places of origin of the others are much disputed. There is dispute, also, about the nature of the Dorian comedy that developed into the dramatic part of Old Comedy. Little is known of Megarian farces or of farces that supposedly existed in other Dorian regions; apparently they were rude improvisations, mere comic sketches, without chorus. Not much definite information emerges until the fifth century B.C., when EPICHARMUS turned this kind of thing into literature.

Aside from the many disagreements about details, there are three glaring difficulties in the Composite theory: Why should there have been Dorian importations into Attica? How, when, and why were all the disparate elements combined into Old Comedy? Where is the evidence that Dorian farce existed early enough to have had an influence on Athens? Puzzlement over these questions has led to a minority reaction in favor of the Unitary theory: that is, that classical Athenian comedy originated in Athens alone. As yet, however, no satisfactory line of descent has been traced.

OLD COMEDY. In Athens, comedy was first performed in connection with
the festival of the Lenaea. Most scholars agree that comedy was admitted as
part of the City Dionysia around 486 B.C. but that it did not receive official
financial support until some twenty years later. State support was granted to
the comedies of the Lenaea in 400 B.C., though comic performances in this
festival had long been made possible by volunteers. It seems that before the
Peloponnesian War the chief archon for the City Dionysia licensed five comedies
every year, and that the chief archon for the Lenaea also licensed five. During
the war, the number was reduced to three but was increased later. The poet
might produce his own comedy, but production under another's name was
common.

Aside from such shadowy figures as Susarion, the earliest known writers of
Old Comedy were Magnes, Chionides, and Ecphantides. With Crates (1) and
Cratinus the genre attained to literary stature. Other older writers were Callias
(2) and Teleclides. A "younger generation," flourishing during the Pelopon-
nesian War, included Pherecrates, Hermippus, Eupolis, Phrynichus (2),
Ameipsias, Plato (1), Philonides, Aristophanes (1), Aristomenes, Aristonymus,
Archippus, Alcaeus (3), Strattis, Theopompus, Apollophanes, Nicochares, and
Nicophon. Of these only Aristophanes is represented by complete extant plays.

Characteristics of Old Comedy in respect to form were its rather rigid
framework involving the chorus (see above under *Origins;* see also CHORUS;
EPIRRHEMATIC AGON; PARABASIS) and its loose plot construction. Its formal
elements, more or less freely combined by the poet, were the prologue, the
parados, the parabasis, the agon, the kommos, "battle scenes" (a series of episodes showing clashes between principal characters and minor characters), and
the exodus. In content, Old Comedy exhibited three peculiarities. The first was
extensive use of personal, political, and cultural satire, expressed in speech so
outspoken that there were various legislative attempts to control it. These
attempts were never very successful, and there is no reason to believe that they
killed the genre as such. The second peculiarity evident in Old Comedy was a
tendency to base plots on folk tale, fairy tale, myth, and free fantasy. The third
was the interspersion of realistic characters, speech, and situations. Old Comedy
titles were likely to be in the plural number, designating the chorus, who were
often animals or personifications, either of political entities or of abstractions.

MIDDLE COMEDY. A transitional type between Old and New, Middle
Comedy may be assigned to an approximate period between 400 and 320 B.C.
The only extant comedies of this type are Aristophanes' *Ecclesiazusae* and
Plutus, written after 400, and Plautus' *Amphitryon* and *Persa,* which were
possibly imitations of Middle Comedy originals; these plays are all that remain
to give an idea of a period that saw the production of comedies by the hundred.
Characteristics of Middle Comedy were: the lessened use of the chorus, which
functioned mostly in the performance of interludes; a change from political
satire to ridicule of courtesans, intellectual leaders, and other nonpolitical figures; increased emphasis on parody of myth and parody of tragedies based on
myth; the emergence of the well-made plot, with love stories and stories of

everyday life becoming ever more prominent; the trend toward realism in language and costume and the trend away from metrical variety and verbal inventiveness. Some writers of the period were Alexis, Amphis, Anaxandrides, Anaxilas, Antiphanes, Eubulus, Philetaerus, and Timocles.

N E W   C O M E D Y. Throughout the fourth century B.C., a rise in the general standard of living, an increasing Panhellenism and cosmopolitanism, and a decreasing scope for individual political activity combined to bring about the breakdown of Old Comedy, the transitional period of Middle Comedy, and the final emergence of the New. The chorus continued only as a device to mark divisions in the action; personal satire and metrical variety disappeared; the speech became standard Attic; and the line became the standard iambic six-footer of dramatic dialogue. Above all, New Comedy was drama of domestic intrigue, with the ever-recurring plot motifs of love, seduction, long-lost children, and recognitions—all descended from the melodrama of Euripides. Constantly appearing characters were the young man, the young girl, the tricky slave, the irate father, the braggart soldier, the parasite, the rapacious courtesan, the goodhearted courtesan, the shrewish old wife, the nurse, the cook, and the mild-mannered old lady. (New Comedy might well be called the prevalent literary form today, thanks to television.) Farcical and broadly comic episodes were only incidental, for the prevailing tone was often sober, sentimental, and even melancholy. The chief writer of Greek New Comedy was Menander, who is represented by one complete extant play, *Dyskolos,* and several others that can be reconstructed from fragments. Other writers were Philemon, Diphilus, Philippides, Posidippus, Machon, and Apollodorus (1 and 2). All of the plays of Terence, and practically all those of Plautus, were adaptations of Greek New Comedy originals.

R O M A N   C O M E D Y. Literary comedy, like tragedy, was brought to the Roman stage in about 240 B.C. by Livius Andronicus, who wrote a Latin adaptation of the Greek New Comedy. This kind of FABULA PALLIATA flourished in Rome for more than a century. All extant examples are by Plautus and Terence; other playwrights were Ennius, Caecilius, Turpilius, Naevius, and Atilius. There was a pro-Roman reaction against these Greek importations which was especially strong in the latter part of the second century B.C. It resulted in the production of FABULA TOGATA, original comedy in Roman settings. All of this kind of comedy is lost; its most prominent exponents were Afranius and Atta.

For minor types of comedy, see ATELLAN FARCE; MIME; PANTOMIME; PHLYAKES.

Comedy of Asses, The. See ASINARIA.

comitium. Meeting place of the Roman Assembly.

Confidentia. Roman deity, the personification of confidence, faith, and trust.

Conisalus (Gk. **Konisalos**). *Myth.* Minor deity attendant on Priapus, the god of male sexual excitation.

Conjurors of the Dead, The (Gk. **Psychagogoi**). Lost play by Aeschylus. It treated Odysseus' visit to the land of the dead (compare the *Odyssey,* Book

XI) and the prophecy of his death by Tiresias. Doubtless the play was part of an Odysseus tetralogy (with *Penelope, The Bone-Gatherers,* and *Circe*).

Connas (Gk. **Konnas**). Flute player and drunkard mocked by Aristophanes in *The Knights* (line 534). Connas won several first prizes at Olympia playing the flute but was poor in his old age. Perhaps the name is a diminutive of Connus, who was Socrates' music teacher and the butt of comic plays by Ameipsias and Phrynichus.

Connus. See CONNAS.

contamination (Lat. **contaminatio,** "spoiling"). A charge was brought against Terence by his literary enemies, principally Luscius Lanuvinus, that he had "spoiled" Greek plays by adapting parts of several in order to make one Latin play. Terence answered the charge in several of his prologues. The term "contamination" is used by modern scholars to mean the general practice, not necessarily bad, of blending several stories.

Conthyle (Gk. **Konthyle**). Attic deme.

Copais (Gk. **Kopais**). Large lake in Boeotia noted for its eels.

Copreus (Gk. **Kopreus**). *Myth.* Henchman of King Eurystheus, whose oppressive commands Copreus transmitted to Heracles. He appears in Euripides' *Heraclidae* as the king's herald.

Coprus (Gk. **Kopros**). Attic deme whose name suggests the Greek word for "dung." Aristophanes puns on the name in *The Knights* (line 899).

Cora or **Core** (Gk. **Kore,** "maiden"). Persephone.

Corcyra (Gk. **Kerkyra**). Large island, with a city of the same name, off the coast of central Epirus. It is now called Corfu. The words "Corcyraean wings" are used by Aristophanes in *The Birds* (line 1463) to refer to a kind of double-thonged whip.

cordax (Gk. **kordax**). Lively dance in comedy, usually vulgar and indecent. It seems that the cordax was originally connected with the cult of Artemis and perhaps, also, with the satyr cult of Dionysus.

Core. See CORA.

Coroebus (Gk. **Koroibos**). *Myth.* Son of the Phrygian king Mygdon. Coming to the help of the Trojans because he wished to marry Cassandra, Coroebus was killed when Troy was taken.

Corus. Personification of the northwest wind.

Corybantes (Gk. **Korybantes**). *Myth.* Members of the retinue of Cybele. As celebrants of Cybele's orgiastic rites, the Corybantes worked themselves into a frenzy to the sound of flute, tambourine, and timbrel. In function they were similar to maenads, and the Curetes and were often confused with them.

Corycus (Gk. **Korykos**). 1. Promontory in Cilicia. On it was a famous cave called the Corycian Cave.

2. A similarly named cave on Mt. Parnassus near Delphi. It was supposedly inhabited by nymphs.

coryphaeus (Gk. **koryphaios,** "at the head"). The leading member of the dramatic chorus. The coryphaeus probably occupied the central position in the front row of dancers. He must often have taken the short speeches assigned to the chorus, but it is not known whether, in any particular case, a speech was voiced by him alone or by the whole group.

costume. See CENTUNCULUS; COTHURNUS; EMBATES; MASKS; ONKOS; PHALLUS; SOCCUS; SOMATION; SYRMA.

Cothocidae (Gk. **Kothokidai**). Attic deme.

cothurnus (Gk. **kothornos**). A kind of soft buskin or boot reaching almost to the knee. The term probably included both the loose-fitting boot, which would go on either foot, and the laced boot. Its toe often curled slightly upward. The cothurnus seems originally to have been a female article of dress and then appropriated for Dionysiac dances. Aeschylus is credited with making it a regular part of the costume of tragedy. The elevator sole was introduced in late Hellenistic times; late, also, was the application of the term cothurnus exclusively to the boot used on the stage.

cottabus (Gk. **kottabos**). Game common at banquets. Its object was the throwing of wine left in the cups into floating saucers so as to sink them.

Cranaus (Gk. **Kranaos**, "rocky"). *Myth.* Early king of Attica. Cranaus was said to have founded Athens, the "rocky" city. Hence Attica was "Cranaa," the Acropolis was "the Cranaan city," and the Athenians were "Cranaids."

Crates (Gk. **Krates**). 1. Writer of Old Comedy (fl. c. 450–425 B.C.). Before becoming a writer Crates was an actor in Cratinus' plays. Aristotle calls him the first writer of comedy to design well-constructed plots. Crates seems not to have gone in for personal or political invective. Fragments from his plays are not numerous, and only a few titles are certainly his: *The Neighbors, The Heroes, Lamia, The Pastimes, The Samians, Daring Deeds, The Animals;* in the last-named play a chorus of animals protested against being eaten by men.

2. Academic philosopher (fl. beginning 3rd century B.C.). Crates wrote a treatise entitled *On Comedy.*

3. Crates of Mallos. Critic (c. 197–159 B.C.). Crates commented on Aristophanes' work.

Cratinus (Gk. **Kratinos**). 1. Writer of Old Comedy (510?–c. 422 B.C.). Cratinus was ranked by the ancients with Aristophanes and Eupolis. He was older than the other two, beginning his career in about 456 B.C. Cratinus appears to have been the playwright who gave Old Comedy its characteristic form and style. In Aristophanes' *The Knights, Peace,* and *The Frogs* he is ridiculed for drunkenness; Cratinus returned the compliment in *The Wine Flask.* It must have been particularly galling to Aristophanes when Cratinus, whom he had portrayed as out of public favor in an alcoholic old age, won first prize with *The Wine Flask* in 423 B.C., in a contest where *Clouds* came out third. In all, Cratinus won six first prizes at the City Dionysia and three at the Lenaea. Some twenty-odd titles of his works are known, the fragments of some of them complete enough to allow reconstruction.

The *Archilochus Comedy* (performed soon after 449 B.C.) may have depicted a contest between the satirical poet Archilochus and certain epic poets who were conjured up as ghosts.

The plot of *Dionysus as Alexander* (c. 430 B.C.) is summarized on a recovered papyrus. In it Dionysus, taking the part usually assigned to Alexander (Paris), judges the beauty contest of the three goddesses (Hera, Athena, and Aphrodite). Dionysus runs away with Helen, but Paris discovers them and is about to give them over to the Greeks, when he is overcome with pity for Helen and makes her his wife. In this satire Dionysus, who causes the Trojan War, represents Pericles, whose ambitions led to the Peloponnesian War.

Nemesis dealt with the wooing of Leda (also called Nemesis) by Zeus in the guise of a swan. Zeus probably represented Pericles and Leda his mistress, Aspasia. The result of the affair was the Trojan (*i.e.*, Peloponnesian) War.

The plot of *The Odysseus Comedy* was the blinding of Polyphemus. At the play's beginning, Odysseus and his crew sailed into the orchestra on a Dionysian ship-wagon; at the end they sailed out again. This play was said to foreshadow Middle Comedy in that it had no parabasis, no choric odes, and no attacks on individuals. It simply parodied a myth.

The See-Everythings satirized philosophers. It was written considerably earlier than Aristophanes' *Clouds*.

The Plutuses probably had a chorus of wealth gods. It was the first known comedy to depict the Golden Age as an era of abundance.

The Tempest-Tossed won second prize at the Lenaea of 425 B.C., and *The Satyrs* won first prize in 424.

The Wine Flask makes fun of Cratinus himself. The poet is married to Comedy but is busy chasing after Methe (Drunkenness). His friends, who form the chorus, go around breaking all the wine containers they see, but Cratinus manages to keep one wine flask from them. He delivers a spirited speech defending the service of Dionysus; two lines from it became famous:

> Wine is a speedy horse for an agile singer,
> But your drinker of water produces nothing good.

Commentaries on Cratinus' works were written by Callistratus, Galen, and Symmachus. His plays were still being read in the fifth century A.D.

2. Writer of Middle Comedy (fl. middle 4th century B.C.). This Cratinus was probably a descendant of the foregoing playwright. Plato was one of the butts of his ridicule. Some of the titles of his lost plays are *The Giants, Omphale, The Pseudo-Changeling,* and *The Pythagorean Philosopheress.*

Crenaean, or **Krenaian Gate** (From Gk. *krenaios,* "pertaining to a fountain"). One of the seven gates of Thebes.

Creon (Gk. **Kreon**). **1.** *Myth.* King of Corinth. Creon granted Jason and Medea asylum when they fled from Iolcus after Medea's murder of Pelias. In both Euripides' and Seneca's *Medea* Creon, having betrothed his daughter to Jason, determines to banish Medea, whose mischief-making he fears. He makes the mistake of granting Medea a day's respite, and she takes the opportunity to send Jason's intended bride a robe and crown, which consume her in flames. In trying to rescue his daughter, Creon suffers her fate.

2. *Myth.* Brother of Jocasta. In Sophocles' *Oedipus the King* and Seneca's

Oedipus, Creon brings the pronouncement from Delphi that the plague in Thebes was brought about by the unpunished murder of Laius. In Sophocles' play, Oedipus accuses Tiresias of being the instrument of Creon who, he suspects, is trying to unseat him by arranging that the seer charge him with Laius' murder. In Seneca's version, Creon himself brings the charge against Oedipus, after having called up the ghost of Laius under Tiresias' direction. Seneca consigns Creon to prison, but Sophocles makes him reappear to take control of affairs at the end of the play, when Oedipus is blinded and broken.

In Sophocles' *Oedipus at Colonus,* Creon appears in a much darker light, for although he had long before cast out Oedipus as a beggar, he comes now to fetch him by force, having learned that Oedipus' presence will bring good fortune. Creon's men seize Oedipus' daughter Antigone, who accompanied her father into exile; his insolence is, however, thwarted by Theseus' intervention. Euripides' *Phoenician Women* portrays Creon supporting Eteocles against the attack of the Seven against Thebes; his son Menoeceus sacrifices himself so that the Thebans may win. After Eteocles and Polyneices have killed each other, Creon becomes king. In Sophocles' *Antigone,* Creon opposes Antigone's wish to bury her brother and sends her to her death for disobeying his decree. In consequence, he loses his son Haemon and his wife Eurydice. Legend adds that Lycus later killed Creon, last ruler of the house of Cadmus, and usurped the throne.

Cresphontes (Gk. **Kresphontes**). 1. *Myth.* Son of Heracles. With his brothers, the other Heraclidae, Cresphontes led an expedition against the Peloponnesus and conquered the whole peninsula. When the brothers cast lots to divide the land, Cresphontes slipped a lump of clay, instead of a potsherd, into the urn, so that when the urn was whirled around the clay would remain inside. By this trick he became king of Messenia.

2. *Myth.* Son of the preceding. The younger Cresphontes' uncle Polyphontes murdered the elder Cresphontes, seized the throne, married Queen Merope, and forced the son to flee. Cresphontes took refuge in Aetolia with an old family servant and years later returned to Messenia under another name. Pretending to be the killer of young Cresphontes, he was welcomed into the palace by the usurping Polyphontes. But his mother, Merope, indignant at the supposed murder of her son, stole into his room with an axe, and only the intervention of the old servant and his revelation of the youth's true identity averted another killing. Merope and her son then plotted revenge, and at the feast next day, when Cresphontes' supposed murderer was given the honor of dispatching the sacrificial animal, he suddenly turned on Polyphontes and killed him.

A lost play by Euripides called *Cresphontes* was produced not long before 424 B.C.; it was based on this myth. Euripides' play served as the model for Ennius' *Cresphontes,* and the same story formed the plot of Voltaire's *Mérope* (1743).

Cretans, The (Gk. **Kretes**). Lost play by Euripides. It told the story of Pasiphaë's mad love for the bull, the birth of the Minotaur, and the latter's concealment in the labyrinth (see PASIPHAË). An extant fragment found on a parchment leaf contains the scene where Minos discovers the Minotaur and Pasiphaë defends herself, pointing out that her unnatural love was Poseidon's retribution for Minos' offense. The chorus seems to have consisted of initiates into the mysteries of the Cretan Zeus.

Cretan Women, The (Gk. **Kressai**). 1. Lost play by Aeschylus, based on the myth of Glaucus, son of Minos, and POLYIDUS.

2. Lost tragedy by Euripides (produced 438 B.C.). Of it only twenty-odd lines are extant. *The Cretan Women* told the story of the Cretan princess Aërope, who was detected in a love affair with a slave by her father Catreus and given to Nauplius to be drowned. Nauplius, however, took Aërope to the mainland, where she married Pleisthenes and became the mother of Agamemnon and Menelaus. According to this play, her sons were adopted by Atreus after their father's death.

Creusa (Gk. **Kreousa**). 1. *Myth.* Daughter of Creon, king of Corinth; she was also called Glauce. Creusa was affianced to Jason. Her fate is described in Euripides' and Seneca's plays entitled *Medea*.

2. *Myth.* Daughter of Erechtheus, wife of Xuthus, and mother of Ion. Creusa is one of the chief characters in Euripides' *Ion*. A lost play by Sophocles called *Creusa* has the alternate title of *Ion*. Its plot is in general the same as Euripides' *Ion*. Whether the Sophoclean or the Euripidean play came first is unknown.

Crisa (Gk. **Krisa**). City near Delphi.

Crispinus, Rufus. First husband of Poppaea. He was prefect of the praetorian guard under the emperor Claudius.

Critias (Gk. **Kritias**). Athenian poet and politician (c. 460–403 B.C.). Born of a noble and wealthy family, Critias reached the logical culmination of his career after the Peloponnesian War, when he became the most tyrannical of the Thirty Tyrants. He was killed during the re-establishment of the democracy. A sometime disciple of Socrates, Critias was, however, associated with ethical principles far from Socratic. He turned his hand to all sorts of literary composition. One dramatic trilogy, *Tennes, Rhadamanthus,* and *Pirithous,* is well-attested as being his; but all that survives of Critias' work is a long fragment from a doubtfully assigned satyr play, *Sisyphus.* The latter contains the earliest appearance, in Western writing, of the theory that religion is an invention— and a necessary one—of the shrewd and powerful ruling class to keep the masses in line.

Crius (Gk. **Krios**). 1. Attic deme.

2. Wrestler who was defeated in the Olympic Games in the time of Simonides. Because *krios* meant "ram," the poet wrote a poem beginning, "The ram has been shorn."

Cronus (Gk. **Kronos**). *Myth.* Second in the Greek series of supreme gods. Having emasculated and overthrown his father, Uranus, Cronus tried to escape being overthrown himself by swallowing his children. But Zeus (called ("Cronion" or "Cronides"—son of Cronus) escaped his father and defeated him, binding him and casting him down into Tartarus. When Cronus reigned, he was associated with the abundance of the Golden Age but also with simple-mindedness, since there was no need of guile in that time.

Ctesias (Gk. **Ktesias**). Glutton, poet, and informer of Aristophanes' time.

cunei (Lat. "wedges"). Latin for KERKIDES.

Cupid (Lat. **Cupido**, "desire"). *Myth.* Roman equivalent of Eros. Cupid was, however, usually conceived of as only a mischievous boy who provoked both love and repulsion with his arrows. In *Phaedra* (line 275) Seneca says that "the twin Cupid [Eros and Anteros] calls Venus mother."

Curculio. Extant comedy by Plautus (c. 200 or c. 193 B.C.). The Greek play from which *Curculio* was adapted is unknown. Translations: Henry T. Riley, 1852; Paul Nixon, 1917. Works influenced by *Curculio:* Shevelove, Gelbart, and Sondheim, *A Funny Thing Happened on the Way to the Forum,* 1962.

S C E N E. Epidaurus.

S U M M A R Y. Phaedromus meets his sweetheart, the slave girl Planesium, surreptitiously at night while her master, the pimp Cappadox, tries to cure his many ills at the Temple of Aesculapius. Only the pimp's preoccupation with his ailments has prevented him from making a prostitute of the girl, who is still chaste. Since Cappadox seems willing to sell her, Phaedromus has sent the parasite Curculio, the "Weevil," to borrow money for him in Caria. Curculio returns to report that he has been unsuccessful but that he has managed to steal the signet ring of a soldier, Therapontigonus, who claims that he has bought Planesium for himself.

Curculio forges a letter containing instructions that Planesium be given to him and seals it with Therapontigonus' ring. Then, posing as the soldier's freedman, he carries off the girl. But on the way home, Planesium recognizes Curculio's ring as one that was worn by her father before she was kidnapped in childhood; she wrests it from him. When Therapontigonus, full of somewhat ineffectual bluster, comes to demand the return of his property, he and Planesium discover by way of the ring that they are brother and sister. Planesium is accordingly given to Phaedromus as his bride, and the pimp is made to return her purchase price as the penalty for having sold a freeborn woman.

C O M M E N T A R Y. The shortness of this play has led to some theorizing about revision, actors' changes, and mutilation of text. Perhaps, however, Plautus sacrificed everything to rapid action and lively character portrayal: Curculio is the most outstanding member of a vivid group. The story is of only routine interest, aside from the local color given it by the features of the Aesculapius cult. The device, traditional to comedy, of skirting the abyss of incest without falling into it demonstrates the closeness of both comedy and tragedy to their mythical-ritual beginnings. The strange little speech of the wardrobe manager (beginning Act Four) is not so much a bridge across a gap in the action (Plautus never minded gaps), nor a kind of Old Comedy parabasis, as it is the age-old trick, now dear to television, of raising a laugh by breaking the dramatic illusion.

Curetes (Gk. **Kouretes**). 1. *Myth.* The young men, demigods, who danced a war dance, clashing their shields and weapons together at the mouth of the cave in Crete where the infant Zeus was hidden. In this way the Curetes drowned out the baby's cries and kept Cronus from finding and swallowing him. They were sometimes confused with the Corybantes.

2. Priests of Zeus in Crete.

Curmudgeon, The. See DYSKOLOS.

Curotrophus (Gk. **Kourotrophos**, "child-nourishing"). Epithet of several deities, especially of Athena as protectress of the sons of early Attic kings.

curtains. Curtains seem to have been used as part of the backdrop in Athenian, Megarian, and Sicilian comedy, and a curtain or screen (*parapetasma*) occasionally blocked out part of the scene. However, the use of the curtain to conceal the whole acting space and to mark a pause in the drama was not known to the Greeks until they borrowed it from Rome, and this practice did not begin until after the time of Plautus and Terence (the traditional date was 133 B.C.).

During the first century B.C. the *aulaeum,* or front curtain, was used; it perhaps originated in mimes. At the play's beginning it was lowered into a deep groove at the front of the stage and raised again at the end of a performance or act. By the second century A.D. the *aulaeum* was manipulated like the curtain in the modern theater: it was raised at the play's beginning, held suspended, and lowered at the end.

There was another kind of curtain, the *siparium,* which was a portable affair originally used by mime actors as both a front curtain and a backdrop. It was not raised or lowered, but drawn aside or folded up. Occasionally a combination of *aulaeum* and *siparium* was used: the *aulaeum* was raised, and the *siparia* were drawn to the sides.

Cyanean or **Kyanean Rocks.** Two rocky islands at the entrance to the Bosporus, identified with the SYMPLEGADES.

Cybele or **Cybebe** (Gk. **Kybele** or **Kybebe**). *Myth.* Great goddess of Phrygia and the mountain ranges of Asia Minor. Cybele was called the Mountain Mother and identified by the Greeks with Rhea, the great Mother of the Gods. Her rites were orgiastic. The Corybantes were her mythical attendants, but her actual servitors were eunuch priests. Cybele's lover was Attis, whose death through emasculation she caused. In 204 B.C. the cult was imported into Rome, where, in Cybele's honor, were celebrated the Megalensian Games (from Gk. *Megale Meter,* "Great Mother"). These games were held in early April and were marked by performances of plays.

Cychrea or **Cychreia** (Gk. **Kychreia**). City on the island of Salamis; by extension, the whole island.

Cyclades, sing. **Cyclad** (Gk. **Kyklades,** from *kyklos,* "circle"). Aegean islands which encircle the holy island of Delos.

cyclic chorus. See CHORUS.

Cycloborus (Gk. **Kykloboros**). So-called Attic stream which was actually only a flash flood coming down from Mt. Lycabettus after a rain.

Cyclops, pl. **Cyclopes** (Gk. **Kyklops, Kyklopes,** "circle-eyed"). *Myth.* Giant with one eye in the middle of his forehead. One group of Cyclopes were depicted as helping Hephaestus in his volcano smithies, especially in the forging of thunderbolts. They were also thought to have helped build the massive walls of certain cities, for example, Corinth. Another group of Cyclopes were described by Homer as living on a faraway island, tending flocks, and caring for neither gods nor men. Of this latter group was Polyphemus.

Cyclops (Gk. **Kyklops**). Extant satyr play by Euripides (produced c. 425 B.C. or between 415 and 409). *Cyclops* is the only satyr play that has been preserved intact. Translations: Percy B. Shelley, 1819; E. P. Coleridge, 1891; Arthur S. Way, 1912; J. T. Sheppard, 1923; William Arrowsmith, 1956; Roger Lancelyn Green, 1957; P. D. Arnott, 1961.

S C E N E. The Sicilian coast near Mt. Aetna.

S U M M A R Y. Silenus, alone, bewails his lot and that of his companions, the Satyrs; for when Hera in her hatred of Dionysus arranged for Etruscan pirates to carry off the god, the Satyrs had set off in search of him. But their ship came too near the foot of Mt. Aetna, where the Cyclops Polyphemus lived, and the monster enslaved them. The Satyrs now come in, driving flocks of sheep and goats and grieving for their past revels with the bacchanals.

A Greek ship is sighted, and men come up the strand looking for food. They are Odysseus and his crew. Thinking he must have landed at Dionysus' home, Odysseus introduces himself to Silenus, who informs him about the Cyclopes and their cannibalistic habits. Odysseus brings out a wineskin to exchange for the roast lamb and cheeses which Silenus carries from Polyphemus' cave. Suddenly the Cyclops looms into view. He catches sight of the Greeks, and Silenus pretends that they have beaten him and stolen the food. Polyphemus prepares for a supper of man meat. When Odysseus appeals to justice and the gods, the Cyclops answers that he cares nothing for gods and that his only god is his belly. He herds the Greeks into his cave, while the Satyrs sing of his brutality.

Stealing out, Odysseus, horrified, describes the monster's feast on two of his men. He goes on to tell how he himself offered Polyphemus cup after cup of wine until the Cyclops was in a drunken stupor. Odysseus then asks the Satyrs to join him in his plan of revenge, which is to heat an olive stake and plunge it into Polyphemus' one eye. The Satyrs express enthusiasm for the plan.

The Cyclops comes from his cave still drinking. When he asks the Greek's name, Odysseus tells him "Nobody." Polyphemus grants his new friend, Nobody, the favor of being the last to be eaten. As the drinking bout continues, there is much horseplay between the Cyclops and Silenus; finally the two disappear into the cave. Odysseus proceeds with his scheme, but the fearful Satyrs refuse to help him in the act of blinding.

The stake plunged into Polyphemus' eye, he writhes and roars, "Nobody has ruined me!" The Satyrs tease and distract him, while the Greeks escape from the cave. As Odysseus departs, he shouts out his real name to the Cyclops, who repeats the prophecy that Odysseus will wander for many years. Odysseus heads for his ship, accompanied by his men and the Satyrs.

C O M M E N T A R Y. The idea of giving a comic turn to the grisly Polyphemus episode from the *Odyssey* was not original with Euripides. Epicharmus had produced a *Cyclops*, Aristias had even written a satyr play of that name, and Cratinus had treated the story in his *Odysseus Comedy*. Euripides' version has been criticized as being no more than an earnest effort, too serious and too much influenced by tragic diction. Yet the characters of Silenus and Polyphemus are amusing enough. The criticism probably arises from the notion that the satyr play was primarily intended to provide comic relief; this function was, however, only secondary. The satyr play served primarily to connect the whole tetralogy to which it belonged with the Dionysus cult and thus to contribute to the spirit of the festival. Euripides makes this connection in the *Cyclops* by importing from the *Homeric Hymn to Dionysus* the motif of the god's sea voyage which led to the enslavement of his followers. Hence at the play's end, when all are freed, the appropriate note of liberation is struck, ending one day's celebration in honor of Dionysus Eleutheros, "the Free One" or "the Liberating One," whom the Romans knew as Liber.

Cycnus. See CYGNUS.

Cydathenaea or **Cydathenaeum** (Gk. **Kydathenaia** or **Kydathenaion**). Attic deme, the home of Aristophanes' enemy Cleon. Cydathenaea was directly north of the Acropolis.

Cydoemus (Gk. **Kydoimos**, "uproar, tumult"). Personification of the servant of War in Aristophanes' *Peace*.

Cydon or **Cydonia** (Gk. **Kydon** or **Kydonia**). City on the north coast of western Crete.

Cygnus or **Cycnus** (Gk. **Kyknos**, "swan"). *Myth.* Several heroes of this name have been inextricably confused with one another: (a) Son of Poseidon and an ally of the Trojans. Cygnus was defeated by Achilles, but since he could not be killed because of his divine invulnerability, he was changed into a swan. (b) Father of TENES. (c) Son of Ares. This Cygnus was a ruffian who attacked, robbed, and killed pilgrims on the way to Delphi. Apollo inspired Heracles to kill him, and when Ares intervened on Cygnus' behalf, either Heracles wounded the god or Zeus stopped the fight with a thunderbolt. It is thought that Aeschylus wrote a play called *Cygnus;* its existence is, however, doubtful.

Cyllarus (Gk. **Kyllaros**). *Myth.* Wonder horse given by Poseidon to Hera and by Hera to Castor.

Cyllene (Gk. **Kyllene**). 1. Mountain in Arcadia on which Hermes was born.

2. *Myth.* Nymph of the mountain. Cyllene took care of Hermes when he was an infant.

3. Port in Elis.

Cynalopex (Gk. **Kynalopex**, "dog-fox"). Nickname for Philostratus, a pimp of Aristophanes' time.

Cynna (Gk. **Kynna**). Notorious courtesan, a contemporary of Aristophanes.

Cynosura (Gk. **Kynosoura**). *Myth.* One of the nurses of Zeus. Cynosura was transformed into a constellation, usually said to be the Little Bear.

Cynthus (Gk. **Kynthos**). Hill on Delos, birthplace of Apollo and Artemis. Cynthus was a favorite haunt of the latter.

Cypris (Gk. **Kypris,** "she of Cyprus"). Epithet of Aphrodite.

Cyrene (Gk. **Kyrene**). **1.** Greek colony in Libya in northern Africa.

2. Notorious courtesan of Aristophanes' time.

Cyrus (Gk. **Kyros**). Founder of the Persian empire; called "the Great" (died 529 B.C.).

Cythera (Gk. **Kythera**). Island off the southern coast of the Peloponnesus. Aphrodite was supposed to have landed there after springing from the foam of the sea.

Cytherea (Gk. **Kythereia,** "she of Cythera"). Epithet of Aphrodite.

Cyzicus (Gk. **Kyzikos**). Greek colony on the south shore of the Propontis. When Aristophanes (*Peace,* line 1176) speaks of "Cyzicene yellow," he refers to the Cyzicenes' reputation for cowardice and, possibly, to a dye made there. He also puns on the word *chezikenikon,* which means "of dung."

D

Daedalus (Gk. **Daidalos**). *Myth.* Athenian inventor and handicraftsman. Envious of the skill of his nephew Perdix (also called Talos), Daedalus pushed the boy off the Acropolis. For this deed he was banished and retired to Crete. There he devised a gigantic bronze robot called Talos, who guarded the island. Daedalus also built the Labyrinth, in which was concealed the MINOTAUR, the offspring of Queen Pasiphaë's unholy love for a bull. For some reason King Minos imprisoned the inventor and his son, Icarus, in the Labyrinth—some say that it was because Daedalus contrived the scheme whereby Theseus found his way out of the maze after killing the Minotaur (see THESEUS). Daedalus constructed wings of feathers and wax for himself and his son, and they escaped. But as they made their way over the sea, Icarus flew too near the sun, which melted the wax. He fell to his death.

The father flew on to Italy, where, on the headland near Cumae, he founded a temple to Apollo and provided it with doors on which was carved the whole story of Minos' and Pasiphaë's shame. The vengeful Minos still in pursuit, Daedalus took refuge at the court of Cocalus, king of the Camicans in Sicily. Minos, however, dispatched messengers bearing the promise of a reward to anyone who could thread a seashell. Daedalus disclosed his identity when he bored a hole in the apex of the shell, tied a thread to an ant, and sent him through the whorls. When Minos came with his soldiers to claim the inventor, the daughters of Cocalus, who were fond of Daedalus, took the king to give him a bath and poured scalding water over him. This was the end of Minos.

Daedalus was the title of a lost play by Sophocles. Whether it dealt with the hero's adventures in Crete or (less probably) in Sicily is not known; nor is it known whether it was a tragedy or a satyr play. A lost comedy by Aristophanes, probably performed in 414 B.C., was also called *Daedalus*. It apparently satirized Alcibiades' disastrous participation in the Sicilian expedition. In one scene Alcibiades-Icarus soared aloft with the aid of the *mechane*.

Dahae (Gk. **Daai**). Scythian nomadic tribe in the region east of the Caspian Sea.

Danaäns or **Danaï** (Gk. **Danaoi**). Homeric and general poetic term for the Greeks.

Danaë. *Myth.* Daughter of Acrisius. The latter immured Danaë in a brass tower (or an underground chamber) when it was prophesied that a son of hers would kill him. But Zeus came to Danaë in the form of a shower of gold, and she bore Perseus. When Acrisius learned of Perseus' existence, he put his daughter and grandson in a chest, which he cast adrift in the sea. The chest was washed shoreward at Seriphos, where Dictys caught it in his fishing net. Dictys' brother Polydectes, the king of Seriphos, fell in love with Danaë. His unwelcome advances were forever repelled when Perseus, grown to manhood, turned him to stone with the Gorgon's head.

Danaë was the title of a lost play by Euripides (performed before 411 B.C.). It dealt with the maiden's imprisonment and Acrisius' discovery of the birth of Perseus. There survive about sixty-six lines in thirteen moralizing passages. In it there is much talk of wealth and its corrupting effect; perhaps Acrisius believed that Danaë's story of the shower of gold meant that she had actually surrendered to a wealthy lover.

Danaïdes. *Myth.* Danaüs' fifty daughters. The Danaïdes fled with their father from Egypt to avoid marriage with their cousins, the sons of Aegyptus (see DANAÏD TETRALOGY). Forced nevertheless to marry Aegyptus' sons, forty-nine of the Danaïdes killed their bridegrooms on the wedding night. After they died, the sisters were pictured as in the underworld, endlessly trying to fill a leaky jar. Their fate may have been in punishment for their crime, or it may have symbolized to the Greeks the forlorn state in the afterlife of those who, because they reject marriage, were uninitiated into the mystery religions. *Danaïdes* was the title of lost plays by Aeschylus and Aristophanes. The latter's play, written perhaps about 413 B.C., was possibly a parody of some similarly named tragedy. It has been suggested that it satirized the proposal to reinforce the Sicilian expedition, comparing it to the Danaïdes' attempt to fill a leaky jar.

Danaïd Tetralogy. A trilogy of tragedies by Aeschylus, *The Suppliants, The Egyptians,* and *Danaïdes,* followed by the satyr play *Amymone.* Only *The Suppliants* is extant. The tetralogy has been shown, by a fragment of the Oxyrhynchus Papyri published in 1952, to have been produced most probably in 463 B.C. Aeschylus won first prize with it in the dramatic contest. Sophocles won second prize, and Mesatus third.

1. **The Suppliants** or **The Suppliant Maidens** (Gk. **Hiketides;** traditional Latin title, **Supplices**). Extant tragedy. Translations: Robert Potter, 1777; J. A. Giles, 1839; F. A. Paley, 1864; Edward H. Plumptre, 1868; E. D. A. Morshead, 1881; John D. Cooper, 1890; Lewis Campbell, 1890; Arthur S. Way, 1906; Walter and C. E. S. Headlam, 1909; G. M. Cookson, 1922; H. Weir Smyth, 1922; S. G. Bernardete, 1956; Philip Vellacott, 1961.

S C E N E. A sacred precinct on the shore not far from Argos, with many images of gods and a common altar.

S U M M A R Y. The fifty daughters of Danaüs, loathing the notion of incestuous marriage with their first cousins, the fifty sons of King Aegyptus, have fled from Egypt with their father and have arrived in Argos, the land of their ancestor Io. It was from Argos that Io, favored with Zeus's love, set out in the form of a heifer to endure wanderings and persecutions at the hands of the jealous Hera, until finally, on the banks of the Nile, she regained human form and at Zeus's touch bore Epaphus, great-grandfather of Danaüs and Aegyptus.

The Danaïdes (the Chorus) are appealing to their kinsmen, the Argives, and to the Argive gods for protection against the certain pursuit of their uncle and his sons. Their passionate refusal to marry their cousins verges on a resolution to preserve perpetual virginity; their hope for aid is, however, darkened by the knowledge that Zeus's execution of justice is often incomprehensible to men.

At the approach of an armed band led by Pelasgus, the king of Argos, the frightened flock of exiles take sanctuary around an altar. From its vantage point they convince the king that they are indeed related to him and threaten to hang themselves at the altar if he should refuse them asylum. Pelasgus is thus presented with a dilemma: he must choose between, on the one hand, committing a breach of hospitality and causing the city to be polluted by the suppliants' deaths, and, on the other, risking war with the Egyptians. He chooses the latter course but sends Danaüs to win the support of the Argive people. Pelasgus then follows, and the maidens, left alone, beseech Zeus to end the sufferings of Io's descendants.

On Danaüs' return his daughters learn that the men of Argos have voted to espouse the women's cause, but their rejoicings and blessings on the Argives are cut short by the arrival of an Egyptian Herald and his armed guards. The Egyptians, disregarding the sanctuary because it is sacred to alien gods, try to force the shrieking Danaïdes on board their ship, but their attempt is foiled by Pelasgus and his men, assisted by Danaüs, who has been granted a guard of honor.

At the play's finale, the Egyptians threaten war and Pelasgus defies them. Danaüs' daughters pray to the virgin goddess, Artemis, while Argive handmaidens sing a kind of counterpoint, reminding their kinswomen that Aphrodite, goddess of love, and Hera, goddess of marriage, must also have their due.

2. *The Egyptians.* Lost play. It may have preceded *The Suppliants* in Aeschylus' trilogy, but scholars are inclined to think that *The Egyptians* was the second play and that it depicted the following: a battle between Argives and Egyptians; the death of Pelasgus; a siege of Argos; a peace arranged with the condition that Danaüs surrender his daughters; Danaüs' succession to the throne of Argos; and his plot with his daughters to murder all their bridegrooms on the wedding night. The Chorus were probably the Danaïdes, and the sons of Aegyptus appeared perhaps only at the end. One of them, Lynceus, probably acted as negotiator during the peacemaking, and one of the Danaïdes, Hypermnestra, fell in love with him.

3. *Danaïdes.* Lost play. Its contents are much subject to conjecture. Some scholars have thought that in it Hypermnestra was put on trial for not obeying her father's command. More probably, however, it was Danaüs and the other forty-nine sisters who were tried (perhaps not formally), rather than Hypermnestra, who had spared her bridegroom. Danaüs must have been repudiated by the Argives for bringing on the land the very pollution that was feared in *The Suppliants,* since his offense against Zeus, the Lord of Hospitality, was greater than Pelasgus' would have been. Aphrodite appeared at the play's end and

effected some kind of reconciliation, voicing in her speech some famous lines, still extant, about the sacred marriage of Heaven and Earth.

4. *Amymone.* Lost satyr play. (See AMYMONE.)

COMMENTARY. Before 1952 the Danaïd Tetralogy was confidently assigned to Aeschylus' early career, and *The Suppliants,* with its large proportion of choric odes and an integral role assigned to the Chorus, was confidently pronounced the earliest extant Greek drama. However, the discovery of the tetralogy's late date now renders all such theories obsolete. Some attempts have been made to show that it was written thirty years earlier, and not performed because of adverse circumstances, but these seem desperate expedients.

Assuming the work to be representative of Aeschylus' maturity, one can accept the probability that the themes of the three tragedies were closely interwoven throughout. Male versus female, foreign barbarism versus Hellenic civilization—these themes are Aeschylean favorites. The motif of violence versus persuasion is one often elaborated, here in connection with sexuality: lust versus love. The Danaïdes and their murderous rejection of sexuality are played off against their violently attacking cousins, the sons of Aegyptus; this motif is reiterated in the satyr play, where Poseidon's wooing is counterpointed against the satyr's assault. The idea of reconciliation is embodied in Hypermnestra and given final voice by Aphrodite. It has already been adumbrated in the story of the ancestress Io, whose unwished-for contact with heaven seemed at first violent and productive only of great suffering, but for whom that violent contact was transformed into a "gentle touch," which resulted in the fruition of birth.

Danaüs (Gk. **Danaos**). *Myth.* Son of Belus and brother of Aegyptus. Danaüs refused to wed his fifty daughters, the Danaïdes, to Aegyptus' fifty sons. Leading his daughters to refuge in Argos, Danaüs begged the protection of the Argives; he appears in this role in Aeschylus' *Suppliants* (see DANAÏD TETRALOGY). According to Euripides (*Orestes,* line 871), Danaüs was made to stand trial on a hill in Argos for inciting his daughters to murder their husbands. He was sometimes regarded, because of his name, as the ancestor of the Danaäns, that is, the Greeks.

Dardanus (Gk. **Dardanos**). *Myth.* Son of Zeus and Atlas' daughter Electra. According to one story, Dardanus' native country was central Italy, which he left for the Troad and to which his posterity was destined to return. In the Troad Dardanus built the citadel of Troy and ruled over the whole region; hence "Dardanian" means "Trojan," the "Dardanidae" are the "Trojans," and "Dardania" is "the Troad." Dardanus stole the ancient statue of Athena, the Palladium, from Arcadia and placed it in the Trojan citadel. His son was Ilus.

Darius (Gk. **Dareios**). King of Persia (c. 550–485 B.C.). Darius seized control of the kingdom after the suicide of Cambyses in 522 B.C. Although he was an able ruler and commander, Darius' expedition against Athens failed at the battle of Marathon in 490 B.C. The Persian coin called the Daric was erroneously thought to have been named for him.

Datis. Persian general (5th century B.C.). Although Datis took pride in his ability to speak the Greek language, he made such absurd blunders that from his name was formed the Greek word *datismos,* meaning "a barbarism, a piece of bad Greek." Aristophanes mocks him in *Peace* (line 289). Xenocles, son of Carcinus, may have been nicknamed Datis.

Daulis or **Daulia.** City in Phocis at the foot of Mt. Parnassus. Thracians at one time inhabited the region, which became famous as the locale of the Procne-Philomela-Tereus myth.

Deianira or **Dejanira** (Gk. **Deianeira**). *Myth.* Daughter of King Oeneus of Calydon and sister of Meleager. When Heracles went to the underworld to fetch Cerberus, he encountered the soul of Meleager and learned of his beautiful sister. On emerging into the daylight, Heracles went to look for Deianira. Finding that she was being wooed by the monster river-god Achelous, Heracles fought with Achelous and overcame him. As he was leaving Calydon with his bride, Heracles entrusted her to the centaur Nessus to be carried across a river. But the centaur tried to run off with her, whereupon Heracles shot him with an arrow poisoned with the venom of the Hydra. The dying Nessus advised Deianira that a tunic dipped into his bood would provide her with an infallible love charm. Believing Nessus, the girl acted on his instructions, and when Heracles was later enamored of the captive Iole, Deianira sent him the charmed tunic to wear. The result was such agony to Heracles that he mounted a great pyre on Mt. Oeta and was burned alive. The remorseful Deianira committed suicide. She appears, in this last episode of her life, in Sophocles' *Trachiniae* and Seneca's *Hercules on Oeta.*

Deidamia. See LYCOMEDES.

Deiphobus (Gk. **Deiphobos**). *Myth.* Son of King Priam and Queen Hecuba of Troy. Deiphobus was Hector's favorite brother. After the death of Paris he married Helen, but during the sack of Troy she removed his weapons and led Menelaus to their bedroom. Menelaus murdered Deiphobus and mutilated his body.

Delos. Aegean island in the midst of the Cyclades. Delos was regarded as the birthplace of Apollo and Artemis and as sacred to Apollo. Hence "Delia" is Artemis and the "Delian shepherd" is Apollo. (See also ORTYGIA.)

Delphi. City on the slope of Mt. Parnassus, on the northern shore of the Gulf of Corinth. Here was the famous sanctuary and altar of Apollo. According to myth, the sanctuary first belonged to Gaia (Earth), who was the mother of all and knew all secrets. Delphi was considered the center of the earth, and the stone omphalos, the navel of the earth, was located there. Gaia then delegated her oracular powers to Themis. In one variant of the myth, Apollo, while a mere infant, killed the guardian serpent, Python, with his arrows and wrested the oracle from Themis, whereupon Gaia discontinued the oracle and sent prophecies directly to men in the form of dreams. But Zeus, on Apollo's appeal, restored prophecy to Delphi. According to another version, Themis bequeathed the oracle to Phoebe, who in turn gave it to Phoebus Apollo when he came over the seas from Delos and was welcomed by Delphos, the ruler of the land. At any rate, Apollo at Delphi was known as Loxias, "He Who Speaks Forth." His priestess was the Pythia, a woman who mounted the bronze tripod of the god, was possessed by him, and in a trance delivered his answers to the questions asked. The Greeks believed that in the three winter months Apollo retired from Delphi and allowed Dionysus to take possession of the sanctuary. Every three years orgiastic rites were held in honor of Dionysus on the heights above the city.

Delphos. *Myth.* King of the country around Delphi. Delphos welcomed Apollo into the land and instituted honors to him there.

deme (Gk. **demos**). Political subdivision of Attica. In accordance with the democratic constitution of Cleisthenes, each of the ten tribes of Attica was subdivided into a varying number of demes, or townships.

Demeter (Gk. "grain mother"). *Myth.* Greek goddess of the cultivated earth and its crops. Demeter was the daughter of Cronus and Rhea and the sister of Hera, Hestia, Zeus, Hades, and Poseidon. In some parts of Greece (for example, Arcadia), she was conflated sometimes with Hecate and sometimes with Erinys and was said to have coupled in the form of a mare with the horse god Poseidon.

Demeter was, however, most commonly associated with her daughter, Persephone, whose father is not named in drama. The principal myth of the goddess had to do with the abduction of Persephone by Hades, Demeter's mourning and search for her daughter (an annual event, during which the earth's vegetation died), Persephone's partial restoration, and the establishment of the Eleusinian mysteries (see PERSEPHONE; ELEUSIS). Demeter and her daughter, called "The Two Goddesses," "The Twain," "The Mother and The Maid," were the chief objects of veneration in Athens at the women's festival, the Thesmophoria.

Demophilus (Gk. **Demophilos**). Writer of New Comedy. Nothing is known of this playwright beyond the fact that Plautus, in the prologue to his *Asinaria*, cites Demophilus' *Onagos* as the Greek play on which his comedy is based.

Demophon. *Myth.* Son of Theseus. Demophon succeeded his father on the throne of Attica. He appears in Euripides' *Heraclidae*, where he champions the sons of Heracles, defeating and capturing their enemy, Eurystheus.

Demos. 1. Rich Athenian of Aristophanes' time. Demos was admired for his good looks and ridiculed for his stupidity. He is alluded to in *The Wasps* (line 98).

2. Personification of the citizenry of Athens. This Demos is a character in Aristophanes' *Knights* and appeared in several lost pieces of Old Comedy.

Demosthenes. Athenian military and naval commander in the Peloponnesian War. Demosthenes appears in the earlier part of Aristophanes' *Knights* as a slave of Demos and the chief opponent of the new slave, Paphlagon, or the Paphlagonian (Cleon).

Demostratus (Gk. **Demostratos**). Athenian demagogue during the Peloponnesian War. Demostratus was the prime mover of the Sicilian expedition in

415 B.C. He came of the ancient family of Bouzyges. In *Lysistrata* (line 391 ff.)
Aristophanes calls Demostratus "Cholozyges" (from *cholos*, "bile") because of
his bad temper.

Deo. Epithet of Demeter as grain mother.

Despoina (Gk. "mistress, queen"). Epithet of several goddesses, especially
Athena, Artemis, Demeter, and Hecate.

Deucalion (Gk. **Deukalion**). *Myth.* Son of Prometheus and husband of
Pyrrha. Warned by Prometheus that Zeus was about to flood the earth to rid
it of mankind, Deucalion built an ark for himself and his wife. After the waters
subsided, the couple disembarked and sacrificed to Zeus, who granted their
request that they might repeople the earth. Deucalion and Pyrrha accomplished
this by throwing stones over their shoulders, those flung by Deucalion becoming
men, and those flung by his wife becoming women.

deus ex machina (Latin for Gk. *theos ek mechanes* or *apo mechanes theos*,
"the god from the machine"; see MECHANE). A deity, or some other deliverer,
introduced to solve the plot complications of a play. Disapproval of such a
device was a commonplace of ancient criticism. Aristotle censured the appearance of Aegeus in Euripides' *Medea*, saying that there was insufficient motivation for it (*Poetics*, 1461b). Horace explicitly advised: *Nec deus intersit,
nisi dignus indice nodus / Inciderit:* "Do not make a god intervene unless the
plot complication calls for such a solution" (*Ars Poetica*, lines 191–92).

deuteragonist (Gk. **deuteragonistes**). The second actor in Greek drama.
(See ACTORS AND ACTING.)

Dexion (Gk. "receiver, welcomer"). Title given to the poet Sophocles in
the cult of Asclepius because he welcomed the god into Athens.

Dexitheos. Athenian harpist of Aristophanes' time. Dexitheos won a musical
contest in the Pythian Games.

Diaconus, Johannes. See JOHANNES DIACONUS.

Diacrians (Gk. **Diakrioi**). The poorest of the three opposing parties in
Athens in Solon's time.

Diagoras. Philosopher, contemporary with Aristophanes. Diagoras was
called "the Atheist" because of his expressed contempt for the gods. He wrote
Phrygian Discourses, making fun of Dionysus and Cybele, and because of his
ridicule of the Eleusinian mysteries, he had to flee from Athens to escape
execution.

Diallage (Gk. "reconciliation"). Personification of reconciliation in Aristophanes' *Acharnians*.

Diana. *Myth.* Roman goddess identified with the Greek ARTEMIS.

Diasia. Athenian festival in honor of Zeus Meilichios, the Chthonian Zeus.
The Diasia was celebrated outside the city with a sacrifice for the public
welfare. Sheep or swine were offered up, and the poorer people threw into the
flames effigies of animals made of dough.

diazoma. Semicircular horizontal aisle separating a lower tier of seats from
a higher tier in a Greek theater.

Dicaearchus (Gk. **Dikaiarchos**). Peripatetic philosopher (late 4th century

B.C.). Dicaearchus wrote, among other works that have been lost, *Analyses (Hypotheses) of Euripides' and Sophocles' Plays*. In it he seems to have been concerned with the plays' deviations from traditional myth. Traces of this work appear in extant hypotheses of some of Euripides' plays.

Dicaeogenes (Gk. **Dikaiogenes**). Writer of tragedies and dithyrambs (apparently late 5th century B.C.). Scanty fragments and two titles—*The Cyprians* and *Medea*—remain.

dicasts (Gk. **dikastai**). Citizen jurors of the Athenian law courts. Juries often contained hundreds of members.

Dictynna (Gk. **Diktynna**). *Myth.* Cretan maid, later deified. While escaping the unwelcome advances of Minos, Dictynna fell into the sea and was rescued in a fisherman's net (whence her name, supposedly, from *diktyon*, "net"). She was taken to Aegina, where she disappeared into a grove, and was worshiped as the goddess Aphaea (identified with Artemis or Hecate).

Dictys (Gk. **Diktys**, "fisherman"). *Myth.* Brother of Polydectes, the tyrant of Seriphos. While fishing on the shore, Dictys pulled up in his net the chest in which Danaë and the infant Perseus had been cast adrift. *Dictys* was the title of a lost play by Euripides (431 B.C.). It presumably told of Polydectes' attempt to force his love on Danaë after Perseus had been sent to fetch the Gorgon's head and of Danaë's flight to an altar, where she remained under Dictys' protection until Perseus returned and petrified the tyrant with the Gorgon's head. Some sixty scattered lines survive.

Dictyulci (Gk. **Diktyoulkoi**, "The Net-Pullers" or "The Fishermen"). Lost satyr play by Aeschylus. *Dictyulci* formed the afterpiece to a trilogy consisting of *Polydectes, Phorcides,* and an unknown tragedy. About ninety fragmentary lines have been recovered from papyri, so that the plot can be fairly well pieced together. In it Dictys is fishing with an old companion; finding the net too heavy to handle, they call for help. Silenus promises the help of his Satyrs, who form the Chorus, on condition that he is given part of the catch. There follows an elaborate pulling scene, with much clowning on the part of the Satyrs. At its climax a large chest is brought to land. A noise from inside it frightens the Satyrs, and when the chest is opened, Danaë and her child are revealed. Telling her sad story, Danaë wins Dictys' sympathy, and when Silenus steps forward to claim her, a quarrel ensues. Dictys then goes off for reinforcements, while the Satyrs dance in triumph and Danaë fights off Silenus. Just as mother and child are about to be dragged away, Dictys returns with help and drives off the Satyr band.

didascaliae, sing. **didascalia** (Gk. **didaskaliai**, sing. **didaskalia**, "instruction" or "training," that is, of actors and chorus, hence "play production"). 1 (*Didascaliae*). Lost work by Aristotle, doubtless compiled from official records that may have been kept from the time of the Persian wars. The work was essentially a list of the annual dithyrambic and dramatic performances at the Athenian festivals, and it included the names of actors and prizes awarded. Carystius of Pergamum wrote a supplementary work similar to that of Aristotle.

2. Notices that appear in the manuscripts of all of Terence's plays and of

Plautus' *Stichus* and *Pseudolus*. The *didascaliae* list title, festival, festival officials, play director, type of flute music, composer, playwright, Greek original,
chronological order of the play in the poet's works, and the year as indicated
by the consuls. The ultimate source of this information may have been the
Roman scholar Varro.

Didymus (Gk. **Didymos**). Scholar at Alexandria near the beginning of the
Christian era. Didymus wrote, among other works that have been lost, commentaries on Aeschylus, Sophocles, Euripides, Aristophanes, and other writers
of tragedy and comedy, as well as a *Lexicon for Tragedy* and a *Lexicon for
Comedy*.

Diitrephes. Athenian political and military man of Aristophanes' time. Originally a manufacturer of baskets, Diitrephes had become a cavalry commander.
He was gibed at by Aristophanes, Plato Comicus, and Cratinus.

Dike. Personification and deification of justice.

Dikephoros (Gk. "bringer of justice"). Epithet of Zeus.

Dinos (Gk. "whirling"). The rotational universal motion produced, according to Anaxagoras' system, by the Supreme Mind, or Nous. In Aristophanes'
Clouds (line 380 ff.), Socrates calls it the chief deity. The playwright doubtless
intended to suggest other meanings of the word, such as "dizziness" and "wine
bowl."

Dio Chrysostom (Gk. **Dion Chrysostomos**). Greek rhetorician from Prusa
famed throughout the Roman empire for public speaking (c. A.D 40–c. 112).
Among his eighty extant orations and essays is a comparison of how Aeschylus,
Sophocles, and Euripides handled the story of Philoctetes.

Diocles (Gk. **Diokles**). *Myth*. Hero who had a cult and festival at Megara
and whose name the Megarians used to swear by.

Diomedes or **Diomede**. 1. *Myth*. King of the Bistonians in Thrace. Diomedes compelled strangers to sleep with his daughters and then threw them to be
devoured by a stable of man-eating mares. One of Heracles' labors was to
bring back the mares to Greece; this he did, having first fed them King Diomedes.

2. *Myth*. Hero from Aetolia, son of Tydeus, and grandson of both King
Oeneus of Calydon and King Adrastus of Argos. A distinguished fighter in the
Trojan War, Diomedes usually assisted Odysseus in his exploits. Together they
surprised and killed the Trojan spy Dolon (the story is dramatized in Euripides'
Rhesus), and together they stole into Troy and carried off the Palladium. The
expression "Diomedean necessity," that is, irresistible necessity, was said to
come from the latter episode; for Odysseus, in order to get sole credit for re-
trieving the Palladium, tried to murder Diomedes, who was accordingly forced
to bind his companion and beat him back to camp with the flat of his sword.
(But some said that the phrase described the methods of Diomedes the Thracian king.) In Euripides' *Orestes* Diomedes is reported to have spoken at Orestes' trial in Argos and to have proposed exile for Orestes and Electra.

Diomeia. Attic deme, where an annual festival in Heracles' honor was held.
The celebration was suspended during the Peloponnesian War.

Dione. *Myth.* Goddess mother of Aphrodite.

Dionysia. Name of several festivals in honor of Dionysus. Plautus' *Cistellaria* (line 89) refers to such a festival at Sicyon, but the two principal Dionysia were in Attica.

1. The Great, or City, Dionysia, was given in honor of Dionysus Eleuthereus and was instituted when the god's statue was permanently moved from Eleutherae to Athens. This happened comparatively late in the development of Attic religion, and the festival became important only in the sixth century B.C. under Pisistratus. Its celebration was open to participants from all over Greece; many were attracted by the dramatic performances. The *archon eponymos*, after whom the year was named, directed the whole festivity. He was helped by two assistants and ten overseers.

In late March there was a ceremony of escorting the image of Dionysus back into the city from a hearth altar on the road to Eleutherae. This was followed by the elaborate Dionysiac procession, the *pompe*, which involved basket-bearers, phallus-bearers, the choregi, and other gorgeously gowned marchers; the procession paused for dances at various altars. Next came a *komos*, a revel procession. At some time in the festival the PROAGON, the dramatic rehearsal, was held, and the ten dithyrambic choruses performed. Then dramatic performances were given, either, as some think, throughout a three-day period, when a tetralogy followed by a comedy was presented each day, or, according to others, throughout a four-day period with three days of tragic tetralogies and five comedies on the fourth day. The whole was concluded by a meeting of the Assembly, which reviewed the conduct of the festival. The approximate dates of the institution of various activities follow:

c. 534 B.C.—the contest in tragedy
c. 486 B.C.—the contest in comedy
449 B.C.—the contest for tragic actors
Between 329 and 312 B.C.—the contest for comic actors
386 B.C.—revival of older tragedies
339 B.C.—revival of older comedies

2. The Rural Dionysia was much older than the city festival. It was held in December and was organized separately by each Attic deme. The original rite seems to have been the carrying around of a phallus image to encourage the fertility of the fields. Doubtless there were feasting, drinking, and games. In Aristophanes' *Acharnians* Dicaeopolis has his daughter parade as basket-bearer, followed by his slave carrying an upright phallus on a pole; a band of revelers bring up the rear and sing a hymn to Phales, the phallus personified. Dramatic contests differed in the various rural festivals; many demes had theaters, but not much is known about specific situations. Poets could produce original plays outside of the city, and revivals of plays already produced in Athens were common.

Dionysiskos (Gk. "Little Dionysus"). Lost satyr play by Sophocles. It treated of the child Dionysus' discovery of wine and the first intoxication of the satyrs.

Dionysius (Gk. **Dionysios**). 1. Tyrant of Syracuse. Dionysius seized control of the city in 405 B.C. and ruled until his death in 367. Amidst a vigorous political and military career he found time to write tragedies, which were ridiculed by the poets of Middle Comedy. Besides an *Adonis,* Dionysius wrote a *Ransom of Hector,* which won the prize at the Lenaea of 367.

2. Greek grammarian of unknown date. Dionysius was the author of a lost commentary on Euripides and a lost treatise on comedy.

Dionysodorus (Gk. **Dionysodoros**). Scholar of Alexandria, pupil of Aristarchus (2) (2nd century B.C.). Dionysodorus wrote, among other works that have been lost, *Errors of the Tragedians.*

Dionysus (Gk. **Dionysos**). *Myth.* Son of Zeus and Semele, Cadmus' daughter. When Zeus fell in love with Semele, the jealous Hera visited the girl in disguise and prompted her to beg Zeus to appear to her in all the glory that he displayed in Hera's presence. Zeus, having given his word that he would do whatever Semele asked, was forced to comply with her request, and in consequence Semele was consumed by lightning. The unborn Dionysus was blasted from her womb by the thunderbolt, but Zeus, in order to conceal his son from Hera, fastened him with a golden pin to his own thigh, where Dionysus remained until ready for birth. The baby was born with bull horns and garlanded with serpents. Again to deceive Hera, Zeus carried Dionysus to Nysa, in India or Arabia, where he gave the child to the nymphs to rear as a girl; Silenus became his foster father. However, Ino, another daughter of Cadmus, was often called his foster mother, or nurse.

Hera eventually discovered Dionysus and drove him mad. Leaving the nymphs, he wandered in many lands, accompanied by Silenus and a train of satyrs and maenads. He became involved in the battle against the Giants, taking the side of the gods and defeating Enceladus with Silenus' help. Hera next sent a band of Etruscan pirates to kidnap Dionysus, but their bonds fell off him. They nevertheless carried him out to sea. Suddenly the waves seemed to turn to meadow and grove, the mast was hung with grapes, the oars sprouted ivy, and a lion and a tiger appeared on board; the frightened pirates leaped into the water and became dolphins (from Seneca's *Oedipus,* line 449 ff.).

Dionysus went to Phrygia, where Rhea purified him and initiated him into her rites. He then began his triumphal progress, bringing the cult of the vine to all the ancient world. He traveled through India, the Red Sea, Lydia, the land of Amazons, across Thrace, and into Greece. Everywhere in Greece there was initial opposition, followed by divinely inspired madness and the destruction of Dionysus' enemies (see LYCURGUS 1; PENTHEUS; PROETIDES). Finally his divinity was everywhere acknowledged, and even Hera became reconciled to his entrance into Olympus. There he made Ariadne his bride, having found her on Naxos deserted by Theseus. Dionysus presented her with a bridal diadem that later became the constellation of the Northern Crown.

Dionysus was represented by the Greeks as attended by SILENUS; his characteristic emblem was the THYRSUS, and he was thought of as the leader of a riotous group (the THIASUS) made up of MAENADS and SATYRS. Hence rituals in his honor often took the form of processionals that represented the revelry of a thiasus. In Delphi and its environs, Dionysus' cult was distinctly subordinate to Apollo's but was nevertheless significant. In Attica his festivals, the Dionysia and the Lenaea, were the seedbed out of which every kind of ancient drama grew.

Dionysus was the god of intoxication, whether it resulted from wine or communal revelry or was self-induced frenzy; he seemed to assault from without and take possession of the psyche. He was the many-named: Bromius, Iacchus, Nyctelius, Bacchus, and Zagreus, among others. Euripides' BACCHAE remains the most complete and profound study of all phases of Dionysianism.

Dionysus Shipwrecked (Gk. **Dionysos Nauagos**). Lost comedy doubtfully ascribed to Aristophanes. Of it one line survives.

Diopeithes. Athenian soothsayer of Aristophanes' time. Diopeithes was Nicias' adviser and Anaxagoras' bitter opponent. He stood against the new philosophy and everything that tended to weaken traditional belief. Aristophanes was hostile to Diopeithes because, like all soothsayers, Diopeithes found a source of profit in war.

Dioscuri (Gk. **Dioskouroi** or **Dioskoroi**, "Zeus's boys"). *Myth.* Castor and Polydeuces (Latin, Pollux), twin sons of Zeus and Leda. Zeus having wooed Leda in the guise of a swan, the twins were sometimes said, like their sister Helen, to have been hatched from an egg. Their mortal father was Tyndareus (though the usual story was that Tyndareus was father only of Castor, who was therefore mortal), and they were sometimes called Tyndaridae. The Dioscuri were hero gods of Greece and Rome, but were especially worshiped in Sparta. Being excellent horsemen, they were sometimes referred to as "the Foals" or the "White Horses." Polydeuces was also an outstanding boxer.

Exploits of the Dioscuri included participation in the expedition of the Argonauts. They clashed with Theseus several times, and made war on Agamemnon after he had killed their sister Clytemnestra's first husband, forcing Agamemnon to marry Clytemnestra. Their most spectacular encounter was with their cousins, Idas and Lynceus, over the daughters of LEUCIPPUS. This duel was said to have ended in the deaths of all except Zeus's son, the divine Polydeuces, who refused to become immortal while his brother was subject to death. Zeus accordingly arranged that the twins should in turn descend to the underworld on alternate days, spending the other days in heaven. To signalize their fraternal devotion, the Dioscuri were translated to the skies as the constellation called by the Romans Gemini, "the Twins." In this aspect they became patrons of sailors and were sworn by in common Roman oaths, for example, *ecastor! edepol! pol!* They appear as a double *deus ex machina* at the end of Euripides' *Helen,* forbidding the Egyptian king to go in pursuit of the fleeing Helen and Menelaus. At the end of Euripides' *Electra,* they arrange for Electra to marry Pylades and prophesy Orestes' torment and its cure.

Diphilus (Gk. **Diphilos**). Writer of New Comedy (fl. c. 300–290 B.C.). Diphilus wrote approximately one hundred plays, of which only sixty titles and a few fragments survive. Plautus' *Casina* was based on Diphilus' *Allotment,* Plautus' *Rudens* on an unknown play of his. Diphilus' *Suicide Pact (Synapoth-*

neskontes) was the original of Plautus' lost *Commorientes* and furnished one scene (Act II, scene 1) for Terence's *Adelphoe*.

Dipolieia or **Dipoleia**. Midsummer Athenian festival in honor of Zeus Polieus, "Zeus of the City." Its principal feature was the ritual of the BOUPHONIA.

diptych. Term used by some modern scholars to characterize certain Greek plays which, in their opinion, fall into two distinct halves.

Dirce (Gk. **Dirke**). 1. *Myth*. Queen of Thebes, daughter of Achelous, and wife of Lycus. Dirce persecuted ANTIOPE.

2. Spring near Thebes. In a cave nearby lived the dragon which Cadmus killed; hence, "Dircean teeth" were the teeth of this dragon. The ashes of Dirce (1), after her death at the hands of Amphion and Zethus, were thrown into the spring, which was named after her.

Dirphys. Mountain on the island of Euboea.

Dis. *Myth*. Roman god identified with HADES.

distegia. Small upper story on the main stage building of the Greek theater. Here the actors could appear to be gazing from city walls and other heights.

dithyramb (see also DITHYRAMBUS). Hymn in honor of Dionysus. The singing of dithyrambs by choruses of men and boys formed an important part of the celebration of the Dionysia. Dithyrambs were not strictly dramatic, but that they were connected with drama is indicated by Aristotle's much-discussed and much-disputed statement that drama developed thanks to the leaders (*exarchontes*) of the dithyramb (*Poetics*, 1449a). (See TRAGEDY.)

Dithyrambus (Gk. **Dithyrambos**). Epithet of Dionysus. The word Dithyrambus was erroneously construed by the Greeks to mean "he who came twice (*dis*) through the door (*thyra*) of birth," with reference to the god's rebirth from Zeus's thigh. The true etymology is uncertain.

Dius Fidius. Roman god of truth and honor, invoked in oaths. Dius Fidius was probably an aspect of Jupiter.

Dodona. Ancient Greek city in the mountains of Epirus, noted for its oracle of Zeus. Dodona was located in a sacred grove centered around the famous "talking oak."

Dolios (Gk. "trickster"). Epithet of Hermes.

Dolon. *Myth*. A Trojan sent by Hector to spy out the Greek encampment by night. While on this mission Dolon was seized by Odysseus and Diomedes, who were also reconnoitering. Dolon gave much information to the two Greeks, who afterward killed him. His story forms part of Book X of the *Iliad* (the *Doloneia*), and he appears as a character in Euripides' *Rhesus*, which dramatizes the incident.

Dolopes or **Dolopians** (sing. **Dolops**). Tribe in Thessaly. *Dolopes* was the the title of a lost play by Sophocles. Of it nothing certain is known. Its subject may have been either the concealment of Achilles at the Scyrian court (see ACHILLES) or the fetching of Neoptolemus to the Trojan War (see NEOPTOLEMUS).

dominus gregis (Lat. "master of the flock"). Director of a troupe of actors in Rome.

Domitius Ahenobarbus, Gnaeus. First husband of the younger Agrippina and father of Nero.

Donatus, Aelius. Latin grammarian (4th century A.D.). Donatus was the teacher of St. Jerome. Besides works on grammar, his *Commentary on Terence* survives, though in somewhat altered form. It seems to have been largely based on the commentary of Aemilius Asper of two centuries before.

Donoessa. See GONOESSA.

Doric farce. See COMEDY.

Doris. Small inland region of Greece between the two divisions of Locris. Doris was east of Aetolia and west of Phocis.

Dorotheus (Gk. **Dorotheos**). Greek scholar of Ascalon just before the beginning of the Christian era. Dorotheus was the author of an extensive lexicon, now lost. *Antiphanes and the Ragout in the New Comedy Playwrights* (the import of the title is unclear) may have been a part of it.

Dorus (Gk. **Doros**). *Myth.* Son of Xanthus and Creusa and ancestor of the Dorian, or Doric, branch of the Greek race.

Dossenus. Stock character in ATELLAN FARCE. The name Dossenus has been connected with *dorsum,* "back," and it is thought that he was a hunchback, but the evidence is scanty.

Draco (Gk. **Drakon**). Scholar of the Alexandrian age. Draco wrote, among other works that are lost, a book on the satyr play.

Dracontides (Gk. **Drakontides**). Athenian politician and military commander. Dracontides was a bitter opponent of Pericles.

Dramas or Niobus. Lost comedy by Aristophanes (written perhaps 412 B.C.). Judging from the alternate title, *Dramas* parodied some tragedy called *Niobe.* Yet there is some evidence that it was a revision of Aristophanes' *Dramas or The Centaur.* The suggestion has been made that in the play Demos (Athens) bewailed, like Niobe, the loss of his children (allies) after the failure of the Sicilian expedition.

Dramas or The Centaur. Lost comedy by Aristophanes, (c. 426 or 425 B.C.). It seems to have dealt with Heracles' visit to Pholus the centaur and perhaps with his visit to the underworld.

dramatic contest. See AGON.

Drusus, Marcus Livius. Roman tribune. By his advocacy of citizenship for the Italian allies and by other schemes of reform, Drusus alienated both the senatorial and the popular parties. He was killed in a riot in 91 B.C.

Drusus Caesar. Son of the emperor Tiberius. Drusus was thought to have been poisoned by his wife, Livia, at the instigation of her lover, Sejanus, in A.D. 23.

Dryads (Gk. **Dryades**). *Myth.* Nymphs of the woods; tree spirits.

Dryas. *Myth.* Thracian hero, father of the Lycurgus who opposed Dionysus.

Duris (Gk. **Douris**). Historian and scholar of Samos (4th century B.C.). Besides his better-known histories, Duris wrote *On Tragedy, On Euripides and Sophocles,* and *On the Contests.* All of these works are lost.

Dyskolos(Latinized, **Dyscolus; The Curmudgeon, The Grouch,** etc.; see

other titles under Translations). Extant comedy by Menander (produced 317
B.C.). First printed edition March 1959, ed. by Victor Martin. Translations:
Gilbert Highet, *The Curmudgeon,* 1959; W. G. Arnott, *Dyskolos, or The Man
Who Didn't Like People,* 1960; W. H. Hewitt and M. W. M. Pope, *The Angry
Old Man,* 1960; Philip Vellacott, *The Bad-Tempered Man,* 1960; Lionel Casson,
The Grouch, 1960; J. H. Quincey, *The Old Curmudgeon,* 1962.

S C E N E. Phyle, in Attica.

S U M M A R Y. Pan, speaking the prologue, enters from the Cave of the
Nymphs and tells the audience that the farm on his right belongs to Cnemon,
a morose and unsociable man who lives with his daughter, Myrrhine, and one
old maidservant, Simice. The farm on the left is worked by Gorgias, Cnemon's
stepson, aided by his aged slave, Daos. Here Cnemon's wife has fled to escape
her husband's bad temper.

Sostratos, a wealthy landowner's son who had come hunting in the area,
has seen Myrrhine and fallen in love with her. He has sent a Slave to speak to
the girl's father. In the first scene, the Slave runs in and reports that the farmer
cursed, stoned, and beat him off the land before he could say a word. Cnemon
himself then appears, grumbling that there are too many people in the world; he
becomes even angrier when he sees Sostratos standing by his front door and
rudely dismisses the young man's appeal for a talk. As Cnemon goes into his
house, Myrrhine comes out to fetch water, and Sostratos insists on helping her.
The encounter is witnessed by Gorgias' slave, Daos, who reports it to his master.

Gorgias fears that the stranger's intentions are dishonorable, but he is
considerably softened when Sostratos vows in the name of Pan and the nymphs
that he wishes to marry Myrrhine. Although Gorgias doubts that Cnemon will
regard Sostratos' suit with favor, he promises to discuss the matter with the
old curmudgeon in the fields and invites Sostratos to accompany him. Daos
points out that Cnemon will be hostile if he sees Sostratos idling in his elegant
cloak but that he may be more favorably disposed toward the latter if he
believes him to be a poor farmer like himself. At this Sostratos agrees to pick
up a mattock and dig along with them, while Daos explains privately to Gorgias
that they can work harder than ever that day and so exhaust Sostratos that he
will pester them no longer. Sostratos, for his part, is willing to do anything to
win a girl so pure and unworldly as Myrrhine.

Sicon, a cook in the service of Sostratos' mother, enters dragging a sheep to
be sacrificed at the shrine. It seems that his mistress, who makes a hobby of
visiting sanctuaries, has been alarmed by a dream in which she saw Sostratos
tilling land; she has planned the sacrifice to ward off the evil portent. Cnemon
emerges from his house and is immediately surrounded by the oncoming crowd
of worshipers. He retreats, damning the Cave of the Nymphs and all its visitors
but is again brought to the door when Getas, a slave in the household of
Sostratos' mother, knocks and asks for the loan of a pot. Cnemon answers with
further curses and a slammed door. The cook makes the same attempt as the
slave and is received with deadly rage.

Sostratos is aching all over from his unaccustomed physical labor. He has failed to see Cnemon but is still friendly toward Gorgias, whom he invites to the sacrificial banquet. Cnemon's old maidservant, Simice, now runs in; having dropped her bucket into the well, she tried to get it out with a mattock, only to lose the mattock as well. Cnemon pursues her furiously offstage.

Suddenly Simice raises a cry: Cnemon himself is now in the well! Although Sicon suggests that a millstone be dropped on the old man, Gorgias and Sostratos rush to the rescue. Cnemon is brought in bedraggled and self-pitying but much sobered by his narrow escape from death. Although he had long been convinced that no man was capable of a disinterested act, he was impressed by the fact that Gorgias, whom he had often abused, had gone to his rescue. In gratitude he adopts Gorgias as his son and asks him to find a husband for Myrrhine. Gorgias promptly betroths Myrrhine to Sostratos, who returns the favor by offering one of his own sisters to him. Unwilling to marry a rich woman because of his own poverty, Gorgias at first refuses but is persuaded by Sostratos' father, Callipides, who has arrived to join the feast and who urges him to use common sense.

All join in the ensuing festivities except Cnemon, who has taken to his bed inside and is relishing his loneliness. But he is brought out asleep by the cook and slave whom he had insulted. They revenge themselves on him by beating on his door and shouting demands to borrow hearth rugs, Persian hangings, and other unlikely objects. The two servants then crown the old man with a garland and pull him into the dance.

COMMENTARY. Until 1957 only twelve fragments remained of this play, but in that year Professor Victor Martin of the University of Geneva announced that the Swiss collector Martin Bodmer had acquired a third century A.D. papyrus manuscript containing the complete text. Jubilation among scholars was only slightly tempered by the consideration that *Dyskolos* had never been reckoned among Menander's masterpieces, since it was known to have been written at the very outset of his career.

The play has proved to be just about what scholars might have expected: while it is full of charm and freshness and abounds in liveliness and good humor, it is somewhat stereotyped in setting and characterization, though not as stereotyped as might have been feared. *Dyskolos* displays some very obvious defects. Although Cnemon, who is given full play, is a vivid enough character, he is not unusual; the roles of the young people, who are far more interesting than nine-tenths of their counterparts in Roman comedy, are somewhat small; and the author falls back on stock characters—the usual cooks and slaves. Most serious of all is that the plot runs out before the end of the fourth act and farce must take over until the close. It is almost as if the Aristophanic tradition still persisted of tacking on slapstick scenes after the main theme was exhausted.

Of considerable importance are the indications for interludes by the Chorus after lines 232, 426, 619, and 783. They tend to confirm the theory that the five-act division was standard before the end of the fourth century B.C.

E

Ecbatana (Gk. **Ekbatana**). Principal city in Media. Ecbatana was one of the residences of the Persian kings. Because of the city's remoteness and legendary wealth, its name became synonymous with luxury and happiness.

Ecclesiazusae (Gk. **Ekklesiazousai, The Women in the Assembly**). Extant comedy by Aristophanes (produced 392 B.C. or, according to a few scholars, at the Lenaea of 393 or 391). Translations: Benjamin B. Rogers, 1924; Arthur S. Way, 1934; Jack Lindsay, 1962.

S C E N E. A street in Athens.

S U M M A R Y. Shortly before dawn, Praxagora comes out of her house dressed in the clothes of her husband, Blepyrus. She calls together the neighbor women, who are similarly disguised and who wear beards in preparation for their planned attendance at the Assembly. Praxagora rehearses her speech proposing that the government be turned over to the women; then they all go off, carefully correcting one another for any slip of the tongue that would show them to be women.

Blepyrus comes out of the house dressed in his wife's clothes because he couldn't find his own. He is joined by neighbors, one of whom, Chremes, tells of the strange meeting of the Assembly that has just taken place. In it a great crowd of pale-faced fellows, who outnumbered the rest, voted to put the women of Athens in power on the ground that everything else had been tried.

Praxagora, returning from the Assembly, is stealing into the house when Blepyrus sees her; he accuses her of having visited a lover, but she convinces him that she has been helping a woman in childbirth. When Blepyrus informs his wife that the women have taken over the government, Praxagora expresses her surprise and joy. She then proceeds to outline her own projects for reform: all property will be held in common, including gold, food, wives, and husbands; before a man can make love to an attractive woman, he must first embrace a plain one, and the women must likewise first accept the ugly men. Chremes prepares to cede his goods to the common store, but another citizen chides him for being a fool and obeying the new law too quickly. Their chatter is interrupted by a Herald, who bids everyone come to the public feast.

There follows a scene in which three old women, in accordance with the new decree, fight over a young man. Two of them finally tear him away from a young girl, to whom he would much prefer to make love. As the play closes, everyone proceeds to the banquet, dancing and singing, and the Chorus appeal to the judges of the play to award it a prize.

COMMENTARY. *Ecclesiazusae* labors under a certain disadvantage in that most readers come to it with the information that it is a piece of Middle Comedy and a work of the author's old age; hence they expect to find the inevitable symptoms of decline. Actually, the spirit of the piece is that of Old Comedy, and individual scenes differ little in style from those of earlier pieces, although the reduced importance of the chorus and the absence of parabasis and agon are obvious. Yet even when one grants that *Ecclesiazusae* has many fine touches, the meager interest it has aroused in both ancient and modern times seems to correspond to a lack of interest on the part of the author himself. Everything begins well enough, but the play somehow runs down: the theme changes from matriarchal rule to communistic reform; the heroine disappears; and the plot dribbles away. All that is left is a pallid burlesque of the kind of political theorizing that Plato and his followers were probably indulging in at the time and that was expressed twenty years later in the *Republic*. The verdict that *Ecclesiazusae* is a tired refashioning of *The Birds* and *Lysistrata* appears just.

eccyclema (Gk. **ekkyklema**, "something rolled out"). Low platform on rollers, used for scenes such as the one involving Agathon in *Thesmophoriazusae*. The exact nature of the mechanism is much disputed, as is the question of whether the device was a convention representing interior scenes.

Echidna. *Myth.* Monster, half maiden, half serpent. Echidna was the mother of Cerberus.

Echinad Isles (Gk. **Echinades**). Group of very small islands off the coast of Acarnania.

Echinus (Gk. **Echinos**). Small town near the north shore of the Malian Gulf. In *Lysistrata* (line 1169) Aristophanes uses the name, making a pun on *echinos*, "hedgehog" or "sea urchin."

Echion. *Myth.* One of the five survivors of the armed men who grew from the earth when CADMUS sowed the dragon's teeth. Echion married Evadne and became the father of Pentheus.

Echo. *Myth.* Nymph of the woods and mountains. While Hera was spying on certain nymphs with whom she suspected Zeus of dallying, Echo detained her in conversation as the nymphs made their escape. In punishment, Hera took from Echo her power of speech except the ability to repeat the last words of another's speech. When Echo fell in love with the beautiful young man Narcissus, he repulsed her and she wasted away, only her voice remaining. (See also Euripides' ANDROMEDA.)

Ecphantides (Gk. **Ekphantides**). One of the earlier writers of Old Comedy. In later antiquity Ecphantides was the earliest known comic playwright represented by an extant play. Only one title, *The Satyrs*, and five fragments are known now. Ecphantides was nicknamed Kapnias, "Smoky," allegedly because he could write nothing bright or clear.

Edonians (Gk. **Edones**). Tribe on the border between Thrace and Macedonia. *The Edonians* was the title of a lost play by Aeschylus. (See LYCURGEIA.)

Eëtion. *Myth.* King of Thebe in the Troad and father of Andromache. Eëtion and all his sons were killed by Achilles in an assault on the town.

Egyptians. The. Lost play by Aeschylus. (See DANAÏD TETRALOGY.)

Eido. *Myth.* Name of Theonoë as an infant.

Eileithyia. *Myth.* Goddess of childbirth. Eileithyia was the daughter of Zeus and Hera.

eiron (Gk. "dissembler"). One of the three basic types of comic character. The *eiron* differs from the ALAZON in that the latter pretends to more knowledge than he has, whereas the *eiron* hides his knowledge. He differs from the BOMOLOCHOS in that the latter is merely an honest buffoon. More specifically, the *eiron* takes forms such as the swindler, the trickster, the hypocrite, and the picaresque rogue. His pretended stupidity is intended to trick the *bomolochos* into some ludicrous action and to prick the *alazon's* conceits. When, in drama, the consequences of deceit are more serious, the role of *eiron,* as in the case of Hamlet and Mephistopheles, turns toward tragedy, though it still retains a suggestion of the comic.

Electra (Gk. **Elektra**). *Myth.* Daughter of Agamemnon and Clytemnestra. After the murder of her father, Electra was grossly maltreated by her mother and Aegisthus. According to some versions of the myth, Electra was responsible for sending away her young brother Orestes to safety in a foreign land; this is her function in the last scenes of Seneca's *Agamemnon.* Electra's part in helping the grown-up Orestes to kill Aegisthus and Clytemnestra is delineated in Aeschylus' *Choephori* and in the *Electra* of Sophocles and that of Euripides. She also appears as a character in Euripides' *Orestes,* which takes place after the killings. (A further adventure of Electra is told under ALETES.)

Electra (Gk. **Elektra**). Extant tragedy by Euripides. Although the date of production is not absolutely certain, critics agree on 413 B.C. Translations: Edward P. Coleridge, 1891; Gilbert Murray, 1911; Arthur S. Way, 1912; Moses Hadas, 1950; D. W. Lucas, 1951; Emily Townsend Vermeule, 1958; Philip Vellacott, 1963.

S C E N E. A poor hut on the outskirts of Argos.

S U M M A R Y. A yeoman Farmer explains how he came to be married to the princess Electra. He tells how Clytemnestra and her lover, Aegisthus, fearing that a noble offspring might avenge Agamemnon's murder, forced Electra to marry a peasant. The Farmer has, however, respected his wife's virginity. Electra now enters carrying a water jar and, to her husband's plea that she not do menial labor, replies that she does it in gratitude for his kindness. The pair go out.

Orestes and his cousin Pylades appear, having come from Agamemnon's grave, where Orestes made a stealthy sacrifice and an offering of his hair. From a distance they overhear Electra speaking with a Chorus of Argive Women, lamenting her misfortunes and praying for the appearance of her brother, Orestes, to be her vindicator. The two young men come forward, and Orestes informs Electra that her brother is alive and asks after her. Electra tells the strangers of her humble life and of her husband's respectful treatment. She vows that she would gladly help Orestes kill her mother and stepfather. Presently the Farmer re-enters and offers the two men the hospitality of his hut; praising his nobility of character, they accept.

Electra, ashamed to entertain such distinguished visitors in so poor a place, sends the Farmer to her father's old Servant to bid him bring suitable food for them. On his arrival the Servant, who had rescued Orestes as a child from his murderous mother, tells Electra that he has found on Agamemnon's tomb a lock of hair and near it a footprint, both seeming to match her own. He concludes that Orestes must be in the land. She scoffs at the idea that brother's and sister's hair or footprints might match, but, when Orestes steps from the hut, the Servant recognizes him and proves his identity by pointing out the scar on his forehead.

The reunited brother and sister embrace joyfully and then plot their vengeance on Clytemnestra and Aegisthus. The latter, who is away from the palace sacrificing to the Nymphs, may be easily killed at the banquet. Clytemnestra may be brought to the Farmer's hut by the report that Electra has borne a child.

Orestes and Pylades set out on their mission, and soon afterward a Messenger brings the report that Aegisthus, after inviting the strangers to assist at the sacrifice, was himself killed on top of the victim. Presently Orestes and Pylades reappear, bringing Aegisthus' body. Electra pours bitter reproaches upon it, after which it is carried into the hut.

Now Clytemnestra approaches, intending to make a sacrifice for Electra's newborn child. Feeling guilty at the sight of her daughter's humble surroundings, she tries to justify her past conduct to Electra, who replies with scorn. Clytemnestra then enters the hut, and at once her dying screams are heard. Orestes and Electra emerge, much shaken by their deed and by their mother's pleas for mercy. Suddenly over the rooftop are seen Castor and Polydeuces, the twin star gods who are Clytemnestra's brothers. While acknowledging Clytemnestra's death to be just, they condemn Orestes' act as wrong. They order that Electra be married to Pylades and predict for Orestes a long pursuit by the Furies until he finds acquittal at last on the Areopagus at Athens.

COMMENTARY. As far back as 1809, the great German critic A. W. Schlegel, in his *Lectures on Dramatic Art and Literature,* used Sophocles' *Electra* as a stick to beat Euripides' play, finding the latter "a monument of poetic perversity." Subsequent discussions have chiefly been defenses against this attack, the most common contention being that Euripides' reason for stripping his characters of nobility, grandeur, and even dignity was to show up the shabbiness of the gods who had brought them to this pass. But such a defense presupposes a view of the gods that is very doubtfully Euripidean. It is far more likely that the playwright was interested in the kind of situation where human beings are led to degenerate tragically under the pressure of mutual hatred and reciprocal retaliation.

In this regard, some illumination might be forthcoming from Euripides' contemporary, Thucydides, in his *Peloponnesian War*. Thucydides was a thinker having little feeling either for or against the gods; yet his work was, like that of Euripides, a study of tragic degeneration. In Thucydides' view, the degeneration during the war consisted of the successive abandonment of one civilized amenity after another, as first one side, then the other, slipped lower in the scale of values.

This process of reciprocal decivilization had interested Euripides from the earliest days of the Peloponnesian War, when he composed his *Heraclidae*. The subject of *Electra* is the degenerative feud between Clytemnestra and Electra, but its treatment is analogous to that in Aeschylus' *Agamemnon* rather than that in *Choephori* (see ORESTEIA). In both *Electra* and *Agamemnon*, the justice of the gods is done, but the sorry nature of the justicers and the sorry spirit of the deed will require further justice.

Electra (Gk. **Elektra**). Extant tragedy by Sophocles. Although most critics assume that Sophocles' play was written earlier than Euripides' *Electra* (c. 413 B.C.), a very few think that it was written later. Translations: Lewis Campbell, 1883; Richard C. Jebb, 1904; F. Storr, 1912; Francis Fergusson, 1938; E. F. Watling, 1953; David Grene, 1957; H. D. F. Kitto, 1962. Adaptations and works influenced by *Electra:* Voltaire, *Oreste,* 1750; Vittorio Alfieri, *Orestes,* 1786; Johann Jakob Bodmer, *Electra,* 1760; Hugo von Hofmannsthal, *Elektra,* 1904, set to music by Richard Strauss, 1909.

S C E N E. Mycenae, the palace.

S U M M A R Y. Orestes, exiled son of the murdered Agamemnon, slips into the city with his friend Pylades and his old Body Servant. Orestes intends to make offerings at his father's tomb and to execute the task of retribution, ordered by the Delphic oracle, on his murderess mother, Clytemnestra, and her paramour, Aegisthus, who now rule Mycenae. It is planned that the rulers will be lulled into a feeling of security by a message that Orestes has been killed in a chariot race at the Pythian Games.

As these three retire, Electra, Orestes' sister, comes out bewailing the death of her father and her own wretched lot. She tells how she is kept unmarried and childless and how her mother hates her daughter for her continued loyalty to Agamemnon's memory; she curses the murderers. The Chorus of Mycenaean Women gently reprove Electra for her excessive hatred and violent words, as does Chrysothemis, her milder sister. Chrysothemis is on her way to make a propitiatory offering at Agamemnon's grave, for Clytemnestra has dreamed that her husband's ghost took the scepter from Aegisthus and planted it at the hearth, whereupon the rod burst into bloom and overshadowed the whole land. Chrysothemis also warns Electra that, because of her intemperate behavior, her mother and stepfather are thinking of throwing her into prison.

Clytemnestra now enters, and she and Electra begin to quarrel. They are interrupted by Orestes' old Servant, who brings a vivid, but false, story of Orestes' death. Clytemnestra acknowledges a pang of maternal pity, but her real feeling is one of relief. She takes the Messenger inside.

Electra cries out in despair. Presently Chrysothemis returns to say joyfully that she found an offering on the tomb that could only have been put there by the long-lost Orestes. Electra tells her sister the news of Orestes' death and begs Chrysothemis to help her avenge their father's murder, but Chrysothemis refuses. Electra then resolves to accomplish the deed herself.

At this juncture Orestes enters, carrying the urn that purportedly contains his ashes. Listening to his sister's piercing lamentation over the remains and pitying her, Orestes reveals himself and tells her of his plan to kill Aegisthus and Clytemnestra. He and Pylades then enter the palace and kill Clytemnestra. Soon afterward Aegisthus, who has been away from the palace, approaches. Lifting the shroud that supposedly covers the body of the dead Orestes, he sees Clytemnestra's face. At the play's end, Aegisthus is driven inside to meet his death, while the Chorus raise a cry of freedom.

COMMENTARY. There has been much ink spilt over the question whether Sophocles' version of the Electra story was a retort to Euripides, whose version was in turn intended as an improvement on Aeschylus', or whether Euripides was retorting to Sophocles' intended improvement on Aeschylus. Until somebody establishes a relative dating of the plays, it is better to judge them on their intrinsic merits. Not many have found in Sophocles' version "the celestial purity, the fresh breath of life and youth" that A. W. Schlegel (in *Lectures on Dramatic Art and Literature*) found in it. On the contrary, attempts to follow Schlegel's approach have ended in a critical impasse, for the play's apparent combination of "homicide and high spirits," in Gilbert Murray's phrase, is the very thing that must be explained away.

It used to be said that in *Electra* Sophocles was archaizing, deliberately presenting the myth as it would have been presented in the conscienceless minds of the mythical period. This theory cannot be given much credit, for the existence of such a mind and such an era is most doubtful; moreover, it cannot be believed that Sophocles would have descended below his own level of conscience.

Perhaps the most pertinent suggestion to make is that, whichever *Electra* came first, Sophocles' play is fundamentally Euripidean in that it portrays a psychological tragedy, a breakdown of character under the pressure of intolerable circumstance. This would clarify the general attitude of the play, in which the subject of Orestes' guilt is avoided. One might well hesitate to go further, as do some interpreters, who assert that Electra attains to some kind of superhuman heroic stature and quasi divinity by the sacrifice of her own nobility and womanliness under the stress of an overwhelming passion for one particular enactment of justice. (See also Euripides' ELECTRA and Aeschylus' ORESTEIA: *Choephori*.)

Electran, or **Electra's, Gates.** One of the seven pairs of gates in Thebes, supposedly named after a daughter of Amphion.

Electryon (Gk. **Elektryon;** also, Lat., **Electrus**). *Myth.* Son of Perseus and Andromeda and father of Alcmena. Electryon was accidentally killed by his son-in-law Amphitryon.

Eleusinians, The (Gk. **Eleusinioi**). Lost tragedy by Aeschylus. *The*

Eleusinians dealt with the peaceful recovery by Theseus of the bodies of the Seven against Thebes and with their burial (compare Euripides' *Suppliants*). This must have been one of the earliest appearances in literature of Theseus as the embodiment of Athenian enlightenment and humaneness.

Eleusis (adj. **Eleusinian**). Small town on the Attic coast west of Athens. Here Demeter is supposed to have stayed and become nurse to the king's son during her search for the kidnaped Persephone; here she established the Eleusinian mysteries; and from here she sent forth Triptolemus to spread the knowledge of agriculture over the earth.

The mysteries, famous throughout the Greco-Roman world, involved lengthy and elaborate preparatory rites and a climactic *epopteia*, a seeing or revelation, at which it is thought that the initiate witnessed some kind of dramatic performance depicting Demeter's loss and retrieval of her daughter. The *epopteia* was undoubtedly a death-and-resurrection ceremony which conferred immortality on the initiates, employing the symbolism of a seed, its death in the earth, and its subsequent flowering. The theory that such ritual drama exercised any extensive influence on the development of tragedy, or on the work of Aeschylus in particular, has been generally discounted by scholars.

Eleutherae (Gk. **Eleutherai**). Town on the border of Attica and Boeotia, on the south slope of Mt. Cithaeron. In the middle sixth century B.C. Pisistratus transplanted the cult of Dionysus Eleuthereus from Eleutherae to Athens. Out of this cult grew Greek drama.

Eleutheria. Any of a number of "festivals of freedom" in honor of Zeus Eleutherios, especially the one established by Miltiades to commemorate the victory over the Persians at Plataea in 479 B.C.

Eleutherios (Gk. "the deliverer"). Epithet of Zeus.

Elis (spelled Alis in Plautus' *Captives;* adj. **Elean**). District in the northwest corner of the Peloponnesus. Elis' chief city, Olympia, was sacred to Zeus and was the seat of the Olympic Games.

Elymnium (Gk. **Elymnion**). Island north of Euboea.

Elysium (Gk. **Elysion**). *Myth.* Tranquil and happy region of plains and groves where blessed spirits retired after death. Elysium was located usually in the underworld but was sometimes placed on the rim of the earth or in the Isles of the Blessed.

embates. Buskins worn by tragic actors. *Embates* had soles consisting of wooden blocks several inches high. They did not come into use until quite late.

embolium (Lat. word from Gk. *emballein,* "to throw in"). An intermezzo performance in a drama, usually a dance or a pantomime.

emmeleia. Solemn dance characteristic of tragedy.

Empolaios (Gk. "concerned with trade"). Epithet of Hermes as patron of business.

Empusa (Gk. **Empousa**). *Myth.* Cannibalistic bogey in the retinue of Hecate. Empusa frightened women and children in the night. She could assume many forms; according to Aristophanes (*The Frogs,* line 293), Empusa had one leg of bronze, one of cow dung.

Enagonios. Epithet of Hermes as god of games and contests.

Enceladus (Gk. **Enkelados**). *Myth.* Giant said to have been overcome by Dionysus in the war between the Giants and the gods.

Enetans. See HENETANS.

Englottogastores (Gk. "in-tongue-bellies"). Imaginary tribe in Aristophanes' *Birds* (lines 1695–96) who "feed their bellies with their tongues," that is, earn their living as informers.

Enispe. Town in Arcadia.

Enna or **Henna.** City in central Sicily noted for its cult of Demeter and Persephone. It was from a plain nearby that Hades was said to have abducted Persephone into the underworld.

Ennius, Quintus. Roman poet and playwright (239–169 B.C.). Of Southern Italian background, Ennius spoke Greek, Oscan, and Latin, a fact that prompted him to say that he had "three souls." He was brought to Rome by Cato the Elder. Although he became intimate with the Scipios, the Fulvii, and other noble families, Ennius was himself always poor, sharing a house with the poet Caecilius. He was fond of his wine, claiming that he wrote best when in his cups and that he never composed poetry unless laid up with gout. Extensive fragments, but no complete works, survive. The "Father of Latin Poetry," Ennius won most fame from his epic poem, *The Annals.* He translated Euhemerus' rationalization of myth, *The Sacred History,* into Latin and wrote *Epicharmus,* a dream fantasy in which the Sicilian playwright learned philosophy from Pythagoras. Of the twenty known titles of Ennius' tragedies, most (like *Andromeda, Andromache, Hecuba,* and *Medea*) suggest Euripides as a model. Two comedy titles are known, *Mine Hostess* and *The Winner of the Pancratium,* as well as two dramas on Roman subjects (*fabula praetexta*), *Ambracia* and *The Sabine Women.*

Enodia (Gk. "on or by the road, pertaining to a journey"). Epithet of Hecate as patroness of journeys and highways. Her statue was erected at cross-ways, and many shrines to her were built along roads and streets.

Enyalius (Gk. **Enyalios**). *Myth.* God of war. Although Enyalius was usually identified with Ares, he was sometimes considered a separate god.

Enyo. *Myth.* Goddess of war, usually called a daughter of Ares.

Eos. *Myth.* Goddess of the dawn.

Epaphus (Gk. **Epaphos**). *Myth.* Son of Io by Zeus. Epaphus was conceived at the breath or touch of the god and born at one of the mouths of the Nile when Zeus touched Io again to deliver her from her bovine form (see 10). Hence his name was explained as meaning "born of the touch" (from *epaphan,* "to touch" or "stroke"). Epaphus was the grandfather of Belus, who was the father of Danaüs and Aegyptus.

Epeians (Gk. **Epeioi**). Ancient inhabitants of Elis and the district to the north of it.

Epeios or **Epeos.** *Myth.* Hero of Phocis and builder of the Trojan horse. Of a lost play by Euripides called *Epeios* nothing is known.

Ephesus (Gk. **Ephesos**). Greek city on the coast of Lydian Asia Minor. Its chief cult figure was an unchaste Oriental goddess who was, nevertheless, some-times identified with the virginal Artemis or Diana.

Epicharmus (Gk. **Epicharmos**). Early Sicilian writer of comedy. His birth date has been placed from 555 to 528 B.C., and he is said to have lived to be nearly a hundred. Epicharmus resided chiefly in Syracuse. At least part of his career antedated the formal introduction of comedy into Athens in the 480's B.C. Other statements about Epicharmus found in ancient sources have been much disputed: that he was a pupil of the philosopher Pythagoras; that he worked at Sicilian Megara before coming to Syracuse; and that he began writing comedy long before its beginnings in Athens. It is said that Epicharmus influenced Athenian Old Comedy through his plays (which were no doubt read in Athens) in such a way as to aid the emergence of Middle Comedy; this may or may not be true.

Epicharmus was active under Hieron, the tyrant of Syracuse. Ancient mention of rival playwrights makes it likely that he was working in a tradition that was at least somewhat well developed: there was probably no chorus, but masks, music, and dancing were doubtless a part of the drama. Since the Dionysus cult was not yet flourishing in Sicily, the performances may have been attached to the cults of Artemis or Demeter. Extant fragments of Epicharmus' work show that he was witty, had considerable rhetorical skill, and wrote for a cultivated audience. Such perennial comic figures as the country bumpkin, the parasite, the braggart, and the pedant are evident in his writings. He produced some forty or fifty plays of which thirty-odd titles are known. They indicate mostly parodies of myths: *Amycus, Busiris, Bacchae, The Sirens, The Sphinx, Philoctetes;* one may even have been a parody on Aeschylus' *Persians,* which was produced in Sicily. Numerous spurious works, however, crept into the corpus quite early. Epicharmus was the subject of considerable editing and commentary in antiquity. In later centuries he was valued chiefly for his quotable sayings, which were collected.

Epicrates (Gk. **Epikrates**). 1. Demagogue in Aristophanes' Athens nick-named the "Beard-Wearer." Epicrates was suspected of traitorous sympathies, both for Sparta and for Persia.

2. Writer of Middle Comedy (4th century B.C.). Of Epicrates' plays only a few titles are known. Some examples are: *The Amazons, The Merchant, The Chorus,* and *Anti-Lais* (satirizing a well-known courtesan).

Epidamnus (Gk. **Epidamnos**). Greek city on the southeastern coast of the Adriatic Sea, also called Dyrrhachium.

Epidaurus (Gk. **Epidauros**). City in Argolis on the southern coast of the Saronic Gulf. Epidaurus was a center of the cult of Asclepius. Its ancient theater is one of the best preserved in Greece.

Epidicus. Extant comedy by Plautus (variously dated 201 B.C. or after 195 B.C.). *Epidicus* was adapted from an unknown Greek play. Its title role was acted by Titus Publilius Pellio. Translations: Henry T. Riley, 1852; Paul Nixon, 1916.

S C E N E. Athens.

SUMMARY. Young Stratippocles, on leaving for the wars, has asked the slave Epidicus to trick his father, Periphanes, into buying the music girl Acropolistis, with whom the young man is very much in love. Epidicus accomplishes this by telling Periphanes that Acropolistis is his long-lost daughter, Telestis. On his return from the campaign, Stratippocles confides to Epidicus that he has transferred his romantic interest to a female captive whom he has bought with forty borrowed minae, a sum that the usurer is demanding.

Again obliged to help his master, Epidicus tells Periphanes in great alarm that his son is planning to buy freedom for a prostitute in order to marry her. Much disturbed by this news, Periphanes gives Epidicus money to buy the woman, who will then be brought back to the house and subsequently removed from the scene. Epidicus promptly passes on the money to Stratippocles and hires a woman to play the part of the prostitute he has supposedly bought.

Complications increase when Philippa, a woman whom Periphanes seduced long before, comes looking for Telestis, her daughter by him. When Acropolistis appears, Philippa denies that the girl is her daughter.

When, finally, Epidicus' many deceits are brought to light and he is tied up ready for punishment, it is found that the captive girl brought back by Stratippocles is really the lost Telestis. Stratippocles must now transfer his affections away from his sister. Periphanes, overjoyed at the discovery of his daughter, forgives the slave and frees him; but Epidicus, sulking, forces Periphanes to beg his forgiveness.

COMMENTARY. Plautus seems to have felt a fondness for this play (compare *Bacchides*, line 214 ff.), but it has never struck critics as being especially outstanding. The plot development is unclear and the unfinished love intrigue is unsatisfying. The character of Epidicus is, however, one of the more interesting examples of the scheming slave, and the work as a whole has sufficient distinction and cohesion to save it from too low a valuation.

Epigenes. Presumed early writer of tragedy from Sicyon. According to ancient sources, Epigenes antedated Thespis. His existence is, however, seriously doubted by modern scholars.

Epigoni (Gk. **Epigonoi,** "after-born" or "posterity"). *Myth.* The sons of the Seven against Thebes. Ten years after their fathers' unsuccessful assault on the city, the Epigoni mounted a new expedition, which succeeded. They were led by Aegialeus, son of Adrastus, and by Alcmeon, who afterward killed his mother, Eriphyle, for sending his father to his death in the earlier campaign.

Epigoni was the title of a lost tragedy by Aeschylus; only a few lines survive. A lost tragedy of the same name by Sophocles included the killing of Eriphyle by Alcmeon; in it Apollo appeared as *deus ex machina*. Accius made a Latin adaptation of Sophocles' play.

epiparodos. Second entrance of the chorus, when the action of a play had necessitated their leaving the stage; also, the ode they sang while re-entering.

epirrhematic agon or **epirrhematic syzygy.** One of the constituent formal elements of Old Comedy. The epirrhematic agon was in essence a debate (see AGON) between opposed characters in the drama or between allegorized characters introduced for that purpose. It comprises the following sections, each in a different meter:

The *strophe* or *ode:* this is sung by a half-chorus and serves to arouse the audience's interest in the matter at issue.

The *katakeleusmos* (Gk. "word of command"): the coryphaeus orders the first debater, who is destined to be the loser, to speak.

The *epirrheme* (Gk. *epirrhema*, "speech" or "address"): the first debater presents his argument; there may be interruptions.

The *pnigos* (Gk. "choking" or "choker"): the first debater reaches the climax of his presentation in a final breathless appeal.

The whole is then repeated for the second debater, the parts being called the *antistrophe* or *antode,* the *antikatakeleusmos,* the *antepirrhema,* and the *antipnigos.* Thus a syzygy (Gk. *syzygia,* "yoking together") is formed.

The chorus then passes judgment on the dispute in the *sphragis* (Gk. "seal" or "stamp").

The epirrhematic agon may not appear in its entirety; in *The Acharnians, Peace,* and *Thesmophoriazusae* there is none, properly speaking. Scholars are in considerable disagreement about the ritual origins of the epirrhematic agon and about its part in the development of comedy.

episode (Gk. **epeisodion**). Scene, consisting of action and dialogue that took place between two choric odes in a Greek drama, especially in tragedy. In comedy the term was sometimes used to denote a scene that had only a tenuous connection with the main action.

Epitherses. Scholar from Nicaea (1st century A.D.). Epitherses was the author of a lost *Attic Diction in Comedy and Tragedy.*

Epitrepontes. See THE ARBITRANTS.

epode. See STASIMON.

Epops (Gk. "hoopoe"). The Hoopoe, a character in Aristophanes' *Birds.*

Erasinides. Prominent military commander for Athens in the Peloponnesian War. Erasinides had democratic sympathies. Toward the end of the war he was among those executed for failing to save the shipwrecked sailors at the battle of Arginusae.

Erasinus (Gk. **Erasinos**). Stream in Argolis. Erasinus springs violently from underground at the foot of Mt. Chaon.

Eratosthenes. Greek scholar and director of the Library at Alexandria (c. 276–c. 192 B.C.). Although Eratosthenes was best known for his measurement of the earth's circumference, he wrote widely in many fields. He pioneered in establishing literary chronology and produced a *Treatise on Old Comedy,* which is lost.

Erebus (Gk. **Erebos**). *Myth.* Region of eternal darkness in the underworld.

Erechtheus. *Myth.* Son of Pandion (1) and king of Athens. When war broke out between the Athenians and the Eleusinians, the latter aided by Eumolpus, Erechtheus was told by the Delphic oracle that he would win if he sacrificed one of his daughters. Erechtheus did so, whereupon his two remaining daughters leaped off the Acropolis. They joined their sister in the sky as the constellation of the Hyades. In the ensuing battle, the Athenian king killed Eumolpus, in spite of the fact that the lower part of Erechtheus' body changed into a serpent. Poseidon then killed Erechtheus in revenge for the death of his son Eumolpus.

Euripides' lost *Erechtheus* is variously dated between 423 and 411 B.C. Its time of composition is thought by some to be near that of *The Suppliants*, which it must have resembled in patriotic fervor. Among fairly extensive surviving fragments are a long speech in which the Athenian queen resigns herself to the sacrifice of her child and a speech of advice from Erechtheus to his son. Athena must have appeared at the play's end to establish the Athenian cult of Erechtheus and his daughters. (Hence Erechtheides meant "Athenians.")

Eriboea (Gk. **Eriboia**). *Myth.* Wife of Telamon and mother of Ajax.

Erichthonius (Gk. **Erichthonios**). *Myth.* Child of the Earth. Athena, who was very fond of the infant, put Erichthonius in a covered basket and set two snakes to guard him. According to some versions of the story, he himself was partly serpent. The goddess entrusted the basket to the daughters of Cecrops (see CECROPIDAE). In most respects Erichthonius is scarcely to be distinguished from Erechtheus.

Eridanus (Gk. **Eridanos**). *Myth.* River mentioned in several stories. Eridanus appeared, for example, in the myths of Heracles and the Argonauts. It was later identified sometimes with the Po and sometimes with the Rhone.

Erigone. 1. *Myth.* Daughter of Icarius and beloved of Dionysus. When Dionysus made Icarius a present of wine, the latter shared it with his neighbors. After drinking the strange beverage and feeling its effect, the neighbors imagined that they had been poisoned and so beat Icarius to death. Erigone hanged herself.

2. *Myth.* Daughter of Aegisthus and Clytemnestra. According to one version of the story, Erigone was responsible for bringing Orestes to trial before the Athenian Areopagus for the murder of Clytemnestra. After Orestes was acquitted, Erigone committed suicide.

Erigone was the title of a lost tragedy by Sophocles. Its surviving fragments are not sufficient to show whether the heroine was the daughter of Icarius or of Aegisthus and Clytemnestra.

Erinyes (less correctly, **Erinnyes**), sing. **Erinys**. *Myth.* Ancient Greek female divinities of retribution. The Erinyes were invoked by curses and aroused by unavenged crimes. Denizens of the underworld, these fiery-eyed creatures were pictured as having fangs, birds' bodies, bats' wings, and as waving torches. When Aeschylus' *Eumenides* was first performed, their portrayal by the chorus caused a sensation. Represented in Aeschylus' day as being quite numerous, the Erinyes were later thought of as only three in number and named Allecto, Tisiphone, and Megaera. Because of the ill omens associated with them, the Erinyes were often euphemistically called the Nameless Ones, or the Dread Ones (Semnai), or the Kindly Ones (Eumenides). For Aeschylus' use of this last euphemism to symbolize the transformation of the Erinyes, primitive spirits of retribution, into Eumenides, social guardians of justice, see ORESTEIA.

Eriounios. Epithet of Hermes. It is not known what the word means.

Eriphyle. *Myth.* Sister of Adrastus, wife of Amphiaraus, and mother of Alcmeon. Eriphyle was induced, by the gift of Harmonia's necklace, to send her husband to certain death in the campaign of the Seven against Thebes. She was again bribed, this time by the gift of Harmonia's robe, to persuade her son to take part in the later expedition of the EPIGONI. On returning from this campaign, Alcmeon killed his mother. *Epriphyle* was the title of a lost tragedy by Sophocles based on the foregoing myth.

Eris. *Myth.* Greek goddess of quarrels and dissension. *Eris* was the title of a lost play by Sophocles, probably a satyr play. Perhaps it dealt with the golden apple that Eris, or Discord, threw into the midst of the marriage feast of Peleus and Thetis, thus causing the Judgment of Paris and the Trojan War. (See PARIS.)

Eros (often pluralized as **Erotes**). *Myth.* Greek god, the personification of love. After the 5th century B.C. Eros was sometimes pictured as a mischievous boy with bow and arrows (see CUPID). He was, however, generally regarded as a powerful but somewhat impersonal divinity.

Erycina. Epithet of Venus, who had a shrine on Mt. Eryx.

Erymanthus (Gk. **Erymanthos**). Mountain range in Arcadia. One of Heracles' labors was to subdue the Erymanthian boar.

Erythaea or **Erytheia.** *Myth.* Fabulous land of the sunset, the home of Geryon.

Erythrae (Gk. **Erythrai**). Town in southern Boeotia at the foot of Mt. Cithaeron.

Eryx. 1. *Myth.* Sicilian hero who challenged Heracles to a fight for Geryon's oxen when Heracles was returning from the west, bringing the animals to King Eurystheus. Eryx was killed in the fight.

2. City in northwestern Sicily. In Roman times Eryx was a center of the cult of Venus.

Eteocles (Gk. **Eteokles**). *Myth.* Son of Oedipus and Jocasta and brother of Polyneices. According to one story, Eteocles and Polyneices expelled Oedipus from Thebes after his disgrace. Oedipus put a curse on his sons, praying that they might die by each other's hands. To avoid this fate, the brothers agreed to alternate in the kingship, but when Polyneices came to Thebes to claim his turn on the throne at the end of the first year, Eteocles refused to yield. With the help of his father-in-law Adrastus, Polyneices set afoot the expedition of the Seven against Thebes, which ended in the killing of the two brothers, each by the other. Eteocles appears as defender of Thebes in Aeschylus' *Seven Against Thebes,* Euripides' *Phoenician Women,* and Seneca's *Phoenician Women.*

Eteoclus (Gk. **Eteoklos**). *Myth.* Argive hero, poor but honorable. Eteoclus was one of the leaders in the expedition of the Seven against Thebes.

Etesian Winds. Winds that blow in the Aegean and eastern Mediterranean seas for about forty days after the rising of Sirius.

Ethiopians. Mythical race (see AETHIOPES). *The Ethiopians* was the title of a lost play by Sophocles. It may have had for its subject the career of Memnon.

Euaeon or **Evaeon** (Gk. **Euaion**). Skillful, popular, but penurious orator. Euaeon was contemporary with Aristophanes.

Euathlus or **Evathlus** (Gk. **Euathlos**). Blustery demagogue in Aristophanes' Athens. Euathlus harassed many prominent political leaders. A pupil of the Sophist Protagoras, he had wide influence.

Euboea (Gk. **Euboia**). Large island that hugs the eastern shores of central Greece. Euboea lies northwestward beside the coastlines of Attica, Boeotia, and Locris.

Eubulus (Gk. **Euboulos**). Poet of Middle Comedy. Eubulus was enormously productive, writing 104 plays, all of which are lost. His career began in the 370's B.C. Most of the known titles of his plays indicate that they were travesties of myth.

Eucrates (Gk. **Eukrates**). Oakum-seller in Aristophanes' Athens. After the fall and death of Pericles, Eucrates became a prominent demagogue.

Eudemus or **Eudamus** (Gk. **Eudemos** or **Eudamos**). Seller of charms, drugs, and antidotes. Eudemus was a contemporary of Aristophanes. He had reportedly made himself immune to poisons.

Eugenius. Teacher in the imperial school at Constantinople (c. A.D. 400). Eugenius was the author of a work, now lost, on the meters used by the three great tragedians (Aeschylus, Sophocles, and Euripides).

Euhoe. Shout emitted by the celebrants of bacchanalian orgies.

Euios (Lat. **Evius**). Epithet of Dionysus as god of the orgies. (See EUHOE.)

Eulyras (Gk. "good harpist"). Epithet of Apollo.

Eumelus (Gk. **Eumelos**). **1.** *Myth.* Son of Alcestis and Admetus. In Euripides' *Alcestis*, Eumelus sings a brief lament for his mother. *Eumelus* was the title of a lost play by Sophocles of which nothing is known.

2. Peripatetic philosopher (dates unknown). Eumelus was the author of a *Treatise on Old Comedy*, now lost.

Eumenides (Gk. "the kindly ones"). Euphemistic name for the ERINYES. *Eumenides* is the title of an extant play by Aeschylus (see ORESTEIA).

Eumolpus (Gk. **Eumolpos**). *Myth.* Thracian king. Eumolpus took the side of the people of Eleusis when they were attacked by King Erechtheus of Athens. He was killed in the war. The Eumolpidae, a family of hereditary priests in Eleusis, claimed descent from him.

Eunuch, The (Lat. **Eunuchus**). Extant comedy by Terence. *The Eunuch* was produced by Ambivius Turpio and Antilius of Praeneste, with music by Flaccus, at the Megalensian Games in April 161 B.C. It was based on Menander's Greek play of the same name, with additional material from Menander's *Colax.* Translations: John Sargeaunt, 1959; Robert Graves and Laurence Echard, 1962; Frank O. Copley, 1963; Betty Radice, 1965.

S C E N E. Athens.

S U M M A R Y. As is usual in his prologues, Terence is occupied with literary disputes. His most persistent critic, the old poet Luscius Lanuvinus, who,

Terence says, made bad adaptations of at least two plays of Menander, *The Ghost* and *The Treasure*, had heard that Terence's adaptation of Menander's *Eunuch* had been bought by the aediles for production at the festival. Lanuvinus had interrupted a rehearsal with the accusation: "This is the work of a thief, not a poet! He stole his parasite and his soldier from Naevius' and Plautus' *Bootlicker!*" Terence admits that Naevius and Plautus had already adapted Menanders' *Colax (The Bootlicker)*, but he declares that he was ignorant of the existence of these adaptations when he imitated the Greek original. Terence goes on to argue that the features of comedy are quite stereotyped and demands to know whether an author is a plagiarist if a bustling slave, or a good old lady, or an unscrupulous prostitute, or a hungry parasite, or a bragging soldier appears in his play. Is it plagiarizing to introduce a supposititious child, or an old master tricked by his slave, or love affairs, feuds, and intrigues? he asks. Nothing is said now that has not been said before, Terence concludes: let the audience judge with open mind.

As the play begins, the young man Phaedria is angry with Thais, a courtesan, because, in spite of his having offered her a eunuch as a slave, she appears to prefer Thraso, a soldier, to him (Phaedria). Thais explains to Phaedria that while in Rhodes the soldier had purchased a music girl called Pamphila, not knowing that the girl, the kidnaped daughter of a prominent Athenian family, had been raised by Thais' mother and had been sold as a slave after the mother's death. Thais wants Thraso to make her a gift of the girl, whom she regards as a sister, but the soldier has thus far refused to do so because he suspects Thais of having a new lover. Now she persuades Phaedria to give her two days in which to convince Thraso of her affection and to cajole him into parting with Pamphila.

As Pamphila is led through the streets by Thraso's parasite, Gnatho, she is seen by Chaerea, Phaedria's brother, who immediately falls in love with her. On the advice of Parmeno, the family slave, Chaerea presents himself to Thais as Dorus, the eunuch sent by his brother. Put in charge of the music girl, Chaerea rapes her and runs off. When Phaedria is told that his supposed eunuch has raped Pamphila, he goes to punish him, and Dorus is forced to betray Chaerea.

Meanwhile, Thais has discovered that Pamphila is the sister of a young Athenian called Chremes. She is on the point of surrendering the girl to Chremes when Thraso, still jealous of Phaedria and determined to reclaim his property, appears with Gnatho and a band of slaves to storm Thais' house. The attack is halted when Chremes declares that Pamphila is his sister and a citizen of Athens who cannot be held as a slave.

Chaerea returns and convinces Thais of his love for Pamphila; and since she is a citizen, he also expresses a desire to marry her. The affairs of the two brothers are put in order with the return of their father, Laches, from the country. Chaerea is betrothed to Pamphila, and Thais accepts the protection of Laches so that Phaedria may have free access to her and Thraso can be excluded. Gnatho, however, advises Phaedria to let Thraso share in Thais' love, pointing out that Phaedria's income is limited and that the soldier is not only generous but stupid and unlikely ever to become a real threat.

C O M M E N TA R Y. This play was Terence's greatest success in his lifetime. At its first performance the audience called for a repetition, and most critics since that time have been approving. *The Eunuch* is generally considered the most Plautine of Terence's plays, by which is meant that it is the most lively and vivid. There are, however, typically Terentian elements—the double plot and the unexpected twists on stereotyped themes and characters. Although the play is noted for certain bawdy scenes, its vulgarity is much minimized by Terence's tasteful treatment.

Euphemius (Gk. **Euphemios**). Corrupt politician in Aristophanes' Athens.

Euphorion. Son of Aeschylus and a tragic dramatist in his own right. Euphorion's play won over those of both Sophocles and Euripides in 431 B.C.

Eupolis. Writer of Old Comedy. In ancient times Eupolis was considered, with Cratinus and Aristophanes, to be one of the three major writers of Old Comedy. His career began in 429 B.C., but there is no evidence that he lived into the fourth century. Many absurd stories are told of Eupolis' death: that he drowned at sea in the Peloponnesian War; that he ridiculed Alcibiades' lisp in *The Dippers,* with the result that Alcibiades, his ship captain at the time, ordered Eupolis dipped in the sea until he died; and that he was buried on Aegina, where his faithful dog expired on his grave.

According to all accounts, Eupolis was as bitterly satirical as Aristophanes. His *Toadies* won first prize, in 421 B.C., over Aristophanes' *Peace.* Aristophanes, however, contrasted Eupolis' coarseness and dullness with his own refinement and ingenuity. Yet there was an ancient tradition that Eupolis wrote lines 1288 through 1315 of Aristophanes' *Knights.* Known titles of Eupolis' comedies follow:

Autolycus. This play was written in two versions. In one or both, Autolycus was the athlete friend of the rich Callias. Doubtless there was included some reference to the mythical trickster of the same name.

The City-States (probably 422 B.C.). It portrayed the Athenian allies bringing their tribute to Athens; they were perhaps represented by women bringing dowries. The play's subject must have been Athenian exploitation of the other members of the so-called Delian League.

The Demes (412 or 411 B.C.). Extensive fragments of the play, found on papyri, were published in 1911. These fragments, when added to bits otherwise preserved, add up to about two hundred scattered lines. Scholars have accordingly attempted reconstruction of *The Demes.* Its chief character seems to have been an old Athenian citizen, its setting the festival of the Anthesteria at Athens, when the spirits of the dead supposedly walked abroad. The old citizen and a magistrate discussed the degenerate politicians of their own day, contrasting them with the politicians in the good old days of Pericles. The ghost of Nicias, who had recently been killed in the Sicilian expedition, appeared. Twenty-four Attic demes formed the chorus, deploring Athenian degeneracy. Statues of great statesmen of the past were carried in, given a rejuvenating bath, and brought to life. They were: Solon, Pisistratus, Harmodius, Aristogeiton, Cleisthenes, Miltiades, Aristides, and Pericles. These heroes may have been chosen archons, after which they revised the city's laws and tried notable offenders. Alcibiades was prominent in the latter part of the play.

The Dippers. In it was a chorus of female worshipers who baptized Alcibiades into the cult of the barbarian goddess Cotytto.

Exempt from the Draft, or The Men-Women. Its content is unknown.

The Friends. It contained some ridicule of Pericles' mistress Aspasia.

The Girl of Naxos. This play was perhaps based on the story of Theseus' desertion of Ariadne.

The Goats. In it was a chorus of goats, who at one point sang of the variety of plants they could eat.

The Golden Race. The play contained something about Cleon, Odysseus and the Cyclops, and a golden age.

The Helots. It seemingly dealt with a revolt of these Spartan serfs.

The Laconians. Content unknown.

Maricas (421 or 420 B.C.). The play's title was a foreign word meaning "pervert"; it was a nickname for the demagogue Hyperbolus. In *The Clouds* (lines 553–55), Aristophanes says that the play was an unskillful imitation of his *Knights.*

The New Moon (425 B.C.). Content unknown.

Officers of Infantry (427 B.C.). Content unknown.

The Prospaltians. A papyrus fragment of twenty-two lines of this play has recently been found. The inhabitants of the deme Prospalta were notorious for litigation. In the fragment someone seems to be on trial; if this person was Pericles, the play was Eupolis' first, produced in 429 B.C. If the person on trial was Heracles, he may have represented Cleon and the play might then have been written later.

The Referee. Content unknown.

The Scofflaws. Content unknown.

The Toadies (Gk. *Kolakes*). This drama won first prize in 421 B.C. It established parasites as stock comic figures. The play was a satire on the rich Callias, Alcibiades' brother-in-law, who bankrupted himself by keeping open house for philosophers and other hangers-on.

Euripides. 1. Last of the three greatest Athenian writers of tragedy. According to one ancient source, Euripides' birth date was 485 or 484 B.C.; according to another, it was 480. He died in the spring of 406 B.C.

L I F E. Euripides' parents seem to have been respectable enough, since they owned property on the island of Salamis, but poets of Old Comedy called the father a peddler and the mother a market-woman. There is no reason to doubt that the names of Euripides' two wives were Melito and Choirile (the latter was the daughter of Mnesilochus, who appears as Euripides' father-in-law in Aristophanes' *Thesmophoriazusae*) or that the names of his three sons were Mnesarchides, Mnesilochus, and Euripides. There is every reason, however, to be skeptical of the story that a favorite slave, Cephisophon, helped the poet with his plays and helped himself to one of the poet's wives.

Euripides was said to have been a disciple (he was probably at least an acquaintance) of the philosophers Anaxagoras, Prodicus, Protagoras, and Socrates. Nothing is known of a military or political career. Of his literary career the following dates are certain: 455 B.C., debut with *Peliades;* 442, first dramatic victory; 438, a tetralogy, *The Cretan Women, Alcmeon in Psophis, Telephus,* and *Alcestis;* 431, a tetralogy, *Medea, Philoctetes, Dictys,* and *The Reapers;* 428, the extant version of *Hippolytus;* 415, a tetralogy, *Alexander, Palamedes, The Trojan Women,* and *Sisyphus;* 412, the tragedies *Helen* and *Andromeda;* 408, *Orestes.*

The last year and a half of his life Euripides spent at the court of King Archelaus of Macedonia. The story that he was torn to pieces by dogs is scarcely credible. After Euripides' death, the younger Euripides produced his father's plays *Iphigenia at Aulis* and *Bacchae.* The poet was said to have written ninety-two plays in all.

E X T A N T   W O R K S (see under individual entries). Sixteen tragedies, undoubtedly written by Euripides, survive: *Andromache, Bacchae, Electra, Hecuba, Helen, Heracles, Heraclidae, Hippolytus, Ion, Iphigenia among the Taurians, Iphigenia at Aulis, Medea, Orestes, The Phoenician Women, The Suppliants,* and *The Trojan Women.* To these should probably be added *Rhesus,* long considered spurious. One satyr play, *The Cyclops,* has been preserved, as well as a play, *Alcestis,* which took the place of a satyr play in a tetralogy.

L O S T   W O R K S (see under individual entries): *Aegeus, Aeolus, Alcmena, Alcmeon in Corinth, Alcmeon in Psophis, Alexander, Alope* or *Cercyon, Andromeda, Antigone, Antiope, Archelaus, Auge, Autolycus, Bellerophon, Busiris, Cadmus, Chrysippus, Cresphontes, The Cretans, The Cretan Women, Danaë, Dictys, Epeos, Erechtheus, Eurystheus, Hippolytus Veiled, Hypsipyle, Ino, Ixion, Lamia, Licymnius, Melanippe Captive, Melanippe the Wise, Meleager, The Mysians, Oedipus, Oeneus, Oenomaus, Palamedes, Peleus, Peliades, Phaethon, Philoctetes, Phoenix, Phrixus* (two versions), *Pirithous, Pleisthenes, Polyidus* or *Glaucus, Protesilaus, The Reapers, Rhadamanthus, Sciron, Scylla, The Scyrians, Sisyphus, Stheneboea, Syleus, Telephus, Temenidae, Temenus, Tennes, Theseus,* and *Thyestes.*

C R I T I C I S M. To believe Aristophanes' *Acharnians, Thesmophoriazusae,* and *Frogs,* in all of which Euripides appears, the latter was, even during his lifetime, the most controversial of ancient dramatists. He has certainly been so since. Aristophanes obviously regarded Euripides as a dangerous exponent of the "new thought," as, for instance, one who advocated removing controls on women while showing the depths to which women would descend when out of control. Aristophanes seems to have thought Euripides technically inclined toward the commonplace rather than toward bold innovation.

What Aristotle meant by calling Euripides the "most tragic" of poets is still open to question. Perhaps he meant what modern critics mean when they describe him as "more psychological," namely, that in Euripides' drama the tragedy is chiefly inward and that corruption and destruction occur in the souls of women like Medea, Hecuba, and Alcmena, rather than in the outward events in which they are involved. (Aristotle probably did not think, as so many moderns do, that man's tragic destiny might be cured by a good psychiatrist.)

Critics in the Romantic era found Euripides guilty of not being Aeschylus or Sophocles, hence not "classic" in the Romantic definition, that is, calm and lucid. (Neither Aeschylus nor Sophocles was "classic" in that sense, either.) In the last century and a half, controversy about Euripides has been chiefly concerned with his dramaturgy and his theology. With regard to the former, he has been accused of having used certain dramatic devices less meaningfully than his predecessors (see CHORUS and PROLOGUE). His predilection for the *deus ex machina* has been disapproved, though few critics have shown the introduction of the god to be unworthy in any particular play. Much more perplexity has been provoked by the tragedies that are not tragedies: *Iphigenia among the Taurians, Helen, Ion,* and perhaps even *Iphigenia at Aulis.* These were written toward the close of the poet's career. As with the last works of Shakespeare and with Verdi's *Falstaff,* Euripides' late tragedies show an aged artist turning to a kind of romantic comedy beyond tragedy to voice his basic— and much qualified—philosophic optimism.

A by-product of Euripides' late work was its influence on New Comedy. As a fragment of Satyrus' *Life* says: "Rapes of maidens, substitutions of babies, recognition scenes involving rings and necklaces: all these tricks are the stock-in-trade of New Comedy, and they all were brought to perfection by Euripides."

As for the playwright's theology, all critics come out by the same door wherein they went. The misguided attempt to make the poet out to be a Thomas Henry Huxley in a chiton has not yet run its course; but it seems absurd to use a Greek of the classical age as a bolster for nineteenth-century agnosticism. Less simple-minded interpreters have pointed out that the quest for a divinity worthy of belief and a consequent emphasis on the difficulty of belief is not a denial of belief itself. To these latter critics Euripides' constant theme appears to be: "God is seldom what he seems, but to ignore him is to risk being strewn over the landscape with Pentheus and Hippolytus."

2. Euripides the Younger, son of the preceding. Shortly after his father's death, the young Euripides produced the former's *Iphigenia at Aulis* (to which he probably added finishing touches), *Alcmeon in Corinth,* and *Bacchae.*

3. Athenian politician (active in early 4th century B.C.). This Euripides proposed a tax on property.

Euripus (Gk. **Euripos**). Narrow strait between Euboea and Boeotia where the island comes closest to the mainland. Through the Euripus run swift currents.

Europa or **Europe.** *Myth.* Daughter of Agenor, king of Phoenicia (though Seneca, in *Hercules Furens,* line 553, calls her "the Assyrian girl"). While playing on the seashore, Europa was attracted by a beautiful white bull that came up out of the sea. She wreathed the animal with garlands and climbed on its back. At once the bull plunged into the waves and swam to the island of Crete, where it revealed itself to be Zeus in disguise. To the god Europa bore three sons: Minos, Sarpedon, and Rhadamanthus.

Eurotas. River flowing past Sparta southward through Laconia.

Eurus (Gk. **Euros**). The southeast wind.

Euryalus (Gk. **Euryalos**). 1. *Myth.* Illegitimate son of Odysseus and the

Epirote princess Evippe. When Euryalus came of age, his mother sent him with tokens to Ithaca so that his father would recognize and acknowledge him. But Penelope was the first to learn who he was, and she told Odysseus that the youth was coming to murder him. Euryalus was consequently killed by his own father. A lost tragedy by Sophocles called *Euryalus* was based on the foregoing myth.

2. One of the Epigoni.

Eurybates. *Myth.* Agamemnon's herald. Eurybates appears in this capacity in Seneca's *Agamemnon.*

Eurycles (Gk. **Eurykles**). Well-known ventriloquist in Aristophanes' Athens.

Eurydice (Gk. **Eurydike**). *Myth.* Wife of the Theban Creon and mother of Haemon. In Sophocles' *Antigone,* Eurydice, on hearing of her son Haemon's death, goes offstage to commit suicide.

Eurypylus (Gk. **Eurypylos**). *Myth.* Son of Astyoche, who was sister to King Priam of Troy. When Zeus carried off Ganymede to Olympus, he gave in compensation to Laomedon, Ganymede's father, a golden vine. This vine Priam gave to Astyoche so that her son would support him against the Greeks attacking Troy. But though Eurypylus fought bravely, he was eventually killed by Neoptolemus, Achilles' son.

Eurypylus was the title of a lost tragedy by Sophocles. Of it two fragments of some seventeen lines each have been recovered from papyri, one from Astyoche's speech of lament, one from a messenger's description of Eurypylus' death.

Eurysaces (Gk. **Eurysakes**). *Myth.* Son of Ajax the Greater and his Phrygian concubine Tecmessa. Eurysaces was named for Ajax's famous shield (*eury sakos,* "broad shield"). He appears as a mute character in Sophocles' *Ajax* (for his name, see lines 575–76). After his father's suicide, Eurysaces returned to Salamis, where he eventually took over the kingship, succeeding his grandfather, Telamon.

Eurysaces was the title of a lost play by Sophocles. It may have told how Telamon was driven off the throne in his old age and how he was reinstated by Eurysaces and Teucer, the latter having been unjustly banished by Telamon.

Eurystheus. *Myth.* Descendant of Perseus and cousin of Amphitryon and Alcmena. When Alcmena was about to bear Heracles, Zeus's child, Zeus declared that the next child born of the Perseid line would reign in Tiryns and Mycenae. Hera then arranged to have Heracles' birth delayed and that of Eurystheus hastened. Thus Heracles became the subject of the weak and cowardly Eurystheus.

When Heracles killed his children in a fit of insanity caused by Hera, he was bidden by the Delphic oracle to become Eurystheus' servant for twelve years. The result was Heracles' twelve labors. After they had been successfully accomplished, Eurystheus drove Heracles from Mycenae, and when the hero died, the king pursued his sons. Eurystheus appears in Euripides' *Heraclidae* as the persecutor of Heracles' children, but he is killed by their protectors, the

Athenians. Afterward, according to a prophecy, he is to be buried in Attica and to become a tutelary spirit.

Eurystheus was the title of a lost satyr play by Euripides. It may have portrayed Heracles bringing in some monster, perhaps Cerberus, and Eurystheus taking refuge in a large jar.

Eurytion. *Myth.* Centaur who tried to run off with the daughter of King Dexamenus of Olenus during her wedding feast. Eurytion was killed by Heracles. A lost satyr play by Aeschylus may have been called *Eurytion*. There is, however, some uncertainty about the title.

Eurytus (Gk. **Eurytos**). *Myth.* King of Oechalia, a city said by some to be on Euboea, by others to be in Elis. When Heracles was Eurytus' guest at a banquet, Eurytus taunted the hero, saying that he was inferior to his (the king's) sons and scorning him for being Eurystheus' slave; he then ejected Heracles from the banquet hall. When, later, Eurytus' son Iphitus was searching for strayed horses, Heracles treacherously threw him off the battlements of Tiryns. For this deed Heracles was forced to endure servitude to Omphale, queen of Lydia. Afterward, however, he sacked Oechalia, killed Eurytus and his other sons, and carried off his daughter Iole.

Euthymenes. Athenian archon in 437–436 B.C.

Evadne (Gk. **Euadne**). *Myth.* Wife of Capaneus, one of the Seven against Thebes. In Euripides' *Suppliants,* Evadne appears at her husband's funeral and throws herself onto his flaming pyre.

Evanthius. Grammarian at Constantinople in the early fourth century A.D. Evanthius' commentary on Terence influenced that of Donatus.

Evenus (Gk. **Euenos**). River flowing through eastern Aetolia southward into the Corinthian Gulf.

exarchos (Gk. "leader" or "chief"). Leader of any kind of choric group. The *exarchos* walked at the head of the choric procession. Dionysus is so called, as leader of the thiasos, in Euripides' *Bacchae* (line 142).

Execestides (Gk. **Exekestides**). Lyre player contemporary with Aristophanes. Execestides won many contests throughout Greece. He had obtained Athenian citizenship, allegedly through fraud.

exodium (Lat.). Originally the final song in a performance of any kind; later, in Rome, an independent comic afterplay, especially following a tragedy. An ATELLAN FARCE was often used for this purpose, but probably other kinds of sketches were also used.

exodus (Gk. **exodos**, "the way out"). Song sung by the chorus as it went out at the end of a play.

Ezekiel. Jewish writer of tragedies in the Greek language (variously dated in the 2nd or 1st century B.C.). More than 250 lines of one play, *Exagoge,* "The Exodus," are quoted by Eusebius (*Evangelical Preparation,* Book IX). Though of no high artistic merit, the work is interesting for its Biblical plot and for its proof of the spread of Hellenism as shown in its adherence to the five-act and three-actor rules of Greek drama. Since about one-fourth of the play is extant, a reconstruction is possible:

Act One: Moses delivers a monologue on the past of the Jews and protects the daughters of the Priest of Midian against shepherds.

Act Two: Moses receives the priest's daughter, Sephora, in marriage.

Act Three: Moses sees the burning bush on Mt. Horeb.

Act Four: After the last of the ten plagues, Pharaoh releases the Jews. A Messenger relates how the Egyptian army later took off in pursuit of them and perished in the Red Sea.

Act Five: Murmurs of the Children of Israel in the desert are stilled by the miracle of waters gushing from the rock and by the report of a nearby oasis inhabited by a marvelous Phoenix. As they leave for the oasis, there is delivered a prophecy of the Promised Land.

F

fabula Atellana. See ATELLAN FARCE.

fabula crepidata (Lat. "drama in Greek shoes"). Another name for FABULA PALLIATA.

fabula palliata (Lat. "drama in Greek robes"). Roman comedy adapted from Greek plays and having Greek names, dress, and settings. All extant Roman comedy is of this type.

fabula praetexta or **praetextata** (Lat. "drama in official robes"). Roman tragedy based on themes from Roman history or legend.

fabula saltica (Lat. "dance drama"). A written text of some kind that established the plot of a pantomime and made the action clear to the audience. Such texts were written by the poets Lucan and Statius, among others.

fabula tabernaria (Lat. "drama of the tavern"). Another name for FABULA TOGATA.

fabula togata (Lat. "drama in the toga"). Roman comedy with Roman dress and settings. No complete play of this kind survives, and fragments are scanty. The setting seems usually to have been a small Italian town; the characters were of the lower class, and there was much emphasis on domestic scenes and female roles.

Faliscus, Cincius. See CINCIUS FALISCUS.

Farmers, The (Gk. **Georgoi**). Lost play by Aristophanes (produced 424 B.C.). It is known from some thirty brief surviving fragments that the general Nicias was satirized for proving inferior to Cleon in the capture of the Spartans at Pylos.

fasces (Lat. "bundles"). Bundles of sticks tied together and enclosing an axe. The fasces, symbols of authority, were borne in public before certain high-ranking Roman officials. The number of fasces preceding an official indicated his position.

Fates (Lat. *fatum*, "what has been spoken"). Roman equivalent of MOIRAE.

Festus, Sextus Pompeius. Roman grammarian (fl. c. A.D. 150). Festus' works contain many quotations from early Roman drama.

Fides. Roman deity, the personification of honor, loyalty, and integrity.

Fons (Lat. "fountain" or "spring"). Personification of water.

Fortuna. Roman goddess of fortune also called Fors Fortuna and Bona ("good") Fortuna.

Friers, The (Gk. **Tagenistai**). Lost comedy by Aristophanes (sometimes dated 422 B.C., sometimes later). Not even the meaning of the title is clear, though both "The Breakfasters" and "The Parasites" have been suggested as possible interpretations. The sophist Prodicus seems to have been satirized, and Alcibiades and his smart set may have figured in the play. Almost all the fragments concern food.

Frogs, The (Gk. **Batrachoi;** traditional Latin title, **Ranae**). Extant comedy by Aristophanes (produced at the Lenaea in January 405 B.C.). Translations: John Hookham Frere, 1839; Benjamin B. Rogers, 1924; Arthur S. Way, 1934; Gilbert Murray, 1938; Dudley Fitts, 1955; Peter D. Arnott, 1961; Richmond Lattimore, 1962; Robert Henning Webb, 1962; David Barrett, 1964.

S C E N E. The underworld.

S U M M A R Y. Dionysus, patron god of drama, has disguised his usual effeminate costume with an overlay consisting of Heracles' lionskin and club. Accompanied by his slave, Xanthias, who is loaded with luggage and mounted on an ass, Dionysus is on his way to the land of the dead. At Heracles' house they pause to consult the hero about the best route to take, since Heracles has been to Hades before. Dionysus confesses that the object of his journey is to bring back the recently deceased Euripides.

When the travelers arrive at the shores of a great lake to which Heracles has directed them, they call out to Charon, who brings his skiff ashore. Charon refuses passage to Xanthias, who, being a slave, must walk around the lake; Dionysus is made to row. An offstage Chorus of Frogs start up their croak of "Brekekekex koax koax!" and refuse to stop when Dionysus protests their singing. They are silenced when he joins in. (Since this Chorus proclaim themselves as favorites of Pan, Apollo, and the Muses, they doubtless represent the voices of all the bad poets who infested the dramatic festivals of Dionysus.)

After disembarking in Hades, master and slave take fright at a glimpse of the monster Empusa. A Chorus of male initiates into the Dionysiac mysteries enter, dressed in white, led by the coryphaeus as their hierophant, or initiator. They sing a hymn in praise of Dionysus, Demeter, and Persephone.

Knocking at the door of Pluto's palace, Dionysus is rudely received by Aeacus, the doorkeeper, who takes him for Heracles and severely upbraids him for having carried off Cerberus. Unnerved, Dionysus makes Xanthias put on the Heracles costume, but when one of Persephone's maids invites Xanthias in for feasting and dalliance, Dionysus snatches back the lionskin, only to be threatened by an infernal Landlady—Heracles evidently having left Hades without paying his bills. Dionysus again exchanges clothes with his slave.

Now Aeacus returns intending to arrest Heracles; he seizes Xanthias. When Dionysus reveals his identity and that of his slave, the suspicious Aeacus, hoping to determine once and for all which is divine, beats them both, on the supposition that a god, will not cry out because he is immune to pain. Both master and slave howl, whereupon Aeacus takes them in to the king and queen of Hades for investigation.

The Chorus of Initiates, left alone onstage, chide the Athenian people for an unforgiving spirit toward their allies and for preferring base men to noble.

Presently Aeacus and Xanthias return. They are on the best of terms now that Aeacus is certain of Dionysus' divinity. A dispute is heard from inside, and Aeacus explains that Euripides is making a fuss and challenging Aeschylus' right to the throne of tragedy at Pluto's table, a seat of which Sophocles was awarded half, though he refused to claim it. Pluto has arranged a poetic contest to decide the issue. The poetry is to be weighed line by line, and Dionysus is to be referee.

The two poets enter, furiously bickering. Euripides accuses Aeschylus of bombast and resorting to such stage trickery as pregnant silences and monster costumes. Aeschylus accuses Euripides of overrealism, overskepticism, and a weakening influence on the moral fiber of the nation. Euripides then voices his scorn for certain of Aeschylus' passages, and the latter retaliates by demonstrating that the phrase "lost his oil-flask" could be inserted at pleasure into any Euripidean prologue. Each parodies the other's lyrics, until at last the scales are brought in and verse is weighed against verse.

In general, Aeschylus' lines are weightier, but Dionysus likes both poets and cannot decide which is the better. He then asks each to give advice to the city of Athens and, finding Aeschylus' counsel preferable, chooses to take him back to the upper world, rather than Euripides, the poet for whom he made the journey. Aeschylus consigns his place at the throne of tragedy to Sophocles.

COMMENTARY. Written at the very time that Athens was faced with utter defeat in the Peloponnesian War, when the whole meaning of Athenian culture was undergoing a kind of death, *The Frogs* had as its framework the common myth of the resurrection of the dead. As Heracles rescued Theseus from the underworld—Theseus, the Athenian hero above all others—so Dionysus undertakes his journey to Pluto's realm on a mission to revive Athenian society through the rescue of a poet who might be a fitting prophet for that society. That Dionysus is not a Herculean figure and that his is not precisely a Herculean task is shown by his quest for identity in the early change-of-costume scenes; the god must be initiated into his own mysteries to discover his true self.

By means of his two-obol fee—the entrance fee both to Hades and to the theater—Dionysus is ferried across to the land of death, the land of Never-Was and Always-Is, the mythical land of dramatic illusion and hence of eternal truth. Here, just as Zeus weighed the souls of Achilles and Hector at the end of the *Iliad*, Dionysus, the spirit of literature, participates in a *psychostasia*, a soul-weighing, involving Euripides and Aeschylus. He learns that his companion is not to be Euripides, the elegant, clever, superficial questioner of all values, but Aeschylus, the austere and somewhat repellent exponent of all that is morally substantial. This preponderance of the spirit in spite of all misleading appearances is the heartening truth that Dionysus and Aristophanes are prepared to snatch for the Athenian citizenry out of the very jaws of annihilation.

Furies (Lat. **Furiae**). Roman equivalent of ERINYES.

G

Gaetulia. Desert section south of Mauretania and Numidia in North Africa.

Gaia or **Ge** (Gk. "earth"). *Myth.* Mother Earth as goddess. Gaia was one of the oldest of Greek divinities. She was conceived of as the source of all prophecy and was sometimes identified with THEMIS.

Galen (Gk. **Galenos**). Greek physician (2nd century A.D.). In addition to extensive writings on medicine, Galen produced several works, now lost, on Old Comedy, including three on the political names in the plays of Cratinus, Eupolis, and Aristophanes.

Galeneia (Gk. "calm"). *Myth.* Sea goddess, personification of calm weather.

gamos (Gk. "marriage"). A wedding scene such as forms the climax of some Old Comedies, for example, Aristophanes' *Birds.* Some modern theorists assert that the *gamos* was a feature surviving from the spring fertility ceremonies out of which comedy emerged.

Ganymede (Gk. **Ganymedes**). *Myth.* Trojan prince, son of Laomedon, according to Euripides. Because of Ganymede's great beauty, Zeus sent an eagle to carry him to Olympus, where he became cupbearer to the gods. To compensate Laomedon for the loss of his son, Zeus gave him some horses or, as others say, a vine made of gold.

Garamantians (Lat. **Garamantes**). Inhabitants of the desert regions of Africa below Libya.

Gargara. City on the southern coast of the Troad in Asia Minor.

Gargettus (Gk. **Gargettos**). Attic deme.

Ge. See GAIA.

Gela. Greek city on the southeastern coast of Sicily. In *The Acharnians* (line 605) Aristophanes plays on the name to suggest *gelos,* "laughter."

Geleon. One of the four original tribes of Athens.

Gelonians (Lat. **Geloni**). Barbarian tribe, in the country that is now Russia, near the River Don.

Genetyllides, sing. **Genetyllis.** *Myth.* Goddesses of birth and fertility. The Genetyllides were closely associated with Aphrodite.

Geraestus (Gk. **Geraistos**). Southern promontory of the island of Euboea. Geraestus was noted for its sanctuary of Poseidon.

Gerenia. Supposedly a city in Messenia in the southwestern Peloponnesus.

Geryon (Gk. **Geryoneus**). *Myth.* Three-headed, three-bodied, winged giant of the far west. Geryon was killed by Heracles, who came to steal his cattle as one of the labors ordered by Eurystheus.

Gerytades. Lost comedy by Aristophanes (variously dated 408, 407, and 403 B.C.). The plot apparently included a delegation to some dead poets in the underworld (the word Gerytades suggests "singer" or "son of a singer"). Among the poets satirized were Euripides and Agathon.

Getae. Barbarian nation living north of Thrace.

Giants (Gk. and Lat. **Gigantes**). *Myth.* Monsters born of the earth, often represented as having abundant hair and beards and serpents' legs. The Giants were defeated by the Olympian gods in a great battle, the Gigantomachy, which was often confused with the similar Titanomachy, since both battles represented the defeat of the forces of disorder by the forces of order.

Girl from Andros, The. See ANDRIA.

Girl from Samos, The. See SAMIA.

Girl with Her Hair Cut Short, The. See PERIKEIROMENE.

Glanis. Fictional soothsayer in Aristophanes' *Knights.* The playwright calls Glanis a brother of BACIS (line 1004 ff.).

Glauce. See CREUSA.

Glaucetes (Gk. **Glauketes**). Glutton of Aristophanes' time. Glaucetes was nicknamed "the Turbot" because of his inordinate fondness for fish.

Glaucus (Gk. **Glaukos**). 1. *Myth.* Son of Sisyphus, king of Corinth, and father of Bellerophon. Glaucus was accustomed to feed his horses on human flesh. When he took part in the races at Pelias' funeral games, not only did he lose, but his own horses turned on him and devoured him.

2. *Myth.* Boeotian fisherman. By chance Glaucus ate an herb that gave immortality, whereupon he plunged into the sea and became a sea god. When Menelaus was sailing from Troy, it was Glaucus who rose from the waves and told him that his brother Agamemnon had been murdered in his bath.

3. *Myth.* Son of Minos. (See POLYIDUS.)

4. Scholar from Rhegium (latter 5th century B.C.). Glaucus wrote *The Plots of Aeschylus,* now lost.

Glaucus of Potniae (Gk. **Glaukos Potnieus**). Lost tragedy by Aeschylus It was produced in 472 B.C. as part of a tetralogy that included the extant *Persians.* About ten fragments (several gleaned recently from papyri) show that it told the story of GLAUCUS (1).

Glaucus the Sea God (Gk. **Glaukos Pontios**). Lost play by Aeschylus based on the story of GLAUCUS (2). A fifteen-line papyrus fragment seems to be part of a speech by an old countryman describing the marvelous sight of the transformed Glaucus rising from the waves.

Gonoessa, more correctly **Donoessa.** Town in Argolis.

Gorgias. Sophist of Leontini in Sicily (c. 480–c. 376 B.C.). Gorgias was considered the founder of systematic rhetoric.

Gorgolopha. Epithet of Athena, derived from *gorgos,* "fierce."

Gorgons (Gk. **Gorgones**; adj. **Gorgonian** or **Gorgoneian**). *Myth.* Bird-women with serpents' hair, daughters of the sea demons Phorcys and Ceto. There were usually said to be three Gorgons. Their glance turned all living creatures to stone. "Gorgon" in the singular referred either to Medusa, whose head was cut off by Perseus, or to the creature overcome by Pallas Athena during the Gigantomachy. (See AEGIS; PERSEUS.)

Gorgopis. 1. Epithet of Athena.

2. Lake or marsh near Corinth.

Gortyna. City on the southern coast of Crete.

Gouneus. *Myth.* King of the Aenianes. Gouneus was a suitor of Helen and a warrior against Troy.

Gracchi. Two Roman brothers, Tiberius and Gaius, who advocated popular reforms and were killed in riots in 133 and 121 B.C., respectively. Their mother, Cornelia, was famous as a model of the old Roman virtues.

Graces (Lat. **Gratiae**). Roman equivalent of CHARITES.

Gradivus. Byname of Mars.

Graeae. See PHORCIDES.

Grouch, The. See DYSKOLOS.

Gyas. One of the Giants.

Gyges. King of Lydia (7th century B.C.). Most of the stories about Gyges are legendary. In Plato's *Republic* (359) the author recounts a fairy tale about Gyges' discovery of a ring of invisibility. Herodotus (Book I, 7–13) relates how Gyges, at that time a member of King Candaules' bodyguard, was invited by the king to view the nude beauty of the queen. The latter caught sight of the intruder but said nothing to her husband. The following day, however, she called Gyges and told him that he must either seize the throne and marry her or die. Gyges chose the former course and became king.

In 1950 a papyrus was found that contained three columns of a Gyges play. Only the middle column, about sixteen lines, was susceptible of reconstruction. It is an excerpt from the Lydian queen's speech after she has seen Gyges in her bedroom. Two controversies have raged about the fragment. First: Was the play a dramatization of Herodotus' account, or was Herodotus' account a prose summary of the play, or did both come from a common source of legend and tradition? Second: Was the play an historical drama of the early fifth century B.C. in the manner of Aeschylus' *Persians,* or was it an archaizing work of the fourth century or later?

H

Hades. *Myth.* God of the underworld and the dead. The underworld was consequently called "the house of Hades," or "the land of Hades," or "Hades." Hades was the son of Cronus and Rhea and the brother of Zeus and Poseidon. The chief story in which he figured was the rape of PERSEPHONE. His cap of invisibility was occasionally referred to.

Haemon (Gk. **Haimon**). 1. *Myth.* Son of Creon and lover of ANTIGONE.

2. *Myth* (adj. Haemonian). Hero who gave his name to Haemonia, old name for Thessaly.

Haemus (Gk. **Haimos**). Mountain range running east to west across northern Thrace.

Halae (Gk. **Halai**). Deme on the east coast of Attica.

Halcyon or **Halcyone.** See ALCYONE.

Halimus or **Alimus** (Gk. **Halimous**). Attic deme.

Halirrhothius (Gk. **Halirrhothios**). *Myth.* Son of Poseidon. Halirrhothius attempted to assault Alcippe, daughter of Ares, and was killed by the latter.

Halys. River flowing into the Black Sea through northeastern Asia Minor.

hamartia. A term used by Aristotle in his POETICS and defined by him (chapter 13) as that essential feature in the tragic hero which leads to his misfortunes. The word *hamartia* is best neutrally translated as "tragic flaw." Later discussions in the *Poetics* apparently support the theory that *hamartia* is a mere lack of information or an error in judgment. This theory, however, seems out of harmony with Aristotle's emphatically ethical conception of tragedy and the tragic hero, and some critics accordingly prefer to define *hamartia* as an "immoral act" or a "defect of character."

A compromise theory might be that the tragic flaw is a culpable ignorance, a blindness to an essential phase of reality, such as Hippolytus' rejection of the gods' arrangements in regard to reproduction in *Hippolytus* or Oedipus' assumption of a purely intellectual noninvolvement in *Oedipus the King.* For such a blind spot the catastrophe itself would constitute the only means of correction.

Harmodius (Gk. **Harmodios**). Athenian youth who, with his friend Aristogeiton, attempted in 514 B.C. to assassinate the tyrants Hippias and Hipparchus. The friends succeeded in killing only the latter and were themselves killed. Although the planned assassination was the result of a personal feud, Harmodius and Aristogeiton were honored as champions of liberty and became the subject of a famous drinking song.

Harmonia. *Myth.* Personification of harmony, daughter of Ares and Aphrodite. All the gods attended Harmonia's wedding with Cadmus, bringing gifts, especially a robe and a necklace (see ERIPHYLE). Harmonia and Cadmus were changed into serpents in their old age.

Harpies (Gk. **Harpyiai**). *Myth.* Monstrous bird-women. The Harpies' favorite trick was to swoop down and either befoul a meal or snatch it away. They are especially prominent in the story of PHINEUS.

Haunted House, The. See MOSTELLARIA.

Heautontimorumenos. See THE SELF-TORMENTOR.

Hebe (Gk. "youth"). *Myth.* Deification of youth, daughter of Zeus and Hera. Hebe was cupbearer to the gods until she was displaced by Ganymede. When Heracles was admitted to Olympus, she became his bride.

Hebrus (Gk. **Hebros**). River in Thrace, flowing into the northeastern Aegean. The Hebrus was noted for its swift current; down this river the head of Orpheus floated to the sea after his dismemberment by the maenads.

Hecate (Gk. **Hekate**). *Myth.* Goddess of magic and witchcraft. Hecate was closely associated with nocturnal darkness and the moon. She was sometimes regarded as only an aspect of Artemis; in this role she was called the offspring of Leto and was appealed to in childbirth. Hecate's function as moon goddess may have partly accounted for the fact that she was often represented as having three bodies and three heads, in accordance with the moon's three phases. As a moon goddess she guarded the house at night, and there were shrines built to her at many house doors in Greece. There were also shrines to her at crossroads, where, on the thirtieth of every month, food was placed for the poor.

In Euripides' *Ion* (line 1047) Hecate is called "guardian of roads, Demeter's daughter" (apparently an identification with Persephone), and her aid is invoked in the poison plot, since she was the archetype of the witch.

Hector (Gk. **Hektor**). *Myth.* Greatest of the Trojan warriors, son of King Priam and Queen Hecuba. Hector's wife was Andromache and his son was Astyanax, or Scamandrius. After killing Achilles' friend Patroclus, Hector was himself killed by Achilles. His body was ransomed by Priam. Hector appears in Euripides' *Rhesus* as leader of the Trojan forces.

Hecuba (Gk. **Hekabe**). *Myth.* Queen of Troy and wife of Priam. Hecuba was sometimes said to have borne Priam fifty children, among them Polyxena, Cassandra, Hector, Paris, Deiphobus, Helenus, Polites, Polydorus, and Troilus. Many of her sons were killed in the Trojan War. After the fall of the city, Hecuba's daughter Polyxena and her grandson Astyanax were torn from her and sacrificed by the victorious Greeks. Hecuba appears in both Euripides' and Seneca's *Trojan Women,* where she witnesses the sack of the city and the tragic destinies of her loved ones.

After these events, according to one story, Hecuba ran along the seashore howling with grief and was changed into a dog. This metamorphosis was said, in another story, to have occurred on the coast of Thrace, where Odysseus had taken Hecuba, and where she had revenged herself on King Polymestor for the murder of her son Polydorus. Her revenge is the subject of Euripides' *Hecuba.*

Hecuba or **Hecabe** (Gk. **Hekabe**). Extant tragedy by Euripides (generally thought to have been produced c. 425 B.C. but dated by a few scholars near the time of *The Trojan Women,* 415 B.C.). Translations: Edward P. Coleridge, 1891; Arthur S. Way, 1912; J. T. Sheppard, 1927; Hugh O. Meredith, 1937; William Arrowsmith, 1956; Philip Vellacott, 1963. Adaptations and works influenced by *Hecuba:* Ennius (lost play); Accius (lost play); Erasmus, Latin version, 1507.

S C E N E. The Thracian coast.

S U M M A R Y. The ghost of Polydorus, son of King Priam and Queen Hecuba, appears above the tents of the Greeks. He tells how, in Troy's last days, his father sent him to King Polymestor of Thrace with treasure so that, should Troy fall, Priam's sons would be provided for. When news came of Troy's defeat, Polymestor killed Polydorus for his gold and threw his body into the sea. The ghost goes on to explain that the Greek fleet has been becalmed by the ghost of Achilles, who is demanding that the Trojan princess Polyxena be sacrificed on his grave. He prophesies that Hecuba will this day see her daughter killed and his own body washed up on the shore.

At this point the aged and grief-ravaged Hecuba is helped from her tent. She tells of having had terrifying dreams concerning her son and daughter and prays to the gods that they may be spared. Her dreams begin to be realized, however, when the Chorus of Captive Trojan Women inform her that Polyxena is to die.

When Odysseus comes to take the girl away, Hecuba recalls to him that she once spared him when he stole, disguised, into Troy and was recognized by Helen. She begs him to reciprocate, but Odysseus answers that he must keep his promise to Achilles to give him Polyxena. The young girl, refusing to beg for her own life, goes off with him.

Her dignified death is described by the herald Talthybius, who soon arrives to bid Hecuba bury her dead. When a Serving Woman brings in a body wrapped in a shroud, Hecuba thinks it is her daughter, but when the shroud is removed, the corpse of Polydorus is revealed. Hecuba cries out in anguish and horror, guessing that King Polymestor was the perpetrator of the crime. Presently Agamemnon comes to summon Hecuba to her daughter's burial. Learning of the new calamity and pitying the former queen, he promises to let her wreak vengeance on the treacherous Polymestor.

Hecuba accordingly sends a message to the unsuspecting king asking him to come and see her and to bring his two sons. When the three arrive, Polymestor pretends sympathy for Hecuba's losses, and to her questions about Polydorus and the Trojan gold he returns lying answers. Hecuba then lures him and his sons into her tent with the promise of treasure. Screams are heard from inside, and soon Hecuba emerges to say that Polymestor has been blinded and his children killed with the help of her women.

Polymestor stumbles out of the tent, bleeding and raging in pain. Hearing the uproar, Agamemnon returns and, listening to Polymestor and Hecuba give arguments for their actions, declares that justice has been done. Polymestor then prophesies that Hecuba will turn into a dog and drown and that both Cassandra and Agamemnon will be murdered by Clytemnestra. Agamemnon indignantly orders that Polymestor be marooned on a desert island and tells Hecuba that she must bury her dead children before sailing from Thrace.

COMMENTARY. *Hecuba* has been picked to pieces by the critics on the charge that it lacks unity; yet most of those who have analyzed it thoroughly conclude that it is still a great play. Not only does the tremendous emotional drive of the main character provide a unifying element, but her emotional deterioration is consistently drawn. This portrait of Hecuba ranks almost with that of Euripides' Medea as a study of the inner tragedy that occurs when a noble nature, or one that is at least strong, fierce, and capacious, is dragged down by the unworthy conventions and crass persecutions of others to a level of beastlike passion that astounds and horrifies. Doubtless the deterioration portrayed in *Hecuba* reflects Euripides' observations on the contemporary effects of the Peloponnesian War.

This emotional theme is complemented by the intellectual theme, the study of *nomos* (law) and *peitho* (persuasion). *Nomos,* in Hecuba's first conception, is the preserve of the gods, a universal pattern of law. It dictates that Polyxena be spared—in return for Hecuba's having spared Odysseus' life, and in acknowledgment of a suppliant's rights, as Hecuba herself had acknowledged the supplication of Odysseus. But Odysseus persuades the Greeks to acknowledge a rival *nomos,* namely, the convention that a hero's ghost must be propitiated by the sacrifice of an enemy. Thus Hecuba loses her profounder conception; even the noble example of submission to necessity set by Polyxena is not enough to prevent the queen's conclusion that law is merely the product of *peitho,* the glib and persuasive tongue. So she blinds Polymestor, kills his innocent children, and justifies herself glibly. If *nomos* in the deeper sense disappears, man becomes mere animal: the animal in Hecuba has already been released, and it will not be long before she fulfills her enemy's prediction that she will run up and down the shores of Thrace, a howling bitch.

Hecyra. See THE MOTHER-IN-LAW.

Hegelochus (Gk. **Hegelochos**). Actor of Aristophanes' time. Hegelochus made himself a laughingstock in a performance of Euripides' *Orestes* by pronouncing the line *"Galen horo,"* "I see a calm," in such a way that it sounded like "I see a weasel." He is mocked for this in *The Frogs* (line 303).

Hegemonios (Gk. "guide"). Epithet of Hermes.

Helen (Gk. **Helene**). *Myth.* Wife of King Menelaus of Sparta and mistress of Paris. Helen's adulterous flight to Troy occasioned the Trojan War. Although she was called the daughter of Tyndareus, Helen was actually the child of Zeus, who wooed Tyndareus' wife Leda in the guise of a swan. But some said that the goddess Nemesis was really her mother and that Leda simply tended the egg that the goddess had laid until Helen was hatched.

On reaching maturity, Helen was so beautiful that Tyndareus feared a general war if he gave her to any one of her many suitors. Therefore, before the choice was made, he forced them all to take an oath to uphold Helen's marriage. The choice then fell on Menelaus, and to him Helen bore a daughter, Hermione.

When Paris came to Sparta to claim Helen as his prize, she ran off with him in Menelaus' absence, stripping the Spartan palace of treasure. According to another tradition, Hera, annoyed at losing the beauty contest to Aphrodite (see PARIS), fashioned a phantom Helen to accompany Paris, while the real woman was conveyed to Egypt. In still another version, it was Zeus who sent Helen to Egypt. The story of her stay there is the basis of Euripides' *Helen*.

After the capture of Troy, Helen's fate hung in the balance. In Euripides' *Trojan Women*, she begs Menelaus to spare her life and wins him over with her beauty and her persuasiveness. In Seneca's *Trojan Women*, she declares her lot, that of the hated seductress dragged away by her husband for judgment, to be worse than that of the Trojan captives. It is clear from other sources that Helen was forgiven and became a queen again in Greece. In Euripides' *Orestes*, she is about to be murdered by Orestes in punishment for all the mischief she has caused, when she disappears, saved by Apollo, to be transported to the skies as a goddess.

Helen actually originated as a vegetation goddess, and her cult was widespread throughout the Greek world. Her brothers were the twins Castor and Polydeuces (the DIOSCURI), who became the constellation Gemini and the patrons of sailors.

Helen (Gk. **Helene**). Extant play by Euripides (produced 412 B.C.). Translations: Edward P. Coleridge, 1891; Arthur S. Way, 1912; Philip Vellacott, 1955; Richmond Lattimore, 1956. Adaptation: Richard Strauss, opera, *Die Aegyptische Helena*, 1928, libretto by von Hofmannsthal.

S C E N E. The palace of the king of Egypt.

S U M M A R Y. Helen has taken sanctuary at the tomb of Proteus, former king of Egypt, to escape the attentions of his son Theoclymenus, the present ruler. Speaking aloud to herself, she recalls Paris' judgment of the beauty of Hera, Aphrodite, and Athena, how Paris chose Aphrodite as the most beautiful goddess on her promise of Helen as a bride. When Paris came to Sparta to carry her off, Helen continues, Hera gave him a woman made of air, while she sent Hermes with the real Helen to Egypt. Now the Trojan War is over, but she is still far from home, ruined in reputation, beset by the lustful Theoclymenus, and waiting for Menelaus.

Teucer presently arrives; he is a Greek hero who was exiled by his father because he did not die with his brother Ajax. Teucer is amazed to see a woman who looks exactly like the hated Helen but does not know that it is really she. He tells Helen that seven years have passed since the fall of Troy, that Menelaus dragged away his wife by the hair, and that her mother and brothers have killed themselves for shame of her. Menelaus' fleet is thought to have been lost on its way back from Troy.

Helen counsels Teucer to leave Egypt at once, since King Theoclymenus kills every Greek who comes there. Teucer blesses her for her kindness and leaves. Lamenting her sad plight, Helen is advised by the Chorus of Captive Greek Women to consult the seeress Theonoë, sister of the king. They accompany her into the palace.

Now Menelaus wanders in, his clothes in tatters. He tells how he was blown off course by storms and shipwrecked and how he managed to save himself and his wife, Helen, the cause of all his misfortunes. She is now in a coastal cave, along with a few other survivors. When Menelaus knocks at the palace door to ask for help, the old Portress recognizes him as a Greek and tells him to go away, for her master has hated all Greeks since Zeus's daughter Helen came there from Sparta.

As Menelaus ponders this puzzle, Helen returns to her place at Proteus' tomb, having learned from Theonoë that Menelaus is alive. At once recognizing her husband, she explains to him that the woman whom he carried from Troy was only a phantom. Menelaus has difficulty in believing this until one of his men comes from the coast to report that the Helen in the cave has declared that her destiny was fulfilled and has disappeared into heaven. Husband and wife joyfully embrace; Helen tells Menelaus the true story of her abduction by Hera, and Menelaus tells her briefly of his own sufferings.

The problem of escape remaining, it is decided that Helen will confide their secret to Theonoë, who, being a seeress, might otherwise see through their plot and detain them. Theonoë agrees to keep silent. Helen then tells Theoclymenus that the Greek stranger has come to bring tidings of Menelaus' drowning and that it is a Greek custom to sail out to sea and to throw offerings overboard for those who have been lost. Theoclymenus consents to furnish ship and gifts, and as Helen and Menelaus embark, the unsuspecting king makes preparations for his marriage to Helen.

Soon one of Theoclymenus' crewmen returns to report that, as they were leaving the shore, a number of Greek castaways came aboard, and when they were well away from land, fighting broke out; he alone of the Egyptian crew was able to escape. Theoclymenus, realizing that Theonoë has betrayed him, announces his intention of killing her, but Castor and Polydeuces, Helen's divine twin brothers, appear in mid-air. They sternly bid the king yield to fate and foretell Helen's eventual destiny as a goddess.

C O M M E N T A R Y. The older criticism, which found *Helen* a monstrosity and an unpleasant surprise for an audience expecting tragedy, has given way to an indulgent acceptance of the play as a comic piece of escapism and a beautifully constructed bit of theatrical melodrama. Yet a case can be made for its being much more than this. It would be hard to find another play, ancient or modern, that could match this one in its emphasis on the theme of illusion versus reality, or in the almost inexhaustible variety with which this theme is presented.

Since such a theme is, however, implicit in every plot, Euripides obviously has deeper concerns. In the earlier parts of the play suspicions, misapprehensions, false rumors, misevaluations, and phantoms produce pathos, misery, war, and suicide; the whole maze of misunderstanding ends, nevertheless, in the salvation of true love.

Theonoë, a pivotal character, exemplifies the human side of what, externally considered, seems to be only an abstract scheme of divine providence. By a judicious temporary concealment of the truth, she behaves as the gods do and effects Helen's restoration and Theoclymenus' enlightenment.

The poet is bold enough to suggest that death, too, may be a gentle deception. The central choric ode (lines 1301–68), often thought irrelevant, tells how Zeus sends the Muses to cheer Demeter as she lies in the snow, despairing of her daughter, whom she thinks irretrievably in the power of the lord of death. At the play's end the Dioscuri, Helen's deified brothers, prophesy their sister's future divinity and Menelaus' immortality in the Islands of the Blessed.

Helena (Gk. **Helene**). Small island off the coast of Attica. It was supposedly named for Helen, who was said to have stopped there with Paris on the way to Troy.

Helen Claimed (Gk. **Helenes Apaitesis**). Lost play by Sophocles. It apparently told how Odysseus and Menelaus went to Troy to claim Helen before the outbreak of the Trojan War, how the Trojans threatened to kill them, and how they were protected by Antenor and his sons.

Helen Seized (Gk. **Helenes Harpage**). Lost play doubtfully ascribed to Sophocles. The title, dubious in itself, may simply be a variant of *Helen Claimed*.

Helen's Marriage (Gk. **Helenes Gamos**). Lost satyr play by Sophocles. It dealt with Paris' pseudomarriage to Helen and no doubt included various lustful capers by satyrs.

Helenus (Gk. **Helenos**). *Myth.* Son of King Priam and Queen Hecuba of Troy. Helenus was Cassandra's twin brother and, like her, endowed with the gift of prophecy. At the fall of Troy he became a slave of Neoptolemus. After the latter's death Helenus took over his kingdom and married Andromache.

Heliades. *Myth.* Daughters of the sun god Helios and sisters of Phaethon. When their brother fell into the river Eridanus, the Heliades mourned him so persistently that they were changed to poplars on its banks and their tears turned to amber. Their name was given to a lost tragedy by Aeschylus that dealt with Phaethon and his fall. One remaining fragment is the famous couplet:

> Zeus is the Aether, Zeus the Earth, and Zeus the Heavens,
> Zeus is indeed the All, and all that stands above.

Heliasts. Six thousand Athenians chosen by lot to be liable for jury duty in the Heliaea, the law courts.

Helice (Gk. **Helike**). City in Achaea on the southern shore of the Gulf of Corinth.

Helicon (Gk. **Helikon**). Mountain in western Boeotia near the Corinthian Gulf and southeast of Delphi. Helicon was associated with Apollo and the Muses.

Heliodorus (Gk. **Heliodoros**). Writer of works on metrics (1st century A.D.). These works, now lost, included metrical analyses of Aristophanes' plays.

Helios (Gk. "sun"). *Myth.* Greek god of the sun. Helios drove across the sky each day in his golden chariot. Because he saw everything, he was sometimes appealed to for information about missing persons.

Hellanios or **Hellenios.** Epithet given to Zeus by the inhabitants of the island of Aegina.

Helle. *Myth.* Daughter of ATHAMAS and sister of PHRIXUS. Helle fell off the golden ram and was drowned in the strait that was subsequently called the Hellespont, "Helle's Sea."

Hellen. *Myth.* Son of Deucalion and ancestor of all the Greeks, the "Hellenes."

Hemera (Gk. "day"). *Myth.* Greek goddess of day, virtually equivalent to Eos, the dawn.

Henetans or **Enetans** (Gk. **Enetoi**). Tribe in Paphlagonia.

Heniochians (Gk. **Heniochoi**). Tribe in the Caucasus, on the shores of the Black Sea.

Henna. See ENNA.

Hephaestion (Gk. **Hephaistion**). Greek scholar (2nd century A.D.). Hephaestion was the author of an extant work, *On Meters,* and of lost works, *Solutions to Problems in Comedy* and *Solutions to Problems in Tragedy.*

Hephaestus (Gk. **Hephaistos**). *Myth.* Greek god of fire (with which element he was sometimes simply identified) and archetypal metalworker. Hephaestus was usually said to be the son of Zeus and Hera, though some said that he was the child only of Hera, who produced him in retaliation for the birth of Athena from Zeus.

Like all spirits of the forge, Hephaestus was generally pictured as ugly and misshapen. According to one story, Hera, offended at the sight of the deformed child she had borne, dropped him from Olympus. Hephaestus fell into the sea and was rescued by Thetis and Eurynome, who cared for him for nine years. According to another story, Hephaestus was thrown from Olympus by Zeus in a quarrel with Hera. He fell on the island of Lemnos and was lamed in both legs.

As archetypal blacksmith Hephaestus produced marvelous works of metal, including intricately designed ornaments, useful objects, suits of armor, and even robots. Using volcanoes as his smithies and the Cyclopes as his helpers, Hephaestus also fashioned Zeus's thunderbolts. His cult flourished in Athens; Erechtheus or Erichthonius, ancestor of the Athenians, was accounted his son. Like Prometheus and Hermes, Hephaestus was something of a trickster. He appears in the first scene of Aeschylus' *Prometheus Bound,* reluctantly fettering the Titan to the crag.

Hera. *Myth.* Principal Olympian goddess, daughter of Cronus and Rhea, sister and wife of Zeus. Hera's marriage with Zeus was the archetype of all marriages, and her particular function as a goddess was to be guardian of matrimony and protectress of the family. She bore four deities to her husband: Hephaestus, Ares, Eileithyia (goddess of childbirth), and Hebe. When Zeus was unfaithful to her, Hera relentlessly harassed his mistresses and their offspring. She appears as a persecutor in the myths of Heracles, Io, Semele, Ino, Dionysus, Callisto, and Leto; she was, on the other hand, the patroness of Achilles, the Atreidae, and Jason. Hera's cult was especially strong in Argos and Samos.

Heracleidae. See HERACLIDAE.

Heracles (Gk. **Herakles**). *Myth.* Most popular Greek hero, son of Zeus and Alcmena. After his death, Heracles became a god. (For details of his birth, see EURYSTHEUS and Plautus' AMPHITRYON.) He was often called Amphitryonides after his mortal father, Amphitryon (Alcmena's husband), and also Alcides, after Amphitryon's father, Alcaeus. Heracles was educated by CHIRON and LINUS (2).

Various stories were told to explain why he came to be a slave to King Eurystheus of Argos. One was that, driven mad by Hera, he killed six of his own children and two sons of his brother Iphicles. After regaining his sanity, Heracles was purified by King Thespius. He then asked the Delphian oracle what he should next do and was told to serve Eurystheus for twelve years. Another explanation of Heracles' servitude was that he offered his services in order to terminate the exile of his father and his family. For the spiteful and cowardly Eurystheus Heracles performed his twelve labors, ridding the earth of sundry pests.

Lists of these labors differ; that in Euripides' *Heracles* (line 348 ff.) is as follows: one, the slaying of the lion that inhabited the grove of Zeus at Nemea; two, the subduing of the wild centaurs; three, the hunting of the golden-horned Cerynian hind; four, the capture of King Diomedes' man-eating mares; five, the killing of Cygnus, who murdered his guests; six, the fetching of the dragon-guarded golden apples from the enchanted garden of the Hesperides; seven, the clearing of pirates from the sea; eight, the supporting of the sky for Atlas; nine, the capture of the girdle from Hippolyta, queen of the Amazons; ten, the disposal of the many-headed, dragonlike Hydra in the swamp of Lerna (from whom he took poison to smear on his arrows); eleven, the conquest of the three-bodied Geryon, monster-herdsman of the West; and twelve, the bringing to the upper world of Cerberus, three-headed dog of Hades (during this exploit the hero brought Theseus back to the land of the living). For the episodes involving Cygnus, Atlas, and the pirates (which were either independently told or made subordinate to other labors) were usually substituted Heracles' victories over the bronze-winged birds of Lake Stymphalus and over the Cretan bull, as well as his cleansing of King Augeas' stables by diverting rivers through them.

According to Euripides' *Heracles* and Seneca's *Hercules Furens*, the hero's madness occurred after his labors were completed.

Other feats accomplished by Heracles were his dispatching of Giants in the war between the gods and the Giants, his rescue of Alcestis, his sack of Troy (see HESIONE), and his liberation of Prometheus (see PROMETHEIA: *Prometheus Unbound*). For the murder of Iphitus (see EURYTUS), he was forced to serve the Lydian queen, Omphale, from whose domain he cleared various ruffians, among them Syleus. Other pests eliminated by Heracles were Antaeus and Busiris. He also took part in the Argonautic expedition (see HYLAS).

The story of Heracles' death and apotheosis forms the subject of Sophocles'

Trachiniae and Seneca's *Hercules on Oeta*. After death he was reconciled with Hera, admitted to Olympus, and married to the goddess of youth, Hebe. Heracles appears as *deus ex machina* in Sophocles' *Philoctetes*. He was a favorite figure in comedy (for example, Aristophanes' *Birds* and his *Frogs*) and satyr play, being portrayed as always gluttonous and boisterous but goodhearted (compare Euripides' *Alcestis*). In Greek art he is easily recognized by his club, lionskin, and bow. Sophocles' lost play *Heracles* was probably identical with HERACLES AT TAENARUM.

Heracles (also called in Greek: **Herakles Mainomenos, The Madness of Heracles** or **Mad Heracles**). Extant tragedy by Euripides (variously dated from 422 to 416 B.C.). Translations: Edward P. Coleridge, 1891; Arthur S. Way, 1912; Hugh O. Meredith, 1937; William Arrowsmith, 1956; Philip Vellacott, 1963. Adaptation: Seneca, *Hercules Furens*.

S C E N E. Thebes, the palace.

S U M M A R Y. Lycus of Euboea, who has murdered King Creon and usurped the throne of Thebes, now prepares to kill the surviving members of the royal house: Megara, Creon's daughter and Heracles' wife; their three small sons; and the aged Amphitryon, Heracles' mortal father. In order to save themselves they have taken refuge at the altar of Zeus the Savior, Heracles' divine father. The hero, whose twelfth labor had been to fetch the three-headed dog Cerberus from Hades, is long overdue; his children, Megara says, inquire anxiously about his return. She despairs of rescue, but Amphitryon, refusing to resign himself to death, expresses his hope that Heracles will soon appear.

A Chorus of Old Men enter, hail the royal family, and lament the loss to Thebes of Heracles' noble sons. Lycus approaches and, remaining merciless despite the plea of Amphitryon for mercy, orders large fires to be built and his victims burned out of their sanctuary. The Chorus chant their censure. Megara requests that she be permitted to garb her sons properly for death and, her request granted, she and the children retire from the altar. The Chorus then sing of the twelve labors of Heracles.

As Megara bids a last farewell to her sons, she sees Heracles, who had remained in the underworld after completing his last labor in order to rescue Theseus, king of Athens. Heracles, learning of Lycus' crimes, kills the unsuspecting usurper, while the Chorus joyously celebrate Thebes' deliverance. Suddenly a crash of thunder interrupts their song as Lyssa (Madness) appears on the roof of the palace, accompanied by Iris, the messenger of the gods. Iris reveals that the implacable Hera, Heracles' lifelong enemy, has devised a new torment for him: Lyssa, daughter of Uranus and Night, is to confound the hero's senses and make him kill his own children. Lyssa is reluctant to undertake this task, but Iris is adamant.

Iris and Madness disappear into the palace, while the weird strains of a flute are heard and are suddenly stilled. The cries of Amphitryon puncture the Old Men's lamentations. A Messenger then emerges from the palace and reports that, as Heracles was making an offering to Zeus, he was stricken with madness and, thinking that he was revenging himself on Eurystheus, the imposer of the twelve labors, murdered his wife and sons. He was prevented from killing Amphitryon only by the appearance of Athena, who knocked him senseless with a stone. Amphitryon then bound Heracles to a broken pillar against which he had fallen.

After the doors of the palace are opened, Heracles awakens, his sanity restored. He is baffled by the scene of destruction before him. Stunned by Amphitryon's account of his actions, Heracles expresses his wish to expiate his guilt by self-destruction. At that moment he sees Theseus, who has come to Thebes to take part in the war against Lycus. Heracles covers his face with his robe so that the Athenian will not behold his shame and be contaminated by it. Theseus, however, urges Heracles to share his sorrow with his friend and condemns the hero's plan to commit suicide as the recourse of an ordinary man. Heracles retorts that he is accursed and that his life is useless, for Hera has succeeded in destroying him. Theseus replies that Heracles, like the gods, must accept his fate with dignity and patience; he offers him a haven in Athens, where his hands can be cleansed of their blood. Admitting that suicide would be the act of a coward, Heracles accepts the invitation of Theseus and departs, his heart still heavy with grief. Amphitryon stays behind to bury the dead.

C O M M E N T A R Y. For a time most critics gave political interpretations of *Heracles.* Some thought that Euripides was trying to contrast the unsatisfactory Dorian-Spartan hero, Heracles, whose insane violence was the outbreak of a natural animality, with the more nearly adequate Athenian hero, Theseus, who was the embodiment of philosophical reason and moral bravery. Others felt that Euripides was proposing a reconciliation between Spartans and Athenians by a sympathetic and symbolical treatment of both heroes. Although there is more to the play than politics, the second of these theories should not be discounted.

Euripides was much occupied with the opposing themes of divinity and humanity, mortality and immortality, death and the possibility of surmounting death. From the play's beginning Heracles' double paternity, both divine and human, is emphasized. By the favor of the gods, it seems, he arrives just in time to preserve his own offspring, but immediately afterward, lest all distinction between men and gods be erased, he destroys these same children in madness. Thereafter, Heracles is comforted by his mortal father and befriended by the mortal Theseus, whom he takes to himself as a son.

In the famous exchange about the gods (line 1313 ff.), when Theseus advises Heracles to emulate the Olympians, who sin, suffer, and yet endure, Heracles rejects the notion of divine sin and suffering but accepts that of divine patience. His direct conquest of death in the capture of Cerberus has been shown to be illusory, for man cannot transcend his human limitations by direct attack; his only opportunity to reach divinity lies in the conquest of his own soul.

Heracles at Taenarum. Lost satyr play by Sophocles. It perhaps told of Heracles' journey to the underworld to bring back Cerberus.

Heraclidae (Gk. **Herakleidai**). *Myth.* Sons and descendants of Heracles. After their father's death the Heraclidae were pursued by Eurystheus from city to city until they were given protection by the Athenians, who killed Eurystheus in a battle. The Heraclidae then made several unsuccessful attempts to re-establish themselves in the Peloponnesus. Finally, in the third or fourth genera-tion, Temenus led them to victory in a campaign known as the "Return of the Heraclidae."

Aeschylus' lost play *Heraclidae* apparently treated the same material as Euripides' extant play of the same name.

Heraclidae (Gk. **Herakleidai, The Children of Heracles** or **The Sons of Heracles**). Extant play by Euripides (usually dated 429–427 B.C., but placed by a few scholars late in the 420's). Translations: Edward P. Coleridge, 1891; Arthur S. Way, 1912; Ralph Gladstone, 1955.

S C E N E. Marathon, the Temple of Zeus.

S U M M A R Y. Heracles is dead, but King Eurystheus of Argos and Mycenae, who had persecuted the hero while he was alive, now pursues his children, hounding them from city to city. In desperation they have come to Attica, led by Iolaus, Heracles' aged squire and kinsman, who has taken charge of the younger sons. Alcmena, Heracles' mother, protects his daughters in the Temple of Zeus, and Hyllus, the eldest son, has sought refuge with his older brothers nearby.

Copreus, an Argive emissary, arrives before the temple, where Iolaus and his charges are sitting. He tries to seize the children, and, on the arrival of Demophon, king of Athens and the son of Theseus, demands that the king surrender Heracles' children to him as Argive natives who have been con-demned to death in their homeland. Copreus menacingly boasts of Eurystheus' military might, adding that no Greek state has hitherto dared to defy his master's will. Iolaus, stating his conviction that the Athenians will not allow themselves to be bullied, reminds Demophon of his obligation to those who seek refuge before God's altar, adding that Heracles has been the friend and kinsman of Theseus. Moved by Iolaus' arguments, Demophon dismisses Copreus and begins preparations for the Argive attack that is sure to come.

Iolaus' hopes of safety are, however, apparently to be doomed, for Demophon reports that the oracles have revealed that the campaign against Eurystheus will fail unless a maiden of noble blood is sacrificed to Persephone. Acknowledging that the Athenians cannot be expected to kill one of their own daughters, Iolaus offers to give himself up to Eurystheus. At this point Heracles' daughter (Macaria) emerges from the temple and states her willingness to die for the sake of her brothers. Iolaus proposes that she and her sisters draw lots to determine which one of them will be sacrificed, but Macaria angrily spurns this suggestion.

After Macaria is led to her death amid the admiration of all, an Attendant reports that Hyllus has gathered an army which he has stationed alongside Demophon's forces. Ignoring the protests of Alcmena and the Attendant, Iolaus, who can barely walk unaided because of his great age, leaves to take part in the battle. Shortly afterward, the Attendant returns to declare that the Athenians have been victorious. Eurystheus had shrunk from Hyllus' challenge to single combat, and Iolaus, with two stars (representing the deified Heracles and his goddess-wife, Hebe) glowing on his chariot, had been miraculously rejuvenated and had captured Eurystheus alive.

When the prisoner is brought in, Alcmena demands that he be put to death immediately, but the Chorus of Old Men of Marathon protest that it is unlawful to kill a prisoner of war. Though he says that Hera inspired his actions, Eurystheus refuses to beg for his life, remarking that his persecution of Heracles and his sons had stemmed from an old feud, and that their survival would have meant his own ruin. He resolves the Athenians' dilemma by recalling an old oracle which had prophesied that, if he were properly buried before Athena's shrine, his spirit would guard the city when the descendants of Heracles' children turned upon their former benefactors. To the grim satisfaction of Alcmena, the citizens grasp at this solution and order the execution of Eurystheus.

C O M M E N T A R Y. The play's unusual shortness, the quotation by the ancient anthologist Stobaeus of passages not in the existing text, and the strange omission of any reference later in the play to Macaria's sacrifice, have led to speculation that the version now extant may have been a late acting script that was much tampered with. Although this particular theory has fallen out of favor, most scholars go so far as to say that the play seems to have been hastily written.

In it Euripides is concerned with several favorite themes—the clash of right and might, the voluntary sacrifice of a young person, the corrosive effects of persecution on the moral fiber of the persecuted, the example that Athens should set in the matter of Hellenic humaneness. His concern is, however, not steady enough to enable him to fashion a coherent whole. Moral issues are confused; Macaria appears and disappears abruptly; Iolaus' heroic rejuvenation verges on the comical; choral comment is skimped; Alcmena's vindictiveness is too little prepared-for to be dramatically convincing; and Athenian integrity is fatally compromised when Eurystheus is executed at the end. Those critics may be right who say that the play was turned out in passion when Euripides rushed to reprove his fellow citizens for the treacherous murder of Peloponnesian ambassadors early in the war.

Heraclides (Gk. **Herakleides**). Scholar from Pontus. Heraclides came to Athens in about 365 B.C. and studied under Plato and Aristotle. Among his numerous writings, all lost, were *The Plots of Euripides and Sophocles* and *The Three Tragic Poets*.

Herakleiskos (Gk. **Little Heracles**). Lost satyr play by Sophocles, probably identical with HERACLES AT TAENARUM.

Heralds, The (Gk. **Kerykes**). Lost play by Aeschylus, presumably a satyr play. Two meager fragments show only that Heracles was a character.

Hercules. Roman form of HERACLES. Although Hercules was imported from Greece, he was a favorite Roman deity. His name was often used in oaths, such as *Hercule!* and *Mehercule!* In Rome a tithe, or a tenth, was called "Hercules' part."

Hercules Furens (Lat. **The Madness of Hercules** or **Mad Hercules**). Extant tragedy by Seneca. It was based largely on Euripides' *Heracles*. Translation: Frank Justus Miller, 1917.

SCENE. Thebes.

SUMMARY. In a bitter monologue, Juno says that she has left heaven, overfilled as it is with constellations that are reminders of Jupiter's amours, and has come to Thebes for a last attempt at crushing Hercules before he takes possession of Olympus itself. But recalling that even Hercules' twelve labors, which culminated in his victory over Cerberus, the hound of death, did not overwhelm the hero, Juno realizes that he must be made to destroy himself; accordingly, she summons the Furies of madness from the depths of the underworld.

Juno withdraws as a Chorus of Theban Maidens greet the morn, a day that will bring serenity to those who are content with little, while the covetous and the proud, who cannot wait for the Fates to dispense their lots, will find but slight repose. Megara, wife of the long-absent Hercules, enters with her children and expresses to the hero's mortal father, Amphitryon, her hope that he will soon return to Thebes, whose throne has been usurped by the detested Lycus. She is fearful, however, that her husband is dead after a life of persecution and suffering. Megara is sought in marriage by the usurper, who wants to strengthen his position in Thebes, but she proudly rejects his offer, pointing out that he is the murderer of her father and brothers. At this Lycus orders his servants to set fire to the sanctuary where Megara and her children have taken refuge.

They are saved by the sudden appearance of Hercules, dragging Cerberus and accompanied by Theseus, whom he has just released from the underworld. Upon hearing of Lycus' crimes, Hercules immediately leaves to kill him. Meanwhile, Theseus describes the capture of Cerberus and his own rescue. His narrative is interrupted by a Chorus of Thebans, who express their joy over the death of Lycus.

As Hercules himself raises his voice in prayer, the madness sent by Juno takes possession of him. Gripped by a delirious sense of power, he takes his own children to be Lycus' offspring and kills them all at the shrine where they have taken refuge; he is about to kill Megara as well when he falls into a deep stupor. Awakening with his sanity restored, Hercules gradually realizes what he has done and is prevented from committing suicide only by the threat of Amphitryon to take his own life. Hercules doubts that he can find a haven in any land, but Theseus invites him to accompany him to Athens.

COMMENTARY. The general agreement is that in *Hercules Furens* Seneca followed Euripides' *Heracles* quite closely. Hercules was the favorite mythological character of the Stoics: his sense of duty, his labors beneficial to mankind, and his conquest of self made him an epitome of Stoic ideals. Unlike Euripides, who was concerned with the relationship of man to god, Seneca emphasized the human hero's merits, sufferings, and final resolution to endure his appointed lot.

In the matter of structure, Seneca is usually said to have produced a better play than Euripides. He tightened and unified the plot by introducing Juno and Theseus early in the play, by making Lycus' motivation more plausible, and by making Hercules suffer the delusion that he is killing Lycus' children, rather than those of Eurystheus, as in Euripides' play.

Hercules on Oeta (Lat. **Hercules Oetaeus**). Extant tragedy by Seneca, based to some extent on Sophocles' *Trachiniae*. Translation: Frank Justus Miller, 1929.

S C E N E. Oechalia and Trachis.

S U M M A R Y. Because Eurytus, king of Oechalia, refused to give Hercules his daughter Iole as a bride, Hercules has sacked the city and killed the king. Yet the hero is filled with weariness at his own deeds; addressing Jupiter, he reviews his many exploits and wonders why he is still denied a place in the heavens. The lovely Iole also laments her fate, for she is to be taken to Trachis as a captive.

Meanwhile in Trachis, Deianira, Hercules' wife, fears that her husband will make Iole his concubine and is wild with jealousy. Ignoring the remonstrances of her Nurse, Deianira is at first determined to kill him but then recalls a love charm given her by the centaur Nessus, who had tried to abduct her and was killed by Hercules' poisoned arrow. Before dying, Nessus had wrenched off a hoof, catching in it some of his poisoned blood, and had told Deianira that if her husband should ever take a mistress, she should give him a garment smeared with the blood; but until that time, the charm must be kept in a dark place lest it lose its potency.

When the blood-soaked robe is ready, Deianira asks Hercules' comrade Lichas to take it to him. But her trials are not yet ended. She informs the Nurse that, suddenly assailed by misgivings, she had daubed the blood on some wool by daylight, whereupon the fleece had withered and disintegrated, while the ground below foamed and quivered. Deianira's fears are confirmed when her son Hyllus runs in to report that, upon donning the robe, his father had filled the air with terrible cries. He had then turned on Lichas and killed him and, in his frantic efforts to shed the garment, had torn off his own flesh. On hearing the dreadful news, Deianira expresses her longing to die in punishment for the crime that she has perpetrated. Heedless of Hyllus' contention that an offense committed in error is no sin, she flees in the belief that she is being pursued by the Furies.

Hercules, convulsed by pain and suffering, begs Jupiter to end his misery; he does not fear death but feels dismay at the thought of having been felled by a woman's hand. He is joined by his mother, Alcmena, and shortly afterward by Hyllus, who announces Deianira's suicide. Acknowledging that the centaur's vengeance is now complete, Hercules begins the preparation for his own death by asking his friend Philoctetes to cut wood for a funeral pyre on Mt. Oeta. He instructs Hyllus to marry Iole, and goes off to die.

Philoctetes, who witnesses the hero's final moments, later relates that after mounting the great pyre, Hercules had given him his bow. Hercules then prayed to Jupiter to be admitted to the stars, ordered Philoctetes to start the blaze, and stood fearlessly amid the smoke and flame until his very face and beard were consumed. Alcmena, carrying her son's ashes in an urn, mourns for him at length, but suddenly she hears his voice from above telling her to lament no longer. Hercules himself appears fleetingly in a vision and proclaims that all that was mortal of him has been consumed by fire. He then vanishes and is borne to heaven.

    C O M M E N T A R Y. By actual line count, *Hercules on Oeta* is longer than any other ancient play. Its overfullness and its formlessness (Friedrich Leo called it "the most shapeless art-work from all antiquity") have occasioned controversy over its authenticity; many a page has been written denying that Seneca wrote the play or ascribing to him only certain passages.

    On the other hand, the theory has been advanced that the play was intended as a summation of all of Seneca's dramatic work: in it each Stoic virtue and each culpable passion of the preceding dramas is epitomized. Without pressing this theory too far, one might agree that the story detailing the apotheosis of Hercules, the Stoic ideal incarnate, might very well strike a Stoic philosopher-dramatist as being worthy of his most lavish treatment. It is obvious that Seneca, in deliberate contrast to Sophocles' *Trachiniae,* vulgarizes and minimizes the character of Deianira so as to throw full light on Hercules. The latter's deification is carefully presented as an illustration of the ancient death-and-immortality mystery cult, but his resurrection is by no means like that of Christ, as some critics have thought. Hercules makes it clear that his humanness has perished with the fire and that only his divine spark ascends to heaven.

    Herkeios (Gk. "pertaining to the courtyard"). Epithet of Zeus as god of the household.

    Hermaeum (Gk. **Hermaion**). Hill or crag on the island of Lemnos, named after Hermes.

    Hermes. *Myth.* Greek god of boundaries, and both the archetypal herald and the archetypal trickster. Hermes' father was Zeus and his mother was Maia, youngest of the Pleiades; he was born in a cave of Mt. Cyllene in Arcadia. Soon after birth, Hermes sprang from his cradle and stole the cattle of Apollo, putting shoes on their feet and pulling them backward by the tails to deceive pursuers. When Apollo finally confronted him with the crime, Hermes succeeded in appeasing the god with the gift of the lyre which he had just devised from a tortoise shell (see *Ichneutae*). And when the precocious infant promptly made himself a shepherd's pipe, Apollo wanted it too, giving in exchange his golden staff and sending Hermes to his old nurses, the Thriae, to learn the art of divination from pebbles.

    Hermes became the messenger of the gods, especially of Zeus. His equipment included a winged cap, winged sandals, and the herald's staff, or caduceus. As the god of boundaries he was patron of heralds, promoter of commerce, and escort of the dead to the underworld; as a trickster he was appealed to in matters of chance and deceit. Hermes was also a fertility god. Stone pillars, called herms, representing only his head and genitals, stood at street corners. His statues were also common in gymnasia.

Hermion or **Hermione.** City on the coast of Argolis.

Hermione. *Myth.* Daughter of Helen and Menelaus. Hermione was betrothed to her cousin Orestes before the Trojan War, but while Menelaus was at Troy, he promised his daughter to Achilles' son Neoptolemus. Hermione appears as a young maiden in Euripides' *Orestes,* where she is used as a hostage by Electra, Orestes, and Pylades. In Euripides' *Andromache* she is the vengeful wife of Neoptolemus, jealous of Andromache and murderously cruel to her. At the end of this play Orestes achieves Neoptolemus' death at Delphi. He afterward married Hermione and had a son by her. *Hermione* was the title of a lost play by Sophocles. It evidently dealt with the rivalry of Orestes and Neoptolemus. Livius Andronicus imitated it in Latin.

Hermippus (Gk. **Hermippos**). Writer of Old Comedy. Hermippus was a contemporary of Aristophanes, who attacked him in *The Clouds* (line 539 ff.). A bitter enemy of Pericles, Hermippus called him "king of satyrs." He brought an indictment of impiety against Pericles' mistress, Aspasia, but Pericles won her an acquittal by weeping before the jury. Of Hermippus' work fairly extensive fragments and ten titles remain. The plays of most interest are *The Birth of Athena, The Bakers' Wives,* and *Moirae,* all of which are represented by fragments.

Hero, The, or **The Demigod** or **The Household God** (Gk. **Heros**). Comedy by Menander (probably written before 315 B.C.). A papyrus containing a synopsis of the play, as well as the text of the opening scenes, was discovered in 1905. This material, in addition to a few more lines subsequently recovered, provides a fair idea of the play. Translation: Francis G. Allinson, 1921.

In the only extant fragment of any length, Davus, a slave, tells how an old freedman had gone heavily into debt to his master, Laches. After the freedman's death, his twin son and daughter, Gorgias and Plangon, became bondservants to Laches to work off their father's debt. Davus has fallen in love with Plangon and has secured his master's consent to the marriage, but now he discovers that Plangon is pregnant.

The rest of the story can be reconstructed with reasonable accuracy from other much shorter fragments, from the extant cast of characters, and from the twelve-line metrical synopsis:

A delayed prologue is spoken by the Hero of the title, the tutelary god of the household (as in Plautus' *Aulularia*). He reveals that the twins are really the children of Myrrhina, mistress of the household, who was attacked by an unknown man at a festival. Myrrhina had exposed the children, along with some belongings of her own and an object that she had torn from her unseen attacker. In subsequent developments it will be found that Laches is the unknown father. Although Davus is willing to claim responsibility for Plangon's condition, she will be able to marry Pheidias, the freeborn man who actually seduced her.

The Hero must have been an unusual play in that it portrayed a noble slave in the character of Davus.

Herodas. See HERONDAS.

Herodicus (Gk. **Herodikos**). Greek scholar from Babylon (middle 1st century A.D.). Herodicus wrote *People of Comedy,* now lost, which was probably the indirect source of much information about the persons satirized in Old and Middle Comedy.

Heroes. Lost comedy by Aristophanes (produced between 413 and 409 B.C.). The play seems to have had something to do with a meal commemorative of the dead; perhaps the souls of the dead appeared.

Herondas or **Herodas.** Author of *mimiamboi,* mimes in the "limping iambic" meter (3rd century B.C.). Herondas was virtually unknown, only thirteen fragments of his work surviving, until the publication of a newly discovered papyrus in 1892. As a result of this and later discoveries, seven complete mimes, as well as parts of others, are now available. Translations: W. Headlam and A. D. Knox, 1922; A. D. Knox, 1929.

Majority opinion inclines to the view that these mimes were intended to be acted, not merely read. All but one have settings on the island of Cos.

The Incantation: A young wife's old nurse tries to persuade her to yield to a young athlete, her husband having been away in Egypt for ten months.

The Pimp: Battaros complains because a rich merchant has stormed into his brothel and carried off one of the girls.

The Schoolmaster: A mother brings her lout of a son to the teacher for instruction; she asks that special emphasis be given to beating.

Women in Asclepius' Temple: Two women chatter about the works of art and rituals in the temple.

Jealousy: Bitinna quarrels with her slave-lover, Gastron, and almost succeeds in getting him flogged.

The Self-lovers: Metro drops in on her friend Koritto to find out where she bought her artificial leather phallus.

The Cobbler: Metro goes to Kerdon's cobbler shop, where there is much inspection of shoes but no purchase.

The Dream (incomplete): The poet tells a slave girl of a dream he had in which some goatherds tore his goat to pieces and in which, afterward, he had to contend against an old man who threatened him with death. The dream was evidently a reference to a contest for poetical fame; in it may have been allusions to literary circles at Cos.

Hesiod (Gk. **Hesiodos**). Boeotian didactic poet (8th–7th centuries B.C.). Hesiod was the author of *Works and Days* and *Theogony.*

Hesione. 1. *Myth.* Daughter of Oceanus and wife of Prometheus.

2. *Myth.* Daughter of King Laomedon of Troy. When Laomedon neglected to pay Apollo and Poseidon for having built the walls of Troy, Apollo sent a plague on the people and Poseidon sent a sea monster to destroy the countryside. Laomedon was forced to make reparation by chaining Hesione to a rock for the monster to devour. The maiden was rescued by Heracles, but when Laomedon cheated the hero out of his reward, Heracles sacked Troy and gave Hesione to Telamon, who had helped him. By Telamon Hesione became the mother of Teucer.

Hesperia. *Myth.* Land of the evening and sunset, sometimes identified with Spain.

Hesperides. *Myth.* Three nymphs, daughters of Atlas. The Hesperides lived in a garden of the gods in the far west, where they watched over the tree of golden apples that Earth gave to Hera on her marriage to Zeus.

Hesperus (Gk. **Hesperos**). *Myth.* Son or brother of Atlas. Hesperus was the spirit of evening embodied in the evening star.

Hestia (Gk. "hearth"). *Myth.* Virgin goddess of the hearth, sister of Zeus, Poseidon, Hades, Hera, and Demeter. Hestia was thought of as the eldest of deities and was often invoked in prayers and oaths.

Hesychia. Personification of peace and quiet.

Hiero (Gk. **Hieron**). **1.** Tyrant of Syracuse from 478 to 467 B.C. Hiero was the patron of Pindar, Bacchylides, and Aeschylus.

2. Athenian auctioneer of Aristophanes' time.

Hieronymus (Gk. **Hieronymos**). **1.** Athenian tragedian and dithyrambist. Hieronymus was contemporary with Aristophanes.

2. Scholar from Rhodes (3rd century B.C.). Hieronymus wrote many works, all lost, on Peripatetic philosophy and literary history, including *The Tragic Poets.*

Hikesios (Gk. "supplicating"). Epithet of Zeus as patron of suppliants.

hilarotragedy (Gk. **hilarotragoidia**). Rare term for the parody of tragedy common among the PHLYAKES of southern Italy.

hipparch (Gk. **hipparchos**). Commander of cavalry.

Hippias. Son of Pisistratus and, after his father's death in 527 B.C., ruler of Athens with his brother Hipparchus. When Hipparchus was assassinated, Hippias became very tyrannical and was driven out in 510 B.C.

Hippios (Gk. "pertaining to a horse"). Epithet of Poseidon.

Hippocrates (Gk. **Hippokrates**). Nephew of Pericles. Hippocrates was a successful military commander during the early part of the Peloponnesian War until he was defeated and killed at the battle of Delium in 424 B.C.

Hippodamia (Gk. **Hippodameia**). *Myth.* Daughter of King Oenomaus, wife of Pelops, and mother of Atreus and Thyestes. Hippodamia was the heroine of a lost tragedy by Sophocles which perhaps told of the murder of her stepson Chrysippus. For Hippodamia's story, see OENOMAUS; CHRYSIPPUS.

Hippodamus (Gk. **Hippodamos**). Architect from Miletus who became an Athenian citizen during Pericles' time. Hippodamus was the originator of city planning.

Hippolyta (Gk. **Hippolyte**). *Myth.* Queen of the Amazons, also called Antiope. Heracles robbed Hippolyta of her golden belt and killed her. According to another story, Theseus fell in love with the Amazon and carried her to Athens, where she bore his son Hippolytus.

Hippolytus (Gk. **Hippolytos**). *Myth.* Illegitimate son of Theseus and the Amazon queen Hippolyta (or Antiope). For Hippolytus' story, see Euripides' HIPPOLYTUS and Seneca's PHAEDRA.

Hippolytus (Gk. **Hippolytos**). Extant tragedy by Euripides (produced 428

B.C.). This play was called in ancient times *Hippolytos Stephanephoros* ("Hippolytus the Garland-Bringer"), in reference to the hero's entrance scene, to distinguish it from an earlier version, *Hippolytos Kalyptomenos* ("Hippolytus Veiled"), now lost (see the *Commentary* below). Translations: Edward P. Coleridge, 1891; Gilbert Murray, 1911; Arthur S. Way, 1912; Augustus T. Murray, 1931; David Grene, 1942; Rex Warner, 1949; Philip Vellacott, 1953; Donald Sutherland, 1960; Kenneth Cavander, 1962. Adaptations and works influenced by *Hippolytus*: Seneca, *Phaedra;* Racine, *Phèdre,* 1677; Robinson Jeffers, *The Cretan Woman,* 1954.

S C E N E. Troezen, before the palace of Theseus.

S U M M A R Y. In the prologue, Aphrodite expresses her hatred for Hippolytus, son of Theseus and the Amazon Hippolyta, who reviles her and honors only the virgin Artemis, forswearing love and marriage. But Aphrodite plans to punish Hippolytus that very day by bringing about his death at Theseus' hands. Phaedra, Theseus' young wife, exiled from Athens with her husband and Hippolytus, is sick with unfulfilled love for her stepson and has even dedicated a shrine to that love. Since Theseus is absent from Troezen, expiating his killing of the Pallantides, Aphrodite's plans have scope to mature.

As Aphrodite disappears, Hippolytus enters with his huntsmen, singing the praises of Artemis. On the altar of the virgin goddess he lays a garland culled from the virgin countryside and vows lifelong devotion. An old Servant suggests that Hippolytus perform some corresponding act of reverence at Aphrodite's altar, observing that honor is due to all the gods. Hippolytus, remarking that a deity worshipped in the night does not please him, passes Aphrodite's altar by as he leaves.

A Chorus of Troezenian Women express their bewilderment at Phaedra's strange malady and at her refusal to accept food. Phaedra herself is brought in on a couch, accompanied by her distracted old Nurse, who presses her to disclose the source of her affliction. Phaedra seems to be raving as she speaks of her longing to join the hunters in their mountain woodlands. Suddenly realizing the implication of her words, she asks that her face be covered to hide her shame and states her desire to end her sufferings by death. The Nurse continues to question her mistress, pointing out that if she dies, her orphaned children may be deprived of their birthright by the bastard Hippolytus. At this name Phaedra starts violently and permits the Nurse to elicit from her the secret of her incestuous love for the young man. When the Nurse and the Chorus recoil in horror from her confession, Phaedra explains that human beings sometimes go astray even though they know the right. Since she is unable to stifle her passion for Hippolytus, *aidos* (shame, modesty, respectability) has made her choose to kill her guilty self lest she dishonor her husband and children, like the secret adulteresses she so despises. Shocked at this determination, the Nurse makes light of Phaedra's woes and advises her to yield to divinely ordained fate, offering to cure her ailment with magic love charms. Even as Phaedra admits the wickedness of the Nurse's plans, she allows herself to be convinced.

Shortly afterward Phaedra hears Hippolytus berating a servant for betraying her mistress and immediately realizes that the Nurse has revealed to him the story of her love. While Phaedra listens unnoticed, Hippolytus delivers a diatribe against all women, expressing his wonder that Zeus has devised so poor a means of reproduction. He is especially rancorous toward the clever ones who enlist their servants' aid in carrying out their lustful schemes. He has given the Nurse his word not to divulge her propositions, but he leaves to join Theseus so as to return with him and witness Phaedra's behavior when she welcomes her husband home. Rejected and despairing, Phaedra angrily upbraids the Nurse for violating her trust and, bent on suicide, meditates on how she may still preserve her reputation.

On returning from his journey, Theseus is greeted by the wails of the women, who have just discovered the queen; she has hanged herself. On her body Theseus finds a tablet that accuses Hippolytus of having assaulted her. Invoking one of three curses once granted to him by Poseidon, Theseus prays for Hippolytus' death. Hippolytus reacts to his father's wrathful accusations by protesting his innocence but, because he has sworn not to betray the Nurse's confidence, does not tell Theseus the full truth. Theseus, taking his son's protestations for hypocrisy, pronounces sentence of banishment.

Hippolytus leaves. A Messenger soon reports that the youth has been fatally hurt in an accident. As he drove along the beach in his chariot, a thundering came from the earth and a huge wave towered out of Poseidon's sea. From the top of it a monstrous bull drew near the land. The chariot team was thrown into such panic that the car overturned, and Hippolytus, tangled in the reins, was dragged over the rocks.

Artemis now appears to Theseus and, rebuking him for his hasty and ill-considered action, tells him of Phaedra's passion for Hippolytus and of the latter's nobility in refusing to break his vow of silence. When the dying Hippolytus is carried in, Artemis promises to avenge him by harming the next mortal to be loved by Aphrodite (a veiled reference to Adonis). Henceforth, Troezenian maidens will sacrifice their hair to Hippolytus before marriage and he and Phaedra will become a theme of song. Withdrawing so that her eyes will remain unpolluted by death, Artemis leaves Theseus and Hippolytus to their tearful reconciliation.

C O M M E N T A R Y. The lost first version of the story, *Hippolytus Veiled*, was possibly written between *Alcestis* and *Medea* and seems not to have been successful. From the available evidence the following can be gleaned: Phaedra appeared as a shameless woman (an ancient commentator suggests that her behavior was inspired by the poet's faithless wife), and her love for her stepson was chiefly in revenge for her husband's infidelities. She made advances directly to Hippolytus, at which he covered his face for shame (whence the title); she then accused him to Theseus and, after Hippolytus' death, hanged herself. The hero was then probably revived by the god Asclepius. This play passed as one of the chief evidences of Euripides' misogyny.

Some of the themes suggested by these fragments—the meaning of *aidos* (sense of shame) and the contrast between men's appearances and their real natures—appear again in the extant *Hippolytus,* which is by all critics ranked with the *Bacchae* as a supreme masterpiece. *Hippolytus* is a tragedy of moral ignorance; no other play, except Sophocles' *Oedipus the King,* provides more pertinent grounds for the theory that Aristotle's *hamartia* is best defined as a culpable ignorance—or rather, ignoring—of an essential phase of reality (see HAMARTIA). Under the sway of passion Theseus believes what he wants to believe, ignoring Hippolytus' character and his strong denial of guilt, jumping to regrettable conclusions. Hippolytus ignores one whole side of life, falling into a veritable *hybris* of virginity; his chastity easily turns into a blasphemous rejection of Aphrodite and Zeus. Phaedra, most complex of the three, chooses not to know what she very well knows, or to act as though she did not know what she knows. In her famous monologue about why human beings go wrong in spite of all their knowledge (lines 373–430), in spite of her own knowledge that language may have a double meaning she deliberately prefers *aidos* as outward respectability to *aidos* as inward purity. The choice in favor of tragic ignorance is also made between the two goddesses who enclose the play, which is introduced by Aphrodite, who represents the single-mindedness of passionate sexuality, and concluded by Artemis, who represents the opposing coldness of detached inexperience.

Hippomedon. *Myth.* One of the Seven against Thebes. Hippomedon came from Lerna, was a son of Talaus, and was a mighty hunter. He was killed in battle by Ismarus.

Hipponax. Greek lyric poet of Asia Minor (6th century B.C.). Hipponax composed satirical and colloquial verse.

Hipponicus (Gk. **Hipponikos**). Father of Callias. Hipponicus was called the richest Greek of his time. He died soon after 426 B.C.

Hipponous (Gk. **Hipponoos**). *Myth.* King of Olenus in Achaea. Discovering that his daughter Periboea was with child, he sent her to King Oeneus of Calydon to be put to death. But the latter, having recently lost his wife Althaea, fell in love with Periboea and married her, and eventually it was discovered that the stranger who had ravished her was Oeneus himself. The child of this union was Tydeus. Hipponous gave his name to a lost play by Sophocles, which was doubtless the model for Pacuvius' *Periboea.*

Homaimon (Gk. "of the same blood," or "related"). Epithet of Zeus.

Homer (Gk. **Homeros**). Oral poet (probably 8th century B.C.). Homer composed the *Iliad* and the *Odyssey.*

Homole. City in Magnesia on the slope of Mt. Ossa.

Homoloides Gates. One of the seven pairs of gates at Thebes, named either because of a neighboring hill called Homole or after a child of Niobe.

Hopletes. One of the four original tribes of Athens.

hoplites. Heavily armed Greek infantrymen.

Horace (Lat. name: **Quintus Horatius Flaccus**). Roman lyric and satiric poet (65–8 B.C.). Horace composed *Odes, Epodes, Satires, Epistles,* and ARS POETICA, all of which are extant.

Horae (Gk. **Horai**). *Myth.* Goddesses of the seasons. The word *horae,* which was used to denote all kinds of time divisions, is sometimes translated as "the Hours."

Horkios (Gk. "pertaining to oaths"). Epithet of Themis.

Hosia. Greek deity, personification of holiness.

Huntresses, The (Gk. **Toxotides**). Lost tragedy by Aeschylus. Extant fragments indicate that its plot was based on the fate of ACTAEON and that the chorus consisted of huntress nymphs, followers of Artemis.

Hyacinthus (Gk. **Hyakinthos**). *Myth.* Favorite of Apollo. The latter accidentally killed Hyacinthus when throwing a discus.

Hyades (Gk. "the rainy ones"). A constellation, said to be the metamorphosis of various female groups, especially of Erechtheus' daughters.

Hybla. City in southeastern Sicily.

hybris or **hubris** (Gk. "wanton violence, insolence," or "outrageous behavior"). The kind of shameless behavior that results from a feeling of pride, especially the effect of success that causes the individual to suppose that he is above the rules applying to others and is approaching the status of a god. (Compare the third choric ode in Aeschylus' *Agamemnon*.) The conception in modern criticism has been extended far beyond the simple meaning of the Greek term.

Hybris was the name of a lost satyr play by Sophocles. Since Hybris was sometimes called Pan's mother, the play perhaps dealt with the birth of Pan.

Hybristes. Scythian river flowing out of the Caucasus. Aeschylus, in *Prometheus Bound* (line 717), calls the Hybristes "truly named" because of its violence. (See HYBRIS.)

Hydaspes. River in India, a tributary of the Indus.

Hydra. *Myth.* Many-headed serpent monster of the swamp of Lerna. Heracles killed the Hydra and thereafter used its poison on his arrows. The Hydra was later depicted as one of the monsters of the underworld.

Hylas. *Myth.* Handsome squire of Heracles. Hylas accompanied Heracles on the voyage of the *Argo*. When the ship stopped at Mysia, Hylas was sent to fetch water, but the nymphs of the spring fell in love with him and pulled him in. Heracles wandered from the *Argo*, searching in vain for the boy, and the ship sailed on without the pair.

Hyllus (Gk. **Hyllos**). *Myth.* Most renowned of Heracles' sons. In Sophocles' *Trachiniae* and in a closely parallel role in Seneca's *Hercules on Oeta*, Hyllus tells of Heracles' sufferings caused by the poisoned robe and denounces his mother, Deianira. Afterward he learns that Deianira is innocent and brings the news to the dying Heracles. At the latter's urging, he promises to marry the captive Iole. According to one myth, Hyllus killed Eurystheus when the Athenians defended the Heraclidae against the Argive king. He himself was finally killed when attempting to regain possession of the Peloponnesus, his father's old home, in an attack by way of the Isthmus of Corinth.

Hymen or **Hymenaeus** (Gk. **Hymen** or **Hymenaios**). *Myth.* God of marriage, son of Dionysus and Aphrodite.

Hymettus (Gk. **Hymettos**). Mountain near Athens, to the south of the city.

Hyperbius (Gk. **Hyperbios**). *Myth*. A Theban hero in the battle of the Seven against Thebes.

Hyperbolus (Gk. **Hyperbolos**). Athenian politician. Originally a lampseller, Hyperbolus entered politics in the middle 420's B.C. and was very much in favor of the Peloponnesian War. He was violently attacked, with the usual charges ranging from treason to obesity, by Eupolis, Hermippus, Plato, and Aristophanes. Later he became a rival of Alcibiades, was ostracized, and died in exile.

Hyperboreans (Gk. **Hyperboreioi**). *Myth*. A people who inhabited a land which, according to the etymology of their name, lay "beyond the North Wind." This land was always happy and sunny. Apollo retired there every year during the winter months, returning to Delphi in the spring.

Hypermnestra or **Hypermestra**. *Myth*. The only one of the Danaïdes who did not kill her husband (Lynceus) on their wedding night. See DANAÏDES; DANAÏD TETRALOGY.

hyporchema. Originally a lyric composed as an accompaniment to the Cretan dance in armor, the *pyrrhiche*. The hyporchema became a feature of satyr play and dithyramb and even appeared occasionally in tragedy and comedy. In later antiquity it was defined as a "song in which the singer also dances."

hyposcenium or **hyposcaenium** (Gk. **hyposkenion**). The space below the raised stage.

hypothesis. The information contained in manuscripts prefacing the text of Greek dramas; particularly, a synopsis of the plot. In addition to plot summaries, hypotheses usually contained some or all of the following: the setting, the *didascalia* about the first performance (see DIDASCALIAE), a brief critical judgment, and a statement about other dramatists' handling of the same story.

Hypsipyle. *Myth*. Daughter of Thoas, king of Lemnos. When the Lemnian women decided to murder all their menfolk (see THE LEMNIANS), Hypsipyle preserved her father by concealing him in a chest and launching it into the sea. She was afterward chosen queen of the island. Aeschylus' lost play *Hypsipyle* told how the ship *Argo* was blown to the island of Lemnos, how the manless women threatened the Argonauts with war, and how finally all were mated, Hypsipyle falling to the lot of Jason. For the Lemnian queen's further adventures, see Euripides' HYPSIPYLE.

Hypsipyle. Lost play by Euripides (produced between 412 and 406 B.C.). Extensive fragments recovered from papyri contain 350 lines, or at least one-fifth of the original play. Reconstruction can therefore be fairly accurate.

S C E N E. The palace of King Lycurgus and Queen Eurydice at Nemea.

S U M M A R Y. The women of Lemnos, discovering that their queen, Hypsipyle, had failed to kill her father, killed him themselves and sold Hypsipyle into slavery. She is now at the court of King Lycurgus and Queen Eurydice, serving as nurse to the royal infant Opheltes.

Two young strangers enter, and Hypsipyle offers them the hospitality of the house. As they disappear inside, the Chorus of Nemean Women come in. They chide Hypsipyle for continually singing of the far-off days when she was a queen and the beloved of the leader of the Argonauts (Jason). Far more exciting events are at hand, they tell her: at this very moment the seven chieftains are marching through Nemea on their way to attack Thebes.

Amphiaraus, one of the Seven against Thebes, leads his men on the scene, asking for water for his army. While Hypsipyle takes him to a spring, a fearful serpent kills her nurseling, Opheltes. Queen Eurydice is about to put Hypsipyle to death when Amphiaraus comes to her defense, avowing that not even he and his men could fight off the serpent's attack. He speaks lines which have become famous (Cicero quotes them in Latin in *Tusculanae Disputationes,* 3.25.59):

> No man born but he must suffer;
> He buries children and gets others;
> He dies himself. Yet men complain,
> Bearing dust to dust. Then let a man
> Reap life like ripened grain: one is,
> And one is not. Why do we groan
> To pass on through to nature's end?

Amphiaraus announces that the baby's death foreshadows the fate of the Seven and decrees that in the child's honor the Nemean Games are to be established. Hypsipyle's life is spared. At the end of the play she is reunited with the two strangers of the first scene; they turn out to be her twin sons by Jason, torn from her arms in infancy.

The play was evidently very popular. The scene in which Hypsipyle shakes a rattle and sings a lullaby must have been famous: In Aristophanes' *Frogs* (lines 1304–06), Aeschylus refers to the "Euripidean Muse, who accompanies herself on the bones."

Hyrcania. Region south of the Caspian Sea.

Hysiae (Gk. **Hysiai**). Village at the foot of Mt. Cithaeron.

I

Iacchus (Gk. **Iakchos**). Epithet of Dionysus.

Iambe. *Myth.* Daughter of Pan and Echo. When Demeter paused at the palace of King Celeus and Queen Metaneira in Eleusis while searching for Persephone, Iambe, a serving maid, told ribald jokes that made Demeter laugh. Sophocles' lost satyr play *Iambe* must have been based on this myth.

Iapetus (Gk. **Iapetos**). *Myth.* A Titan, father of Prometheus.

Iaso. *Myth.* Goddess of healing, daughter of Asclepius.

Iberians, The. Lost play by Sophocles. It may have treated one of Heracles' exploits in Spain—the fetching of the golden apples from the garden of the Hesperides or the capture of Geryon's cattle.

Ibycus (Gk. **Ibykos**). Greek lyric poet (6th century B.C.).

Icarus (Gk. **Ikaros**). *Myth.* Son of Daedalus. When Icarus escaped from the Labyrinth with his father, he flew too near the sun, and the heat loosened the wax in his wings. Icarus fell and drowned in the sea, thereafter called the Icarian Sea (the southeastern Aegean).

Ichneutae (Gk. **Ichneutai, The Trackers,** or **The Searching Satyrs**). Satyr play by Sophocles. Nearly four hundred lines, presumably almost one-half of the play, were published in 1912 in Volume IX of the papyri recovered from Oxyrhynchus in Egypt. Translations: Denys L. Page, 1950 (in *Greek Literary Papyri*, Loeb Classical Library); Roger Lancelyn Green, 1957.

S C E N E. Mt. Cyllene in Arcadia.

S U M M A R Y. The fragment begins as Apollo promises a reward to anyone who can recover his stolen cattle. Silenus offers his services and those of his sons, the Chorus of Satyrs, on Apollo's promise that, if they are successful, they will win a golden wreath and freedom from servitude. The searchers soon discover the cattle tracks, which are, however, confused and reversed. As they listen for the lowing of the cattle, they hear an unidentifiable sound, one never heard before. By now the Satyrs are so unnerved that they are prevented from abandoning the search only by the remonstrances of Silenus, who berates them for their cowardice.

Coming to the mouth of a cave, the Satyrs sing and dance in front of it, making such an uproar that the mountain nymph Cyllene emerges and angrily chides them for being so noisy. When they ask her about the source of the strange sound, she first swears them to secrecy and then tells them that, without the knowledge of Hera, Zeus has had a love affair with the daughter of

Atlas. An extraordinary child was born of the illicit union and was given to Cyllene to rear. In the six days of his life, he has shown incredible development, and it was he who was responsible for the new and mysterious sound, produced from the body of a dead animal. Cyllene teases the Satyrs as they try to unravel the meaning of these words and finally reveals that the child had used a tortoise shell for his invention, the lyre. An oxhide stretched over the lyre leads the Satyrs to assume that the clever infant was the thief of Apollo's cattle. Cyllene is, however, indignant to hear such an accusation directed against a son of Zeus.

Here the manuscript ends. Undoubtedly Apollo confronted the marvelous child, Hermes, was won over by the gift of the lyre (as in the *Homeric Hymn to Hermes*, which tells the same story), and rewarded the Satyrs for their discovery.

Ida (adj. Idaean). Mountain range in the Troad. Euripides fancifully called Mt. Ida the eastern boundary of the world (*The Trojan Women*, lines 1067–69).

Idaea (Gk. **Idaia**). *Myth.* Daughter of Dardanus and second wife of PHINEUS.

Idas. *Myth.* Son of Aphareus and brother of Lynceus (3). (See LEUCIPPUS.)

Idmon. *Myth.* Soothsayer of the Argonautic expedition. Idmon went along even though he foresaw that in the course of the return voyage he would be killed by a snake bite in Libya.

ikria (Gk.). Wooden temporary stands or bleachers said to have been used for early dramatic performances.

Ilione. *Myth.* Eldest daughter of Priam and Hecuba and wife of Polymestor.

Ilissus or **Ilisus** (Gk. **Ilissos**). Stream in Attica flowing through the southern part of Athens.

Ilium (Gk. **Ilion**). Troy.

Illyria or **Illyricum.** Region along the eastern coast of the Adriatic Sea, north of Epirus.

Image-Bearers, The (Gk. **Xoanephoroi**). Lost play by Sophocles. There is considerable doubt as to its content. The only reference to it in ancient literature describes the gods as carrying their own statues out of doomed Troy.

Imbros. Island in the northern Aegean Sea, northeast of Lemnos.

Inachus (Gk. **Inachos**). 1. River in Argolis.

2. *Myth.* God of the river Inachus, primeval king of Argos, and father of Io. Sophocles' lost play *Inachus* (probably produced before 425 B.C.) dealt with the tale of Io. There is a papyrus fragment in which Hermes comes to kill Argus and frightens the satyrs; if the fragment is from Sophocles' drama, it would show *Inachus* to have been a satyr play. Other fragments seem, however, to indicate that *Inachus* was a tragedy dealing with the metamorphosis of Io, the blasphemous reaction of her father Inachus, and the consequent tribulations of the Argives.

Inarime. Poetical name for Ischia, an island off the coast of Campania.

Ino. *Myth.* Daughter of Cadmus, wife of Athamas, and nurse of Dionysus. (See ATHAMAS.)

Ino. Lost tragedy by Euripides (produced before 425 B.C.). Its plot was as follows: After Ino had joined a maenad band and had disappeared into the wilderness, her husband, Athamas, gave her up for lost and married Themisto, having two children by his second wife. Later Ino came back, and Athamas, wishing to conceal her, made her the nurse of both Themisto's two children and of her own two. The wicked Themisto determined to kill the children of the former marriage. Taking the nurse into her confidence, Themisto told her to dress her (Themisto's) two children in white and Ino's children in black, so that she might steal into the bedroom in the gloom and stab the two latter. The unrecognized Ino naturally did exactly the opposite, and Themisto stabbed her own children. When Themisto learned what she had done, she committed suicide. Athamas then went mad, killed his eldest son, Learchus, and pursued Ino and her other child, Melicertes, into the sea, where they became the sea goddess and sea god Leucothea and Palaemon. (See ATHAMAS.)

Inopia (Lat. "want" or "lack"). Personification of poverty. Inopia speaks the prologue of Plautus' *Trinummus*.

Io. *Myth.* Daughter of Inachus, priestess of Hera at Argos, and beloved of Zeus. Io was ordered in a dream to go to the meadows of Lerna, and there the god made love to her. To conceal Io from the jealous Hera, Zeus changed her into a white cow, but Hera divined the secret and asked that the animal be given to her. She then set the many-eyed Argus to guard Io. But Hermes, at Zeus's command, lulled Argus to sleep and killed him. Hera then pursued Io all over the earth, sending a gadfly to goad and torment her. She appears in this painful condition in Aeschylus' *Prometheus Bound,* where Prometheus foretells her further wanderings and sufferings. Io recovered her human form on the banks of the Nile, where, at Zeus's touch, she bore Epaphus.

Iobates. *Myth.* King of Lycia, father-in-law of Proetus. It was to Iobates that Proetus sent Bellerophon with a sealed message instructing the king to put the bearer to death (see BELLEROPHON). Sophocles' lost play *Iobates* was probably a treatment of the Bellerophon story.

Iocles (Gk. **Iokles**). *Myth.* Father of Amphiaraus. There may have been a lost play by Sophocles called *Iocles,* but not even the title is definitely known.

Iolaus (Gk. **Iolaos**). *Myth.* Son of Iphicles and nephew of Heracles. Iolaus helped the latter in many of his feats, and after Heracles' death, he protected the hero's sons. Iolaus appears as an old man in Euripides' *Heraclidae.* Having led Heracles' children to refuge at an Attic altar, he appeals to the Athenians for aid against their pursuer, King Eurystheus. In the battle with the Argives, Iolaus miraculously becomes young again and captures Eurystheus himself.

Iolcus (Gk. **Iolkos**). City in Thessaly on the northern shore of the Pagasaean Gulf.

Iole. *Myth.* Daughter of EURYTUS, king of Oechalia. When Heracles sacked the city, he took Iole, whom Eurytus had formerly denied him. This aroused the jealousy of Heracles' wife, Deianira, who sent her husband the robe that killed him. Iole appears as a mute character in Sophocles' *Trachiniae* and has one speech in Seneca's *Hercules on Oeta*. In both plays Heracles, as he lies dying, tells his son Hyllus to marry her.

Ion. *Myth.* Son of Xuthus and Creusa and ancestor of the Ionians. A lost play by Sophocles called *Ion* was probably the same as his *Creusa*. Euripides' *Ion* is extant.

Ion. Extant play by Euripides (variously dated between 421 and 408 B.C.). Translations: Arthur S. Way, 1912; H. D. [Hilda Doolittle], 1937; D. W. Lucas, 1950; Philip Vellacott, 1955; Ronald F. Willetts, 1958.

S C E N E. Delphi, the Temple of Apollo.

S U M M A R Y. Speaking the prologue, Hermes reveals that Apollo once forced his attentions on Creusa, daughter of King Erechtheus of Athens, who secretly bore him a child but abandoned the infant in her shame. At the request of Apollo, Hermes carried the child to Delphi, where a priestess reared the foundling, who has now reached manhood and is serving as a temple attendant, still ignorant of his parentage. Creusa, meanwhile, married Xuthus, a foreigner who had come to Athens' aid in time of war. Their marriage being childless, they have now come to Delphi to consult the oracle.

Ion, emerging from the temple, sings a morning hymn to Apollo and expresses his joy in serving the god. When a Chorus of Creusa's Slaves arrive, Ion invites them to admire the beautiful ornamentation of the temple. They are soon joined by their mistress, who tearfully recalls the wrong done her by Apollo long ago. Unburdening herself, she tells Ion that a friend had been ravished by the god and had given birth to a child whom she had exposed; now she would like to know whether the child is still alive. After Creusa departs, Ion discloses that, despite his devotion to Apollo, he is disturbed by the god's irresponsibility; if men are held accountable for their misdeeds, it is not just that the gods who make the laws should go unpunished for similar transgressions.

Xuthus, who has been within the temple, suddenly rushes out and embraces Ion, addressing the youth as his son. He explains that, according to the oracle, the first person he would meet upon leaving the temple would be his son. Xuthus adds that he has never been unfaithful to Creusa and that Ion was undoubtedly the fruit of some youthful escapade. Although Xuthus wants Ion to return with him to Athens, where riches and a throne await him, the young man fears that he will be resented as a foreign upstart by the Athenians and especially by the childless Creusa. He does agree, however, to let Xuthus offer a great feast in his honor.

After they leave the temple precincts, Creusa returns, accompanied by her aged Tutor. Although Xuthus, fearful of hurting his wife, had sworn Creusa's servants to secrecy, one of them reveals to her the meeting between Ion and his supposed father. Creusa is deeply offended and angry, both at the god and at her husband, while the Tutor contends that Xuthus had undoubtedly known of the boy's existence and had long been planning to seat his baseborn son on the throne of Athens. At length Creusa decides to avenge herself on Apollo by poisoning Ion in the god's own city with a drop of Gorgon's blood which she has in her possession. But the attempt miscarries. A Messenger reports that as Ion was about to drink from the poisoned cup, an ill-omened word made him pour the liquid away. When a sacred dove fell dead after sipping the wine, Creusa's plot was disclosed, and the Delphians decreed that she be hurled off Mt. Parnassus.

Pursued by Ion and the Delphians, Creusa seeks sanctuary at the temple. They are about to pull her away from the altar when the priestess intervenes, bearing the chest in which Ion was left as a baby. Creusa recognizes it and, by correctly identifying its contents, proves to Ion that she is his mother, though the youth is reluctant to believe that Apollo is his father. Athena suddenly appears, having been sent by Apollo, and declares that Ion is indeed the god's son. She urges them on to Athens, where Ion will become the ancestor of the Ionians, while Creusa and Xuthus will become the parents of two sons who will found the races of Dorians and Achaeans.

C O M M E N T A R Y. Here is a play that has won almost everyone's approval, though for a variety of contradictory reasons. Interpretation has proceeded on three levels.

One: *Ion* was a pleasant piece of political propaganda, intended to raise Athenian spirits during the Peloponnesian War with a reminder, or perhaps a newly invented theory, about the divine origin of all Ionian stock. This theory seems unobjectionable as far as it goes, but it goes only an inch.

Two: The knowing spectator was supposed to take in unquestioningly, literally, and wholesale all the complaints against the gods, particularly against Apollo, that were made by the human characters in the play. This interpretation has become, to a large extent, the orthodox one. Apollo is shown up by the playwright as a lecher, a liar, a child-deserter, and a coward; he is so timid and so conscious of his own shiftiness that he must send out his sister Athena to face the audience at the denouement. Since this Apollo is, however, the guarantor and author of Athenian divinity, it can be seen that Theory Two demolishes Theory One. The advocates of Theory One reply that the play's antireligionism was a kind of private joke between the author and the superior members of his audience (who were also above patriotism, one supposes) and between him and his later superior critics. But the jokes may possibly exist only between Euripides and the advocates of Theory One.

Theory Three turns Theory Two upside down. According to it, Apollo's wooing of a mortal is to infuse the human with the divine. Apollo's lies turn out to be deeper truths than the truth, for Xuthus gains a son and the Athenians gain assurance of their high origin and destiny; and Ion, far from having been deserted by his father, is proved to have had the best of childhoods in his own home. In the play's final scene the god, just as he has generously surrendered his charge to Athens, delicately turns over the task of final explanation to Athena, lest he should be a reproach to those who have so crudely misunderstood him. *Ion*'s meaning dictates its form: instead of tragedy there is melodramatic comedy. In it mortal misapprehensions and suspicions are skillfully brought to enlightenment, and the stupidities and selfish aims of human beings are guided to a happy conclusion by the wisdom and kindliness of the god.

Ionia. Specifically the central western coast and adjacent islands of Greek-colonized Asia Minor. The area was settled by the Ionians, a major branch of the Greek nation that included the Athenians. The adjective "Ionian" or "Ionic" characterized a certain musical mode, a certain style of architecture, certain dances, and the sea between Greece and Italy (said to have been named from Io).

Ion of Chios. Greek tragedian, poet, philosopher, and autobiographer (born between 492 and 480 B.C.; died c. 422 B.C.). Ion was a friend, or at least acquaintance, of Aeschylus, Sophocles, Cimon, Themistocles, and Pericles. He spent much time in Athens, where he exhibited his first play around 450 B.C. It is known that Ion won at least one first prize in the dramatic contest and that in 428 B.C. his play was defeated by Euripides' *Hippolytus*. The Alexandrians ranked Ion as a tragedian just below the three giants (Aeschylus, Sophocles, and Euripides). Of his works many fragments and nine tragedy titles are known: *Agamemnon, Alcmena, The Argives, The Great Drama, The Guards, Laertes, Phoenix* (two versions), *The Sons of Eurytus,* and *Teucer.* Much can be reconstructed of a satyr play, *Omphale,* which depicted Heracles as the slave of the Lydian queen; Omphale herself, a ridiculous figure in male dress, displayed a gargantuan appetite.

Besides many kinds of shorter poems and a philosophical treatise, *On the Three Primal Powers,* Ion wrote the first known memoirs, *Travels* (Gk. *Epidemiai*). Extant fragments from the latter work include anecdotes about Aeschylus and Sophocles.

Iophon. Son of Sophocles and a tragedian in his own right. Of fifty tragedies only two fragments survived. In 428 B.C. Iophon's play took second prize in the dramatic contest, Euripides' *Hippolytus* taking first. The story of Iophon's attempt to have his father declared senile by the courts is much doubted (see SOPHOCLES).

Iphianassa. *Myth.* Daughter of Agamemnon, usually identified with IPHIGENIA.

Iphigenia (Gk. **Iphigeneia**). *Myth.* Daughter of Agamemnon and Clytemnestra. In the year that Iphigenia was born, Agamemnon vowed to sacrifice to Artemis the fairest product of his land but ignored his vow. Years later, when the Greek fleet was assembled at Aulis, Artemis caused the winds to fail and demanded as propitiation her overdue sacrifice. Iphigenia's death is the subject of Euripides' *Iphigenia at Aulis.* In another version of the myth a doe was substituted at the sacrificial altar, while Artemis whisked the girl away to the land of the Taurians. Her experiences there are recounted in Euripides' *Iphigenia among the Taurians.* (For still further adventures, see CHRYSES 2; ALETES.) Iphigenia was the subject of lost tragedies by Aeschylus and Sophocles, both of which dealt with her sacrifice.

Iphigenia among the Taurians or **Iphigenia in Taurica** (Gk. **Iphigeneia he**

en Taurois; traditional Latin title, **Iphigenia in Tauris**). Extant play by Euripides (dated between 414 and 412 B.C.). Translations: Arthur S. Way, 1912; Augustus T. Murray, 1931; Philip Vellacott, 1953; Witter Bynner, 1956; Gilbert Murray, 1956. Adaptations and works influenced by *Iphigenia among the Taurians:* Naevius, *Iphigenia* (lost); Gluck, *Iphigénie en Tauride* (opera), 1779; Goethe, *Iphigenie auf Tauris*, 1779.

S C E N E. The land of the Taurians (Crimea), before the Temple of Artemis.

S U M M A R Y. In the garb of a priestess, Iphigenia recalls how she came to the land of the uncouth Taurians long ago: When the Greek fleet was becalmed at Aulis, Agamemnon was forced to propitiate Artemis by sacrificing his daughter Iphigenia, whom he had failed to sacrifice at birth to the goddess, though he had promised to offer up the fairest product of his land. Now it is Iphigenia's cruel duty, in turn, to preside over the sacrifice of any foreigner who comes to the Taurian land. At the moment she is troubled by a dream of the night before, which has convinced her that her brother, Orestes, is dead.

After Iphigenia retires, Orestes and his friend Pylades cautiously approach the temple. As partial expiation for his crime of matricide, Orestes has been ordered by Apollo's oracle to steal the image of Artemis from the temple and to present it to the Athenians. Momentarily discouraged by the difficulty of the task, Orestes speaks of returning to their ship, which lies anchored nearby, but Pylades bolsters his courage, proposing that they hide in a cave until nightfall.

As Iphigenia performs a rite in memory of her presumably dead brother, assisted by a Chorus of Captured Greek Maidens, a herdsman runs in to report that two prospective victims, both Greeks, have managed to pass between the Clashing Rocks and reach the Tauric land. Before the Taurians captured them, one was seized by a fit of madness and thrashed about wildly, as if pursued by visions. Iphigenia observes that, now Orestes is dead, her heart can feel nothing, not even pity for the victims, though they will be the first Greeks to be sacrificed at the Taurian shrine. She cannot, however, believe that Artemis demands the spilling of human blood and concludes that the Taurians are attributing their own savage inclinations to the goddess.

When the captives are brought to the temple, Iphigenia questions them about the Trojan War and the family of Agamemnon. From the curt answers of Orestes, who refuses to reveal his name, she realizes that her dream was false and that her brother is still alive. Iphigenia promises to spare Orestes if he will take a letter to Argos, but Orestes insists that Pylades go in his place. Pylades points out that the letter may be destroyed, an event that would force him to break his oath to deliver it at all costs. Iphigenia then begins to recite its contents so that he can commit them to memory. When it becomes apparent that the letter is addressed to Orestes, he convinces Iphigenia that he is himself her beloved brother and relates to her the woes that have befallen their house.

Believing that Artemis herself will favor their enterprise, brother and sister try to devise a plan that will enable the three of them to escape with the image of the goddess. Orestes proposes that they kill King Thoas lest he prevent their flight, but Iphigenia refuses to offend the gods further, citing the king's kindness to her. Presently Iphigenia hits on a ruse that she feels certain will deceive the Taurians, even their king. She will say that, since both prisoners are be-smirched by the crime of matricide, they must be cleansed in salt water before their sacrifice; even the image has been defiled by their presence and must be purified. Once they are at the water's edge, Iphigenia continues, they can flee to the waiting ship.

Iphigenia easily dupes the king, who agrees to advise the Taurians to stay indoors to protect themselves from contamination, while he also remains behind to purify the temple. After Iphigenia, Orestes, and Pylades have departed with the image, one of the soldiers accompanying them rushes back to report to Thoas that the priestess and her prisoners have succeeded in eluding their guards and have taken refuge aboard Orestes' ship. He adds that it seems likely that they can be recaptured, for their ship has not been able to sail because of unfavorable weather.

While Thoas is giving orders for the pursuit of the Greeks, Athena appears and informs him that Poseidon has stilled the sea at her request. She orders Orestes (gods can be heard afar off) to take the image of Artemis to a spot near Athens. There he is to erect a temple to the goddess and to name it for its Taurian origin, but the goddess' priest will shed no more than a single drop of blood in her rites. Iphigenia is to continue serving Artemis at a shrine at Brauron. Athena then instructs Thoas to free the captive maidens, who raise their voices in joyful song. The king, realizing the futility of defying divine edicts, submits to the will of the goddess.

C O M M E N T A R Y. This play has always gained the applause of critics for its faultless construction, which is especially noteworthy for its use of suspense and dramatic irony. Aristotle singled out the recognition scene for praise. *Iphigenia among the Taurians* belongs with *Ion* and *Helen* in the group of plays (melodramatic comedies that are tragedies in name only) which have as a common theme the mystery of divine guidance that leads through ill-under-stood mazes of circumstances to the ultimate salvation of man. Here the salva-tion is threefold: not only are Orestes and Pylades saved, but with their rescue Iphigenia is won back from the brutalizing and embittering effects of a long barbarian exile, and the cult of Artemis is uprooted from a savage soil to be transplanted, ennobled, and purified in the civilized soil of Attic Greece. So Athena, the embodiment of divine wisdom and most Greek of goddesses, fittingly speaks the final word.

Iphigenia at Aulis (Gk. **Iphigeneia he en Aulidi**). Extant tragedy by Euripides (produced posthumously by his son in 406 or 405 B.C.). Translations: Arthur S. Way, 1912; Florence M. Stawell, 1929; Charles R. Walker, 1958. Adaptations and works influenced by *Iphigenia at Aulis*: Ennius, lost play; Racine, *Iphigénie*, 1674.

S C E N E. The Greek camp at Aulis.

S U M M A R Y. Although it is late at night, Agamemnon, commander in chief of the Greek armies en route to Troy, emerges from his tent in great distress and gives an aged Servant a letter to deliver to Argos. This letter, he explains, revokes an earlier message in which he asked his wife, Clytemnestra, to send their daughter Iphigenia to Aulis, ostensibly to be married to Achilles but actually to be sacrificed to Artemis. Agamemnon had been told by the prophet Calchas that if the sacrifice were not made, the Greek fleet, detained at Aulis by lack of a wind, would not be able to sail to Troy. Now, however, Agamemnon regrets his decision to kill Iphigenia.

As the letter carrier leaves, a Chorus of Women who have stolen over from Chalcis out of curiosity creep in; they express their wonderment at the impressive Greek military equipment and describe the heroes they have seen. The sudden noise of a scuffle brings Agamemnon from his tent again; his brother Menelaus has caught the old Servant and is wresting the letter from him. Having read its contents, Menelaus berates Agamemnon for his indecisiveness, while the latter retorts that Menelaus was not even capable of keeping his wayward wife, Helen, in check. The quarrel is interrupted by the news that Iphigenia has already arrived, accompanied by her mother and her infant brother, Orestes. Now that the dreadful deed is so close at hand, even Menelaus is filled with pity and urges his brother not to carry out the sacrifice, but Agamemnon replies that the troops will force him to go through with it once they learn of Calchas' prophecy. Upon being greeted by his family and hearing Iphigenia's protestations of love for him, Agamemnon is unable to restrain his tears; nevertheless he leaves to begin preparations for the sacrifice.

Achilles, who comes in complaining about the delay in sailing, is bewildered when Clytemnestra refers to him as her daughter's prospective husband. Both Achilles and Clytemnestra are stunned to learn from the old Servant that Iphigenia is really marked for death. Clytemnestra appeals to Achilles for protection, and he promises support if Agamemnon should prove obdurate.

Clytemnestra implores Agamemnon to spare their daughter, and Iphigenia, who is by now aware of the fate in store for her, adds her own entreaties to her mother's. But Agamemnon refuses to yield, maintaining that his duty to Greece transcends his personal feelings; in any case, he concludes, the army is so maddened with bloodlust that everyone will be killed unless Iphigenia dies. Achilles attempts to defy the general will, but even he is threatened by the soldiers with stoning.

Although Achilles offers to defend her to the end, Iphigenia now realizes the hopelessness of her plight. She goes out to her death with dignity and courage, confident that she will be recognized as a benefactress of Greece. A Messenger reports the final event: when Agamemnon struck the death blow, the girl suddenly vanished and a mountain doe appeared on the altar, bleeding its life away.

COMMENTARY. Evaluation of this play is particularly difficult because the text has suffered many changes. Some of them were, according to tradition, made by Euripides the Younger, who was said to have put the finishing touches to his father's work, which was produced after his death.

These factors have, however, afforded scope for conflicting opinions. Not many protests are made to those who call *Iphigenia at Aulis* pure melodrama.

Like other Euripidean melodramas, such as *Ion* and *Iphigenia among the Taurians,* it is not a nineteenth-century thriller but a seriocomic treatment of a theme that requires a happy ending.

The happy ending, in which an animal is substituted for the human victim, is said not to have been in the original version. There is, nevertheless, evidence that Artemis appeared in some way, and it seems hardly likely that the goddess came just to smack her lips over a bloodletting. One might conjecture that the divine purpose throughout the action was to bring forth, from the cruelty, ambition, passion, and vacillation of the older generation, the chivalry and nobility of the younger. The honorable behavior of Achilles and the self-sacrifice of Iphigenia (whose character Aristotle thought inconsistently drawn, but who makes an impression as fine as any in Greek drama) seem a kind of human manifestation of the splendid innocence of Artemis herself.

Iphigone. Iphigenia.

Iphis. *Myth.* Father of Eteoclus and Evadne. The latter was the wife of Capaneus. Iphis appears in Euripides' *Suppliants,* where he tries to dissuade Evadne from leaping onto her husband's funeral pyre.

Iphitus (Gk. **Iphitos**). *Myth.* Son of EURYTUS.

Iris. *Myth.* Goddess of the rainbow and messenger of the gods, especially of Hera. Iris appears in Euripides' *Heracles,* where, at Hera's command, she brings Lyssa, "Madness," to afflict the hero. In Aristophanes' *Birds,* Iris comes from Olympus to protest the blockade of the sky; she is received with insults and rudely dismissed.

Islands, The (Gk. **Nesoi**). Lost comedy doubtfully ascribed to Aristophanes. Its chorus consisted of the various Aegean islands that were unwilling vassal states of Athens before and during the Peloponnesian War.

Islands of the Blessed. *Myth.* A kind of heaven for the souls of departed heroes. These islands were vaguely located in the River Ocean, beyond the Pillars of Hercules. The idea was parallel to that of the fields of Elysium in the underworld.

Ismara or **Ismaros.** City on the Thracian coast. In Greek poetic usage, "Ismarian" often meant "Thracian."

Ismene. *Myth.* Daughter of Oedipus and Jocasta. Weaker in character than her sister Antigone, Ismene always appears as a foil for Antigone, or as her companion or attendant. Examples of this can be found in Sophocles' *Oedipus the King* (mute character), *Oedipus at Colonus,* and *Antigone* and in Aeschylus' *Seven Against Thebes.*

Ismenus (Gk. **Ismenos**). Stream in Boeotia.

Ister or **Hister.** The lower Danube River.

Isthmian Games or **Isthmia.** Contests held on alternate years at Corinth (on the Isthmus). The games were open to all Greeks.

Isthmiasts, The (Gk. **Isthmiastai**). Lost satyr play by Aeschylus, also called *Theoroi,* "The Spectators." About one hundred lines have been recovered from papyri, enough to give a fair idea of some of the action:

A group of satyrs, led by Silenus, have come to the Isthmus of Corinth for the Isthmian Games. In one scene they bring votive offerings, probably masks exactly like the ones they are wearing, to the Temple of Poseidon. Dionysus enters and reproaches them for deserting him to become participants in the games. He replies to some charge implying that he is effeminate, providing only for tragedies and comedies in his own celebrations, and excluding athletics. Later on the satyrs are apparently offered the Dionysiac ship-wagon to use in the sporting events. At this point the fragments end. All experts agree that this piece was the satyr play to a trilogy of which *Athamas* was one tragedy, but there is no agreement as to what the other two were.

Istria or **Histria**. Peninsula at the northeastern corner of the Adriatic Sea.

Ithaca (Gk. **Ithake**). Island off the coast of Acarnania. Ithaca was the homeland of Odysseus.

Itys. *Myth.* Son of Tereus and Procne. Itys was killed by his mother, who served him up to his father at a meal. When Procne was subsequently changed into a bird, she mourned Itys constantly. (See TEREUS.)

Iugulae. A constellation consisting of the belt of the constellation Orion. It is referred to in Plautus' *Amphitryon* (line 275).

Ixion. *Myth.* King of the Lapiths. When Ixion's father-in-law came to collect the bride price for his daughter, Ixion pushed him into a pit of burning coals. Becoming thus the first murderer of a kinsman, Ixion could find no absolution on earth and was finally purified by Zeus himself. Ixion returned Zeus's kindness by attempting to seduce Hera, who reported the attempt to her husband. To find out whether Hera's story were true, Zeus created a cloud in the shape of his wife. When Ixion subsequently boasted of having enjoyed Hera's favors, Zeus bound him to a flaming wheel to circle the sky forever. In due time the cloud (Nephele) gave birth to the first of the race of Centaurs.

Aeschylus' lost play *Ixion* was probably a sequel to *The Perrhaebians,* telling of Ixion's wicked deeds in heaven. Of Sophocles' lost *Ixion* only one word survives. Euripides also wrote an *Ixion,* which was produced soon after 411 B.C. It is clear, from its four extant fragments, that Euripides' play concluded with the punishment on the wheel of fire.

J

Janus. *Myth.* Two-faced Roman god of doors, bridges, and beginnings.

Jason (Gk. **Iason**). **1.** *Myth.* Son of Aeson. Although Aeson was the rightful heir to the throne of Iolcus, his half brother Pelias seized the throne and imprisoned him in the palace. Aeson's son Jason was secretly taken from the city and was reared on Mt. Pelion by the centaur Chiron. When Jason returned to Iolcus to claim his heritage, he was charged by Pelias, who hoped to rid himself of the young man, to fetch the golden fleece from Colchis (see PHRIXUS).

Jason accordingly built the *Argo* and assembled heroes (the Argonauts) from all over Greece to accompany him on his voyage. After many adventures (see HYPSIPYLE; PHINEUS; SYMPLEGADES) they reached Colchis. But King Aeëtes was determined not to give up the fleece and set Jason impossible tasks to perform in order to win it. Jason nevertheless performed them with the aid of the king's daughter Medea, who had fallen in love with him. When Aeëtes remained unwilling to part with the fleece, Medea helped Jason to steal it from the dragon that guarded it and to escape from Colchis.

On the Argonauts' return to Greece, Medea, who had accompanied them, plotted the death of Pelias. After this deed Jason and Medea (now married) were forced to flee to Corinth. Their experiences in that city are the subject of Euripides' *Medea*, in which Jason is a very unsympathetic character. It was said that afterward Jason went out and sat under the *Argo*. Its rotten prow fell and killed him.

2. Tyrant of Pherae. This Jason was murdered in 370 B.C.

3. Actor from Tralles. When in 53 B.C. the Romans were defeated at Carrhae, Jason was playing the role of Agave in the *Bacchae* at the Parthian court. The head of the triumvir Crassus was brought in and Jason used it in the last scene of the play.

Jocasta (Gk. **Iokaste**). *Myth.* Daughter of Menoeceus, sister of Creon, and wife of King Laius of Thebes. Laius was warned by the oracle that a son of his would kill him, but Jocasta lured him to her bed by making him drunk and he begot Oedipus. Jocasta pierced the child's feet and gave him to a shepherd to expose on Mt. Cithaeron. But he was saved by the shepherd and was brought up by King Polybus and Queen Merope (or Periboea) of Corinth as their own. Years later, after the murder of Laius and the conquest of the Sphinx, Jocasta unwittingly married Oedipus. They had four children: Eteocles, Polyneices, Antigone, and Ismene.

In Sophocles' *Oedipus the King* and in Seneca's *Oedipus* Jocasta plays a leading role. On learning that she is married to her first husband's murderer and her own son, she commits suicide—by hanging in the former play, by the sword in the latter. In Euripides' *Phoenician Women* Jocasta lives until the war of the Seven against Thebes. She goes to prevent her sons from fighting, but finding that they have killed each other already, she stabs herself. Jocasta has several long speeches in Seneca's *Phoenician Women* when on a similar mission before the duel, but the play breaks off before anyone dies.

Johannes Diaconus. Medieval writer (fl. between A.D. 1000 and 1200). Johannes' commentary on Hermogenes has, in this century, been found to contain information on ancient drama and fragments from it not known before.

Juba. King of Numidia and historian (c. 50 B.C.–c. A.D. 23). Juba married Cleopatra Selene, daughter of Antony and Cleopatra, and ruled in Africa as an ally of Augustus. Among his numerous lost works was a *History of the Theater.*

Judgment, The (Gk. **Krisis**). Lost satyr play by Sophocles based on the story of the Judgment of PARIS.

Julia. 1. The Elder (39 B.C.–A.D. 14). Only daughter of the emperor Augustus. Julia was banished for immorality in 2 B.C.

2. The Younger. Daughter of the above and banished for the same reason.

Juno. Roman goddess identified with HERA. In Terence's *Andria* (line 473) Juno is identified with Lucina, Roman goddess of childbirth. In Seneca's *Hercules Furens* Juno appears as Hercules' persecutor.

Jupiter (also, in English, **Jove**). Roman god identified with Zeus. Jupiter's temple on the Capitoline Hill was the most important in Rome; there he was called *Optimus Maximus,* "the best and greatest." He appears in Plautus' *Amphitryon,* taking the form of Amphitryon and seducing Alcmena.

K

katablemata. Backdrops or painted screens that could be thrown over the permanent stage setting of a Greek theater.

katakeleusmos. See EPIRRHEMATIC AGON.

Ker, pl. **Keres.** *Myth.* Goddess of death or evil, equated with the Sphinx or with the Erinyes (compare Aeschylus' *Seven Against Thebes,* lines 775 and 1061).

keraunoskopeion. Device in the Greek theater, probably some kind of revolving prism, to give the effect of lightning.

kerkis, pl. **kerkides** (Gk. "shuttle" or "tapering rod"). Section or block of seat rows in a Greek theater.

Klerios or **Klarios** (Gk. "pertaining to the casting of lots"). Epithet of Zeus as apportioner of fate.

Knights, The (Gk. **Hippes;** traditional Latin title, **Equites**). Extant comedy by Aristophanes (produced at the Lenaea of 424 B.C.). *The Knights* took first prize. Translations: John Hookham Frere, 1839; Benjamin B. Rogers, 1924; Arthur S. Way, 1934; Robert Henning Webb, 1962.

S C E N E. Athens, a street by the Pnyx, meeting place of the Assembly.

S U M M A R Y. The Athenian generals Nicias and Demosthenes are represented as slaves in the household of Demos ("the people," or "the democracy"). Their life has recently been made unbearable by the appearance of a new slave, Paphlagon (who represents the demagogue Cleon), a tanner who lies, steals, curries favor with the master, and takes credit for the achievements of others. Having learned from an oracle that Paphlagon will be supplanted by a Sausage-Seller, Nicias and Demosthenes light upon the first one they meet and urge him to try his hand at statecraft since he possesses the principal qualifications: ignorance and impudence.

With the help of a Chorus of Knights (young men who form the cavalry corps in the Athenian army), the Sausage-Seller engages Paphlagon in a contest of abuse. The former accuses the latter of dishonesty, and the latter boasts of his own guile and his skill in manipulating the Athenians. The verbal fireworks end as each runs off to denounce the other to the Boule, the deliberative body of the state.

During their absence, the Knights address the audience, explaining why Aristophanes has as yet never brought out a play under his own name; among other reasons, they mention the fickleness of the public, which deserted Magnes

and Cratinus in their old age. They praise the valor of their forefathers and celebrate the exploits of the current war.

The Sausage-Seller and Paphlagon continue their mudslinging match, each
trying to win the favor of Demos with oracles and gifts of food and drink. While
the Sausage-Seller promises peace and prosperity, Paphlagon makes much of
his services to the state and presents one of his rival's offerings as his own,
imitating the example of his real-life counterpart in claiming the Athenian
victory at Pylos. Paphlagon is, however, forced to retire in defeat when one
of his own oracles, describing his successor, turns out to fit the Sausage-Seller
perfectly. The latter, who reveals that his name is Agoracritus ("choice of the
market place"), takes over the care of Demos, rejuvenating him by a magical
process. At the play's end the Sausage-Seller gives Demos advice on how to
resist the wiles of demagogues.

COMMENTARY. *The Knights* was Aristophanes' first comedy to be produced under his own name. Its vehement and sustained attack on Cleon was
made openly, soon after Cleon had prosecuted the poet for his criticism in
The Banqueters and directly after Cleon had returned to Athens covered with
the glory of his accidental military victory over the Spartans at Pylos. There is
no sparing of invective, and the poet's intense passion of hatred and contempt
lends the play a tightness and a drive that are unique, though the variety and
lyricism of the other comedies are missing.

The play's underlying theme is that of a cycle of ages which proceed
through successive stages of degeneration until the cycle ends in utter chaos and
the Golden Age begins anew. Hence there is much reliance on interpretation of
oracles to arrive at the fulfillment of the cycle and the nadir of degradation.
This is discovered in the person of the Sausage-Seller, whose name is Agoracritus, "choice of the market place," and who, as the lowest point of democratic
vulgarity, forms a basis for the upward turn in the fortunes of Demos. Cleon,
who can swallow only bribes, is outdone by the Sausage-Seller, who, as a
"stuffed gut," in Cedric Whitman's phrase, prefigures the plenty and content-
ment of the Golden Age.

kommos, pl. **kommoi** (Gk. "beating of the breast, dirge"). Dramatic song,
usually a lament, sung by some character in the play in alternation with the
chorus. Kommoi could therefore usually be distinguished from monodies (solos
without chorus) and from duets and trios.

komos, pl. **komoi** (Gk.). A parade of merrymakers through the streets.
There were both informal and formal *komoi*. The informal kind came as a
climax to a drinking session or arose in connection with a wedding celebration
or a serenade of a ladylove. More formal *komoi* ranged from the *quête*, connected with a seasonal festival (going from house to house in the village and
demanding a treat), to the phallophoric and dithyrambic processions forming
part of the ritual of Dionysus. (See DIONYSIA; PHALLOPHORIA.)

Kophoi (Gk. "The Mute Ones" or "The Stupid Ones"). Lost satyr play by
Sophocles. Various conjectures have been made as to the content of *Kophoi*, the
most interesting being that it was the old fable of the Serpent and the Ass:

In reward for betraying Prometheus, Man was given by Zeus the gift of immortal youth. Man loaded the gift on an ass, and in the course of his journey came to a spring guarded by a serpent. The thirsty ass traded its burden to the serpent for a drink. As a result, Man grows old and dies, while the serpent sheds its skin and stays forever young.

Kratos (Gk. "strength" or "violence"). Personification of power. Kratos appears in the first scene of Aeschylus' *Prometheus Bound,* where he orders Hephaestus to enchain Prometheus.

Ktesios (Gk. "pertaining to property or to the household"). Epithet of Zeus as protector of the household.

L

Labdacus (Gk. **Labdakos**). *Myth*. King of Thebes, grandson of Cadmus, and father of Laius. Labdacus' descendants were called the Labdacidae or Labdacids.

Laberius, Decimus. Writer of mimes. A contemporary of Cicero, Laberius died in the same year as the statesman, 43 B.C. Of his works only fragments and forty-odd titles remain. Some typical titles are: *The Painter, The Fisherman, The Saturnalia, The Gauls.* Laberius' language seems to have been colloquial, clever, and racy. In his writings there were many allusions to philosophy and politics. The great disgrace of his life occurred in 46 B.C. when Caesar forced him to appear against the professional actor Publilius Syrus in a mime of his own composition. Since acting was considered a disreputable profession, an appearance on the stage was certain to cost Laberius his position as an *eques,* a knight. He lamented his misfortune in the prologue to the mime, and in the play inserted the line: "Up, Romans! Your freedom is slipping away!" Caesar gave Laberius a small fortune in compensation for his humiliation and personally restored to him the gold ring of the equestrian class.

Labes. A dog in Aristophanes' *Wasps* who is put on trial for stealing. The name means "snatcher" and is a pun on LACHES.

Lacedaemon (Gk. **Lakedaimon**). LACONIA. Because Sparta was in Laconia, the adjective "Lacedaemonian" usually meant "Spartan."

Laches. Athenian naval commander in the early part of the Peloponnesian War. After an expedition to Sicily in 427 B.C., Laches was recalled to Athens. There, it is thought, he was brought to trial by Cleon, who apparently charged him with peculation.

Lachesis (Gk. "allotter"). *Myth*. One of the MOIRAE.

Laconia (Gk. **Lakonia** or **Lakonis**). Section of the Peloponnesus around Sparta. The adjective "Laconian" or "Laconic" characterized a kind of key that locked doors from the outside, and also a type of red shoes that were fashionable and of high quality.

Laconian Women, The (Gk. **Lakainai**). Lost play by Sophocles. Its title doubtless derived from the chorus of Spartan handmaidens who, in the play, attended Helen at Troy. With Helen they assisted Odysseus and Diomedes, who had slipped into the city disguised as beggars in order to steal the sacred image of Athena, the Palladium, on which Troy's fate depended. Probably included in the play was the quarrel between the two Greeks on their way back to camp. (See DIOMEDES 2.)

Laertes. *Myth.* Father of Odysseus. The latter was sometimes called Laertiades. While Odysseus was absent at Troy, and while he wandered afterward, Laertes lived in poverty on a farm to which he had withdrawn. (According to some, Odysseus' real father was SISYPHUS.)

Laespodias (Gk. **Laispodias**). Athenian politician. Although Laespodias came from an aristocratic family, his sympathies were at first democratic. He was one of the main supporters of the Sicilian expedition. In 411 B.C., however, he joined the oligarchic faction and was probably executed in the reaction that followed.

Lais. Notorious courtesan of Aristophanes' time. Lais was the mistress of a certain Philonides.

Laius (Gk. **Laios**). *Myth.* Son of Labdacus, king of Thebes, and father of OEDIPUS. Inspired with an unnatural passion for Pelops' young son Chrysippus, Laius kidnaped the boy and was consequently cursed by Pelops. Apollo's oracle warned Laius that a son of his would kill him and that he should therefore die childless, but Laius became drunk and sired Oedipus. Aeschylus' lost play *Laius* was a part of the THEBAN TETRALOGY.

Lamachus (Gk. **Lamachos**). Distinguished Athenian military commander. Lamachus was a colleague of Nicias in the Sicilian expedition, where he lost his life. He appears in Aristophanes' *Acharnians.*

Lamia. *Myth.* Libyan daughter of Belus. Because Lamia was loved by Zeus, Hera caused her children to die as soon as they were born. Lamia consequently retired to a cave, becoming a monster who revengefully killed other women's children at night. She had removable eyes which she kept in a jar when not in use. A lost play by Euripides was called *Lamia.* It has been suggested, however, that the work was not a separate play but a prologue to *Busiris* spoken by Lamia.

Lampon. Soothsayer who prophesied the rise of Pericles and the fall of his rival Thucydides. Lampon played a prominent role in the founding of the Athenian colony at Thurii. The comic poets made fun of his avarice and gluttony.

Lanuvinus, Luscius. Comic playwright in Rome (early 2nd century B.C.). Lanuvinus is the "malevolent old poet" whose criticisms Terence counters in the prologues to all of his plays except *The Mother-in-Law.* Only two of Lanuvinus' plays are known: In *The Ghost,* adapted from a play by Menander, the plot turns on the device of a hole in the common wall of two houses. In *The Treasure,* a tomb that has been bought by a miser is found to contain money which was left there purposely by the dead man, who foresaw the eventual bankruptcy of his spendthrift son.

Laocoön (Gk. **Laokoon**). *Myth.* Priest of Apollo in Troy. Laocoön had offended the god, either by making love to his wife in the temple or by begetting children against the god's command. Two serpents appeared out of the sea, therefore, and swallowed his sons. Anchises and his son Aeneas interpreted this event as a portent of the fall of Troy and left the city with a group of followers. Sophocles' lost tragedy *Laocoön* was based on this story.

Laomedon. *Myth.* King of Troy, father of Ganymede, Hesione, and Priam. Laomedon was notorious for his dishonesty. He refused to pay Apollo and Poseidon for building the walls of Troy and denied Heracles his reward for rescuing Hesione from the sea monster sent by Poseidon. Heracles accordingly took Troy and killed Laomedon.

Lapiths (Gk. **Lapithai**, Lat. **Lapithae**). Tribe in Thessaly. The Lapiths were said to have had a murderous battle with the drunken Centaurs at the wedding feast of PIRITHOUS.

lar, pl. **lares** (Lat.). *Myth.* Deified soul of an ancestor that acted as tutelary spirit of a household. The household lar speaks the prologue to Plautus' *Aulularia* and appears throughout the first act of the anonymous *Querolus*.

Larissaeans, The (Gk. **Larisaioi**). Lost play by Sophocles. Its plot was probably based on the story of Perseus' accidental killing of Acrisius.

Lasus (Gk. **Lasos**). Lyric poet from Hermione (late 6th century B.C.) Lasus was Pindar's teacher. He was one of the first to use non-Dionysian subjects in the dithyramb.

Latona. Latin form of LETO.

Laurium (Gk. **Laurion**). Mountainous district in southeastern Attica. Here was mined the silver used in the owl coins of Athens.

Leda. *Myth.* Wife of Tyndareus and mother of Helen, Clytemnestra, Castor, and Polydeuces. According to one version of the story, Leda, wooed by Zeus in the guise of a swan, produced an egg. From it were hatched Helen and Polydeuces. She bore Clytemnestra and Castor to Tyndareus. In another version, however, Leda laid two eggs, one of which yielded Helen and Clytemnestra, the other Castor and Polydeuces (see DIOSCURI). When Helen eloped with Paris, Leda hanged herself for shame.

Leipsydrion. Fortified place on Mt. Parnes. In 513 B.C. bloody strife occurred there between Athenian political factions.

Leitus (Gk. **Leitos**). *Myth.* Boeotian hero. Leitus was a prominent warrior at Troy, where he was wounded by Hector.

Lemnians, The (Gk. **Lemnioi**). Lost play by AESCHYLUS. Probably it described how the men of Lemnos offended the goddess Aphrodite and how she caused them to chase after the women of Thrace, with the result that their own women plotted to kill them. The sequel to all this was the subject of Aeschylus' *Hypsipyle* and Sophocles' *Lemnian Women*.

Lemnian Women, The (Gk. **Lemniai**). 1. Lost play by Sophocles. *The Lemnian Women* existed in two versions (or there may have been two plays). It is probable that in it the Argonauts landed on Lemnos after a battle with the women there. The play may have concluded with the departure of the Argonauts, followed by the discovery of Hypsipyle's preservation of her father and her sale into slavery as punishment. (See HYPSIPYLE.)

2. Lost comedy by Aristophanes (produced c. 412–408 B.C.). This play seems to have been a parody on the foregoing story.

Lemnos. Large island in the northern Aegean Sea. Lemnos was famous for wine, for fires that rose out of the ground (said to have sprung up when Hephaestus, god of fire, fell to earth from Olympus), and for the legend that its women once killed all of their men (the "Lemnian crime" or "Lemnian evils").

Lenaea (Gk. **Lenaia,** from *lenai,* "maenads"). Annual Athenian festival in honor of Dionysus, occurring in January. The Lenaea was marked by a procession in which jesters on wagons mocked at the crowd as they went by. There were also dramatic performances, both comic and tragic, which none but Athenian citizens could attend. Two tragic poets competed, each with two plays, and five comic poets (three during the Peloponnesian War) each entered one play. These contests were held under the supervision of the *archon basileus* (king archon). They did not receive state support until the middle of the fifth century B.C. and were never as important as those held at the City Dionysia.

leno (Lat. "pimp"). The pimp who was a stock character—always detestable—in New Comedy.

Leonidas. Spartan king. Leonidas led the three hundred Spartans who, in 480 B.C., died at Thermopylae while heroically opposing the Persians. Leonidas was himself killed.

Lepreum (Gk. **Lepreon** or **Lepreos**). Town in southern Elis. In *The Birds* (line 149), Aristophanes puns on the name to suggest *lepra,* "leprosy."

Lerna. Marsh in Argolis. Its spring was said to have emerged at Poseidon's command for the benefit of AMYMONE. It was here that Heracles killed the Hydra.

Lesbos. Large island in the Aegean Sea, off the Aeolian coast of Asia Minor. Lesbos was famous for its wine and for its poet-singers Arion, Alcaeus, and Sappho.

Lethe (Gk. "oblivion"). *Myth.* River in the underworld. A taste of Lethe's waters caused complete forgetfulness of the past.

Leto. *Myth.* Goddess loved by Zeus. Hera pursued Leto over the earth until, at last, Leto came to the island of Delos, where she gave birth to the twin deities Artemis and Apollo.

Leucas or **Leucadia.** Island off the coast of Acarnania.

Leucate. Promontory at the southern tip of Leucas.

Leucippus (Gk. **Leukippos**). *Myth.* Father of Phoebe and Hilaira, who were called the Leucippides. Leucippus' daughters were engaged to be married to their cousins Idas and Lynceus, but Castor and Polydeuces (see DIOSCURI) carried them off and married the maidens themselves. Idas and Lynceus pursued their successful rivals and fought with them. In the duel all of the men were killed except the divine Polydeuces. Phoebe and Hilaira bore their husbands' sons.

Leucothea (Gk. **Leukothea**). *Myth.* A sea goddess, the deified form of INO after she leaped into the sea.

Libation-Bearers, The. See CHOEPHORI.

Liber (Lat. "free"). Roman name for DIONYSUS, often used simply to mean "wine."

Lichas. *Myth.* Companion and herald of Heracles. In Sophocles' *Trachiniae* Lichas leads in the captives from conquered Oechalia and reluctantly confirms the messenger's story that Heracles sacked the city for love of the Oechalian princess Iole. Deianira asks Lichas to give to Heracles the box containing the fatal robe. Later in the play Hyllus reports that Heracles, in his agony, caught the innocent Lichas and hurled him to death on the rocks.

Licinius, Porcius. See PORCIUS LICINIUS.

lictor. One of the attendants who bore the fasces for a Roman official.

Licymnius (Gk. **Likymnios**). *Myth.* Illegitimate son of Electryon and brother of Alcmena. Licymnius assisted his nephew Heracles in various adventures. He gave his name to a lost tragedy by Euripides, which was produced probably about 450 B.C. Of it a half-dozen brief fragments that survive are not enough to show which of Licymnius' adventures furnished the subject. It is, however, likely that the play dealt with Licymnius' son Argeius, who accompanied Heracles on his expedition against Troy. On the way to or from Asia Minor the ship was struck by lightning, and Argeius was half-consumed. Heracles burned the young man's body (the first known cremation) to conceal his fate from his father.

Liguria. Region of Italy along the northwestern coast adjacent to Gaul.

Limnae (Gk. **Limnai**, "swamps" or "marshes"). See ANTHESTERIA.

Linus (Gk. **Linos**). 1. *Myth.* Son of Apollo and the Argive princess Psamathe. The child was eaten by dogs, and his fate was commemorated in an annual festival of lamentation.

2. *Myth.* Musician, son of Amphiaraus and a Muse. Linus, in attempting to teach music to Heracles, corrected the boy harshly and repeatedly. He was killed by his pupil.

Lion, The (Gk. **Leon**). Lost play by Aeschylus. *The Lion* was most probably a satyr play that dealt with the story of Heracles' conquest of the Nemean lion.

Livia. Wife of Drusus, the son of the emperor Tiberius. It was said that, at the instigation of her lover Sejanus, Livia poisoned her husband. The matter came to light after Sejanus' fall, and she was put to death in about A.D. 31.

Livius. See DRUSUS.

Livius Andronicus, Lucius. Founder of Roman literary drama (c. 284– c. 204 B.C.). Brought to Rome as a captive after the war with Tarentum (272 B.C.), Livius became the slave of a certain Lucius Livius. When his master freed him, he taught school, and it was probably in this connection that he translated the *Odyssey* into Latin. In 240 B.C., during the games celebrating the end of the First Punic War, Livius introduced the first Latin adaptation of a Greek comedy and a Greek tragedy. His career as dramatist, director, and producer continued for several decades. Although Livius was also an actor, his voice was so weak that he employed a boy to sing his arias backstage while he went through the motions. In 207 B.C. the College of Playwrights was founded, mainly in his honor. It grew into the College of Poets and met in the specially built Temple of Minerva.

Only fragments are left of Livius' work, and even some of the titles are doubtfully ascribed. Of comedies there are *The Dagger* and *The Gambler;* of tragedies, *Achilles, Aegisthus, Ajax the Whip-Bearer, Andromeda, Danaë, Hermione, Tereus,* and *The Trojan Horse.*

Locris (Gk. **Lokris**). Section of Greece north of Boeotia, extending along the coast opposite northern Euboea. This region was called Opuntian Locris, because it contained the city of Opus, to distinguish it from another Locris on the Corinthian Gulf.

logeion (Gk. "speaking-place"). In the Greek theater, the stage proper, or the "boards"—the raised platform for the actors—as opposed to the orchestra. (See RAISED STAGE.)

Loxias (Gk. "speaker"). Epithet of the Delphic Apollo as speaker of prophecy.

Lucania. Section of Italy at the "instep of the boot," north of Bruttium, the "toe of the boot." Elephants, first seen here by the Romans in the war with King Pyrrhus, were called "Lucanian bulls" or "Lucanian oxen."

Lucifer (Lat.). The morning star.

Lucina. *Myth.* Roman goddess of marriage and childbirth.

Lucretia. Legendary Roman heroine (said to have lived in the late 6th century B.C.). When Lucretia was raped by Sextus, son of King Tarquinius, she committed suicide to prove her virtue. Tarquinius was expelled from Rome with his whole family. Thus ended the Roman monarchy.

ludi (Lat. "games"). Festivals in Rome. The ludi were celebrated by theatrical performances and other entertainments. These festivals were:

Ludi Romani, "Roman Games." The games were held in September, under the direction of the curule aediles (see AEDILES). Beginning in 240 B.C. plays were presented, and beginning in 214 B.C. there were four days of performances.

Ludi Plebei, "Plebeian Games." This festival was held in November, under the direction of the plebeian aediles. It was introduced in 220 B.C., and plays were first staged in about 200 B.C.

Ludi Apollinares, "Games of Apollo." These games were held in July, under the direction of the city praetor. They were introduced in 212 B.C., and plays were presented almost from the beginning.

Ludi Megalenses, "Games of the Great Mother (Cybele)." These games were held in April, under the direction of the curule aediles. They were introduced in 204 B.C., and plays began to be staged ten years later.

The Floralia, "Festival of Flowers." At this celebration there were presented mimes only, and the practice did not begin until 173 B.C.

Although the government gave the directing officials money for play productions, it was never enough. Ambitious politicians gave lavish sums out of their own pockets. They paid the poet for his work, using as intermediary a *dominus gregis* (actors' troupe director), who was afterward given the play as his own property. The best actor was given a palm branch as a prize. Plays were also presented in connection with special ludi given by private individuals. These ludi were funeral, votive, dedicatory, and triumphal.

Luna. Roman deity, the personification of the moon. The Nemean lion and other monsters were thought by some to have fallen to the earth from Luna.

Luxuria. Personification of wealth or luxury. Luxuria appears, with Inopia, "Poverty," in the prologue of Plautus' *Trinummus.*

Lyaeus (Gk. **Lyaios,** "freer" or "loosener"). Epithet of Dionysus.

Lycabettus (Gk. **Lykabettos**). Conical hill to the northeast of Athens.

Lycaon (Gk. **Lykaon**). *Myth.* Son of Ares. Lycaon was killed by Heracles.

Lyceum (Gk. **Lykeion**). Gymnasium near the Temple of Apollo Lyceus in Athens. The Lyceum was later the site of Aristotle's school of philosophy.

Lyceus, Lyceius, or **Lycius** (Gk. **Lykeios** or **Lykios**). Epithet of Apollo as god of wolves (from Gk. *lykos*) or, some think, as god of light (from obsol. Gk. root *lyke*).

Lycia (Gk. **Lykia**). 1. Region near the southwestern corner of Asia Minor. 2. Fountain on the island of Lemnos.

Lycis (Gk. **Lykis**). Playwright of Aristophanes' time. In *The Frogs* (line 14 ff.) Aristophanes gibed at Lycis for his use of comic clichés. None of Lycis' works were extant even in later classical times.

Lycomedes (Gk. **Lykomedes**). *Myth.* King of Scyros and father of Deidamia. When Achilles was in concealment at the court of Lycomedes, he made love to Deidamia, who bore him Neoptolemus.

Lycon (Gk. **Lykon**). 1. Athenian of Aristophanes' day. Lycon was accused by writers of Old Comedy of being a traitor. He was one of the indicters of Socrates. His wife, Rhodia, was notorious for her debauchery.

2. Actor (4th century B.C.). Lycon was considered unmatched in comedy. He was a favorite of Alexander the Great and performed in Tyre and Susa during the conqueror's Asian campaigns.

Lycophron (Gk. **Lykophron**). Tragic playwright, member of the Alexandrian Pleiad (see PLEIAD, TRAGIC). Born before 310 B.C., Lycophron probably lived to a considerable age. He died, while acting in a tragedy, *cothurnatus,* "with his buskins on." Of the forty or sixty plays that he wrote, very few fragments and only twenty titles survive. Most have mythical subjects, for example: *Aeolus, Laius, Oedipus.* A few, however, such as *Men of Marathon, The Orphan,* and *The Allies,* may represent historical material. One or two critical works on comedy are also mentioned in ancient writings, as well as a satyr play, *Menedemus.* There is a dispute whether the author of the extant poem *Alexandra* was this Lycophron or a different one.

Lycormas. Older name for the Evenus River in Aetolia.

Lycurgeia (Gk. **Lykourgeia**). Lost tetralogy by Aeschylus. The *Lycurgeia* consisted of the following: (a) A tragedy, *The Edonians,* based on the opposition of Lycurgus to Dionysus (see LYCURGUS 1). (b) A tragedy, *Bassarae*, or *The Bassarids*, which told of Orpheus' disregard of Dionysus in favor of Helios, whom he worshiped under the name of Apollo. For his disbelief Orpheus was torn to pieces by the foxskin-wearing maenads of Thrace, the Bassarae, as he climbed Mt. Pangaeum to greet the rising sun. (c) A tragedy, *The Youths*, of which the fragments are too scanty for reconstruction. (d) A satyr play, *Lycurgus*, also represented by very scanty fragments.

Lycurgus (Gk. **Lykourgos**). 1. *Myth.* King of the Thracian Edonians. Opposing the worship of Dionysus, Lycurgus imprisoned maenads and satyrs and chased the god into the sea. For this he was driven mad and, mistaking his own son for a vine, chopped him up with an axe. Later Lycurgus was immured in a cave or, according to another version, torn to pieces by horses. *Lycurgus* was the title of a lost play by Aeschylus. (See LYCURGEIA.)

2. Legendary Spartan reformer. Lycurgus was the founder of the Spartan military constitution and his name became a byword for sternness and austerity.

3. Athenian of Aristophanes' time. This Lycurgus was nicknamed "Ibis," either because he was of Egyptian origin or because he had thin legs.

4. Famous Athenian orator and statesman (c. 396–325 B.C.). Lycurgus was noted for his opposition to Philip of Macedonia and for his management of finances. He rebuilt the great Theater of Dionysus, authorized standard texts of the works of the three great tragedians (Aeschylus, Sophocles, and Euripides), and erected their statues in the theater.

Lycus (Gk. **Lykos**). 1. *Myth.* Uncle of ANTIOPE (2). When Antiope was seduced by Zeus, Lycus was charged by her father to punish the young woman. He accordingly carried her by force from Sicyon, where she had taken refuge, and abandoned her to the cruelty of his wife, Dirce. After Antiope's sons, Amphion and Zethus, had killed Dirce, they dethroned Lycus.

2. *Myth.* Usurper of the throne of Thebes. Lycus secured the kingdom for himself by murdering Creon. In Euripides' *Heracles* he threatens to kill Megara, Heracles' wife, and her children; in Seneca's *Hercules Furens* he tries to force Megara to become his wife. In both plays the hero returns unexpectedly and kills Lycus.

3. *Myth.* Brother of Aegeus. The latter banished Lycus to Messenia. There he became skilled at soothsaying and the law. After visiting Asia Minor, where he gave his name to Lycia, Lycus returned to Athens and forced Theseus into exile. He became the patron-hero of Athenian law courts.

Lydia. Central section of the western coast of Asia Minor. The Lydians were once the rulers of a widespread empire. After their defeat by the Persians, they became notorious for their cowardice and their luxurious mode of living.

Lydias. River in Macedonia.

Lynceus (Gk. **Lynkeus**). 1. *Myth.* Son of Aegyptus. Lynceus was the only one of the fifty bridegrooms of the DANAÏDES to be spared on the wedding night. (See also DANAÏD TETRALOGY: *The Egyptians*.)

2. *Myth.* One of the Argonauts. Lynceus was noted for his keen eyesight.

3. *Myth.* Brother of Idas. (See LEUCIPPUS.)

Lyrnessus or **Lyrnesus** (Gk. **Lyrnesos**). City in Mysia, the home of Briseis.

Lysicles. Athenian military commander. Lysicles was a friend of Pericles. After the latter's death he married Aspasia. Lysicles was killed in Caria in 428 or 427 B.C.

Lysistrata (Gk. **Lysistrate**). Extant comedy by Aristophanes (produced under the name of his friend Callistratus in 411 B.C.). Translations: Benjamin B. Rogers, 1924; Arthur S. Way, 1934; Henry B. Lister, 1938; Charles T. Murphy, 1944; Doros Alastos, 1953; Dudley Fitts, 1954; Patric Dickinson, 1957; Robert Henning Webb, 1963; Douglass Parker, 1964.

S C E N E. Athens, near the Acropolis.

S U M M A R Y. As Lysistrata ("Disband-the-Army") impatiently awaits the women she has called together from all parts of Greece, she explains to her friend Calonice that she has devised a plan to save the country. The women begin to stream in, among them Myrrhine, another Athenian, and the Spartan Lampito. When Lysistrata asks the women whether they want to end the war that has taken their husbands from their sides, she receives an emphatic yes for an answer. She then reveals her scheme: to deprive the menfolk of sex until the fighting stops. Although the women are at first reluctant to make the sacrifice, they are eventually persuaded to take an oath—on penalty of drinking water instead of wine—that they will make themselves as alluring as possible, but will deny themselves to their husbands; if taken by force, they will not cooperate in any way.

Meanwhile, the older women have accomplished their assignment of occupying the Acropolis, where they are joined by Lysistrata and the others. A Chorus of Old Men now appear. They are carrying sticks and fire pots and intend to smoke the women out of the Acropolis, but their preparations are interrupted by a Chorus of Old Women armed with pitchers of water. After the two groups trade insults and epithets, the women pour water over their adversaries. Just then a Magistrate enters, accompanied by four Scythian policemen, whom he orders to pry open the locked doors of the treasury so that he can withdraw funds to hire rowers for the galleys.

After the doors are opened, Lysistrata and some of her followers emerge. The Magistrate tries to arrest them, but the fearless matrons completely rout the Scythians. Lysistrata informs the Magistrate that henceforth the women will administer the treasure so as to prevent the wars and other evils provoked by men's folly; the men can take on the domestic chores. After enduring a great deal of abuse, the Magistrate angrily stalks off. The Old Men express their amazement at the women's insolence and perfidy, but the Chorus of Women retort that they contribute their children to the state, while the foolish men merely squander its wealth. Only a short time elapses, however, before the women try to slip away from the Acropolis; one informs Lysistrata that she must attend to her wool, another to her flax, and a third inserts a helmet under her tunic to convince Lysistrata that she is about to give birth at any moment. Lysistrata manages to rally her followers by producing an oracle stating that only birds which band together will be successful.

As Cinesias, the husband of Myrrhine, approaches, laboring under considerable strain from his enforced chastity, Lysistrata instructs Myrrhine to tease him but not to yield. The seemingly complaisant Myrrhine discards her garments, but keeps going off, first to fetch a bed, then a mattress, a pillow, a coverlet, and a bit of perfume; finally she runs back to the Acropolis, leaving her husband with his passion unsatisfied. He rushes off in search of a harlot. A harried Spartan Herald now arrives to report the great distress in that land on account of the frigidity of the Spartan wives; it seems that the women will not allow their husbands to touch them until peace is restored to Greece. Realizing that a nationwide conspiracy is afoot, the Magistrate requests that ambassadors be sent from Sparta so that a settlement can be arranged. The Choruses of Old Men and Women make a truce of their own. When the Spartan emissaries meet with their Athenian counterparts, Lysistrata scolds them for making war on one another while the enemies of Greece are nearby with their armies. She invites them to the Acropolis, where they can exchange pledges and be entertained and feasted by their wives. After the banquet, Spartans and Athenians, each man with his wife, dance and sing to celebrate the restoration of peace.

C O M M E N T A R Y. In *Lysistrata* there is comparatively little personal or political satire. Aristophanes' emphasis on Panhellenic reconciliation was probably due to outward circumstances at the time that he wrote the play—the utter failure of the Sicilian expedition and the temporary overthrow of the Athenian democratic constitution. His sense of comic absurdity remained, however, unimpaired. The play's action exhibits undiminished high spirits and its plot has unusual tightness. The latter feature may have contributed to its continuing popularity, but the main attraction has doubtless been its unabashed sexuality.

In rival plays and adaptations (including Aristophanes' own adaptation in *Ecclesiazusae*) the main point, or rather the main counterpoint, is usually missed: love versus war, creation versus destruction, the battle between the sexes as the solvent of the battles between nations. Sex in all its absurdity is, after all, in all senses, what holds the human race together. In *Lysistrata* the women's sex strike reaches its logical conclusion when they seize the Acropolis, both a military fortress and the epitome of civilization. This logical conclusion can be dissolved only by less-than-logical appetites, with whose triumph the bonds of society are re-bound.

Lyssa (Gk. "madness"). Personification of madness. Lyssa was called the child of Uranus and Nyx.

M

Macaria (Gk. **Makaria**). *Myth.* Only daughter of Heracles. Macaria's mother was Deianira. In Euripides' *Heraclidae* Macaria (though she is not named) offers herself as a human sacrifice so that her brothers and the Athenians may successfully repel the assault of Eurystheus.

Maccus. Stock character in ATELLAN FARCE.

Machon. Writer of New Comedy in Alexandria (3rd century B.C.). Of Machon's plays only two titles have survived, *Ignorance* and *The Letter*. He is best known for *Chreiai*, a collection of clever sayings and anecdotes, mostly about courtesans.

Macistus (Gk. **Makistos**). Mountain usually identified with the modern Kandhili on Euboea.

Mad Hercules. See HERCULES FURENS.

Maeander or **Meander** (Gk. **Maiandros**). River flowing through Phrygia and Caria into the Aegean Sea near Miletus.

maenads (Gk. **mainades**, "madwomen"). Female followers of Dionysus. Possessed by the spirit of the god and inspired by the music of flute and tambourine, the maenads danced violently with heads thrown back and hair flying. They were wreathed with ivy and carried the thyrsus.

Maenalus (Gk. **Mainalos**). Mountain in Arcadia.

Maeonia (Gk. **Maionia**). Northeastern section of Lydia.

Maeotis (Gk. **Maiotis**). Inlet on the northeast shore of the Black Sea. Called Lake Maeotis by the ancients, it is now known as the Sea of Azov.

Magar, Magara or **Megara.** Suburb of Carthage, later considered a quarter of the city and called New City. Magar was noted for its beautiful gardens.

Magnes. One of the earlier writers of Old Comedy (active c. 480–c. 450 B.C.). According to Aristophanes (*The Knights*, line 518 ff.), Magnes won many dramatic contests, but was ignored in his old age. Of his plays only a half-dozen lines and a few titles remain. Examples are: *The Birds, The Gallflies, Dionysus, The Herb-Gatherer.*

Magnesia. Region along the coastline of Thessaly, terminating in the peninsula that forms the eastern side of the Pagasaean Gulf.

Magus or **Magian** (Gk. **Magos**). Member of a Median tribe.

Maia. *Myth.* Daughter of Atlas and mother of Hermes by Zeus.

Malea (adj. Malean or Maliac). Promontory at the southeastern tip of the Peloponnesus.

Malis or **Melis.** Small region at the western end of the Maliac or Malean Gulf. The latter is an inlet west of the upper end of Euboea.

Manducus. Stock character in later ATELLAN FARCE. Manducus developed from the character Bucco of earlier times. He wore a mask with enormous teeth.

Manto. *Myth.* Daughter of Tiresias. Like her father, Manto was adept at soothsaying. She often led her blind father around and described the omens to him. In this role she appears in Seneca's *Oedipus.*

Marathon. Town near the Attic coast northeast of Athens. The Persian invasion forces were defeated here in 490 B.C.

Mardi or **Mardians** (Gk. **Mardoi**). Tribe inhabiting the mountains south of the Caspian Sea.

Mariandyni (Gk. **Mariandynoi**). Tribe in Bithynia on the Black Sea. The Mariandyni were famous for their dirges.

Maricas (Gk. **Marikas**). Lost comedy by Eupolis.

Marmarica. Section of North Africa west of Egypt, now the northeast section of Libya.

Marmor Parium. The "Marble of Paros." On it is an inscription listing important events in Greek history from mythical times to about 263 B.C., including the dramatic victories and death dates of many playwrights. There are pieces of this marble in various museums.

Maron or **Maro.** *Myth.* Priest of Apollo in Thrace. Maron was a son, or grandson, of Dionysus. He presented Odysseus with the wine that was later used to make Polyphemus drunk.

Mars. *Myth.* Roman god of war, identified with the Greek ARES. Whereas Ares often appeared in an unfavorable light, Mars was revered by the Romans as father of Romulus and Remus and ancestor of the race. The month of March was named after him, and on the Calends of Mars (March 1) there was an important festival of Roman matrons called Quinquatrus Martis.

Marsyas. See MIDAS.

masks. Because masks were widely worn in primitive ritual, and because they were a prominent feature of the Dionysus cult in particular, their use in Greek tragedy, comedy, and satyr play was a natural development. In early times, celebrants of vintage festivals smeared their faces with grape juice; it was said that Thespis, the originator of Greek tragedy, did the same. Later, white lead was used and, still later, a covering of linen. Linen continued as the common material for theatrical masks, though thin wood and cork are occasionally mentioned in ancient writings.

It is thought that by the time of Aeschylus (who was called, with little justification, the introducer of masks), and perhaps due to his efforts, dramatic masks were fairly elaborate and fairly standardized. The spectator in the large Greek theater was thus able to tell at a glance what sort of character was performing. According to Pollux, tragedians had at their disposal twenty-eight different types of masks. Actors in satyr play used only four, and doubtless there were special masks for unusual characters, such as blind prophets and mythological monsters. In Old Comedy a variety of animal masks must have been worn, as well as masks representing stock comic figures.

It was, however, in New Comedy that there was the highest development of specialization and stereotype. Pollux lists forty-four standard New Comedy masks: nine kinds of old men (for example, the grandfather and the pimp), eleven kinds of young men (for example, the bumpkin, the lover, the parasite, and the soldier), seven kinds of slaves (for example, the old slave and the tricky baldhead), and seventeen kinds of women, including six varieties of prostitutes.

As for Roman drama, ancient evidence seems to indicate that masks were not used at first and were not brought in until shortly before 100 B.C. Yet some scholars have argued, first, that it would have been strange to borrow Greek plays in Greek dress and leave off the masks; second, that certain phrases in Plautus and Terence imply the use of masked actors; and third, that the different ancient sources contradict one another. The problem is among the most baffling in literary history, and so far no consensus has emerged.

Massagetae. Tribe living in central Asia, north of the Oxus River.

Massicus. Mountain in Campania famous for its wine.

Massilia. Greek colony on the southern coast of Gaul—modern Marseille.

mechane (Gk. "device"; in Lat. *machina*). Large crane, "the machine," used to represent characters as flying or gods as appearing in the sky.

Mecisteus (Gk. **Mekisteus**). *Myth.* Father of Euryalus (2).

Medea (Gk. **Medeia**). *Myth.* Daughter of King Aeëtes of Colchis and granddaughter of Helios the sun god. In common with many descendants of the sun and in conformity with the reputation of Colchis, Medea had great ability in witchcraft. She fell in love with Jason when he came to get the golden fleece. After making Jason swear to marry her, Medea gave him a magic balm that kept him invulnerable in the trials prescribed by Aeëtes. She then led him to the golden fleece and charmed its serpent guardian to sleep so that Jason was able to seize his prize. Medea afterward escaped with the Greeks in the *Argo*. To delay her father's pursuit, she killed her young brother Absyrtus and dropped pieces of his body at intervals in the water. While Aeëtes gathered them, the *Argo* slipped away.

After the Argonauts had returned to Jason's native Iolcus, Medea brought about the murder of PELIAS. She and Jason were consequently banished from the city. When, after some years of exile in Corinth, Jason proposed to divorce Medea and marry the Corinthian princess Creusa (also called Glauce), Medea caused the deaths of Creusa and her father Creon, afterward killing her own children. This story is told in both Euripides' and Seneca's *Medea*. Forced to flee from Corinth, Medea took refuge in Athens with King Aegeus, whom she married. When her plot to poison THESEUS miscarried, she again fled. For Medea's last adventure, see MEDUS.

Medea (Gk. **Medeia**). Extant tragedy by Euripides. *Medea* was produced in 431 B.C. with Euripides' *Philoctetes, Dictys,* and *The Reapers.* It was awarded last place. Translations: Edward P. Coleridge, 1891; Arthur S. Way, 1919; Augustus T. Murray, 1931; Robert C. Trevelyan, 1939; Rex Warner, 1944; D. W. Lucas, 1950; Peter D. Arnott, 1951; Philip Vellacott, 1963. Adaptations and works influenced by *Medea:* Neophron, lost play; Ennius, *Medea Exul* (lost); Ovid, lost play; Seneca, *Medea;* George Buchanan, *Medea* (in Latin), 1544; Pierre Corneille, *Médée,* 1635; Friedrich Wilhelm Gotter, *Medea* (Cherubini's opera was based on this play), 1775; Franz Grillparzer, *Medea,* 1821; Henri René Lenormand, *Asie,* 1931; Jean Anouilh, *Medea,* 1946; Robinson Jeffers, *Medea,* 1946.

S C E N E. Corinth, before the house of Medea.

S U M M A R Y. Emerging from the house, Medea's old Nurse laments in the prologue, "If only the trees had never fallen on the mountain and the ship *Argo* had never been built nor gone to Colchis to bring Medea to Greece!" Then Medea, daughter of Aeëtes, king of Colchis, would not have fallen in love with Jason and helped him to steal the golden fleece, even though it meant murdering her own brother. Returning with Jason to his native Iolcus, Medea caused the death of his uncle Pelias, who had unjustly deprived him of the throne. For this crime the two were banished from Iolcus and found a haven in Corinth. But now Jason is deserting Medea and their children to marry the daughter of the king of Corinth, Creon. Medea has withdrawn into her house, where she eats nothing, weeps, and broods over vengeance, refusing even to see her two boys.

The boys enter with their Tutor (guardian-slave, *paidagogos*), who brings word that the king has just decreed banishment for Medea and her children. Medea's cries are heard in the house as the Nurse discusses her plight with a Chorus of Corinthian Women. Medea herself appears and delivers to them a speech on the wrongs of women: they must buy a husband with a dowry; must marry a man chosen for them, knowing little whether he is good or bad; must keep to the house while their husband roams abroad. As for their freedom from danger, she declares, "I would rather stand in battle thrice than labor once in childbirth." And to add to her misery, Medea is not only a woman but a foreigner in an alien land, with no one to turn to in her extremity.

King Creon draws near and orders Medea to leave Corinth with her children at once; he readily admits that he fears her resentment and her cunning. All Medea's pleas for mercy are unavailing, but she gains a reprieve of one day by appealing to Creon's affection for his own child and begging that she be given time to provide for her sons. As soon as the king is out of sight Medea reveals her true intent: to murder Jason, his bride, and Creon by means of poisons, in the uses of which she is skilled. Her remaining problem is to find a place of refuge for herself.

Medea's next visitor is her husband, who declares that her own evil tongue and stubborn temper have brought the sentence of exile upon her. In a seething reproach for his ingratitude, Medea reminds Jason that she has abandoned her family and country for his sake; now all the world's doors are barred to her.

Jason's retort is simply that she should be grateful for having been made acquainted with Greek civilization and for having won fame through him. With a final offer of money and aid, he withdraws.

A third visitor to Medea is Aegeus, king of Athens. Having consulted the Delphic oracle about his childlessness, he is on his way to Troezen, whose king may be able to help him unravel the god's response. Medea wins Aegeus' sympathy with a recital of her wrongs and promises that with the aid of her magic powers he will be able to have sons. In return he vows to receive Medea in Athens and never to expel her from his realm.

Now that Medea is assured of a haven, she can put into execution her plot against Jason and his bride. She will send Creon's daughter a fine robe and a golden diadem on which poison has been smeared. Medea's one bitter grief is that she must also kill her own children, for she is determined that Jason's house shall be totally destroyed. Sending for Jason, she puts on an air of humility and gains his acquiescence in a plan to send the children with the gifts to Creon's daughter so that, by ingratiating themselves, they may have their banishment revoked.

When they are gone, Medea, torn between maternal love and hatred for Jason, gives voice to the conflict that rages within her. One of Jason's men rushes in and warns Medea to flee: the Corinthian princess, having put on the robe and crown, was struck with agony and enwrapped in flame. As her father embraced her, he too was consumed. Realizing that she must now kill her children to save them from a worse death, Medea enters the house. The children's pleas for help are heard, but the Chorus cannot save them; they can only wonder at a woman who can murder her own offspring. Jason runs in with his servants to capture the murderess, but the doors are barred. Medea appears on the roof in a dragon-drawn chariot, a gift of her grandfather Helios, the sun. In the chariot are the bodies of the dead boys. After exchanging insults with Jason, she says that she, not he, will bury the children and institute rituals in their memory. Leaving her husband broken and despairing, Medea flies away in her chariot.

COMMENTARY. One might say that the quintessence of Ibsenism first appeared on the Western stage with Euripides' *Medea*. Here, if anywhere, it is demonstrated that simpleminded ethical judgments will not pass muster. The play is not merely a deliberate assault on the fatuously complacent convictions of its audience: it is a deliberately treacherous assault, so constructed as to lure the philistine into an emotional and philosophical ambush.

It is evident why Euripides became for the Greeks an object both of excited interest and of aversion. Even Aristotle fell into the trap with his famous criticism that Aegeus was dragged into the story as a kind of extraneous *deus ex machina*. At that point in the play, the audience must have felt that Medea would go away happily to Athens and they themselves would go home feeling cheerful. But instead of a happy ending there is child murder—in an episode that prolongs the play beyond normal length and that may have been Euripides' own invention. The murderess then makes her escape, but the spectator is left with nagging problems.

The Greek playgoer must have asked himself: What is the justification for my pride in being a civilized Greek, when Jason's civilization is the very thing that evokes Medea's barbarism? What are the claims of love, and what are the conditions of social justice? How far can retaliation against social injustice be justified? How are Medea's motives to be evaluated? With the enactment of the struggle in Medea's breast between her feelings as spurned wife and as loving mother the audience was presented with the first complete revelation of inner conflict in world literature.

The plays of Euphorion, the contest winner in 431 B.C., are gone; the trilogy submitted by Sophocles, who won second place, is unknown. The outraged feelings of the judges probably led them to award *Medea* last place. Posterity has awarded it immortality.

Medea (Gk. **Medeia**). Extant tragedy by Seneca, based largely on the *Medea* of Euripides. Translations: Frank Justus Miller, 1916; Moses Hadas, 1956.

S C E N E. Corinth, the courtyard of Jason's house.

S U M M A R Y. As Medea calls all the curses in heaven, earth, and the underworld upon the head of Jason, who has deserted her for a Corinthian princess, the Chorus enter singing a marriage hymn. Creon, king of Corinth, reveals that, fearing the guile and cruelty of Medea, he had wanted to put her to death but had been prevailed upon by Jason to spare her life. Now he orders her to leave Corinth at once; against his better judgment, however, he grants her the rest of the day so that she may take leave of her sons. Later Medea tells Jason that she wishes to take the children with her, but he refuses, declaring that they are his only solace. Thus he discloses to her his most vulnerable spot.

Although Medea tells Jason that she no longer harbors any ill-feeling against him, as soon as she is alone she begins to plan her revenge by calling for a robe and necklace which she will have her children present to Jason's bride. But first, before the altar of Hecate, Medea asks the gods to endow the robe and necklace with magical, death-dealing properties. She soon learns that her plot has been successful: a Messenger reports that her gifts have caused the deaths of Creon and his daughter and that the royal palace has been consumed by a fire that is now threatening the city.

To make her vengeance complete, Medea strengthens her resolution to kill her children. After she has slain one of them, Jason and an angry crowd burst into the courtyard, but Medea eludes them, appearing out of reach on the roof with the dead body and the remaining child. She kills her second son and throws both bodies down to Jason, then flies away in her dragon-drawn chariot.

C O M M E N T A R Y. Seneca was not interested in the ethical questions raised by Euripides, nor in his casuistry—to use the word in the old sense. The audience is not particularly invited to weigh Medea's case against Jason's, to balance Medea's motives one against another, or to consider the problem of whether social injustice should be privately rectified. Playgoers are instead treated to some stunning passages of poetic richness and some theatrically exciting displays of passion. In the latter Seneca falls into few of his clichés. These passages could, however, be imagined as the result of Medea's magic, since she has never made an appearance in art, either in ancient or in modern times, without exercising a powerful effect.

Media. Inland region of Asia, north of Persia. To the Greeks the Medes were indistinguishable from the Persians, and the Persian wars were sometimes called the "Median wars."

Medus (Gk. **Medos**). *Myth.* Son of Medea and Aegeus. When Medea fled from Athens after Theseus' arrival, Medus went with her, but the two became separated in Asia. Medus wandered to Colchis, which was ruled by Perses, who had dethroned his brother, Medea's father Aeëtes. Perses was, however, fearful that some descendant of Aeëtes would unseat him. Knowing this, Medus pretended to be Hippotes, son of Creon of Corinth, and alleged that he was seeking revenge on Medea for the deaths of his father and sister.

When a famine arose in the land, Medea, having returned home, and having disguised herself as a priestess of Artemis, promised to end the dearth. Her remedy was the sacrifice of Hippotes, who she had heard was in the palace. Medus was made ready for sacrifice and brought out, but at this point mother and son recognized each other. Medea then gave the sacrificial sword to her son, who killed Perses, took over the kingdom himself, and called it Media. The foregoing story is the plot of Pacuvius' lost tragedy *Medus*, which was probably based on an unknown Greek play.

Medusa (Gk. **Medousa**). *Myth.* Chief of the GORGONS. Medusa was beheaded by Perseus.

Megabazus (Gk. **Megabazos**). Name of several Persian generals and satraps (governors of provinces).

Megaera (Gk. **Megaira**). *Myth.* One of the three Erinyes, or Furies. Megaera appears, with the ghost of Tantalus, at the beginning of Seneca's *Thyestes*.

Megara. 1. City of the city-state Megaris. Megara lay next to Attica on the west, occupying the upper part of the Corinthian Isthmus. It was noted for its dramatic farce, which consisted of crudely humorous and realistic sketches. Megarian farce had some influence on Old Comedy.

2. *Myth.* Wife of Heracles. In his madness Heracles killed his children by Megara, then killed his wife too. She appears in Euripides' *Heracles* and in Seneca's *Hercules Furens*.

Megareus. *Myth.* Son of Creon and Eurydice. Megareus was killed while defending Thebes against the Argives led by Adrastus in the expedition of the Seven against Thebes.

Meges. *Myth.* Nephew of Odysseus and outstanding warrior with the Greeks at Troy.

Melanion, Meilanion, or **Milanion.** *Myth.* Husband of Atalanta and sometimes said to be the father of Parthenopaeus. Atalanta, the swiftest of runners, consented to marry only the suitor who could win against her in a foot race. Melanion therefore enlisted the help of Aphrodite, who gave him three golden apples. When, during the race, the young man dropped the apples, Atalanta stopped to pick them up and lost to him. After their marriage, the couple lay together in a place sacred to Zeus, who punished them by turning them into lions.

Melanion was probably, in early myth, a male counterpart of Atalanta, that is, one who was passionately fond of hunting and who shunned the opposite sex. He was later confused with Hippomenes, who was also said to be Atalanta's husband and the father of Parthenopaeus.

Melanippe. *Myth.* Daughter of Aeolus and Hippo, Chiron's daughter. While her father was away from home, Melanippe bore twins to Poseidon. She concealed them in a stable, where they were suckled by cows. The differing stories of what happened after Aeolus' return formed the subjects of two lost plays by Euripides: *Melanippe Captive* and *Melanippe the Wise*.

Melanippe Captive (Gk. **Melanippe Desmotis**). Lost play by Euripides. A parchment leaf and papyrus containing lines from *Melanippe Captive* were published early in the twentieth century. When this text is added to the extant fragments quoted in ancient writings, more than a hundred lines are furnished. There is, however, still much disagreement about the plot. This much is certain:

Melanippe was imprisoned for her fall from virtue (see MELANIPPE). Her twin sons, Aeolus and Boeotus, were exposed but were eventually adopted by the king of Metapontum in Italy. Theano, the queen, formed a plot to kill them, but it failed. After the twins had liberated Melanippe, she learned their identity and revealed that she was their mother. Poseidon appeared at the play's end, designating the young men ancestors of the Aeolians and Boeotians. Somewhere in the play was a famous speech maintaining that women are superior to men.

Melanippe the Wise (Gk. **Melanippe he Sophe**). Lost play by Euripides (produced before 411 B.C.). Johannes Diaconus' *Commentary on Hermogenes,* recovered early in the twentieth century, gave a summary of *Melanippe the Wise* and quoted twenty-two lines from its prologue. The plot was as follows:

When Aeolus returned (see MELANIPPE), the twin sons of his daughter Melanippe were brought to him, with the report that they had been found suckled by cows. Thinking that the cows must have given birth to the children, Aeolus determined to burn such monstrous offspring. They were given to Melanippe to deck out for the sacrifice. After failing to persuade her father not to believe in omens and to spare the children, Melanippe admitted that they were hers. She herself was saved from death only by the intervention of a *deus ex machina*—either Hippo, her mother, or Poseidon, her lover.

Melanippus (Gk. **Melanippos**). *Myth.* Theban hero in the war of the Seven against Thebes. Melanippus was killed by Amphiaraus and his brain was eaten by Tydeus. It is thought that perhaps Accius used this story in a lost play.

Melanthius (Gk. **Melanthios**). Writer of tragedies (late 5th century B.C.). Melanthius was a great-nephew of Aeschylus and the brother of Morsimus. Only a short fragment of his *Medea* (c. 421 B.C.) is extant. Melanthius was a favorite target of ridicule for almost all the writers of Old Comedy. In Archippus' *Fishes* he was bound and thrown into the pond as fish food.

Meleager (Gk. **Meleagros**). *Myth.* Son of King Oeneus and Queen Althaea of Calydon. (According to some, Meleager was Althaea's son by Ares.) When Meleager was a week old, the Fates appeared to his mother and revealed that his life would end when a certain piece of wood on the hearth was entirely consumed. Althaea beat out the fire and locked the wood away in a chest.

After Meleager was grown, King Oeneus summoned heroes from all over Greece to rid the land of a monster boar sent by Artemis because Oeneus had slighted her at the sacrifice. Among those who answered the king's summons was the maiden huntress Atalanta. Meleager fell in love with Atalanta and at the killing of the boar awarded her the animal's skin. When his mother's brothers criticized him for giving the trophy to a woman, there ensued a brawl in which he killed them. At this deed, the angry Althaea threw the enchanted piece of wood into the flames, and when it burned away, Meleager fell dead.

Sophocles' lost *Meleager* was apparently based on the Homeric version of this story (*Iliad*, Book IX). According to Homer, a war broke out between the Calydonians and the Curetes (Aetolians) over the hide of the slain boar. After killing his uncles in battle, Meleager was cursed by his mother. He consequently withdrew from the fight until the city of Calydon was about to be taken. At that juncture, his wife, Cleopatra, appealed to him. Meleager went out and saved the city, but he himself was killed. At the end of Sophocles' play, Cleopatra and Althaea hanged themselves and were changed into guinea fowl.

Of Euripides' lost *Meleager* about sixty lines survive. It is clear, from these fragments, that its plot centered around the Calydonian hunt, Meleager's love for Atalanta, and the conflict between Meleager and his mother.

Meletus (Gk. **Meletos**). Writer of tragedies (5th century B.C.). Meletus was ridiculed by Aristophanes in *The Frogs* (line 1302). It is not clear whether it was he or his father who was one of the accusers at Socrates' trial in 399 B.C.

Melicertes or **Melicerta** (Gk. **Melikertes**). *Myth.* Son of INO. When Melicertes' mother leaped with him into the sea, he became the sea god Palaemon. (See also ATHAMAS.)

Melite. Attic deme. In Melite there was a well-known temple to Heracles.

Melos. Island in the southwestern Aegean Sea. In 415 B.C. Melos was blockaded by the Athenians under Nicias. When, at last, it surrendered as a result of famine, its men were killed and its women and children were sold into slavery.

Memnon. *Myth.* Prince of Ethiopia. Memnon was the son of Tithonus and the dawn goddess Eos and the nephew of Priam. In the Trojan War he came to the aid of the Trojans. After killing Antilochus, Nestor's son, Memnon was faced with Achilles. While Zeus weighed the lots of the two heroes on the Scales of Fate, their goddess mothers, Eos and Thetis, stood by in suspense. Memnon lost, but he was granted immortality after death.

Aeschylus' lost tragedy *Memnon* was based on this myth. Sophocles' lost *Memnon* was probably the same as his *Ethiopians*.

Memphis. Capital of ancient Egypt.

Menaechmi (Lat. **The Menaechmus Twins** or **The Twin Menaechmi** or **The Brothers Menaechmus**). Extant comedy by Plautus of uncertain date (conjectures range from 215 to 186 B.C.). *Menaechmi* was adapted from a doubtfully ascribed Greek play, perhaps by Posidippus. Translations: Henry T. Riley, 1852; Benjamin B. Rogers, 1908; Paul Nixon, 1917; Edward C. Weist and Richard W. Hyde, 1942; Frank O. Copley, 1949; Palmer Bovie, 1962; Lionel Casson, 1963; Samuel Lieberman, 1964; E. F. Watling, 1965. Adaptations and works influenced by *Menaechmi*: Giangiorgio Trissino, *I Simillimi*, 1547; Shakespeare, *The Comedy of Errors*, 1592–93; Jean de Rotrou, *Les Ménechmes*, 1636; Carlo Goldoni, *I Due Gemelli Veneziani*, 1748; Rodgers, Hart, and Abbott, *The Boys from Syracuse*, 1938.

S C E N E. Epidamnus (Dyrrhachium).

S U M M A R Y. The speaker of the prologue tells the audience that, many years earlier, a Syracusan merchant took Menaechmus, one of his identical twin sons, to Tarentum. There the boy was lost in a crowd at a festival and subsequently abducted by a rich, childless merchant of Epidamnus. Menaechmus' father died in despair and the twins' grandfather memorialized the lost boy by changing the remaining brother's name from Sosicles to Menaechmus (II). When the Epidamnian, who had adopted Menaechmus I, died, he left him a large fortune. As the play opens, Menaechmus I is living in Epidamnus with his wife; his twin has been searching for him for six years.

Peniculus, a parasite, enters first, declaring his intent to sponge on Menaechmus I for a meal. The latter, leaving his house with one of his wife's dresses under his coat and cursing her for prying, tells the audience he has stolen the dress for his mistress, Erotium. Peniculus receives promise of his meal. Erotium appears, takes the dress delightedly, and promises to prepare a dinner for her lover. As Menaechmus I and Peniculus leave for the forum, Erotium sends her cook, Cylindrus, for provisions.

Meanwhile, Menaechmus II has reached Epidamnus with his slave, Messenio, who warns his master of the town's swindlers, spongers, and women. First Cylindrus, then Erotium, take Menaechmus II for his twin. Thinking both mad, he holds back, but then decides to make the most of his opportunities. He filches Erotium's new dress, promising to have it embroidered for her, and despite Messenio's concern, enters her house.

On his way back from the forum where he has lost Menaechmus I, Peniculus sees the drunken Menaechmus II leaving Erotium's house with the dress and thinks himself tricked out of a meal. When Menaechmus II insults him, he leaves, promising to inform Menaechmus I's wife about the theft. Just then Erotium's maid brings out a bracelet and tells Menaechmus II to take it to the jeweler. But, congratulating himself on his fortune, Menaechmus II heads for the harbor.

Menaechmus I is charged by his wife and Peniculus with stealing the dress. After feigning ignorance, he admits taking it, but only to lend to Erotium. When his wife demands its return, he goes after it, but Erotium, thinking he is trying to cheat her of both dress and bracelet, angrily closes the door on him.

Menaechmus II passes by with the dress just as his twin's wife is leaving her house. The two shout insults, and she sends for her father and complains; but Menaechmus II denies her charges and feigns madness. Frightened, she goes inside, her father goes for a doctor, and Menaechmus II leaves again for his ship. In his absence, his twin, confused and angry at having been turned out by wife and mistress, is met by his wife's father and the Doctor. He threatens the Doctor, who sends for some slaves to hold him, but Messenio, thinking his master is in danger from robbers, fights them off. Dazed, Menaechmus I goes into Erotium's house for the dress and comes out again. At this point Menaechmus II appears, arguing with Messenio, whom he has just met.

Messenio resolves the play by observing the likeness between the two men and inferring the truth. When the twins' identities are finally revealed, Messenio is given his freedom, and Menaechmus I decides to auction his property and return to Syracuse with his brother.

C O M M E N T A R Y . Hardly a word of censure has ever been uttered against *Menaechmi*. It is universally praised, both in its entirety and in detail. The episode of the Doctor—whose tribe was a traditional target of satire even in ancient Rome—is usually singled out for special commendation. Furthermore, there is general agreement that the play's most famous imitation, *The Comedy of Errors,* is inferior to it. (The latter has the complication of a double set of twins, the identical servants having been borrowed from Plautus' *Amphitryon.*) To be considered the superior of Shakespeare, even in one work, seems accolade enough for any writer.

Menander (Gk. **Menandros**). Most important writer of New Comedy (see COMEDY: *New Comedy*).

L I F E . Menander was born in Athens in 343 or 342 B.C. and died during a swim in the sea between 292 and 290 B.C. He came of a prominent and wealthy family, his uncle being the comic playwright Alexis. Menander's writing career began early: his first comedy, *Anger,* went on the boards in about 324 B.C., and his first dramatic victory (see AGON) came in 315. Menander must have written about three plays a year; he is credited with having produced between 105 and 109 comedies in all.

Little seems to have marred the felicity of the playwright's existence. He was the constant lover of the courtesan Glycera, who had been the mistress of Harpalus, the treasurer of Alexander the Great. His literary reputation was, however, overshadowed by that of Philemon, and he won only eight drama contests. Nevertheless Menander was recognized, after his death, as the leader in the field. His pre-eminence was summed up in the famous saying of the critic Aristophanes: "Menander and Life! Which of you two copied the other?" Quotable lines were gathered from his works to make a collection called *Menander's One-Line Sayings* (758 in number). Until the twentieth century, this collection and the usual random fragments were all that survived.

E X T A N T   W O R K S (see under individual entries). One complete comedy, *Dyskolos* (*The Curmudgeon*), was discovered in 1957. Considerable sections of four others had been found in 1905; their titles are: *The Arbitrants*

(Gk. *Epitrepontes*), *The Hero* (Gk. *Heros*), *Perikeiromene* (*The Girl with Her Hair Cut Short*), and *Samia* (*The Girl from Samos*).

L O S T   W O R K S. Of the following plays fragments survive, or there exists information about them: *Anger* (Gk. *Orge*), *Brotherly Love* (Gk. *Philadelphoi*), *The Brothers* (Gk. *Adelphoi;* there were apparently two different plays by this name), *The Carthaginian* (Gk. *Karchedonios*), *The Changeling* (Gk. *Hypobolimaios*), *The Charioteer* (Gk. *Heniochos*), *The Coppersmiths' Holiday* (Gk. *Chalkeia*), *The Cousins* (Gk. *Anepsioi*), *The Doorkeeper* (Gk. *Thyroros*), *The Double Deceiver* (Gk. *Dis Exapaton*), *Drunkenness* (Gk. *Methe*), *The Eunuch* (Gk. *Eunouchos*), *The False Accuser* (Gk. *Katapseudomenos*), *The Farmer* (Gk. *Georgos*), *The Fishermen* (Gk. *Halieis*), *The Flatterer* (Gk. *Kolax*), *The Ghost* (Gk. *Phasma*), *The Girl from Andros* (Gk. *Andria*), *The Girl from Boeotia* (Gk. *Boiotia*), *The Girl from Cnidus* (Gk. *Knidia*), *The Girl from Leucas* (Gk. *Leukadia*), *The Girl from Olynthus* (Gk. *Olynthia*), *The Girl from Perinthus* (Gk. *Perinthia*), *The Girl in the Arrhephoria* (Gk. *Arrhephoros*), *The Girl Twins* (Gk. *Didymai*), *The Harpist* (Gk. *Kitharistes*), *The Hated Man* (Gk. *Misoumenos*), *The Heiress* (Gk. *Epikleros*), *The Hired Mourner* (Gk. *Karine*), *The Hirer of Mercenaries* (Gk. *Xenologos*), *Hymnis*, *The Imbrians* (Gk. *Imbrioi*), *The Kerchief* (Gk. *Kekryphalos*), *The Ladies' Luncheon* (Gk. *Synaristosai*), *The Man from Ephesus* (Gk. *Ephesios*), *The Man from Sicyon* (Gk. *Sikyonios*), *The Marriage Broker* (Gk. *Demiourgos*), *The Mistress* (Gk. *Pallake*), *The Necklace* (Gk. *Plokion*), *The Noise-Shy Man* (Gk. *Psophodees*), *The Nurse* (Gk. *Titthe*), *Phanium* (Gk. *Phanion*), *The Pilots* (Gk. *Kybernetai*), *The Pitcher* (Gk. *Hydria*), *Poisoned* (Gk. *Koneiazomenai*), *The Priestess* (Gk. *Hiereia*), *The Promiser* (Gk. *Epangellomenos*), *The Pseudo-Heracles* (Gk. *Pseuderakles*), *The Ring* (Gk. *Daktylios*), *The Self-tormentor* (Gk. *Heautontimoroumenos*), *She Who Gets Slapped* (Gk. *Rhapizomene*), *The Shield* (Gk. *Aspis*), *The Shipowner* (Gk. *Naukleros*), *The Slave* (Gk. *Paidion*), *Sold* (Gk. *Poloumenoi*), *The Soldiers* (Gk. *Stratiotai*), *The Stable-Boy* (Gk. *Hippokomos*), *The Superstitious Man* (Gk. *Deisidaimon*), *Thais*, *Thrasyleon*, *The Treasure* (Gk. *Thesauros*), *Trophonios*, *The Widow* (Gk. *Chera*), *The Woman-Hater* (Gk. *Misogynes*), *The Woman Possessed* (Gk. *Theophoroumene*), *The Woman Set Afire* (Gk. *Empimpramene*).

The following are doubtfully ascribed or are little more than titles: *Aphrodisia*, *The Basket-Bearer*, *The Begging Priest*, *The Common-Law Husband*, *The Dagger*, *Dardanus*, *The Dedicated Girl*, *The Deposit*, *The Girl from Thessaly*, *In Service Together*, *The Lawgiver*, *The Love-Sharer*, *The Man-Hater*, *Of the Same Father*, *Self-aggrieved*, *Summoned Beforehand*, *The Suspicious Man*.

C R I T I C I S M. Until there is more text to work on—and recent discoveries encourage hopes—it would be dangerous to judge how well deserved was Menander's ancient fame. *Dyskolos* was, after all, an early play and was never counted among the best. New Comedy as an art form seems, like Western movies, to have rigidified almost at birth. Within its limitations Menander gives the impression of endless ingenuity, a rather surprising avoidance of cliché, an elegant virtuosity, and a kindly and optimistic interest in the vagaries of human behavior.

Menelaus (Gk. **Menelaos**). *Myth.* Son of Atreus and brother of Agamemnon. Having been reared during part of his boyhood by Tyndareos, Menelaus was given the hand of Helen in preference to many other suitors; he also succeeded Tyndareos on the throne of Sparta. All of Menelaus' appearances in extant ancient drama are connected with the Trojan War, and he is nearly always an unsympathetic character.

In Euripides' *Iphigenia at Aulis* Menelaus is the chief advocate of Iphigenia's sacrifice. In Sophocles' *Ajax* he joins with his brother Agamemnon in trying to deprive Ajax of burial rites. In Euripides' *Trojan Women* he is stern toward his erring wife, Helen, but it is obvious that he will not punish her. Only in Euripides' *Helen* does Menelaus win the audience's sympathy, but this is because the play is based on the story that a phantom Helen went to Troy, while the real woman was carried, on Zeus's orders, to Egypt. In Euripides' *Orestes* Menelaus is again an unworthy character, vacillating and untrustworthy. And in Euripides' *Andromache* he joins with his daughter Hermione in cruelly persecuting the heroine.

Menoeceus (Gk. **Menoikeus**). **1.** *Myth.* Father of Creon and Jocasta.

2. *Myth.* Son of Creon. In the war of the Seven against Thebes, Tiresias prophesied that victory could be won only if Menoeceus were sacrificed. Although Creon tried to persuade his son to flee, Menoeceus killed himself at the gates of the city. He appears in this role in Euripides' *Phoenician Women.*

Mercator (Lat. **The Merchant**). Extant comedy by Plautus (date uncertain). *Mercator* was based on Philemon's Greek play *Emporos* (*The Merchant*). Translations: Henry T. Riley, 1852; Paul Nixon, 1930; Charles T. Murphy, 1942.

S C E N E. Athens.

S U M M A R Y. Young Charinus, in a soliloquy that serves as prologue, relates that he has just returned from a business trip to Rhodes, where he was sent by his father, the merchant Demipho, to get him out of the clutches of harlots, pimps, and moneylenders. While away, he acquired and has brought back a slave girl, Pasicompsa, who caught his fancy.

When Demipho espies the girl, he is told that she was bought as a maid for his wife. Falling in love with Pasicompsa himself, he tells his son that she will be unsuitable as a maid and persuades his old friend Lysimachus to purchase her. Pasicompsa is accordingly installed in Lysimachus' house, where Demipho intends to visit her, but Lysimachus' wife returns unexpectedly from the country, discovers her, and threatens divorce.

Charinus, on learning that Pasicompsa has been sold, decides to go into exile. When, however, Demipho is informed that the girl is his son's mistress, he willingly gives her up.

C O M M E N T A R Y. Psychologists might find something sinister in the interest that Plautus shows in father-versus-son rivalries (compare *Bacchides* and *Casina*). Literary critics might, however, point out that it is of the essence of comedy to depict a victory of the young and vital over the old and obstructive. *Mercator* has received some decidedly adverse verdicts to the effect that it is feeble and dull. Most critics commend it, but not warmly. The comparative quietness of the action, the simplicity of the plot, and the lack of metrical complexity are due to its being an early work of Plautus, or an unusually faithful copy of the Greek original, or both.

Merchantmen, The (Gk. **Olkades**). Lost comedy by Aristophanes (produced probably in January 423 B.C.). Although almost all of the many citations from *The Merchantmen* are given in illustration of unusual words, it is said to have contained a plea for peace.

Mercury (Lat. **Mercurius**). Roman god identified with Hermes. Mercury appears as a character in Plautus' *Amphitryon,* where he takes on the guise of the slave Sosia in order to assist Jupiter in the seduction of Alcmena.

meretrix (Lat.). The courtesan or prostitute, a stock character in New Comedy.

Meriones. *Myth.* Cretan hero, a distinguished fighter with the Greeks at Troy.

Merope. 1. *Myth.* Queen of Corinth and foster mother of Oedipus.

2. *Myth.* Wife of CRESPHONTES (1) and mother of CRESPHONTES (2).

Merops. *Myth.* King of Cos, father of Titanis.

Mesatus (Gk. **Mesatos**). Writer of tragedies (middle 5th century B.C.). The papyrus (published 1952) that dates Aeschylus' *Danaïd Tetralogy* probably in 463 B.C. also indicates that Mesatus won third place in the dramatic contest that year, after Aeschylus and Sophocles.

Messalina. Mother of Octavia and wife of the emperor Claudius. Messalina was put to death in A.D. 48 on a charge of immorality.

Messapius or **Messapium** (Gk. **Messapios** or **Messapion**). Mountain in Boeotia now called Ktypas.

messenger (Gk. **angelos**). Stock character in tragedy. The messenger was usually introduced for the sole purpose of narrating scenes of violence and bloodshed that were thought unfit for portrayal on the stage.

Meton. Athenian astronomer and engineer (active from the 430's B.C.). Meton devised a nineteen-year calendar cycle harmonizing the solar and lunar calendars. He appears briefly in Aristophanes' *Birds.*

Micon (Gk. **Mikon**). Greek sculptor and painter (middle 5th century B.C.). Micon painted the murals for the Stoa Poikile (Painted Porch) and the Theseum in Athens.

Midas. *Myth.* Phrygian king. Midas was the subject of several stories. In one myth, he favored Marsyas over Apollo in the contest of flute versus lyre. The angered god punished Midas by giving him ass's ears.

Middle Comedy. See COMEDY.

Midias (Gk. **Meidias**). Athenian of Aristophanes' time. Midias was accused by writers of Old Comedy of stealing public money. Judging by Aristophanes' reference to him in *The Birds* (line 1297), Midias either bred quail or resembled one in his walk.

miles gloriosus (Lat.). The braggart soldier, a stock character in New Comedy. The *miles gloriosus* was probably already developed in Middle Comedy in such plays as Antiphanes' *Tychon* (c. 360 B.C.) and Alexis' *The Soldier* (c. 342 B.C.). The type reappeared in Renaissance literature.

Miles Gloriosus (Lat. **The Braggart Soldier** or **The Braggart Warrior** or **The Swaggering Soldier**). Extant comedy by Plautus (produced c. 206–204 B.C.). *Miles Gloriosus* was based on a Greek play, *Alazon*, of unknown authorship. Translations: Henry T. Riley, 1852; Robert Allison, 1914; Paul Nixon, 1924; George E. Duckworth, 1942; Erich Segal, 1963; E. F. Watling, 1965. Adaptations and works influenced by *Miles Gloriosus:* Nicholas Udall, *Ralph Roister Doister*, 1553; Lodovico Dolce, *Il Capitano*, 1560; Jean Antoine de Baïf, *Le Brave*, 1567; Ben Jonson, *Every Man in His Humour*, 1598; Pierre Corneille, *L'Illusion Comique*, 1636; Ludvig Holberg, *Jacob von Tyboe*, 1724; Shevelove, Gilbert, and Sondheim, *A Funny Thing Happened on the Way to the Forum*, 1962.

S C E N E. Ephesus.

S U M M A R Y. Pyrgopolynices, a mercenary soldier full of boasting and bluster, has carried off the courtesan Philocomasium from Athens while her lover, Pleusicles, was away on government business. Pleusicles' faithful slave Palaestrio, who has given chase, now also belongs to Pyrgopolynices, having been captured by pirates and given to the soldier. But by means of a letter, Palaestrio has brought Pleusicles to Ephesus, where he is staying with Periplectomenus, an old family friend who owns the house next door. Through a hole dug in the common wall by Palaestrio, the lovers, abetted by Periplectomenus, have been secretly meeting.

When another of the soldier's slaves, chasing a monkey onto the neighboring roof, sees Pleusicles and Philocomasium together, Periplectomenus thinks their affair ruined. But Palaestrio devises a plan to save the situation: Philocomasium will pretend that she is her twin sister who has just arrived from Athens with her own lover. In accordance with this plan, the girl cleverly plays two roles, appearing first at the door of one house, then at the door of the other. Finally the stubborn slave is convinced that it was the twin sister, rather than Philocomasium, that he had seen embracing Pleusicles.

Palaestrio next devises a scheme to enable them all to get free of the soldier and at the same time bring about his ruin. Borrowing Periplectomenus' ring, the slave persuades him to hire a prostitute to pose as his wife and to pretend that she passionately desires the soldier. Palaestrio himself will present Pyrgopolynices with the ring on the pretense that it signifies the woman's passion. The soldier's ruin, Palaestrio is confident, will follow from his lecherous, vainglorious nature.

Pyrgopolynices is thoroughly deceived by the acting of the prostitute and her maid. When Palaestrio suggests that he send Philocomasium away to make room for his new lover, Pyrgopolynices immediately agrees, even to letting Philocomasium leave with the jewelry and fine clothes he had previously given her. When he hears that Periplectomenus' supposed wife has received a divorce and a dowry, he is the more eager to go to her.

Philocomasium, pretending to be heartbroken, prepares to sail for Athens along with Pleusicles, who is disguised as a ship captain; Palaestrio, who has been given his freedom; and, ostensibly, her twin sister and sick mother. The lovers almost give away the ruse by forgetting themselves and kissing in the soldier's presence, and Palaestrio overplays his reluctance to go. Pyrgopolynices is, however, finally left alone, and the prostitute entices him inside Periplectomenus' house. He is immediately carried out again by slaves, who beat him as an adulterer and threaten him with castration. The soldier is more than willing to give them money and to swear that he will never injure them for having beaten him. When he learns at last how he has been tricked, he repents his past actions.

COMMENTARY. This play is unusual for the elaborateness of its intrigue. Opinions differ greatly as to Plautus' success in handling it: some critics think the plot threads neatly interwoven, others find the connections crude. The obvious reason for the play's success, both in ancient and later times, is its classic portrait of the central figure. In *Miles Gloriosus* the braggart soldier steps definitively onto the stage of world literature.

Miletus (Gk. **Miletos**; adj. **Milesian**). Greek city on the western coast of Asia Minor. Miletus was noted for its woolens. The cowardice of the inhabitants was proverbial. In 413 B.C. Miletus defected from Athens.

Miltiades. Athenian statesman and general (c. 550–489 B.C.). Miltiades was an influential leader in the victory at Marathon.

Mimas. 1. *Myth.* One of the Giants in the battle against the gods. Depending on the version of the myth, Mimas was pitted against Zeus, Ares, or Pallas. He was defeated.

2. Mountain range near Erythrae in Ionia.

mimes. Short dramatic sketches of realistic farce. Mimes were originally staged for an essentially uneducated audience. Scenes and characters from the lower classes were accordingly given emphasis in them. Mimes differed from PHLYAKES plays and ATELLAN FARCE in that no use was made of masks or of stock figures with traditional names. Unlike comedy, the mime was improvised, and instead of a connected plot it had a single scene; in addition, women were allowed on the stage.

The foregoing type of mime is impossible to separate from the primitive Dorian farce (see COMEDY), out of which it must have grown. The term "mime" first appeared, however, in Sicily, and the first important mime writer was Sophron in the late fifth century B.C. If the term had existed half a century earlier, some of the comic pieces of Epicharmus would have been classified as mimes.

In the Hellenistic age the mime attained real literary and poetic status with such writers as Herondas and Theocritus. Transplanted to Rome at least as early as the second century B.C., it became enormously popular there also.

In Rome mimes, as well as Atellan farces, were common as interludes and after-plays. Outstanding mime writers of Cicero's day were Laberius and Publilius Syrus. Actresses in mime, such as Cytheris, Mark Antony's mistress, acquired widespread, though unsavory, reputations. The popularity of mime, both Greek and Roman, increased in imperial times; Philistion was the pre-eminent writer in this period. All indications show that the mime flourished until the empire fell. It doubtless left a considerable legacy in the popular drama of the Middle Ages.

mimologoi. Actors in mimes.

Minerva. *Myth.* Roman goddess identified with the Greek ATHENA. Minerva's festival, the Quinquatrus Maiores, was celebrated in Rome on March 19–23.

Minos. *Myth.* King of Crete, son of Zeus and Europa. For the numerous myths connected with Minos, see EUROPA; PASIPHAË; DAEDALUS; NISUS; SCYLLA; THESEUS; POLYIDUS; CAMICANS; CRETANS. After his death, Minos became a judge in the underworld.

Sophocles' lost *Minos* has been identified by some scholars with *Daedalus,* by others with *The Camicans.*

Minotaur (Gk. **Minotauros**). *Myth.* Monster, half man and half bull. When King Minos prayed to Poseidon that a bull might come from the sea, the god answered his request, but Minos failed to sacrifice the bull. In revenge, Poseidon caused Queen Pasiphaë to fall in love with the animal, and the result of their unnatural union was the Minotaur. Minos, greatly embarrassed, instructed Daedalus to build the Labyrinth, and in it he concealed the monster, which was supplied with human victims until Theseus killed it.

Minucius Prothrymus. Roman actor. Minucius was said, with Cincius Faliscus, to have introduced masks into Roman drama. (See MASKS.)

Minyans or **Minyae** (Gk. **Minyai**). The inhabitants of Boeotian Orchomenus in early times, and the noble families that traced descent from them.

Mnemosyne (Gk. "memory"). *Myth.* Goddess of memory. Because early poetry was oral, dependent on the bard's memorized stock of formulae, Mnemosyne was the Mother of the Muses.

Mnesilochus (Gk. **Mnesilochos**). Father-in-law of Euripides. In Aristophanes' *Thesmophoriazusae* Mnesilochus appears as Euripides' ally.

Moirae, sing. **Moira** (Gk. **Moirai,** sing. **Moira**). *Myth.* The Fates, or Fate, considered sometimes as three goddesses, sometimes as one. The Moirae were thought of as daughters of Night and hence as sisters of the Erinyes. They were represented as spinning and cutting the destinies of men. Their names were Clotho, "the Spinner"; Lachesis, "the Allotter"; and Atropos, "She Who Cannot Be Turned Aside."

Molon. Actor of huge size who appeared in the premieres of several Euripidean plays, among them probably *Andromeda* and *Phoenix.*

Molossia or **Molossis.** Region of southern Epirus. Molossia gave its name to a breed of sheep dogs.

Molossus (Gk. **Molossos**). *Myth.* Son of Neoptolemus and Andromache.

Molossus appears as a child in Euripides' *Andromache,* where Thetis prophesies that he will become a king and ancestor of the Molossians.

Momus (Gk. **Momos**). *Myth.* God of criticism and sarcasm. When Earth was groaning from overpopulation and Zeus was preparing to use flood and lightning as remedies, Momus advised him to beget Helen and arrange for Thetis' marriage, thus starting the Trojan War.

Sophocles' lost play of this name was probably a satyr play; its plot is unknown.

monody (Gk. **monoidia**). Solo song in drama (especially in tragedy) as opposed to choric song or ensemble.

Mopsus (Gk. **Mopsos**). *Myth.* Soothsayer of the Argonauts. Mopsus' myth was confused with that of Idmon, who was also an Argonaut.

Morsimus (Gk. **Morsimos**). Tragedy writer and eye doctor (late 5th century B.C.). Morsimus was a great-nephew of Aeschylus and brother of Melanthius. As a poet he was considered unmetrical, formless, and frigid. In *The Frogs* (line 151) Aristophanes consigns Morsimus' admirers to Hades.

Moschion. Writer of tragedy (late 4th or early 3rd century B.C.). A few fragments exist of Moschion's *Telephus* and of two plays based on history, *Themistocles* and *The Pheraeans.* The latter apparently dealt with the murder of Alexander of Pherae by his wife and her brothers.

Mostellaria (Lat. **The Haunted House** or **The Ghost**). Extant comedy by Plautus (produced perhaps between 200 and 194 B.C.). *Mostellaria* was in all probability based on Philemon's Greek play *Phasma* (*The Ghost*). Translations: Henry T. Riley, 1852; Paul Nixon, 1930; Frank O. Copley, 1955; Lionel Casson, 1960; E. F. Watling, 1964. Adaptations and works influenced by *Mostellaria:* Shakespeare, *The Taming of the Shrew,* 1593–94; Thomas Heywood, *The English Traveller,* 1633; Henry Fielding, *The Intriguing Chambermaid,* 1733; Ludvig Holberg, *A Ghost in the House or Abracadabra,* 1752; Shevelove, Gilbert, and Sondheim, *A Funny Thing Happened on the Way to the Forum,* 1962.

S C E N E. Athens.

S U M M A R Y. In the absence of his father, Theopropides, who has been in Egypt for three years, Philolaches has borrowed from a moneylender and purchased and freed the slave girl Philematium, whom he loves. The entire household, assisted by his father's roguish slave Tranio, his own friend Callidamates, and assorted harlots and hangers-on, have been carousing night and day.

On Philolaches' first appearance he is seen drunkenly comparing a man to a house and noting his own dissipation. Overhearing Philematium avow her constancy toward him, he greets her, and the two are joined by the drunken Callidamates and Delphium, his courtesan. But Tranio interrupts their merriment with news that Philolaches' father has returned.

Promising to rescue them all from the compromising situation, Tranio orders everyone into the house with the door locked and, when Theopropides appears, frightens him off with news that the deserted house is haunted by the ghost of a man murdered by the previous owner. At this point the moneylender comes for Philolaches' interest payment, and to complicate matters, Theopropides returns. Tranio tells the moneylender that Theopropides will pay him and tells Theopropides that his son borrowed in order to buy the house of their neighbor Simo. Pleased, Theopropides promises to pay but insists on inspecting his new property. Tranio lies to Simo that Theopropides wants ideas for remodeling his own house and manages to preserve both fictions, slyly mocking the two men.

Theopropides learns the truth about his son from two of Callidamates' slaves and the truth about Simo's house from Simo. Borrowing some slaves, he sets a trap for Tranio, but the latter overhears the plan. Failing to bluff his way out of the situation, Tranio dashes to the safety of an altar and calmly mocks while Theopropides rages at him. At this point Callidamates returns as peacemaker for the penitent revelers and mediates between Theopropides and Tranio, who is pardoned along with Philolaches.

COMMENTARY. To censure *Mostellaria* would be like kicking a frisky dog: though the goings-on are by no means innocent, the spirit of innocent fun that keeps this rapid play on the move has won the favor of all critics. The worst that has been said of it is that the later scenes do not completely live up to the promise of the earlier.

Mother-in-Law, The (Lat. **Hecyra**, Latinized form of Gk. *Hekyra*). Extant comedy by Terence (first staged in April 165 B.C.). *The Mother-in-Law* was again produced in 160 B.C. at the funeral games for Lucius Aemilius Paulus. Having failed the first two times, the play was successfully produced by Ambivius Turpio at the Ludi Romani of 160 B.C. Translations: John Sargeaunt, 1925; Frank O. Copley, 1962; Robert Graves and Laurence Echard, 1962; Betty Radice, 1965.

SCENE. Athens.

SUMMARY. (There are two prologues extant, one written for the second production, one for the third.) The first prologue explains that the play's first production lost its audience to a dancer on the tightrope. Terence, rather than repeat it, had waited and later sold it to the city officials a second time. The second prologue, originally spoken by Lucius Ambivius Turpio at *Hecyra's* third trial, attributes the second failure to an uproar about gladiatorial games, though there are hints that a clique hostile to Terence caused most of the trouble. Ambivius says that he carried the plays of Caecilius to success in the teeth of similar opposition, and he hopes to achieve the same favor for Terence.

As the play opens, Pamphilus, a young Athenian, is returning from Imbros where he was sent by his father, Laches. Parmeno, slave to father and son, gives the background. Deeply in love with the courtesan Bacchis, Pamphilus had been forced by his father to marry Philumena. Instead of consummating the marriage, he had continued to see Bacchis. But after a time she grew cold, and he grew to love his wife's good, gentle nature. It was then, unwillingly, that he went to Imbros, leaving his wife with his mother, Sostrata. But Philumena began strangely to avoid his mother and finally went back to her own parents.

Laches blames Sostrata for the rift, but Pamphilus, on returning, discovers the truth. Two months before marrying him, Philumena had been raped by a stranger who, moreover, stole a ring from her finger. When she could no longer hide her pregnancy, she ran to her mother. Pamphilus has promised not to expose his wife but feels that he cannot take her back with another man's child. Parmeno, the only one who knows of the unconsummated marriage, is sent on a false errand so that he will not learn of the birth.

Pamphilus, concealing the truth, pretends to accept the story of a quarrel between his wife and mother. But his father-in-law, Phidippus, learns of the child's existence and, assuming that Pamphilus is the father, blames Philumena's mother for snatching her daughter away.

Sostrata, believing herself the cause of Philumena's estrangement, generously offers to leave in order that Philumena may return, but Pamphilus will not hear of it. Then Phidippus informs Pamphilus and Laches that Philumena's mother is really to blame. But when Pamphilus is still unwilling to take wife or child, Laches and Phidippus lay the blame in turn at Bacchis' door.

Bacchis convinces Laches of her innocence and, overcoming her shame, agrees to go and ease the minds of the other women. Parmeno, returning from his futile errand, meets her just as she is leaving Philumena's house. Bacchis bids him hurry and tell Pamphilus that the ring he gave her ten months ago has been recognized as the very one the ravisher pulled off Philumena's hand. Still ignorant of the situation, Parmeno goes off, and Bacchis reveals to the audience that Pamphilus is both ravisher and father. Pamphilus is overjoyed to learn the news, and he and Bacchis become friends. Parmeno remains in the dark.

C O M M E N T A R Y. *Hecyra's* two prologues make it known that the play had the distinction of emptying the theater at its first two trials. The audience, which must have been avid "for a jig or a tale of bawdry," streamed away to see boxers and rope dancers, the bustle of the patricians' entourages and the women's squeals drowning out the actors.

Some modern critics are equally unsympathetic: they carp at the use of monologue where they would prefer dialogue, at a lack of a comic element, and at the incredibility of the dénouement. This last detail seems, however, to come straight out of Menander, in whose play *The Arbitrants* the husband is discovered to be his wife's former unknown violator. Euripides' *Oeneus* might be given as an even earlier instance of this turn in plot. *Hecyra* seems peculiarly Menandrian in its gentle judgments on human nature, its quiet tone, and its emphasis on character portrayal rather than rapid dramatic narration.

It has been pointed out that the prolongation of suspense until the very end of the play is unusual; equally unusual is the character Sostrata, the antithesis of the mother-in-law of popular jesting. And although the bad girl with a heart of gold was not at all uncommon in ancient comedy, she receives in the person of Bacchis her classic formulation.

Mothone or **Methone.** City in Messenia.

Mothones. Group of Spartans sprung from citizen fathers and helot mothers. The term was used as an insult. In *The Knights* (line 635) Aristophanes calls some imaginary spirits of bestiality by this name.

Mounichion. Tenth month of the Attic calendar corresponding to the end of April and the beginning of May.

Mulciber. Byname of the Roman god Vulcan, who was identified with HEPHAESTUS.

Munichia (Gk. **Mounichia**). Harbor and promontory east of, and adjoining, the Piraeus.

Musaeus (Gk. **Mousaios**). *Myth.* Musician reared by the Muses. Musaeus was said to have been a pupil of Orpheus or of Linus (2).

Muses (Gk. **Mousai**). *Myth.* Nine daughters of Zeus and Mnemosyne. The Muses were goddesses of song, of intellectual inventiveness, and of poetical and musical inspiration. They were, however, sometimes thought of as one: the Muse. The goddesses were localized either in Pieria in Thrace, whence their name "Pierides," or on Mt. Helicon in Boeotia. They were closely associated with Apollo, the Graces, and certain fountains. Although systematic mythographers have tried to assign to each Muse a certain sphere, they were fairly interchangeable in ancient literature.

In Euripides' *Rhesus,* a Muse of the Mountains appears as Rhesus' mourning mother. Sophocles' lost play *The Muses* was perhaps identical with his *Thamyras.*

Mycale (Gk. **Mykale**). *Myth.* Witch of the Thessalian Lapiths. Mycale could charm the moon down from the skies.

Mycenae (Gk. **Mykenai**). City in Argolis. In the second millennium B.C. Mycenae was the leading power in Greece. Its walls were said to have been built by the Cyclopes.

Myconus (Gk. **Mykonos**). Island in the southern Aegean Sea northeast of, and very near to, Delos.

Mygdon. *Myth.* Father of Coroebus and an ally of King Priam in the Trojan War.

Mynniscus (Gk. **Mynniskos**). Actor (fl. middle 5th century B.C.). Mynniscus was said to have acted for Aeschylus. He called his rival Callippides an ape because of his exaggerated style of acting.

Myrmidons (Gk. **Myrmidones**). *Myth.* Achilles' soldiers. The Myrmidons gave their name to a lost tragedy by Aeschylus, probably the first play of an Achilles trilogy, the other two being *The Nereids* and *The Ransom of Hector.* A papyrus fragment possibly from *The Myrmidons* indicates that in it the Greeks threatened to stone Achilles for withdrawing from the fight at Troy. Judging from Accius' *Myrmidons* and *Achilles,* lost Roman adaptations of Aeschylus' play, its plot culminated in the death of Patroclus.

Myronides. Athenian general. With an army of old men and boys Myronides defeated both Corinthians and Boeotians in the 450's B.C.

Myrrha. *Myth.* Daughter of Cinyras, king of Cyprus. Fired by an incestuous passion for her father, Myrrha managed to disguise herself and to lie with him. When Cinyras discovered the identity of his bedfellow, he pursued her with a sword, but the gods changed the pregnant girl into a myrrh tree. When Cinyras' sword tore open the bark, the child Adonis was born.

Myrtilus (Gk. **Myrtilos**). *Myth.* Charioteer of King Oenomaus. When Pelops challenged Oenomaus to a chariot race for the hand of his daughter Hippodamia, he promised Myrtilus the first night with the bride if the charioteer would help him to win. Myrtilus accordingly removed the lynchpins from Oenomaus' chariot. After Pelops' victory, Myrtilus tried to rape Hippodamia, but Pelops threw him into the sea, which was thenceforward called Myrtoan. As he drowned, Myrtilus put a curse on Pelops and his descendants.

Mysia. Region in the northwestern corner of Asia Minor.

Mysians, The (Gk. **Mysoi**). Lost tragedy by Aeschylus based on some story about Telephus. Conjectures vary: *The Mysians* may have dealt with the Aleadae or with Auge or with Telephus' injury at the hands of Achilles. Sophocles' *Mysians* dealt with the story of Telephus and Auge. It is doubtful that Euripides wrote a tragedy of this name. (See TELEPHUS; AUGE; ALEADAE.)

mysteries. Secret death-and-resurrection cults into which an individual had to be initiated. There were several mystery cults in the Greek world, such as those connected with Dionysus, the Cabiri, and other deities. By far the best known were the Eleusinian mysteries. (See ELEUSIS.)

Mytilene. City of eastern Lesbos. During the Peloponnesian War in 428 B.C., Mytilene defected from Athens. Cleon proposed that all the male citizens be put to death, but this order was not carried out.

N

Nabataei. Tribe in Arabia that inhabited the northeast shore of the Red Sea.

Naevius, Gnaeus. Roman writer from Campania. Naevius' dramatic career extended from 235 B.C. until his death in 201. He was imprisoned around 206 B.C. for his attack on the powerful Metelli and allegedly wrote two plays in prison: *The Soothsayer* and *The Lion.* Soon after his release, Naevius was banished from Rome. He withdrew to Africa, where he died.

Naevius' chief work was his lost epic *The Punic War,* but he also wrote plays of various kinds and was said to have initiated the national Roman tragedy, FABULA PRAETEXTA, with his *Clastidium.* To Naevius are attributed also, on shaky grounds, the introduction of "contamination" (combining and adapting the plots of two or more Greek plays) and the first use of *cantica* (solo songs) in Roman comedies. Besides numerous fragments there survive titles of thirty-odd comedies. Typical are: *The Madmen, Speared, The Sleepless Ones, The Potter, The Cloak Comedy, Glaucoma, The Comedy of Masks.* There exist also the titles of about nine tragedies, some of which are: *Danaë, Hector's Farewell, Romulus,* and *The Trojan Horse.*

Naiads or **Naids** (Gk. **Naiades** or **Naides**). *Myth.* Nymphs who were spirits of streams, pools, and fountains.

Naupactus (Gk. **Naupaktos**). Seaport in Locris on the north shore of the Corinthian Gulf.

Nauplia. Seaport on the Gulf of Argolis.

Nauplius (Gk. **Nauplios**). *Myth.* Son of Poseidon and Amymone and father of Palamedes. A noted sailor, Nauplius was entrusted by Aleos with the task of drowning his erring daughter Auge. Catreus similarly gave him Aërope to drown because the oracle had said that he would be killed by one of his own children. Out of pity Nauplius spared both daughters; he married Aërope's sister Clymene.

When he learned of the unjust death of his son Palamedes at the hands of his Greek fellow soldiers at Troy, Nauplius sailed to Troy to demand satisfaction, but Agamemnon refused to uphold his claim. Nauplius took vengeance in two ways. First he went to the wives of the absent kings, told them stories of their husbands' infidelities, and incited them to take lovers. In this Nauplius succeeded best with Clytemnestra, the wife of Agamemnon. Later, when the homecoming Greek fleet was nearing Caphareus, on the southern cape of Euboea, he lit a number of misleading beacon fires. The result was that innumerable ships were wrecked on the rocks.

Nauplius the Fire-Kindler (Gk. **Nauplios Pyrkaeus**). Lost tragedy by Sophocles. It told how Nauplius took vengeance on the Greeks by wrecking their returning fleet with false beacons.

Nauplius' Voyage (Gk. **Nauplios Katapleon**). Lost play by Sophocles. It is not certain whether the work dealt with Nauplius' voyage to Troy in an attempt to save Palamedes or with his vengeful wanderings in Greece, poisoning the minds of the women against their absent husbands.

Nausicaa (Gk. **Nausikaa**). *Myth.* Daughter of King Alcinous and Queen Arete of Phaeacia. In obedience to a dream, Nausicaa went down to the seashore with her handmaidens to wash her clothes in preparation for marriage. After finishing their task, the girls played with a ball and aroused the sleeping Odysseus, who had been cast up on the shore in his wanderings. Nausicaa, much attracted by the handsome stranger and fancying him for a husband, gave him directions for finding her father's palace. But Odysseus, after recounting his adventures to the assembled Phaeacians, continued his voyage home.

Sophocles' lost play *Nausicaa* was perhaps a satyr play, since there is nothing inherently tragic in Nausicaa's story. It had an alternate title, *Plyntriai*, "The Washers." Sophocles himself was said to have played the leading role.

Nausicydes (Gk. **Nausikydes**). Wealthy but dishonest grain dealer in Aristophanes' Athens.

Naxos. Island in the South Aegean Sea southeast of Delos.

Neistian Gates. One of the seven pairs of gates at Thebes. The word "neistian" probably meant the "lowest."

Neleus. *Myth.* King of Pylos and father of Nestor.

Nemea. Locality southwest of Corinth. It was at Nemea that Heracles' encounter with a monster lion took place. Nemea was also the site of the Nemean Games, which were held every other year.

Of Aeschylus' lost play *Nemea* no fragment remains. It possibly related the death of Opheltes. (See Euripides' HYPSIPYLE.)

Nemesis. *Myth.* Goddess of divine vengeance. Nemesis kept all things in their proper places and in right order. According to one myth, she was the real mother of Helen.

Nemetor (Gk. "awarder, dispenser of justice"). Epithet of Zeus.

Neophron. Writer of tragedies from Sicyon. A few ancient authorities called Neophron the real author of Euripides' *Medea*. There is, however, no substance to this claim, and Neophron probably lived about a century later than Euripides. Three fragments of his *Medea* indicate that Neophron tried to meet Aristotle's criticism that Aegeus' entrance lacked motivation. In the play Aegeus came to consult Medea about the meaning of a Delphic oracle. One line spoken by Medea before killing her children calls to mind Lady Macbeth: "O hands, hands! for what a deed I have armed you!" These fragments are all that remain of tragedies by Neophron allegedly numbering 120.

Neoptolemus (Gk. **Neoptolemos**). 1. *Myth.* Son of Achilles and Deidamia. Neoptolemus was also known as Pyrrhus. Reared on the island of Scyrus by his mother and his grandfather Lycomedes, Neoptolemus was persuaded by the Greek delegates Odysseus and Phoenix to enter the Trojan War after Achilles' death. He himself was sent with Odysseus to obtain the services of Philoctetes, who was in possession of Heracles' bow and arrows. This is Neoptolemus' role in Sophocles' *Philoctetes*. At the sack of Troy he behaved with great brutality, killing Priam at the altar of Zeus, sacrificing Polyxena on the tomb of Achilles, and taking as his concubine Andromache, Hector's wife. In Seneca's *Trojan Women* Neoptolemus (called Pyrrhus in the play) makes an appearance to demand Polyxena for the sacrifice.

After returning to Greece, he succeeded to the throne of his grandfather Peleus at Iolcus and married Helen's daughter Hermione. But Hermione had no children, whereas Andromache bore Neoptolemus a son, Molossus. This aroused Hermione's jealousy, and the complications that followed form the plot of Euripides' *Andormache*. During the action of the play Neoptolemus is absent in Delphi, where his death is brought about by Orestes, who had originally intended to marry Hermione. According to another tradition, however, Neoptolemus went to Epirus after the Trojan War and at his death was succeeded by Helenus, his Trojan captive, who married Andromache.

2. Actor from Scyrus (fl. middle 4th century B.C.). Neoptolemus was a great favorite of Philip of Macedon, who made him his confidant and ambassador. According to some authorities, Philip was murdered while attending one of Neoptolemus' performances.

Nephele (Gk. "cloud"). **1.** *Myth.* Wife of Athamas.

2. *Myth.* The cloud that Zeus fashioned in the image of Hera to find out whether IXION had made advances to her.

Nephelococcygia (Gk. **Nephelokokkygia**). Cloudcuckooland in Aristophanes' *Birds*.

Neptune (Lat. **Neptunus**). Roman god identified with Poseidon.

Nereids (Gk. **Nereides**). *Myth.* Sea nymphs, daughters of Nereus. Their number was generally given as fifty; one of the Nereids was Thetis.

A lost tragedy by Aeschylus called *The Nereids* is thought to have been part of an Achilles trilogy, preceded by *The Myrmidons* and followed by *The Ransom of Hector*. It probably told how Thetis brought new armor to Achilles, who then returned to battle and killed Hector.

Nereus. *Myth.* Sea divinity, the Old Man of the Sea. Nereus was sometimes identified with Proteus and sometimes called his father. He was the father of numerous sea nymphs, the Nereids.

Neriene (Sabine word meaning "bravery"). Roman deity, the personification of bravery. Neriene was sometimes called the wife of Mars.

Neritos. Small island near Ithaca.

Nero. Roman emperor from A.D. 54 to 68. Nero appears as a character in the pseudo-Senecan play *Octavia*.

Nessus (Gk. **Nessos**). *Myth.* Centaur, son of IXION and Nephele (2). For the story of his poisoning of Heracles, see DEIANIRA.

Nestor. *Myth.* King of Pylos. Nestor was the oldest of the Greek chieftains at Troy and their most respected adviser.

New Comedy. See COMEDY.

Nicanor (Gk. **Nikanor**). Scholar of Alexandria (2nd century A.D.). Among Nicanor's lost works was one called *Plots of Comedy*.

Nicias (Gk. **Nikias**). Distinguished Athenian general and statesman (c. 470–413 B.C.). Nicias was an associate of Pericles and an opponent of Cleon, in which latter capacity he appears in Aristophanes' *Knights*. Having negotiated the "Peace of Nicias" in 421 B.C., he was reluctantly drawn into the Sicilian expedition of 415. In Sicily Nicias' cautious generalship resulted in disaster, and he was captured and executed by the Syracusans.

Nicochares (Gk. **Nikochares**). Writer of Old Comedy (fl. c. 400 B.C.). Nicochares was the son of Aristophanes' friend Philonides. His *Laconians* came out in 388 B.C., in the year of Aristophanes' *Plutus*. Only scanty fragments and a few titles survive, among them *Galatea, Heracles the Play Producer*, and *Amymone*.

Nicomachus (Gk. **Nikomachos**). 1. Athenian scribe. Nicomachus was chosen in about 410 B.C. to record and codify the laws; it was commonly thought that he altered them to his own advantage.

2. Playwright from the Troad (dates unknown). Nicomachus wrote tragedies and comedies, all of which are lost. About eighteen titles survive.

Nicophon (Gk. **Nikophon**). Writer of Old Comedy (early 4th century B.C.). Nicophon's works were also probably transitional to Middle Comedy. Twenty-nine fragments remain, as well as a few titles, such as *Pandora, Adonis, The Sirens, Aphrodite's Birth*, and *The Man Who Came Back from Hades*.

Nicostratus (Gk. **Nikostratos**). 1. Son of Aristophanes and writer of Middle Comedy. There is some confusion between Nicostratus and PHILETAERUS.

2. Tragic actor (fl. c. 425 B.C.). This Nicostratus was ranked at the top of his profession. He was especially good in messenger roles.

Nike (Gk. "victory"). *Myth.* Goddess of victory, often depicted as winged.

Niobe. *Myth.* Daughter of Tantalus and wife of Amphion, king of Thebes. Niobe bore to her husband seven handsome sons and seven beautiful daughters. She boasted that she was due more honor than Leto, who had borne only Apollo and Artemis, whereupon the two latter, at their mother's request, shot down all of Niobe's children. The weeping mother turned into a rock from which flowed a fountain.

Aeschylus' lost *Niobe* was one of his most famous plays. Throughout much of the action the grief-stricken Niobe sat silent on her children's tomb, but at last she broke out dramatically. A papyrus fragment published in 1933 may be part of her speech; in it Niobe says that she has mourned for three days and that she expects the arrival of her father, Tantalus. These curious lines occur: "When God wants to obliterate a household, he plants a fault in men; but still, a mere mortal who enjoys prosperity from the gods should keep his tongue from rash speech." Tantalus seems to have appeared, and Amphion's house seems to have been struck by lightning and burned. Reconstruction of the play has, however, been the source of much dispute.

Apparently Sophocles' lost *Niobe* differed from Aeschylus' version in that it dealt directly with the deaths of Niobe's children and had Niobe transported to Lydia after the catastrophe. It is not clear whether Aristotle's criticism (*Poetics*, 1456a) that "too much material is crammed into one plot" refers to this play or to that of Aeschylus. Some papyrus fragments discovered in the lining of a mummy case in the British Museum describe a terrified girl fleeing from a deadly danger while the chorus look on horror-stricken. This description may refer to one of Niobe's daughters being pursued by Artemis.

Niptra. See ODYSSEUS AKANTHOPLEX.

Nireus. *Myth.* Suitor of Helen and warrior against Troy. Nireus was noted for his handsome appearance.

Nisus (Gk. **Nisos**). *Myth.* King of Megara. Nisus had a purple (or gold) lock of hair on his head. According to an oracle, the king would die when this lock was cut off. When the city was besieged by Minos, Nisus' daughter Scylla fell in love with the enemy leader. Knowing that the safety of the city depended on her father's purple lock, Scylla snipped it off. But though Minos took the town, he was filled with horror at her deed and bound her to the prow of his ship, where she was either drowned or transformed into a monster. (See SCYLLA.)

Nocturnus. *Myth.* Roman god of night.

Nomios (Gk. "pertaining to shepherds"). Epithet of Hermes.

Notus (Gk. **Notos**). *Myth.* God of the south wind.

Novius. Writer of ATELLAN FARCE. Novius was a contemporary of Cicero. Of his works about forty-four titles remain; they are typical of the genre. Some examples are: *The Ass, The Dowry, The Two Dossenni, The Fullers' Holiday, The Chicken Comedy, Maccus the Innkeeper, Contest of Life and Death, Stingy, The Trial, The Vintage, The Pregnant Virgin.*

Nox. Latin equivalent of NYX.

Nurses, The (Gk. **Trophoi**). Lost play by Aeschylus. The nurses of the title were those of Dionysus. There is dispute as to the content of the play. Perhaps it was a satyr play in which Medea performed magical rites and rejuvenated the nurses and their husbands, the satyrs.

Nyctelius (Gk. **Nyktelios**, "nocturnal"). Epithet of Dionysus, some of whose ceremonies took place at night.

nymphs. *Myth.* Demigoddesses, spirits of the woodland and of nature, especially of trees, mountains, springs, and the sea. The nymphs of the land were especially associated with Pan, with the satyrs, and with Artemis.

Nysa. Mountain where Dionysus was nursed by the nymphs (hence his epithet Nysius). Nysa was probably a mythical mountain at first. In historical times it was located in various places but usually in India.

Nyx (Gk. "night"). *Myth.* Goddess of night and the primeval darkness. Nyx was the mother of many monsters and deities, including Nemesis, Moira, and Eris.

O

obolus (Gk. **obolos**). Small coin worth one-sixth of a drachma.

Oceanides. See OCEANUS.

Oceanus (Gk. **Okeanos**). *Myth.* The water that girdled the earth. Oceanus was personified as a god. He was regarded as a river and was called the father of all other rivers. With Tethys, a primeval sea goddess, Oceanus produced the water nymphs, the Oceanides. He appears in a scene of Aeschylus' *Prometheus Bound;* his daughters, the Oceanides, form the chorus.

Octavia. Extant tragedy ascribed to Seneca (see *Commentary* below). Translation: Frank Justus Miller, 1917.

S C E N E. Rome, the imperial palace in A.D. 62.

S U M M A R Y. Octavia, alone, sadly recalls the execution of her mother, Messalina, the past cruelty of her stepmother, Agrippina, the murder of her father, the emperor Claudius, and her own forced marriage to her stepbrother, the present emperor, Nero. Octavia's Nurse tries unsuccessfully to placate her as she continues to express loathing for Nero, who killed her brother, Britannicus, and later dispatched Agrippina; moreover, Nero's new mistress, Poppaea, threatens Octavia's own position. Half longing to die, she briefly contemplates killing Nero.

After Octavia and her Nurse have withdrawn, a Chorus of Courtiers provide an interlude. They review the crimes of the imperial house, especially Nero's attempt to have his mother drowned at sea in a ship that fell apart, and her escape and subsequent death by an assassin's sword. The philosopher Seneca then appears, deploring the undesired prominence into which his former position of tutor to Nero has forced him. He is soon joined by Nero, who cynically describes the servility of the people, asserts that imperial fortunes are founded on bloodshed and not mercy, and, over Seneca's repeated counsel of clemency and restraint, states that Octavia will die and he will marry Poppaea. When the two men have left, Agrippina's ghost enters briefly, cursing her son and his coming marriage.

Two nights and a day pass, during which time Nero has divorced Octavia and married Poppaea. Octavia consoles a grieving Chorus of Romans with the reminder that she has at last been separated from the man she detests, but they go off angrily to seize Poppaea and attack the palace.

Meanwhile Poppaea reveals to her Nurse a portentous dream and, despite the Nurse's favorable interpretation of it, leaves to make a sacrifice. A Chorus of

Women sympathize with Poppaea and praise her beauty. At this point a Messenger rushes in with news that a mob has revolted in favor of Octavia, demolishing Poppaea's statue and threatening the palace. The Chorus sing that it is futile to strive against the weapons of Cupid. Now Nero enters, enraged. Toying with the idea of setting fire to Rome in order to crush the people, he gives orders that the riot be put down and Octavia executed. The efforts of Nero's Prefect to mitigate his wrath go unheeded.

The Chorus of Romans deplore the danger of being loved by the people, after which Octavia enters under guard. Sadly she wishes to be able to grieve in peace. The Chorus sing that human beings are marshaled by the Fates, but Octavia, not content, prays to her father's soul for revenge on Nero. When she is taken away, the Chorus recall other imperial women who have met similar fates and call on the winds to bear away Octavia just as Iphigenia was borne from her punishment. In other lands, they say, the gods are appeased by the blood of strangers, but Rome revels in her citizens' blood.

C O M M E N T A R Y. *Octavia* is the only extant Latin tragedy on an historical theme, hence the only example of *fabula praetexta*. The vast majority of scholars hold that it was not written by Seneca, to whom manuscripts ascribe it, but that it was written soon after Nero's death by a poet working in the Senecan tradition. The unexampled appearance of the author in the play and the accurate details of Nero's death are enough to rule it out as Seneca's. As for the play itself, opinions range from severe condemnation to lukewarm defense. There are fine passages, and the effect of the whole is by no means contemptible, but true dramatiç conflict is conspicuously absent. Seneca himself would never have neglected the opportunity of a confrontation scene between Poppaea and Octavia or between Octavia and Nero.

Odeum (Gk. **Oideion**). Hall in Athens used for musical events, lawsuits, and the PROAGON.

Odomantians (Gk. **Odomantoi**). Tribe in Thrace whose territory extended from the lower Strymon River to Mt. Pangaeum.

Odrysae. Tribe in central Thrace. Hence *Odrysian* means "Thracian."

Odysseus. *Myth.* King of Ithaca, son of Laertes (or of Sisyphus), and husband of Penelope. Odysseus was tricked into going to the Trojan War by PALAMEDES, on whom he later wreaked a treacherous vengeance.

In all the extant ancient plays in which he appears, Odysseus is a model of shrewdness, eloquence, and trickery. A character in Euripides' *Rhesus*, he goes, accompanied by Diomedes, on a night expedition behind the Trojan lines. Together the Greeks deceitfully kill the Trojan spy Dolon and the Trojan ally Rhesus. It was also with Diomedes that Odysseus slipped disguised into Troy and stole the Palladium, Pallas' statue. Although the men were recognized by Helen and Hecuba, they were allowed to leave. In Sophocles' *Philoctetes* Odysseus is accompanied by Neoptolemus on a successful mission to win the aid of Philoctetes for the Greeks. And in Sophocles' *Ajax*, Odysseus has won by his eloquence the arms of Achilles, thus inspiring Ajax to rage and madness.

After the fall of Troy Odysseus received Queen Hecuba as his slave. In Euripides' *Hecuba* he is deaf to the queen's appeal to spare the life of her daughter Polyxena. Odysseus' many adventures and sufferings on his way home to Ithaca are the subject of Homer's *Odyssey*. One episode, his blinding of the Cyclops Polyphemus, is portrayed in Euripides' *Cyclops*. On arriving home, Odysseus killed his wife's insolent suitors and re-established his household and kingdom. He was subsequently killed by TELEGONUS, his son by Circe (see ODYSSEUS AKANTHOPLEX).

Odysseus Akanthoplex (Gk. "Odysseus Wounded with the Spine of a Sting Ray"). Lost play by Sophocles. *Odysseus Akanthoplex* is thought to be identical with another lost play, *Niptra*, "The Washing," which was imitated by Pacuvius. It told how Odysseus was forewarned by the oracle that he would be killed by his own son. He therefore avoided Ithaca for years. On returning home in disguise, Odysseus was discovered by a maidservant who, when washing his feet, recognized the scar on his leg. When some strangers attacked the island, Odysseus went out to help repel the invaders but was mortally wounded by a spear tipped with the poisonous spine of a sting ray. His killer turned out to be Telegonus, his son by Circe.

Odysseus' Madness (Gk. **Odysseus Mainomenos**). Lost play by Sophocles. It told how Odysseus feigned madness to avoid going to the Trojan War, yoking together an ox and an ass and throwing salt over his shoulder as he plowed. His fraud was uncovered by Palamedes, who placed the infant Telemachus in the furrow, causing Odysseus to turn aside.

Oea (Gk. **Oia**). Attic deme. Oiatis was a section of pastureland in Oea.

Oeagrus (Gk. **Oiagros**). Actor who played the role of Niobe, probably in Sophocles' *Niobe*.

Oeax (Gk. **Oiax**). *Myth.* Son of Nauplius and Clymene and brother of Palamedes. To avenge Palamedes' death, some say, Oeax urged Clytemnestra to kill Agamemnon. In Euripides' *Orestes* he is reported as proposing that Orestes be exiled.

Oechalia (Gk. **Oichalia**). City or cities located by various writers in Messenia, western Thessaly, or Euboea.

Oecleus or **Oecles** (Gk. **Oikles**). *Myth.* Father of Amphiaraus, who was also called Oecleides.

Oedipus (Gk. **Oidipous**, "swollen foot"). *Myth.* King of Thebes, son and murderer of Laius, son and husband of Jocasta. When he solved the riddle of the Sphinx, Oedipus became famous for his cleverness. He appears in Sophocles' *Oedipus the King* and *Oedipus at Colonus*, in Euripides' *Phoenician Women*, and in Seneca's *Oedipus* and *Phoenician Women*. (See these entries for his story.)

Aeschylus' lost *Oedipus* formed part of the THEBAN TETRALOGY. Euripides' lost *Oedipus* was produced after Sophocles' *Oedipus the King* but was completely eclipsed by it in later times. Recently discovered fragments make it certain that in Euripides' play Oedipus was blinded by the servants of Laius, perhaps at the time that he killed Laius.

Oedipus. Extant tragedy by Seneca based largely on Sophocles' *Oedipus the King*. Translations: Frank Justus Miller, 1916; Moses Hadas, 1955.

S C E N E. Thebes, before the palace.

SUMMARY. Thebes has been devastated by drought and plague. Before dawn in front of the palace, King Oedipus communes with himself, wondering why he alone seems to be spared. He reveals his continuing fear of the Delphic oracle's prophecy that caused him to leave his supposed parents, King Polybus and Queen Merope of Corinth, namely, that he would kill his father and marry his mother. (After leaving Corinth, Oedipus came to Thebes, solved the riddle of the Sphinx, married Jocasta, the widowed queen of the former king, Laius, and took over the rule.) Jocasta draws near to comfort him, after which the Chorus of Theban Elders enter and describe the plague's devastation.

With the coming of day, Jocasta's brother Creon returns from Delphi with an oracle indicating that Laius' murderer, not discovered at the time because of the menace of the Sphinx, must be found out and banished before the plague will cease. In response, Oedipus puts a curse on the unknown murderer, promising him unpardoned exile.

After Creon describes the spot where Laius was killed, the blind prophet Tiresias enters, led by his daughter Manto. Asked to interpret the oracle, the prophet orders a bull and a heifer to be sacrificed. As his daughter describes the flame, the blood, and the entrails, Tiresias realizes that the omens are dire. To obtain their precise meaning, he leaves with Creon and Manto to call up Laius' soul from the dead.

The Chorus sing a long hymn praising Bacchus, after which Creon returns. He tells how Tiresias summoned with elaborate rites the ghosts of famous Thebans and, last, the ghost of Laius, who denounced Oedipus as the killer. Since the revelation seemingly does not coincide with the oracle he heard long ago at Delphi, Oedipus refuses to believe it. He charges Creon with plotting with Tiresias to put him off the throne. Creon defends himself, but the adamant king orders him taken away to prison.

Oedipus reveals to Jocasta that he did in fact kill an old man many years ago. Learning that Laius' appearance at the time and place of the murder tally with his own recollection, he fears the worst. At this point an Old Man arrives from Corinth with the news that Polybus has died. Saddened by the death of his supposed father, Oedipus is nevertheless heartened at the apparent refutation of the oracle. To quiet his remaining fear of incest, the Corinthian tells the king that Merope is not really his mother. The infant Oedipus, the Old Man explains, was in fact given to him, years ago, by one of Laius' shepherds who had disobeyed his master's order to expose the baby, with its ankles pinned together, on Mt. Cithaeron.

The Old Man counsels Oedipus to keep the truth concealed, but the king sends for the shepherd who received the baby from Laius. When the shepherd, Phorbas, admits that he disobeyed Laius and gave a child of Jocasta's to a Corinthian, Oedipus realizes that he has indeed killed his father and married his mother, as was prophesied. Cursing himself, he rushes into the palace.

A Messenger reports that Oedipus has torn out his eyes. After the Chorus sing of the power of fate, the king emerges, followed by Jocasta. Each of the two is torn between pity and horror at the other's presence. Jocasta, overcome by self-revulsion, bids Oedipus kill her, then takes a sword and stabs herself. As she dies, Oedipus cries that he is a double parricide, then gropes his way out, bidding the plague leave Thebes with him.

C O M M E N T A R Y. Granted at the outset that Seneca's *Oedipus* is much inferior to its model, lacking the subtleties of plot and profundities of meaning found in Sophocles' play, it is still of some interest to comment on certain of Seneca's changes. Oedipus, instead of being a man whose pride of intellect is brought low in order that he may learn wisdom, becomes simply a tyrant who falls. Instead of the portrayal of a struggle against divine revelation that leads to the divulgence of a deeper secret, there is simple propaganda for the art of divination, a favorite Stoic rite. And instead of the depiction of gods as instructors of man, teaching him by calamity that his knowledge is only ignorance by their standards, the emphasis is placed on man, who can achieve virtue by meeting with fortitude the extremes of circumstance. The play is uneven in quality and has never been reckoned among Seneca's better efforts.

Oedipus at Colonus (Gk. **Oidipous epi Kolonoi**; traditional Latin title, **Oedipus Coloneus**). Extant tragedy by Sophocles (produced posthumously in 401 B.C. by the poet's grandson Sophocles). Translations: Thomas Francklin, 1759; Richard C. Jebb, 1904; F. Storr, 1912; Gilbert Murray, 1948; Theodore H. Banks, 1953; Robert Fitzgerald, 1956 (revised); Paul Roche, 1958.

S C E N E. Colonus, near Athens; by the Grove of the Eumenides.

S U M M A R Y. As the play opens, Oedipus, old, blind, and exiled, led by Antigone, comes to the outskirts of Athens and stops to rest in the sacred grove. Realizing that he has reached his destined place of burial, he bids a stranger summon King Theseus of Athens. When the man has left, Oedipus reveals to Antigone that Apollo's oracle prophesied that in such a place he would find peace, at the same time conveying a blessing to those who received him and a curse to those who banished him.

Soon the Chorus of Elders of Colonus enter and insist that Oedipus step down from the holy precinct. At first sympathetic, they show fright when they learn his identity and start to drive him away. But Antigone succeeds in gaining a hearing for her father. Oedipus maintains that his crimes were committed unawares, then hints of the blessing he brings. Moved by his words, the Chorus declare that Theseus must judge his cause.

Oedipus' other daughter, Ismene, appears with news from Thebes. She reports that Eteocles and Creon have expelled Polyneices in a quarrel over the kingship, and that Polyneices has gone to Argos and formed an army. Creon, according to Ismene, will soon come to take Oedipus back, for he has heard from oracles that her father's presence will guarantee Thebes's safety; his plan is to keep Oedipus just outside Thebes's boundary, so as to have his blessing without the pollution of his body. When Oedipus learns that his sons have heard the oracles and evidently prefer the kingship to their father's return, he curses them and Creon and declares he will never return to Thebes.

The Chorus instruct Oedipus how to propitiate the Eumenides, whose grove he has violated, and Ismene goes to perform the rites for him. Then

Theseus enters. Already acquainted with the story of Oedipus' suffering, the king hears his suit, learns of the gift he brings Athens, promises him protection, and leaves. While he is away, Creon attempts to carry off Oedipus, having already seized Antigone and Ismene. But Theseus returns in time to prevent the seizure and, upbraiding Creon for mocking his rule and Athenian law, declares that he will not be allowed to leave Athenian soil until the daughters are released. Then he and Creon go out.

After the Chorus sing of Theseus' might, he returns with Antigone and Ismene, as well as the news that one of Oedipus' kinsmen is begging a word with him. Knowing the kinsman to be his exiled son Polyneices, Oedipus recoils from the meeting but finally bows to Antigone's plea that he see him. The Chorus sing of the afflictions of old age, and then Polyneices appears. He relates his struggle for power and banishment by his brother, his subsequent marriage to the daughter of King Adrastus of Argos, and the formation of an army, under seven leaders, to drive Eteocles from Thebes. But when he begs his father's blessing, knowing the oracle's prediction that the side favored by Oedipus will win, he receives instead Oedipus' curse, a pronouncement that the expedition will fail and that he will kill, and be killed by, his next of kin. Oedipus will not forget that, when Polyneices sat on the throne, he drove his father out. Although Antigone pleads with her brother not to undertake the foredoomed struggle against Thebes, he leaves determinedly.

Oedipus hears the thunder presaged by the oracle of Apollo as the signal for his death, and he summons Theseus. He directs the king to accompany him to his secret burial ground but to conceal its location forever. Then the two men, with Oedipus' daughters, enter the grove. The Chorus pray for Oedipus' peaceful death, after which a Messenger describes the ritual performed by Oedipus, his commendation of his daughters to the king, the voice from heaven that told him not to tarry longer, and his final disappearance before the eyes of Theseus alone. As he promised, he has become a guardian spirit to Athens. Finally Antigone and Ismene emerge, grieving. They are followed by the king, who sends them to Thebes where they will try again to forestall their brothers' fated struggle.

COMMENTARY. In *Oedipus at Colonus*, which is the most mysterious of Greek tragedies and which might be considered the last will and testament of a poet on the edge of the grave, Sophocles has deliberately deviated from his earlier version of the Oedipus story in order to make the old man all sinned against and not at all sinning. Some critics carelessly describe Oedipus as portrayed in this play as a kind of saint, purified and gentle, but aside from the love between father and daughters, there is not much trace of gentleness here. Other commentators have pointed out more perspicaciously that if Oedipus is a saint he is far from being a Christian one.

The general impression of the old king's character is not of gentleness, but of weakness that turns into a mysterious kind of power. The power is that of justification, patience, and self-sufficiency. When the man most accursed of all men comes to the grove of the goddesses of curses, and when the man most offended against is housed in the sanctuary of the deities of retribution and by divine dispensation takes on the aspect of a spirit of retribution himself, then the pattern of his life is seen in all its completeness, and, in Yeats's words, "a terrible beauty is born."

Thus the view that the violent scenes with Creon and Polyneices are an interpolation, marring the serenity of the whole, is ill-founded. The men who are so pitifully and despicably grasping at the obvious powers of this world are overwhelmed by the power of the man who has suffered everything, who desires nothing but death, and who has something to give but can himself be given nothing. "Best it is never to be born, and next best is to go to the land of death as quickly as possible." Oedipus goes willingly into the transcendence of death, and Theseus and Oedipus' two daughters, three of the noblest of characters in terms of this life, are left behind in grief and bewilderment.

Oedipus the King (Gk. **Oidipous Tyrannos;** Latinized, **Oedipus Tyrannus;** traditional Latin title, **Oedipus Rex**). Extant tragedy by Sophocles (generally dated in the early 420's B.C.). Translations: Thomas Francklin, 1759; Richard C. Jebb, 1904; F. Storr, 1912; David Grene, 1942; Dudley Fitts and Robert Fitzgerald, 1949; Theodore H. Banks, 1956; Albert Cook, 1957; Paul Roche, 1958; Bernard M. W. Knox, 1959; H. D. F. Kitto, 1962. Adaptations and works influenced by *Oedipus the King:* Seneca, *Oedipus;* Pierre Corneille, *Oedipe,* 1659; John Dryden and Nathaniel Lee, *Oedipus,* 1679; Voltaire, *Oedipe,* 1718; Jean Cocteau, *La Machine Infernale,* 1934.

S C E N E. Thebes, the palace.

S U M M A R Y. Plague, failure of crops, disease in the flocks, and barrenness of women afflict the city of Thebes. A group of Suppliants, with a Priest as their spokesman, appeal to Oedipus, their king, for help. They have come to him, the Priest explains, not because they consider him a god, but the first of men, and because formerly the god had put into his mind the means to set straight all their lives—saving the city by solving the riddle of the Sphinx. Oedipus declares that the present affliction is especially painful to him since, while each of the Suppliants suffers only a private grief, he must grieve for himself, for them, and for the city as a whole. The king tells the people that he has sent his brother-in-law, Creon, to consult the Delphic oracle.

Returning, Creon offers to deliver his news to Oedipus in private, but the king bids him speak out. Creon reveals that Apollo has commanded them to drive forth the pollution, the miasma, that they have been nurturing in their land. The unpunished murderer of Laius, the former king, who was killed with all his attendants save one while traveling to Delphi, is polluting the land with his presence, and must be expelled. The surviving attendant, Creon says, reported that Laius was killed by robbers, but no further investigation was made at the time because the city was being harassed by the Sphinx.

Oedipus points out that it is in his own interest to discover the murderer, for he himself might be the next victim. At the king's summons, the City Council of Elders assemble as a chorus, praying to the gods, particularly Apollo, for deliverance. Oedipus makes the following declaration: As "a stranger to the report and to the deed" he must turn to them for information. If the murderer confesses, the penalty will be exile only; but if he does not, he will be cursed and thrust from the land; no one will receive him or speak to him or let him share in worship. Oedipus himself, as Laius' successor and husband to Laius' queen, will take on the avenging role of next-of-kin, as if Laius were his own father.

When the Chorus advise Oedipus to seek the help of the blind prophet Tiresias, the king replies that he has already summoned him. But Tiresias, entering, exclaims, "How terrible is knowledge when it brings no good to the knower!" and asks the boy who leads him to take him home. Oedipus at first reproaches him courteously for not revealing what he knows, but quickly falls into an intense rage at what appears to him to be treachery. Finally, he accuses Tiresias of having planned Laius' murder. The prophet is stung into shouting, "You are yourself the unholy defiler of this land! You yourself are the murderer whom you seek!" Oedipus retorts that Tiresias is blind and in fact no prophet at all, for he had to wait for the stranger Oedipus to solve the Sphinx's riddle. The king accuses the prophet of plotting with Creon to usurp the throne. In an answering fury, Tiresias declares that Oedipus has sight, but cannot see in what misfortune he is or where he lives or with whom he houses or from whom he has his being; he is enemy to those below and those on earth. Tiresias predicts that the "terrible-footed curse" of Oedipus' mother and father will hound him out of the land, and the eyes that see light will soon see darkness. "This day will bring you to birth and will destroy you!" the prophet says. "This murderer here, though a stranger, will be shown to be a Theban born; seeing, he shall be blind; rich, he shall be poor; he shall make his way to a foreign land groping with his staff, being brother and father to his children, son and spouse to his wife, co-husband and murderer to his father." Tiresias withdraws amid general alarm.

When Creon comes to acquit himself of the charge of treason, Oedipus refuses to be convinced. Creon, he says, is the one who suggested calling in Tiresias in the first place, and further, the prophet waited years before revealing what he presumably knew all along. Oedipus' wife, Queen Jocasta, separates her husband and brother at the height of their quarrel. After Creon has left, Jocasta learns of the horrible prophecy and consoles Oedipus. Soothsayers, she says, cannot be believed: although prophets of Apollo told Laius that he would be killed by his own son, he actually died at the hands of highwaymen at a place where three roads meet. His three-day-old son he had exposed years before, with his ankles pinned together, on a mountain.

Oedipus is, however, not reassured. He presses Jocasta for details, then asks her to call in Laius' lone surviving servant. The truth is, he says, that long before, at a banquet in Corinth, a drunken companion taunted him with not being the real son of King Polybus and Queen Merope, as he thought. When the rumor spread, he consulted the Delphic oracle, only to hear that he would have children by his mother and would kill his father. Horrified, Oedipus left Corinth in order to be far away from his parents. Arriving at the place where three roads meet, he had killed an angry old man in a chariot who had almost ridden him down. Oedipus concludes that his only hope lies in the testimony of Laius' servant, who had said expressly that the old king was killed by robbers. Jocasta reiterates her belief that their son died long ago in infancy. The two then go into the palace.

After a Choral ode, Jocasta emerges to pray to Apollo but is interrupted by a Messenger from Corinth, who reports that King Polybus has died of old age and that Oedipus is to be his successor. Jocasta thinks the divination conclusively disproved, but Oedipus remains troubled by the oracle's words that he would marry his mother; he says he will not return to Queen Merope at Corinth. To reassure Oedipus, the Messenger reveals that Polybus and Merope are not his real parents. He himself, the Messenger says, took the infant Oedipus from one of Laius' shepherds on Mt. Cithaeron, loosed the spikes from his ankles, and gave him to the king and queen of Corinth. When Oedipus asks about Laius' shepherd, the Chorus identify him as the servant already sent for. Jocasta, realizing the truth, begs Oedipus not to inquire any more, but he continues, thinking that she may be ashamed to have married a man of low descent. Jocasta goes into the palace.

At this point the Shepherd appears. Extremely reluctant to speak, he is forced by Oedipus to tell how he received Laius' child from Jocasta, pitied it, and handed it over to the Corinthian. Finally aware of the whole truth, Oedipus rushes into the palace.

The Chorus lament the king's fate, after which a Second Messenger comes out to describe the sequel: Oedipus broke into the royal bedroom to find that Jocasta had hanged herself. Taking down her body, he struck out his eyes with her golden brooches so that they might no longer see the misery of his life. Oedipus now gropes his way out, supported by attendants. With the Chorus, who regard him with pity and horror, he chants of his doom. Creon, now in charge of the city, enters and announces that Oedipus cannot be exiled until they learn Apollo's instructions. Oedipus' two young daughters, Antigone and Ismene, are brought to him for a last farewell and embrace. He leaves as the Chorus sing: "Natives of Thebes, behold this Oedipus, who knew the famous riddle and was most powerful of men, whose lot no one looked upon without envy, to what a sea of terrible calamity he has come! Do not consider blest anyone who is a mortal until he has passed the term of his life without suffering."

COMMENTARY. Aristotle's implicit opinion that *Oedipus the King* is the perfect tragedy has commanded universal assent, but it has also given rise to endless discussion: What is the tragic flaw (see HAMARTIA) of a hero whose offenses were foredoomed before his birth? Not his rashness, his suspiciousness, his irascibility, nor even his intellectual pride. Some critics, abandoning the theory of the tragic flaw, say that Oedipus is merely an awesome example of the power of the gods and that his fate is a demonstration of the utter helplessness of man.

Utter helplessness is not culpable, but Oedipus *is* culpable. In trying to cure the plague without realizing that he himself is the plague, Oedipus attempts to handle the problem without becoming personally involved in it. The disengagement caused by intellectual pride is Oedipus' flaw, just as it was the besetting sin of the clever Greek and the clever Athenian and is now the besetting sin of modern Western man. In *Oedipus the King* this sin is cured by the gods in the only way possible: the king is shown that he himself is both the problem and the answer, that knowledge is not wisdom, that the solution must not merely be known but lived, and that evil is not an exterior problem but an inner mystery and it begins at home.

So the confrontation of Oedipus, the clever man who knows all the answers, and blind Tiresias, the wise vessel of divine wisdom, is crucial. Oedipus boasts that he solved the riddle of the Sphinx: What goes on four legs in the morning, on two legs at noon, on three legs in the evening? But Tiresias indicates that Oedipus did not then really know the answer. The one who gave to the Sphinx the response, "Man," must now live it; that is, he who stands on two feet in the noon of his glory must in this day of his life learn that he was an infant with wounded and hobbled feet, and he must go out into the darkness of this very evening, groping his way with a staff. *Oidipous,* "Swollen Foot," must become *Oidipous,* "He Who Knows His Feet."

Oedipus is perhaps not the most pitiful of tragedies, but it is by all odds the most fearful. It says to the spectator in clearly ringing tones, "*De te fabula,*" "This is your story." And the most ironical scene in this masterpiece of tragic irony is the last, when Creon and the Chorus look on Oedipus as a being different from themselves, complacently viewing his problem as one in which they are not involved and congratulating themselves that their fate is not his.

Oeneus (Gk. **Oineus**). *Myth.* King of Calydon. By his first wife, Althaea, Oeneus became the father of Meleager and of Deianira, who married Heracles. Tydeus was his son by his second wife, Periboea. Oeneus' sons and descendants were called Oeniadae. When, one year, he failed to make sacrifice to Artemis, the goddess sent a gigantic boar to ravage the land. Oeneus summoned all the strong young men of Greece to kill it, promising the boar's skin to the one who dispatched the monster. It was over a quarrel concerning the prize that Meleager lost his life (see MELEAGER). In his old age Oeneus was dethroned and mistreated by his nephews, but his grandson Diomedes avenged him.

Sophocles' lost *Oeneus* possibly treated the king's misfortunes in old age. The play's existence rests, however, on slender evidence. Euripides' lost *Oeneus* (produced before 425 B.C.) told how Diomedes rescued and avenged his grandfather.

Oenoe (Gk. **Oinoe**). City on the island of Icaria.

Oenomaus (Gk. **Oinomaos**). *Myth.* King of Pisa in Elis. Either because he loved his daughter Hippodamia unnaturally, or because an oracle had prophesied that a son-in-law would kill him, Oenomaus contested all the girl's suitors in a chariot race to the Isthmus of Corinth. If overtaken, the suitor would be put to death. Because Oenomaus' horses were the offspring of the wind, he had never lost a race. Hippodamia, in addition, was made to ride with the suitor and was supposed to distract him.

When Pelops came wooing, Hippodamia fell in love with him and persuaded Myrtilus, her father's charioteer, to remove the lynchpins from the chariot axles. (In some versions of the story it was Pelops who persuaded Myrtilus to help him win by offering the charioteer the first night with the bride.) Oenomaus' chariot consequently fell to pieces in the race, and he was dragged to his death.

Sophocles' lost *Oenomaus*, produced before 414 B.C., was apparently a success and was revived in the next century. The start of the chariot race may have taken place in the orchestra of the theater. It is uncertain whether Accius' Latin *Oenomaus* was modeled on Sophocles' or Euripides' play. Of Euripides' lost tragedy (produced 409 B.C.) the twenty-odd extant lines tell very little about the plot. It is, consequently, hard to say how this version differed from Sophocles'.

Oenone (Gk. **Oinone**). Old name for the island of Aegina.

Oenops (Gk. **Oinops**). Father of Hyperbius.

Oeta (Gk. **Oite**). Mountain ridge along the southern border of Thessaly near the Maliac Gulf.

Ogygus or **Ogyges** (Gk. **Ogygos** or **Ogyges**). *Myth.* First king of Boeotia, which was also called Ogygia after him. During Ogygus' rein the country was flooded when Lake Copais overflowed its banks. The word Ogygian referred to Boeotia and to Thebes.

Oiatis. See OEA.

Oïleus or **Ileus.** *Myth.* King of Opuntian Locris. Oïleus was the father of Ajax (2).

Old Comedy. See COMEDY.

Old Curmudgeon, The. See DYSKOLOS.

Olenus (Gk. **Olenos**). City in Aetolia. The Olenian Goat, which was raised here, suckled the infant Zeus and was set in the sky as the star Capella.

Olophyxus (Gk. **Olophyxos**). Town on the Acte peninsula, where Mt. Athos stands. In *The Birds* (line 1041) Aristophanes uses the town's name in a pun on *olophyromai*, which means "lament."

Olympia. City in Elis on the river Alpheus. Olympia was the chief site of the cult of Zeus. The Olympic Games were held there in his honor.

Olympus (Gk. **Olympos**). 1. Mountain on the northern border of Thessaly.

2. *Myth.* The same mountain thought of as the home of the heavenly gods, crowned with their palaces. Olympus was hence equated with the sky itself.

3. *Myth.* Famous flutist, usually called the son of Marsyas. The latter contended against Apollo in music.

Omphale. *Myth.* Queen of Lydia. Heracles was made to serve Omphale in punishment for having killed Iphitus (see EURYTUS). The queen was said to have fallen in love with Heracles, who was reported to have exchanged his lionskin for a Lydian robe. According to some, the lovers exchanged clothes, Heracles wearing a woman's gown and jewelry and Omphale dressing in the lionskin and brandishing Heracles' club. She bore him several sons.

Onca (Gk. **Onka**). *Myth.* Phoenician goddess identified with Pallas Athena.

onkos. Style of coiffure, the piling up of the hair in front. The onkos was used in tragedy and adopted as a feature of the tragic mask.

Ophion. *Myth.* Originally the great world serpent. In some cosmogonies Ophion was said to be the world ruler before Cronus. In later myth he was either confused with Cadmus, who was changed into a serpent, or regarded as one of the Giants who attacked Olympus.

Ophiuchus (Gk. **Ophiouchos,** "serpent-holder"). Constellation, sometimes said to represent Asclepius.

Opora (Gk. "the latter part of summer"). *Myth.* Personification of the fruit season and harvesttime. Opora appears as an attendant of Peace in Aristophanes' *Peace.*

Ops. Roman goddess of wealth and abundance.

Opuntius (Gk. **Opountios**). Stupid, one-eyed Athenian of Aristophanes' time.

Opus (Gk. **Opous**). City in LOCRIS.

orchestra (Gk. "dancing place"). Area in the Greek theater where the chorus performed. The orchestra was a circular space between the spectators and the raised stage. (See also ALTARS; THEATER; THYMELE.)

Orcus. 1. Roman equivalent of HADES, god of the underworld.

2. Roman underworld and land of the dead.

Oreithyia. *Myth.* Daughter of King Erechtheus of Athens. Oreithyia was carried off by Boreas, the north wind. She bore him twin sons, Zetes and Calais. In Aeschylus' lost tragedy *Oreithyia* Erechtheus seems to have rejected Boreas' suit. His daughter was nevertheless carried off. Sophocles wrote a play called *Oreithyia* which is lost. So little is known about it that its content cannot be distinguished from that of Aeschylus' play.

Oresteia. Tetralogy by Aeschylus of which the tragic trilogy, *Agamemnon, Choephori,* and *Eumenides,* is extant; the satyr play, *Proteus,* is lost. The *Oresteia* was produced in 458 B.C. and was awarded first prize. Translations of the complete trilogy: Robert Potter, 1777; F. A. Paley, 1864; Edward H. Plumptre, 1868; Lewis Campbell, 1893; E. D. A. Morshead, 1904; Arthur S. Way, 1906; Walter and C. E. S. Headlam, 1909; H. Weir Smyth, 1922; Robert C. Trevelyan, 1923; Gilbert Murray, 1925; Richmond Lattimore, 1953; G. M. Cookson, 1956; Philip Vellacott, 1956; Paul Roche, 1963; Peter D. Arnott, 1964. Adaptations and works influenced by the *Oresteia:* Sophocles, *Electra;* Euripides, *Electra;* Seneca, *Agamemnon;* Voltaire, *Oreste,* 1750; Vittorio Alfieri, *Oreste,* 1786; Eugene O'Neill, *Mourning Becomes Electra,* 1931; Jean-Paul Sartre, *Les Mouches,* 1943; Gerhart Hauptmann, *Die Atriden-Tetralogie,* 1949. (For other works influenced by the *Oresteia,* see Sophocles' ELECTRA.)

Agamemnon. Translations of this play alone: H. S. Boyd, 1823; Thomas Medwin, 1832; Henry Hart Milman, 1865; Edward Fitzgerald, 1876; Robert

Browning, 1877; W. Watson Goodwin, 1906; Locke Ellis, 1920; Louis MacNiece, 1951; John Sheppard, 1952.

S C E N E. Argos, the palace.

S U M M A R Y. In the darkness before dawn, a Watchman stationed on the roof of the royal palace describes his year-long wait for the bonfire that will flame out in the night to signal Troy's fall. His bed has been drenched with dew, he has been too fearful to sleep or dream, and his sorrow over the misfortunes of the royal house has prevented him from singing. As the Watchman speaks, the light flares at last. Joyfully he goes to wake the queen, executing a little dance of jubilation, but he cannot dismiss a feeling of foreboding as he reflects on what the walls of the palace might tell—things about which he himself prefers to remain silent.

A Chorus of Elders file in. It is the tenth year, they say, since the sons of Atreus (Agamemnon and Menelaus), like eagles whose nest has been robbed, sailed against Troy, leaving the old men at home, too feeble to fight. They recall an omen that appeared at the outset of the expedition—two birds devouring a pregnant hare—which was interpreted by the seer Calchas as symbolizing Artemis' anger against the Greeks for attacking the Trojans, the strong preying on the weak and timid. Calchas ended his interpretation with a prayer that Artemis should not cause unfavorable winds or demand a terrible countersacrifice.

The Chorus break off to address Zeus: "Zeus, whoever he is, if it is pleasant to him to be named this, this we call him." They recall his predecessors, Uranus and Cronus, without naming them: "He, blossoming in all manner of warlike audacity, who will not even be said to have existed, and he who later was and is gone away. But whoever whole-heartedly gives the victor's crown to Zeus fashions wisdom in all things." Zeus, they say, has ordained that men learn through suffering (*mathos* is achieved through *pathos*). Yet wisdom comes to men against their wills, and the grace of the gods is filled with violence. The Chorus then continue their description of the prelude to the Trojan War: The Greek force was, as feared, delayed by a great calm. Calchas determined that Iphigenia, the daughter of Agamemnon and Clytemnestra, must accordingly be sacrificed to Artemis. After agonizing indecision, Agamemnon consented, despite his daughter's pleas, and she was fettered in her own robes and gagged. Able to plead only with her eyes, Iphigenia was done away with. The sequel, the Chorus conclude, they do not know.

Clytemnestra, glimpsed briefly before, now comes forward. Having set the whole city astir with rituals of thanksgiving she confirms the report of Troy's capture and describes how the first beacon fire on Mt. Ida kindled a chain of others, like a relay race of torch-bearers, on peaks around the rim of the Aegean, up to the last one, visible in Argos. The queen goes on to picture the chaos and horror within the captured city. The Greeks, she hopes, will reverence the Trojan shrines, in order that they may return safely, for even if there is no sacrilege the suffering of the slain may not be lulled to sleep. The Chorus sing exultantly that Zeus and Night have thrown the all-encompassing net of

Ate over the towers of Troy, the punishment of those who are led by prosperity into succumbing to temptation. But with the example of Paris before them, they reveal premonitions about the vengeance enacted by the Erinyes on the great and arrogant.

A Herald from Troy enters, greets his homeland after a ten-year absence, and bids the people prepare to receive their lord Agamemnon, who has utterly uprooted Troy, with all its altars and its shrines and the whole country's seed. Noting the Chorus' melancholy, he tells them to rejoice at the good fortune, although he himself could complain of a soldier's suffering from weather and sky. Clytemnestra again passes across the scene, proclaiming her faithfulness to Agamemnon—she knows "no more pleasure from another man than how to dye bronze"—and her eagerness for his return. The Chorus inquire about Menelaus and learn that he, along with most of the army, was lost to the others in a great storm, from which Agamemnon's ship was saved by Fortune, the Savior. Again the Chorus deplore marriage that brings misery, like that of Paris and Helen, and the nurturing of evil in one's own house. They liken Paris to a pet lion cub who, when fully grown, devoured the substance of those that reared him. *Hybris* (overweening insolence and unscrupulousness), they declare, reproduced itself in unbroken sequence. The old proverb that prosperity produces insatiable woe should be corrected to mean that the impious deed begets another of its kind.

Agamemnon enters in a triumphal chariot with Cassandra, the Trojan princess and prophetess, at his side. He thanks the gods of Argos for aiding his safe return and sharing in the justice done at Troy. Listening to no tongue of man, they tossed their verdicts into the bloody urn of condemnation, while Hope alone approached the opposite urn. As Agamemnon prepares to take over the reins of management, Clytemnestra interrupts with a description of her own melancholy years of waiting, the rumors that would have had Agamemnon more full of holes than a net and the numberless disasters that he suffered in her dreams, which made her weep till the sources of her tears ran dry. She bids her servants spread a royal purple carpet for him, so that, as she says, Justice may bring him to his unexpected home. Agamemnon comments drily on her long speech and reproaches her for offering him such homage as belongs to gods and not to men. Nevertheless, she persuades him to tread on the carpet, though he prays to be spared the envy of heaven for doing so. Instructing his wife to welcome Cassandra, whom the army has awarded him as booty, Agamemnon enters the palace.

Clytemnestra orders Cassandra into the palace, but the prophetess remains in the chariot and the queen angrily hurries off, remarking that the victims are ready for the sacrifice. Alone with the Chorus, Cassandra is overcome by the spirit of Apollo, who, when she rejected his love, condemned her gift of prophecy (which she had wheedled from him) to go unbelieved. She sees visions of the past—among them Agamemnon's uncle, Thyestes, eating the flesh of his own children unawares, after it had been served him by his brother Atreus. She foresees the net of death thrown over Agamemnon, his murder in the bath, her own murder, and the eventual return of an exile (Orestes) to enact vengeance.

Immediately after Cassandra goes inside, Agamemnon cries out twice that he is being murdered. The Chorus mill about ineffectually until Clytemnestra is disclosed, blood on her forehead, standing over the bodies of her husband and the captive prophetess. Graphically the queen describes how she threw a wicked wealth of robe, like a net for fish, around her husband, struck him three times, and rejoiced like the earth under spring rains as blood spurted over her from his final gasps. To the Chorus' protestations that she will bring on her the hatred of all, she answers that Agamemnon was not hated for sacrificing his child, and she challenges them to punish her by force if they dare. They bewail the *daemon* that haunts the house of Atreus. Finally Aegisthus, Clytemnestra's lover and Thyestes' sole surviving son, enters, rejoicing that at last justice has been enacted for Atreus' cannibal feast of his two brothers. His response to the Chorus' taunts is to order his men to attack, but Clytemnestra intervenes. Although further insults are exchanged, it is clear that, as the queen says, she and Aegisthus rule the house and will manage all things as they see fit.

Choephori (Gk. *Choephoroi, The Libation Bearers.*) Translations of this play alone: Verrall, 1893; Tucker, 1901.

S C E N E. Argos, the tomb of Agamemnon.

S U M M A R Y. Orestes, son of Clytemnestra and the murdered King Agamemnon, enters with his friend Pylades. He has spent his entire life in exile, unrelenting in his purpose to take vengeance on his mother and her lover, Aegisthus, for his father's murder. Stealthily Orestes lays a lock of hair on Agamemnon's tomb. At the sound of voices, he and Pylades move to the background.

A Chorus of Slave Women enter, led by Orestes' sister Electra, bearing appeasing libations from Clytemnestra for the tomb. They sing sadly of the crime that has fouled the house of Atreus and declare that nothing can atone for the shedding of blood. As Electra pours the libations on the grave, she prays to her father's soul for Orestes to appear and avenge his murder. Suddenly she notices the lock of hair; its resemblance to her own hair, coupled with a footprint strangely like her own, suggests that Orestes may possibly be near.

Orestes, who has overheard Electra, makes his presence known. He tells her that Apollo's oracle has threatened him with a loathsome disease unless he placates their murdered father's blood. Electra, Orestes, and the Chorus then alternate in a kind of war chant around the tomb, exhorting one another, denouncing the murderers, recalling the outraging of Agamemnon's body and Electra's ill treatment. Orestes declares that he is willing to die if he can be the instrument of his mother's death.

Although the Chorus repeatedly encourage the brother and sister to carry out their resolve, Orestes asks first to know the meaning of Clytemnestra's libations. The Chorus explain that the queen has been driven to appease her husband's ghost by a dream in which a serpent to which she had given birth drew blood when she offered it her breast. Interpreting the dream as a favorable omen referring to himself, Orestes declares himself ready for revenge. He instructs his sister to return to the palace but to conceal what she has learned. He and Pylades, speaking as strangers from Phocis, will gain entrance and will kill Aegisthus. After the three have left, the Chorus ruminate on legends of wicked women.

The scene shifts to the palace, where Orestes and Pylades demand entrance. Delivering the false message that Orestes is dead, they are received by the insincerely grieving queen. While they are inside, Orestes' aged Nurse comes by to call Aegisthus to greet the two strangers. Grief-stricken, she informs the Chorus that the queen is secretly glad at her son's death. The Chorus persuade her to have Aegisthus come without attendants, and, when she leaves, pray to Zeus and bid Orestes be firm.

Aegisthus soon arrives and goes into the palace. Almost at once his dying cries are heard, and a servant summons Clytemnestra to his aid. She calls for a weapon, but her son emerges, sword in his hand. She pleads with him, recalling her early care for him, the evil of matricide, and Agamemnon's bad treatment of her. Orestes wavers, but recalls Apollo's warning, and pursues his mother into the palace. She recognizes her own son as the serpent in her dream.

The Chorus sing of the triumph of justice, and the palace doors open to show Orestes standing over the bodies of his mother and her paramour. Grieving rather than exultant, Orestes holds up the robe in which his father was snared and murdered and speaks at length to justify his own deed. But as he announces his intention of going to Delphi and throwing himself on the mercy of Apollo, who has promised him absolution, Orestes is pressed by a crowd of Erinyes, who are visible only to him. As he rushes out, driven by the loathsome creatures, the Chorus chant of the history of the curse and wonder what will follow.

Eumenides (Gk. *The Furies*). Translations of this play alone: Bernard Drake, 1853; John F. Davies, 1885; Francis G. Plaistowe, 1901.

s c e n e. Delphi, the Temple of Apollo; later, Athens.

s u m m a r y. The Priestess of Apollo at Delphi, after praying to the deities who preside or have presided over the sacred shrine, enters the innermost sanctuary to receive the oracular revelation. Immediately she rushes out in horror and describes what she has seen. Orestes is stretched as a suppliant on the holy navel stone of the earth, while around him sleep the loathsome Erinyes (the Chorus), who present a horrible spectacle. The temple doors are then opened to reveal Orestes and his pursuers. Apollo and Hermes now emerge from the sanctuary, and Apollo promises Orestes his protection, instructing him to go to the shrine of Pallas at Athens where he will find justice.

Orestes leaves under the conduct of Hermes, after which Clytemnestra's ghost comes to waken the Erinyes and spur them on. Gradually rousing, they complain that Apollo, a younger divinity than they, has snatched away their rightful prey. Apollo at this point commands the Erinyes to leave his holy shrine, but they reply that matricide cannot go unpunished. Denying Apollo's contention that the marriage pact is more sacred than blood relationship, of which they are the guardians, they take up the chase again.

The scene changes to Athens, where Orestes is seen clasping the image of Athena at her temple on the Acropolis. While he is begging the goddess to receive him, Orestes is discovered by the Erinyes, who chant exultantly of their ancient prerogative of retribution, assigned to them prior to the reign of the Olympian gods. Orestes claims that he has expiated his guilt through a long penance and calls on Athena to champion him. But the Erinyes persist, chanting that they will make sure that blood atones for blood, even though they are despised by Zeus. They claim that the younger gods have no right even to submit to trial the question of the guilt of their appointed victims.

When Athena appears, the Erinyes identify themselves as children of Night, called Curses in their home beneath the earth; they present their charge against Orestes, granting Athena power to arbitrate. Orestes defends himself, declaring that Apollo shares responsibility for the murder. Athena then reveals that she alone cannot judge issues of blood guilt. A dilemma faces her: Orestes has come to her as a purified suppliant, and she must therefore take him in; on the other hand, she is not permitted to banish the Erinyes. Further, if the latter lose their case. they will poison her land. What she will do, Athena says, is to ordain a court to settle this and all future questions of blood guilt.

After the goddess leaves, the Erinyes proclaim that the loss of their case will mean the end of all justice and the endangering of all society; they prophesy doom for the unjust. Athena returns with a jury of twelve Athenian citizens for the court, which will serve as a model for all time—the prototype of all law courts. Apollo then enters as Orestes' advocate, and the trial begins.

As the Erinyes question the defendant as his accusers, it becomes clear that Clytemnestra escaped their vengeance because she did not kill a blood relation, the only crime that concerns them. Apollo, on Orestes' behalf, maintains that the mother is no kin to the son, since she merely receives the seed from the father and nurtures it until birth. He says, further, that the command to kill Clytemnestra came ultimately from Zeus.

Athena delivers the charge to the jurymen, directing them to be just. Since she herself is sprung from Zeus alone, the goddess says, she favors the male and will vote for Orestes in the event of a tie. The votes are indeed equal, and Orestes is acquitted. After Apollo retires, Orestes leaves, promising eternal friendship between his country, Argos, and Athens.

Orestes' acquittal provokes an outburst of indignation from the Erinyes. Heedless of Athena's reasonable and soothing words, they maintain that they have been robbed of honor, that justice has been flouted, and that now they will be a heavy burden to Attica. Athena reminds them that the vote was fair and the decision ultimately Zeus's. When the Erinyes continue their protests, the goddess offers them an honorable place of worship in her city. This they at first refuse, but Athena points out that it would hardly be just of them to refuse her offer of hospitality, then to afflict the country because it did not honor them. Finally, assured that no house or society will prosper without their grace, the

Erinyes are persuaded to take their place in the framework of the polis and become beneficent deities of Athens. The assembled citizens then form a triumphal procession to escort the Furies to their new underground shrine below the Areopagus, the Hill of Ares. The Erinyes, or spirits of retribution, thus become the *Semnai,* the Venerated, and the *Eumenides,* the Well-disposed.

Proteus. This satyr play is lost, only four lines and a few isolated words remaining. Probably it told how Menelaus, on his way home from Troy, was blown to the island of Pharos off the coast of Egypt. There he met Eidothea, a sea goddess, learned from her of the fate of Agamemnon and others, and, following her instructions, caught the sea god Proteus and forced him to reveal the way to reach Greece.

COMMENTARY. In richness of poetry and complexity of meaning the *Oresteia* takes its place among the top handful of masterpieces in world literature. Its subject is a threefold theme of justice: justice working itself out in the particular case of the house of Atreus, the establishment of justice in human society, and the justification of the ways of God to man.

These three aspects of justice, manifested in an extraordinarily complex system of symbolism, are ultimately only one. The justice achieved by Clytemnestra and Aegisthus in the first play, and even the justice executed by Orestes in the second, are shown to be incomplete until they are taken up into the divine order of justice as revealed to man in the third play. The chain of evil appears to be endless and meaningless until it is finally woven into this pattern. Thus the gods use the evil deeds of mankind to turn darkness into day, barbarism into civilization, and ignorance into wisdom. The order of retribution, which decrees punishment for crime and reward for virtue, is not discarded but is made part of a larger whole, and this whole is greater than the sum of its parts.

Orestes' deed is deliberately juxtaposed with that of Clytemnestra in the tableaus where both murderers stand over their handiwork, she exultant, he tormented. Justice demands that he be punished less than she. But the gods do not deal in mere retributive equations; they add something from above. The suffering that comes from the sky, like rain and dew, like Agamemnon's blood that falls on Clytemnestra, brings the harvest of wisdom. This wisdom is not merely the wisdom to bear suffering, as some critics captiously suggest, but a wisdom that transcends suffering in that it views human justice as a right and beautiful part of the universal order. Thus the Erinyes become the Eumenides, dispensing blessing as well as punishment. Clytemnestra's fructifying baptism with her husband's blood, the mythical union of sky-father and earth-mother, prefigures the ultimate marriage of heaven and earth.

Orestes. 1. *Myth.* Son of Agamemnon and Clytemnestra and brother of Electra and Iphigenia. In Seneca's *Agamemnon* Orestes, a child, is secretly sent away by Electra for his safety. In Aeschylus' *Choephori* it is said that he was sold as a slave by Clytemnestra. According to the usual version of the story, Orestes grew up at the court of Strophius, king of Phocis, where he became the good friend of Pylades, Strophius' son.

In Aeschylus' *Choephori,* Sophocles' *Electra,* and Euripides' *Electra* Orestes returns to Argos, when he is grown, to avenge his father's death by killing his mother, Clytemnestra, and her lover, Aegisthus. Euripides' *Orestes* portrays his ensuing madness. In Aeschylus' *Eumenides,* Orestes is tormented by the Erinyes but gains eventual release at Athens.

In Euripides' *Iphigenia among the Taurians,* he wanders to the Tauric peninsula before his acquittal in Athens. (For Orestes' further adventures, see ALETES; CHRYSES.)

In Euripides' *Andromache* Orestes causes the death of Neoptolemus, his successful rival for the hand of Hermione, Helen's daughter. After Neoptolemus' death he married her.

2. A highwayman of Aristophanes' time who robbed travelers of their clothes.

Orestes. Extant play by Euripides (produced 408 B.C.). Translations: Edward P. Coleridge, 1891; Gilbert Murray, 1911; Arthur S. Way, 1912; William Arrowsmith, 1958.

S C E N E. Argos, the palace.

S U M M A R Y. Orestes has been tormented by the Erinyes for six days following his murder of his mother, Clytemnestra, and her lover, Aegisthus, in revenge for their murder of his father, Agamemnon. While Orestes sleeps, exhausted, his sister Electra keeps watch and meditates on the misfortune of their house, revealing that the townspeople are to decide the fate of brother and sister that day. Electra, who was a party to the crime of matricide, places her hope in Menelaus; the latter is shortly to arrive from Troy.

Menelaus' wife, Helen, secretly sent ahead for fear of the Greeks' revenge, asks Electra to take offerings for her to the tomb of her sister, Clytemnestra. When Electra refuses, telling her to send her daughter Hermione, Helen leaves. Electra comments that Helen is as vain as ever. The Chorus of Argive Women enter and speak with Electra of her brother's plight. Orestes awakes, momentarily sane, but the Erinyes again invade his brain and he falls into delirium. The Chorus sing of avenging spirits and fortune's reversals.

When Menelaus arrives, Orestes pleads for his help against the people of Argos, who are about to stone him and Electra as matricides. Clytemnestra's father, Tyndareus, then enters and denounces his grandson as a murderer. Orestes defends himself, maintaining that if he had let his mother go unpunished, no husband would ever be safe. Tyndareus leaves unmoved. Orestes again turns to Menelaus, but the latter consents only to try to persuade the people to be lenient.

Orestes' friend Pylades now enters; he has been driven into exile by his father for assisting in Clytemnestra's murder. Hearing of Orestes' predicament, Pylades advises him to stand trial and, if condemned, to die a hero's death. After the two friends leave, the Chorus bewail Orestes' deed.

Presently a Messenger informs Electra that, despite Orestes' plea to the Argive Assembly not to embolden their women to commit crime, she and Orestes have been sentenced to die. The Assembly's only concession is that they may take their own lives. Orestes, returning, chides his sister for lamenting. Pylades insists he will die with them and urges that they punish Menelaus, who maintained indifference to their misfortune throughout the trial. In revenge against him, and on behalf of all Greece, Orestes and Pylades decide to kill Helen. At Electra's suggestion, they plan to take Hermione as a hostage. Calling on the soul of Agamemnon for aid, Orestes and Pylades enter the palace, while Electra watches for Hermione.

Just as Helen's cry is heard from inside, Hermione returns from her mission to Clytemnestra's grave. Convinced by Electra that the cry was Orestes', Hermione enters the palace. A Phrygian Slave soon rushes out panic-stricken; he describes Helen's near death and sudden disappearance and the seizure of Hermione.

As Menelaus approaches, Orestes and Pylades appear on the roof holding Hermione, having barred the palace gates. Orestes threatens to kill Hermione and set fire to the palace unless Menelaus persuades the Argives to spare his and his sister's lives. When Menelaus defies him, Orestes calls to Electra and Pylades to kindle the fires. At this point, Apollo appears from above and proclaims the destiny of each: Helen, Zeus's divine daughter, snatched away from Orestes' sword by Apollo, has ascended to heaven to become a goddess of the sea and patroness of sailors. Orestes, after suffering and exile, is to be tried in Athens and freed by verdict of the gods; he will then wed Hermione and rule Argos. Electra is to marry Pylades, and Menelaus is to get himself another wife and go home to Sparta. Apollo himself will effect a reconciliation between Orestes and the people of Argos.

COMMENTARY. In spite of admiring words for Euripides' portrayal of Orestes' madness, for his masterly delineation of Helen's character, and for the theatrical brilliance of the play, Orestes has generally been considered dramatically defective, psychologically faulty, and ethically repellent. In the words of Wilhelm Schmid (History of Greek Literature): "All the ethical valuations, all the emotions, excitements, sorrows, and disappointments depicted so vividly are converted into a senseless puppet play, with an irresponsible god pulling the strings."

Besides the objection to Apollo as a *deus ex machina* of the worst kind, there have been criticisms as to the inappropriateness of Helen's deification, to the psychological unlikelihood of Orestes' and Hermione's marriage, and to the meanness of behavior, not only of Menelaus (whose portrait Aristotle censured as unduly base), but of the central trio, Orestes, Electra, and Pylades.

Various rebuttals have been made to the foregoing criticisms: that Orestes' madness strikes the keynote in a drama of a world gone mad; that Menelaus and Helen represent a debased society in which the only steadfast and ennobling relationships are those of brother and sister (Orestes and Electra) and of friends (Orestes and Pylades); that, even in these relationships, the interaction of evil deeds is shown to produce deterioration—a favorite Euripidean theme; and that the playwright is pointing out that, when human wickedness has descended to a chaos of desperation, the only hope is for forceful intervention from above.

Oreus (Gk. **Oreos**). Town on Euboea once called Histiaea. When in 445 B.C. its inhabitants massacred the crew of an Athenian ship, Athens expelled them and recolonized the town with its own citizens.

Orion. *Myth.* One of the Giants and a hunter. Invited by Oenopion of Chios to rid the island of wild beasts, Orion tried to assault the king's daughter. In revenge, Oenopion plied him with wine and blinded him. Orion then went to Hephaestus' smithy and carried off the child Cedalion, whom he set on his shoulders as a guide. Bidding Cedalion lead him to the east, Orion faced the sun, whose rays restored his sight. When, later, Orion offered violence to Artemis, he was stung to death by a scorpion which the goddess sent. Both the scorpion and the mighty hunter became constellations.

Orneae (Gk. **Orneai**). Town in Argolis. Orneae was unsuccessfully besieged by Athens in 416 B.C. Its name suggests *ornis*, "bird."

Orpheus. *Myth.* Son of Oeagrus and one of the Muses. Calliope was usually said to be Orpheus' mother. He was so great a harpist and singer that wild beasts followed him and trees bent down to hear him. On the voyage of the Argonauts, Orpheus outsang the Sirens. When his wife, Eurydice, died of snake bite, he sang so sweetly that Pluto let him take her back to the light of day on condition that he not look at her on the return journey. But Orpheus disobeyed and lost Eurydice forever. In his grief, the young husband ignored the charms of some maenads, who, in revenge, tore him to pieces and threw his head into the Thracian river Hebrus. The head floated to sea and became an oracle on the island of Lesbos.

Orpheus appears in no extant plays and very few lost ones, but there are references to Orphism, a mystical death-and-resurrection cult allied with Dionysianism (compare Euripides' *Hippolytus*, line 953 ff.).

orthian nome. Spirited type of song associated with the poet Terpander.

Ortygia. Epithet of Artemis. Her birthplace, Delos, was once called Ortygia, "Quail Island." In *The Birds* (line 870) Aristophanes calls Artemis' mother Leto "Mother of Quails."

Ossa. Mountain in northern Magnesia. The giant Aloadae, Otus and Ephialtes, piled Mt. Pelion on Mt. Ossa in their unsuccessful attempt to storm Olympus.

Othrys. Mountain in southern Thessaly north of the Maliac Gulf.

P

Pactolus (Gk. **Paktolos**). River in Lydia. The Pactolus was said to have gold-bearing sands.

Pacuvius, Marcus. Called by Cicero the greatest Roman writer of tragedy (c. 220–130 B.C.). Pacuvius was the nephew of Ennius and the friend of Accius. He was a painter as well as a poet, having a famous mural in the Temple of Hercules. Pacuvius was probably a member of the literary circle of the younger Scipio, to which Terence belonged. Of his works about four hundred fragments survive. These fragments have been used in the reconstruction of the lost Greek plays on which they were modeled. Some titles of Pacuvius' plays were: *Antiope* (after Euripides), *Award of Armor* (after Aeschylus), *Atalanta, Chryses* (probably after Sophocles), *Hermione, Ilione, Medus, Niptra, Orestes as Slave, Pentheus, Periboea, Teucer,* and *Paulus* (a *fabula praetexta*). For unusual versions of myth surviving in Pacuvius' writings see MEDUS; PARTHENOPAEUS; POLYDORUS.

Paean (Gk. **Paian**). 1. Epithet of Apollo as healer.

2. (paean). Hymn to Apollo or victory hymn or war song, or any solemn choric song.

Paeonia (Gk. **Paionia**). 1. Region in northeastern Macedonia.

2. Festival of Apollo as healer.

Paetians or Paeti (Gk. **Paitoi**). Thracian tribe that lived near the Hebrus River.

Palaechthon (Gk. **Palaichthon**). *Myth.* Father of Pelasgus.

Palaemon (Gk. **Palaimon**). *Myth.* God of harbors and patron of sailors. After INO leaped into the sea with her child Melicertes, the child was transformed into this divinity. (See also ATHAMAS.)

Palamedes. 1. *Myth.* Son of Nauplius and Clymene. Palamedes was known for his shrewdness and was sometimes said to have invented letters and numbers. When Agamemnon, Menelaus, and Palamedes went to fetch Odysseus to accompany them to Troy, the latter feigned madness in order to avoid going, yoking together an ass and an ox and flinging salt over his shoulders as he plowed. But Palamedes set down Odysseus' son Telemachus in front of the oncoming team, and Odysseus turned aside, thereby proving his sanity. Odysseus avenged himself on Palamedes at Troy by convincing the Greeks that Palamedes was in correspondence with King Priam. A forged letter, in addition to a sack of gold planted in Palamedes' quarters, led to his condemnation. He was stoned to death.

In Aeschylus' lost tragedy *Palamedes,* the hero defended himself against Odysseus' unjust accusations. After Palamedes' death, Nauplius came to investigate the matter.

Sophocles' lost tragedy *Palamedes* seems to have dealt mainly with the plot against the hero. In it Odysseus caused the Greek camp to be moved for a day because of an alleged dream; he buried gold on the site of Palamedes' tent and then arranged for the interception of a slave who bore a forged letter confirming Palamedes' treacherous negotiations with the enemy.

Euripides' lost *Palamedes* was produced in 415 B.C., with *Alexander, The Trojan Women,* and *Sisyphus.* In it the hero's brother Oeax wrote the news of Palamedes' condemnation on oars and threw them into the sea, so that at least one would float to Greece and inform Nauplius, their father. This device was parodied by Aristophanes in his *Thesmophoriazusae* (line 770 ff.).

2. Lexicographer (perhaps 2nd century A.D.). Palamedes was the author of *Lexicon to Comedy* and *Lexicon to Tragedy,* both of which are lost.

Pallas. Epithet of Athena.

Pallene. 1. Attic deme where there was a shrine to Athena. Hence she was called the "Pallenian virgin."

2. Westernmost peninsula jutting down from the region of Chalcidice in Macedonia.

pallium. Greek cloak. The pallium was the characteristic dress of *fabula palliata,* Latin comedy adapted from Greek.

Pamphilus (Gk. **Pamphilos**). Politician and military commander in Athens (early 4th century B.C.). Pamphilus was punished for dishonest conduct with confiscation of his property. He either painted a picture or wrote a play, called *Heraclidae,* that depicted a group of suppliants.

Pamphylia. Coastal region along the southern shore of Asia Minor.

Pan. *Myth.* Greek god of the wilderness, probably in origin a pasture god. Pan had goatlike features, as well as the horns and legs of a goat. His arms and torso were those of a man. Pan was usually called the son of Hermes, but occasionally the son of Zeus. Like Silenus, he was sometimes thought of as not one being but many, and Pans were confused with satyrs. The Panpipes were his instrument and Arcadia was his particular haunt. His cult was connected with that of the nymphs, though he was often included in the entourage of Dionysus. In Menander's *Dyskolos* he appears in front of a grotto of Pan and the Nymphs and speaks the prologue. Pan was known for producing sudden fears or panics. As a spirit of trickery, and also as god of flocks, he brought the golden lamb to the flock of ATREUS.

Panacea (Gk. **Panakeia**). *Myth.* Goddess of healing, daughter of Asclepius.

Panathenaea (Gk. **Panathenaia**). Annual birthday festival of Athena, held at Athens in August. The Panathenaea was marked by sacrifices, athletic contests, and a famous processional which included youths on horseback, maidens carrying baskets, and a ship-wagon bearing the embroidered robe to be presented to the goddess.

pancratium (Gk. **pankration**). Contest in the athletic games. The pancratium combined boxing and wrestling.

Pandateria or **Pandataria.** Island off the southeastern coast of Italy. Pandateria was used by the Roman emperors as a place of banishment.

Pandemos (Gk. "of all the people"). Epithet of Zeus and Aphrodite.

Pandion. 1. *Myth.* Son of Erichthonius and king of Athens. Pandion was the father of Erechtheus, Procne, and Philomela. The Athenian tribe Pandionis was named after him.

2. *Myth.* Son of Cecrops, grandson of Erechtheus, and king of Athens. Overthrown by the sons of Metion, Pandion fled to Megara, where he married Pylia, the daughter of King Pylas. He himself eventually became king of Megara. Pandion was the father of Aegeus, Pallas, Nisus, and Lycus (3).

Pandora. *Myth.* The first woman. After Prometheus had stolen fire from the gods, Zeus ordered Hephaestus to create Pandora in order to bring unhappiness to mankind. This beautiful but frivolous woman, made from earth, was given to Prometheus' brother Epimetheus as his wife. Soon afterward Pandora opened a jar which she had been warned to keep closed, and immediately there swarmed out all the miseries that have plagued humanity ever since that time. Pandora's name, meaning "she who gives all gifts," shows that she was essentially a form of Mother Earth.

Sophocles' lost satyr play *Pandora,* also called *The Hammerers,* depicted either the creation of Pandora by Hephaestus, with satyrs as helpers, or her awakening as Mother Earth in the springtime, with mallet-bearing satyrs breaking up the frozen clods.

Pandrosus (Gk. **Pandrosos**). *Myth.* One of the daughters of Cecrops. (See CECROPIDAE.)

Pangaeum or **Pangaeus** (Gk. **Pangaion, Pangaios**). Mountain near the coast in southeastern Macedonia.

Panopeus. See PHANOTEUS.

Panoptes (Gk. "all-seeing"). Epithet of Argus.

Panthous (Gk. **Panthoos**). *Myth.* Trojan elder and priest of Apollo. In Euripides' *Rhesus* (line 28) Panthoides ("Panthous' son") could have been either Polydamas, a warrior skilled in prophecy, whose advice Hector ignores in the *Iliad,* or Euphorbus, who wounded Patroclus in the back.

pantomimes. Dramatic performances consisting of the dancing and acting of stories, usually by one dancer, sometimes by several. At times the libretto was sung by a chorus as the dancer performed. Pantomime undoubtedly originated in cult ritual; it first became an art form in Sicily and was then imported into Greece. It was enormously popular in Rome, where something resembling pantomime appeared as early as the third century B.C., but it did not reach the height of success until imperial times, when its popularity probably owed something to Oriental influence.

Paphlagonia. Region on the southern shore of the Black Sea. Paphlagonia was a fertile source of slaves. "Paphlagon," Aristophanes' name for Cleon in *The Knights,* was both a slave name and a pun on *paphlazon,* "spluttering, blustering."

Paphos. City on Cyprus associated with the worship of Aphrodite.

Papposilenus. Silenus, especially in his role of father or leader of the satyrs.

Pappus (Gk. **Pappos**). Gray-haired slave, a stock figure in comedy.

parabasis. Principal song of the chorus in Old Comedy, addressed directly to the audience. The parabasis was one of the most striking formal components of Old Comedy. After a *kommation,* a short passage to command the audience's attention, the poet used the chorus to address the public, defending himself, upbraiding his rivals and critics, or appealing to the judges; this part of the parabasis was called "the anapests." The second part consisted of lyric strophes sung and danced by the chorus in their character as birds, clouds, etc. The original core of this part was a ritual song to the gods, to which general or personal ridicule was added.

Paralia. Coastal section of Attica between the Piraeus and Phalerum.

Paralus (Gk. **Paralos**). One of the Athenian state galleys. The *Paralus* carried official messages and official delegations to festivals.

parasite (Gk. **parasitos,** Lat. **parasitus**). Stock character in New Comedy. The parasite was a shameless rascal who would do anything to get an invitation to a meal. Originally the term referred to a priest whose meals were furnished at public expense, whereas a toady or flatterer was a *kolax* (see EUPOLIS, whose *Kolakes, The Toadies,* was produced in 421 B.C.). Presumably Alexis, in his play *Parasitos,* made "parasite" the more common term.

paraskenion, pl. **paraskenia. 1.** One of two projecting rooms or structures on either side of the skene.

2. (sing.) The use of a member of the chorus as a fourth actor.

paratragedy. Burlesque or parody of tragedy. Paratragedy was common in Old Comedy and was one of the chief types of Middle Comedy. The term could also be used for the more serious kind of comedy, such as Euripides' *Helen* or *Ion.*

Parcae. Roman equivalent of the MOIRAE.

Paris. *Myth.* Prince of Troy and lover of Helen. Paris was also called Alexander (see ALEXANDER 1). When Peleus and Thetis celebrated their marriage, Eris (Discord) was not invited to the feast. She thereupon threw among the assembled guests a golden apple bearing the inscription "For the Fairest." The three goddesses Hera, Athena, and Aphrodite claimed the apple, and Zeus sent them to Paris to judge among them. On Aphrodite's offer of Helen as a bride, Paris awarded her the apple. Helen's abduction caused the Trojan War. In drama, Paris appears in Euripides' *Rhesus.*

Parnassus (Gk. **Parnasos**). Mountain in Phocis. On its southern slope was Delphi. Also on Parnassus was a Temple of Dionysus in which a vine was said to grow, yielding a grape cluster every day for a libation to the god.

Parnes. Mountain in the northern part of Attica. On its slopes wood was gathered for charcoal.

parodos (Gk. "side passage"). The passageway on both sides of the skene, between it and the rows of seats. Because the chorus made its entrance through the parodos on the spectator's right, the entrance song of the chorus was called by this name.

Paros. Island in the southern Aegean directly west of Naxos. Paros was noted for its marble.

Parrhasia. Section of southern Arcadia on the border of Messenia.

partheneion. Choric song performed by young girls.

Parthenius (Gk. **Parthenios**). Mountain between Arcadia and Argolis.

Parthenopaeus (Gk. **Parthenopaios**). *Myth.* Son of Atalanta by either Meleager or Melanion. One of the Seven against Thebes, Parthenopaeus died in battle. In Pacuvius' lost *Atalanta,* he and his friend Telephus came to race against Atalanta, who had exposed her son as an infant and therefore did not know him. Parthenopaeus won the race and was about to claim Atalanta as his prize when she recognized him by an armlet that he was wearing.

Parthia. Region in Asia northwest of Persia. The Parthians were noted archers.

Pasiphaë. *Myth.* Wife of King Minos of Crete. When Minos angered Poseidon, the god caused Pasiphaë to fall in love with a bull. From the unnatural union that ensued came the MINOTAUR.

Patroclus (Gk. **Patroklos**). *Myth.* Friend of Achilles. When Achilles withdrew from the fighting in the Trojan War, Patroclus borrowed his armor and accomplished many feats of valor until he was killed by Hector. Achilles rejoined the Greek army to avenge the death of Patroclus.

Peace (Gk. **Eirene;** traditional Latin title, **Pax**). Extant comedy by Aristophanes (produced at the Dionysia of 421 B.C.). *Peace* was awarded second prize, Eupolis' *The Toadies* winning first. Translations: Benjamin B. Rogers, 1924; Arthur S. Way, 1934; Doros Alastos, 1953; Patric Dickinson, 1957; Robert Henning Webb, 1964.

S C E N E. The house of Trygaeus on one side of the stage, the house of Zeus on the other, and between them a cave.

S U M M A R Y. Two slaves of Trygaeus are feeding dung cakes to an enormous beetle, which is hidden from view inside Trygaeus' stable. They explain that their master has been supplicating Zeus for peace and, having fallen and broken his head while attempting to climb to heaven on a ladder, has now brought back the stinking beetle, on which he hopes to ascend. Trygaeus himself now appears, riding the creature up into the air. As he rises, he explains to the slaves and to his daughters, who have come running out, that he is going to consult Zeus about the god's plans for Greece.

Landing by Zeus's house, Trygaeus is gruffly received by Hermes, who tells him that all the gods have gone off to the ends of heaven in disgust at the Greeks, who refuse to make peace although they have had every opportunity to do so. War, who is in control of Zeus's household, has thrown Peace into a cave and blocked it with stones. At this point War enters and Trygaeus, hiding, observes the god tossing into a huge mortar various Greek cities represented by leeks, garlic, cheese, and honey. War then sends his assistant, Uproar, to earth for a pestle. Uproar soon returns to report that Athens has lost her pestle (Cleon the Tanner) and Sparta hers (the general Brasidas).

When War and Uproar go inside, Trygaeus calls to Greeks of all cities and classes, to come to Peace's rescue. Those who come in response form the Chorus. As the Greeks set to work to clear away the stones, Hermes interrupts with threats that Zeus has decreed death for anyone caught freeing Peace. But Hermes is easily bribed and persuaded to assist.

Following some bickering among the various Greek factions, Peace is at last drawn by a rope from the deep cave; also rescued are her two attendants, Opora (Harvest) and Theoria (Holiday). After the goddesses are welcomed, Trygaeus and the Chorus alternate in a hymn to the land and its peaceful uses. Hermes recounts the background of Peace's banishment, blaming the politicians and the recalcitrance of both Athens and Sparta; he then assigns Opora as a mate for Trygaeus. The latter agrees to conduct Theoria to her former home in the Senate. In the absence of his beetle which, he learns, has been harnessed to Zeus's chariot, Trygaeus flies home with Opora and Theoria. During the journey earthward, the Chorus make the customary appeal to the audience on behalf of the poet, pointing out his services in ridding the comic stage of vulgar stereotypes and in castigating the pests of society, Cleon in particular.

Once home, Trygaeus orders preparations for his marriage to Opora and hands over Theoria to the officials of Athens. The preliminary sacrifice to Peace is interrupted by the soothsayer Hierocles, who declares that the time has not yet come for Peace to be freed. He then asks for some meat but is beaten away by Trygaeus' servant. A Sickle-Maker is welcomed to the feast, but various makers of armor, who complain that their business is ruined, are forced to leave. In the finale, all join in the nuptial song.

C O M M E N T A R Y. Ancient testimony and the existence of fragments that cannot be fitted into the present play prove that there was a second version of *Peace,* though some scholars think it is the same play as Aristophanes' lost *Farmer.* At any rate, this first version could only be the dramatization of the Athenian mood that was to result in the Peace of Nicias a short time later. Aristophanes' own particular blend of fantasy and farce is nowhere better realized than in the first part of this play. Although the momentum somewhat slackens, the audience can nevertheless enjoy the author's usual high spirits and unusual sunny optimism.

Pegasus (Gk. **Pegasos**). *Myth.* The winged horse ridden by Bellerophon when he vanquished the Chimera.

Peitho. *Myth.* Greek goddess of persuasion.

Pelargicum or **Pelasgicum** (Gk. **Pelargikon** or **Pelasgikon**). Wall atop the northern slope of the Acropolis supposedly built by the Pelasgians. The name suggests *pelargos,* "stork."

Pelasgia. Greece. (See PELASGUS.)

Pelasgus (Gk. **Pelasgos**). *Myth.* Son of Zeus and brother of Argus. Pelasgus was the mythical ancestor of the Pelasgians, a vague term used for the earlier inhabitants of Argolis and other regions of Greece.

Peleads (Gk. **Peleiades**). Two priestesses at the sanctuary of Zeus in Dodona. Their name suggests "doves."

Peleus. *Myth.* King of Phthia and son of Aeacus. Peleus was the father of Achilles, who was called "Peleides" or "Pelides." Peleus and his brother Telamon, either accidentally or because of jealousy, caused the death of their half brother Phocus. For this deed they were sent into exile. Peleus went to the court of King Acastus in Iolcus, where he was purified. He repulsed the advances of Acastus' wife, who slandered him to the king, whereupon Acastus took Peleus hunting and abandoned him without a weapon in the wild Centaur country. But Hephaestus gave him a sword, and the kind centaur Chiron took him to his cave. Later Peleus captured Iolcus and killed Acastus and his wife.

Meanwhile, Peleus had been given shelter by Eurytion, king of Phthia, and made his heir. Peleus took part in the hunt for the Calydonian boar, in Heracles' sack of Troy, in the battle of Centaurs and the Lapiths, and in the Argonautic expedition. While sailing on the *Argo*, he glimpsed the Nereids sporting in the sea and fell in love with one of them, the goddess Thetis. Zeus also loved her but, having been warned by Prometheus that a son of Thetis would be greater than his father, approved Peleus' suit. Chiron showed Peleus how to catch Thetis as she basked on the shore, warning him to keep his hold on her, even though she took the form of fire, water, wind, lion, or serpent. Peleus was successful, and when the wedding was celebrated, almost all the gods came bringing gifts; Poseidon's present was a team of marvelous horses, which Achilles later used at Troy. But Eris, goddess of discord, who had not been invited, threw among the assembled guests the golden apple that was to cause the Trojan War (see PARIS).

After several children of the marriage had been killed by Thetis in her attempts to make them immortal, Peleus snatched the infant Achilles away from her, and Thetis returned to the sea in anger. In his old age, during the Trojan War, Peleus was dethroned and imprisoned by the sons of Acastus. He was eventually freed by his grandson Neoptolemus.

In Euripides' *Andromache* Peleus is an old man; he protects Andromache against Hermione and Menelaus. At the play's end Thetis makes an appearance, telling Peleus to bury the murdered Neoptolemus and then to await her in a cave by the sea until she and her sisters come to escort him to immortality in the submarine palace of Nereus.

Sophocles' lost *Peleus* (produced before 424 B.C.) seems to have been well known. Aristophanes parodied many of its lines. It is thought that the play recounted Peleus' expulsion by Acastus; his dethronement and flight to the island of Icus, where he encountered the homecoming Neoptolemus; their recognition scene and the killing of Acastus' sons by trickery; and the prevention of Acastus' death by the appearance of Thetis.

There are indications that Euripides' lost play *Peleus* (produced before 423 B.C.) dealt with the story of Peleus and Acastus' wife.

Peliades (Gk. **The Daughters of Pelias**). Lost play by Euripides, part of his first trilogy, produced in 455 B.C. Its plot dealt with Medea's dispatching of Pelias. (See PELIAS.)

Pelias. *Myth.* Son of Tyro and Poseidon. Pelias had a twin brother, Neleus. Becoming king of Iolcus, he was warned to beware of a man wearing one sandal. Soon afterward Jason, the son of Pelias' half brother Aeson, arrived in the city, having lost one sandal while crossing a stream. Pelias rid himself of Jason by sending him in quest of the golden fleece, and in his absence the king caused the deaths of Aeson, Aeson's wife, and a younger son. When Jason returned, accompanied by Medea, the latter went to the palace in disguise and persuaded the daughters of Pelias that she had magical powers of rejuvenation. Cutting up an old ram, she boiled it in a pot, after which a young lamb leaped out. The Peliades, all but Alcestis, accordingly cut up their father and threw him into the pot. This was the end of Pelias.

Concerning Sophocles' lost play *Pelias* nothing is known.

Pelion. Mountain in Magnesia. Chiron the centaur lived in a cave here.

Pella. City in Macedonia.

Pellene. 1. Village in Achaea.

2. Another form of PALLENE (1 and 2).

Pellio, Titus Publilius. Roman actor (early 2nd century B.C.). Pellio took the leading role in Plautus' *Stichus* and *Epidicus.*

Pelopia. *Myth.* Daughter of Thyestes, by whom she had a child, AEGISTHUS.

Peloponnesus (Gk. **Peloponnesos**). See PELOPS.

Pelops. *Myth.* Son of Tantalus. After winning Hippodamia from her father, OENOMAUS, Pelops became lord of the southern peninsula of Greece, called after him the Peloponnesus, "Pelops' Island." Pelops was the father of Atreus, Thyestes, and Chrysippus.

Pelorum or **Pelorus.** Promontory at the northeast tip of Sicily.

penates. The gods of the pantry and food supply in a Roman household.

Peneius or **Peneus** (Gk. **Peneios**). River in Thessaly flowing northeastward through the Vale of Tempe into the Aegean Sea.

Penelope. *Myth.* Wife of Odysseus and mother of Telemachus. Penelope faithfully waited twenty years for the return of her husband, who spent ten years at Troy and another ten wandering the seas. But her many suitors, who took up residence at Odysseus' palace, demanded that Penelope remarry. Promising that she would choose one of them as a husband when she had finished making the shroud of Laertes, Odysseus' father, Penelope wove it during the day and undid it at night. When Odysseus returned, he went to the palace in disguise and, learning of the state of affairs there, killed the suitors.

The one-line fragment that survives of Aeschylus' lost *Penelope* seems to be part of a lie that Odysseus told in order to maintain his disguise.

Penestae (Gk. **Penestai**). The class of serfs in Thessaly, originally a conquered tribe.

Penia. Personification of poverty.

Penthesilea. *Myth.* Queen of the Amazons. Penthesilea fought in the Trojan War as an ally of the Trojans. She was killed by Achilles.

Pentheus. *Myth.* Grandson of Cadmus and king of Thebes. Pentheus opposed Dionysus and was consequently torn to pieces by his mother and her sisters. This story is the subject of Euripides' *Bacchae.*

Aeschylus wrote a lost tragedy *Pentheus,* of which only a line survives. Obviously it told the same story as Euripides' *Bacchae;* in it Dionysus may have appeared in bull form. Both Thespis and Pacuvius wrote plays on this theme.

Peparethus (Gk. **Peparethos**). Aegean island off the southern tip of Magnesia.

peplos (Gk.; Lat. **peplum**). Woman's garment resembling a large shawl. A special embroidered peplos was carried in the procession of the Panathenaea to be presented to Athena.

Pergama or **Pergamus.** The citadel of Troy, or, by extension, the whole city.

Pergasae (Gk. **Pergasai**). Attic deme.

periaktos, pl. **periaktoi.** Movable flat or screen with scenery painted on it. *Periaktoi* were used at the sides of the Greek stage.

Periboea (also called **Merope**). Queen of Corinth and foster mother of Oedipus.

Pericles (Gk. **Perikles**). Famous leader of the Athenian democracy (c. 495–429 B.C.).

Periclidas (Gk. **Perikleidas**). A Spartan. When in 464 B.C. the helots revolted after an earthquake, Periclidas went as an envoy to Athens and obtained Athenian aid.

Periclymenus (Gk. **Periklymenos**). *Myth.* Son of Poseidon and a Theban hero. In the battle of the Seven against Thebes, Periclymenus killed Parthenopaeus. He pursued Amphiaraus, but the latter vanished into the earth when Zeus cracked it open with a thunderbolt.

Perikeiromene (Gk. **The Girl with Her Hair Cut Short;** or **She Who Was Shorn;** or **The Rape of the Locks;** or **The Shearing of Glycera**). Comedy by Menander (produced c. 302 B.C.). Translations: Francis G. Allinson, 1921; L. A. Post, 1929; Gilbert Murray, 1942; Lionel Casson, 1960. Of an estimated thousand lines of the original play, about 450 have been recovered.

s c e n e. A street in Corinth: before the houses of Polemon and Pataecus.

s u m m a r y. Apparently there was a delayed prologue after an initial scene in which Glycera, deeply offended by her lover, the soldier Polemon, prepared to leave his house. In this prologue Agnoia, the personification of ignorance or misunderstanding, explains to the audience that many years ago a merchant named Pataecus, being nearly bankrupt, had exposed his twin children, a boy and a girl. The boy, Moschion, had eventually been adopted by a wealthy woman, Myrrhina, who had by chance married Pataecus after his first wife's death. Pataecus then proceeded unwittingly to adopt his own son.

The girl Glycera had been reared in poverty, finally becoming Polemon's

mistress. She had long tried to trace her real parentage through certain belongings left with her when she was exposed. Her search has led her to the
knowledge that Moschion, her next-door neighbor, is her brother; therefore,
when the boy steals up to her and gives her some flirtatious kisses, Glycera is
more amused than alarmed. But unfortunately Polemon comes on the scene
and in a jealous rage cuts off her hair. This is the undeserved abuse that causes
Glycera to leave the house. She takes refuge with her neighbors, Pataecus and
Myrrhina.

Polemon is at first remorseful but then suspects that Glycera has gone to
join her supposed lover, Moschion. Meanwhile the latter, also believing that
she has come to him through love, makes further advances until he is smartly
repulsed.

Polemon organizes an assault on the house but is convinced by Pataecus
that only gentle methods will win a woman. Pataecus undertakes to plead the
soldier's cause. When he does so, Glycera declares that she is freeborn and not
to be treated so shamefully. As proof she shows Pataecus her birth tokens,
which he recognizes as belonging to his late wife. Moschion, eavesdropping,
learns that Glycera is his twin sister and Pataecus his real father. Polemon,
thoroughly chastened and repentant, is forgiven by Glycera, and they prepare
for marriage.

peripety (Gk. **peripeteia**). Change of a situation to its opposite, a reversal
of fortune. Peripety was called by Aristotle one of the three elements of plot,
the other two being recognition and suffering. (See POETICS.)

Perrhaebians, The (Gk. **Perrhaibides**). Lost play by Aeschylus. Its few
surviving lines relate to Ixion (king of the Lapiths in Perrhaebia, northern
Thessaly) and his murder of his father-in-law. (See IXION.)

Persa (Lat. **The Persian** or **The Girl from Persia**). Extant comedy by
Plautus (between 200 and 194 B.C.). *Persa* was evidently adapted from a Greek
play written in the period of Middle Comedy. Line 506 refers to the Persian
empire as still in existence, which dates the original play before Alexander's
time and hence before the age of New Comedy. Translations: Henry T. Riley,
1852; Paul Nixon, 1930; Charles T. Murphy, 1942.

S C E N E. Athens.

S U M M A R Y. The slave Toxilus tells his fellow slave Sagaristio that he
needs money to buy and free the courtesan Lemniselenis, whom he loves, from
her owner, the pimp Dordalus. Sagaristio promises to try to help. When the two
leave, the parasite Saturio enters and boasts of his family's successful parasitism.
He is interrupted by Toxilus, who returns with a plan to trick the pimp into
providing the money he needs. Promising Saturio free run of his master's
kitchen, Toxilus begs the loan of the parasite's daughter, who will masquerade
as a kidnaped Persian and be "sold" to Dordalus, who does not know her. Later
Saturio will claim her as a freeborn girl.

After repartee between Lemniselenis' Maid and the young slave Paegnium,
Sagaristio returns and jubilantly reveals that he has appropriated money given
him by his master for the purchase of oxen; he gives it to Toxilus instead.

Toxilus says happily that he will free his sweetheart and repay his friend after they have tricked Dordalus.

Saturio's daughter objects to the deception but is willing to obey her father. After the pimp gets his money for Lemniselenis, Toxilus hides Sagaristio and Saturio's daughter, both dressed as Persians, and lays the bait. Telling Dordalus he has a great opportunity for him, Toxilus shows the pimp a letter, ostensibly from his master, which says that a highborn Persian girl has been brought from Arabia and that she is to be sold as a slave in Athens without a legal title. Saturio's daughter now appears with Sagaristio, her presumed seller. Though Dordalus balks at the illicit sale, the girl's acting and Toxilus' subtle goading combine to whet his appetite for her. Hearing that her father will soon come to ransom her, he leaves to get his money.

Soon Dordalus returns and buys the girl and, when Sagaristio pretends to leave for his ship, goes back into his house. But when he comes out again, pleased with his purchase, Saturio rushes on, pretending to be the Persian girl's father; he snatches her away and threatens to hale the pimp into court.

The play ends with Toxilus, Lemniselenis, Sagaristio, and Paegnium celebrating their successful ruse. When Dordalus appears and inveighs against them for depriving him of both girl and money, they jeer at him mercilessly.

C O M M E N T A R Y. Critics agree that *Persa* is an amusing trifle, but it is doubtful that the general burlesque atmosphere is a holdover from the habit of parody so characteristic of Middle Comedy. The play would seem to be more of a parody on New Comedy, with the usual New Comedy plot transferred to the lower classes. The high percentage of lyric passages contributes to what many call an ancient equivalent of *opera buffa*.

Persephassa. Persephone.

Persephone (Lat. **Prosperpina**). *Myth.* Daughter of Demeter and queen of the dead. Hades fell in love with Persephone and abducted her. Demeter wandered the earth in search of her daughter, and when she learned of the abduction, she was so angry that she refused to return to heaven and caused the earth's crops to fail. Zeus then sent Hermes to ask Hades to restore Persephone to her mother, and Hades replied that the girl might return if she had not yet tasted the food of the dead. Persephone prepared to leave, but because it was found that she had eaten a pomegranate seed, Hades decreed that she must return to him for three months every year.

On Persephone's return to earth, Demeter established the Eleusinian mysteries. (See DEMETER; ELEUSIS.)

Perses. *Myth.* King of Colchis and father of Hecate.

Perseus. *Myth.* Son of DANAË, grandson of ACRISIUS. Sent by King POLYDECTES to behead the Gorgon Medusa, Perseus accomplished his mission with the aid of the PHORCIDES and the Stygian nymphs, the latter providing him with winged sandals, a wallet, and Hades' cap of invisibility. On his return journey to Seriphos, Perseus rescued ANDROMEDA and turned Phineus to stone. He arrived at the court of Polydectes just in time to save his mother from the king's advances, turning him to stone also. Later, Perseus accidentally killed

Acrisius, who had lived in fear of a prophecy that such an event would come to pass. Perseus, Andromeda, and her parents, Cepheus and Cassiopeia, became constellations. (See also DICTYS.)

Persians, The (Gk. **Persai**). Extant tragedy by Aeschylus. *The Persians* was produced in 472 B.C. as the second play of a tetralogy. It was preceded by *Phineus* and followed by *Glaucus of Potniae* and the satyr play *Prometheus the Fire-Kindler;* all of these plays are lost. The tetralogy won first prize. Scholars have made various attempts to exhibit a theme common to the four plays, but there has been little agreement as to what the theme might be. Translations of *The Persians:* Robert Potter, 1777; W. Palin, 1829; Edward H. Plumptre, 1868; Lewis Campbell, 1893; E. D. A. Morshead, 1908; Walter and C. E. S. Headlam, 1909; H. Weir Smyth, 1922; S. G. Bernardete, 1956; Philip Vellacott, 1961.

S C E N E. Susa. A council hall; later, at the tomb of Darius.

T I M E. 480 B.C., soon after the battle of Salamis.

S U M M A R Y. The Persian Elders (the Chorus), appointed to oversee the empire in the absence of King Xerxes, are filled with foreboding. Xerxes has taken a vast Asiatic host to Greece to avenge the defeat of his father, the dead King Darius, at Marathon. The Elders' anxiety is intensified by the queen mother, Atossa, who tells of a dream in which her son, having yoked a Persian woman and a Dorian Greek woman to his chariot, was thrown to the ground by the recalcitrant bucking of the Greek; then Xerxes saw his father before him and tore the king's royal robes. This dream was reinforced by Atossa's vision at the sacrificial altar of a falcon attacking a frightened eagle.

After the Elders advise Atossa to sacrifice further and to summon the soul of her husband, she questions them about this distant, insignificant Attica that has claimed her son's attention and learns of its wealth, might, and democracy. Their replies are interrupted by a Messenger who announces that Xerxes' forces have been destroyed except for a handful of men. The Elders chant of Persia's doom, but Atossa is somewhat comforted by the news that her son is alive. The Messenger goes on to describe in detail the disastrous sea battle around Salamis, naming the fallen Persian leaders and praising Greece's cunning: Before the fight a Greek informed Xerxes that the Greeks meant to flee as soon as night came, and Xerxes accordingly placed his ships to guard the narrow sea outlets; when the Greeks instead attacked, the crowded Persians ships were destroyed. While waiting to ambush the returning Greeks, a group of Persia's greatest warriors were themselves surprised and defeated, and Xerxes, tearing his royal robes, was forced to signal retreat.

After the Elders lament the defeat, hinting of the imprudence of their king, Atossa invokes the spirit of Darius; the Elders chant of Darius' glorious rule. The dead king, rising from his tomb, learns of the ruin of Persia and his son's impious yoking of the Hellespont, and he reveals that an oracle had foretold vengeance on Xerxes for his pride. Atossa explains that Xerxes had been taunted by men around him with his father's exploits. Darius then reviews the glorious history of the Persian dynasty, which has ended with Xerxes' folly and recklessness.

He tells the Persians never again to attack Greece. Prophesying the further defeat of the Persians at Plataea, brought on by their blasphemous destruction of Greek shrines and temples, Darius tells Atossa to wear her best robes and to comfort her returning son. He then sinks again below the earth.

The Chorus' song in praise of their land's former prosperity ushers in the defeated and broken Xerxes, who recalls bitterly his dead comrades and expresses his own self-disgust. Then Xerxes and the Chorus join in a long lament for the slain.

C O M M E N T A R Y. Because of the recent discovery that Aeschylus' *Suppliants* was produced in the late 460's B.C., *The Persians* emerges as the earliest extant Greek drama. It is the only surviving play on an historical subject, but even greater interest lies in the fact that it is a prime example of the Hellenic spirit, that humane cosmopolitanism that enhances a local patriotic fervor. While Aeschylus portrays the enemy with sympathy, he points to the lust for wealth and the presumptuous and barbarous deeds with which Xerxes over-stepped the bounds of prudence, illustrating the eternal lesson that pride goeth before a fall. Thus the play was more of a warning to the Greeks than a cry of triumph over the Persians. Its second performance in Sicily (some scholars suggest a premiere there) might have carried the same message to the western Greeks, who had just repulsed another Oriental power, the Carthaginians.

Phaeacians, The. Lost play by Sophocles. It has been conjectured that the subject was either the encounter of Odysseus and Nausicaa or the episode, in the voyage of the *Argo*, in which the Phaeacian king and queen protected Medea and the Argonauts against King Aeëtes, Medea's father.

Phaedra (Gk. **Phaidra**). *Myth.* Daughter of Minos and Pasiphaë and wife of Theseus. For her story, see Euripides' HIPPOLYTUS and Seneca's PHAEDRA.

Sophocles' lost *Phaedra* is thought by some to have been a kind of retort to Euripides' first version (see HIPPOLYTUS: *Commentary*), presenting Phaedra more sympathetically. If so, it must have been written between c. 435 and 429 B.C.

Phaedra (also called *Hippolytus*). Extant tragedy by Seneca, based on the lost first version of Euripides' *Hippolytus* called *Hippolytus Veiled*. Translation: Frank Justus Miller, 1916.

S C E N E. Theseus' palace at Athens.

S U M M A R Y. Hippolytus, son of King Theseus of Athens and the Amazon Antiope, has sworn himself to a life of chastity. As the play opens, he leaves with his followers for the hunt. His stepmother, Phaedra, enters with her Nurse and bemoans her passion for her stepson, made more perilous now that her husband, Theseus, is away trying to help his friend Pirithous carry off Proserpina, queen of the underworld. Phaedra is at first reproached by her old Nurse for her impious, incestuous love, but the Nurse, soon realizing that the queen is on the point of suicide, resolves to aid her.

The Chorus of Athenian Citizens sing of Cupid's might. Then the Nurse, who has been ministering to Phaedra, emerges from the palace and describes her mistress' lovesickness. Advised by the Chorus, she prays to Diana. Presently Hippolytus returns. The Nurse suggests that he renounce his chaste life and enjoy his youth, but the young man praises the solitary life of the woods, free from the crimes of society, free especially from the bane of women.

Phaedra re-enters and faints on seeing Hippolytus. When he lifts her, she gradually makes clear her feelings for him. Uncomprehending at first, Hippolytus reacts with horror on realizing the truth and draws his sword to kill Phaedra. But when she expresses her willingness to die by his hand, he flings away the sword and runs off. While Phaedra lies in a swoon, the Nurse decides to put the blame on Hippolytus and cries out that the queen has been attacked by him.

After the Chorus praise Hippolytus' manly virtues, Theseus returns, weary from his quest, having been rescued from Hades by Hercules. When Phaedra tells her husband that Hippolytus has dishonored her and shows him his son's sword, Theseus is horrified and prays to Neptune, his divine father, to grant him the last of three promised services: to kill Hippolytus. The Chorus declare that blind fortune rules human life, after which a Messenger enters and describes in detail the horrible death of Hippolytus: as the boy rode along the coast, a tempest rose and a monster bull coming out of the great waves caused his horses to bolt, wrecking the chariot and dragging him over the rocks.

Phaedra, filled with remorse, declares the guilt to be hers and not Hippolytus' and falls on the sword. Theseus is left to lament the dead and, crying for vengeance on himself for having killed his son, arranges for Hippolytus' funeral. As for Phaedra's corpse, he directs only that it be covered with earth.

C O M M E N T A R Y. It would be clearly unfair to compare Seneca's *Phaedra* with Euripides' extant *Hippolytus,* since all indications point to the fact that it was the lost version which Seneca followed. One might very well suspect, however, that Seneca's elimination of all action by gods was a departure from his model. It is evident that his chief purpose was a psychological-ethical study of the destructive power of love. Considered only as such, the play seems finely done; it had considerable influence on Racine's *Phèdre,* which is perhaps the most powerful of French classical tragedies.

Phaethon. *Myth.* Son of Helios and Clymene. Phaethon was permitted by his father to drive the chariot of the sun. Unable to control the horses, he let the fiery car come so near Mother Earth that she was in torment. At her appeal, Zeus smote Phaethon with a thunderbolt, and he fell into the river Eridanus. His mourning sisters, the Heliades, were changed into poplars, which stood on the river banks.

Fairly extensive fragments of Euripides' lost *Phaethon* have been accumulated from various sources, making reconstruction possible. The scene was the palace of Merops, king of the Ethiopians and husband of Clymene. Merops intended to marry his supposed son Phaethon to a daughter of Aphrodite. Phaethon, anxious about this exalted match, was secretly told by Clymene that he was really the son of Helios. Probably he went to get proof of his parentage, and a messenger must have told of his wild ride in the sky. Phaethon's smoking body fell out of the sun chariot into the courtyard of Merops' palace just before the king entered with a chorus of maidens chanting a marriage hymn. When Merops discovered the body, Clymene probably confessed everything.

Phaethontiades. Another name for the HELIADES.

Phalerum (Gk. **Phaleron**). Harbor in Attica slightly east of the Piraeus.

Phales. Demigod, personification of the phallus.

phallophoria. Procession bearing the phallus as a symbol of fertility, particularly in the rituals of Dionysus. Such rituals, with obscenities and insults exchanged between performers and spectators, may have had some influence on the development of comedy.

phallus (Gk. **phallos**, "male organ"). Although the artificial oversized phallus seems to have been a regular feature in the costumes of the satyr choruses and the buffoons of *phlyakes* plays, its use in Old Comedy is involved in much dispute. Some authorities think that it appeared only rarely, others that it was always worn but was often tied up so as to be almost out of sight.

Phanae (Gk. **Phanai**). Promontory at the southern tip of Chios. In *The Birds* (line 1694) Aristophanes puns on the name to suggest *phainein*, "to reveal, inform on."

Phanoteus. Variant of Panopeus, a city in Phocis.

Phaon. *Myth.* A ferryman of Lesbos, supposedly made young and handsome by Aphrodite. The comic poets made much of the legend that the poetess Sappho fell in love with Phaon and committed suicide when he spurned her.

Pharae. See PHARIS.

Pharis. Older name of Pharae, a town in Laconia.

Pharnaces (Gk. **Pharnakes**). Name of several prominent Persian generals and governors.

Pharos. Island off the coast of Egypt near one of the western mouths of the Nile.

Pharsalia or **Pharsalus** (Gk. **Pharsalos**). City in central Thessaly.

Phasis. River in Colchis.

Phayllus (Gk. **Phayllos**). Famous athlete (early 4th century B.C.).

Phelleus. Hilly section of Attica.

Phenakes. Greek word meaning "tricksters." It was applied by Aristophanes (*The Knights*, line 634) to mean spirits of trickery.

Pherae (Gk. **Pherai**). City in Thessaly not far from the Pagasaean Gulf.

Pherecrates (Gk. **Pherekrates**). Writer of Old Comedy (probably active c. 435–415 B.C.). Pherecrates was known for his imaginative and original plots and for his pure Attic diction. His chief interests were social satire, realistic comedy, and subjects drawn from folklore; he was the first to use courtesans as characters (as shown in the titles *Corianno* and *Petale*). Of Pherecrates' works about 275 fragments survive. Some of his plays were: *The Savages* (staged at the Lenaea of 420 B.C.); *The Flounders* (probably c. 427 B.C.), set in the underworld—in one fragment the dead Aeschylus defends his own work;

The Miners, who, it seems, dug through to the underworld, where they found a land of plenty; *The Ant Men;* and *The Tyranny,* which dealt with rule by women.

Pherephatta. Persephone.

Pheres. *Myth.* Son of Tyro and Cretheus, founder of Pherae, and father of Admetus, Idomeneus, and King Lycurgus of Nemea. Pheres' descendants were called Pheretids. He appears in Euripides' *Alcestis,* where he defends himself for not giving up his life for his son Admetus.

Phibalus (Gk. **Phibalos**). District in Megara famous for figs.

Phidias (Gk. **Pheidias**). Great Athenian sculptor. Phidias was a protégé of Pericles, who commissioned him to erect buildings on the Acropolis and to execute the statue of Athena in the Parthenon. He was also famous for his statue of Zeus in Olympia. In the 430's B.C. the enemies of Pericles accused Phidias of fraud, and he was exiled and died shortly thereafter.

Philammon. *Myth.* Poet and prophet, son of Apollo and father of Thamyris.

Philemon. Probably the most prominent writer of New Comedy after Menander (see COMEDY: *New Comedy*). Philemon lived almost a century, from about 364 to 264 B.C. Although he often defeated Menander in dramatic contests, it was generally agreed that Philemon was really inferior. He was said to have written ninety-seven plays; there survive sixty-odd titles and more than two hundred fragments. Typical titles are: *The Stateless Man, Kidnaped, The Claimant, The Doorkeeper, Neaera, The Pancratiast, Palamedes, The Soldier, The Suicide Pact, The Changeling.*

Plautus' *Mercator* and *Trinummus* were adapted from Philemon's *Merchant* and *Treasure* respectively, and Plautus' *Mostellaria* may have been based on Philemon's *Ghost.* About one hundred extremely mutilated lines from papyri have been thought to come from a play by Philemon that was used by Plautus as the model for his *Aulularia,* but the only feature common to both works is the name of the slave, Strobilus.

Philepsius (Gk. **Philepsios**). Politician in Aristophanes' Athens who made a living by telling stories.

Philetaerus (Gk. **Philetairos**). Writer of Middle Comedy (fl. middle 4th century B.C.). Philetaerus was sometimes said to be the third son of Aristophanes, rather than NICOSTRATUS (1). Furthermore, two plays, *Antyllus* and *Oenopion,* were attributed both to Philetaerus and Nicostratus. Perhaps they were one and the same poet.

Philip (Gk. **Philippos**). King of Macedonia, father of Alexander the Great (c. 382–336 B.C.). The coin named after him, the *philippos,* was current throughout the Greek world.

Philippi (Gk. **Philippoi**). City in northern Macedonia.

Philippides. Writer of New Comedy (active c. 335–c. 286 B.C.). Philippides was prominent in politics and through his connection with Lysimachus won many benefits for Athens. For this he was voted a gold crown, a bronze statue in the theater, and other honors. He died of sudden joy in his old age on learning that he had won the drama contest. Of Philippides' works about twenty fragments and fifteen titles survive. Some examples are *The Women at the Adonis Feast, The Money Disappears, The Miser, The Euripides-Lover.*

Philistion. Writer of mimes (early 1st century A.D.). Philistion was called the inventor of mime, but this is absurd. Although none of his works remain, he was often referred to, and many anecdotes were told of him. In this way he came to represent the archetypal mime writer.

Philocles (Gk. **Philokles**). Writer of tragedies. Philocles was a nephew of Aeschylus. He was accused of plagiarizing Sophocles' *Tereus* in his *Pandionis.* His works were considered so harsh that he was nicknamed Chole, "gall;" but one of them won first prize over Sophocles' *Oedipus the King.*

Philocrates (Gk. **Philokrates**). Athenian poultry dealer of Aristophanes' time.

Philoctetes (Gk. **Philoktetes**). *Myth.* Son of Poeas. Philoctetes assisted the dying Heracles by lighting his funeral pyre. In reward he was given the hero's famous bow and arrows, which were tipped with the poison of the Hydra. (This episode is narrated by Philoctetes himself in Seneca's *Hercules on Oeta.*) Having been a suitor of Helen, Philoctetes embarked on the expedition against Troy. But on the way he violated the sanctuary of the island deity Chryse and was bitten by a serpent. Because his wound was incurable and his cries of pain unbearable, the Greeks, prompted by Odysseus, deserted Philoctetes on the uninhabited island of Lemnos. After ten years of fruitless siege at Troy, the Greeks learned that in order to take the city they must have Philoctetes and his bow and arrows. Odysseus and Neoptolemus thereupon set out to fetch him; their visit to Lemnos forms the plot of Sophocles' *Philoctetes.* At Troy Philoctetes was healed by the sons of Asclepius and joined in the fighting. He shot down Paris.

Knowledge of Aeschylus' lost tragedy *Philoctetes* comes from a few fragmentary lines and the essay of Dio Chrysostom comparing the treatment by the three tragedians (Aeschylus, Sophocles, and Euripides) of the Philoctetes story. In Aeschylus' version the chorus consisted of Lemnians; Neoptolemus perhaps spoke the prologue but played a very subordinate role. The chief task of persuading Philoctetes to go to Troy was performed by Odysseus, who employed disguise, falsehoods, and finally the trick of stealing Heracles' bow, which was Philoctetes' only means of getting food.

Euripides' lost *Philoctetes* was produced in 431 B.C. In it Diomedes and Odysseus were sent to get Philoctetes. At the same time, a Trojan delegation was dispatched with instructions to offer Philoctetes the sovereignty of the city if he would bring with him Heracles' bow, on which, Helenus had prophesied, Trojan survival depended. Odysseus, disguised by Athena, represented himself as persecuted by Odysseus, in this way gaining Philoctetes' sympathy as a fellow sufferer. Eventually his arguments prevailed. Dio Chrysostom particularly praises the choric odes of the play.

Philoctetes (Gk. **Philoktetes**). Extant tragedy by Sophocles (produced

409 B.C.). *Philoctetes* was awarded first prize in the dramatic contest. Translations: Thomas Francklin, 1759; Richard C. Jebb, 1904; F. Storr, 1912; Kathleen Freeman, 1948; E. F. Watling, 1953; David Grene, 1957; Kenneth Cavander, 1965; Theodore H. Banks, 1966.

S C E N E. The coast of the island of Lemnos.

S U M M A R Y. Having learned the god's decree that Troy cannot be taken without the help of Neoptolemus, son of the dead Achilles, and Philoctetes, Heracles' former comrade and inheritor of his marvelous bow and arrows, the Greeks at Troy have recruited Neoptolemus and have sent him with Odysseus to fetch Philoctetes from the island of Lemnos. There Philoctetes was marooned by the Greek army on its way to Troy, at the advice of Odysseus, when, after he had suffered an incurable snake bite, the army was no longer able to bear the sound of his cries and the sight and stench of his wound.

As the play opens, Odysseus and Neoptolemus have reached Lemnos. When they discover Philoctetes' cave, Odysseus instructs his companion to pretend to have sailed away from Troy because Achilles' armor, promised to him, was awarded instead to Odysseus; otherwise Philoctetes, who hates the Greeks for what they did to him, will never consent to go with him. Neoptolemus balks at the dishonesty, but Odysseus convinces him that the deception is in the general interest of Greece, as the war cannot be won without Philoctetes' bow and arrows. Odysseus then retires.

After Neoptolemus and the Chorus speak of Philoctetes' misfortune, the latter appears, suffering greatly. Learning Neoptolemus' identity, Philoctetes receives him and describes his abandonment, as well as the desolate existence he has led for the last ten years; he curses the Greeks, particularly Odysseus. Neoptolemus tells the lie as directed, speaks of the war, and starts to leave, ostensibly for Greece. When Philoctetes begs the young man to take him along, Neoptolemus pretends to consent.

Two Sailors sent by Odysseus, one disguised as a merchant, appear with the warning that Odysseus is on his way to take Philoctetes by force, having heard from the captured Trojan prophet Helenus that Philoctetes' presence is necessary for a Greek victory. When the Sailors leave, Philoctetes swears he will never return to the Greek army. He then brings out the bow and arrows and grants Neoptolemus, who has begun to feel qualms about the deception, the right to hold them. The two go into the cave and presently emerge.

Seized by an overwhelming pain in his foot, Philoctetes gives the bow and arrows to Neoptolemus to hold, then falls asleep. When he awakes, eager to leave, as he thinks, for Greece, Neoptolemus is overcome with doubts about the rightness of his actions and pity for his new friend's agony. He finally confesses the truth. Philoctetes cries miserably that he is betrayed and demands the return of his bow. Before Neoptolemus can decide what to do, Odysseus enters and declares that they will take Philoctetes by force if necessary. At this Philoctetes moves as if to commit suicide, and when the Chorus manacle him, he curses Odysseus and the Greek army and cries for vengeance. Odysseus declares he will take the bow and arrows for someone else to use and orders Neoptolemus to leave with him, but the latter, pitying Philoctetes, bids the Chorus watch over him for the time.

The Chorus, chanting that the gods, and not Odysseus or the other Greeks, are responsible for Philoctetes' misfortune, urge him to go to Troy, but he persists in bewailing his fate and finally goes into the cave. At this point, Neoptolemus, still in possession of the bow, reappears with Odysseus and, despite the latter's protests, says he will give it back to Philoctetes. When Odysseus leaves, Neoptolemus gives the bow to his friend, but soon has to prevent him from killing Odysseus with it.

When he and Philoctetes are alone, Neoptolemus reveals that Philoctetes will be healed, but only if he goes to Troy to help the Greeks. Philoctetes wonders if he is again being deceived, then declares that he cannot help those who did him such injustice and begs Neoptolemus to take him to Greece instead. Neoptolemus has at last consented, when suddenly Heracles, now a god, appears with a decree from Zeus: Like Heracles, Philoctetes will win glory as recompense for past suffering; the healer Asclepius will cure him, and the bow will be the instrument of Troy's fall. Heracles then commands the two to go to Troy, where they will together take the city. Philoctetes submits and bids farewell to Lemnos.

COMMENTARY. That the death of innocence is a tragedy no less poignant than any other death, and that it can be transcended as well as any other death, is what Sophocles makes clear in *Philoctetes*. Interest centers on the development of Neoptolemus, young, inexperienced, and eager to take his place in the world of practical affairs. He is flanked by two dark figures: Odysseus, his mentor, the essence of practicality, to whom any end justifies any means, and Philoctetes, unjustly treated and imbued with so great a sense of injustice that he cannot yield himself to any practical end, with the result that his uselessness is more pitiful than his pain. Yet the justice of the divine scheme, the punishment of Troy, is larger than Philoctetes' personal grievance. Neoptolemus is aware of this but is faced by the dilemma of a noble aim and an ignoble method of achieving it. His self-sacrificing decision to share Philoctetes' suffering rather than Odysseus' deceit is the action that sets the stage for Heracles' appearance. Heracles, the man who became a god by sacrificing himself for man, is the right person to reveal that the noble plan of the gods must be nobly fulfilled.

Philoctetes at Troy. Lost play by Sophocles. Its plot must have dealt with the healing of Philoctetes and his victory over Paris. (See PHILOCTETES: *Myth.*)

Philomela. *Myth.* Daughter of King Pandion (1) of Athens and sister of Procne. For Philomela's story, see TEREUS. According to one version of the myth, Philomela became a nightingale rather than a swallow; this version became traditional in later classical times.

Philonides 1. A rich and stupid Athenian. The lover of the courtesan Lais, Philonides was satirized by Aristophanes in *Plutus* (lines 179 and 303).

2. Writer of Old Comedy. Philonides is known by only a dozen fragments and a few titles, *The Buskins, The Mule-Car, The True Friend*. His *Rehearsal* was said to have won first prize at the Lenaea of 422 B.C. over Aristophanes' *Wasps*, but in fact Philonides was probably producing Aristophanes' play under his own name, as he did for the same author's *Dramas or The Centaur, Amphiaraus*, and *The Frogs*.

Phineus. *Myth.* Thracian king and seer. Phineus put away his first wife, Cleopatra, daughter of Boreas, and married Idaea (called also Eidothea and Eurythia), the daughter of Dardanus. Idaea falsely accused Cleopatra's two sons of trying to assault her virtue, and she blinded them, or caused Phineus to do so. Zeus thereupon blinded Phineus and sent the Harpies to harass him, whenever he sat at table, by carrying off a portion of the food and polluting the remainder. When the Argonauts came past, two of them, Zetes and Calais, who were brothers of Cleopatra, undertook to chase the Harpies away. But in *Hercules Furens* (line 750 ff.) Seneca depicts Phineus in the underworld, still tormented by the creatures.

Aeschylus' lost *Phineus* was produced in March 472 B.C., with *The Persians, Glaucus of Potniae*, and *Prometheus the Fire-Kindler*. Fragments indicate that it told how the sons of Boreas pursued and overcame the Harpies and how Phineus used his prophetic powers to warn the Argonauts of future dangers. Various ingenious guesses have been made as to the possible link between *Phineus* and the extant *Persians*. Perhaps in both plays were sung the praises of Boreas, the North Wind, who had helped the Greeks against the Persian fleet in 480 B.C.; or perhaps this Phineus was identified with another Phineus, Andromeda's wicked suitor, who had been turned to stone by Perseus, father of Perses, who was in turn the mythical ancestor of the Persians.

It is impossible to distinguish between Sophocles' two lost plays called *Phineus*. They probably told how Phineus' two sons, after being healed by Asclepius, put their wicked stepmother to death.

Phlegethon. *Myth.* One of the rivers of the underworld, the river of fire.

Phlegra. Plain in Macedonia said to be the place where the gods fought the Giants.

Phlya (Gk. **Phlye**). Attic deme.

phlyakes (Gk. "prattlers of nonsense"). Actors in a form of Dorian farce that flourished in the Greek cities of southern Italy, especially Paestum and Tarentum. The genre had definitely taken form by the third century B.C. and had probably been much influenced by Epicharmus some time earlier. Little written material survives on the subject of *phlyakes* plays; most information comes from paintings on vases and other art objects. The male performers wore an enormous phallus and costumes grotesquely padded in belly and buttocks; masks seem also to have been used. The stage seems to have been a temporary platform. Play plots were sketches from everyday life or burlesques of tragedy and myth. Names of several writers are preserved, the most important being RHINTHON. There must have been constant interaction of influence among formal comedy, mime, and the *phlyakes* plays. The *fabula Atellana* must have been largely modeled on this type of farce.

Phobos (Gk. "rout" or "fear"). *Myth.* Personification of panic and fear, a son of Ares.

Phocis (Gk. **Phokis**). Section of Greece on the northern coast of the Corinthian Gulf west of Boeotia. Delphi was located here.

Phocus (Gk. **Phokos**). *Myth.* Son of Aeacus. Phocus founded the kingdom of Phocis. He was killed by his jealous half brothers, Peleus and Telamon.

Phoebe (Gk. **Phoibe**). 1. *Myth.* Titaness, mother of Leto. Phoebe gave the oracular shrine of Delphi to her grandson Apollo.

2. Epithet of Artemis and of Hecate, as goddess of the moon.

3. *Myth.* Daughter of Leda and sister of Helen and Clytemnestra.

Phoebus (Gk. **Phoibus**, "shining"). Epithet of Apollo.

Phoenician Women, The (Gk. **Phoinissai**). Lost comedy by Aristophanes (produced perhaps March 409 B.C., perhaps in 407). In this play Aristophanes may have used the fratricidal strife of Eteocles and Polyneices (see Euripides' PHOENICIAN WOMEN: *Summary*) to symbolize the civil strife in Athens between the oligarchical Four Hundred of 411 B.C. and their democratic opponents.

Phoenician Women, The (Gk. **Phoinissai**). Extant tragedy by Euripides (produced c. 411–409 B.C.). The play was awarded second prize in the dramatic contest. Translations: Edward P. Coleridge, 1891; Arthur S. Way, 1912; Elizabeth Wyckoff, 1958. Adaptations and works influenced by *The Phoenician Women:* Accius, lost play; Seneca, *Phoenissae;* Jean de Rotrou, *Antigone,* 1638; Jean Racine, *La Thébaide,* 1663; Vittorio Alfieri, *Polinice,* 1782.

S C E N E. Thebes, the palace.

S U M M A R Y. The first to enter is the aged queen Jocasta, who relates the story of the curse on the family of Laius. Jocasta tells of her marriage to Laius, king of Thebes, and the birth of a son, Oedipus, despite the oracle's warning that Laius would be killed by his child. She recounts the events that resulted from Laius' transgression against the oracle: Oedipus' exposure and rescue, his childhood in Corinth, his murder of his father, marriage to his mother, and eventual self-blinding upon learning the truth about his deeds. The queen continues, telling of Oedipus' curse on his sons Eteocles and Polyneices, their agreement to alternate in ruling Thebes, Eteocles' subsequent banishment of his brother, and of Polyneices' emigration to Argos where he married into the royal family. Polyneices, having formed an army led by seven chieftains, is now about to attack Thebes.

Jocasta reveals that she has summoned Polyneices within the walls to discuss a truce. She then retires, and her daughter Antigone appears on the roof with an old Servant who describes the enemy to her. When they leave, a Chorus of Phoenician Maidens enter, singing of their pilgrimage to Delphi and deploring the war they have come upon. Presently Polyneices enters, followed by his mother; he describes to her the difficulties of exile, his marriage to a daughter of King Adrastus, and his formation of an army.

When Eteocles appears, Jocasta tries to reconcile her sons, but Eteocles knows no value but a ruler's glory and Polyneices will not be deterred from winning justice for himself. Jocasta says that the only possible issue of the war is evil, but her sons vow to kill one another. After the queen and Polyneices leave, the Chorus sing of the founding of Thebes; then Creon, Jocasta's brother, appears. Eteocles consults his uncle about the defense of the city and is advised to deploy seven of his own chieftains at the city's seven gates. He in turn gives his uncle instructions in the event of his death: Antigone must marry Creon's son Haemon, and Polyneices, should he die, must remain unburied. Eteocles then goes to summon the seer Tiresias.

The seer soon appears, led by his daughter and accompanied by Creon's son Menoeceus. He tells Creon the only way to save Thebes is to propitiate the war god Ares by sacrificing a descendant of one of the original Thebans, all of whom sprang to life from the teeth of Ares' sacred dragon, killed by Cadmus. When Creon hears that Menoeceus is the only one eligible, he immediately decides to send the boy away to safety. But after he leaves, Menoeceus reveals his intention to kill himself for the sake of the city.

Presently a Messenger arrives; he informs Jocasta that because of Menoeceus' self-sacrifice the city has thrown back all the enemy's assaults. The Messenger discloses that Jocasta's sons are alive but that they have resolved to decide the struggle by meeting in single combat. At this Jocasta hurries off with Antigone to try to prevent the fight.

Creon, mourning his dead son, learns from another Messenger that the brothers have killed each other and that Jocasta, coming upon her dying sons, committed suicide. The Messenger then describes the final Theban victory over the Argives.

Now Antigone enters, chanting a dirge, followed by servants bearing the corpses of her kin. She is joined by her blind father, Oedipus, who also laments the deaths. Creon orders Oedipus into exile so that the land may be freed of his curse. He then makes the pronouncement that whoever gives Polyneices burial rites shall die. Defying him, Antigone declares that she will not marry Haemon and indicates that she will secretly bury her brother's body. After Creon leaves, Oedipus reveals the prophecy, made by the oracle, that he will have final peace at Colonus, near Athens. Antigone leads her father out into exile.

C O M M E N T A R Y . *The Phoenician Women* was popular with ancient audiences. It has, however, been generally unpopular with modern critics, who have found it more of a mythical pageant than a unified play. Written in the pessimistic mood of *The Trojan Women*, it lacks the profound irony of that play and suffers from the need of a central character like Hecuba through whom the impact of the successive calamities might be transmitted to the audience. Various attempts have been made to discover a unifying theme, for example: the malevolence of the gods (but it has never been proved that Euripides thought them malevolent); the Theban polis as a hero (a fanciful idea, not conferring unity); the fall of the house of Oedipus (again not a unifying theme). In spite of the effectiveness of individual scenes, it is hard to challenge the opinion of an ancient commentator that the play is "episodic and overfull."

Phoenician Women, The (Lat. **Phoenissae;** also called **Thebais** or **The Thebaid**). Tragedy by Seneca based on Euripides' *Phoenician Women*. It was apparently never completed. Translations: Frank Justus Miller, 1917; Ella I. Harris, 1942. Work influenced by Seneca's *Phoenician Women:* Thomas Sackville and Thomas Norton, *Gorboduc*, 1561.

S U M M A R Y. There are two pairs of scenes, which constitute about half a play; possibly these fragments are, however, parts of more than one unfinished play. In the first scene Oedipus, blind and exiled, longs for death and tries to persuade Antigone to leave him. She replies that Oedipus is needed to quell the war that has broken out in Thebes between his sons, Eteocles and Polyneices, who are quarreling over the kingship. Antigone's plea wins her father back to life. In the scene pendant to the first, Oedipus is summoned to the city and rages at his sons for their folly.

The third scene finds Antigone and her mother, Jocasta, in Thebes. Polyneices has gathered together the army, which is about to attack the city. Jocasta is urged to use her influence against this fratricidal war. In the last scene Jocasta is on the battlefield, pleading first with one son, then the other. Eteocles is moved by her appeal, but it is clear that Polyneices is as determined as ever to make war. At this point the fragments end. There are no choruses.

Phoenix (Gk. **Phoinix**). *Myth.* Son of Amyntor. His father's concubine made advances to Phoenix, but he repulsed her, whereupon she slandered him to Amyntor, who put out his eyes. Phoenix fled to the court of Peleus, who took him to the centaur Chiron, the great physician. Chiron restored his sight. Phoenix thereafter became the guardian of Peleus' son, Achilles.

Sophocles' lost *Phoenix* was perhaps based on the foregoing myth. (If so, Ennius' *Phoenix* was modeled on Sophocles' play.) Some scholars think, however, that a papyrus fragment in which some satyrs describe their qualifications as suitors comes from this play. If so, *Phoenix* was a satyr play, probably telling how King Oeneus held a contest for the hand of his daughter Deianira and how Phoenix came as a suitor but married Deianira's sister Perimede. But Ion of Chios wrote two plays called *Phoenix*, and the fragment may therefore be his.

Euripides' lost tragedy *Phoenix* (produced before 425 B.C.) dealt with the hero's blinding. The play was often cited in ancient writings. It was revived in the fourth century B.C.

Pholoe. Highland in southeastern Elis near the border of Arcadia.

Phorbas. 1. *Myth.* Teacher of Theseus, and his charioteer. Phorbas reputedly invented wrestling.

2. *Myth.* Aged shepherd, a character in Seneca's *Oedipus*.

Phorcides (Gk. **Phorkides**); also called **Graeae.** *Myth.* Daughters of Phorcys, or Phorcus, a primeval sea deity. In *Prometheus Bound* (line 794 ff.) Aeschylus describes the Phorcides as "three aged swan-shaped virgins, on whom neither sun nor moon ever shines, having among them a single eye and a single tooth." They were the guardians of Medusa. While the Phorcides were passing around their eye and tooth, Perseus stole them, promising to return them if the sisters would show him the way to the Stygian nymphs.

Aeschylus' lost tragedy *Phorcides* probably formed part of a trilogy to which *Dictyulci* was the satyr play. Although only one line survives, the play doubtless treated Perseus' killing of the Gorgon. (The Gorgons were also daughters of Phorcys.)

phorminx. The seven-stringed lyre, Apollo's instrument.

Phormio (Gk. **Phormion**). Capable Athenian naval commander during the Peloponnesian War.

Phormio. Extant comedy by Terence, based on the Greek play *Epidikazomenos* (*The Lawsuit*) by Apollodorus (1). *Phormio* was produced by Ambivius Turpio, with music by Flaccus, in September 161 B.C. Translations: John Sargeaunt, 1912; Barrett H. Clark, 1915; W. Ritchie, 1927; F. Perry, 1929; Frank O. Copley, 1958; Lionel Casson, 1960; Robert Graves and Laurence Echard, 1962; Samuel Lieberman, 1964. Work influenced by *Phormio*: Molière, *Les Fourberies de Scapin,* 1671.

S C E N E. Athens.

S U M M A R Y. The prologue is part of the running literary feud between Terence and Luscius Lanuvinus, who had criticized Terence for the thinness of his plots and style. By way of reply, Terence makes a mild gibe at Luscius' love for the melodramatic and denies that he ever wanted to quarrel.

As the action begins, the brothers Demipho and Chremes are away from Athens, having left their sons, Antipho and Phaedria, respectively, in the care of the slave Geta. Phaedria has fallen in love with a music girl, Pamphila, but cannot afford to buy her from the rapacious pimp Dorio. Antipho, in love with a recently orphaned and penniless girl, Phanium, has married her. Because his father would never have let him marry without receiving a dowry, Antipho allowed the parasite Phormio to work a deception: pretending to be a friend of Phanium's dead father, the parasite brought suit against Antipho on the pretext that Antipho was the orphaned girl's next of kin and therefore legally bound to marry her. The young man promptly carried out his duty.

Both Geta and Antipho fear Demipho's return. Hearing that he has indeed come back, Antipho runs off, leaving the slave and Phaedria to defend him. Demipho is, as expected, furious at the marriage and insists that Phormio take Phanium off his hands. When Phormio refuses, Demipho seeks advice from lawyers, but he receives such varied advice that he decides to wait for the opinion of his brother Chremes.

Antipho returns, ashamed at having run away, and learns that Phormio has temporarily pacified his father. Then Phaedria learns that Dorio has found a buyer for his girl friend. Although Antipho and Phaedria beg the pimp not to sell Pamphila, he remains firm. Finally Geta declares that with Phormio's help he will get the money so that Phaedria can buy the girl himself.

Meanwhile Chremes, who has also returned to Athens, tells Demipho that he went to Lemnos to bring back his daughter, whom he had by a mistress, but that both had lready left the island in search of him. Demipho repeats a long-standing promise to save his brother the embarrassment of anyone's discovering the mistress and daughter and assures Chremes that Antipho will marry the girl.

Following Phormio's instructions, Geta tells Demipho that the parasite has consented to marry Phanium, provided she is divorced from Antipho and furnished with a dowry of thirty minae (the sum Phaedria needs to buy his sweetheart). Demipho is at first indignant, but when Chremes, eager to free Antipho to marry his own daughter, offers to pay the dowry himself, Demipho agrees. Antipho, who has overheard the agreement, thinks Geta and Phormio have tricked him out of his wife; he is not wholly placated by Geta's assurance that this is not so.

Presently Sophrona, the former nurse of Antipho's wife, enters. Chremes recognizes her as the nurse of his own daughter in Lemnos and learns that the girl his nephew married is in fact his daughter. An amusing scene follows, in which Chremes tries to hint to his brother what he has learned without disclosing his secret to his wife, Nausistrata, who is also present.

Antipho, still unaware that Phanium is his uncle's daughter, discusses Phaedria's good fortune with Phormio, who has given Phaedria the thirty minae. When Geta, having overheard Chremes and Demipho, tells Antipho and Phormio the truth, Antipho is overjoyed. But Phormio now sees a way to enable Phaedria to keep the thirty minae.

Demipho and Chremes demand that Phormio give back the money for the dowry, but the parasite says he has already spent it. When they threaten him, he in turn threatens to reveal Chremes' scandalous secret to his wife. The brothers try to drag Phormio off to court, but the parasite shouts for Chremes' wife and, when she comes, manages to get out the truth. By informing Nausistrata that the money he gained from his trickery went to help her son, Phormio gains her protection and an invitation to dinner. Chremes, in order to win his wife's forgiveness, must submit to her wish.

C O M M E N T A R Y. Aside from *Adelphoe, Phormio* has earned more praise than any other Terentian comedy. It is more comical than the others; the handling of the improbable plot is masterly; the characters, as is usual with Terence, are complex and sympathetic; and in the endless variations on a theme that is the essence of New Comedy, it is interesting to see the parasite, rather than the slave, carry the burden of intrigue.

Phormis or **Phormos.** Syracusan writer of comedy. Phormis was a contemporary of Epicharmus. Of him nothing is known but these titles: *Admetus, Alcinous, Alcyoneus, Cepheus* or *Perseus, The Fall of Troy* or *The Horse.*

Phoroneus. *Myth.* Considered by the Peloponnesians as the first man. Phoroneus was son of the river god Inachus. In *Thyestes* (line 115) Seneca calls the Inachus River the "Phoronean stream."

Phosphorus (Gk. **Phosphoros**). The morning star.

Phrixus (Gk. **Phrixos**). *Myth.* Son of Athamas and Nephele, and brother of Helle. When, according to one version of the myth, Athamas' second wife,

Ino, contrived that Phrixus and Helle should be sacrificed, Nephele sent a golden ram, on which brother and sister were carried to the sky (see ATHAMAS). As the ram flew over the sea, Helle fell off its back, but Phrixus was carried to Colchis on the eastern shore of the Black Sea. Here he married the daughter of King Aeëtes, sacrificed the ram to Zeus, and gave its fleece to the king, who nailed it to a tree in the grove sacred to Ares. But Aeëtes, learning from an oracle that he would perish at the hands of a descendant of Aeolus, put Phrixus to death. Of Sophocles' lost *Phrixus* nothing is known.

Phrixus was the title of two lost tragedies, presumably two versions of the same story, by Euripides. One or both may have been produced late in the dramatist's career, probably after 412 B.C. In them Ino, the wicked stepmother, contrived to get rid of Nephele's children, persuading the women of the land to parch the seed corn before it was planted. When the crops failed to grow, Athamas sent to Delphi to inquire of the oracle what should be done, and Ino induced the returning messengers to demand the sacrifice of Phrixus and Helle as propitiation. A papyrus fragment published in 1919 shows that in the course of the play Athamas discovered Ino's perfidy.

Phrygia. Interior section of western Asia Minor. Phrygia extended up toward the Aegean Sea and the Propontis, so that even the Trojans were called Phrygians. The region was noted for its archers, sheep, wool, and flutes. In classical times the name Phrygian was a byword for cowardice and effeminacy.

Phrygians, The (Gk. **Phryges**). 1. Alternate title of THE RANSOM OF HECTOR.

2. Lost play by Sophocles. In a fragment from *The Phrygians*, Cassandra prophesies a marriage. It has accordingly been conjectured that the play dealt with the murder of Achilles in the ambush to which he was lured on promise of marriage to Polyxena.

Phryne. Name of a prostitute. The word also means "toad" (*Ecclesiazusae*, line 1101).

Phrynichus (Gk. **Phrynichos**). 1. Writer of tragedies (c. 540–c. 470 B.C.). Phrynichus was highly regarded throughout the fifth century B.C. but was largely forgotten thereafter. His plays seem to have consisted mostly of choric odes. He was said to have introduced feminine roles. Of several of Phrynichus' works only the names remain: *Actaeon, Antaeus, Just Men, The Danaïdes, Tantalus, Troilus, The Women of Pleuron* (about Meleager and his mother), and *The Egyptians* (about Aegyptus and his sons). In his *Alcestis*, perhaps a satyr play, Apollo got the Fates tipsy at Admetus' wedding feast and made them promise that they would accept a substitute for Admetus; Death appeared on the stage to snip off a lock of Alcestis' hair; and Hercules wrestled with Death. Phrynichus' *Phoenician Women* (c. 476 B.C.) resembled Aeschylus' *Persians* in that in the first scene a eunuch prepared seats for a meeting of the Persian council, and news arrived, later, of Xerxes' defeat. His most famous play, *The Capture of Miletus*, produced soon after 494 B.C., offended the Athenian audience by treating an event that they wished not to be reminded of, and the poet was fined. In 467 B.C., Phrynichus' son produced his father's Theban tetralogy, probably after the latter's death.

2. Writer of Old Comedy (active c. 430–c. 405 B.C.). Of Phrynichus' works many fragments and ten titles are known: *The Incubus, Cronus, The Satyrs, The Tragedians, The Muses* (405 B.C., won second prize), *The Hermit* (414 B.C.), *The Initiates* (407 B.C.), *The Herb-Gatherers.* Two plays, *Connus* (which won second prize in 423, outranking Aristophanes' *Clouds*) and *Members of the Komos* (which won first prize in 414, outranking Aristophanes' *Birds*) may perhaps have been by Ameipsias. Phrynichus was interested in political satire, metrics, and music. In *The Frogs* (line 12 ff.) he is censured for using stale comic tricks.

3. Athenian general of oligarchic sympaties. Phrynichus was a bitter opponent of Alcibiades. He was assassinated 411 B.C.

4. Actor contemporary with Aristophanes. This Phrynichus was a skillful dancer.

Phthia. Southeastern section of Thessaly. Phthia was the home of Peleus and Achilles.

Phthian Women, The (Gk. **Phthiotides**). Lost play by Sophocles. If *The Phthian Women* was not merely an alternate title for *Hermione,* the play must have dealt with Neoptolemus' homecoming to Phthia.

Phyla (Gk. **Phyle**). Deme in northwest Attica. Phyla was the base of operations for Thrasybulus and the returning democrats during the overthrow of the Thirty Tyrants in the last years of the fifth century B.C.

phylarch (Gk. **phylarchos**). The commander of the cavalry contingent furnished by each Athenian tribe.

Phyleus. *Myth.* Son of Augeas and father of Meges. When Augeas refused to pay Heracles for cleaning his stables, Phyleus took Heracles' side and was banished.

Pieria. Section on the border of Thrace and Macedonia. Pieria was associated with the Muses, who were often called Pierides.

Pindar (Gk. **Pindaros**). Lyric poet of Boeotia (518–438 B.C.). Pindar was noted for his still extant choric odes in honor of athletic victors.

Pindus (Gk. **Pindos**). Mountain range between Thessaly and Epirus.

Piraeus (Gk. **Peiraeus**). Port city of Athens. In classical times Piraeus was connected with Athens by the Long Walls.

Pirene (Gk. **Peirene**). Spring on the citadel of Corinth, associated with the Muses.

Pirithous (Gk. **Peirithoos** or **Peirithous**). *Myth.* Son of Ixion, prince of the Lapiths, and bosom friend of Theseus. At the feast celebrating the marriage of Pirithous and Hippodamia, the centaur Eurytion got drunk and tried to carry off the bride. This act caused the famous battle between the Lapiths and the Centaurs.

Scholars, both ancient and modern, have disputed the authorship of the lost play *Pirithous;* while some have claimed it was written by Euripides, others have assigned it to Critias. It seems that in the play Heracles rescued both Theseus and Pirithous from the land of death. (See THESEUS.)

Pisa. City in Elis.

Pisander or **Peisander** (Gk. **Peisandros**). Follower of Cleon who later supported the oligarchical party. Pisander was a butt of writers of Old Comedy because of his ostentation, dishonesty, and warmongering.

Pisias (Gk. **Peisias**). Father of Melus. The latter was a bad harpist in Aristophanes' Athens.

Pistorium. City in Etruria. The name suggests *pistor*, "baker."

Pitane. Aeolian city on the coast of Asia Minor.

Pittalus (Gk. **Pittalos**). Athenian physician of Aristophanes' time.

Pittheus. *Myth.* Son of Pelops and Hippodamia. Pittheus was king of Troezen, father of Aethra, and grandfather of Theseus.

Placentia. City in the Po valley. The name suggests *placenta*, "cake."

planipedes (Lat. "flat-footed"). Performers in pantomime, who danced without sock or buskin.

Plataea (Gk. **Plataia** or **Plataiai**). City in southern Boeotia near the Attic border.

Plato (Gk. **Platon**). 1. Writer of Old Comedy, called Plato Comicus to distinguish him from the philosopher. Plato was active from about 425 to about 385 B.C. He was fond of writing political satire and parody of myths. Of his works more than 250 fragments and 28 titles are extant, among them *Adonis, Daedalus, Zeus's Troubles, Laius, Phaon, Peisander, The Envoys, Cleophon, Hyperbolus, The Property Dresses,* and *The Long Night* (dealing with the begetting of Heracles and proposed by some as the original of Plautus' *Amphitryon*).

2. Great Athenian philosopher (c. 428–c. 347 B.C.). Plato was often satirized by writers of Middle Comedy.

Platonius (Gk. **Platonios**). Writer on comedy, of unknown date. Two excerpts, "The Different Types of Comedy" and "The Different Types of Characters," have been preserved from the preface to his commentary on Aristophanes.

Plautus, Titus Maccius. One of the two writers of Roman comedy whose works are extant (born c. middle 3rd century B.C.; died 184 B.C.).

L I F E. Born in the town of Sarsina in Umbria, not far from Rimini, Plautus seems to have come to Rome in his youth. There he worked in the theater, but it is not known in what capacity. He saved enough money to embark on a mercantile career, but his lack of succes was so great that he was reduced to pushing a millstone. In his leisure hours Plautus produced three comedies, all now lost: *The Bondsman, Saturio,* and a play of unknown title. Presumably these plays brought him literary fame some years before the turn of the century. Devoting himself wholly to writing, he continued to be prolific and successful for the twenty years preceding his death. Only two of Plautus' plays can be definitely dated: *Stichus* in 200 B.C. and *Pseudolus* in 191.

E X T A N T   W O R K S (see under individual entries). *Amphitryon* (Lat. spelling, *Amphitruo*), *Asinaria* (*The Comedy of Asses*), *Aulularia* (*The Pot of Gold*), *Bacchides* (*The Two Bacchises*), *Captivi* (*The Captives*), *Casina, Cistellaria* (*The Casket Comedy*), *Curculio, Epidicus, Menaechmi, Mercator*

(*The Merchant*), *Miles Gloriosus* (*The Braggart Soldier*), *Mostellaria* (*The Haunted House*), *Persa* (*The Girl from Persia*), *Poenulus* (*The Little Cartha-ginian*), *Pseudolus, Rudens* (*The Rope*), *Stichus, Trinummus* (*The Three-Penny Day*), *Truculentus*, and *Vidularia* (*The Tale of a Traveling Bag*, very fragmentary). More than a century after Plautus' death the critic Varro settled on twenty-one Plautine plays as unchallengeably authentic. It is likely that the twenty-one listed above, which are more or less complete, are these same "Varronian plays."

L O S T   W O R K S. It is said that more than one hundred other plays were variously ascribed to Plautus in ancient times. Varro was willing to admit that some of them were probably Plautus' work. The names of thirty-four are known, but only twelve are held by scholars to be possibly authentic: *Bacaria, The Bagatelle Comedy, The Lady Banker, The Blind Man, The Bondsman, The Flatterer, The Girl from Boeotia, Lipargus, Nervolaria, The Rustic, Saturio*, and *The Strait*.

C R I T I C I S M. All critics have appreciated Plautus' verve and verbal vir-tuosity. His delineation of character, when well thought out (as it usually was), was excellent; his management of plot ranged from superb to very bad. Critics in earlier centuries objected to Plautus' occasional coarseness and immorality, but modern critics think that the general high spirits of the proceedings render all this innocuous. The Romanization of the Greek originals is marked, for Plautus obviously remolded his models with a free hand. The most striking technical feature of his plays is the reintroduction into comedy of the lyrical element; for the possible precedents of this, see CANTICUM.

Pleiad, Tragic. Seven minor writers of tragedy in the Alexandrian age. Listings of the members of the Pleiad vary, but always included are: Lyco-phron, Sositheus, Alexander the Aetolian, Homer the Tragedian, and Philiscus (or Philicus), as well as two of these three: Sosiphanes, Dionysiades, and Aiantides.

Pleiads (Gk. **Pleiades**). *Myth.* Seven daughters of Atlas. Pursued by the mighty hunter Orion, they were turned by the gods into doves and placed among the stars.

Pleisthenes. *Myth.* According to one story (followed by Seneca in his *Thyestes*), the son of Thyestes, killed by Atreus and fed to his father (see ATREUS; THYESTES). According to another story, Pleisthenes was actually the son of Atreus, but was carried off by Thyestes when he went into exile and represented as Thyestes' son. The latter groomed his nephew to become Atreus' murderer, but when Pleisthenes made an attempt on Atreus' life, he was killed. The father then learned that he had killed his own son. Atreus reared Pleisthenes' sons, Agamemnon and Menelaus, who were therefore sometimes called Pleisthenids.

Euripides' lost *Pleisthenes* (produced before 414 B.C.) apparently dealt with the protagonist's unsuccessful attempt on Atreus' life.

Pleistus (Gk. **Pleistos**). Small stream near Delphi.

Pleuron. City in Aetolia near Calydon.

Pluto (Gk. **Plouton**). Another name for Hades. Pluto appears at the end of Aristophanes' *Frogs*, instructing Dionysus to choose between Aeschylus and Euripides.

Plutus (Gk. **Ploutos**). *Myth.* Greek god of wealth. Plutus was often represented as blind. He has the title role in a comedy by Aristophanes.

Plutus (Gk. **Ploutos**). Extant comedy by Aristophanes (produced in 388 B.C.). Translations: Benjamin B. Rogers, 1924; Arthur S. Way, 1934.

S C E N E. A street in Athens.

S U M M A R Y. Chremylus and his slave Cario return from the oracle at Delphi following a ragged, old, blind man. When Cario objects to what he considers a senseless pastime, Chremylus discloses that he consulted the oracle about converting his only son into a complete rascal so that he might succeed in life. The oracle told Chremylus to attach himself to the first person he met on emerging from the shrine and to win that person's friendship.

The blind man, after being threatened by Cario, reveals that he is Plutus, the god of wealth, blinded by Zeus who was jealous of the just and wise humans to whom Plutus had been in the habit of going. Learning that Plutus would return to the just if given back his sight, Chremylus says he will help him. Then he and Cario overcome the god's fear of Zeus by convincing him that he is the most powerful god of all, for money is the basis of Zeus's rule, as well as of all things men prize.

Chremylus tells Cario to call in his neighbors (the Chorus) to share the new wealth; the latter rejoice at their fortune. Chremylus' friend Blepsidemus suspects him of having acquired his wealth by robbery or some other crime, but on hearing that Plutus is actually in the house, Blepsidemus becomes eager to help restore the god's sight. The two men decide to take him to the Temple of Asclepius, god of healing.

Just as they are leaving, Penia (Poverty), a gigantic, terrifying female, rushes in and protests that they are plotting her abolition. In a debate with Chremylus, she undertakes to prove that she is better than Plutus on the ground that she is the only incentive to progress and industry, that wealth breeds vice and dishonesty, and that without her there would be no servant class or workers to produce luxuries. But Chremylus and Blepsidemus refuse to be persuaded, and they drive her off.

After Chremylus, Blepsidemus, and Cario lead Plutus away to the Temple of Asclepius, there is a lengthy interlude of Choral dancing. Then Cario returns with news that Plutus has regained his sight, and he describes to Chremylus' wife the ritual at the temple. The Chorus dance again, and soon the happy Plutus returns, proclaiming that he will never again leave the virtuous. He enters Chremylus' house, which is now filled with good things.

The play closes with the appearance of five typical persons whose lives have been changed by the sudden wealth. A Just Man, formerly poor, gives thanks for his new prosperity, and an unprincipled Informer protests his loss of fortune. Next an Old Woman complains that since her young lover has acquired money he has fallen out of love with her. She is followed by Hermes, god of luck, who is starving because no one sacrifices to him any more; a priest of Zeus, who also arrives, is out of business for the same reason. Chremylus admits Hermes and the Priest to his house, promises the Old Woman she will have her lover back, and the play concludes with a procession to Athena's treasury on the Acropolis, where Plutus is to be installed in permanent residence.

C O M M E N T A R Y. Until comparatively recent times *Plutus* ranked high among Aristophanes' plays; it is hard to say why. It now is sent to the bottom of the list. One would almost rather have the lost version of 408 B.C. than this tired performance of twenty years later. All that remains here of the Old Comedy chorus is the indication of song-and-dance interludes, and all that remains of Old Comedy satire are the few watered-down scenes at the play's close. Probably the audience was at fault; money-grubbing ages are not pleased to be satirized. Hence Aristophanes' shift to the milder and more abstract Middle Comedy. But the inevitable reaction to *Plutus* is: "If this is what is left of Middle Comedy, then the loss of the rest is bearable."

pnigos. See EPIRRHEMATIC AGON.

Pnyx. Semicircular terrace on the slope of a hill west of the Acropolis in Athens. The Pnyx was the meeting place of the Athenian Assembly.

Poeas (Gk. **Poias**). *Myth.* One of the Argonauts and father of Philoctetes.

Poenulus (Lat. **The Little Carthaginian**). Extant comedy by Plautus (date uncertain). *Poenulus* was based probably on Alexis' *Karchedonios* (*The Carthaginian*). Translations: Henry T. Riley, 1852; Paul Nixon, 1932; George Duckworth, 1942.

S C E N E. Calydon.

S U M M A R Y. The speaker of the prologue gives the background: A wealthy Carthaginian lost his seven-year-old son, Agorastocles, through a kidnaping, and he died of grief. The boy was taken to Calydon and sold to a rich old man who wanted a child but hated women. The old man adopted Agorastocles, who, when the old man died, became his heir. Agorastocles' father's cousin, also a wealthy Carthaginian, similarly lost his two young daughters and their nurse, who were subsequently sold to the pimp Lycus and brought to Calydon. At the time of the play, many years later, Agorastocles is madly in love with the elder daughter, Adelphasium, unaware that they are related. He is, however, kept from her by the pimp. As the play opens, the girls' father, who has been searching for them ever since they were lost, has just arrived in Calydon.

Agorastocles' slave Milphio presents a plot to enable his master to obtain Adelphasium from the pimp. Agorastocles will give a large sum of gold to his overseer, Collybiscus, who will pretend to be a stranger eager to have a good time and will enter the pimp's house. Agorastocles will then appear and ask whether his slave is inside. When Lycus denies it, thinking that it is Milphio who is meant, he will be guilty of theft and, unable to pay the fine, forced to forfeit his entire household to Agorastocles.

Adelphasium and her sister emerge from Lycus' house on their way to the Temple of Venus where they are to make offerings in honor of the Aphrodisia.

Agorastocles praises his ladylove to Milphio, greets her, and, when the sisters have left, goes to get the counselors who are to witness Lycus' undoing. The pimp, who has just heard a soothsayer predict his misfortune, appears briefly with a braggart soldier who desires the younger daughter.

Agorastocles returns with Collybiscus and the counselors, who, according to plan, inform Lycus that a wealthy mercenary soldier desires his services. The greedy pimp welcomes the stranger royally but is immediately called out by Agorastocles who declares that his slave has brought Lycus money and is at that moment inside the pimp's house. Lycus denies it, but the counselors rush up and denounce him.

One of the pimp's slaves reveals to Milphio that the two sisters are actually freeborn Carthaginians, whom Lycus bought from a man who stole them. Milphio reveals his own master's similar background, and the two slaves decide to ruin the pimp completely.

In the meantime Hanno, the girls' father, appears, seeking the adopted son of a friend who has just died. Accosted on the street by Agorastocles and Milphio, Hanno speaks in his native Punic, which Milphio pretends to understand. Changing to Latin, he learns that Agorastocles is the young man he seeks, then that Agorastocles is a Carthaginian. Through the latter's recollections and childhood scar caused by a monkey's bite, Hanno identifies him as his kinsman and the two happily embrace. Hanno is then persuaded to enter the plot against the pimp by pretending to be the sisters' Carthaginian father and claiming them as freeborn. When Hanno is overcome by the gradual realization that the girls are actually his daughters, Milphio attributes his emotion to clever acting.

On seeing his daughters' old nurse, Hanno is certain of their identity and, overjoyed, promises Adelphasium to Agorastocles. Milphio is somewhat sorry that his scheme has proved to be the truth. Then Adelphasium and her sister appear and are reunited with their father. All the pimp's objections are stopped by the threat of prosecution for kidnaping, and he turns himself over to Agorastocles and promises to return the gold. At the play's end, Agorastocles and Adelphasium are to be married, and all the Carthaginians prepare to sail for Carthage.

COMMENTARY. Nobody apparently finds *Poenulus* very interesting except the student of ancient Semitic, who is grateful for Hanno's speeches in Carthaginian. The various inadequacies of plotting have been explained as the result of the contamination of two Greek plays (see CONTAMINATION), careless revision for revivals, and Plautus' own makeshift contributions. Most scholarship is devoted to these problems. The general judgment on *Poenulus* is: "Dull and poorly constructed."

Poetics (Gk. **Peri Poietikes**). Treatise by Aristotle. The *Poetics* is the earliest extant piece of systematic literary criticism and probably the most influential ever written. As with all the works of Aristotle, the text and baffling manner of composition have provided a battleground for critics and scholars. Key words are left unexplained or are explained in contradictory fashion; the progress of the argument is at times haphazard; and promised discussions, for example, the treatment of comedy, never materialize. Also typically Aristotelian is the resolute avoidance of the religious aspect.

The first three chapters and part of the fourth take up the general nature of literature and poetry, with some incidental remarks on the origin of drama. The latter part of chapter 4, and chapter 5, contain very controversial observations on the origins of comedy and tragedy.

In chapter 6 is the famous definition of tragedy: "Tragedy is a literary imitation of a sequence of actions, a sequence that is serious, complete in itself, and large in scope; its language is rendered pleasant sometimes by metrical means alone and sometimes by the addition of music; it is dramatic and not narrative; and by pity and fear it brings about a catharsis of these emotions" (see CATHARSIS). The components of tragedy are listed: plot, characterization, diction, sentiments and arguments expressed in the dialogue, visual effects, and music. Emphatically the most important of these, Aristotle insists, is plot.

Chapters 7 through 11 treat the prerequisites of a good plot: It should be neither too short nor too long; it should begin with a situation of which the antecedent action can be easily grasped; it should develop this situation in accordance with probability and inevitability, that is, the plot should be free from the interference of accidents or irrelevancies characteristic of ordinary life and of history; and it should bring the sequence of events to its logical conclusion. Plots may be simple or complex; complex plots involve PERIPETY, preferably accompanied by ANAGNORISIS.

Chapter 12 lists the divisions of a tragedy: prologue, episodes, exodus, and choric odes, this last category being subdivided into parodos and stasima.

Chapter 13 presents the necessary characteristics of the truly tragic hero. Here occurs the discussion of the "tragic flaw" (see HAMARTIA).

Chapter 14 discusses the kinds of incidents that arouse pity and fear; chapter 15, the rules for characterization; chapter 16, the varieties of recognition, or anagnorisis; chapter 17, rules to keep in mind while plotting; chapter 18, the classification of tragedies according to their chief elements of effectiveness.

Chapters 19 through 22 are a rather technical (and from the modern point of view highly unsatisfactory) treatment of diction, including a discussion of metaphor. The rest of the treatise has to do with the epic and other matters only incidentally related to drama.

Poetry (Gk. **Poiesis**). Lost comedy, ascribed by some ancient sources to Aristophanes, by others to Archippus.

Poinai. Goddesses of vengeance, the personification of punishments for evildoers.

polemarch (Gk. **polemarchos**). One of the nine Athenian archons. Originally a battle commander, the polemarch was later a judge.

Polias. Epithet of Athena as guardian of the polis, or city-state.

Pollux 1. Latin form of Polydeuces. (See DIOSCURI.)

2. Julius Pollux, Greek orator and rhetorician (late 2nd century A.D.). Pollux was the author of *Onomasticon,* an extant work that contains many definitions of technical terms pertaining to the stage.

Polus (Gk. **Polos**). One of the most famous of tragic actors in ancient times (fl. late 4th century B.C.). Polus was best known for his performances in revivals of classics; he was especially applauded in Sophocles' *Electra*.

Polybus (Gk. **Polybos**). *Myth.* King of Corinth. Polybus reared Oedipus as his own son.

Polydectes (Gk. **Polydektes**). *Myth.* Ruler of Seriphos. Here Perseus and his mother, Danaë, were brought ashore by Polydectes' brother Dictys. Desiring Danaë, Polydectes sent Perseus on the seemingly hopeless quest of killing the Gorgon. Danaë rejected Polydectes' advances and appealed to Dictys for help. On Perseus' return, the hero was able to save both his mother and her protector by showing Polydectes the Gorgon's head, thus changing him into stone.

Of Aeschylus' lost tragedy called *Polydectes* only the title is known. It must, however, have been part of a Perseus tetralogy (which included *Phorcides* and the partially extant *Dictyulci*. The play must have told of Perseus' revenge on the king of Seriphos.

Polydeuces. One of the DIOSCURI.

Polydorus (Gk. **Polydoros**). 1. *Myth.* Son of Cadmus and Harmonia and father of Labdacus.

2. *Myth.* Son of Priam and Hecuba of Troy. In the last days of Troy, the youth was sent with the family treasure to the protection of King Polymestor in Thrace, but the greedy Polymestor murdered him. Polydorus' ghost makes an appearance in Euripides' *Hecuba*. In Pacuvius' and Accius' lost plays named *Ilione*, Ilione, Polydorus' sister and Polymestor's wife, substitutes for Polydorus her own son Deipylus, who is killed by his father. Polydorus learns of the fate of Troy at Delphi, and on his return he helps his sister to blind Polymestor. Horace mentions a notorious performance in which the ghost of the murdered Deipylus came to his mother in a dream and begged piteously for burial, but the drunken actor playing Ilione had passed out on the stage.

Polyidus (Gk. **Polyidos** or **Polyeidos**). *Myth.* Famous seer connected with King Minos of Crete. When Minos' son Glaucus disappeared, the oracle said that the boy could be found only by the seer who could invent the most apt comparison for Minos' marvelous cow, which turned from white to red to black every day. All the soothsayers of Crete suggested metaphors, but Polyidus compared the cow to a mulberry and was proclaimed the winner. By his divining art he then proceeded to discover that Glaucus had accidentally drowned in a large jar of honey. When the boy could not be revived, Minos enclosed Polyidus in the tomb with his body. A snake crept into the tomb, and Polyidus killed it, but shortly afterward the snake's mate brought it back to life by covering it with a certain herb. Polyidus used the same herb on Glaucus with equal success. When Minos heard noises from the tomb, he opened it, releasing both boy and seer.

Sophocles' lost *Polyidus* is usually identified with his *Soothsayers*. The chorus must have consisted of Cretan diviners.

Euripides' lost *Polyidus* (produced perhaps between 414 and 410 B.C.) was also known as *Glaucus*. Fragments amounting to about thirty lines indicate that in it Polyidus, by means of omens from birds, discovered that Glaucus had been drowned, but not at sea. The often-quoted lines "Who knows but that to live is but to die, / While death is the only life to those below?" are parodied by Aristophanes in *The Frogs* (line 1477).

Aristophanes' lost comedy *Polyidus* (dated between 418 and 408 B.C.) may have used the myth of this seer as a basis for an attack on warmongering soothsayers.

Polymestor. *Myth.* Wicked Thracian king, husband of the Trojan princess Ilione. For Polymestor's story, see Euripides' HECUBA, in which he is a character, and POLYDORUS.

Polyneices, Polynices (Gk. **Polyneikes**). *Myth.* One of the two sons of Oedipus and Jocasta. Polyneices arranged with his brother Eteocles to alternate in the rule of Thebes, but Eteocles refused to yield at the end of his term. Polyneices then went to Argos, married one of King Adrastus' daughters, and mounted the expedition of the Seven against Thebes in order to regain his rights. He appears in Sophocles' *Oedipus at Colonus,* trying to win Oedipus' support, but his father curses him. In Euripides' and Seneca's *Phoenician Women* he appears as Eteocles' opponent. The brothers killed each other in the attack on Thebes, and against Creon's orders Antigone buried Polyneices' body. In Aeschylus' *Seven Against Thebes* (lines 577 and 658) and Euripides' *Phoenician Women* (line 1493), Polyneices' name is interpreted as meaning "much strife."

Polyphemus (Gk. **Polyphemos**). *Myth.* One of the Cyclopes, a son of Poseidon. In Euripides' *Cyclops* Polyphemus is blinded by Odysseus.

Polyphontes. *Myth.* Theban hero. In the attack of the Seven against Thebes Polyphontes defended the Electran Gates, near which there was probably a shrine of Artemis.

Polyphrasmon. Writer of tragedies, son of the tragedian Phrynichus, and rival of Aeschylus. Polyphrasmon's tetralogy *Lycurgeia* won third prize in the dramatic contest of c. 468 B.C. when Aeschylus' *Theban Tetralogy* placed first.

Polyxena (Gk. **Polyxene**). *Myth.* Daughter of Priam and Hecuba of Troy. Chancing to see Polyxena, Achilles fell in love with her. He came secretly to the Temple of Apollo Thymbraeus to arrange a marriage but was ambushed and killed by Paris. After the fall of Troy, Polyxena was sacrificed either immediately on Achilles' tomb (as intimated in Euripides' *Trojan Women* and dramatized in Seneca's, where Pyrrhus takes her away for execution), or later, to appease Achilles' ghost, during a landing of the Greek fleet in Thrace. This latter version of the story was used in Euripides' *Hecuba,* where Polyxena goes bravely to her doom. In Sophocles' lost tragedy *Polyxena,* Achilles' ghost appeared, demanding the sacrifice of the girl.

Pompaios (Gk. "escorting"). Epithet of Hermes as guide of the souls of the dead to the underworld.

Pomponius, Lucius. Writer of ATELLAN FARCE (fl. c. 89 B.C.). Pomponius was the first to raise this type of comedy to the level of literature. He wrote FABULA TOGATA also. The fragments from Pomponius' works show that he was fond of puns, crude witticisms, obscenities, and everyday diction. Seventy titles are extant. Of them the following may serve to indicate the range of this kind of comic skit: *The Marriage, The Counterfeit Agamemnon, Ariadne, Bucco's Adoption, The First of March, The Pimp, The Maccus Twins, The Doctor, Farmer Pappus, The Baker,* and *Pappus' Bride.*

Pomponius Secundus. Most important Roman writer of tragedy in the 1st century A.D. Pomponius was in disgrace during Tiberius' reign, but was politically prominent under Caligula and Claudius. Scanty fragments and two titles, *Aeneas* and *Atreus,* are ascribed to him.

Pontus (Gk. **Pontos**). Region on the south shore of the Black Sea east of Paphlagonia.

Poppaea. Second wife of the emperor Nero. Poppaea appears in the pseudo-Senecan play *Octavia.*

Porcius Licinus. Author of a lost Latin poem on literary history (late 2nd century B.C.). A few fragments from Porcius' work survive; they give a very unfavorable view of Terence.

Porphyrion. 1. *Myth.* Giant (or Titan) who tried to storm Olympus.

2. Species of sea bird .

Porthaon. *Myth.* King of Calydon and grandfather of Deianira.

Portus Persicus (Lat. "Persian Harbor"). Anchorage on the Greek coast opposite Euboea where the Persian fleet once landed.

Poseidon. *Myth.* Greek god of the sea, brother of Zeus and Hades. Poseidon must originally have been a god not only of the sea, but of the earth and sky, since he was associated with the horse, was called the Earth-Shaker, and carried the trident (probably a thunder symbol in the beginning, though later identified as a fish spear). With Apollo Poseidon built the walls of Troy but was defrauded of his payment by the king (see LAOMEDON). He appears at the beginning of Euripides' *Trojan Women* after the fall of Troy, and he is one of the gods who come to Cloudcuckooland to sue for peace in Aristophanes' *Birds.*

Posidippus (Gk. **Poseidippos**). Writer of New Comedy. Posidippus' first play was produced in 291 B.C. There survive about a hundred scattered lines from seventeen plays, for example: *The Man Who Regained His Sight, Hermaphrodite, The Ant, The Pimp, The Dancing-Girls.*

postscaenium (Lat.). Section of theater behind the facade of the skene.

Pothos. Greek deity, the personification of amorous desire. Pothos was an attendant of Aphrodite.

Potidaea (Gk. **Potidaia**). City on the isthmus of the westernmost Chalcidic peninsula in Macedonia.

Potnia (Gk. "mistress" or "queen"). Title given to several goddesses, especially Hera or one of the Erinyes.

Potniae (Gk. **Potniai**). Town in Boeotia.

Pot of Gold, The. See AULULARIA.

praecinctio. Latin equivalent of DIAZOMA.

Praeneste. Town in Latium a few miles east of Rome.

praetor. High official in Rome having mainly judicial duties. Praetors ranked directly below consuls.

Pramnion. Place of unknown location mentioned by Homer and later writers as being famous for its wine.

Prasiae (Gk. **Prasiai**). Town on the eastern coast of Laconia. Prasiae was sacked by the Athenians in 430 B.C. In *Peace* (line 242) Aristophanes puns on the name to suggest *prason,* "leek."

Pratinas. Lyric poet and writer of satyr plays and tragedies (c. 540–470 B.C.). Probably already a successful poet at Phleius, Pratinas moved to Athens in about 500 B.C. and was credited with introducing the satyr play there. He was said to have written thirty-two satyr plays and about eighteen tragedies, rivaling Aeschylus during the early part of the century. The longest fragment from his works deals with a contention between satyrs and flute players over different types of music. After Pratinas' death, his son won a second prize in 467 B.C. with his father's *Perseus, Tantalus,* and a satyr play, *The Wrestlers.*

Priam (Gk. **Priamos**). *Myth.* King of Troy, son of Laomedon. When Heracles sacked Troy and killed Laomedon, Priam was only a child, but Hesione ransomed him and he regained the throne. At the time of the Trojan War Priam was very old. His chief act was to go to Achilles' encampment and ransom the body of his son Hector; this story is told in the last book of the *Iliad.* At the sack of Troy, Priam was killed by Achilles' son Pyrrhus, and his headless body was thrown out on the shore. His sons and descendants were called Priamidae.

Of Sophocles' lost tragedy *Priam* nothing is known. Some have thought it to be only another title for *The Phrygians.*

Priestesses, The (Gk. **Hiereiai**). Lost play by Aeschylus. Three scanty fragments from it refer to some sort of mystic rites conducted by priestesses of Artemis, called "Beekeepers."

proagon (Gk. "preliminary contest"). Competitive rehearsal of plays to be entered in the City DIONYSIA at Athens. The plays were performed without masks or costumes.

Processional, The (Gk. **Propompoi**). Lost play by Aeschylus of which nothing except the title is known.

Procne (Gk. **Prokne**). *Myth.* Wife of TEREUS and sister of Philomela. Procne appears as the Hoopoe's wife in Aristophanes' *Birds.*

Procris (Gk. **Prokris**). *Myth.* Daughter of King Erechtheus of Athens and wife of Cephalus. Growing suspicious and jealous because her husband spent so much time hunting, Procris hid in a thicket to spy on him. Cephalus threw his spear at the rustling underbrush and unwittingly killed his wife. Afterward he was tried by the Areopagus and condemned to exile. A lost tragedy by Sophocles was called *Procris.*

Procrustes (Gk. **Prokroustes**). *Myth.* Robber chieftain. Procrustes forced passers-by to lie on his bed; if they were too short to fit it, he stretched them; if too long, he lopped off the excess length. Theseus killed Procrustes on his way from Troezen to Athens.

Prodicus (Gk. **Prodikos**). Sophist (late 5th century B.C.). Prodicus was well known as a traveling teacher in the Greek world.

proedra or **proedria.** Front-row seat in a Greek theater, reserved for officials and distinguished guests. (See AUDIENCE.)

Proetides (Gk. **Proitides**). *Myth.* Lysippe, Iphinoë, and Iphianassa, the three daughters of Proetus. Because the Proetides opposed the worship of Dionysus, the god drove them mad. The seer Melampus offered to heal them, demanding in payment a third of Proetus' kingdom for himself and an equal share for his brother Bias. After Proetus had reluctantly agreed to pay the price, Melampus, aided by some stalwart young men, chased the mad women from the mountains. In the pursuit Iphinoë died, but the other two sisters were cured and afterwards married to Melampus and Bias.

Proetus (Gk. **Proitos**). *Myth.* King of Tiryns, twin brother and bitter enemy of Acrisius. In a quarrel over the throne of Argos, Acrisius expelled Proetus, who went to Lycia and married Stheneboea, the daughter of King Iobates. The latter sent an army to Argos and won the throne for his son-in-law. When Stheneboea falsely accused BELLEROPHON of making improper advances, Proetus sent the young man to Iobates to be put to death. One of the sets of gates at Thebes was called the Proetid Gates, or Gates of Proetus, supposedly because the king was expelled from Argolis and forced to take refuge in Thebes. (See also PROETIDES.)

prologue (Gk. **prologos,** Lat. **prologus**). Originally the part of a play spoken before the entrance of the chorus. The prologue was later used, also, to designate an address by an actor to the audience at or near the beginning of a play (as well as the actor making this address). Ancient critics noted that prologues of this second kind served several purposes: to commend the play to the audience; to defend the poet against criticism (this use of the prologue was associated with Terence, though it probably did not originate with him); and to outline the plot or fill in the necessary background (this use was associated with Euripides and the writers of New Comedy).

Prometheia. Trilogy by Aeschylus (variously dated c. 479–478 B.C., c. 469 B.C., and c. 458–456 B.C.). Of the *Prometheia* only one play, *Prometheus Bound,* is extant. (The theory of Wilhelm Schmid that the extant play is not by Aeschylus but is an anonymous work written one or two generations later under the influence of the Sophists has found little support.) The two lost plays were *Prometheus Unbound* and *Prometheus the Fire-Bringer;* they are generally thought to have followed *Prometheus Bound* in the foregoing order. A few scholars still think, however, that the *Fire-Bringer* was first in the trilogy. The satyr play is unknown.

Prometheus Bound (Gk. *Prometheus Desmotes;* traditional Latin title, *Prometheus Vinctus*). Translations: T. W. C. Edwards, 1823; Elizabeth Barrett (Browning), 1833; Henry David Thoreau, 1843; E. Lang, 1870; John D. Cooper, 1890; Janet Case, 1905; Robert Whitelaw, 1907; E. D. A. Morshead, 1908; Walter and C. E. S. Headlam, 1909; Edward G. Harman, 1920; G. M. Cookson, 1922; Clarence W. Mendell, 1926; Lewis Campbell, 1938; Robert C. Trevelyan, 1939; David Grene, 1942; Marjorie L. Burke, 1961; Philip Vellacott,

1961; Warren D. Anderson, 1963; Paul Roche, 1964. Work influenced by *Prometheus Bound:* Shelley, *Prometheus Unbound,* 1820.

SCENE. The Scythian mountains.

SUMMARY. On the rim of earth, Hephaestus, god of fire and metalworking, assisted by the personifications of Power (*Kratos*) and Force (*Bia*), reluctantly rivets his fellow-god Prometheus to a mountain crag. By suffering indefinite exposure, Prometheus is to learn to bear the rule of Zeus, who alone is free, and to check his own favoritism toward mankind. It is a heavy thing to transgress against Zeus's laws, Hephaestus says, yet Prometheus, though a son of Themis ("she of the right plan"), has overstepped the bounds of Dike ("that which has been spoken"). He has stolen Hephaestus' own element, fire, and given it to man. Prometheus' punishment will be of indefinite duration: the one who will release him has not yet been born, and Zeus's purpose is scarcely to be modified, since whoever has newly achieved power is harsh in its exercise. Power hurls a last taunt: Prometheus ("Forethought") is a misnomer for one who has let himself come to such a pass. The hero, with arms and legs fettered and chest pierced, is left alone to bewail the injustice of his fate. He declares, in reply to the taunt, that he in fact has foreseen his suffering but has chosen to suffer it out of friendship for man.

A Chorus of Nymphs, daughters of Oceanus, fly in drawn by the sound of Hephaestus' hammer. They join Prometheus in denouncing Zeus's cruelty. Prometheus confides to them his private consolation: one day Zeus himself will need him to reveal the new scheme of things by which an unknown man or god will strip Zeus of his royal honors. Prometheus vows that he will be neither coaxed nor threatened into speech.

The daughters of Oceanus, counseling moderation, ask for Prometheus' story. He tells them that, when war broke out among the gods, he had supported the party of Zeus against Cronus and the Titans, knowing through his mother Themis (who is also called Gaia, or Earth) that trickery would win over brute force. The victorious Zeus had parceled out spheres of power and duty to his fellow divinities, but had decided to supplant the human race with some other kind of creature. Prometheus alone in pity had saved mankind, settling blind hopes in them so that they might not see clearly their limited lot, and giving them fire, the source of all arts and crafts.

At this point the Nymphs' father, Oceanus, enters and, while offering to try to obtain Prometheus' release, advises him to learn humility. When he leaves, Prometheus recalls the dreamlike confusion in which man, like a cave dweller, previously existed, looking yet not seeing, perceiving sound yet not hearing. From him, he says, man learned the cycle of the year, building, writing, agriculture, carriage-making and sailing, as well as the arts of medicine, augury, and metallurgy. When the Nymphs wonder why Prometheus has not acted in his own behalf, he declares that Necessity, which is stronger even than Zeus, has decreed his eventual release. The Chorus then comment that Prometheus, overly concerned for men, has still not greatly improved their lot, for life still amounts to little more than a dream.

Next Io enters. Because she was loved by Zeus, she has been persecuted by Hera. Exiled by her own father on command of an oracle, Io was changed by Zeus into a heifer, but Hera sent the myriad-eyed herdsman Argus to guard her. On his death, Io was pursued all over the earth by his ghost, a relentless gadfly. Io is, in fact, a perfect example of the undeserved misery that comes from encounters with the gods. After she relates her story to the Chorus, Prometheus, in response to her pleading, discloses her future torments, but prophesies final peace for her in Egypt on the banks of the Nile, where she will bear Zeus's son, Epaphus ("Born from the touch of God"). Prometheus assures Io that one day Zeus's tyranny will be ended, for from a future marriage Zeus will produce a son (a descendant of Io) who, though he must endure torments worse than Prometheus' own, will be greater than his father. This offspring will also be Prometheus' deliverer.

Stung by the gadfly, Io departs, and the Oceanides sing fearfully of the dangers of union with a divinity. Prometheus then reveals that Zeus's eventual destruction will result from the curse of Cronus, whom Zeus overthrew. Hermes now arrives. He informs Prometheus that Zeus has overheard his prophecy and demands to know who it is that Zeus must not marry. Prometheus greets the question with hatred and defiance. Hermes warns that if Prometheus does not reveal the answer he will be thrown into Hades by a thunderbolt, buried for ages, and emerge only to have his liver repeatedly devoured by Zeus's eagle, until such time as one of the gods voluntarily inherits his suffering and goes down to Hades and Tartarus. All Hermes' threats are received defiantly by Prometheus, who declares that he would rather be imprisoned than serve the new gods. Then Hermes leaves. Crying to Themis to behold injustice, Prometheus vanishes with the nymphs in a violent thunderstorm sent by Zeus.

Prometheus Unbound (Gk. *Prometheus Lyomenos*). A few fragments, a few ancient references, and a Latin translation of some lines by Cicero make possible a limited reconstruction of this lost tragedy. Its action took place tens of thousands of years after that of *Prometheus Bound.* The chorus consisted of Prometheus' defeated brothers, the Titans, now released by Zeus and reconciled to his rule. Gaia apparently persuaded the hero to disclose the secret prophecy that Zeus would be dethroned if he should mate with Thetis. Heracles, Prometheus' deliverer, then appeared; he received advice from Prometheus on how to obtain the apples of the Hesperides. At the play's end a divine messenger brought the news that Zeus had decreed Prometheus' release.

Prometheus the Fire-Bringer (Gk. *Prometheus Pyrphoros*). The longest surviving fragment from this play consists of about forty mutilated lines from a choric ode. The general opinion has been that *Prometheus the Fire-Bringer* represented the complete reconciliation of Zeus and the persecuted Titan, as well as the establishment of the Prometheus cult in Athens.

C O M M E N T A R Y. Few plays have been more discussed than *Prometheus Bound,* and few more fruitlessly. All evidence indicates that the *Prometheia* was as profound and complex a work as the *Oresteia* and just as impossible to grasp in its entirety until the last ode of the concluding play was sung. Yet scholars persist in basing their theories about Aeschylus' characterization of Zeus on the harsh portrait in *Prometheus Bound,* forgetting that Zeus is absent from the play and that "the absent are always wrong." It is usually allowed that Prometheus is partly wrong, too, and that he and Zeus must have learned a lesson in the course of the trilogy. Zeus is thus a "developing god." But it is doubtful that any Greek, especially Aeschylus, would have countenanced such a theological absurdity.

Aeschylus' steady insistence, in the *Oresteia,* on the unchanging justice of Zeus and on the educative value of human suffering favors the entirely different interpretation put forward by a few critics. In this view, the cruel Zeus of the extant play is only an illusion of Prometheus, the representative of mankind. Prometheus' concealment of his secret here resembles his deception of Zeus in Hesiod's *Theogony,* where Zeus divines the trick but decides to act as though he were ignorant of it. The introduction of Io might be analogous to the use of the Io myth in the *Danaïd Trilogy,* where she serves to illustrate the idea that God's cruelty may be kindness in disguise, a necessary spurring-on of mankind to the goal to which God knows he must arrive.

In the absence of the two concluding plays, a loss as deplorable as any in ancient literature, even this interpretation must be looked on as tentative.

Prometheus. *Myth.* Son of the Titan Iapetus and called a Titan and a god himself. Prometheus was the father of Deucalion and Hellen. He was the patron deity of the potters at Athens, and at his annual festival there was a torch race to relight the fires of the kilns. For his principal myth and principal dramatic appearance, see PROMETHEIA. Prometheus was sometimes said to have freed Athena from Zeus's head, though this action was usually attributed to Hephaestus. In Aristophanes' *Birds* he appears in his traditional trickster role, slipping down from Olympus to encourage the birds to hold out for extreme terms in their peace pact with the gods.

Prometheus Bound. See PROMETHEIA.

Prometheus the Fire-Bringer. See PROMETHEIA.

Prometheus the Fire-Kindler (Gk. **Prometheus Pyrkaeus**). Lost satyr play by Aeschylus. It was produced in 472 B.C. as the last play of the tetralogy of which *The Persians* was a part. Pandora and her jar of evils may have entered into the plot. In the thirty mutilated lines that have been recovered, a satyr who has never seen fire before tries to kiss it; Prometheus, calling him "My goat," warns him against singeing his beard.

Prometheus Unbound. See PROMETHEIA.

Propontis. The body of water between the Hellespont and the Bosporus, now called the Sea of Marmora.

Propylaea (Gk. **Propylaia**). A complex of structures forming the elaborate gateway to the Athenian Acropolis.

proscenium (Gk. **proskenion**). Literally, "something in front of the skene," that is, in front of the facade of the skene, and hence a movable flat or screen. Even in ancient times, however, the term was used to mean the stage itself or the facade of the skene below the stage or sometimes the whole of the theater exclusive of the auditorium.

Proserpina. Latin for PERSEPHONE.

protagonist (Gk. **protagonistes**). Chief actor. (See ACTORS AND ACTING.)

protatic character. Character appearing only in the opening scenes of a play for purposes of exposition.

Proteas. Military commander in Aristophanes' Athens.

Protesilaus (Gk. **Protesilaos**). *Myth.* King of Phylace in Thessaly. Immediately after Protesilaus' marriage to Laodamia, he sailed for the Trojan War. According to a prophecy, the side that lost the first man would win the war; at the landing, Protesilaus leaped from his ship and was killed by the Trojans. Laodamia persuaded the gods to let her husband out of the underworld for one last meeting, and afterward she had a wax figure of him made, which she was in the habit of caressing. A slave told her father, Acastus, that she had a lover, whereupon Acastus burned the wax figure, and Laodamia threw herself into the flames. *Protesilaus* was the name of a lost tragedy by Euripides.

Proteus. *Myth.* In the *Odyssey,* a sea god who shepherded flocks of seals, driving them up on the island of Pharos off the Egyptian coast. According to Homer, Proteus' daughter Eidothea gave advice to Menelaus when he was lost in Egypt on the way home from Troy. Eidothea told Menelaus that he could force Proteus to reveal the course he must take to return to Greece, that he and his men must hide under sealskins and catch the sea god after he came up from the waters, and though Proteus would change into many shapes, Menelaus, if he kept his grasp on the old man, would gain his wish. This incident must have formed the plot of Aeschylus' lost satyr play *Proteus* (see ORESTEIA).

In Euripides' *Helen,* Proteus is referred to as a former king of Egypt, the father of Theonoë and Theoclymenus.

Prothous (Gk. **Prothoos**). *Myth.* Leader of the contingent of Greeks from Magnesia in the Trojan War.

Prothrymus, Minucius. See MINUCIUS PROTHRYMUS.

proxenoi. Public guest-friends. Proxenoi were individuals from a foreign state who enjoyed a kind of hereditary bond of hospitality with the citizens of the state which they were visiting. Hence they became representative agents of the foreign state, similar to modern consuls.

prytanes (Gk. **prytaneis**). Fifty members of an executive council in Athens whose chief duty was to preside over official meetings. The prytanes ate together at public expense in the prytaneum (Gk. *prytaneion*), where ambassadors and specially honored citizens shared their meals.

Psamathe. *Myth.* Nereid who became the wife of Aeacus and the mother of Phocus. Psamathe later married Proteus, king of Egypt.

Pseudolus. Extant comedy by Plautus (produced in 191 B.C.). *Pseudolus* was based on an unknown Greek play, perhaps Menander's *Thesauros.* Translations: Henry T. Riley, 1852; Paul Nixon, 1932; Charles T. Murphy, 1942; Lionel Casson, 1963; E. F. Watling, 1965. Work influenced by *Pseudolus:* Shevelove, Gilbert, and Sondheim, *A Funny Thing Happened on the Way to the Forum,* 1962.

S C E N E. Athens.

S U M M A R Y. Calidorus has received a note from his sweetheart, the courtesan Phoenicium, saying that Ballio, the brothelkeeper who owns her, has sold her to a Macedonian soldier. The soldier has made a down payment of fifteen minae and left the impression of his seal in wax; he is to send a messenger the following day, carrying the identical impression, to pay the balance of five minae and take the girl away. In despair Calidorus confides in his father's slave Pseudolus, who promises to present him with the girl or the twenty minae before the day is over. Pseudolus adds that he will get the money from Calidorus' father if necessary.

The two are interrupted by Ballio, who emerges from his house abusing a group of slaves and courtesans. They beg him to wait a few days before selling Phoenicium so that Calidorus can obtain the money to buy her, but Ballio refuses, and they shower him with invective. When the pimp leaves, Pseudolus hints that he has a scheme and orders Calidorus to find him a shrewd man. But when Calidorus leaves, the slave reveals that in fact he has no idea what to do.

Calidorus' father, Simo, enters with his neighbor, Callipho. Simo has heard that his son intends to swindle him out of the twenty minae, and, to Pseudolus' momentary chagrin, charges him with intent to defraud. But the slave defies Simo and wagers a whipping against twenty minae that he will get the money from Simo and the girl from Ballio before nightfall.

As Pseudolus, alone, considers his tactics, Harpax, the Macedonian soldier's messenger, appears. Pseudolus pretends that he is Ballio's steward, but Harpax refuses to trust him with the soldier's money. He does, however, ask Pseudolus to deliver a letter containing the soldier's seal of identification. When Harpax leaves, Pseudolus, overjoyed, states that he had conceived that very means of tricking Ballio but had needed the aid of Fortune.

When Calidorus brings his friend Charinus, the shrewd man requested by Pseudolus, the slave hints of his good fortune, then obtains Charinus' promise to lend him five minae, a soldier's costume, and a clever slave. The latter, impersonating Harpax, will hand over the seal of identification and the five minae to Ballio and will take away the girl.

Ballio discloses that Simo has warned him that Pseudolus means to swindle Phoenicium from him. When Ballio goes inside, Pseudolus returns with Simia, the slave whom Charinus has provided. Simia has no difficulty in trading the token and money for the girl. Ballio, having (as he thinks) concluded his business, is so happy that he insists on betting Simo twenty minae that Simo's wager with Pseudolus is already won. No sooner are the words out of the pimp's mouth than the real Harpax enters, demanding Phoenicium. Thinking him an impostor, Ballio treats him with scorn, until Harpax describes Pseudolus as the slave to whom he gave the letter. Thoroughly swindled, Ballio pays Simo his twenty minae. Simo, acknowledging Pseudolus' cunning, pays the slave, who, drunk from the victory dinner, promises to give at least half of it back.

COMMENTARY. It is said that Plautus liked *Pseudolus* very much, and practically all critics have agreed with him, commending the play's humor and rapid action. Pseudolus, the tricky slave, and Ballio, the pimp, can lay claim to being definitive specimens of these two New Comedy stereotypes.

Pterelas or **Pterelaus**. *Myth.* King of the Teleboans. Pterelas was defeated and killed by Amphitryon.

Publilius Syrus. Writer of mimes. Publilius was a contemporary of Cicero. Born in Syria, a country famous for its actors, he came to Rome as a slave and soon attracted attention by his handsome looks and his wit. He won fame by writing mimes and acting in them throughout Italy. Publilius reached the height of his career when he won a contest for mime actors in 46 B.C. Of his works only three titles are known, and even they are doubtfully ascribed to him; they are *The Myrmidons, The Pruners,* and *Sowbelly.* Publilius' works appealed to the educated class. Soon after his death more than seven hundred of his *sententiae,* quotable sayings, were collected. The collection is extant.

pulpitum (Lat.). The stage in the Roman theater.

Punic (Lat. Punicus, "Phoenician"). Carthaginian. A "Punic lantern" seems to have been one made with glass.

Pylades. 1. *Myth.* Son of King Strophius of Phocis. Pylades was the cousin and friend of Orestes; in this role he appears in Seneca's *Agamemnon* (as a mute character), Aeschylus' *Choephori,* Euripides' *Electra,* Sophocles' *Electra* (mute), Euripides' *Orestes,* and Euripides' *Iphigenia among the Taurians.* Pylades eventually married Electra.

2. Pantomimist and freedman of the emperor Augustus. Pylades began his career in about 22 B.C., becoming very rich and popular. He had a large repertory of roles and excelled in tragic pantomime. One of his pantomimes, mentioned in ancient writings, was "Semele's Death and the Birth of Dionysus."

Pylae (Gk. **Pylai**). Thermopylae, a pass on the Maliac Gulf. There, in 480 B.C., the Spartan army was completely annihilated while defending the pass against the Persians. Commemorative games were afterward held at Thermopylae.

Pylaemachus (Gk. **Pylaimachos**). Epithet of Athena, invented by Aristophanes (*The Knights,* line 1172), meaning both "fighter at the gates" and "fighter at Pylos."

Pylatides. Gathering place of the amphictyonic assembly at Thermopylae.

Pylos. Coastal city of the southwestern Peloponnesus.

Pyrrha. *Myth.* Daughter of Epimetheus and Pandora and wife of Deucalion. With her husband, Pyrrha survived the great flood. She helped to repeople the earth by throwing stones, which became women. (See DEUCALION.)

Pyrrhus (Gk. **Pyrrhos**). 1. Another name for NEOPTOLEMUS (1).

2. King of Epirus. Pyrrhus fought the Romans on behalf of Tarentum early in the third century B.C.

Pytho (adj. Pythian). Older name for the part of Phocis where Delphi was situated and for Delphi itself.

Python. 1. *Myth.* Monster serpent that lived at the foot of Mt. Parnassus. Apollo killed the Python before establishing his oracle at Delphi.

2. Reputed author of the satyr play *Agen.* Python was possibly the same person as the distinguished orator of that name from Byzantium, who was a pupil of Isocrates and acted as an ambassador for Philip of Macedon.

Q

Querolus. Extant anonymous comedy in Latin prose (4th or 5th century A.D.). Translation: George Duckworth, 1942. *Querolus* was based largely on Plautus' *Aulularia.* Its preface says that it was written for the author's friends and not for the stage. The plot deals with the unsuccessful attempt of Mandrogerus to defraud Querolus of a buried treasure which the latter's father had left him before going on a journey. *Querolus* is a unique specimen of the Christianization of classical Roman comedy.

R

raised stage. Whether the actors performed on a raised stage in classical Greek drama, or whether they were in the orchestra on the same level as the chorus, is a controversy of long standing. Scholars now incline to agree with certain ancient writers in supporting the former view; communication and interaction between actors and chorus were made possible by steps leading up from the orchestra to the stage.

Ransom of Hector, The (Gk. **Hektoros Lytra**). Lost tragedy by Aeschylus, also called *The Phrygians* (who attended King Priam as a chorus). *The Ransom of Hector* formed the conclusion of a trilogy; it was preceded by *The Myrmidons* and *The Nereids.* The play was famous for the long, typically Aeschylean silence preserved by Achilles at its beginning, when Hermes came to prepare the way for King Priam. It was marked also by some odd dances by the chorus.

Rape of the Locks, The. See PERIKEIROMENE.

Reapers, The (Gk. **Theristai**). Lost satyr play by Euripides. *The Reapers* was produced in 431 B.C., with *Medea, Philoctetes,* and *Dictys.* No fragment remains.

Rehearsal, The (Gk. **Proagon**). Lost comedy by Aristophanes. *The Rehearsal* was produced under the name of Aristophanes' friend Philonides at the Lenaea of 422 B.C. It was awarded first prize. For the meaning of the title, see PROAGON.

revivals. Beginning in 386 B.C., an old play was revived every year at the City Dionysia. Later on, after the works of Aeschylus, Sophocles, and Euripides had been established as "classics," revivals became ever more common. From 341 to 339 B.C., for example, only revivals are recorded as having been staged. Euripides was by far the favorite in this respect, though Sophocles was also popular.

Rhadamanthus (Gk. **Rhadamanthys**). *Myth.* Cretan hero, son of Zeus and Europa, and sometimes said to have been the husband of Alcmena. Because of his upright character Rhadamanthus became a judge of the dead in the underworld. A lost play called *Rhadamanthus* was doubtfully attributed to Euripides.

Rhamnus (Gk. **Rhamnous**). Attic deme on the northeast coast of Attica.

Rhea (Gk. **Rheia**). *Myth.* Daughter of Uranus and Gaia and wife of Cronus. Rhea was called the Great Mother and the Great Mother of the Gods. She was sometimes identified with Cybele.

rhesis (Gk. "speech"). The speeches and dialogue in Greek drama, as distinguished from the lyric parts of the play. (See THESPIS.)

Rhesus (Gk. **Rhesos**). *Myth.* Thracian hero. For his story, see the following entry.

Rhesus (Gk. **Rhesos**). Extant tragedy by Euripides (thought to be one of Euripides' earlier works, produced between 455 and 441 B.C.). Although it was known that Euripides wrote a *Rhesus,* the play summarized here was long thought not to be his. Opinion has, however, recently shifted in favor of Euripides' authorship. Translations: Gilbert Murray, 1911; Arthur S. Way, 1912; Richmond Lattimore, 1958.

S C E N E. The Trojan camp.

S U M M A R Y. Two prologues, one of them not by Euripides, were current in ancient times, but neither remains. The surviving text, based on the tenth book of the *Iliad*, begins on the night following Hector's forcing the invading Achaean army almost to the sea. It is the fourth watch.

A Chorus of Trojan Guards inform the Trojan general of great activity and all-night fires in the Greek camp, and Hector, leaping to the conclusion that the Greeks mean to retreat, orders pursuit. But Aeneas convinces him that it would be more prudent first to send a spy into the Greek camp to discover whether the Greeks are preparing a trick. Dolon, a man of lower rank, volunteers, upon promise of the horses of Achilles when victory comes. He will bring back the head of Odysseus or Diomedes as proof of the accomplishment of his mission. After Dolon leaves, camouflaged in a wolfskin, the Chorus pray for his success.

A Shepherd informs Hector of the arrival of King Rhesus of Thrace (son of a Muse and the Thracian river god Strymon) with a large army. Hector finds fault with Rhesus for coming only after the Trojan victory is certain, but the Shepherd persuades him to welcome the Thracians as allies. Reproached by Hector for waiting so long to pay the debt incurred when Hector helped him win his kingdom, Rhesus explains that he has been held back by Scythian attacks on his own army. He asserts that he will compensate for his tardiness by defeating the enemy in one day and will make a point of killing Odysseus. Hector then shows Rhesus to a quiet spot and leaves him to sleep.

The Chorus, at watch before Hector's tent, wonder why there has been no word from Dolon, then go off to wake the next watch. Odysseus and Diomedes now appear, carrying the wolfskin and mask of Dolon, whom they captured while on their own spying mission. After inducing the captive to reveal the Trojan password, they killed him. The Greeks enter Hector's tent with swords drawn but find it empty. Leaving the wolfskin, they are about to return to their own camp when the goddess Athena materializes. She tells them to stay but to kill only Rhesus, for his entrance into the war would mean Trojan victory. After Athena directs the Greeks to Rhesus' tent, Paris enters Hector's tent, investigating a rumor that some Achaean intruders are present. But the goddess, changing her form to that of Aphrodite, lulls Paris' suspicions.

Odysseus and Diomedes reappear, having killed Rhesus. Pursued by the Trojan Guards, they are captured, but Odysseus gives the password and pretends to be an ally, and he and Diomedes escape. The Guards go in search of the killer, then return, suspecting Odysseus of the killing. They are followed by Rhesus' wounded Charioteer, who tells how Rhesus was killed on the ground as he slept; he adds that his master's wonderful horses are gone too. Presently Hector appears and angrily blames the Guards for permitting the Greeks to enter the camp, but the Charioteer turns and accuses Hector of treachery in order to obtain Rhesus' horses.

After Hector has placated and ministered to the wounded Charioteer, the Muse who is Rhesus' mother enters, carrying her son's body. Lamenting his death, she reveals Odysseus and Diomedes as the agents and curses them. Rhesus, she says, will not descend to the land of death but will become an oracular spirit enshrined in a faraway cave. After the Muse bears away her son, Hector goes to get his shield. He sees Dolon's bloody wolfskin, but, disregarding it, leads his troops out to what he proclaims will be a decisive victory.

C O M M E N T A R Y. *Rhesus* is a rather ineffective play. This fact, together with its peculiarities of diction and construction (the two goddesses appear only as incidental characters) has made critics reluctant to assign it to Euripides. In addition, it treats pretty much the same story as Book X of the *Iliad*, the "Doloneia," and the doubt that *Iliad* X is by Homer seems to have generated the doubt that *Rhesus* is by Euripides. There is, however, almost no external evidence to prove that Euripides did not write the play. Possibly it represents an early and not very successful experiment.

Rhinthon. Chief writer of the *phlyakes* play or hilarotragedy of Greek southern Italy, the type of drama called by the Romans *fabula Rhintonica*. Rhinthon lived in about 300 B.C. Fragments from his works are scanty, but the titles show that they were parodies of tragedies. Some examples are: *Amphitryon, Heracles, Iphigenia at Aulis, Medea,* and *Orestes.*

Rhipa (Gk. **Rhipe**). Town in Achaea.

Rhium (Gk. **Rhion**). Promontory in Achaea.

Rhodope. Mountain range between Macedonia and Thrace.

Rhoeteum (Gk. **Rhoiteion**). Town on the coast of the Troad northwest of Troy.

Root-Cutters, The (Gk. **Rhizotomoi**). Lost play by Sophocles. In fragments from it, Medea gathers roots and calls on Hecate in preparation for magical rites. Presumably the play's subject was the murder of PELIAS.

Rope, The. See RUDENS.

Roscius Gallus, Quintus. Roman actor (1st century B.C.). Roscius appeared in both comedy and tragedy, and in his own lifetime he came to be regarded as a model of what an actor should be. He was very popular, made a large fortune, and was raised to equestrian rank by Sulla. Many Romans of high rank were his friends, especially Cicero, who defended him in a civil suit (68 B.C.) in a still extant speech, *Pro Roscio Comoedo*. Before he died (62 B.C.) Roscius opened an acting school and wrote a book on acting and speaking.

Rudens (Lat. **The Rope** or **The Cable**). Extant comedy by Plautus (date uncertain). *Rudens* was based on a Greek play by Diphilus (perhaps his *Pera*). Translations. Henry T. Riley, 1852; F. A. Wright and H. L. Rogers, 1924; Paul Nixon, 1932; Cleveland Clark, 1942; C. W. Parry, 1954; Frank O. Copley, 1956; Lionel Casson, 1960; Samuel Lieberman, 1964; E. F. Watling, 1964.

S C E N E. The coast of North Africa not far from Cyrene.

S U M M A R Y. The prologue is spoken by the star Arcturus, who explains that Jupiter regularly sends down stars to walk the earth and report human misbehavior. Near the town of Cyrene on the African coast, Arcturus says, lives Daemones, an Athenian who retired from the world in misery after losing both his fortune and his only daughter. The girl, Palaestra, was kidnaped and sold to a Cyrenian pimp, Labrax. Recently the pimp accepted a down-payment for Palaestra from her lover, Plesidippus, also an Athenian, but after being urged by a Sicilian friend to sell all his girls at a higher profit in Sicily, Labrax broke faith and, with his entire household, set sail for Sicily. Before leaving, he falsely promised Plesidippus that he would meet him for breakfast at the shrine of Venus nearby. Arcturus, enraged at the fraud, has caused a storm to wreck Labrax's ship. As the action begins, Palaestra and her friend Ampelisca have managed to reach shore.

Seeking Labrax, Plesidippus goes to the shrine, where he meets Daemones, who lives next door, and his servant. Daemones informs Plesidippus that a ship has been wrecked below, and the young man hurries off. After Daemones and the servant leave, Palaestra appears, soaked, and is soon joined by Ampelisca. The two kneel at the altar and are given refuge by the priestess of the Temple of Venus.

Plesidippus' slave Trachalio, seeking his master, meets Ampelisca, who tells him of the pimp's attempted flight. Palaestra is heartbroken, she says, for she fears the loss of a small chest containing the only tokens of identification by which she could recognize her father. Trachalio goes into the temple to console Palaestra.

Presently Labrax and his Sicilian friend make their way to the temple, learn that the two girls are inside, and go in after them. Meanwhile Daemones, who has reappeared, reveals a dream in which he chained a she-ape that was attacking two swallows. Then Trachalio rushes out of the temple to report that the pimp has removed the girls forcibly from Venus' statue. At once Daemones calls his slaves and enters the temple.

Palaestra and Ampelisca emerge, frightened, followed by Daemones and the slaves, who are dragging Labrax. The pimp protests that the girls are his, and Trachalio accuses him of illegal possession. Finally Trachalio leaves to summon Plesidippus, who soon returns and hales Labrax off to stand trial for defrauding him.

Daemones' slave Gripus appears next, dragging a huge net containing Labrax's trunk, which he pulled out of the sea. Thinking he has found a treasure that will buy his freedom, Gripus happily approaches Daemones' cottage but is stopped by Trachalio, who recognizes the trunk. When Gripus won't give up the trunk, the two slaves appeal to Daemones to arbitrate the dispute. Palaestra is challenged to name the objects found in a small chest inside the trunk in order to prove they are hers. Daemones, hearing their description, realizes that she is his lost daughter.

Daemones is happy to marry Palaestra to Plesidippus, and he consents to intercede for Trachalio in order that the slave may win his freedom and marry Ampelisca. Labrax then returns, having lost his case to Plesidippus but hoping to reclaim Ampelisca. He promises a reward of one talent to Gripus for the return of his trunk but breaks his bargain. Daemones, however, succeeds in getting the money from the pimp, gives one half of it back in payment for Ampelisca's freedom, and keeps the other half in return for Gripus' freedom.

C O M M E N T A R Y. *Rudens,* named for the two slaves' tug-of-war over the recovered trunk, is unusual for its setting, its extended and clever recognition scene, and its combination of romance and farce. Plautus added a little of the flavor of Euripidean melodrama when he made the gods supervise the human action. Although a few commentators have leveled charges of padding and undue length, most put *Rudens* in the front rank of Plautus' plays.

Rufus. Greek scholar of unknown date. Rufus was the author of a *History of Drama* and a *History of Music,* both lost.

S

Saba. Region in southwestern Arabia.

Sabazius (Gk. **Sabazios**). *Myth.* God of orgiastic rites, imported from Asia Minor. Sabazius was said to have been born to Persephone, to whom Zeus made love in the form of a serpent. He was sometimes identified with Dionysus.

Sacas. (Gk. **Sakas**). Persian word for "Scythian," applied to the tragic poet Acestor. The latter was of foreign extraction but had obtained Athenian citizenship by dubious means.

Saians or **Saii** (Gk. **Saioi**). Thracian tribe living on the coast opposite Samothrace.

Salabaccho. Athenian courtesan of Aristophanes' time.

Salaminia. One of the two Athenian state galleys. The *Salaminia* was used to fetch prisoners for trial. When Alcibiades was indicted after leaving on the Sicilian expedition, he was brought back to Athens on this ship.

Salamis (adj. Salaminian). **1.** Island in the Saronic Gulf.

2. City on the east coast of Cyprus.

Salmoneus. *Myth.* Son of Aeolus and father of Tyro. Salmoneus essayed to imitate Zeus's thunderbolts by hurling lighted torches while riding in a metal chariot, with chains dragging, over a bronze road. For his impious behavior he was annihilated by a real thunderbolt. Sophocles' lost satyr play *Salmoneus* was based on this myth.

Salmydessus (Gk. **Salmydessos**). Thracian city on the coast of the Black Sea.

Salus. Roman goddess, a personification of safety, health, and general well-being.

Samia (Gk. **The Girl from Samos** or **The Woman of Samos**). Comedy by Menander in fragmentary condition. Translations: Francis G. Allinson, 1921; L. A. Post, 1929; J. M. Edmonds, 1951; Lionel Casson, 1960.

S C E N E. Athens, before the houses of Demeas and Niceratus.

S U M M A R Y. Although about a third of this play has been recovered (representing two rather lengthy series of scenes from the three middle acts), no entirely satisfactory reconstruction of the story has been achieved. Chrysis, the girl from Samos, has been virtually taken off the streets by Demeas, a middle-aged Athenian, and made his common-law wife; her foreign origin prevents a legal union. Dameas' adopted son, Moschion, is to marry Plangon, the daughter of their neighbor Niceratus.

As the festivities are being prepared, Demeas overhears some servants identify Moschion as the father of a nameless infant whom Chrysis has taken into the house, and shortly afterward he sees her nursing the child. Thinking that Chrysis has seduced his son, Demeas drives her out of the house; she and the child take refuge with Niceratus.

Later Demeas has reason to think the infant a premarital offspring of Moschion and his bride-to-be, but when he tells this to Niceratus, the latter is so angry that he attacks Chrysis and the child, and Demeas has to protect them. In a still later scene Moschion, reflecting on his father's unjustified suspicions, states his determination to go abroad as a soldier. But presumably all ends happily, and perhaps Chrysis is found to be an Athenian after all and is able to marry Demeas properly.

The puzzling thing in the extant portion of *Samia* is the identity of the baby. Some think it is Chrysis' own child by Demeas and that, for some unknown reason, Chrysis is afraid Demeas will not rear it; others think that Chrysis is passing off the child as Moschion's and Plangon's to bring about their marriage. Some say that the child really belongs to the two latter; and others add to this the idea that Chrysis took it because she had just lost a child of her own. There is even a theory that both of the foregoing conjectures are true and that there are actually two babies. The greatest stumbling blocks to solving the mystery seem to be the fact that Chrysis suckles the child and the fact that Moschion is believed by the servants to be the father; moreover, Demeas learns of this belief by accident and not as a result of a deliberate plot. In default of more evidence, the matter had better be given up.

Samos. Island in the southern Aegean Sea just off the coast of Asia Minor. Samos was noted for its cheap pottery.

Samothrace (Gk. **Samothrake**). Island in the northern Aegean Sea. Samothrace was famous for the mysteries of the Cabiri.

Sappho. Poet of Lesbos (fl. c. 600 B.C.). Her legendary love affair with the ferryman Phaon was a source of ridicule in Old and Middle Comedy.

Sardanapalus (Gk. **Sardanapalos**). Assyrian king whose name became a byword for arrogant luxury.

Sardis. Capital of Lydia. Sardis produced a famous alloy of gold and silver, called electrum, and a purple dye.

Sardo. Sardinia.

Sarmatia. Name for a vague region in north central and northeastern Europe which was inhabited by nomadic tribes.

Saronic Gulf or **Saronic Sea.** Gulf east of the Isthmus of Corinth, between Attica and the Peloponnesus.

Sarpedon. *Myth.* Son of Zeus and Europa and king of Lycia. Sarpedon joined the Trojan War as an ally of Troy. He was killed by Patroclus.

Sarsina. Town in northern Umbria.

Saturn. Roman god identified with CRONUS.

satyr play. The fourth play of a tetralogy, following the tragic trilogy. The chief features of the satyr play were as follows: the chorus consisted of satyrs led by Silenus, the plot was comical, and the action was short and simple. The origins of satyr play are inextricably intertwined with those of tragedy. According to tradition, Pratinas of Phleius introduced this type of play into the Athenian festivals. The ancients considered Aeschylus, Achaeus, and Aristias the masters of the satyr play, but the only complete extant specimen is Euripides' *Cyclops*. Considerable portions of Sophocles' *Ichneutae* have been recovered, as well as enough fragments of Aeschylus' *Dictyulci* and *The Isthmiasts* to permit reconstruction.

The choristers, apparently eleven in number with the Silenus leader making twelve, seem to have worn pelts, phalli, satyr masks, and horsetails. (The combined use of horse features and goat features was presumably a later development, but this is much disputed.) The satyr dance was called the *sicinnis;* the setting of the play was woods or wilderness. Plots often dealt with victory over some villain or monster (*Cyclops, Sciron, Syleus*) or with some invention or discovery (*Prometheus the Fire-Kindler, Ichneutae*). The satyrs often seem to have been inserted arbitrarily by the author into the myths on which the plays were based. It was formerly said that the purpose of the satyr play was the provision of comic relief after three tragedies. A more likely purpose, however, was that of providing a connection between the mythical material of the trilogy on the one hand, and the Dionysus cult on the other, thus ending the whole tetralogy in the proper Dionysiac spirit.

satyrs (Gk. **satyroi**). *Myth.* Demons of the woodland. Satyrs originally had horses' tails, legs, and other horselike characteristics. For the confusion of satyrs, Pans, and Sileni, see SILENUS.

Satyrus (Gk. **Satyros**). Scholar (probably 3rd century B.C.). Portions of Satyrus' life of Euripides, which was part of a *Lives of the Poets* in dialogue form, were discovered on papyrus in 1911.

scaena ductilis (Lat.). Movable flat or screen with scenery painted on it, equivalent to the modern backdrop.

scaenae frons (Lat.). The facade of the skene, rising at the rear of the logeion, facing the audience. The *scaenae frons* constituted a permanent scenic backdrop. Those that have been preserved, or that can be reconstructed, represent a building of one to three storeys having entrance doors, elaborate columns, and statuary.

scaena vertilis or **scaena versilis** (Lat.). Latin equivalent of PERIAKTOS.

Scamander (Gk. **Skamandros**). Small stream near Troy.

Scarphe (Gk. **Skarphe**). Town in Locris near the Maliac Gulf.

Scaurus, Mamercus Aemilius. Roman writer of tragedies (1st century A.D.). A member of a distinguished family, Scaurus became *consul suffectus* (substitute consul) in A.D. 21. Suspected of criticizing the emperor Tiberius with his tragedy *Atreus*, he was accused of practicing magic and of committing adultery with Livilla, a princess of the imperial family, and so was driven to suicide in A.D. 34.

scenery. Ancient authorities credit Aeschylus with being the first to make use of *skenographia*, scene-painting, but all evidence indicates that painted flats or backdrops were never of much importance in the Greek and Roman theater. For items connected with scenery in the modern sense, or with scenic effects in the widest sense, see ALTARS; ANAPIESMA; ANGIPORTUM; CHARONIAN STEPS; CURTAIN; ECCYCLEMA; KATABLEMATA; KERAUNOSKOPEION; MECHANE; PERIAKTOI; PROSCENIUM; SCAENA DUCTILIS; SCAENAE FRONS; THYROMATA.

Scione (Gk. **Skione**). City on the peninsula of Pallene.

Scira or **Scirophoria** (Gk. **Skira** or **Skirophoria**). Athenian festival held in summer in honor of Athena. The chief feature of the Scira was a processional in which the priest of Erechtheus, carrying the sacred parasol, descended from the Acropolis.

Sciron (Gk. **Skiron** or **Skeiron**). *Myth.* Robber chief of the Isthmus of Corinth. Sciron forced passers-by to wash his feet, after which he kicked them down a cliff onto the Scironian Rocks, where a giant tortoise mangled their bodies. Young Theseus, on his way from Troezen to Athens, disposed of Sciron in the same way. This story was the subject of a lost satyr play, *Sciron,* by Euripides.

Scylla (Gk. **Skylla**). *Myth.* Daughter of Nisus of Megara. Scylla fell in love with the invading King Minos and betrayed her father and city (see NISUS). After Scylla was bound to Minos' ship in punishment for her crime, the gods transformed her, either into a bird, or into a monster having the face and torso of a woman but the lower parts consisting of dog-headed snakes. Stationed on a rock in the Strait of Messina, Scylla fed on mariners passing through. On an opposite rock was Charybdis. The existence of a lost play by Euripides called *Scylla* is doubtful.

Scyrians, The (Gk. **Skyrioi**). Lost play by Euripides (probably an early work). A handful of fragments and a summary on a papyrus sheet published in 1933 show that *The Scyrians* dealt with the concealment of Achilles in woman's clothing at the court of King Lycomedes of Scyrus in accordance with a plot of his mother, Thetis, to prevent his going to the Trojan War. Deidamia, the king's daughter, tried to mask her pregnancy under pretense of illness, but in the course of the play she bore Achilles' son. Odysseus and Diomedes, sent to fetch Achilles, succeeded in uncovering his identity by enticing him to try out some weapons. Doubtless much was made of the hero's conflict between love and desire for glory.

Scyrians, The (Gk. **Skyrioi**). Lost play by Sophocles (conjecturally dated before 450 B.C.). Its subject was the fetching of Neoptolemus, Achilles' son, by Odysseus and Phoenix, to fight at Troy. In one nine-line papyrus fragment, Odysseus seems to be trying to palm himself off as a merchant; in another, Deidamia, the boy's mother, seems to be plotting to spirit him away to Euboea to prevent him from suffering his father's fate.

Scyrus (Gk. **Skyros**). Island in the central Aegean.

Scythia (Gk. **Skythia**). Vaguely defined region extending from the northern extremity of Thrace along the north shore of the Black Sea. The region was inhabited by nomadic tribes. Scythians were used as a police force in Athens.

Scythian Women, The (Gk. **Skythai**). Lost tragedy by Sophocles. Scholars agree that the play must have portrayed Medea's murder of Absyrtus in a Scythian setting during the flight of the *Argo* to Greece. Accius' *Medea or The Argonauts* may have been modeled on this play.

Searching Satyrs, The. See ICHNEUTAE.

Seasons, The (Gk. **Horai**). Lost comedy by Aristophanes (variously dated from 421 to 407 B.C., the former date being most probable). *The Seasons* seems to have protested the introduction of foreign cults and to have represented native deities, the Horai and others, repelling an invasion of gods from such places as Thrace and Egypt. The play may also have parodied Euripides' *Erechtheus,* which told of a foreign invasion.

Seat-Grabbers, The (Gk. **Hai Skenas Katalambanousai**). Lost comedy by Aristophanes (date uncertain). Little can be interpreted from the fragments of this play. It is, however, clear that the chorus consisted of women who had secured the best places to watch a festival and that Aristophanes admitted to being influenced by Euripides in his style.

Secundus, Pomponius. See POMPONIUS SECUNDUS.

Selene. *Myth.* Greek deity, a personification of the moon.

Seleucus (Gk. **Seleukos**). Any of several kings of the Greco-Syrian empire during the third and second centuries B.C.

Self-tormentor, The (Lat. **Heautontimorumenos,** Latinized form of Gk. **Heautontimoroumenos**). Extant comedy by Terence. *The Self-tormentor* was produced in April 163 B.C. by Ambivius Turpio, with music by Flaccus. It was based on the Greek play of the same name by Menander. Translations: John Sargeaunt, 1912; W. Ritchie, 1927; F. Perry, 1929; Frank O. Copley, 1963.

S C E N E. A country road in Attica.

S U M M A R Y. Terence, as is his custom, uses the prologue to defend his practice of *contaminatio* (see CONTAMINATION) and to repudiate the charge that he passes off others' work as his own. He claims to avoid both unnatural and trite characterization.

As the play opens, Chremes, an old gentleman of Attica, reproves his neighbor Menedemus for working so hard on his land. When Menedemus tells him to mind his own business, Chremes remonstrates: "I am a man; I consider nothing human alien to me." Menedemus then explains that he is doing penance for his harshness toward his only son, Clinia: when the youth had fallen in love with a poor Corinthian girl, Menedemus had been so outraged and had spoken at such length about his own early hardships as a soldier that Clinia had gone off to join the Persian army.

Chremes soon learns from his son, Clitipho, that Clinia has returned from the wars but, unsure of his reception by father or sweetheart, has taken refuge at Chremes' house. Syrus, a slave in Chremes' household, fetches Clinia's sweetheart, Antiphila, who has preserved both her virtue and her love for him; he discloses that the old woman, now dead, with whom Antiphila had been living was not really her mother. Besides Antiphila, the wily slave has brought to the house Bacchis, a grasping courtesan with whom Clitipho is infatuated. Clitipho is fearful of his father's reaction should he learn of the affair, but

Syrus proposes that Bacchis pretend to be Clinia's mistress. She demands ten minae to act the part. Antiphila is to be passed off as a servant for Sostrata, Chremes' wife. Syrus then tells Clitipho that he has a plan that will enable him to enjoy Bacchis' favors and to obtain the money he has promised her.

Menedemus is overjoyed at the news of his son's return and wants to give Clinia his entire fortune at once, but Chremes warns that this will only spoil him; instead, Menedemus should dole out money through a third person, even allowing himself to be "cheated." Syrus later informs Chremes that Bacchis lent 1,000 drachmas to Antiphila's mother, taking the girl as security. Now that the mother is dead, Bacchis wants Clinia to pay her and take the girl. When Chremes declares that Menedemus will not give him the money, Syrus expresses satisfaction, leaving Chremes thoroughly bewildered.

By a ring Antiphila is wearing, she is recognized as the daughter of Chremes and his wife, Sostrata, who had disobeyed her husband's edict that their baby girl be exposed. Chremes is now happy to have a daughter, but Syrus thinks his scheme has been ruined, for Clinia, free to marry Antiphila, will no longer be willing to pretend to love Bacchis. Nevertheless, the slave is able to persuade Clinia to take part in the deception a little longer. Clinia is now to tell his father the truth—that he wants to marry Antiphila and that Bacchis is Clitipho's mistress. When Chremes hears this news from Menedemus, Syrus is certain, he will not believe it.

As Syrus has foreseen, Chremes refuses to believe the truth and contends that the story of Bacchis being the mistress of Clitipho is merely part of the plot to swindle Menedemus. He himself pays to Syrus the money which Antiphila allegedly owes to Bacchis, and the slave immediately turns it over to Clitipho. Chremes finally realizes that it is he, not Menedemus, who has been duped when he learns that Clinia wants to marry Antiphila immediately and that he has expressed no interest in his father's money. Angry and hurt by Clitipho's deception, Chremes decides to cure his son of his debauchery by pretending to make over his entire estate to Antiphila as her dowry.

Clitipho is crushed by his supposed disinheritance and for a while doubts that he is the real son of Chremes and Sostrata. When Chremes points out that what Clitipho lacks is not parents but the disposition to obey them, the youth becomes thoroughly ashamed of himself. At the close of the play, Chremes is persuaded to pardon his son on condition that he look for a respectable wife.

C O M M E N T A R Y. *The Self-tormentor* is usually considered a less successful *Adelphoe:* its theme is similar and its characterization is almost as good. But Terence is thought to have started weaving more threads than he could effectively manage; some of the strands are left unwoven, and the general pattern, even when completed, is hard to follow. Connoisseurs of plot point out a unique feature: in this play the recognition scene adds to the complication rather than to the denouement.

Selli (Gk. Selloi). Priests of the shrine of Dodona. The Selli slept on the ground.

Sellios or **Sillios**. Greek scholar (1st century A.D.). Sellios composed a *Summary of Menander's Plays*, a few fragments of which have been recovered.

Semele. *Myth*. Daughter of Cadmus and Harmonia and mother, by Zeus, of Dionysus. While Semele was pregnant, the jealous Hera visited her in disguise and incited the girl to beg her lover Zeus to appear to her in his full divine glory. Zeus, having promised to do anything that Semele wished, reluctantly complied with her request, whereupon she was consumed by lightning. The unborn child was, however, rescued (see DIONYSUS). When Dionysus became a god, he descended to the underworld and raised his mother to heaven— a myth partly parodied in Aristophanes' *Frogs*. In Euripides' *Bacchae* Semele's tomb, still smoking, is represented onstage.

Some sixty extremely fragmentary lines from papyri have been identified as belonging to Aeschylus' lost tragedy *Semele*. In it Hera seems to have appeared disguised as a mendicant priestess of the river nymphs of Inachus in Argos. The rest of the play must have shown Semele's self-induced destruction. The play had an alternate title, *The Water Carriers*, an indication that the chorus may have consisted of maidservants bringing water for the ritual purification of Semele after the birth of Dionysus.

Semnai. *Myth*. The "august, awesome ones," a euphemistic name for the ERINYES.

Seneca, Lucius Annaeus. The only writer of Latin tragedies whose works are extant (c. 4 B.C.–A.D. 65). (The anonymous *Octavia* is still ascribed by some scholars to him.)

L I F E. Seneca is one of the few writers whose political careers were as eminent as their literary careers. He is also one of the few playwrights whose dramatic production formed only a minor part of their literary production. Seneca's family was of Spanish origin. His father was a rhetorician whose phenomenal memory was responsible for the many excerpts from famous speakers included in his (the father's) extant *Controversiae* and *Suasoriae;* his nephew was Lucan, author of the extant epic *The Civil War*.

Born in Cordova, Seneca was reared and educated at Rome, suffering through a sickly childhood and youth. At some point he began a lifelong adherence to Stoic philosophy. Legal practice led to a quaestorship, but on the accession of Claudius in A.D. 43, Seneca was banished to Corsica on a trumped-up charge of adultery with a princess of the imperial house. The banishment was brought about through the enmity of Messalina, Claudius' wife. Eight years later, after Messalina's fall and Agrippina's succession as empress, Seneca was recalled and made tutor to the latter's son Nero. The first years of Nero's reign were considered a new Golden Age, for which Seneca was traditionally given much of the credit. After Nero murdered Agrippina, he bade Seneca write a speech, addressed to the Senate, defending his act. Seneca not long afterward retired to his estates. In A.D. 65, Nero, using as an excuse the conspiracy of Piso, sent him the usual imperial notice that his presence on earth was no longer required. Seneca committed suicide with true

Stoic fortitude, dictating his sensations as the blood drained from his wrists.

W O R K S. Most of Seneca's works are philosophical prose: dialogues, letters, treatises, and scientific discussions. The extant corpus bulks larger than that of any other classical Roman writer except Cicero. When and for what purpose the tragedies were written is unknown. The controversy over whether they were intended to be acted is long-lived and rather bootless. Some think the plays were written for the stage, some for declamation; some think they belonged to the old tradition of illustrating philosophical tenets by closet dramas. There are nine tragedies (see under individual entries): *Agamemnon*, *Hercules Furens*, *Hercules on Oeta*, *Medea*, *Oedipus*, *Phaedra*, *The Phoenician Women*, *Thyestes*, and *The Trojan Women*.

C R I T I C I S M. Seneca's repute as a playwright has fluctuated wildly. In ancient times his plays were virtually ignored; only the quotation of a line of *Medea* by a contemporary, Quintilian, saved him from being a hypothetical ghost, Seneca the Dramatist. In the Renaissance and the seventeenth century Seneca became the very model of a tragedian, having as great and deep an influence as any playwright who ever lived. When the Romantics reacted against Latin culture in favor of philhellenism, Seneca was toppled from his pedestal. His rhetoric and sensationalism were execrated, and his unoriginality was thought to be proved by close comparisons with his supposed Greek models.

Recently a readjustment has taken place. Good studies have been made of the plays as illustrations of Stoicism. There is an increasing willingness to judge the tragedies in themselves: tiresome at times, often overstrained, but at their best displaying a verbal brilliance and theatrical power not easily equaled.

senex (Lat.). The old man, a stock character in New Comedy. This character was often *senex iratus*, the bad-tempered old man.

Sepias. Promontory at the southeastern tip of Magnesia.

Septentriones. Latin name for the constellation of the Big Dipper.

Serians (Gk. **Seres**). People supposedly located in India from whom silk was imported; hence possibly the Chinese.

Seriphos. Small island in the southwestern Aegean Sea whose insignificance was proverbial.

servus (Lat.). The slave, a stock character in New Comedy who usually took the form of *servus dolosus*, the tricky slave.

Sestos. City on the north shore of the Hellespont opposite Abydos.

Seven against Thebes. *Myth.* Seven Greek chieftains, one of whom was Polyneices. The latter, with the aid of his father-in-law, Adrastus, led the Seven to battle in order to gain his rightful place on the throne of Thebes. The other six were Tydeus, Capaneus, Amphiaraus, Hippomedon, Eteoclus, and Parthenopaeus. (See individual names, especially Polyneices.)

For Aeschylus' tragedy called *The Seven Against Thebes*, see THEBAN TETRALOGY.

Shearing of Glycera, The. See PERIKEIROMENE.

Shepherds, The (Gk. **Poimenes**). Lost play by Sophocles. Numerous fragments from *The Shepherds* indicate that the chorus consisted of Phrygian shepherds and that the action concerned the Greek landing at Troy. There is mention of Protesilaus and Cygnus, but no reconstruction has been agreed upon.

She Who Was Shorn. See PERIKEIROMENE.

ship-wagon (Lat. **carrus navalis**). Wagon in the form of a ship connected principally with processionals in the cult of Dionysus. Its symbolism has never been satisfactorily explained. The attempt to identify ship-wagons with the carts allegedly used for dramatic performances by Thespis has not found much favor.

Sibyl (Gk. **Sibylle**). *Myth.* Any of several prophetesses connected with several places in the Greco-Roman world, for example, the Troad, Lydia, and Cumae. The Sibyls had superhuman powers and lived for centuries.

Sibyrtius (Gk. **Sibyrtios**). An athletic trainer. In *The Acharnians* (line 118) Aristophanes sarcastically called Sibyrtius the father of the weakling Cleisthenes.

Sicilian expedition. Athenian invasion of Sicily, 415–413 B.C., during the Peloponnesian War. The invaders suffered a disastrous defeat.

sicinnis (Gk. **sikinnis**). Dance imported from Phrygia connected with the cult of Dionysus-Sabazius (see SABAZIUS). The *sicinnis* was the characteristic dance of the satyr play.

Sicyon (Gk. **Sikyon**). City-state west of Corinth.

Sidon. City in Phoenicia noted, among other things, for the manufacture of a delicate kind of cloth. Sidon was the original home of Cadmus, the founder of Thebes; hence "Sidonian" sometimes meant "Theban."

Sigeum or **Sigeium** (Gk. **Sigeion**). Town and promontory at the northwestern corner of the Troad.

Silanus, Lucius Junius. Roman nobleman betrothed to Octavia. Silanus was put to death so that Nero could marry her.

Sileniae (Gk. **Sileniai**). Rocky coastal section of Salamis.

Silenus, pl. **Sileni** (Gk. **Seilenos,** pl. **Seilenoi**). *Myth.* In preclassical times, the Sileni were horse demons of the woodlands, especially in Ionian parts of Greece; they were not necessarily connected with Dionysus. The Sileni came to be confused with the satyrs, who originally were similar horse demons in the Peloponnesus. In the classical period, Silenus was often regarded as one person, the leader of the satyrs and the foster father of Dionysus. He was represented as an aged, fat, snub-nosed, big-bellied drunkard riding on a donkey—more or less as he appears in Euripides' *Cyclops.* Later, both Sileni and satyrs were confused with the Pans, who were goat demons. (See PAN.)

Silvanus. Roman god of forests.

Simois (Gk. **Simoeis**). River near Troy.

Simonides. Lyric poet from Ceos (c. 556–468 B.C.). Noted for his *partheneia* (songs for girls' chorus) and dithyrambs, Simonides also acquired the reputation of being the first poet to write for money.

Sinis. *Myth.* Giant brigand, son of Poseidon. The Isthmus of Corinth was Sinis' habitat. There he tied each passer-by to two pine trees that he bent down to the earth; when he let the trees spring up, his victim was split in two. Theseus, on his way from Troezen to Athens, did the same for Sinis.

Sinon. *Myth.* The Greek who persuaded the Trojans to pull the wooden horse into their city. Allowing himself to be captured, Sinon told the Trojans that he had escaped being sacrificed by the Greeks. He claimed that the horse was an expiatory offering to ensure the Greeks a safe voyage home. During the following night, after the horse had been hauled into the city, Sinon let the Greek chieftains out of their hiding place inside it.

Sinon was a lost play by Sophocles; plays by Naevius and Livius Andronicus, both titled *The Trojan Horse,* may have been modeled on it.

Sinope. Greek colony on the southern shore of the Black Sea.

siparium. A kind of stage curtain. (See CURTAINS.)

Sipylus (Gk. **Sipylos**). Mountain in Asia Minor. The weeping Niobe was said to have been transported to Mt. Sipylus and transformed into a stone. It was there, also, that her father Tantalus hid Zeus's golden dog.

Sirens (Gk. **Seirenes**). *Myth.* Bird-women of the sea whose enticing song lured sailors to shipwreck on the rocks of their island.

Sisyphus (Gk. **Sisyphos**). *Myth.* Son of Aeolus and founder of Corinth. According to one myth, Sispyhus seduced Anticleia on the night before her wedding and so was the real father of Odysseus. Later, Sisyphus revealed to Asopus that it was Zeus who had carried off his (Asopus') daughter Aegina. In punishment Zeus sent Death to him, but Sisyphus surprised Death and chained him up. When Zeus noticed that no one was dying, he loosed Death again, whereupon Sisyphus died. But just before dying, he had told his wife to leave his body unburied. When Sisyphus arrived below, he complained to Hades about his wife's outrageous neglect and was allowed to return to life to punish her. Thus he lived to a ripe old age. After his final descent to the underworld, Sisyphus was forced eternally to push a stone up a hill; as he neared the top, the stone always slipped out of his grasp and rolled to the bottom.

Only two words survive of Sophocles' lost satyr play *Sisyphus.* The existence of a satyr play of this name by Euripides is doubtful; there may have been confusion with one of the same name by Critias.

Sisyphus the Runaway (Gk. **Sisyphos Drapetes**). Lost play by Aeschylus. It probably told how Sisyphus outwitted Death. This play was perhaps identical with *Sisyphus the Stone-Pusher.*

Sisyphus the Stone-Pusher (Gk. **Sisyphos Petrokylistes**). Lost play by Aeschylus, probably a satyr play. Nothing is known of it.

Sitalces (Gk. **Sitalkes**). Thracian king who allied himself with Athens at the beginning of the Peloponnesian War.

skene (Gk. "tent" or "booth"; Lat. **scaena** or **scena**). In origin presumably the hut or booth behind the orchestra used for the actors' exits, entrances, and costume changes. By the fifth century B.C. the skene had already developed into a full stage building having logeion (stage proper), *scaenae frons* (rear facade), and paraskenia (side structures). The stone skene probably did not appear until the following century. Elaboration of the building continued throughout the classical period.

skenotheke (Gk.). Small side building or room of the skene used for storage and dressing.

Skiapodes (Gk. "shadow-feet"). Imaginary Libyan tribe. The Skiapodes were web-footed and one-legged or three-legged; they used their gigantic feet as umbrellas. Aristophanes refers to them in *The Birds* (line 1553).

Skitaloi (Gk.). *Myth.* Spirits of shamelessness and deceit.

Smintheus. Epithet of Apollo as mouse god.

soccus. The slipper worn in Roman comedy, the "sock."

Socrates (Gk. **Sokrates**). Athenian philosopher (c. 470–399 B.C.). Socrates was a leading character and the chief target of satire in Aristophanes' *Clouds*.

Sol. Roman deity, a personification of the sun.

Soli (Gk. **Soloi**). City on the northern coast of Cyprus.

Solon. Celebrated Athenian lawmaker (c. 640–c. 560 B.C.). Even in ancient times Solon's name was virtually synonymous with the word "legislator."

somation (Gk. "little body"). Padded bodice or jerkin worn for grotesque effect in Old and Middle Comedy.

Somnus. Roman deity, the personification of sleep. In *Hercules Furens* (line 1066) Seneca calls Somnus the "winged offspring of Astraea."

Sophia. Greek personification of wisdom.

Sophocles (Gk. **Sophokles**). 1. The second of the three great Athenian writers of tragedy (born 500–494 B.C.; died 406–405 B.C.).

L I F E. Sophocles came of a well-to-do family; his father Sophillus was probably the owner of a prosperous manufacturing establishment. He himself was handsome, athletic, witty, and popular. Sophocles' musical and poetical talents were apparent early. His first play, *Triptolemus,* was staged in about 468 B.C. and won first prize in the dramatic contest. He was said to have won first or second prizes twenty-four times, on two of these occasions defeating Euripides' *Alcestis* and *Medea.* In his early plays he took the leading role but retired from acting because of a weak voice. Sophocles' chief contributions to the development of dramatic technique were the introduction of the third actor (see ACTORS AND ACTING), the increase of the tragic chorus from twelve to fifteen members, and the first use of scene painting.

By his first wife, Nicostrata, he had two sons: Iophon, also a tragedian, and Sophocles. His second wife, Theoris, bore him a third son, Ariston. Because of the success of *Antigone* in the late 440's B.C., Sophocles was elected strategos. He was the friend or acquaintance of Aeschylus, Euripides, Herodotus, Pericles, Ion of Chios, and Socrates. After the death of Euripides, he and his chorus appeared in mourning at the official preliminary rehearsal for dramas in 406 B.C.

Sophocles was known for his personal charm and for his piety. He was one of those responsible for introducing the cult of Asclepius to Athens and after his death was honored in a hero cult of his own. The only episode that marred his singular good fortune was the one in which, it was said, his sons sued to have him declared *non compos mentis* in his old age; the suit was dismissed when the old man read his just-completed *Oedipus at Colonus* to the court. It is, however, doubtful that this story is true.

EXTANT PLAYS (see under individual entries). The following seven are extant and complete: *Ajax, Antigone, Electra, Oedipus at Colonus, Oedipus the King, Philoctetes,* and *Trachiniae.* A large portion of *Ichneutae,* a satyr play, has been recovered on papyri. The production dates of only three of the foregoing plays are known with any certainty: *Antigone,* 442 or 441 B.C.; *Philoctetes,* 409; and *Oedipus at Colonus,* in 401 (posthumous).

LOST PLAYS (see under individual entries). In ancient times 130 titles were said to have been the titles of plays by Sophocles. A few of them are thought by scholars to be spurious, and some are doubtless alternate titles of the same play. In addition to the eight named above, they are: *The Achaeans' Banquet, Achilles' Lovers, Acrisius, Admetus, Aegeus, Aegisthus, Ajax of Locris, Alcmeon, Aleadae, Aletes, Alexander, Amphiaraus, Amphitryon, Amycus, Andromache, Andromeda, Antenoridae, The Assembly of the Achaeans, Athamas* (two versions), *Atreus, The Camicans, The Captive Women, Cedalion, Cerberus, Chryses, Clytemnestra, The Colchian Women, Creusa, Daedalus, Danaë, Dionysiskos, Dolopes, Epigoni, Erigone, Eriphyle, Eris, The Ethiopians, Eumelus, Euripylus, Euryalus, Eurysaces, Helen Claimed, Helen Seized, Helen's Marriage, Heracles, Heracles at Taenarum, Herakleiskos, Hermione, Hippodamia, Hipponous, Hybris, Iambe, The Iberians, The Image-Bearers, Inachus, Iobates, Iocles, Ion, Iphigenia, Ixion, The Judgment, The Laconian Women, Laocoön, The Larissaeans, The Lemnian Women* (two versions), *Meleager, Memnon, Minos, Momus, The Muses, The Mysians, Nauplius the Fire-Kindler, Nauplius' Voyage, Nausicaa, Niobe, Odysseus Akanthoplex, Odysseus' Madness, Oeneus, Oenomaus, Palamedes, Pandora, Peleus, Pelias, The Phaeacians, Phaedra, Philoctetes at Troy, Phineus* (two versions), *Phoenix, Phrixus, The Phrygians, The Phthian Women, Polyidus, Polyxena, Priam, Procris, The Root-Cutters, Salmoneus, The Scyrians, The Scythian Women, The Shepherds, Sinon, Sisyphus, Tantalus, Tereus, Teucer, Thamyras, Theseus, Thyestes* (three versions), *Triptolemus, Troilus, The Tympanists, Tyndareus, Tyro* (two versions), and *The Water Carriers.*

CRITICISM. From the days of Aristophanes and Aristotle, Sophocles' literary reputation has been unassailable. If his works were little read or produced in Roman, medieval, and Renaissance times, later attention made up for this neglect. Some of the German philhellenists tried to make the playwright into a classical marble statue, and some British critics, into a pietistic Victorian. These views are, however, easily corrected by a glance at the violence and horror in his plays. Recent studies have concentrated on the imagery, the multiple ironies, and the tragic vision of Sophocles' plays. His uncompromisingly tragic world view still seems surprising in a man whose outward circumstances were so sunny. Some modern attempts to show that this pessimism was assumed for effect, or that it revealed a basic skepticism about religion, have not been very successful.

2. Grandson of the above. Sophocles produced his grandfather's *Oedipus at Colonus* in 401 B.C. He was himself a prolific and popular tragedian.

Sophron. Chief writer of Syracusan mime (later 5th century B.C.). Although his works are lost, Sophron seems to have been influenced by Epicharmus and to have influenced Theocritus in turn. Sophron was much admired by the philosopher Plato and was the subject of a work by Apollodorus. His works were read in schools in the Roman empire, and they remained popular throughout ancient times. Sophron's mimes were divided into "Men's" and "Women's." Some of the "Women's Mimes" were *The Women Who Claim to Call Up the Goddess, The Women at the Isthmian Games, The Stepmother;* some of the "Men's" were *The Messenger, The Tuna Fishers, Fisherman versus Peasant.*

Soter (Gk. "savior" or "preserver"). Epithet of Zeus and, in the feminine form Soteira, of Tyche and Persephone.

Spartoi (Gk. "sown"). *Myth.* The warriors who grew out of the earth when Cadmus sowed the dragon's teeth.

Spercheius or **Sperchius** (Gk. **Spercheios**). River flowing eastward through southern Thessaly into the Maliac Gulf.

Spes. Roman deity, the personification of hope.

Sphettus (Gk. **Sphettos**). Attic deme.

Sphinx. *Myth.* Monster, part woman, part lion. The Sphinx sat on a rock beside the highway west of Thebes and put her riddle to every passer-by: What goes on three legs at morning, two legs at noon, and three legs at evening? She killed all who could not solve the riddle. When Oedipus gave the correct answer, "Man," the Sphinx plunged into a chasm to her death. For Aeschylus' lost play called *The Sphinx*, see THEBAN TETRALOGY.

sphragis. See EPIRRHEMATIC AGON.

Spintharus (Gk. **Spintharos**). Minor writer of tragedies (late 5th century B.C.). Of his works only the titles *The Pyre of Heracles* and *Semele Struck by Lightning* are preserved.

stage. See LOGEION; RAISED STAGE; SKENE.

Stamnios (Gk. "of the wine jar"). Name that Dionysus invents for his supposed father in Aristophanes' *Frogs* (line 22).

stasimon, pl. **stasima** (Gk. "standing still"). In tragedy, the choric ode or odes, particularly the central odes as distinguished from the parodos and exodos. Like all choric odes, the stasimon was made up of pairs of stanzas, usually elaborate, consisting of a "turn" (strophe), followed by its exact metrical equivalent, the "counterturn" (antistrophe). Each pair might or might not be followed by a metrically different "epode."

Statius, Caecilius. See CAECILIUS STATIUS.

Stenia. Athenian festival, celebrated by women at night, on either the first or second day of the Thesmophoria. The Stenia was an occasion of rejoicing over the return of Demeter. Its rites included much abusive and obscene language.

Stheneboea (Gk. **Stheneboia**). *Myth.* Wife of King Proetus of Tiryns. The plot of Euripides' lost *Stheneboea* (produced before 422 B.C.) dealt with Bellerophon's revenge on the queen. (See BELLEROPHON.)

Sthenelus (Gk. **Sthenelos**). 1. *Myth.* Son of Capaneus. Sthenelus was a warrior at Troy.

2. *Myth.* Son of Perseus and father of Eurystheus.

3. Tragic poet and actor of Aristophanes' time. Sthenelus was reduced by poverty to selling his wardrobe. In his *Poetics* (chapter 22), Aristotle cites Sthenelus' poetry as an example of low style.

stichomythy (Gk. **stichomythia**). In dramatic dialogue, an interchange in which each actor spoke only one line at a time. Stichomythy was a striking formal feature of Greek tragedy.

Stichus. Extant comedy by Plautus (produced 200 B.C.). *Stichus* was based on Menander's *Adelphoi*. (The latter play was not the same as the play adapted by Terence for his *Adelphoe*.)

The title role was taken by the actor Pellio. Translations: Henry T. Riley, 1852; Paul Nixon, 1938; John R. Workman, 1942.

S C E N E. Athens.

S U M M A R Y. Panegyris and her sister are being pressed into remarriage by their father, Antipho, their husbands having been away for three years on a trading venture. But the girls choose to remain faithful to their husbands. When the two voyagers return laden with wealth, there follow scenes of farce and merrymaking: A parasite tries unsuccessfully to get a dinner from each of the new arrivals; Antipho tries to wheedle a slave girl from the cargo; and Stichus, the returning slave, celebrates a tipsy feast with his girl friend and his rival.

C R I T I C I S M. *Stichus* seemingly starts out to be a comedy, but all traces of plot promptly disappear. Critics have puzzled over the reason for this, but perhaps there is none. If this play were classified as a mime, it could be enjoyed well enough.

Stilbides. Soothsayer in Aristophanes' Athens. Stilbides was taken by Nicias on the Sicilian expedition.

Storks, The (Gk. **Pelargoi**). Lost comedy by Aristophanes (presumably written in the 390's B.C.). The few surviving fragments are unilluminating, but it can be seen that the playwright made some use of the bit of folklore that storks show filial affection by carrying their aged parents around on their wings.

strategoi. Ten Athenian officials elected every year to serve as military and naval commanders and to supervise military affairs.

Stratonicus (Gk. **Stratonikos**). Famous harpist (4th century B.C.). Stratonicus traveled widely over the Greek world. He was noted for his wit.

Strattis. Writer of Old Comedy (active c. 410–c. 375 B.C.). Of Strattis' works about eighty fragments and seventeen titles remain. He was apparently fond of parodying the tragedians: his *Medea, The Phoenician Women,* and *Chrysippus* parodied those plays by Euripides (and perhaps his *Lemnomeda* burlesqued Euripides' *Hypsipyle* and *Andromeda*); his *Troilus* and *Philoctetes* parodied Sophocles' plays. Strattis' *Callippides* ridiculed the famous actor, and his *Cinesias*, the famous dithyrambic poet. In *Atalanta* was satirized the love of the orator Isocrates for a courtesan.

Strophaios (Gk. "twister" or "turner" or "pertaining to hinges"). Epithet applied to Hermes, both because of his trickiness and because his image commonly stood by the door.

strophe. See STASIMON.

Strophius (Gk. **Strophios**). *Myth.* King in Phocis and father of Pylades. Strophius brought up Orestes, who was his nephew. At the end of Seneca's *Agamemnon* Strophius, appearing in Argos after an Olympic victory, accepts the infant Orestes from Electra and bears him off to safety. In Euripides' *Orestes* he is said to have banished Pylades for assisting in the murder of Clytemnestra.

Strymon 1. River in eastern Macedonia.

2. *Myth.* God of this river, the father of Rhesus.

Stupidus (Lat.). Stock character in mime whose name is self-explanatory. Stupidus was often represented as a baldhead and a cuckold.

Stymphalus (Gk. **Stymphalos**). Mountain and lake in northeastern Arcadia. Stymphalus was the home of the iron-winged, man-eating birds overcome by Heracles.

Styx (adj. Stygian). *Myth.* Boundary river of the underworld. The gods swore their oaths in the name of the Styx. Its waters conferred invulnerability.

Suebi or **Suevi.** Tribe of central Germany.

Sulpicius Apollinaris. Roman poet and scholar (2nd century A.D.). The verse summaries affixed to Terence's plays are the work of Sulpicius.

Summanus. *Myth.* Roman god of nocturnal lightning. Summanus was an aspect of Jupiter.

Sunium (Gk. **Sounion**). Cape at the southeastern tip of Attica.

Suppliants, The. Extant play by Aeschylus. (See DANAÏD TETRALOGY.)

Suppliants, The (Gk. **Hiketides**). Extant tragedy by Euripides (variously dated from 423 to 416 B.C., but usually c. 421 B.C.). Translations: Edward P. Coleridge, 1891; Arthur S. Way, 1912; Frank Jones, 1958.

S C E N E. Eleusis, the Temple of Demeter and Persephone.

S U M M A R Y. As an aftermath of the war of the Seven against Thebes, the victorious Thebans have denied burial to their enemies, and the mothers of the seven dead chieftains have come to Attica to beg for King Theseus' intervention. Adrastus, leader of the defeated armies, is with the group before the temple, as well as Theseus' mother, Aethra, who has been urged to intercede with the king.

When Theseus appears, Adrastus presents their suit and, in response to Theseus' questioning, relates the background of the war. He led the seven armies against Thebes, he says, in order to help his son-in-law, Polyneices, recover his lawful inheritance. Polyneices had voluntarily left Thebes following the curse put on him and his brother Eteocles by their father, Oedipus. Eteocles had then robbed Polyneices of his turn as king. Coming to Argos, Polyneices was received by Adrastus as his son-in-law, in obedience to the oracle's decree that Adrastus wed his daughters to "a lion and a boar" (the other daughter married Tydeus). Adrastus concedes that he flouted the wishes of heaven when he went into battle despite bad omens.

At first Theseus is averse to promising his help. He says that men cannot flout the will of the gods. But when his mother joins her pleas to those of the aged suppliants, reminding her son that burial is the right of all citizens of Hellas, Theseus reconsiders. First, he says, he must present the case to the Athenian Assembly.

After a Choral ode, Theseus returns to dispatch a Herald to demand the bodies of the slain from Thebes. Simultaneously a Theban Herald arrives to demand that Theseus expel Adrastus or face war with King Creon. Theseus defies this Herald and champions Athenian democracy and the right of burial. Warning that Theseus will be defeated, the Herald withdraws, after which Theseus leaves to gather his army.

The Chorus chant of the battle, and then a Messenger appears and describes Theseus' victory. The corpses of the dead heroes are brought back and suitably praised and mourned, while Adrastus laments their misfortune and his own rashness. In response to Theseus' query, he describes the seven fallen chieftains. Two funeral pyres are then kindled, one for the body of Capaneus, the chieftain struck by Zeus's lightning, the other for the rest of the dead. As the Chorus sing the lament, Capaneus' wife, Evadne, appears on a rock above her husband's pyre, chanting that she will join him. Though her aged father, Iphis, attempts to deter her, she throws herself into the flames.

A procession of children carrying the ashes of their dead fathers enter, and they and the Chorus alternate in an extended dirge, which reaches a climax with the epiphany of Athena. The goddess instructs Adrastus to swear that the Argives will never attack Athens, then directs a sacrifice. Adrastus' son, Aegialeus, when he is older, is to attack Thebes and win a great victory, as a result of which he and the chieftains' sons will be known as the Epigoni, or "after-born."

C O M M E N T A R Y. Because of close similarity in theme, *The Suppliants* is inevitably compared with the *Heraclidae* and accounted the superior play. Yet there are defects that keep it from greatness. It contains more political and ethical discussion than any other work by Euripides. Prominent motifs are the ideal of Hellenic unity, the praise of Athenian enlightenment, and the presentation of Theseus as a model leader—but these motifs are never completely integrated into the drama. Typical of its limitations is the fact that its best piece of theatre, the episode where Evadne throws herself into the flames, is without effect on the action and without relevance to the theme.

Susa (Gk. **Sousa**). Royal Persian city in Susiana, a region of the Persian empire south of Media and west of Persia proper, having a coastline on the Persian Gulf.

Susarion (Gk. **Sousarion**). Alleged inventor of comedy (supposedly c. 570 B.C.). Susarion was said by some to have been from Megara, but the evidence for this is poor, and his existence is doubtful.

Sutrium. Town a few miles north of Rome. During a war with the Gauls in the late third century B.C., there was a forced march to this town.

Sybaris. Greek colony on the Bay of Tarentum in southern Italy. Sybaris was noted for the luxurious style in which its inhabitants lived.

Syennesis. Cilician king, a vassal of Xerxes.

Syleus. *Myth.* Thracian chieftain who forced strangers to work in his vineyard and then killed them. When Heracles came to Syleus as a slave (either on loan from Omphale or sold by Hermes for his misdeeds), he tore up the chieftain's vineyard, built a large fire, and roasted Syleus' oxen. When Syleus objected, Heracles killed him with a blow. Euripides' lost satyr play *Syleus* was based on this myth.

Symmachus. Commentator on Aristophanes (fl. c. A.D. 100). Traces of Symmachus' work appear in the ancient scholia.

Symplegades. *Myth.* The "Clashing Rocks," also called the Blue Rocks, at the entrance to the Black Sea. Whenever a ship passed between them they rushed together to crush it. Orestes and Pylades braved the Symplegades on their voyage to the Taurian country (*Iphigenia among the Taurians,* lines 1388–89). The Argonauts also passed through.

Syracusius (Gk. **Syrakosios**). Demagogic orator in Aristophanes' Athens. Syracusius was said to have proposed a law to restrict freedom of speech in comedy.

syrma. Long-sleeved robe worn in tragedy, presumably derived from the cult of Dionysus.

Syrtes. The Syrtis Major and Syrtis Minor, stretches of sandbanks along the coast of North Africa.

Syrus. See PUBLILIUS SYRUS.

T

Taenarum or **Taenarus** (Gk. **Tainaron** or **Tainaros**). City and promontory of the same name located at the tip of the peninsula forming the western side of the Bay of Laconia. A cave in the vicinity was thought to be an entrance to the underworld.

Tagus. River in central Spain and Portugal that flows into the Atlantic Ocean.

Talaus (Gk. **Talaos**). *Myth.* King of Argos, father of Mecisteus, Adrastus, and Eriphyle.

Tale of a Traveling Bag, The. See VIDULARIA.

Talthybius (Gk. **Talthybios**). *Myth.* Herald of Agamemnon. Talthybius appears in this capacity in Euripides' *Hecuba* and *Trojan Women* and in Seneca's *Trojan Women.* Although he does not appear in Euripides' *Orestes,* it is reported that he spoke against Orestes when the Argives considered the latter's fate.

Tanais. River in Russia, now the Don.

Tantalus (Gk. **Tantalos**). 1. *Myth.* King of Phrygia, son of Zeus, and father of Niobe and Pelops. Tantalus was best known for his sufferings in the underworld, variously detailed. According to one tradition, he was fixed under a huge rock that threatened always to fall. According to another, he was put in water up to his neck, and boughs laden with fruit hung near his face; but when he tried to satisfy his hunger and thirst, both water and fruit withdrew from reach.

The offenses against the gods which brought on the punishment were varied. A certain Pandareos, having stolen the golden dog that Zeus had set to guard his temple in Crete, took it to Tantalus on Mt. Sipylus. Tantalus hid the dog and, when Hermes demanded to know where it was, denied that he had seen it. For this lie Zeus buried him under the mountain. Again, after Tantalus had been invited to the banquets of the gods, he showed his gratitude either by stealing nectar and ambrosia or by babbling the secrets confided to him by the gods. In still another story, he served the gods with a dish made of his own son, Pelops. Tantalus' descendants were known as "Tantalids." His ghost appears at the beginning of Seneca's *Thyestes.*

Sophocles' lost tragedy *Tantalus* is represented by scanty fragments. It seems to have dealt with Tantalus' concealment of the golden dog. Two papyrus scraps may come from this play: in one Tantalus contemplates a stone that looks like his daughter Niobe; in the other there is reference to an earthquake, probably the one that destroyed Tantalus' palace and buried him under the mountain.

2. *Myth.* Son of Thyestes. There are two stories of Tantalus' death: either he was killed by Atreus and served up to his father (as in Seneca's *Thyestes*), or he became the first husband of Clytemnestra and was killed by Agamemnon.

Taphos. Island off the coast of Acarnania. The Taphians lived here and in adjacent islands.

Tarentum (Gk. **Taras**). Greek colony inside the heel of the boot of Italy. Tarentum was noted for the production of fine woolen materials.

Tarquin, Tarquinius Superbus. Last king of Rome. Tarquin dethroned Servius Tullius with the help of the king's daughter, Tullia.

Tartarus (Gk. **Tartaros**). *Myth.* Deep abyss of the underworld, the prison of Cronus and the Titans. Tartarus was later thought of as a place of punishment for the wicked.

Tartessus or **Tartesus** (Gk. **Tartessos**). City in southern Spain founded by the Phoenicians.

Taurians or **Tauri** (Gk. **Tauroi**). Scythian tribe that inhabited the Crimean Peninsula.

Tauropolos. Epithet of Artemis meaning "drawn by bulls" or "hunting bulls." In Artemis' honor was celebrated the festival Tauropolia in Attica.

Taurus (Gk. **Tauros**). Mountain range in southern Asia Minor.

Taygetus (Gk. **Taygetos**). Mountain range in western Laconia.

Tecmessa (Gk. **Tekmessa**). *Myth.* Phrygian princess captured by the Greeks. Tecmessa became the concubine of Ajax the Greater; she bore him a son, Eurysaces. Tecmessa appears in Sophocles' *Ajax.*

Teithras. Attic deme.

Telamon. *Myth.* Hero, and ruler of Salamis. Telamon helped Heracles in the sack of Troy. He was the father of Ajax and Teucer.

Teleboans (Gk. **Teleboai**). Tribe in Acarnania.

Teleclides or **Telecleides** (Gk. **Telekleides**). Writer of Old Comedy (probably active c. 445–c. 425 B.C.). Although Teleclides was very successful in his own time, he was soon forgotten after his death. Of his works sixty-odd fragments and about eight titles survive. Examples are: *The Amphictyons,* picturing a kind of Lotus Land, *Eumenides, The Hesiod Comedy, The Non-Liars, Revenge, The Soldiers, The Prytanes,* and *Stubborn Men.*

Teleios (Gk. "perfect" or "full-grown" or "bringing to pass"). Epithet of Zeus. The feminine form, Teleia, was an epithet of Hera.

Telemachus (Gk. **Telemachos**). *Myth.* Son of Odysseus and Penelope.

Telemessians, The (Gk. **Telemesses**). Lost comedy by Aristophanes (produced shortly before 400 B.C.). Telemessus was a city in Asia Minor noted for its soothsayers. In one or two fragments of the play there is depicted a consultation of an oracle or of soothsayers. Certain disciples of Socrates, for example Chaerephon and the young Plato, seem to have been satirized.

Telepheia. A supposed tetralogy by Sophocles. An inscription found at

Aexonae in Attica, dating from perhaps as early as 420 B.C., mentions Ecphantides' *Trials,* Cratinus' *Cowherd,* Timotheus' *Alcmeon* and *Alphesiboea,* and a *Te——* by Sophocles. Many scholars think that Sophocles wrote a tetralogy, *Telepheia,* which was composed of *Aleadae, The Mysians, The Assembly of the Achaeans,* and the satyr play *Telephus.*

Telephus (Gk. **Telephos**). *Myth.* Son of Heracles and Auge, daughter of King Aleos of Tegea. When Aleos noticed that his daughter was with child, he instructed Nauplius to drown her. On the way to the sea, Auge bore Telephus and abandoned him, but he was reared by shepherds, who found him suckled by a doe. Auge herself was spared by Nauplius, who sold her as a slave. She was carried to the court of King Teuthras of Mysia, and the king came to love her like a daughter.

When Telephus grew up, he set out in search of his mother. In his wanderings he came to the palace of King Aleos at Tegea and killed Aleos' sons (see ALEADAE). On finally reaching Mysia, he narrowly avoided an incestuous union with his own mother (see AUGE). After Teuthras' death, Telephus succeeded to the throne. When the Greek armada made their first attempt to reach Troy, they landed by mistake in Mysia, and in the ensuing battle Telephus was wounded by Achilles. After the baffled Greeks had sailed home again, Telephus learned from an oracle that his wound could be healed only by the wounder. He accordingly made his way to Greece and offered to guide the fleet to Troy. His offer was accepted, and Achilles healed his wound with the rust from the spear that had inflicted it.

Aeschylus' lost *Telephus* doubtless told how Telephus was healed. Only about two lines survive. Sophocles' lost *Telephus,* according to some conjectures, was the satyr play of a tetralogy, TELEPHEIA.

Euripides' lost play *Telephus* was produced in 438 B.C. The prologue was spoken by Telephus, who came into the Greek encampment after the fleet had returned from its unsuccessful attempt to reach Troy. Telephus had come across the sea to have his wound cured by Achilles. Disguised as a beggar, he revealed himself to the Greeks but was forced to snatch up and hold hostage the infant Orestes to save himself from being killed. (This scene became quite famous; it is parodied by Aristophanes in his *Thesmophoriazusae,* where Mnesilochus snatches up the woman's wineskin, thinking it a baby. There is a dispute as to whether Aeschylus included a similar scene in his version of *Telephus.*) Because of the intervention of Clytemnestra, Telephus was finally healed. Euripides' play was popular, and Ennius based his *Telephus* on it.

Teleutas. *Myth.* King in Phrygia, father of Tecmessa.

Temenidae (Gk. **Temenidai**). Lost tragedy by Euripides. (See TEMENUS.)

Temenus (Gk. **Temenos**). *Myth.* Descendant of Heracles and ruler of Argos. Because of Deiphontes' military prowess, Temenus favored him as heir over his own two sons (the Temenidae). The latter accordingly attacked their father while he was bathing, but as he lay dying, Temenus consigned his daughter and his kingdom to Deiphontes. Then followed a struggle over the throne of Argos, resulting in the expulsion of the Temenidae. It was said that they went to the north, where they founded the kingdom of Macedonia.

Euripides' lost tragedy *Temenus* was based on the foregoing myth. As the kings of Macedonia claimed descent from Temenus, it has been thought that Euripides wrote a Macedonian trilogy during the last year or two of his life while he was in Macedonia. If so, the plays included were *Temenus, Temenidae,* and *Archelaus.*

Tempe. Valley in Thessaly between Mt. Olympus and Mt. Ossa. Through it flows the Peneius River.

Tenedos. Small island off the west coast of the Troad.

Tenes or **Tennes.** *Myth.* Son of Cygnus. When after Tenes' mother died Cygnus remarried, his new wife made advances to her stepson. Tenes repulsed his stepmother, whereupon she told her husband that he had tried to seduce her. Cygnus put Tenes and his sister into a chest which he threw into the sea, and they floated to a certain island, where Tenes became ruler, calling the island Tenedos after himself. Years later, when the Greek fleet stopped there on the way to Troy, Tenes was killed by Achilles, some say while protecting his sister from the Greek.

A play called *Tenes* was ascribed to Euripides, but the ascription was suspect even in ancient times. The evidence for such a play by Aeschylus is likewise very slight.

Tenos. Island of the southern Aegean Sea southeast of Andros.

Terence (Lat. **Publius Terentius Afer**). One of the two writers of Roman comedy (the other being Plautus) whose works are extant (c. 195–159 B.C.).

L I F E. Born in Carthage, Terence came to Rome as a slave, becoming the property of a senator, Terentius Lucanus. His master noticed his intellectual promise, educated him, and freed him. It is said that when Terence submitted his first play to the aediles for production, he was told to get the opinion of Caecilius, who was then an established author. Going to Caecilius' house, where a dinner was in progress, Terence sat at the side of the room and began reading it aloud; soon he was invited to join the guests on the couches, where he finished reading the play to great applause. Terence was drawn into the intellectual circle centering around the younger Scipio, and there were unfounded rumors that these aristocrats wrote the plays that were produced under Terence's name. *Andria* came out in 166 B.C., the five other comedies following at the rate of about one per year. Terence died during a voyage to Greece.

W O R K S (see under individual entries). All six comedies are extant: *Adelphoe, Andria, The Eunuch, The Mother-in-Law, Phormio,* and *The Self-tormentor.*

C R I T I C I S M. Terence's reputation has never been entirely unassailed. In his own lifetime he had to counter the charges of plagiarism and of clumsily putting together two Greek plays to make one of his own (see CONTAMINATION). Several ancient critics placed Terence very low in the ranks of Roman comedy writers. Julius Caesar called him "half a Menander." But other judges—Cicero,

Varro, Horace, and Quintilian—admired him, and there appeared several commentaries on his works. The best-known literary comedies of the Middle Ages, those of the nun Hrotsvitha of Gandersheim, were intended to be Christian counterparts of Terence's plays. In the Renaissance and neoclassical period he was much imitated.

Most of Terence's present-day enemies have found fault with him for not being Plautus or for reproducing Greek originals (which are, however, all lost). It is true that Terence was more faithfully Greek than Plautus, the taste of his day probably demanding it. It is true also that his plays remind the reader of Menander and that if more of Menander's plays had survived, Terence might seem a minor figure. Nevertheless there is general appreciation for his elegant language, his skillful management of plot (usually a double plot), his quiet humor, and his sympathetic view of human nature.

Tereus. *Myth.* Thracian king, son of Ares. Tereus married Procne, daughter of King Pandion (1) of Athens. Conceiving a desire for her sister Philomela, Tereus raped the girl and cut out her tongue to prevent her from revealing the deed. But Philomela wove a tapestry of the whole story and showed it to Procne, who killed Itys, her child by Tereus, and fed him to his father. When Tereus learned what he had eaten, he pursued the sisters to Daulis in Phocis, where they prayed to the gods and turned into birds: Procne to a nightingale and Philomela to a swallow. Tereus was also changed into a bird, the hoopoe. (Later poets sometimes reversed the roles of Procne and Philomela, the latter becoming a nightingale.)

Sophocles' lost tragedy *Tereus* was one of his most famous plays; of it about fifty-seven lines remain. It was produced before Aristophanes' *Birds*, in which Tereus and Procne appear in bird form. Sophocles' play was the model for Accius' *Tereus*.

Tethys. *Myth.* Wife of Oceanus and his female counterpart as a primeval sea deity. Tethys was regarded as encircling the earth; she was the mother of all streams and fountains.

tetralogy. Group of four plays consisting of three tragedies (the trilogy) and a satyr play. The dramatic poet submitted a tetralogy for performance at a festival. Plenty of evidence exists, however, to show that in all periods a poet might submit only three plays, or even two. Modern scholars classify tetralogies as either "genuine," that is, closely knit and developing a unified theme, or "spurious," that is, pseudotetralogies composed of four plays on different subjects and having no connection, or only a very tenuous one. Both types seem to have been composed in all periods, but the closely knit type is associated especially with Aeschylus.

Teucer (Gk. **Teukros**). *Myth.* Son of Telamon and half brother of Ajax the Greater. Teucer's mother Hesione, daughter of King Laomedon of Troy, was given to Telamon as a concubine by Heracles after the latter's sack of the city (see LAOMEDON; HESIONE 2). Teucer was the best bowman in the Greek army at Troy but was always suspect because of his Trojan blood. After Ajax's suicide, he was able to persuade the Greeks to permit an honorable burial; in this role he appears in Sophocles' *Ajax*.

When Teucer returned to Salamis, he was unjustly banished by Telamon on the ground that he had not prevented Ajax's death, had not avenged him, and had lost touch with Ajax's son Eurysaces on the way home. As Teucer was going into exile, he justified his conduct in a speech made on shipboard to his countrymen on the shore. There followed years of wandering; in Euripides' *Helen*, Teucer makes an appearance in Egypt. Finally Apollo's oracle told him to go to Cyprus and there found a new Salamis. Years later, he was reconciled to the aged Telamon and helped to restore him to his throne.

Sophocles' lost *Teucer* doubtless told the circumstances of Teucer's exile. The play may have been part of a trilogy, preceded by *Ajax* and followed by *Eurysaces*. Pacuvius' Latin *Teucer* was presumably modeled on that of Sophocles.

Teucrians. Name for the Trojans. Teucer was a mythical Trojan king.

Teumessus (Gk. **Teumessos**). Mountain in Boeotia.

Teuthras. *Myth.* King of Mysia. Teuthras bought Auge as a slave and adopted her son Telephus.

Thales. Philosopher of Miletus (early 6th century B.C.). Thales' name became proverbial for "a wise man."

Thamyras or **Thamyris.** *Myth.* Son of Philammon and a nymph. Having gained great renown as a lyre player, Thamyras challenged the Muses to a competition. He was defeated, and the goddesses punished him with blindness because of his insolence.

The lost *Thamyras* of Sophocles was an early work. In it the poet acted the title role and displayed his musical skill. The last scene made a great impression, for Thamyras, defeated and blinded, broke his lyre and sat in despair, surrounded by the fragments.

Thanatos. Personification of death. Thanatos appears at the beginning of Euripides' *Alcestis*.

Tharrhelides. Athenian of Aristophanes' time who had a pert and forward son of diminutive stature.

Thasus (Gk. **Thasos**). Island in the northern Aegean Sea, just off the coast of Macedonia. Thasus was noted for wine and for a kind of fish sauce.

Theagenes. See THEOGENES.

theater (Gk. **theatron**). The Greek word must originally have referred to the crowd of spectators standing around the orchestra—the round dancing place —and watching the chorus perform. It continued to be applied to the auditorium part of the whole theater building, the semicircular hillside where the spectators sat and where they were eventually provided with rows of stone seats. Although there were innumerable minor developments in the theater building throughout classical and Hellenistic Greek times, the theater always consisted of three basic parts: auditorium, orchestra, and skene.

The Roman theater was not essentially different from the Greek. The orchestra was encroached upon by the stage, which became deeper and lower, and there was usually a more elaborate *scaenae frons*. Scholars differ widely as to how much of this development was purely Roman and how much was derived from Hellenistic Greece.

The Roman stage usually (but not always) represented a city street. There are thought to have been three doors behind the stage, though most plays required only two houses. There is much dispute about the convention concerning entrances and exits from the wings; it seems that the exit to the audience's right led to the market place, the one to the left to the harbor. This appears to be the opposite of the Greek convention.

Theban Tetralogy (called also the **Oedipus Tetralogy**). Tetralogy by Aeschylus consisting of three tragedies: *Laius* (lost), *Oedipus* (lost), *The Seven Against Thebes* (extant), and the lost satyr play *The Sphinx*. Produced in 468 (or 467) B.C. at the City Dionysia, the *Theban Tetralogy* was awarded first prize. Remains of a summary of the whole tetralogy have been discovered on a papyrus.

Laius. Of this play only a handful of very short fragments have survived. Laius himself spoke the prologue, announcing his intention to go to Delphi, undoubtedly to inquire about means of ridding Thebes of the Sphinx. The play concluded with a message about Laius' death on the journey. He was lamented by Queen Jocasta and the Chorus of Elders.

Oedipus. In general outline this play must have resembled Sophocles' *Oedipus the King*, beginning with a pestilence at Thebes, continuing with the uncovering of Oedipus' guilt as murderer of his father and mate of his mother, and concluding with Jocasta's suicide and Oedipus' blinding of himself.

The Seven Against Thebes. Translations: Robert Potter, 1777; John S. Blackie, 1850; Frederick A. Paley, 1864; Edward H. Plumptre, 1868; Lewis Campbell, 1890; E. D. A. Morshead, 1904; Arthur S. Way, 1906; Walter and C. E. S. Headlam, 1909; H. Weir Smyth, 1922; G. M. Cookson, 1922; Robert C. Trevelyan, 1923; Gilbert Murray, 1925; David Grene, 1956; Philip Vellacott, 1961.

S C E N E. The Acropolis of Thebes.

S U M M A R Y. Eteocles, ruler of Thebes, informs the citizens that the omens foretell a violent assault on the city that very day; the enemy, who have been long engaged in a siege, are now determined on more active measures. As men are being posted to defend the walls, a Theban Spy enters and reports that Adrastus, leader of the Seven against Thebes, and the other chieftains have sworn to capture the city or die. (They had declared war on Thebes to right the injustice done by Eteocles to his brother Polyneices, son-in-law of Adrastus.)

Eteocles' prayers for protection are taken up by a Chorus of Theban Maidens, who hear the horrid clashes of war in the distance. As they hysterically embrace the images of the gods, Eteocles expresses his contempt for the weakness of women and orders them to be quiet lest they spread panic among the citizens. Vowing to sacrifice abundantly to the guardian gods of Thebes and to deck their shrines with spoils stripped from the enemy, he goes off to station captains at six gates of Thebes while he guards the seventh.

After a choric ode depicting the miseries of a captured city, both Eteocles and the Spy return. There follows a scene of dramatic symmetry as the Spy describes each of the leading assailants of the seven gates, their demeanor and the blazonry of their shields, while Eteocles, commenting scornfully on the pretensions of the enemy, sends a Theban hero to face each of the assailants. Five of the attackers are insolent and blasphemous: Tydeus, who regards the unfavorable omens cited by the seer as proof of the latter's cowardice; Capaneus, who vows to carry out his assault even though Zeus's thunderbolts should block the way; Eteoclus, who shouts that Ares himself could not drive him from the walls; Hippomedon who, full of battle-lust, raves like a bacchant; Parthenopaeus, who threatens the ramparts with the Sphinx as his emblem. In contrast to his comrades the sixth chieftain, the prophet Amphiaraus, goes into battle doubting the justice of their cause and knowing that he will die in the assault. Last of all is Polyneices, instigator of the war, who carries the figure of Justice on his shield. Eteocles declares that he will be his brother's opponent, ignoring the plea of the Chorus that he not shed the blood of a near kinsman.

The Chorus review the curse that has worked in the royal house of Thebes ever since King Laius, father of Oedipus, disobeyed Apollo's injunction not to beget a child; they recall Oedipus' curse on his two sons, Eteocles and Polyneices, who are to die by each other's hands. Presently the Spy returns to report that the enemy has been repulsed at six of the city gates; at the seventh, however, Eteocles and Polyneices lie dead, each the victim of the other.

The bodies of the two brothers are brought in by a group of mourners led by their sisters Antigone and Ismene, who alternate in leading the funeral dirge. A Herald then announces a decree of the Theban councilors: Eteocles, the defender of the city, is to be buried with full honors, while Polyneices, the attacker of his fatherland, is to lie unburied to be devoured by the dogs. Antigone immediately declares that she will defy the edict regardless of the consequences to herself. Half of the Chorus join her in her resolution; the others leave with Eteocles' funeral procession.

The Sphinx. Of this satyr play only three small fragments exist. Presumably it told of Oedipus' solution of the Sphinx's riddle.

COMMENTARY. There is no doubt that a tetralogy written by Aeschylus at the height of his powers developed many themes and contained many subtle meanings which now escape modern readers, since less than one-third of the work survives. Fortunately this third is the last part of the tragic trilogy, bringing the significance of the whole to its conclusion. One obvious theme is the disruption of the cosmos brought about by the transgressions of the house of Laius against the natural order: Laius' own unnatural passion for the boy Chrysippus, whom he kidnaped; his and Jocasta's disregard of the oracle's warning that they should not beget children; Oedipus' murder of his father and incest with his mother; the killing of Eteocles and Polyneices, each by the other's hand; and the unnatural prohibition of Polyneices' burial.

The myth-minded Greek of Aeschylus' day had an unshaken conception that there was an essential continuum linking divine providence, individual morality, social well-being, and natural order (a conviction that later antiquity lost with the decline of mythic thinking and that the Middle Ages and the Renaissance recovered, only to lose it again). To this Greek the symbolism of poetry was not merely a play of fancy and a retreat into the world of imagination, but a direct representation of reality and history above history. Thus *The Seven Against Thebes* is a play "full of Ares," in the words of an ancient commentator—Ares, the god of the curse, who executes the universal command that spiritual disorder must express itself in physical disorder. It follows that in the play the blazonry on the heroes' shields expresses the souls of the men behind them. Moreover, the chaos of the Theban city, caused by the chaos in the souls of its rulers, is brought by the gods into balance by the imposition of its natural result, human suffering.

Such was the conception of the "primitive" Aeschylus, shared by the equally primitive Dante and Shakespeare.

Thebe 1. City in Mysia, the home of Andromache.

2. Another form of the name Thebes.

Themis. *Myth.* Titaness, goddess of law, usually called daughter of Uranus and Gaia (the Earth) and one of the mates of Zeus. Themis was, however, sometimes identified with Gaia and sometimes considered a daughter of Zeus. Oaths were sworn in her name; she was patroness of lawmakers and executors of justice. Themis preceded Apollo as an oracular power at Delphi.

Themiscyra (Gk. **Themiskyra**). City in Pontus on the southern shore of the Black Sea.

Themistocles (Gk. **Themistokles**). Athenian statesman (c. 528–459 B.C.). Themistocles was responsible for building up the fleet that defeated the Persians at Salamis and for fortifying Athens after the Persian wars. He was, however, ostracized and eventually fled to Persia, where he was said to have killed himself by drinking bull's blood.

Theoclymenus (Gk. **Theoklymenos**). *Myth.* King of Egypt, son of Proteus and Psamathe. In Euripides' *Helen*, Theoclymenus presses Helen to marry him.

Theocritus (Gk. **Theokritos**). Author of pastorals and works in other minor poetic genres (fl. first half of 3rd century B.C.). Several of Theocritus' extant pastoral poems are mime-like in form, and certain other pieces, for example, "The Women at the Adonis Festival," are pure mimes.

Theodectes (Gk. **Theodektes**). Orator and writer of tragedies (4th century B.C.). Theodectes was a pupil of Plato, Aristotle, and Isocrates. When asked to write something in praise of King Mausolus, he produced a tragedy, *Mausolus*, which enjoyed a surprising success. Theodectes wrote fifty tragedies in all, but only about a dozen titles and a dozen fragments survive.

Theodorus (Gk. **Theodoros**). Actor (fl. c. 380 B.C.). Known for his fine voice and for his interpretation of female roles in tragedies, Theodorus was called by Plutarch "one of the glories of Athens." The tyrant Alexander of Pherae once left the theater while Theodorus was onstage, explaining that it would be strange for him to be seen weeping over the fate of Hecuba or Polyxena when he had killed so many real people.

Theogenes or **Theagenes**. Politician and military leader in Aristophanes' Athens. Theogenes became one of the Thirty Tyrants. Aristophanes ridiculed his coarseness and superstition. He was known as "Smoke" because most of his grandiose plans disappeared into thin air.

Theognis. Writer of tragedies contemporary with Aristophanes. Theognis was known as "Snow" because his poetry was so cold. Also a corrupt politician, he became one of the Thirty Tyrants of Athens in 404 B.C.

theologeion (Gk. "stage of the gods"). The flat roof of the skene where a god in a drama customarily appeared.

Theon. Scholar, probably in Alexandria, during the age of Augustus. Theon revised the text of Sophocles' plays. Among many works now lost, he produced a *Lexicon to the Comic Poets* and perhaps a *Lexicon to the Tragic Poets.*

Theonoë. *Myth.* Priestess and prophetess, daughter of Proteus and sister of Theoclymenus. In Euripides' *Helen,* Theonoë helps Helen and Menelaus to escape from Egypt.

Theophrastus (Gk. **Theophrastos**). Greek philosopher (c. 370–c. 287 B.C.). A pupil of Aristotle, Theophrastus succeeded his teacher as head of his school. Among voluminous works, he wrote on poetics, especially on comedy, though the gist of what he said is much disputed. Theophrastus may have developed Aristotle's theory of plot (see POETICS), dividing a play into the following parts: prologos (exposition), protasis (posing of the problem), epitasis (intensification), and lysis (denouement). His definition of tragedy was "a reversal of prosperity on the heroic level"; a definition of comedy, probably his, was "a sequence of the affairs of ordinary men, in which there is a distinct change, but no disaster."

Theopompus (Gk. **Theopompos**). Writer of Old Comedy. Theopompus had a long career, which extended from about 415 to about 360 B.C. Of his works only about a hundred fragments and twenty titles remain. His fondness for travesties of myth suggests Middle Comedy; examples of this are: *Althaea, Theseus, Medus, Odysseus, Penelope, Phineus.* Other titles were *The Barmaids, Peace, Pantaleon.*

Theoria (Gk. "a viewing," or "attendance at a festival"). Attendant on the goddess of peace in Aristophanes' *Peace.* Theoria was the personification of a festival or holiday.

Theoroi. See THE ISTHMIASTS.

Theorus (Gk. **Theoros**). Athenian politician, a follower of Cleon. Theorus appears in Aristophanes' *Acharnians.*

Theramenes. Athenian politician (c. 455–404 B.C.). Theramenes was called "Cothurnus" (the boot used in tragedy, which could be worn on either foot) because of his frequent changes of sides. He became one of the Thirty Tyrants but fell out with the leaders and was executed.

Thermodon. River in Pontus. The Amazons supposedly lived on its banks.

Thersites. *Myth.* Soldier with the Greek army at Troy notorious for his sharp tongue.

Theseus. *Myth.* Attic hero, son of Aegeus and Aethra. (For the story of his birth, see AEGEUS.) Some said, however, that on the night when Aegeus made love to Aethra, she had first gone out in obedience to a dream and had been forced by Poseidon, so that Theseus was really the son of the god. Before Aegeus left Troezen and returned to Athens, he buried a sword and sandals and placed a large stone over them, telling Aethra not to let their son come in search of him until he could lift the stone. Theseus accomplished this deed at the age of sixteen and set out for Athens. On the way he disposed of the monster sow of Crommyon and the brigands Cercyon (see ALOPE), SINIS, SCIRON, and PROCRUSTES.

When Theseus arrived in Athens, Aegeus was under the spell of the enchantress Medea, who divined the young man's identity. Two stories were told as to how she tried to get rid of him. One was that she sent him against the monster bull of Marathon; easily overcoming the beast, Theseus was afterward sacrificing it when Aegeus recognized the sword being used. The other story was that Medea convinced Aegeus that the young man was coming to murder him; Aegeus accordingly planned to give Theseus a cup containing poison, but in the course of the banquet Aegeus recognized his sword and overturned the cup. In any case, Medea had to flee.

Shortly afterward Theseus voluntarily joined the group of seven young men and seven maidens who were sent to Crete every year, at King Minos' orders, to be fed to the Minotaur. Minos' daughter Ariadne fell in love with him and held the end of a skein which Theseus unwound while making his way through the Labyrinth. When he came to the monster, he killed it, afterward finding his way out of the Labyrinth by following the thread. Theseus, Ariadne, and the young Athenians then fled Crete, but on the return voyage, Theseus deserted Ariadne while she slept on the island of Naxos. On nearing Athens, he failed to change the black sails of his ship to white as a sign that he was alive. Aegeus, seeing the black sail and believing his son dead, leaped into the sea in despair.

Theseus had, in addition to Ariadne, several other loves and wives. He carried off Antiope, queen of the Amazons, and she bore him Hippolytus. The Amazons invaded Attica to rescue Antiope, but she perished in the fighting. With his Lapith friend Pirithous, whom he helped in the war of the Centaurs and Lapiths, Theseus carried off Helen, but she was soon reclaimed by her brothers, the Dioscuri. Then Pirithous determined with Theseus' help to kidnap Persephone, queen of the dead, and the two friends descended to the underworld. Hades invited them to dine and showed them to the Seat of Forgetfulness. There both would have remained forever if Heracles, coming down to capture Cerberus, had not taken Theseus back with him to earth.

Theseus was regarded by the Athenians as the originator of Attic unity and political institutions. He eliminated the Pallantides, his cousins and rivals to the throne, and in consequence of this he had to retire in penance from Athens for a time. It is during this period that the action of Euripides' *Hippolytus* and Seneca's *Phaedra* takes place; in these plays Theseus is rash and hot-tempered. He is, however, usually represented as the very ideal of Hellenic humaneness: in Euripides' *Heracles* and Seneca's *Hercules Furens* he is the faithful friend of the hero in his darkest hour; in Sophocles' *Oedipus at Colonus* he becomes Oedipus' protector and accompanies him to his apotheosis in the Grove of the Eumenides; and in Euripides' *Suppliants* he upholds the right of honorable burial for the heroes killed in the expedition of the Seven against Thebes. During the Athenian festival honoring Theseus and celebrating the unity of the citizenry, the poorer people were fed bread and barley broth at public expense.

Theseus was the title of a lost play by Sophocles. Since only two words remain, its contents are unknown; even its existence is doubtful.

If Euripides' lost *Theseus* formed a trilogy with *Aegeus* and the first *Hippolytus*, it was produced probably in the late 430's B.C. Its plot dealt with the killing of the Minotaur. Thirty-odd lines is the sum total of the surviving fragments. In the longest, an illiterate herdsman spells out Theseus' name by describing the shape of the letters.

Thesmophoria. Women's festival. The Thesmophoria was celebrated at Athens in the fall, chiefly in honor of Demeter and Persephone.

Thesmophoriazusae (Gk. **Thesmophoriazousai, The Women at the Thesmophoria** or **Ladies' Day** or **The Poet and the Women**). Extant comedy by Aristophanes (produced in 411 B.C.; some say 410). Translations: Benjamin B. Rogers, 1924; Arthur S. Way, 1934; Dudley Fitts, 1959; David Barrett, 1964.

S C E N E. Athens, at first a street, later the Temple of the Twain (Demeter and Persephone).

S U M M A R Y. The poet Euripides and his old father-in-law, Mnesilochus, are seen in front of the house of the poet Agathon. Euripides tells his father-in-law that the matrons of Athens, who are about to gather for the Thesmophoria, their annual festival in honor of Demeter and Persephone, are planning to take action against him (Euripides) for the unflattering portrayals of the female sex in his plays. It is Euripides' hope that Agathon will agree to slip into the meeting dressed as a woman and to speak in his defense.

The two men find Agathon deeply engrossed in the composition of a tragedy, taking all the parts in turn. Mnesilochus is at a loss to know whether he is male or female, but Agathon explains that a poet must live his creations and become a woman if he would write about women. When Euripides makes his request, pointing out that Agathon, with his effeminate features, would be the ideal person to spy on the women's meeting, Agathon flatly refuses because of what the women might do to him if they discovered his presence.

Mnesilochus then volunteers to play the part. After his beard and body hair have been removed, he dons a female costume borrowed from Agathon and makes his way to the temple, where he takes his place among the Women (the Chorus). After the opening prayers, the Women turn to a consideration of the punishment that is to be inflicted on Euripides. The first speaker proposes death by poisoning or some other method, pointing out that Euripides' representations of shrewish, dishonest, and adulterous wives have made husbands unbearably suspicious. A Widow complains that her trade in temple garlands has fallen off since Euripides has convinced audiences that there are no gods.

At this point Mnesilochus rises to the defense. Although he professes to hate Euripides, he asks the ladies to admit that the dramatist has exposed only a few of their faults. Has he ever mentioned the wives who take slaves as lovers or the women who pass off others' babies as their own? As the Women are protesting Mnesilochus' imprudence, the effeminate Cleisthenes, an ally of the women, rushes in to report that Euripides has planted a spy in their midst. When Mnesilochus is questioned, he is somewhat hazy as to his identity, but a close inspection in undress makes it clear that he is not a woman. To protect himself he grabs the baby of the woman nearest him, threatening to stab it, but the baby turns out to be a wineskin smuggled into the meeting. Mnesilochus drinks the wine and, recalling Euripides' promises to protect him, tries to summon the poet by borrowing a device from his play *Palamedes;* but instead of writing a message on oars as did Oeax in the play, he uses some wooden statues, which he scatters about.

The Chorus then address the audience with a heartfelt defense of their sex and an attack on men, whose offenses are far more serious than those of their wives. Since Euripides has not appeared, Mnesilochus decides to attract him by quoting Helen's lines from the poet's play named after her. Euripides promptly arrives disguised as Menelaus, but the two men are unable to escape as do the pair in the play because a Magistrate summoned by Cleisthenes arrests Mnesilochus and leaves him in the custody of a Scythian Policeman, who lashes him to a post. Mnesilochus then voices the laments of Euripides' Andromeda while the poet, as an offstage Echo, repeats the last few words of each of Mnesilochus' lines and confuses the Scythian by echoing his speeches too. Euripides then makes an appearance as the rescuer Perseus, but while the Policeman is willing enough to let him make advances to Mnesilochus, he will not release the old man.

Eventually Euripides, having decided to employ a more mundane strata-gem, reappears dressed as a procuress and accompanied by a Dancing Girl and a Flute Girl. After promising the Women that they will henceforth have no cause to complain of their treatment at his hands, Euripides bids the girls entice the Policeman, who soon goes off with the Dancer. He and Mnesilochus then make good their escape. When the Policeman realizes that he has been outwitted and starts in pursuit of the fugitives, the Women give him wrong directions, thereby indicating that they have made their peace with Euripides.

C O M M E N T A R Y. *Thesmophoriazusae* is a hearty and raucous guffaw at Euripides' metaphysicalism. Some judge it the funniest and cleverest of Aristophanes' plays. At the time, Euripides was in his illusion-versus-reality phase; this was the period of *Iphigenia among the Taurians, Helen,* and the lost *Andromeda.* He was probably trying to reassure his countrymen, who were suffering from external defeat and internal dissension, that the way of escape from such calamities is not merely onward, but upward, since things are not always what they seem. *Thesmophoriazusae* is a Sancho Panza retort to this quixotism: things have a way of being very thingy, and the physical world cannot be left out of account. Place Euripides and his proxy in a situation of real physical danger, and all the tragic posturings in the world cannot effect their deliverance. Flesh cannot be ignored, nor can the coarse perceptions of the fleshly man; it is only when a flesh-and-blood girl walks in and lures the Scythian away that the poet and his helper are able to walk out.

Thespiades. *Myth.* The fifty daughters of Thespius, a Boeotian king. When Heracles was staying with Thespius, the latter, wanting to have descendants from such a hero, slipped each of his daughters by turns into Heracles' room at night. All the Thespiades bore sons.

Thespis. Athenian writer, actor, and chorus leader. At some time between 536 and 532 B.C., Thespis produced the first recorded tragedy at the City Dionysia. He was, more commonly than any other writer, credited with the invention of drama. Not only was he said to have introduced masks, substituting them for the face painting he had previously used, but, most important, he was said to have first included the *rhesis,* lines spoken by a solo actor in conjunction with the original choric ode. There are various theories as to how this may have come about: Thespis may have developed the *rhesis* out of the chorus part; or he may have simply added it from without, as it were, to the chorus-part; or, according to one theory, there may have been a division of the chorus into two responsive groups, one group in the course of time gradually dwindling to one actor. That Thespis took his group from place to place and performed on wagons is mentioned only by Horace (*Ars Poetica,* lines 275 ff.), who is generally thought to have been confused or misinformed.

Four play titles are doubtfully attributed to Thespis: *Pentheus, The Contests of Pelias, The Youths,* and *The Priests.*

Thesprotia. Region in southern Epirus.

Thessalus. See THETTALUS.

Thessaly (Gk. **Thessalia** or **Thettalia**). Section of Greece east of Epirus, north of the Maliac Gulf, and south of Macedonia.

Thestius (Gk. **Thestios**). *Myth.* King of Pleuron in Aetolia. Thestius was the father of Althaea and Leda.

Thestor. *Myth.* Son of Apollo and father of the seer Calchas.

Thetideion. Region in Phthia, in Thessaly, where there was a temple to Thetis.

Thetis. *Myth.* Sea goddess, daughter of Nereus, wife of PELEUS, and mother of ACHILLES. Thetis appears at the close of Euripides' *Andromache.*

Thettalus or **Thessalus** (Gk. **Thettalos** or **Thessalos**). Actor much favored

by Alexander the Great. Thettalus won dramatic victories at the Dionysia of
347 and 341 B.C., but in 332 he lost to Athenodorus in a famous acting contest
at Tyre. In 324 he took part in Alexander's wedding festivities at Susa.

thiasus (Gk. **thiasos**). Procession of Dionysus' followers celebrating the
orgies of the god.

Thoas. *Myth.* King of the Taurians. Thoas appears in Euripides' *Iphigenia
among the Taurians.*

Thoricus (Gk. **Thorikos**). Mountainous section of eastern Attica.

Thracian Women, The (Gk. **Threissai**). Lost tragedy by Aeschylus. *The
Thracian Women* was thought to be second in an Ajax trilogy, following *The
Award of Armor* and preceding *The Women of Salamis.* Apparently it told of
Ajax's suicide. The only authentic fragment from it relates how Heracles made
the infant Ajax invulnerable—except in one shoulder—by throwing his lionskin
over him.

Thrasybulus (Gk. **Thrasyboulos**). Democratic leader in Athens. Thrasybulus helped to overthrow the Thirty Tyrants and to restore the democracy in
403 B.C.

Three-Penny Day, The. See TRINUMMUS.

Three-Phallus Man, The (Gk. **Triphales**, implying "The Man with the
Huge Phallus"). Lost comedy by Aristophanes (c. 411 or 410 B.C.). *The Three-
Phallus Man* satirized Alcibiades, comparing him to the mythical infant Priapus,
who had unusually large genitals.

Thria. Attic deme.

Thronium (Gk. **Thronion**). City in Locris.

Thucydides (Gk. **Thoukydides**). Leader of the oligarchic faction in Athens
and opponent of Pericles. Thucydides was ostracized in 444 B.C.

Thule. Land located vaguely in the northern seas and thought of as the
remotest spot on earth.

Thurii or **Thurium** (Gk. **Thourioi** or 'Thourion'). Greek city on the Gulf of
Tarentum. In 443 B.C. Thurii was colonized by Athens. It had previously been
the site of Sybaris, which was destroyed.

Thyestes. *Myth.* Son of Pelops and Hippodamia. (For myths involving
Thyestes, see AEGISTHUS; ATREUS.) His ghost appears at the beginning of
Seneca's *Agamemnon,* and he is of course the main character in Seneca's
Thyestes.

Thyestes is the title of two (some say three) lost plays by Sophocles. One
version, also called *Thyestes in Sicyon,* must have dealt with the ravishing of
Pelopia by her father. Euripides' lost *Thyestes* was produced before 425 B.C.
It is not known what part of Thyestes' story was treated in this play.

Thyestes. Extant tragedy by Seneca. Translations: Frank Justus Miller,
1917; Ella I. Harris, 1942; Moses Hadas, 1957.

S C E N E. Argos, the palace.

S U M M A R Y. The ghost of Tantalus is conjured up from the underworld
and compelled by a Fury to incite his descendants to monstrous crimes. When
Tantalus and the Fury vanish, the former's grandson Atreus is introduced deep

in meditation. Although he and his brother Thyestes were supposed to share the throne of Mycenae, Thyestes had seduced Atreus' wife and with her help secured the golden lamb that was the symbol of sovereignty. Atreus had been dethroned and expelled. He was able to win back the throne from his brother, whom he banished, but his thirst for revenge has not yet been sated. Recalling the tale of Procne and Philomela, who fed Tereus his own children's flesh at a feast, he plans a similar fate for Thyestes and sends him an invitation to return from exile.

Thyestes, having returned to Argos only at the entreaty of his sons, is given a cordial welcome by Atreus, who insists that his brother share the crown with him. Atreus then takes his brother's sons away on the pretext that he wants to clothe them suitably. But a Messenger soon enters with the report that the king actually dragged them to a gloomy grove, sacrificed them before an altar, and carved up their bodies, using the various parts to prepare a meal for their father. Even the sun is confounded with horror at this deed, and an unnatural darkness falls over the land.

Thyestes, after consuming the dinner provided him by Atreus, tries to be cheerful, but a vague terror oppresses him. At the end of the banquet Atreus brings in a dish and removes the cover to disclose the heads of Thyestes' sons. To the grieving father's request that his sons be given a decent burial, Atreus replies that he has just eaten them. The play ends as Atreus exults over the success of his plot, while Thyestes implores divine vengeance on his brother.

COMMENTARY. This gory tale was a favorite with ancient dramatists, but Seneca's is the only treatment that has survived. Perhaps because there has been no Greek model to compare it to, critics have had to turn their attention to the play itself; they have found much to admire. Playwrights in the English Renaissance particularly loved it, and *Thyestes* became the father of numerous revenge plays, among them *Hamlet*.

Thyiad (Gk. **Thyias**). Maenad or bacchante.

Thymaetadae (Gk. **Thymaitadai**). Attic deme.

Thymbra. City in the Troad. Thymbra was the center of a cult of Apollo.

thymele. Altar in the center of the orchestra of a Greek theater. Not being permanent, it could be replaced by a platform for certain performances. The term also could be loosely used for the entire orchestra or for the stage.

thyroma, pl. **thyromata.** Broad recess in the *episkenion,* or upper section of the skene. In it were set decorations or scene paintings; in addition, interior scenes were staged there.

thyrsus (Gk. **thyrsos**). Symbol of Dionysus. The thyrsus was a staff wound with ivy and vine leaves. It often had a pine cone at the top.

tickets. In the ancient theater tickets were coin-shaped and made of bone, lead, clay, or other cheap material. A ticket indicated a block of seats, but not an individual seat. Numerous tickets have been discovered.

Timocles (Gk. **Timokles**). Writer of Middle Comedy (active at least until 317 B.C.). Of Timocles' works about twenty-five titles and forty fragments have survived. He was unsparing in his ridicule of prominent politicians and notorious courtesans. Judging by one fragment from his *Women at the Adonis Festival,* Timocles appears to be the first to voice the idea that tragedy pleases because the sight of the characters' misfortunes takes the spectator's mind off of his own troubles.

Timolus. See TMOLUS.

Timon. Well-known Athenian of Aristophanes' time. Timon withdrew from the world and refused to see anyone but Alcibiades. He seems to have figured in Phrynichus' *Hermit* (414 B.C.).

Tiphys. *Myth.* Pilot of the *Argo.*

Tiresias (Gk. **Teiresias**). *Myth.* Blind soothsayer. Tiresias' revelations form an important part of the plots of Sophocles' *Oedipus the King* and *Antigone,* Seneca's *Oedipus,* and Euripides' *Phoenician Women.* In Euripides' *Bacchae* he joins with Cadmus in deciding to welcome the cult of Dionysus.

Tiryns. City in Argolis southeast of Argos.

Tisiphone. *Myth.* One of the Erinyes.

Titanis. *Myth.* Daughter of Merops, king of Cos. Titanis joined Artemis' band of followers but was expelled by the goddess and changed into a deer.

Titans. *Myth.* Children of Uranus and Gaia (or Chthon). After Zeus overthrew their brother Cronus, the Titans tried to unseat the Olympian gods. They were defeated and hurled into Tartarus in a cosmic battle called the Titanomachy. In later Roman poetry "Titan" used alone frequently designated Helios, the sun.

Tithonus (Gk. **Tithonos**). *Myth.* Beloved of Eos, the dawn goddess. Eos begged for Tithonus the boon of immortal life but forgot to ask for immortal youth. His name came to mean "a senile man."

Tithras (adj. Tithrasian). Attic deme.

Tityus (Gk. **Tityos**). *Myth.* Giant who tried to assault Leto. Zeus struck Tityus with a thunderbolt and sent him to the underworld, where every day a vulture devoured his inner organs, which grew back by night.

Tmolus or **Timolus** (Gk. **Tmolos**). Mountain range in southern Lydia.

Toxeus. *Myth.* Son of Eurytus of Oechalia and brother of Iole. Toxeus was killed by Heracles.

Trachiniae (Gk. **Trachiniai, The Women of Trachis** or **The Trachinian Women**). Extant tragedy by Sophocles (dated by various scholars from 441 to 413 B.C., most placing it near the latter date). Translations: Richard C. Jebb, 1904; Lewis Campbell, 1906; F. Storr, 1912; Esther S. Barlow, 1938; Gilbert Murray, 1948; E. F. Watling, 1953; Ezra Pound, 1956; Michael Jameson, 1957; Theodore H. Banks, 1966.

S C E N E. Trachis, the house of Heracles.

S U M M A R Y. Because Heracles had treacherously killed Iphitus to avenge the wrongs he had suffered at the hands of Iphitus' father, King Eurytus of Oechalia, the Greek hero and his family had been exiled to Trachis; in addition, Zeus had forced Heracles to become the slave of the Lydian queen Omphale. He has now been absent from Trachis for fifteen months. Heracles' wife, Deianira, is fearful that some evil has befallen him, for he left with her an oracular tablet which she interpreted as meaning that if he did not return in a year and three months he would either die or pass on to a more tranquil life.

At the suggestion of her Nurse, Deianira sends their son Hyllus in search of his father. A Messenger then arrives to report that Heracles is well and is on his way home. The good news is soon confirmed by Lichas, Heracles' herald, who reveals that, upon completing his year of bondage to Omphale, Heracles had killed Eurytus and enslaved the citizens of Oechalia; at present he is in Euboea, consecrating altars and gifts to Zeus.

Lichas has brought with him several captive women from Oechalia, one of whom stirs Deianira's compassion by her grief and her noble bearing. On learning from the Messenger that Lichas has not given a full account of Heracles' deeds, Deianira extracts from his unwilling lips the information that her husband had become infatuated with Eurytus' daughter Iole and had attacked Oechalia only because the king refused to give her up to him. Iole, now destined to become Heracles' mistress, is the very maiden who had attracted Deianira's attention. Deianira tries to restrain her anger at Heracles, for she is familiar with his weaknesses, but the thought that she must share her house with Iole is unendurable. After some hesitation, she decides to recapture her husband's attentions with a love charm given her by the centaur Nessus. When Nessus was mortally wounded by Heracles after attempting to ravish Deianira, he gave her some of his blood with the instruction that she should use it if her husband's affections should stray. Deianira, having kept the blood hidden from the light as the centaur had bidden, now smears it on a new robe which she sends to Heracles by Lichas.

After the gift is dispatched, Deianira has premonitions of disaster, for the tuft of wool with which she daubed the blood on the robe has dissolved to dust and foam upon being exposed to sunlight. With the return of Hyllus, all her forebodings are shown to have been justified. Cursing his mother, Hyllus relates that Heracles was wearing the robe as he made an offering to Zeus and that the warmth and light of the sacrificial flame had caused it to cling to his body and consume his flesh. Half mad with pain and suspicion, he had killed the innocent Lichas and was now being brought to Trachis, barely alive. Deianira rushes away without a word, and as the Chorus bewail the turn of events, the Nurse brings the news that she has stabbed herself.

Heracles is carried in on a litter. He raves wildly in his pain and expresses bitterness that he should have been cut down by a woman; but Hyllus, who is now aware of Deianira's innocence, explains the truth to his father. Heracles, realizing that his fate represents the fulfillment of an old oracle that he would be killed by one who dwells in the land of the dead, commands Hyllus to take him to the sacred peak of Mt. Oeta and to gather wood for his funeral pyre, which the youth is to set afire. In addition, he must marry Iole. Hyllus reluctantly agrees to do his father's bidding, except that he refuses to kindle the pyre. He concludes the scene with a rebuke to the gods, who load men with sorrows and view the result with indifference.

COMMENTARY. It has been suggested that Euripides' works influenced

Sophocles in the *Trachiniae*. This is certainly admissible insofar as Sophocles chose for his subject a love intrigue that would have interested Euripides, but to go so far as to say that the play represents a Euripidean skepticism toward the gods is to assert that Sophocles borrowed an idea that never existed in Euripides' mind. The fact that Heracles' fate was foretold by oracles has thrown modern criticism off balance. Because modern critics do not believe in oracles, they fail to see their one important feature: a man may not deserve his fate when it is foretold, but he may very well deserve it by the time it arrives. Babies do not deserve to be old, but an old man may have earned his old age.

Deianira, in spite of her loving and charming nature, chooses to work through magic, which is a means of playing god and of deceiving men. Heracles, sacking a city from motives of lust and revenge and bringing back a concubine to present to his wife, is scarcely less reprehensible than Agamemnon in Aeschylus' drama. Fate obliterates both of them. At the end of the play, Hyllus gives vent to youthful inexperience and rebellion when he says: "Servants, for my sake grant a great forgiveness for all this, you who have seen the gods' great unforgivingness for the deeds that have been done—the gods, who bring us to life, and are called our fathers, yet look upon such suffering!" But this speech is echoed by the wiser Chorus, who know that fathers must chastise: "Sorrows many, and new, and strangely shaped, and none of them that is not Zeus."

Trachis. City in Thessaly.

Trackers, The. See ICHNEUTAE.

Tractatus Coislinianus. A short Greek outline of a theory of comedy. *Tractatus Coislinianus,* found in a tenth-century manuscript in the De Coislin collection, was first printed in 1839. It shows obvious Aristotelian influence, but the closeness of its relationship to Aristotle's writings is much disputed.

After dividing poetry (or perhaps literature) into mimetic and nonmimetic types, and mimetic poetry into narrative and dramatic types, the outline divides dramatic poetry into comedy, tragedy, mime, and satyr play. The definition of comedy, which is closely modeled on that of tragedy in Aristotle's *Poetics*, is as follows: "an imitation of action involving ludicrous mishaps . . . through pleasure and laughter bringing about a *catharsis* of such emotions." Comic diction is attained by puns, verbal malformations, dialect; comic plots will contain deceptions, unexpected developments, *non sequiturs*, clumsy dances. Comic characters are the *bomolochos*, the *eiron*, and the *alazon*. The language of comedy is realistic; the periods of comedy are Old, Middle and New.

The preceding statements are the most interesting in the *Tractatus*.

Tragasae (Gk. **Tragasai**). Small town in the southwest angle of the Troad. In *The Acharnians* (line 808), Aristophanes puns on the name Tragasae to suggest *tragein*, "to eat."

tragedy. ORIGINS. The Greek word *tragoidia* originally meant "goat song." Tragedy originated in connection with the cult of Dionysus, specifically when a particular form of his cult was imported from Eleutherae to Athens and the City Dionysia was established in the sixth century B.C. (see DIONYSIA). Here all certain knowledge ends. There is no more vexed problem in literary history than the origins of tragedy; there has been much tossing-about of theories, and the end is not yet. Presumably the "goat" in the word "tragedy" referred to Dionysus, or some Dionysiac celebrant, but this does not convey much information. It is undeniable that patterns of primitive ritual can be discerned in extant tragedies, but it is a Procrustean task to fit tragedies to any set ritual pattern, and even if this is done, not much knowledge is gained of the immediate antecedent development of the Greek tragedy that is known today. One of the questions that puzzled the Greeks was why myths about Dionysus appeared so seldom in the plays they saw. In regard to this question dim figures, such as ARION, EPIGENES, and CLEISTHENES of Sicyon, lurk in the background, but they explain nothing and raise the equally insoluble problem of a possible non-Attic source for drama (compare Aristotle, *Poetics*, 1448a).

Aristotle is the chief authority on the beginnings of tragedy, but his statements have only exasperated scholars. In his *Poetics* (1449a) he says that tragedy originated in improvisation; but this is not very enlightening. Immediately thereafter he says that it developed from the satyr play. This is surprising: no two genres could be less compatible in spirit than tragedy and satyr play; moreover, the satyr play as it is known by modern readers gives every indication of being an addition to the tragic trilogy. If satyrs were goatlike, then some etymological connection might be made, but unfortunately satyrs were originally equine. Aristotle also remarks that tragedy came from the *exarchontes* of the dithyramb (*Poetics*, 1449a). There is, however, no agreement as to whether *exarchontes* meant "leaders of the dithyrambic chorus" or "those who delivered a prelude to the dithyramb." Aristotle then blandly states that the stages of development in tragedy are well known.

It is no surprise that some scholars have abandoned Aristotle altogether and have looked for tragedy's beginnings in the ceremonies of mourning at heroes' tombs or in recitations of the rhapsodes at Panhellenic festivals.

About all that can be said is that tragedy developed, somehow, out of choric odes in the ritual of Dionysus. THESPIS produced the first recorded tragedy between 536 and 532 B.C., but there is no reason to think that this was the very first. The figure of Thespis is also surrounded by doubts. For a long time there was only one actor, which meant that although there could be more than one character, thanks to the use of masks, there could be no dialogue between two characters. Aeschylus introduced a second actor, and Sophocles a third.

TRAGEDY IN THE FIFTH CENTURY B.C. The great names of this period are Aeschylus, Sophocles, and Euripides, the only writers whose tragedies are extant. Their careers so overlapped that less than seven decades separate the earliest surviving play and the latest. Aeschylus is identified with the closely knit tetralogy but seems not always to have used it. With Euripides the form tended to burst its bounds; even ancient critics noticed that romantic melodramas like *Helen* and *Ion*, as well as some lost happy-ending plays of reunion and recognition, were the precursors of New Comedy. Yet there is no vast difference in form or spirit between the earliest tragedy, *The Persians,* and the latest, the *Bacchae*. Practically all tragedies were based on myth. There was some experimentation with subjects drawn from contemporary history, such as Aeschylus' *Persians* and Phrynichus' *Capture of Miletus,* but these tragedies failed to please the public. Nevertheless, sporadic examples of historical plays occurred even in the fourth century B.C.

Older than Aeschylus were Choerilus and Phrynichus; Aeschylus' contemporaries were Pratinas and Aristias. Later in the century came Achaeus, Aristarchus of Tegea, Ion of Chios, and Agathon. There were many lesser dramatists, but they are now known chiefly as targets of ridicule in the plays of the comic poets.

LATER GREEK TRAGEDY. The decline of tragedy in Greece began suddenly, but its actual demise was not swift. Tragedies were staged at festivals all over the Greek world, tragic poets made triumphal tours, and tragic actors became famous—but chiefly for their roles in plays by the Big Three (Aeschylus, Sophocles, and Euripides, who had become virtually canonized by the middle of the fourth century B.C.). Revivals, which were not unheard-of in the fifth century, became standard practice beginning in 386 B.C. In the fourth century there were a number of tragedy writers, none outstanding. Many titles survive, but there exist few fragments and no complete plays. In the Alexandrian period there was a minor renascence of tragedy with the Pleiad (see PLEIAD, TRAGIC), but again nothing of permanent value emerged.

TRAGEDY IN ROME. Greek tragedy was first Latinized by Livius Andronicus, who, in 240 B.C., presented both a tragedy and a comedy adapted from Greek plays. Andronicus then proceeded to adapt a number of other tragedies. Ennius and Naevius also produced tragedy as well as comedy, the latter being credited with the invention of the *fabula praetexta,* serious drama on subjects from Roman history. The anonymous *Octavia,* attributed to Seneca, is the only extant specimen of a *fabula praetexta.* The great age of Roman tragedy—insofar as it was ever great, all Roman tragedies being largely adapted from Greek models—came a little later than that of comedy, with the work of Accius and Pacuvius.

Tragedies continued to be written and produced throughout the first century B.C. Both tragedy and comedy were sufficiently vital topics to be treated by Horace in his ARS POETICA. Ovid wrote a famous *Medea,* now lost; and the emperor Augustus produced an *Ajax,* who, he remarked wryly, "fell on his sponge." In the first century A.D. there was also some interest in tragic drama, the best-known writer being Pomponius Secundus. Little is heard of the genre after that time. It seems a mere oddity of fate that the only Roman tragedies to survive are those of Seneca, for they were virtually ignored by his contemporaries.

tragic flaw. See HAMARTIA.

tragicomedy. Same as HILAROTRAGEDY.

Triballi (Gk. **Triballoi**). Barbarian tribe on the borders of Thrace. From their name came Triballus, the barbarian god in Aristophanes' *Birds.*

tribunalia. Balconies or boxes over the side entrances to the orchestra in a

Roman theater. In the *tribunalia* sat the officials who sponsored the presentation of the plays.

Tricca (Gk. **Trikke**). City in central Thessaly.

Tricorythus (Gk. **Trikorythos;** adj. Tricorysian). Attic deme.

trilogy. The three tragedies of the TETRALOGY. The term trilogy is often used where tetralogy would be more accurate.

Trinummus (Lat. **The Three-Penny Day** or **The Three-Dollar Day**). Extant comedy by Plautus (produced after 194 B.C.). *Trinummus* was based on Philemon's Greek play *Thesauros* (*The Treasure*). Translations: Henry T. Riley, 1852; Paul Nixon, 1938; George Duckworth, 1942; C. W. Parry, 1954; E. F. Watling, 1964. Adaptation: Gotthold Ephraim Lessing, *Der Schatz,* 1750.

S C E N E. Athens.

S U M M A R Y. In the prologue Affluence (Luxuria) directs her daughter Poverty (Inopia) into a house which had formerly belonged to Charmides, but which his son Lesbonicus has had to sell because he has squandered Charmides' fortune in his absence. The purchaser of the house was Callicles, a family friend who had promised to look after Charmides' interests; he lets Lesbonicus keep a room in it. When Callicles is reprimanded by his friend Megaronides for taking advantage of Lesbonicus' distress and for helping him to debauch himself further, Callicles reveals in confidence that a sum of money lies hidden in the house which is to serve as a dowry for Charmides' daughter; he had been forced to buy the house lest the money fall into strange hands.

Lysiteles, who is in love with Charmides' daughter, naturally thinks that she is destitute and persuades his father, Philto, to arrange a marriage without demanding a dowry. Lesbonicus agrees only reluctantly, since the family will be dishonored if his sister is a dowerless bride. He determines to provide her with something, even if he must give up the farm that is his sole means of support and become a mercenary soldier.

When Callicles hears of the projected marriage, he decides to put the hidden money to its intended use but fears that he may be accused of withholding some of it or that Lesbonicus' profligate instincts may again be aroused. At Megaronides' suggestion he engages for three pennies a man to pose as a foreigner sent by Charmides to deliver the gold to his daughter. The somewhat disreputable emissary reaches the house just as Charmides himself returns unexpectedly. Charmides is amazed to learn that he has sent money and chagrined to find that he no longer has a home, but with the appearance of Callicles all is explained. During the ensuing reunion Charmides is induced to forgive his son for his dissolute past, while Lesbonicus promises to mend his ways and to marry a daughter of Callicles.

C O M M E N T A R Y. Although *Trinummus* received the flattery of imitation in the Renaissance and neoclassical period, most imitators implicitly voiced a criticism of the play by supplying it with female characters, whose absence is sorely felt in a plot concerned wholly with romantic intrigue. It is usually recognized that the style of *Trinummus* is more Terentian than Plautine but that there is a notable want of Terentian care in the working out of its plot.

Triptolemus (Gk. **Triptolemos**). *Myth.* Prince of Eleusis. Demeter sent Triptolemus through the world on a dragon-drawn chariot to initiate mankind into the secrets of agriculture.

Evidence indicates that Sophocles' lost *Triptolemus,* produced in about 468 B.C., was his first staged play and that it was given the prize on the spot, the ordinary procedures of judging being suspended.

tritagonist. The third actor in Greek drama. (See ACTORS AND ACTING.)

Tritogeneia. Epithet of Athena, who was supposedly born near Lake Tritonis in Libya.

Triton. *Myth.* Sea deity, son of Poseidon and Amphitrite. His name was often pluralized; Tritons were represented as forming Poseidon's retinue and blowing on seashells.

Tritonis. Lake or marsh in North Africa in the southern part of the region that is now Tunisia.

Trivia. Epithet of Diana.

Troad, the. Extreme northwestern corner of Asia Minor, the district around Troy.

Troades. See THE TROJAN WOMEN.

Troezen (Gk. **Troizen**). City in the southeastern peninsula of Argolis.

Troilus (Gk. **Troilos**). *Myth.* Youngest son of Priam and Hecuba of Troy. The oracle said of Troilus that Troy would never be taken if he reached the age of maturity, but he was killed by Achilles while still a mere youth. *Troilus* was the title of a lost tragedy by Sophocles.

Trojan Women, The (Gk. **Troades**). Extant tragedy by Euripides. It was produced in 415 B.C. with the lost tragedies *Alexander* and *Palamedes* and the lost satyr play *Sisyphus;* the tetralogy won second place in the dramatic contest. Translations: Gilbert Murray, 1911; Arthur S. Way, 1912; Edith Hamilton, 1937; Richmond Lattimore, 1947; F. Kinchin Smith, 1951; Isabella K. and Antony E. Raubitschek, 1954; Philip Vellacott, 1955. Adaptations and works influenced by *The Trojan Women:* Accius, lost play; Seneca, *The Trojan Women;* Franz Werfel, *Die Troerinnen,* 1915.

S C E N E. Troy, outside the walls.

S U M M A R Y. As dawn breaks over the blackened walls of Troy, fallen through the trick of the wooden horse, Poseidon reflects on the past glories and present woes of the city, which he had long cherished; now it holds only the captive women who are to be distributed among their Greek conquerors. Poseidon is joined by Athena, who has her own grievance against the Greeks: when Ajax assaulted the Trojan princess Cassandra as she clung to Athena's shrine, not one of the Greeks protested the outrage. The goddess enlists Poseidon's help in wrecking the Greek fleet on its homeward voyage.

After the deities vanish, the Trojan queen, Hecuba, awakens. She mourns her fallen estate, and her grief is echoed by the Chorus of Trojan Women. Presently the Greek herald Talthybius enters to announce that the chieftains have drawn lots to determine the fate of the prisoners. Cassandra, Hecuba's daughter, is to grace the bed of Agamemnon, while her sister, Polyxena, is to guard the tomb of Achilles; Andromache, widow of the Trojan hero Hector, will go to Achilles' son Pyrrhus, and Hecuba will become the slave of Odysseus. Suddenly the half-mad Cassandra appears, garbed in white and brandishing a wedding torch. She prophesies that her becoming Agamemnon's concubine will mark the ruin of his house and that Argos will be unhappier than even Troy, even as the Greek soldiers slain in war far from home had a more miserable end than the Trojans who fell while fighting for their wives and children. Cassandra also foretells Odysseus' ten years of suffering. Coming out of her trance, she bids farewell to her mother and is taken away.

The Chorus recall the bringing of the Trojan horse into the city and the destruction that it poured forth in the night. Andromache now rides in with her small son, Astyanax, on a chariot loaded with the spoils of war. Revealing that Polyxena has been killed and that her body lies over the tomb of Achilles, she expresses her belief that death would be preferable to the existence that lies before her. Hecuba replies that only life can offer hope. As she and Andromache lose themselves in melancholy reminiscence, Talthybius, obviously distressed, returns with sad tidings: the Greek council has decided that Astyanax must be thrown to his death from the towers of Troy lest he grow up to take revenge on his captors. After a tearful leave-taking, the boy is pulled from his mother's grasp.

Menelaus now comes in to remove Helen from among the captives. The Greeks have voted that he be allowed to do with her as he likes: he can either kill her on the spot or take her home to Greece for punishment. When Helen is brought out, she pleads for her life, blaming Aphrodite's vanity, Paris' lust, and Menelaus' neglect for her misdeeds; even Hecuba, who bore Paris, is included in her indictment for having let him live. Hecuba refutes Helen's charges, but Menelaus cannot bring himself to kill his wayward wife and orders her to board the ship for Greece.

Talthybius then brings back the dead Astyanax so that Hecuba can give him decent burial; he himself has washed the body and will dig the grave. The old queen places the child on his father's shield and, aided by the other women, performs the funeral rites. She concludes her sad ceremonies with the words: "If God had not overturned us, throwing that which was exalted beneath the earth, we should have vanished, never hymned by the Muses, never giving songs to those of men who come later."

As the boy's body is borne out, Troy is put to the torch, and Hecuba has to be forcibly restrained from hurling herself into the flames. Against the glowing background, the last dirge for the city is sung, and the women pass down the beach to embark on the Greek ships.

C O M M E N T A R Y. *The Trojan Women* is universally judged one of Euripides' masterpieces. It is obviously a crushing indictment of war and a terrifying portrayal of human brutality and human suffering hardly to be paralleled outside of the pages of the *Iliad*. Yet it is more than that: the successions of unrelievedly piteous scenes are carefully juxtaposed in such a way that clear patterns of irony become apparent.

In the prologue, which is unusual for its dialogue between the gods, the latter are carefully chosen for their roles—Poseidon to recall the past trickery and impiety of Laomedon's city, for which it has now received its due, and Athena to stress the fact that the present trickery and impiety of the Greek nation must be paid for in the future. These points are driven home in Cassandra's speeches.

The miseries of Hecuba, the unifying figure of the drama, are in contrast not only to her past glory but to the beautiful and eternal example in song and story that her fate is to become. Equally impressive is the skillful insertion of the Helen episode between the Astyanax episodes: for fear of future trouble the Greeks eliminate an innocent infant; they then proceed to take home with them the woman who has caused all their past trouble.

Trojan Women, The (Lat. title, **Troades**). Extant tragedy by Seneca, based on Euripides' *Trojan Women* and *Hecuba*. Translation: Frank Justus Miller, 1916.

S C E N E. Outside the walls of Troy.

S U M M A R Y. With a Chorus of Captive Trojan Women, Hecuba stands before the ruins of Troy. She recalls that before giving birth to Paris she dreamed that she had borne a firebrand and foresaw the downfall of Troy; now she blames herself for the city's destruction. All the women mourn for Hector and Priam. Word comes that the ghost of Achilles has demanded Polyxena, Hecuba's daughter, as his bride in death. King Agamemnon, entering, opposes the sacrifice, but Pyrrhus, Achilles' son, claims it as a fitting memorial to his father. After an angry exchange with Pyrrhus, Agamemnon lays the matter before the seer Calchas, who declares that the girl must die; moreover, Astyanax, Hector's son, must be killed as well, so that no future Trojan hero may threaten Greece.

Andromache, the mother of Astyanax, hides him in Hector's tomb and, when Ulysses comes in search of the boy, swears that her child is in the grave. Ulysses is almost convinced, but suddenly becoming suspicious, he orders that the tomb be wrecked and Hector's ashes scattered over the sea. Andromache, torn between love for her son and horror at the sacrilege to Hector's remains, at last brings forth the boy, and he is taken away to be thrown from the walls of Troy. Helen now appears, ostensibly to prepare Polyxena for her marriage to Pyrrhus but in reality to lead her to her death. Overcome by sorrow, Helen reveals the truth to Polyxena, who receives the news with joy. Only Hecuba and Andromache are left at the play's end to hear the Messenger's description of the double sacrifice.

C O M M E N T A R Y. Even those who think little of Seneca admit that his *Trojan Women* falls not far below its Greek models. Although it lacks some of the tragic dimension of Euripides' plays, its portrayal of Stoic fortitude is beautifully done. Critics have especially admired the scenes between Pyrrhus and Agamemnon and between Ulysses and Andromache.

Trophonius (Gk. **Trophonios**). *Myth.* Son of Apollo. Trophonius was renowned as a builder. After his death he had an oracular shrine in a cave near Delphi.

Troy (Gk., Lat. **Troia**). **1.** City in northwestern Asia Minor.

2. An intricate Roman game or ritual, executed by mounted men who wheeled their horses in concentric circles.

Truculentus. Extant comedy by Plautus (variously dated from 191 to 186 B.C.). Translations: Henry T. Riley, 1852; Paul Nixon, 1938; George Duckworth, 1942.

S C E N E. Athens.

S U M M A R Y. Phronesium, an unscrupulous prostitute, has virtually ruined Diniarchus, a young Athenian, and now turns to other lovers who are willing to pay generously for her affection. Strabax, a country boy, is interested, much to the disgust of his bad-tempered slave, Truculentus. But Phronesium's chief victim is Stratophanes, a Babylonian soldier whose child she pretends to have borne; in reality, she has obtained the unknown infant through her hairdresser. When the soldier arrives, Phronesium shows scant interest in the gifts he has brought and plays him off against Diniarchus, who has given her his last cent but presently finds himself shut out of the house.

At this juncture Callicles, to whose daughter Diniarchus was once engaged, appears at Phronesium's door; he is seeking his daughter's illegitimate son, who was carried off soon after birth. It is soon discovered that Diniarchus is the father and that the missing child is the baby in Phronesium's possession. Diniarchus offers to marry the girl and asks Phronesium to return his son; however, he yields to her request that she be allowed to keep him for three more days so that she can continue to fleece the soldier. Promising to pay Phronesium an occasional visit in the future, Diniarchus leaves. Strabax and Stratophanes are left to outbid each other for the courtesan's favors until she declares that she will accept both of them as lovers.

C O M M E N T A R Y. The aged Plautus especially favored *Truculentus* among his works, but many critics take this as proof that parents most love their least attractive children. The play is, however, well turned out, and it is possible to imagine the author's satisfaction at having neatly executed a satirical portrait of human nature at a rather low level.

Tullia. Daughter of Servius Tullius, king of Rome. Tullia was the wife of Tarquinius, Tullius' successor. After she and her husband had murdered her father—according to legend—Tullia drove her chariot over his body, which she denied burial. Tarquinius and his family were eventually expelled.

Turdetani. Tribe in Spain.

Turpilius, Sextus. Writer of *fabula palliata,* Roman comedy freely adapted from Greek originals (c. 185–103 B.C.). Of Turpilius' plays *The Basket-Bearers, The Artisan, The Heiress, Leucadia* (the story of Sappho and Phaon), and *Thrasyleon* were adapted from plays by Menander. Some other titles were *Demetrius, The Helpers, The Courtesan,* and *The Girl from Lindos.* Only 142 short fragments survive.

Turpio, Lucius Ambivius. See Lucius AMBIVIUS TURPIO.

Twin Menaechmi, The. See MENAECHMI.

Two Bacchides, The or **The Two Bacchises.** See BACCHIDES.

Tyche. Greek deity, the personification of fortune.

Tydeus. *Myth.* Son of King Oeneus of Aetolia. After killing his uncle (some say his brother), Tydeus fled to Argos. There he married one of King Adrastus' daughters and became one of the Seven against Thebes. As Tydeus lay mortally wounded in the battle, Athena came to give him immortality but was shocked when she saw him eating the brain of his dead enemy, Melanippus. Athena accordingly withheld her gift, and Tydeus died. His son Diomedes was called Tydides.

Tympanists, The (Gk. **Tympanistai**). Lost play by Sophocles. It is probable that *The Tympanists* portrayed the blinding of Phineus' children by their step-mother Idaea and that it had as chorus the orgiastic devotees of the Great Mother. (See PHINEUS.)

Tyndareus or **Tyndarus** (Gk. **Tyndareos** or **Tyndaros**). *Myth.* King of Sparta. Tyndareus' wife Leda bore Helen and at least one of the Dioscuri to Zeus, but Tyndareus passed as their mortal father. Helen was often called Tyndaris and the Dioscuri Tyndaridae or Tyndarids. Because of the mutual jealousies of Helen's suitors, Tyndareus made them all take an oath to preserve her marriage. He then gave her to Menelaus, whom he had reared, with his brother Agamemnon, in his own house. To Agamemnon he gave his other daughter, Clytemnestra. After the latter was killed by her son Orestes, the aged Tyndareus denounced him to the Argive council; this is the role Tyndareus enacts in Euripides' *Orestes.*

Nothing definite can be learned from the two remaining fragments of Sophocles' *Tyndareus.*

Typhon, Typhos, or **Typhoeus.** *Myth.* Gigantic, hundred-headed monster, a child of Gaia. After some initial successes against the gods, Typhon was finally overcome by Zeus's thunderbolts and crushed beneath Mt. Aetna in Sicily, where he continued to cause earthquakes and eruptions.

Tyre. Chief city of Phoenicia. Tyre was noted for ships and for purple dye.

Tyro. *Myth.* Daughter of Salmoneus. After the death of Tyro's mother, Salmoneus married Sidero, who mistreated the girl cruelly. While Tyro was walking along the banks of the river Enipeus, she attracted the attention of Poseidon, who drew her into the waves and made love to her. Tyro bore him twin sons, Pelias and Neleus, who, when they reached maturity, came to their mother's rescue and put Sidero to death.

Tyro was the title of two lost plays by Sophocles; perhaps the second version was a revision of the first. The second version appeared between 420 and 414 B.C. It contained a famous recognition scene (referred to in detail in Menander's *Arbitrants,* line 109 ff.). Tyro had abandoned her twin sons, wrapped in a goatskin, in a little ark, with a wallet containing tokens. They had been suckled by a mare and reared by a goatherd. When they were grown, the goatherd gave the brothers the ark and tokens and sent them in search of their parents. They found Tyro by a well, where her wicked stepmother had sent her to fetch water. At the end of the play, Poseidon appeared and directed Tyro to marry her uncle Cretheus.

Tyrrhenian or **Tyrrhene.** Etruscan. The Tyrrhenian Sea is directly west of Italy. "Tyrrhenian fish" were dolphins, into which the Etruscan pirates who menaced Dionysus were transformed.

Tzetzes, Johannes. Grammarian (c. A.D. 1112–c. 1185). Author of commentaries on Euripides, Aristophanes, and Aeschylus, which are lost, and of *An Introduction to Dramatic Poetry* in Greek verse, parts of which are extant.

U

Ulysses. Latin form of Odysseus. Ulysses appears in Seneca's *Trojan Women*, where he tricks Andromache into turning over the child Astyanax for execution.

Umbria. District in north central Italy lying toward the Adriatic Sea.

Uranus (Gk. **Ouranos**, "sky"). *Myth*. One of the two primeval deities, the other being Gaia, the Earth, whom Uranus covered in close embrace. To free Earth so that her children could be born, one of them, Cronus, castrated Uranus with a sickle and took his place as supreme god.

V

Varro, Marcus Terentius. Roman scholar and poet (116–27 B.C.). Varro's voluminous works on drama, now lost, greatly influenced later scholars; among them were:

On Poems, which may have defined such genres as tragedy and the varieties of Roman comedy.

On Poets, which gave information on earlier Roman writers.

Stage Origins, on Roman theatrical history.

Dramatic Plots, containing data on dramatic performances and premieres, as well as plot summaries.

On Descriptions, which may have treated character portrayal in drama.

On Masks, which included discussions of stock characters.

Plautine Questions and *The Comedies of Plautus*, which established as authentic the twenty-one Plautine plays now extant, designated nineteen more as probably authentic, and rejected others.

Varro also wrote six books of *Pseudo-Tragedies* intended for reading only. He claimed to have invented this genre, but some of the Cynic philosophers seem to have written *tragoidaria* which presented Cynic teachings in play form.

Velabrum. The market district of Rome, between the Palatine Hill and the Tiber.

Venus. Roman goddess of love, identified with the Greek Aphrodite. As the mother of Aeneas and hence the ancestress and protectress of Rome, Venus was regarded with much respect. All grace, charm, and luck were gifts from her, and the winning throw at dice was called the "Venerium."

Vergiliae. Roman name for the Pleiades.

Vesperugo (Lat.). The evening star.

Victoria. Roman deity, the personification of victory.

Vidularia (Lat. **The Tale of a Traveling Bag**). Fragmentary comedy by Plautus (date uncertain). *Vidularia* was based on a Greek original, *Schedia*, probably by Diphilus. Translation: Paul Nixon, 1938.

S U M M A R Y. Only about a hundred lines of the play, mostly discontinuous, are extant. The central character is young Nicodemus, who is shipwrecked and taken in by a fisherman. He is finally reduced, in spite of his obviously upper-class breeding, to working as a farm laborer for the kindly landowner Dinia. Thanks to the recovery of his luggage (Lat. *vidulus*, "traveling bag"), he is shown to be Dinia's long-lost son.

Virginia. Possibly legendary Roman maiden (5th century B.C.). Virginia's father killed her to prevent her falling into the hands of the tyrannical Appius Claudius.

Virtus. Roman deity, the personification of courage and virtue.

Vitruvius. Author of an extant work *On Architecture*, which contains much information on ancient theater building. Vitruvius has been identified with Lucius Vitruvius Mamurra, Caesar's chief of the engineer corps and the butt of some of Catullus' most satirical poems. This identification is, however, questionable.

Volcacius Sedigitus. Author of a lost Latin poem *On Poets* (late 2nd century B.C.). In one fragment Roman writers of comedy are ranked; Terence is placed sixth, after Caecilius, Plautus, Naevius, and others.

Vulcan (Lat. **Vulcanus**). Roman god identified with Hephaestus.

W

Wasps, The (Gk. **Sphekes;** traditional Latin title, **Vespae**). Extant comedy by Aristophanes. *The Wasps* was produced at the Lenaea of 422 B.C. under the name of the author's friend Philonides; it was awarded second prize. Translations: Benjamin B. Rogers, 1924; Arthur S. Way, 1934; Douglass Parker, 1962; David Barrett, 1964.

S C E N E. Athens, a street.

S U M M A R Y. The old Athenian Philocleon (Cleon Lover) is so addicted to jury service that his son, Bdelycleon (Cleon Loather), has been forced to throw a net around his house and to post two slaves as guards to keep his father from going to court. Philocleon makes several unsuccessful efforts to get out of the house: first he tries to escape through the chimney, declaring that he is the smoke; then he clings to the underside of a donkey being driven to market, like Odysseus escaping from the Cyclops' cave; finally, when the door has been barred and shored up with stones, he crawls under the tiles of the roof in an attempt to fly away like a sparrow. He is awaiting other old men who revel in jury duty. They are as quick to anger as "a nest of wasps," he says. "They have an extremely sharp sting."

Although it is barely dawn, a Chorus of Old Jurymen, dressed like wasps, arrive to summon Philocleon to jury duty. They remind him of the delights of judging and condemning and collecting pay for it all. Philocleon manages to gnaw through the net, but before he can join the Jurors, Bdelycleon and the slaves sally forth and rout the Wasps with sticks and smoke. The Wasps retaliate by raising their stings and denouncing Bdelycleon as a blasphemer and collaborator with the Spartans.

Father and son then engage in a debate on the juror's role in society. Philocleon maintains that the juror is lord of the universe: litigants dance attendance on him, politicians flatter him, he is able to bend or break the law, and he gets his three-obol fee besides. Bdelycleon, on the other hand, proves that the juryman's payment is a trifle compared to the huge sums pocketed by the demagogues, who manipulate juries as they please. Even the Chorus is convinced by Bdelycleon's arguments, but Philocleon still cannot bring himself to forsake the courts. Bdelycleon then offers to support his father in comfort and to set up a courtroom on the spot so that he may judge household disputes. The first case involves the dog Labes ("Grabber," representing Laches, a general who had led an expedition to Sicily), who is accused by another dog, Kyon (representing Cleon), of snatching a Sicilian cheese. Bdelycleon, who speaks for the defendant, introduces the latter's puppies to appeal to the judge's sympathies, but Philocleon is unmoved. The old man is, however, misled into voting for an acquittal for the first time in his life and faints when he learns of his mistake. Bdelycleon consoles his father by promising that henceforth he will lead a life of sheer pleasure.

In the interval the Chorus rebuke the audience for having failed to give first prize to *The Clouds* the year before despite the poet's courageous and imaginative efforts to combat the enemies of society. Recalling their youthful exploits, they declare that they are the true Attic men who, like the wasps, are fearless, irascible, and gregarious; there are, unfortunately, even some drones among them. They conclude with an encomium on the men of old, conquerors in the Persian Wars, who represent the conservative outlook.

Bdelycleon, preparing Philocleon for his new life, attempts with little success to teach him how to behave like a gentleman. When Philocleon attends a fashionable banquet, he gets drunk, insults the other guests, and carries off the flute girl. On his way home he commits further outrages on citizens, who angrily pursue him, demanding redress. Philocleon is unruffled by their accusations, but he is hustled into the house by Bdelycleon, whose conduct earns the praises of the Chorus. The old man's high spirits still undampened, he reappears, dressed as Polyphemus in Euripides' *Cyclops,* and breaks into a comic dance in which he is soon joined by the Chorus, whom he leads away.

C O M M E N T A R Y. Most critics vote for *The Wasps* as a well-made, witty, and amusing play, but some condemn it, saying that its concern with a local institution makes it alien to modern sympathies. This verdict would be hard to justify, for Aristophanes attacks the perennial perils of a democratic society: its meddlesomeness, its tendency to use the judiciary for political ends, and its everlasting inclination to judge all conduct by low and negative standards.

It has been pointed out that the obvious theme of *The Wasps* is the conflict between the generations, which is the basic theme of all comedy, here taking its most familiar form: the search for the right relationship between nature and convention. This theme of *nomos,* convention, versus *physis,* nature, was an inexhaustible source of speculation for the Greeks, as it has been for all later ages. In this play a not unfamiliar variation is presented: the younger generation is somewhat stuffy and conventional and the older generation is uninhibited, naturally wicked, and wickedly attractive. The irrepressible nature of Philocleon is never defeated; he shifts from one tactic to another, always making use of convention to fulfill his wish. Philocleon's final triumph completes his portrait as one of the most likable rogues in comic literature.

Water Carriers, The (Gk. **Hydrophoroi**). 1. Alternate title of Aeschylus' SEMELE.

2. Lost play by Sophocles. Like Aeschylus' play, it probably dealt with the birth of Dionysus.

Weighing of Souls, The (Gk. **Psychostasia**). Lost play by Aeschylus apparently treating the death of MEMNON.

Woman of Andros, The. See ANDRIA.

Woman of Samos, The. See SAMIA.

Women of Salamis, The (Gk. Salaminiai). Lost play by Aeschylus. *The Women of Salamis* is thought to have concluded an Ajax trilogy, following *The Award of Armor* and *The Thracian Women*. It dealt with Telamon's exile of TEUCER.

Women of Trachis, The. See TRACHINIAE.

X

Xantriai. Lost tragedy by Aeschylus of which not even the title is clearly understood. Most likely *Xantriai* means "The Wool Carders." If so, the play probably presented the daughters of King Minyas of Orchomenus, who were diligent spinners. Scorning Dionysus, they were smitten with madness (Lyssa, "Madness," appeared onstage, as in Euripides' *Heracles*) and tore to pieces the child of one of them. Only a half-dozen lines of the play are extant.

Xenarchus (Gk. Xenarchos). Son of Sophron and, like him, a writer of mimes.

Xenios (Gk. "pertaining to a guest"). Epithet of Zeus as guardian of hospitality.

Xenocles (Gk. Xenokles). Writer of tragedies, son of Carcinus. Xenocles was satirized by Aristophanes as a bad poet and a bad man (*Thesmophoriazusae*, line 169). He was called the "Man of Twelve Tricks" because he relied more on spectacle than on poetry.

Xerxes. King of Persia, son of Darius. Xerxes' punitive expedition against Greece was defeated in 480–479 B.C. He appears at the end of Aeschylus' *Persians*.

Xuthus (Gk. Xouthos). *Myth.* Son of Aeolus and husband of Creusa of Athens. Xuthus is a leading character in Euripides' *Ion*.

Y

Youths, The (Gk. Neaniskoi). Lost play by Aeschylus. (See LYCURGEIA.)

Z

Zacynthus (Gk. **Zakynthos**). Island off the west coast of the Peloponnesus.

Zagreus. Deity sometimes regarded as a form of Dionysus, sometimes identified with the Cretan Zeus.

Zephyr or **Zephyrus** (Gk. **Zephyros**). The west, or northwest, wind, often personified.

Zetes. *Myth.* Winged son of Oreithyia and Boreas, the north wind. With his twin brother, Calais, Zetes joined the Argonauts. In the course of the expedition the twins chased off the Harpies, who were plaguing King Phineus.

Zethus (Gk. **Zethos**). *Myth.* Brother of Amphion. (See ANTIOPE 2.)

Zeus. Supreme god of the Greek Olympian pantheon, the "father of gods and men." Zeus attained supremacy by unseating his father, Cronus, and banishing him to Tartarus. Cronus, who had swallowed all of his children as soon as they were born, would have gulped down Zeus if he had not been tricked into swallowing a stone instead. As an infant Zeus was concealed in a cave in Crete, was nursed by nymphs, and suckled by a goat; his cries were drowned out by the clashing spears and shields of the Curetes. On reaching maturity Zeus, properly a god of sky and weather, gained the upper hand of his brother Poseidon, whom he relegated to the sea and whose cult he subordinated to his own in many places. He also overshadowed his brother Hades, who was sometimes called "the Zeus beneath the earth."

In his rise to ascendancy in the Greek world, Zeus came to be associated with many local goddeses and heroines, begetting many gods and heroes. Hera was considered his legal spouse; by her he had Hebe, Eileithyia, and Ares. He was sometimes called the father of Aphrodite by Dione, and of Persephone by Demeter. When Metis was pregnant with Athena, Zeus swallowed her, fearing her power. He then produced Athena from his own head. By Mnemosyne he was father of the Muses; by Eurynome, of the Graces; by Leto, of Apollo and Artemis. With Danaë he begot Perseus; with Aegina he begot Aeacus; with Io, Epaphus; with the nymph Electra, Dardanus; with Europa, Minos, Sarpedon, and Rhadamanthus; with Callisto, Arcas; with Antiope, Amphion and Zethus; with Semele, Dionysus; with Leda, Helen and the Dioscuri (or at least one of them, Polydeuces); with Alcmena, Heracles. There were other descendants of less renown. Many of these ladyloves were persecuted by the jealous Hera.

As god of the sky, Zeus sent clear days and storms, bad weather and good; it was his special prerogative to cast the thunderbolt. As Sky Father, he united with Mother Earth in the sacred marriage of earth and heaven, fertilizing her with rain, lightning, dew, hail, and snow. Because of the natural association of the regular revolution of the skies and the regular progress of the seasons with the conception of cosmic order, he became the embodiment of justice, the overseer of oaths, the dispenser of fate, and the patron of rulers.

Aeschylus expressed a subtle and profound conception of Zeus in the *Oresteia* and apparently did so in other trilogies. The rain, dew, storms, and lightning symbolize the suffering that Zeus inflicts upon mankind, but this suffering is fertilizing and creative: out of it comes the crop of justice on earth. Thus, in the beginning of *Agamemnon,* the chorus appeal to "Zeus, whoever he is," discounting the lesser deities and recognizing him as the one true god.

Zeuxis. Celebrated Greek painter (5th century B.C.).